GUNSMITHING: RIFLES

PATRICK SWEENEY

Published by

**krause
publications**

700 E. State Street • Iola, WI 54990-0001
Telephone: 715/445-2214

Please call or write for our free catalog.
Our toll-free number to place an order or obtain a free catalog is 800-258-0929
or please use our regular business telephone 715-445-2214
for editorial comment and further information.

Library of Congress Catalog Number: 99-61449
ISBN: 0-87341-665-1

Printed in the United States of America

Table of Contents

Chapter 1 Introduction 7

Chapter 2 Requirements for Rifle Gunsmithing 15

Chapter 3 Tools 35

Chapter 4 Trigger Work 54

Chapter 5 Scope Mounting 70

Chapter 6 Barrels: Cleaning, Selection and Installation 92

Chapter 7 Cleaning the Action 126

Chapter 8 Break-in, Cryo and Fire-lapping 143

Chapter 9 Stocks 152

Chapter 10 Wood Repair and Refinishing 177

Chapter 11 Metal Finishes 187

Chapter 12 Accuracy Testing 196

Chapter 13 Recoil Reduction 204

Chapter 14 Buying a Used Rifle 215

Chapter 15 Glass Bedding 226

Chapter 16 Building a Ruger 10/22 235

Chapter 17 Building a Precision/Beanfield Rifle 241

Chapter 18 Working the AR-15 258

Chapter 19 Building a Scout Rifle 293

Chapter 20 Refreshing the Hunting Rifle..310

Chapter 21 A Century and a Half: The Lever-Action Rifle 336

Glossary 343

Suppliers 348

Acknowledgments

At first glance, you might think that writing a book is a simple task: sit down and type out what you know. Sure, and just as easy as "snatch the pebble from my hand, grasshopper...." The only two authors I ever heard of who could write a book entirely out of their own heads were Winston Churchill and Isaac Asimov. The rest of us have to depend on others for information, confirmation and in the case of a gunsmithing book, stuff. I would again like to thank the members of the gunsmithing community who were so free with their time, knowledge and encouragement, and the manufacturers who gladly sent me the toys to photograph and play with.

And for all of her help, strength and belief, Felicia.

The Author

With a lifelong interest in firearms, and experience in many fields, it was inevitable that Patrick Sweeney would end up working in a gun shop. After spending more than two decades in the firearms business at retail and in gunsmithing, he shifted to writing and teaching. This, his second book delves into gunsmithing the tool of the American Mythos, the rifle.

Living in the Midwest, he travels the US competing and teaching, and writing about both.

Dedication

The production of a book requires a team effort. Not to steal any lines from "Bull Durham", but I just want to do my best for the team. I would like to dedicate his book to all my fellow gunsmiths who have been so free with their knowledge, tricks and tips. And to the manufacturers who so kindly sent me the tools and rifles to show you in this book. But most of all, to the one who has always encouraged me, believed in me, and felt that I could do much more than I thought myself capable of. With many thanks, to Felicia.

Foreword

Just about everyone has likely looked at one of his or her rifles and thought, regardless of the malady, "There's got to be something I can do about that."

If you are one of those people, Gunsmithing Rifles is for you. Author Patrick Sweeney brings more than two decades of experience as a professional gunsmith and a competitive shooter to the workbench in this book. He painstakingly details the steps needed to tackle both minor and major gunsmithing problems. Perhaps more importantly, he tells readers what jobs are best left to the professionals and whether the work you're considering is really worth the effort and the cost.

Gunsmithing is not for everyone, but anyone with basic skills and the desire to learn can use this book to rework an aging relic or make an average rifle shoot like a dream.

Sweeney provides intricate detail on every aspect of working on all major rifle types and includes specific information on many of the most popular models in use today. This is a book for the home gunsmith. The information is direct and straightforward and the illustrations clearly define the steps needed to complete the repairs described.

This book alone won't make anyone an expert gunsmith, but it will provide the hands-on practitioner with valuable information and easy-to-follow directions.

Building a better rifle starts with this book.

Good Shooting.

Kevin Michalowski
Firearms Editor, Krause Publications

CHAPTER 1

Introduction

"I have less expensive ways to chop down trees."

The Emperor of China after seeing a Maxim machinegun for the first time. During the demonstration, the gun was used to cut down a mature tree.

Man has been referred to as the tool-using animal. I think it would be more accurate to say man is the tool-building animal, as anthropologists have seen other primates using sticks and rocks as tools.

One category of tool developed by man is the projectile weapon. Rather than jump on his prey or his enemy with a club or sharpened tool in hand, humans set about to invent a tool that would secure prey or stop an enemy without the danger of close proximity. To do so the tool needed to launch a projectile. A rifle is the latest manifestation of the projectile weapon.

What is a rifle? Different shooters will give different examples. A deer hunter would mention his favorite hunting rifle. A veteran (depending on which war he was involved in) might suggest the M-1 Garand, the M-14 or the M-16. To a benchrest competitor, the only rifle worthy of the name is something accurate to the point of being spooky.

Rifles come in various sizes, a huge listing of calibers, and may be richly decorated or strictly utilitarian. Characteristics they all have in common are these: A rifled bore. Each launches a single projectile for each pull of the trigger. All are designed to be used with both hands and fired from the shoulder. Accuracy is paramount.

Can non-rifles have rifled bores? Sure, the proliferation of shotguns with rifled bores for deer hunting is not new. Before the 20th Century, a long gun with a smooth bore that had a cou-

ple of inches of rifling at the muzzle saw some use. The system, called "Paradox" allowed a shooter to use either shot or slug. Today, the screw-in choke tube system allows a shotgun shooter to use a rifled choke tube and shoot slugs with accuracy.

Can we call such firearms rifles? No, if for no other reason than to avoid confusing new shooters. The government will not allow us to call it a rifle, either. A rifle with a bore larger than .50-caliber is classified as a "destructive device" and to own one requires much paperwork. The few rifles chambered in calibers used in dangerous game hunting are exceptions. To avoid that paperwork, we do not call a 12-gauge with a fully rifled bore a ".70-caliber rifle."

Colonel Townsend Whelan has been quoted as saying, "Only accurate rifles are interesting." An inaccurate rifle exists only as a platform upon which to make an accurate one.

Ask a veteran what "a rifle" is, and you'll get an answer that depends on when he was in the service. Ask a hunter, and you'll probably get asked "For what kind of hunting?"

It has a rifled bore, it fires one round at a time, and has a scope. Is it a rifle? No. It is a souped-up shotgun that has lost the capability of shooting birdshot or buckshot in a useful way. By the way, this Remington is accurate even by rifle standards, shooting 3-inch groups with ammo it likes.

The advances in firearms technology have far outstripped the old classifications. This shotgun is more accurate as a rifle than many rifles were a century ago, but it is still a shotgun.

Using both hands to shoot a firearm does not make it a rifle. Even with a rifled bore, this is still a handgun. And no one shot this way in the real Old West, but they didn't shoot like in the movies, either!

Additionally, many competitions encourage handgun shooters to fire using both hands. But a rifled bore and the use of both hands for firing aren't enough to qualify the weapon as a rifle. Adding a stock may push the gun into that category, but it is also against the law. What about something like a Heckler & Koch MP-5 or Colt AR-15/M-16 in 9mm? The use of a pistol caliber is not enough to exclude these from the rifle group.

Rifled bore, shoulder stock, one round per trigger pull when the selector is set on "semi." Even the grumpiest curmudgeon will have to admit that the definition of a rifle will stretch to cover a large number of firearms.

No one knows when or why the first gunsmith cut grooves into the bore of a musket. This was long ago, and there weren't nearly as many gun magazines to trumpet the

If you considered it a "rifle" this would be a .70 caliber one, and prone to classification as a "destructive device." Such are the hazards of letting lawyers who don't know anything about firearms write firearms laws.

On top, a pistol-caliber rifle (9mm Parabellum). In the middle, a rifle-caliber handgun (.30-30 Winchester). On the bottom, a handgun curiosity (Chinese Inglis with issue stock/holster). Neither caliber nor stock alone are enough to get a firearm into the group known as "rifle."

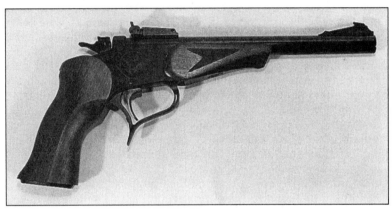

This Thompson/Center Contender is chambered in .30-30 Winchester, a revolutionary cartridge in 1894. Now, it is a hard-kicking hunting caliber in this handgun.

The old Paradox barrels were rifled only in the last few inches. The Hastings Paradox is fully-rifled, and this barrel will keep all of its shots in tight groups for as long as you can stand to shoot it.

latest and greatest advances in technology every month. Looking back, it would seem to be an obvious attempt at creating room for the large amounts of fouling black powder creates. After the first experiment, the next one would be to give the grooves a twist, to increase their volume. At that experiment the rifle was born.

What does the rifling do for us? By imparting a spin to the projectile the rifle stabilizes the bullet for its trip to the target.

A pitcher throwing a knuckleball has figured out how to throw the ball without giving it any spin. Without spin, the ball drifts off of its initial path, buffeted by the slightest breeze or change in atmospheric density. Once thrown, neither the pitcher, catcher nor hitter knows for sure where it will go. So it is with bullets.

In the days of smoothbore muskets for military use, an individual was safe from any particular shooter if he was only 200 yards away. Regardless of his skill the shooter could not guarantee that a fired bullet would pass within 10 feet of the intended target at that range. The poor accuracy of muskets lead armies to develop a great deal of faith in the bayonet. Units would maneuver until they were 50 yards apart, unleash a volley at each other and charge with bayonets. After the initial volley warfare reverted to the combat known since the first phalanx was formed.

So why not issue rifles to the troops? That fouling again. In order to ensure a tight fit between the bullet and the rifling, the bullet would have to be pounded down the bore. Even using cloth or leather as a patch to seal the bore, the fouling would quickly make seating another shot impossible. The gap between the ball and the bore, called windage, was made generous enough on muskets that without the paper wadding the bullet and powder were wrapped in, the ball would roll right out of the bore if it were pointed down.

The most elegant attempt at a fast-loading rifle using black powder was the Ferguson. The trigger guard was attached to a spiral block that ran through the rear of the rifle. Rotating the

The American rifled musket, commonly (and in many cases mistakenly) called the "Zouave," was a muzzleloading single-shot that was responsible for many of the casualties in the Civil War.

trigger guard lowered the block, exposing the breech. The shooter would then put ball and powder into the breech. As the block was rotated up the excess powder could be pushed into the pan, and the flintlock cocked and fired. It could be loaded faster than a regulation musket, and an experienced shooter could easily hit his target at 200 yards. When demonstrating it to British officials of the Royal War Office, then-Captain Ferguson fired four aimed shots a minute in a pouring rain, and hit his target at 200 yards every shot for five minutes straight.

The War Office was so under-enthused by this that they ordered 100 rifles and sent the captain off to the Colonies to try them out. Despite their obvious advantages, the rifles were never adopted, and the American Revolution succeeded. Looking back, it is easy to see that if the Royal War Office had taken the money spent on Hessian mercenaries and spent it on Ferguson rifles, the Americas might still under the control of the British.

The United States did not lack for experimentation in the field of breech-loading rifles. One attempt that got as far as adoption by the Army was the Hall rifle. Not only was the Hall a breech-loading rifle, it used percussion caps instead of flints, and was manufactured on machines, allowing parts to be interchanged. The breech of the Hall lifted in the front, allowing the powder and ball to be inserted. When the breechblock was pivoted back down in line with the bore and fired, the ball would engage the rifling for spin, and also push some of the fouling out ahead of it. The Hall was used for 25 years, finally being retired on account of three main factors: the poor seal between the breechblock and the bore, the fragile stock, and the improvements in other designs.

The next advance in rifle technology came from France. Captain Minie came up with the idea of using a hollow-based bullet with a clay plug in the base. The undersized bullet could easily be rammed down over the powder. On firing, the powder gases would expand the base, the bullet would be gripped by the rifling and rotated on its journey. Experimentation soon showed the clay plug was not needed. This "rifled musket" was the main infantry weapon in the American Civil War, and some say the horrendous casualty rates were a result of common battle tactics not having caught up with the advances in weaponry. Accustomed to the accuracy and range of muskets, officers and soldiers spent too much time in the open, trading rifle fire with opposing units. It was not uncommon for battle summaries to show units that had suffered 40, 50 even 60 percent casualties.

Advances in rifle technology continued. The next step was the fixed cartridge. Unlike the musket, with separate bullet, powder, and cap, the fixed cartridge contained all three in a copper or brass cylinder. The first breechloaders were rimfires, with the priming compound in the edge of the folded head of the case. They were also less powerful than the rifled muskets. For military applications, power didn't really matter for combat. When faced with a unit that could fire 10 shots to their two, the musket-armed soldiers did not care about power. This is a lesson that had to be learned again almost a century later.

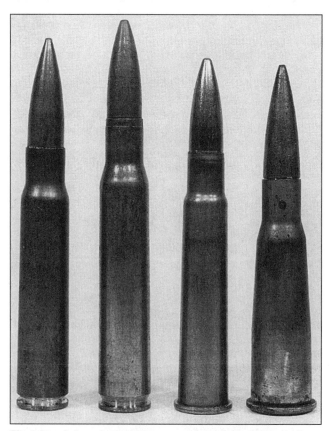

The chemistry of smokeless powder caused the design of new rifle cartridges. Left to right, the German 8mm Mauser, the American .30-06, the British .303, and the French 8mm. The French cartridge was the first, but their initial design caused rifle design difficulties. The large rim and tapered body made for clumsy rifle actions and low magazine capacities.

Even when it was new, the .30-06 was being made by many companies. The War to End All Wars demanded cartridges by the billions. All three of these cases are too old to be safely reloaded. The two made in 1918 were primed with mercuric primers, and are entirely unsuited. Buy new ammo, and save the old stuff as collectors' curiosities.

By the end of the 19th Century rifles had evolved into magazine-fed repeaters using fixed ammunition. The last hurdle was the powder. Black powder is bulky for its power, and has a low burning pressure. The only way to get more power is to use a larger cartridge. Black powder also generates a large amount of smoke outside of the bore, and residue inside. It is sensitive to moisture.

The French, again, led the way to something new. They developed a smokeless powder and teamed it up with a new cartridge, bullet, and rifle. While the powder was fantastic, the bullet was a sensational leap forward. Instead of being a round-nosed solid lead bullet, it was sharply pointed and turned from bronze. Its shape and velocity turned the usual "thrown baseball" trajectory of previous bullets into a nearly flat line. The hard bullet penetrated almost all obstacles. Any military facing it would be at a serious handicap. The Germans, long-time competitors of the French and winners of the last war, began their own work.

In little more than a decade, every major military establishment on the globe, and many minor ones, had changed the rifle they issued to the troops. They had changed from a black-powder single-shot rifle throwing low-velocity lead bullets to a magazine-fed repeater using smokeless powder, with a high velocity "spitzer" bullet. Some, the United States being one, changed their rifle more than once.

In 1892 the United States Army went from the Trapdoor Springfield in .45-70 to the Krag rifle. The Krag was a magazine-fed repeater, and its cartridge was a smokeless round with a copper-jacketed bullet. Still, the advance was not enough. Faced with Mausers in the hands of Spanish defenders in the 1898 war with Spain, the Army wanted better. By 1903 they had the Springfield '03 rifle, and a new cartridge in the .30-03. Even this had to be upgraded in 1906, ending with the now-legendary .30-06. As far as the military was concerned, such rifles were good enough for the next half century.

Hunters and target shooters experimented ceaselessly. The plain bolt-action rifles the military used were too generic, too jack-of-all-trades for these gun lovers. So they went to work. As a result, we have a large variety of rifles and cartridges. Today, the choice is perhaps overwhelming. In Britain, where the expense of owning rifles and going hunting could only be easily borne by the landed gentry, the double rifle arose. An outgrowth of the side-by-side shotgun, it offered a hunter the fastest second shot of any action. For those hunting dangerous game, a heavy double was comforting indeed. Handmade and frightfully expensive, they are rare and beautiful rifles.

The rest of the world went right from single-shot black powder rifles to bolt-action rifles. Once Peter Paul Mauser had refined the Mauser 1898 bolt-action, his marketing department went out and sold it to most of the governments of the world. The Mauser rifle collector has perhaps the richest field to select from, and some collectors sub-specialize in one aspect of Mauser rifles. The United States, after facing Mauser rifles, designed their own rifle, the Springfield. They took so much from the Mauser design the US government had to pay royalties to Mauser.

The sporting use of rifles in the United States went down another path, led by one company, and one designer. Winchester had the exclusive services of the world's best firearms designer in John Moses Browning. Winchester wanted lever-action rifles. Starting with their improvements of the Volcanic Repeater in 1866, Winchester had had a 20-year run of market success. When Browning offered his services, Winchester accepted, and he designed lever-action rifles beyond compare. While the rest of the world was switching to bolt-actions for hunting, the American hunter was using lever-actions. Plenty accurate for hunting, with power to spare for medium game, the lever-action is faster than the bolt for most shooters. The lever-action was found in most American hunting camps until after the American experience in WWI.

The Mauser action swept the armies of the world, and those who did not have one either bought them from Mauser, or made their own copy.

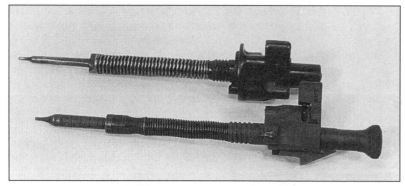

The United States designed its own rifle, and ended up with such a close copy of the Mauser that they ended up making royalty payments on it. The striker assembly of the Mauser (top) and Springfield (bottom) demonstrate the similarity in design.

There many men were exposed to the benefits of the bolt-action rifle. The lever-action held on, but the accuracy, durability and power advantages of the bolt-action were too much. Lever-action rifles, with their tubular magazines, could not use the new pointed bullets. When telescopic sights became inexpensive and durable enough for hunting, the bolt gun surged ahead. The lever-action with few exceptions had no place to easily put a scope.

The size, shape and power of the common military cartridges did not satisfy some hunters and experimenters. At the end of the 20th Century we have hundreds or maybe even several thousand cartridges to choose from. Rifles can be had starting in .22 Short, up to the immense .50 Browning machine gun cartridge. The .22 Short started life during the American Civil War as a handgun cartridge produced by Smith & Wesson. The Big Fifty saw the light of day as a heavy machine gun and anti-tank round, designed by John Moses Browning for use during WWI. In between are a plethora of cartridges designed to bring down every kind of game. The target shooters did not let any moss grow beneath their feet. From BR-50 competitions using .22 rimfire to the 1,000-yard benchrest matches with rifles chambered in .50 Browning, you can have a target rifle made up in the caliber of your heart's content.

Rifles can be single-shots, bolt-actions, lever-actions, pumps, self-loaders or double rifles. Each is favored by some segment of the competition or hunting crowd. There are still black powder rifles, even black powder cartridge rifles. These are not just for nostalgic hunters, but for serious hunters and serious competitors. Despite the differences in caliber, action type or purpose they all are intended to be fired from the shoulder at a particular point on a target.

The design modifications insisted on by sportsmen, hunters and target shooters ended up creating hundreds or thousands of calibers. Each bin and drawer seen here at Loon Lake Precision is one gauge or reamer of one caliber. Each caliber requires a minimum of two reamers and two gauges. It quickly adds up.

Well-kept rifles last a long time. This British Short-Magazine Lee-Enfield was made in 1916, and still works just as designed. Properly treated, it will still work as well in 2099 as it does in 1999.

And what is the measure of success? For some it is an impossibly small group size. For others it is a game animal successfully hunted and brought back. For some competitors, the measure of success is a certain number of hits within a specified amount of time. One standard that all rifles can be measured by is the group size they can shoot (with human guidance) at 100 yards. When I am discussing the performance of a rifle in this book I will use one of two standards. All center-fire rifles will be measured by their performance at 100 yards. All rimfire rifles will be measured at 50 yards. So when I refer to a rifle that "shot 1-inch groups" you will know how far away the target was. Otherwise I will have to write the phrase "...at one hundred yards" several hundred times. For most of the 20th Century the 1-inch group at one hundred yards (see? I did it already!) has been the aspiration of shooters.

To ask "Can your rifle shoot a 1-inch group?" is almost to question a shooter's manhood or veracity. I know shooters who have laminated and framed targets they have shot. When it comes to the minds of some shooters, accuracy is everything.

I think accuracy is important, but not at the sacrifice of comfort, handling ability, and in some cases, looks. To my mind a rifle has to look right, or it just isn't a rifle.

Why all the fuss over rifles? For the simple reason that they last. In this age of disposable goods, a quality rifle that is well-maintained is a lifetime possession. On the southern coast of Turkey, a harrowing 22-kilometer drive east of Antalya is the ancient city of Perge (Pear-gay). Already a going concern by the 3rd Century B.C., it survived through the Roman occupation and much of the Byzantine Empire. Saint Paul preached there after he left Cyprus. If you happen to be there after a rain storm, you will hear the sound of running water. That is the city drain system, still working after the city has been abandoned for 1,000 years. You want quality design and construction? Try to beat that record. A quality rifle that is well-maintained will keep its accuracy for many thousand rounds. For many shooters, 1,000 rounds is a lifetime of shooting.

A rifle represents power and independence. As Jeff Cooper has remarked, "The ability to strike a blow at a distance merely by willing it is a distinctly God-like ability."

Past designs can puzzle current shooters. The lever marked "ON" on this Springfield is a magazine cut-off. Military designers a century ago wanted magazine rifles that could be used as single-shots, with their magazine held in reserve. They were very much afraid of the soldiers using up all their ammo and having none left. Today, the M16A2 has a 3-shot burst. Some things don't change.

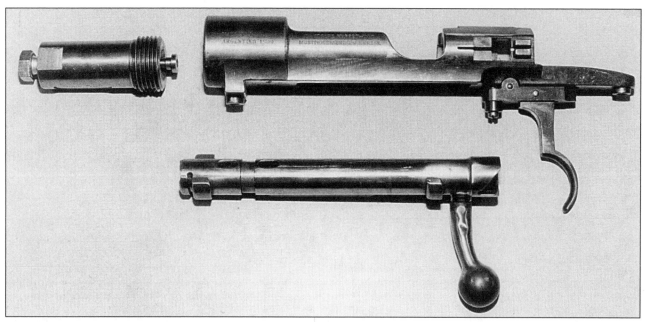

New rifle designs have to contend with the legacy of equipment and expectations. The old rifles can be rebuilt time and again, creating "new" rifles. Shooters tastes change slowly, and what seems like a great idea may take a decade just to build up steam.

An experienced shooter with a rifle has the ability to decide "Hit that, and not the other" for almost anything he can see. Anyone with the will to learn and practice can gain it. Posting a high score on an arcade or computer game is small satisfaction compared to acquiring the skill to use a rifle. But to improve your skill you must have a tool up to the job. A quality rifle is a most valuable tool.

What will rifles be in the future? While there are many technologies that show promise for improving rifles, there are also stumbling blocks. Any new technology must not only offer real and measurable improvements, it has to fit in with the traditional view of a rifle. One case in point from recent history are synthetic stocks. While a stock may be made of space-age materials, it is shaped just like the wooden one it replaced. Another example is that of the new scopes that have a built-in laser rangefinder. A neat idea, but the problem is, it makes the scope so large it looks like a rifle with a goiter. The moment any manufacturer can get the scope/laser combination down to the size of current scopes they will sell truckloads of them. Any improvements to a rifle must fit the image of a rifle, or founder on the rocks of consumer indifference.

The next century should prove to be a grand ride.

CHAPTER 2

Requirements for Rifle Gunsmithing: Skills and a Place to Work

"I'm a gunsmith. I can fix anything."

Anonymous

The wide variety of skills that a general gunsmith must have in order to solve the problems his customers bring to him is enormous. The level of skill and attention to detail he (or she) needs in order to satisfy the picky or discriminating customers is gained the same way you get to Carnegie Hall. Practice. Practice. Practice. The general gunsmith might be called on to cut and file, sand and finish, solder and file, weld and re-blue. The professional gunsmith will also be required to explain the process, hold the customer's hand, and properly fill out all of the mandated government paperwork. If you aspire to work full-time as a gunsmith there is no time to waste; start reading and practicing now.

If you just want to work on your own guns, for fun, to make a change that might be too expensive if shopped out, or to learn at a leisurely pace, then you can get started simply and work your way up. The majority of work you will do on your own rifle can be done with simple hand tools and a stable bench. Do not be hesitant about taking care of your rifle's basic needs, or your desires. Even a serious competitor who puts many rounds downrange each year does not need a fully-equipped machine shop just to clean his rifle after each match. The truly serious competitor will clean his rifle that often. The dedicated hunter who is out in the woods every weekend in the season does not need power tools to keep his hunting rifles in top shape. The fancy gadgets and power tools are nice, but not necessary.

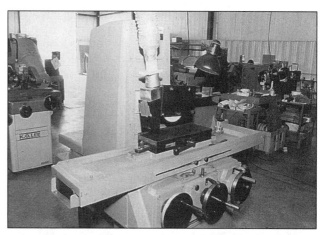

A surface grinder is a neat tool, and a requirement for production work. Even for the single-job gunsmithing pro it is too much machine, too expensive and takes up too much floor space. Lust if you will, but don't buy.

Just what is involved in cleaning and maintaining your rifle? You will spend most of your time taking your rifle apart, cleaning it, and putting it back together. Each rifle (and handgun and shotgun) has a limited capacity for how much shooting you can do and how much neglect it will take before it complains. The complaints might take the form of decreasing accuracy or decreasing reliability. When your rifle reaches its

A solid bench and a medium-sized vise are sufficient to do many gunsmithing tasks. A big stable bench like this one is big enough for anything.

No one can afford to sell a rifle as soon as it gets dirty and then buy another one. No one I know is as rich as the guy in the joke, who bought a new Cadillac as soon as the ashtrays were full. (Photo courtesy of Quality Parts/Bushmaster.)

limit, it stops working. Each time you compete in a match, or go hunting, you use up part of that margin. Sort of like the oil in your car. Every time you drive, you get closer to needing an oil change. Go too long, and the engine wears out faster. Going too long without cleaning your rifle means it will also wear faster, and it also may just quit on you. Cleaning your rifle brings that operational odometer back to zero. If you use that margin up completely but don't realize it, your rifle will malfunction the next time you go to shoot it. If that happens while staring at a big buck through your scope, you will not like it. Failure to clean was the largest single cause of malfunctions that brought rifles and their owners to my shop. Every time I was faced with a rifle that had failed to fire, failed to cycle, or lost accuracy, each was immediately treated to a thorough cleaning and then tested. More than 90 percent of the time, cleaning solved the "problem."

The other common tasks you could need or want to do include mounting a scope or receiver sight on an already drilled and tapped rifle, replacing minor parts that are worn, repairing cracked or dented stocks, and tuning the trigger pull on your rifle.

Mounting a scope is not a difficult job, once you know how and have the right tools. The trick is in getting the scope on straight, securely and undamaged. This does not require expensive tooling, just patience and the right procedure. Installing a receiver sight is simple, if the proper holes are already there in your action. More on these in Chapter Five. In order to replace small parts, you have to be able to disassemble your rifle, which is part of that cleaning we talked about just a moment ago. Replacing parts with new, improved or just different parts does not take a rocket scientist. Repairing dented, cracked or chipped stocks is straightforward with a few supplies and some practice. On some rifles, adjusting the trigger pull is easy, if exacting work. Before you flip ahead to the section on trigger work, which seems to consume much of the interest and passion of shooters, let me give you some advice: You cannot improve your shooting solely by making the trigger lighter! Unless you are a serious benchrest shooter, a trigger lighter than 3-1/2 pounds will not, by itself, do anything good for your shooting. Practice with a rifle until you have worn out the barrel, then start thinking about a lighter trigger pull.

One small tool that is a lifesaver to the professional, but one that you might need only rarely, is the frozen screw

Practice with a rifle until you have worn out the barrel, and only then start worrying about improving the trigger. This is one of a bunch of "worn-out" barrels I salvaged from a police department by welding on flash-hider/extensions. Thoroughly cleaned and properly installed, they deliver under an inch with match ammo.

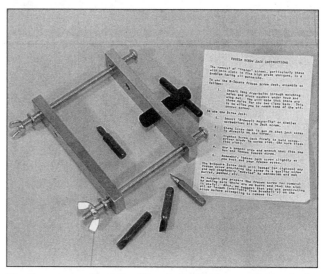

For the screws that won't come out, a frozen screw jack like this one from B-Square is just the ticket. You can generate enough torque on the screw to break the head. Then you'll have to take it to your welder. (Soak the screw in penetrating oil for days and weeks before you use the jack, to avoid the trip.)

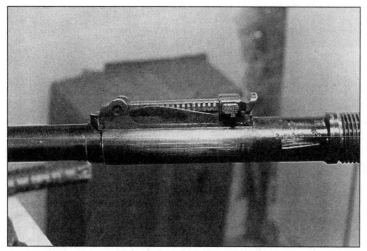

Replacing the rear sight on this Mauser barrel is a good practice project. The bore was rusted, so the vise marks are not a problem. In fact, they would offer you a chance to practice draw-filing and polishing.

You will need tools to work on your rifles, and you'll need a place to store them. This Kennedy box is the best, but expensive.

This little tabletop drill press can do everything you need to do. With it you can drill and tap a rifle for scope mounts. Without it you must send your rifle out to someone else.

jack. Working on a thousand firearms a year, I ran into many screws that defied normal removal. The B-Square frozen screw jack allowed me to remove many of them. The ones that broke off, or resisted even the jack were turned over to my welder.

Involved gunsmithing jobs require an investment in both tools and practice. The first time you glass bed a rifle you will probably have to glass bed it two or three times. This is not a problem, provided you used release agent and can get the action and stock apart. Why twice or thrice? The epoxy may not get everywhere you wanted it to. Or you didn't mix enough. Epoxy doesn't care, just clean the surface to remove the release agent, rough it up to give the next application a place to bite, and start again.

If you are replacing your stock with a new one you'll need files and scrapers. If you are refinishing the old stock or finishing a new one you'll need sandpaper and stock finish. To clean up and repoint checkering requires a magnifying visor and checkering files. Refinishing a stock is not an overnight operation. It will take at least a week of regular shop sessions. After you have refinished the stock, you definitely will want to take your rifle to the range and check your zero. It probably has not changed, but who wants to find out on Opening Day? Replacing the trigger on your rifle may require removing wood from the stock. You'll need the same scrapers, files and chisels that you used for the new stock installation. You may also need drift punches to remove the old trigger mechanism from the action.

While soldering does not involve a larger investment in tools, it takes more practice. If you are planning to solder sights onto a barrel, it is worth the investment in a scrap barrel as a practice bar. Rather than solder your sight onto your one-and-only heirloom hunting rifle several times before it stays on, heat up the practice barrel. If you think

A lathe is a wonderful tool, but a good one costs money and takes up floor space. This Clausing (a popular brand in the Detroit area) has a turret on the tail, for production work. The turret can hold several different tools, a luxury even a professional gunsmith rarely needs.

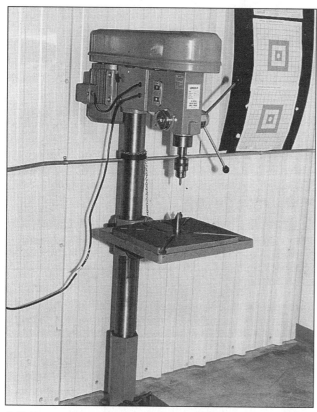

A floor-mount drill press can be larger and have more horsepower. The important benefit of a floor-mount drill press to a gunsmith is the greater available distance between the chuck and the table. Once you clamp a vise to the table, a drilling jig in the vise, a rifle in the jig and a drill bit in the chuck, you need almost 18 inches between chuck and table.

Gunsmiths that do production work buy whatever equipment they need, if it means more work done. These three Bridgeports hold the floor down at Mag-na-Port, and see regular use.

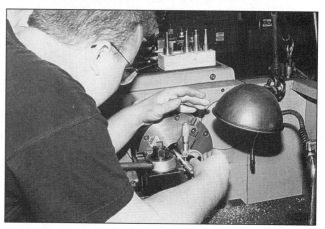

The big advantage of a lathe is precision. The bigger and more expensive the lathe the more precise it can be. But the operator must check it. No tool thinks for itself.

a soldered barrel sling swivel stud is the neatest thing since sliced bread (on the right rifle, I have to agree), then solder it onto your test barrel, then try to pull it off. Once you have the technique down pat you can always heat the stud up, remove it from the practice barrel, and then install in on your hunting rifle. The hardest lesson for some people to learn about soldering is that 90 percent of

the time involved is spent in setup. The actual heating is almost an afterthought.

Larger jobs require even more of an investment in tools. Replacing a barrel is something you can do, within limits. Replacing a barrel requires a barrel vise and action wrench, and a bench sturdy enough to stand still for the wrestling. You'll also need a chambering reamer and headspace gauges.

If you are going to use a lathe (or any machine tool) wisely, you should take notes on each job you do. When you go to do the same job again on another rifle, check your notes to make sure you haven't forgotten anything.

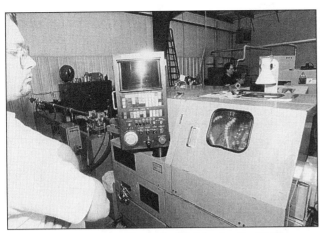

Just when I was saying no tool thinks for itself, along comes this beast. It is an automated lathe at Loon Lake Precision. It feeds in 20-foot bars and turns out ready-to-flute reamers. But can it make a good cup of coffee? I think not.

If the building is big enough, a professional shop can dedicate a room to the messy machines. Grinding, polishing, buffing and sanding all go on in here, and the mess stays.

If you are not starting the job with a pre-threaded, chambered and contoured barrel, then you can't do the job without a lathe. If you want to have your action trued, again you need a lathe. And not just a small hobbyist one, but a large and precise one. If you want such work done professionally, use the information you will gain from this book as a guide in your instructions to your gunsmith. If you need to drill and tap the rifle for a scope mount or receiver sight, you'll need a drill press. A hand-held variable speed drill will not be enough.

These are also jobs complicated enough that you may want to practice on another rifle before you perform the operation on your pride and joy. Practice is easy. For cleaning, you practice by cleaning. As long as you use a bore guide or muzzle cap along with a coated one piece rod, you can only harm your rifle when cleaning it by leaving the most aggressive bore solvents in the barrel overnight. To practice disassembly, again you follow the instructions to disassemble your rifle. Mounting a scope is simple enough that it doesn't require practice to do correctly. It does get faster the more times you do it. The expense of a practice rifle is small, compared to turning your father's hunting rifle over to a professional gunsmith after

This installation is more elegant and efficient than my Shop-Vac/belt sander combo. It also cost a lot more. If you must have a bench grinder, keep it someplace where the mess will not be a problem.

A professional machine shop will solve the problem of dirty machines by installing vacuum-air cleaners. The grindings are sucked up and filtered out. Far too expensive (and large) for your home workshop.

The optimist thinks the bench will always stay half-full. The pessimist knows it will soon be running over. (Photo courtesy Quality Parts/ Bushmaster.)

going ahead and drilling and tapping it without practice.

In case you were wondering, I have seen such rifles. One poor fellow who did this used a hand-held drill. The four holes were not in line, and not straight up and down. The major miracle of his work was that he had not drilled the forward screw hole so deep that it protruded into the chamber! (I have seen holes drilled right into bores and chambers.) I ended up removing the barrel, welding the holes up, and then re-drilling them in my mill. I finished by re-blueing the action and then screwing the barrel back in. All this work cost him more than a practice rifle would have. If you do not want to buy a whole rifle, then buy a scrap barrel and a used stock. Less cost, less paperwork if you live where a rifle requires paperwork, and there is no sentimental attachment. You can practice to your heart's content until the barrel and stock are used up. Then buy replacements.

The top-end of gunsmithing tools are the power tools. The drill press is a compact tool that can fit in the corner. For drilling holes in steel, especially the hardened steel of rifles, you can't beat a drill press. With a drill press and the proper fixture you can drill and tap scope mount holes, install iron sights or put an aperture sight on a rifle that didn't come from the factory ready for one.

Other power tools take up much more room. Even the

smallest mill that can handle gunsmithing work will require at least 12 square feet of floor space. If you add a lathe capable of handling barrels, you will require another 18 square feet, and either a concrete slab floor or reinforcements to a frame floor. What should you consider when looking for a mill or lathe? The mill should have a table at least 2 feet long. Anything shorter and you won't be able to properly clamp and brace a barreled receiver while you work on it. Avoid mills that do not have micrometer vertical adjustments. A good mill will allow you to move the cutting tool up and down by means of a crank, using a scale as your guide. A cheap mill only allows you to move the cutting head up and down in rough increments. To use the cheap one you have to fuss endlessly while you attempt to move the cutting head, measure where it will cut, and re-adjust until it is correct. On a good mill you simply bring the cutting tool down until it touches the top surface, pull the tool to the front or back for clearance, and then lower the tool the precise amount you need to cut.

Do you need CAD/CAM and power-feed capabilities? No. While they are nice to have (along with a digital read-out), you'll pay more for these features than you will for a big mill, let alone a small one.

A lathe suitable for rifle gunsmithing must be larger than the minimum needed for handgun work. The clearance hole

This is a very pessimistic bench, with about 100 square inches of useable space.

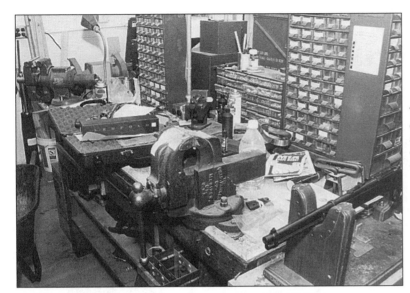

This is a large and useful vise, if you could only get to it. It is so crowded in by other stuff that you can't get close enough to it to do any work. Keep the area around your bench, and its vise, clear.

The cabinet in the corner, and the shelves on top of and next to it contain everything you would need to do pistolsmithing. Rifles are much bigger, and so are their tools. This cabinet could not hold all of the necessary riflesmithing tools mentioned in this book.

through the headstock has to be large enough for a receiver or a barrel blank to fit into it. You'll need at least 1-inch diameter. The lathe must have a four-jaw chuck. A three-jaw chuck is convenient for fast work, but you cannot center a piece as easily with the three-jaw as with the four-jaw chuck. When you go to true the important surfaces on a receiver, you have to be able to center it precisely in the chuck. The bed of the lathe should be long enough to work on a barrel. I have not seen a lathe yet that didn't have power feed. Used to cut threads, your lathe does not have to have quick-change capabilities on either chuck revolutions per minute or thread adjustments. You won't be using it for production, so it doesn't matter if it takes you a minute or two to change from one setting to another.

What about combination tools? By building a machine tool with both the lathe and milling mechanisms as integral parts, you can save a good amount of floor space. But do not trade vertical adjustments on the mill for convenience of shop space. Many of the combo machines are intended for hobbyist work, crafting parts for model trains, radio-controlled aircraft and the like. Not that those aren't satisfying pursuits. They simply do not require the equipment that good gunsmithing does.

Any power tools also take more room than cleaning and

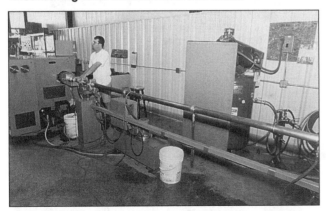

The bar-feeder on the Loon Lake lathe takes up four times as much floor space as my first commercial shop, and 10 times the space of my first home shop! I didn't need this much room, and you probably won't either.

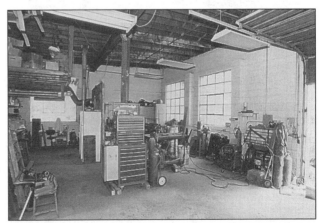

The large windows in this welding shop provide lots of light. The open garage door provides plenty of ventilation. However, it is cold in the winter, hot in the summer, and a bear to keep clean.

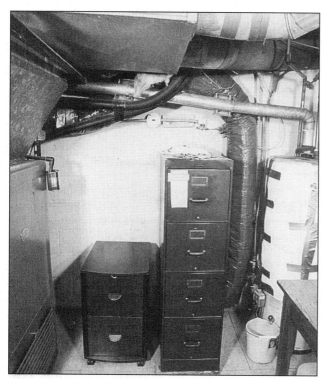

If all you were working on were handguns, then a couple of lockable cabinets like these would be plenty. As a riflesmith, you'll need much larger storage.

A desiccant can will protect your rifles from moisture and rust. A reversible desiccant can like this can be baked dry in the oven and placed back in your gun safe. Get one. Use it. Bake it dry each month.

NEW REMINGTON GUN SAFES
PREMIER SERIES

A gun safe like these Remington models will keep your guns safe even if they are obvious. Just don't write the combination on a nearby surface, thieves know about such memory tricks. (Photo courtesy Remington Arms Co.)

A big honking fire-proof safe, like this one out of an old bank, is great for protecting papers. Unless you can get a used one as a deal, don't spring for a fireproof model. Your rifles don't need it, and your wallet will thank you.

maintenance do. You may be hard-pressed to find enough room for a full-sized lathe, even if you have a burning desire to swap barrels all the time. Some power tools do not take up much space for themselves, but require large amounts of space for the mess they make. Bench grinders, belt sanders and power buffers all take up a small amount of floor space, but throw stuff several feet in every direction. Using a belt sander to install a recoil pad is particularly messy. Professional gunsmiths who spend any time at all (and can arrange

their shop), hide all of these tools in a separate room! Even hooking a Shop-Vac up to my belt sander wasn't enough, I ended up with ground-up rubber all over me and everything else in the shop. Unfortunately my shop was too small to build a separate room, and I had to resort to broom, vacuum and drop cloths. If you are thinking of adding these power tools, you should consider keeping them in the garage, even if your workshop is in the house or basement. You, your workshop and anyone living in your house will be all be happier.

So where to put all the stuff you will accumulate? And just how much room do you need? Optimistic shooters look at the problem as a matter of efficiently storing everything. Optimists think they can store the Library of Congress in their spare bedroom with the right design of shelves. Pessimists look at the problem as a matter of extra space attracting extra stuff. The pessimist thinks that if he could find and heat an aircraft hanger as his workshop, in a short time period it would be so packed with stuff that he couldn't move. I started the business of gunsmithing as an optimist, and in a few years had become a pessimist. I was buried in stuff. It was stuff that I had kept with the thought that it could be "useful someday." My advice on this subject is to be brutal about hanging on to things. If you have concrete plans for a particular part, tool or rifle, do not invest in the rest of the parts or tools until you are ready to begin the job. Otherwise you'll find yourself constantly tripping over the boxes full of tools for "the next job."

During one of my fits of cleaning, I found myself holding a drawer full of parts. Every part in the drawer had been saved from oblivion because it would be "useful someday." I realized that not only had I not used any of the parts, I hadn't opened the drawer and looked inside it for several years. The contents of that drawer and many others were dumped into a box and shipped off to West Hurley, where the Gun Parts Co. could sort through them and store them for the next century. A few weeks later they sent me a check, and a fair one, for the parts. Don't end up buried under your good intentions.

Rifles take up more space than handguns do, and not just in storage of the rifles. If you have a small room already devoted to handgun work, it may not be large enough to work on rifles. Also, drawers will be of limited use for working on a rifle. While almost everything associated with pistolsmithing will fit in a drawer, this is not the case with rifles. Consider cleaning the bore of a rifle. A short-barrel rifle might only have an 18-inch barrel. The cleaning rod has to be at least that long plus its handle. The rifle sits in a cradle that butts against the far wall. The rifle stock and cradle take up another 18 inches. You have to have enough room in front of the muzzle so you can put the rod into it without hitting your elbow on the back wall. You end up with a short rifle needing at least 6 feet of room in which to clean it! A tall shooter cleaning a long-barreled varmint rifle may need 8 feet of elbow room. Moving things to the vertical doesn't help. Once you stand on a chair, the standard 8-foot ceiling of the American home gets a little crowded. Getting onto and off of the chair is a drag, and you will drip cleaning solvent at a faster rate while clambering up and down. And, where are you going to find a drawer to hold that 24-inch cleaning rod? If you clean from the chamber (as you should!) you save some length in the benchtop, but have to lengthen the cleaning rod.

My first home workshop was an old root cellar in the corner of the ground floor. It measured 5 feet by 7 feet. While it was large enough (barely) to work on handguns, it was not sufficient to work on rifles. Every time I wanted to swab out a bore I would find myself standing out in the hallway with a cleaning rod stretching back into the room. Your converted broom closet can get too small to step into once you have stored the rifles and their cleaning tools in it. The ammunition is larger, the gun cases are larger, and the wall racks or gun safe you'll need are larger than handguns require. No, you need a larger room than my first one, or a dedicated bench in the garage or basement.

Let us design an adequate room for storage and cleaning, without going overboard. You will need four things: a place to lock up the rifles and tools; a place to work on them; light and ventilation. First, storage of the rifles and equipment. Rifles take up more room than handguns. As a professional gunsmith and serious competitor, my handguns all fit into a standard gun safe. The same safe will only hold a fraction of my rifles and shotguns. A standard gun safe will store a dozen rifles without too much trouble. If you will never own more rifles or shotguns than that, get a standard safe. Larger is better, and not just because it holds more guns. A larger safe is heavier and thus harder to move. A larger safe will have better air flow. A standard safe with a dozen rifles in it will be tightly packed. If you drop your wet rifle in there after hunting, the moisture will affect the other rifles. A larger safe allows room for air flow around the rifles, lessening moisture exposure. A larger safe also allows room for desiccants, a light bulb or other moisture-reducing gadgets.

Do not spend large amounts of money for a "fire-proof" safe large enough to hold your rifles. Safes that stay cool enough to be called fire-resistant or fire-proof are designed to hold valuable papers. The extra insulation takes up space. A gun-safe sized fire-resistant safe will have half the internal room as the gun safe would. The insulation also costs more. Rifles can withstand more heat than paper, and will do fine in a gun safe. A friend of mine had his house burn down around his gun safes. Once the fire department was done hosing down the safes and the pile of coals they sat in, Jim opened them up to find his rifles, shotguns and handguns soggy but unscorched. He spent that day dipping the guns in a drum of diesel fuel and then storing them in his barn. The diesel protected the guns until he could go through them one at a time and give them a proper cleaning. You should not use diesel fuel as a long-term storage protectant. The petroleum base will soften wood and attack wood finishes if left on too long.

Your safe should be bolted to the floor or wall. This is particularly important if your gun safe sits in the garage, or your house sits on a slab instead of a basement. My brother used to live in Houston, land of hot weather and a high water table. None of the houses had basements. Anyone with a gun

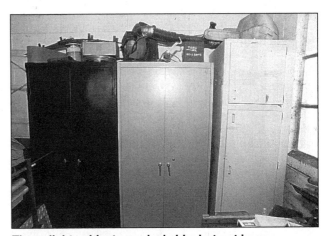

These light cabinets are lockable, but not heavy enough. If you use cabinets like these, bolt them down and add a hardened hasp over the door lock. While they are better than nothing, such cabinets can be opened in a few minutes by determined thieves.

The "belt and suspenders" crowd add gunlocks to their other measures.

The Weatherby horizontal security chest gives you the safety of steel without looking like a safe. Put some cushions on it and it might pass without notice in your den or family room. (Photo courtesy Weatherby)

In the old days people liked to show off their rifles. A classy cabinet like this was the way to keep dust and fingerprints off while showing off. Now you need steel, and you have to hide the safe, too. Such is progress.

safe and common sense bolted the safe to the wall or the slab. Thieves will crash a stolen vehicle into a building to get at guns, and unless your safe is bolted down they will simply wrestle it into a truck and drive off, to open at their leisure. I know personally of four different gun shops in my area that have had vehicles deliberately crashed into them as a means of gaining entry. The gunshop solution in each case was to install modern tanktraps. These are steel pipes set in the ground and filled with concrete. Not only is this unsightly, it may violate the landscaping codes in your neighborhood, and they make it a drag to get into your own garage. Camouflage to hide the safe is an attractive option. One carpenter in our gun club placed his safe in a corner of his basement. Once it was bolted down, he framed it in and then put paneling over the frame and an interior door in front of the safe. If you were to walk into his basement you would think it was just another linen closet. Weatherby makes a gun safe designed to work as a horizontal safe. The door has a pad on it. If your basement is paneled, by extending the paneling around the safe you make it look like a built-in seat. Sure, someone may think it is a storage seat, but one look under the cushions will discourage further searching.

Add weight to your safe. Even if you never plan to load any shotgun ammunition ever, buy 200 pounds of lead shot. Resting in the bottom of your safe, it adds to the burden of hauling it away. Let's total this up. One lightly-built safe at 400 pounds. Two hundred pounds of lead shot. A dozen rifles at ten pounds each. Binoculars, a hunting knife or two, whatever else is valuable enough to store in the safe. This comes to 750 pounds, starting with a light safe. Start with a larger or heavier safe and the total goes up. Can two men move it? Yes, but only barely if it isn't bolted down. If your safe is in the basement, can the stairs hold all the weight? Two husky men plus the safe can total 1,200 pounds. You may have to call the police to your house to deal with the two dead burglars, crushed when the stairs collapsed under them.

Your desiccant canister should be the right size for the safe and guns. This canister is just fine for handguns, but would be overwhelmed in a rifle safe. Bigger is better, and not just in calibers.

Even with all precautions, guns get stolen. If you have an appraisal tucked away someplace else, your insurance company can't make you take ten cents on the dollar as "compensation." Proof in hand, you can get every penny you are owed. You also have a better chance of recovering your firearms.

Place each sheet on the last one.....

and then compress the layers. Shooters have an advantage here because everything we have is heavy. These 500 pounds of bullets produced a tight bond.

This leads to another question. If the safe is so heavy, how do you get it IN the basement? First, take the door off. Put lumber down the stairs, across the treads, as a ramp. Using blankets and ropes, slide the safe down the stairs. Move it to its new location, install the door and add the lead shot. The lead shot also keeps the safe from tipping when the door is open. Why not use sand, which is cheaper? Sand holds moisture. If you use desiccants, the sand will just be adding to their labors. If you do not use dessicants, the sand will promote corrosion. You should store the cleaning supplies, spare magazines, tools and ammunition outside of the safe.

For someone with many firearms, there is another alternative. If you have more rifles than will fit into a couple of safes, or some that are extremely expensive, then you can build a room as a vault. The $3,000 to $4,000 you might spend on multiple safes can be spent on a solid door, deadbolt locks, a stiffened door frame, and even interior protection in the room. If someone breaks into the house they are presented with just another locked door, but one more difficult to break into than the rest of the interior doors. They are not presented with the tempting safe as an object of attention. Also, don't forget to reinforce the window.

Best of all, harden the room, WITH the gun safe in it. One acquaintance who shoots sporting clays with his

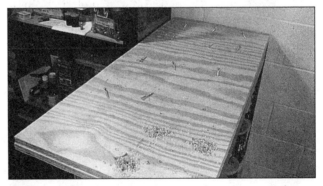

Once the adhesive is set, then wood screws complete the assembly.

favorite London Best double has a store room with gun safes in it. To get into the room, you'd think you were being escorted into the Launch Room at NORAD. He has a keypad for the alarm, two different high-security deadbolt locks in a steel door, and then inside the room are the gun safes themselves.

Second, you need a location in which to work. You should have your workbench near the safe. Locking your rifles in the closet of the master bedroom on the second floor, with your workbench in the basement will soon get to

If your workbench is not stiff or thick enough, you can laminate sheets of plywood to it. Use construction adhesive for a solid bond.

Vise in place and cleaning mat down, this bench is ready to go. Later I'll paint it to keep it from absorbing oils and solvents. The bench is shallow in order to prevent "bench debris" from accumulating on the back and in the corners.

of 2x4's or heavier lumber. It has to stand up to the weight of a heavy vise and even a barrel vise. One way to stiffen a bench is by attaching a sheet of plywood to it as a working surface. Cut the plywood to the table dimensions. Spread construction adhesive onto the table top and place the plywood over the adhesive. If you are the "belt and suspenders" type, use wood screws to pull the plywood and tabletop tightly together. Otherwise just pile several hundred pounds of assorted ammunition and other gear onto the plywood while the adhesive cures.

The bench should be at least 6 feet long, 2 feet deep, and 30 to 34 inches high. A bench shorter than six feet quickly becomes too cramped to be a suitable workspace. By the time you attach a vise and place your rifle cradle on the bench for cleaning, there isn't much room left. Even if you store the cradle off of the bench, there isn't much work space. A bench deeper than 2 feet only encourages clutter. When I moved into my commercial shop there were deep benches already installed. It was too easy to ignore things pushed to the back, and any bench deeper than 2 feet collected too much stuff at the back. When I built my new shop, I made the benches only 24 inches deep.

Then there's the vise. You do not need great precision in a vise, but you do need strength, weight and size. Buy a vise that has at least 4 inches of jaw width and opens at least 4 inches. It's better to have 5 inches on each dimension, but anything more than 6 inches is probably too much. Your vise will have steel jaws. If you do not have some sort of padding, you will damage the gun with the jaws. On some parts the marks will not matter, and on others you won't be clamping hard enough to make a difference. As an example, when you go to bend over a bolt handle on a surplus Mauser, you can

be a real drag. It could become such a drag that you may neglect cleaning a rifle when you know it needs it, and your match scores or hunting trip may suffer. Or, because of the hassle of taking it upstairs, you may leave the rifle on the workbench, open to the view and admiration of your guests or the furnace repair guy. Keep the bench close to the safe and put your rifles away. Build a sturdy bench constructed

The bench is the right height for me (34 inches) and the vise has a post under it for additional support. The reloading components underneath keep the bench from moving.

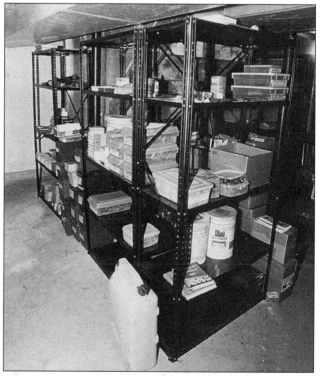

If you have room for them, there is no such thing as too many shelves. Unless you are a pessimist, and feel that empty shelves act to attract clutter.

Basements can be warm and useful work spaces. Tall people should be careful of low beams.

clamp the bolt body in the steel jaws. The bolt is hard enough, and you will not be clamping tightly enough, to mark the bolt. But when you go to clamp the barrel so you can do some work on the trigger, if you do not pad the vise jaws you'll mar the barrel. For padding, you can buy or make copper or lead sheeting as vise jaw covers. An even softer padding method is to use multiple layers of shop cloths. Use only clean and new cloths. If you use a cloth that has been used to wipe off filings or lapping compound, you can find the impression of the filings pressed into your barrel. The cloth pads cannot be used when you are soldering, or when you will be doing energetic work on the rifle. The padding is slightly slippery, and if you work too hard on a rifle padded by cloths, you might loosen it from the vise.

The bench should have storage room built in, on or around it. The storage can be shelves or drawers and cabinets. Store items according to their weight. The heavier it is, the closer to the floor it stays. Do not store objects heavy enough to hurt you higher than chest high. There is a reason your local gym uses racks for their dumbells and free weights that are waist high. Also, do not store chemicals over delicate objects. A leaking bottle of bore solvent or stock dye could ruin a rifle you have worked on for months.

The bench height depends on your height. If you can, before you build a bench, work on tabletops or workbenches of various heights. If you find one that you can work at without bending over, or lifting your hands too high, measure it and duplicate its height. To get a rough idea of bench height, stand next to one with your arm at your side. If the top of the bench is just higher than your wrist, it will be close to the correct height.

In addition to being sturdily-constructed, a good bench has to be heavy. A sturdy but light bench will walk around the room with you if you try to do any heavy work on it. The easiest way I have found to keep a bench in place is with reloading components. A well-built bench with a layer of bullets on the bottom shelf will not go anywhere when you apply torque to the vise. Professional gunsmiths go a step further. My friend Andy Manson of Mountaindog Gunsmithing gave up on benches for his barrel vise. Instead of a bench, he put anchor bolts into the slab of his shop. He then bolted a section of I-beam to the slab, and bolted his barrel vise to the top of the I-beam. If you are going to be replacing a truckload of barrels every year as he does, then you might consider his method.

Install good lighting overhead. Fluorescent fixtures are inexpensive and easy to install. They are cool in operation and will

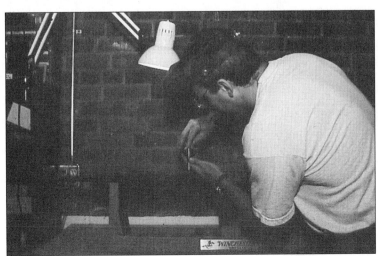

A flexible desk lamp is very useful in getting light to where you need it. Buy several (they're cheap) and clamp them to the bench where and when you need them.

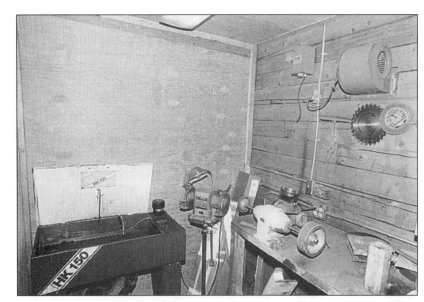

Proper ventilation is a must. The blower on the wall of this shop pumps the smell of the cleaning tank outside.

give you large amounts of even lighting. What fluorescent lights don't like is cold. If your work area will be cold most of the time you aren't in it, you may find your lights buzzing and flickering until you warm the space up. You should have desk lamps with a flexible arm attached to the bench. No matter how bright or even your fluorescent lighting is, you will need to direct light into a job, or into your own shadow from the overheads. A desk lamp does this perfectly. Desk lamps are hot, and will be close to you. Keep flammable items away from them.

An aside on warmth for your space: My first home workshop was in the basement. The old-style low efficiency furnace kicked out enough excess heat in the basement that the tools and I were both warm. I have talked to people with newer, high-efficiency furnaces that do not create excess heat. A cold basement becomes a damp basement (unless you live in Arizona). Dampness is bad. The commercial workshops were both heated and air-conditioned, and the tools led a better life in the summer than I did. The second and the current home workshops were both in block buildings and partly below grade. Both are/were cold. To keep the temperature up to comfortable in the winter I needed an extra source of heat. Since my workshop is also my reload-

ing room, I didn't want anything with an open flame or red-hot electrical heating elements. I use an oil-filled radiant heater. Portable and compact, I don't have to worry about flammable objects or chemicals being ignited by the heater. It puts out plenty of heat, and I can move it around the shop to keep near me while I work on a particular task.

And last, but not least, you must have ventilation. Some bore cleaners have a strong odor to them. Being trapped in a small windowless room with a dozen solvent-soaked cleaning patches can make you dizzy. Opening the door can present problems. If the door leads to the rest of the house, your housemate may rightly object to the odor. If the door leads outside, you may let in unwanted visitors, or get unwanted attention. One of the members of my gun club found the police intensely interested in his activities after he went out onto the porch to spray out his shotgun barrel. He did not have the entire shotgun, but a neighbor called and he got a visit. This is a conversation you do not want to duplicate.

A small window to the outside, covered to block prying eyes, and small enough to prevent entry, will do nicely In a garage, a pair of ventilation fans can serve the same purpose. Arrange the fans so one sucks fresh air in, while the other

Jeff Chudwin blasting away at bowling pins. His rifle and all his ammo came out of a tiny room in his house. Small shops work, if you are clean and efficient.

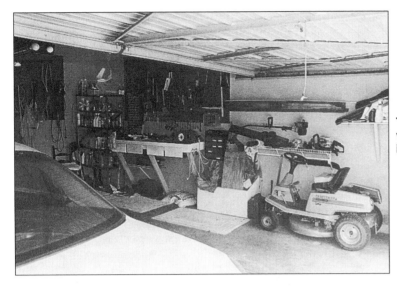

The problem with garages is they are open to view, and they usually have those pesky cars in them, dripping water from rain and snow.

exhausts to the outside. Install them at least ten feet apart, and do your cleaning in between them. You may be cold in the winter, but you can breath fresh air while you quickly clean.

But where to put all this? If you have it, you can turn a spare bedroom into an exemplary gun room. One of the finest rifle shots I have ever competed against, Jeffrey Chudwin, for years did all of his rifle work and his loading in a spare room in his house that measured 8 feet by 12 feet (the room, not the house). In the room he had a loading bench, a workbench, a gun safe and floor-to-ceiling shelves and drawers. When he moved, he built a much larger room for his loading and gunsmithing work, but he won many prizes at bowling pin matches from his work in that monk's cell of a gun room. Converting a spare room on the ground floor calls for curtains and bars on the window. You don't want people to see in and be tempted, and you don't want that to be the easy window to break into. A second-story window is less of a problem, but requires a second-story room.

What if you don't have a spare room? A garage will do, but you must be careful. Garages can be cold and damp. A snow-covered car parked in the garage will quickly overwhelm a safe full of desiccant cans, exposing your rifles to moisture. Also, garages are open to view every time you drive in and out. If you build your workbench in the garage or leave your safe there,

find a way to hide them. Build French doors or a sliding panel to hide the safe, and do not leave anything in view on your workbench that is obviously gun-related. There is one small problem to having your workshop in the garage. If you also use the garage for other things, are the extra tools sitting around? A gun safe is difficult to open, but the crowbars and auto jack you have under the other workbench make opening it a lot easier. If you have tools that might be used to open your gun safe, lock them up in another cabinet.

If using the garage as your gun room, the garage door itself must be secured. If you have a remote door opener, be sure it uses a coded signal to prevent opening by someone with the same brand opener. If you do not have an automatic opener keep your door locked, not just closed.

Basements are another popular choice. A basement can be warm, dry and secure. With the furnace in the basement, excess heat from the furnace ensures a warm basement. Dryness is a matter of good drainage. Basements can be damp. A solution not available to the garage workshop is to install a de-humidifier. With a hose to a floor drain this will not only keep your rifle dry, it will keep mold and mildew off of anything else in the basement, and keep the house drier as well. Another option is to use bags of reversible desiccant. These absorb moisture from

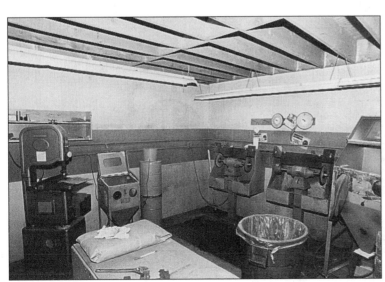

Luckily the rafters here are high enough that even a tall riflesmith can't hit his head. Not all basements are like this, so be careful.

If you find a range that has everything you need, don't mess up a good deal by breaking the rules. This steel target is not supposed to be shot with rifles. Doing so will get you thrown out of the club.

the air. Once they become saturated you steam the water out by cooking the bags in your microwave or regular oven. Once dried, you put them back to repeat the cycle.

You should take mildew seriously. I once stored a bunch of gear, parts and equipment in an unheated storage space. Some of the leather and most of the stocks showed spots of

mildew on them. It took several evenings of scrubbing to be sure I had gotten all of it cleaned up. If you toss your rifle into the safe after a season of hunting, and don't pull it out until after the bowl games are over, you may be shocked and saddened at how it looks when you drag it out.

Burglars do not like going into basements, because there is only one way in or out. They do not like the feeling of being trapped. If you install a lock on the basement door, your rifles in their safe will be behind three locked doors. It takes time to get through three locks. Few burglars like to spend that much time to get their hands on loot. Down in the basement, a gun safe is unlikely to be hauled off for later opening. It would be too heavy and awkward to haul up the stairs, even if you neglected to bolt it to something solid.

One last thing about elbow room for rifles: As well as taking up more room for storage and cleaning, they require more room for practice. If you have been shooting at a shotgun club, or an indoor range for handgun practice, you may have to find another range at which to practice with your rifle. While a line of skeet or trap shooters may only need a few hundred yards downrange for safety, rifles need more. The backstop on an indoor range that easily handles target loads from handguns would be wrecked in short order by even moderate rifle calibers such as the .30-30.

Many private clubs do not advertise or even make themselves easy to find. You may have to search to find a place where you can shoot to your heart's content, or even shoot regularly. As for practicing long-range shooting for your upcoming elk hunt, there may only be a few places in your home state where you can shoot past 100 yards. When you find such a place, be polite and follow the rules or you may not be invited back. Rare commodities often come with high price tags.

Once you have a place to work, you need to gain or improve your skills. Do not start out practicing on your best rifle. Buy a practice rifle, or practice parts. I realize that in some jurisdictions buying an extra rifle may be time- and cost-prohibitive. If you don't have that choice, then buy parts. Buy a worn-out barrel or a used stock, and practice on those.

If buying a practice rifle is not a hassle, then head right out and buy yourself a surplus Mauser. I went out during the production of this book and purchased a pair of 98K Mausers for $60 each. The bores are dark and pitted, but I didn't buy them to shoot them just as they were. For my

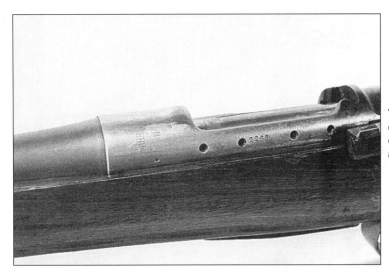

This tired old Mauser is a perfect practice rifle candidate. You can experiment to your heart's content, knowing you'll never be tempted to actually go and shoot it.

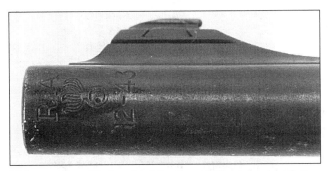

This practice rifle has had the barrel shortened and re-crowned, and the front sight moved back. It was a very good 1943 production 03-A3 Springfield barrel until someone let it rust out.

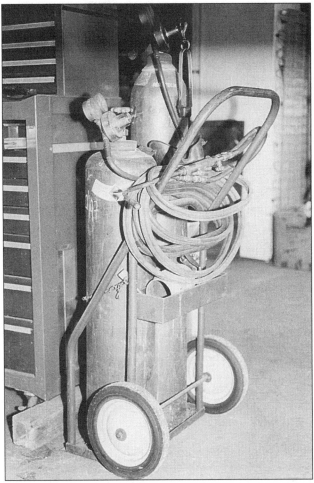

If you want to learn how to use this oxy-acetylene setup, enroll in the local community college metal shop. First learn if you have the touch, and if you do then invest the money in a good rig.

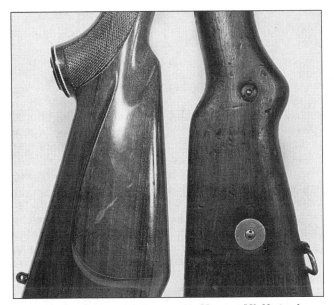

Before you start practicing on the Mauser Mk X stock on the left, practice on the surplus stock on the right.

investment, I can experiment all I want, knowing that I am not risking either a large financial investment or a treasured family memento. You can do the same.

What to practice? On the barrel alone, you can shorten and re-crown the muzzle many times before you even get close enough to worry about making it too short. When being short gets to be a worry, remove the barrel from the receiver and use it for lathe practice. Silver-soldering is a skill that takes some practice and a light touch. You can solder the barrel repeatedly and not worry about looks. You can repeatedly solder the same part, practicing over and over. If you do not use enough heat and the part falls off, then try

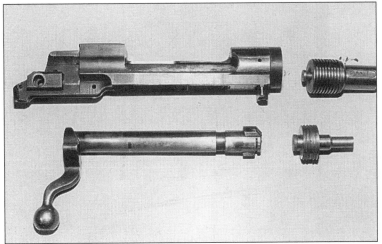

If the action is in good shape, go gently on it when you practice. After all, it is what you attach everything else to in order to make a rifle. You can use it to make another one.

It takes a delicate touch to weld like this without harming the bore. "On the job training" can get expensive if you have to scrap good barrels learning the touch.

again. If you accidentally heat the barrel too much, learn from the experience without cringing at the thought of a good barrel toasted from too much soldering. Practice your steel filing and polishing on the barrel. Even practice checkering on what's left of the barrel.

One of the touchiest tasks on a barrel is drilling and tapping it for sights. If you want to put sights on your hunting rifle, practice putting them on your surplus Mauser. Drill the barrel until the sight is straight. Seven holes? So what? Measure the depth of each to be sure you have left a safety margin and not drilled into the bore.

The stock offers an opportunity to learn many things. First, get the old oil and grease out of the wood. Then sand the stock and raise the dents. Re-finish the stock using one product on one side and another, different one on the other side. Drill and tap the stock for seven or 10 sling swivel studs. Practice until your studs are installed straight up and down. Who cares if the stock has so many holes in it that it looks like a wooden replica of Swiss cheese?

After all this you still have a stock on which you can practice your glass-bedding. Bed the rifle, then grind out the bed-

ding and do it again. Drill the action screw holes out and pillar bed the rifle.

Treat the action gentler than the barrel and stock. After all, you can build the action up into a rifle again. With the barrel in or out, drill and tap the receiver for a scope mount. Take your hand-held grinder and a cut-off wheel and modify the bolt handle to turn the handle down. The actual welding should be done by a professional, but you can do all the preparatory work.

With no barrel in the action, you can experiment on the trigger pull all you want. After all, how can you accidentally shoot your calendar if there is no chamber for the round to rest in? What you will find on the Mauser is that there is no improving the factory military trigger. But by studying the trigger and playing with it you'll understand how the adjustments work on the replacement you'll put in later.

If you can't buy a whole rifle, then a stock and barrel will be enough. Again, practice often and don't sweat the occasional mistake.

One skill you should not worry about developing is welding. While welding is a very useful skill in itself, you will not need it very often in gunsmithing. Even as a pro-

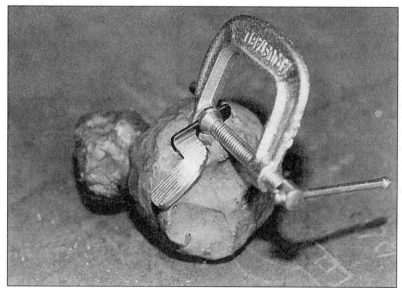

The local community college can also teach you tricks like this, using modeling clay to hold oddly-shaped parts together long enough to tack them before doing the final weld.

If you're serious about doing your 'smithing right, you can't know too much. Buy books. Read them. Knowledge is power, and an old trick can sometimes salvage a broken rifle.

fessional, unless you seek out the kind of work that requires welding, you won't need to do very much welding. But when you need it, nothing else will do. To learn how to weld, solder and braze, go to your local community college and sign up for a course in welding. While the local CC probably doesn't have any courses in gunsmithing, they will have courses in machine shop procedures, welding and soldering, and maybe even woodworking. Under the eye of an accomplished welder you will learn many valuable skills. Gaining the right touch in soldering can take quite a bit of trial and error. With an instructor looking over your shoulder you can learn faster and not pick up bad habits. Depending on the particular college's policy on home projects, you might even be able to bring some of your work in to use the school's torches on. I imagine the policy in Montana or New Mexico might be a bit more lenient than New York or California.

Also, by learning the basics of welding, you'll be better able to describe what you want done when you describe the welding you need to a professional welder.

With the school's mills, lathes and drill presses to work on, you can both gain useful skills and get an idea of the machines themselves. If you think you might want to invest in power tools, you can gauge how often you might need them, and what size to go with, from your use of the school machines.

While sanding a bookcase is not nearly as involved as sanding a rifle stock, the basics are the same. At the CC classes you will learn the look and feel of various finishes and woods, and again learn under the eye of an experienced woodworker.

For specific gunsmithing skills, you need to either get more books on gunsmithing, or attend classes. Krause Publications has a number of gunsmithing titles available. Books are an often overlooked resource. I have been involved with guns most of my life, and have been a gunsmith for myself or as a professional for more than 20 years. I have more books than guns, and I have a shop full of guns. If you are wandering a gun show and see a book that looks interesting or has information on a rifle of interest to you, buy it. You will not be disappointed.

For gunsmithing classes, you can contact the NRA about their classes. Or, the next time you order a part or a new catalog from Brownells, you'll get the NRA schedule.

The Brownells catalog is the greatest boon to mankind since....since... well, ever. If you can't find it in Brownells you'll probably have to make it for yourself. You can learn many useful tricks from the AGA, and by joining you can get insurance if you plan to start doing work for other people.

The NRA classes, and others like them, are usually a week-long affair. I look at it as a vacation, with benefits. If you went on a cruise, or traveled to a theme park, or went to Vegas the time spent would be the same. The cost for the gunsmithing class would be less (a lot less than Vegas, unless your card skills are VERY good!) and you don't have to worry about sunburn or seasickness. At this time, the NRA classes run from $125 to $325 for the class, plus travel and accommodations.

If you want more than just some of the skills then you'll have to get a degree in gunsmithing. One method that used to be more common was to apprentice as a gunsmith. The apprentice method tended to be less expensive (you were either working for free, or making a small wage, instead of paying for tuition) and could be more specific. The advantages to a degree in gunsmithing are several: You'll be instructed on correct business practices, the lack of which is a common failing for beginning 'smiths, and you will be forced to try things you might not have had an interest in. As an example, I know one gunsmith who didn't have any interest in stocks, he only wanted to do metalwork. It turns out he has "the touch" for wood, and now makes more money on stocks than on metal.

If you are planning on getting a degree as the first step to becoming a professional, then you need to contact Yavapai College, the Colorado School of Trades, Lassen Community College or Montgomery Community College.

The money will be well-spent and you will learn many useful things. As a last consideration, the Armed Forces can be a means to your ends. The drawbacks are severe, but the payoff can be great. The limits to using Uncle Sam are simple: You may not get the job you want. While your recruiter can promise you a slot in an armorer's program, if the service you signed up for decides they need your services as a cook at a radar installation on the Arctic Circle, then you'd better pack your long johns. Also, you will learn the skills needed to work on a limited selection of firearms, and not all of those skills may be used in the civilian world. After all, how many belt-fed machine guns are you likely to work on after your stint in the military? However, if you do get an armorer's slot, when you get out you'll have your enlistment bonus and college bonus money to live on while you get a degree in gunsmithing. As a vet with a degree, you will be sought-after by many.

Whatever path you take, good luck in furthering your education, and I know you'll have fun in the years to come.

CHAPTER 3

Tools

Once you have a space where you can do your riflesmithing you will need tools. Even the simplest work will require more than just your bare hands.

But what will you need? The most important tools will be a set of screwdrivers. Screwdrivers are so important that professional gunsmiths make their own, and will grind a set for each type of firearm they work on. With very few exceptions your rifle is held together by screws. Almost everything attached to your rifle will be held on with screws. For disassembly and cleaning you will need screwdrivers to remove the action from the stock. You will need screwdrivers to attach or remove a scope, or even adjust the iron sights. Screwdrivers that are the wrong size or fit the screw slot poorly will mess up the heads of the screws. The term I use is "knarfed." I had occasion to work on customers' rifles that had been attacked so many times with poorly-fitting screwdrivers that the knarfed heads of the screws had been turned up to sharp edges. The edges could cut my hands if I was not careful. On rare or old rifles I would repair the slot and try to bring it back to looking new. For many rifles the solution was to replace the screws. Do not knarf the screws on your rifle.

A first-class screwdriver set is cheap compared to the cost of replacing knarfed screws, or getting your rifle re-blued because the screwdriver slipped and gouged a line across the action and scope. Even in the biggest screwdriver set not all of the screw bits will be a perfect fit. If you have to modify a particular tip to make it fit properly, do so. Use a file or bench grinder. If you use the bench grinder, go slowly to avoid overheating the tip and drawing the temper out of it. You want your bits to be (and remain) hard.

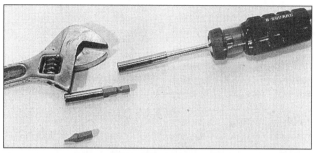

One very useful part of the B-Square screwdriver set is the wrench extender. Stick the extender in the handle, and the tip in the extender. You can now clamp the wrench on the hex shaft of the extender and get more leverage.

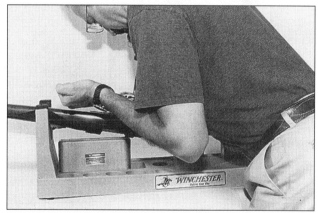

By leaning on the handle and using the wrench to turn the shaft, even stubborn screws can be turned. If this isn't enough, break out the frozen screw jack.

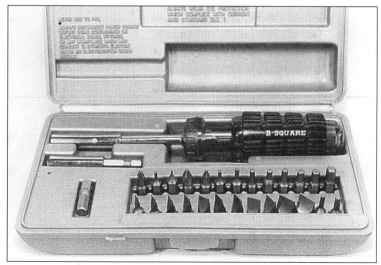

Buy a good set of proper gunsmithing screwdrivers. Treat them well and you'll get good use out of them for many years. Abuse them and your rifles will end up with knarfed screw slots.

Not all rifle screws are slot-head screws. Some are Allen-head. You'll need English Allen wrenches to remove these screws. Many rifles are now coming right from the factory with Allen-head screws, get used to it.

Brownells d'Solve is a water-based cleaning concentrate that doesn't have the unpleasant odor of mineral spirits.

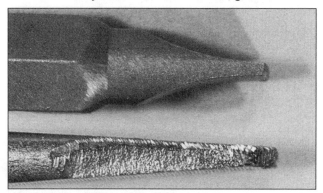

The household screwdriver on the bottom tapers to its tip, so it "fits" all screw slots. It fits them all poorly, that is. The hollow-ground firearms screwdriver on the top will fit only one slot, but it won't mar the slot removing the screw.

If you have a rifle held in its stock by bolts with Allen heads instead of screws with slots, then you'll need Allen wrenches. Shooters who specialize in accuracy and accurate rifles use a torque wrench to tighten the Allen bolts. If you have just invested a couple of thousand dollars for a super-accurate rifle, the investment in a torque wrench is small and worth the price.

The screwdrivers you have around the house are different than screwdrivers designed for use on firearms and you should not use these in your gunsmithing. The household screwdrivers are too thick at the tip, are made too soft for firearms work, and the tip of the blade tapers. Instead of the taper-ground tips, you need screwdrivers that are "hollow-ground." The sides of the blade will be parallel at the tip. The taper-ground tip will lever itself out of the slot, or worse yet, deform the top edges of the screw slot. You can grind or file the tip narrower and parallel, but then the soft metal will deform under the load of firearms work. Buy the real deal, and get gunsmithing screwdrivers.

After you have gotten the neat-o screwdriver set, you have to get the boring, everyday stuff. The stuff to clean your rifle with, and the explanation of how to take it apart. Cleaning solvents come first, and you'll need both bore solvents and a general cleaning solvent. Along with the sol-

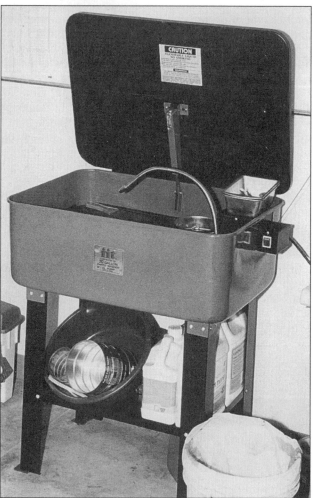

Through some miracle, this parts washer is not in the center of a splattered mess of crusted oils and greases, and powder residue. (It must be brand-new.)

vents, you'll need a tray, pan or tank to clean in. The pros used a parts cleaning tank, but you can get by for a long time with some flat trays and a utility sink such as the concrete one in your laundry room. To clean, you'll need brushes. The bore needs specialized brushes, but the rest of the rifle can be cleaned with a military M-16 brush. In a

Disposable paper cleaning and wiping rags are very handy, and you don't have to worry about contaminating your washing machine trying to clean cloth rags. The "Nubtex" are printing wipes, very absorbent, and the "Wypall" comes from my local Industries for the Blind. Both work well.

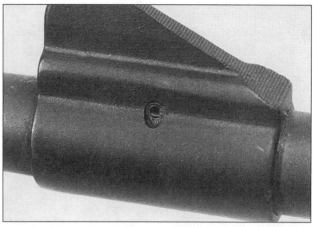

The roll pin on the Ruger can be removed with a standard drift punch, if it fits correctly. If you are not willing to grind a punch to the exact size, use a domed roll pin removal drift punch.

pinch you can use old toothbrushes, but once you've used them on rifles, they are no good for teeth. Along with brushes you'll need cleaning patches for the bore, wiping tools for the action, and wiping cloths for your hands. The patches and action rods are covered in Chapters Six and Seven, respectively. The hand towels can either be disposable paper towels, or "red rags," the standard shop cloth used in machine shops and by mechanics. Everything but the paper towels are available from Brownells, but if you shop at the local machine tool store you might save a dollar or two on the whole shebang.

New rifles will have an owner's manual for disassembly and cleaning. If you plan to disassemble more than one type of rifle, or you acquired your rifle without a manual, then get the NRA disassembly manual or the rifle disassembly book by J.B. Wood. If you've bought a used rifle that is still in production, you can write to the manufacturer and they will be more than happy to send you the owner's manual.

The next tools to obtain are a good dial caliper and a binocular visor. You will have to measure many things while gunsmithing, and a ruler just won't do. Do not try to take the cheap way out and get a plastic caliper. You need precision,

repeatability and durability. Digital is nice, but the old dial style works fine. A micrometer can measure many of the same things a dial caliper can, but it will not span more than an inch. A 5-inch caliper should be enough.

The binocular visor makes small work a great deal easier. It also saves your eyesight and reduces the chances of an error due to fatigue. Along with the binocular visor, get a flexible desk lamp. Rather than peering and squinting, get more light on a job and magnify it. You can do good work without the visor, but you'll do better work with it. You'll also reduce eyestrain, headaches and mistakes. My optometrist feels that I have delayed the onset of middle-aged vision changes by spending so much of my time at the workbench with a visor on, saving my eyes the strain.

Parts not attached to your rifle with screws may be pinned on. A pinned part has a hole drilled through the part and the rifle where the two join. A tightly fitting steel rod is pressed through this hole, fastening the two together. Pinning is commonly done along with some other mechanical attachment, such as a dovetail or slip-over fit. Two examples of this would be the attachment of the stripper clip guide on a Springfield M1A, and the Choate front sight installation

In addition to Brownells for current parts and tools, you'll need a source for used parts and obsolete or out of production rifles. Gun Parts is in West Hurley, NY, and Jack First is in South Dakota.

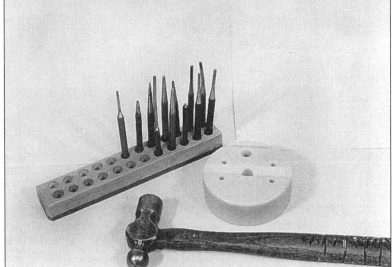

Rather than let your drift punches rattle around in a box or a drawer, keep them so you can see what each one is.

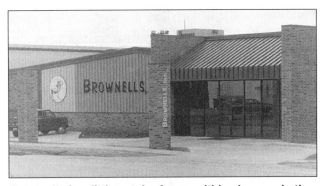

Brownells is a little patch of gunsmithing heaven in the middle of Iowa. If you're driving by Montezuma, drop in and prepare to be amazed.

The B-Square sight pusher is a neat tool both in the shop and the range. It allows you to make small and precise adjustments to a front sight, and to remove one without whacking it with a hammer and drift punch.

The bottom punch is a drift punch. The middle one is a center punch, for marking the location of holes to be drilled. The top one is a tapered punch, for starting stubborn pins.

on a Ruger Mini-14. Or, the pin may be held in place by spring tension and retaining grooves, such as the trigger assembly of an AR-15. To remove such pins you will need drift punches. You will need a selection of sizes. You obviously cannot use a drift punch larger than the pin you are removing. It won't fit in the hole. Less obviously, you cannot use a drift punch that is too much undersized. If you try, you will mar the head of the pin. If the pin is pressed securely in place, you may bend or break a drift punch that is too small.

Flip open your Brownells catalog and get the basic drift punch set. Be sure to buy one or two tapered punches. Use the tapered punch to start moving a pin. A tapered punch is stiffer than a punch of the same tip diameter and will not bend. Once the pin is moved by the first hammer blow switch to a drift punch slightly smaller in diameter than the pin, and tap the pin out. You can also use drift punches to press a sight into or out of its dovetail. The punch set and the tapered punches will be made of steel. If you use a steel punch to drift a front sight blade you will mar the sight. To avoid marring without buying a sight pusher buy a brass drift. This is a section of 1/4-inch or 3/8-inch brass rod that is long enough to grasp and strike with a hammer. Some gunsmiths like to use a brass rod with a nylon tip, or a nylon

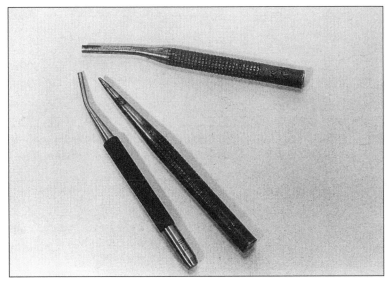

Save your bent drift punches. Not because you can straighten them (you can't, and keep them truly straight) but they are a source of taper punches. straighten the bent punch as best you can, and then use a bench grinder to make a taper punch out of it.

rod. I have found that the all-nylon drifts flex too much. And the nylon-tipped ones get chewed up by the dovetails. A brass drift that gets chewed on by a dovetail can be peened back into shape. A section of brass rod is cheaper than a sight pusher. What the expense of a sight pusher such as the B-Square gives you is better control, and freedom from the vise. With the pusher you can make delicate adjustments to your sights at the range. With a hammer and drift punch you may have to drift and try several times to get the sight just right. If you try to drift a front sight without supporting the base, you could bend or break the base. To support it you need a vise. The sight pusher braces itself against the sight base and prevents the possibility of breaking the base or base screws.

To drive these punches you need a hammer. I use a small ball-peen hammer in my range bag as part of my emergency kit. For bench work I use a medium ball-peen hammer. When you are moving a pin, you need mass, not velocity. If a pin does not move when I first try to drift it out, I do not swing the hammer harder. I get a heavier one. Professionals keep a selection of hammers, some as big as 2 pounds. However, they will have to move anything that comes in the front door. You do not. If you cannot remove a drift pin with

a correctly-fitting punch and an 8- or 12-ounce ball-peen hammer, take the stubborn rascal to a professional.

The file has been referred to many times as a hand-held milling machine. A file is a stick of very hard steel that has cutting teeth formed on one or more sides. A side without cutting teeth is called a "safe edge." In earlier times, an aspir-

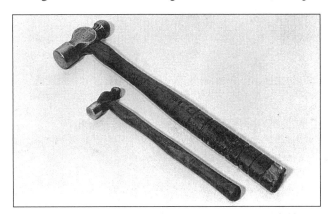

The small hammer can be useful, but the most useful hammer I own is a 12-ounce ball-peen hammer. If it won't move to the 12, don't hit it harder, get a bigger hammer.

The file is a must. Small files for small jobs, big files for big jobs, and always the best you can buy. The small specks are pins that have to be carded out or they will mar the work.

Brownells is so large you could get lost in it. This is one aisle of one building, and it has tens of thousands of parts. The nearest shelf is full of gunsmithing books, one title in each stack.

ing gunsmith was expected to be able to shape all manner of firearms parts from raw stock, using only a file. British gunsmiths still shape the receivers of shotguns with files, and probably will continue doing so until there are no shotguns in Britain. They are an odd lot. One example of the requirements demanded of the British gunsmithing trade is the cube. An aspiring gunsmith is handed a lump of steel and told, "File it to a 1-inch cube." Once turned in for measurement, the cube is expected to measure 1.00 inches in every dimension. You will not need to make parts from scratch, and will not need the large files with coarse teeth (called "cuts") used in parts shaping. What you will need are files in medium and fine cuts, in handy sizes. I found that most of my work could be done with a file in the Swiss #2 cut, which corresponds to the American Smooth Cut. Such a file was aggressive enough that I could remove stock quickly if I had to, while being fine enough to be a finished surface for a lot of jobs. If I needed a finer finished cut, I would pull out a Swiss #4, or use an old file as a backer to emery cloth.

The single file I use most often comes from Brownells. It is an extra-narrow pillar file, 8 inches long in the Swiss #2 cut. It is handy enough to fit almost anywhere you need to file. It is sharp enough to cut hard steel, although no file likes doing that. And it is large enough that I can get a good grip on it. The extra narrow pillar file has two safe edges opposite each other. If you are filing a slot, you will not cut the sides of the slot using this file. The only drawback is that it is slightly flexible. If pressed too hard it will bend, and the resulting cut will be round and not flat. You should have this file if you are serious about doing good work. A good companion to this file is a larger one, a 10-inch American pattern Second cut. It is more coarse than the pillar file. Larger and stiffer, it will not bend under a load. If you need to do large amounts of filing, this one will be up to the task. If you want to polish a surface flat, then use this file as a backer to emery cloth, and your surface will not be rippled or wavy.

Next on your "to-get" list of files is a set of needle files. These are short little files that get into places where big ones can't reach. You'll use them to fit small parts, and do not need to remove large amounts of metal. Get your needle files in a kit, and in a fine cut.

If you are going to install sights you will need a three-sided file. It must have at least one safe edge.

Buy handles for your files. A handle is not only a safer way to hold a file, it also increases your control, reduces fatigue and gives you a place to hang onto for file cleaning.

To maintain your files you will need file chalk and a file card. The little bits of metal cut off of the main piece by your file (called "filings") will not always fall off of the file. They may stick in the teeth of the file. A filing stuck in the teeth of a file is called a "pin." The pin decreases the cutting surface available to you, and mars the work. If you push a file that has a pin in it across your work, the pin will gouge a line on the surface. A file loaded with pins will not cut at all, as the file is held away from the metal by those same pins. The chalk reduces the number of pins but does not eliminate them. File the piece of chalk to fill the teeth with chalk. Then file the metal. When you inspect the file, pick individual pins out with a sharp wire. If you get a number of pins, card the pins out and re-chalk.

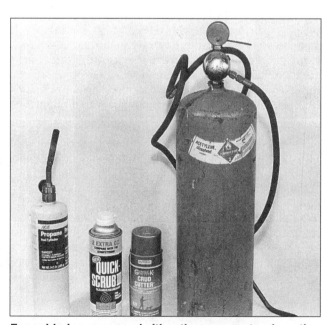

For soldering, you need either the propane torch on the left or the acetylene tank on the right. The degreasers in the middle ensure a good bond between the solder and the metal.

The pressurized tanks used in oxy-acetylene welding are hazardous, and must be secured to a cart or post. Incredibly flammable and under high pressure, they can become bombs or projectiles if not treated correctly.

To file with a large file, grasp the handle with one hand and the tip with the other. Place the file against the work at the correct angle. Check the location and angle, then press down and push forward.

Files do not cut in both directions. They only cut on the push stroke. Pick the file up, pull it back to the start position, place it down and repeat. If you pull the file back across the work you will not cut the metal, but you will prematurely dull the file. Every couple of passes, inspect the work to make sure you are filing where you want to be filing, and at the correct angle. Also inspect the file for pins. I would tap the tip of the file against the anvil of my vise to dislodge the filings. It would also knock chalk out of the file. When the chalk got low, I would inspect for pins and re-chalk. Filing is a messy operation, and you should sweep and vacuum afterwards to keep from tracking the filings and chalk into the house. Filing wood does not create pins. The teeth will become loaded with wood quickly, and will need carding more often. Aluminum is a soft metal, and will load a file with pins quickly. When filing aluminum you may well spend more time cleaning the file than in the filing itself.

For a finer cut on steel than a file can give you, you need to use a stone. Not just any piece of rock picked up from the

parking lot, but a particular bit of rock. The stones used in stoning are graded according to the fineness of their grit. They also come in two types, natural and synthetic. While all stones are fragile and should be treated with care, natural stones tend to be more brittle than synthetics and more likely to break if abused. Natural stones require oil as a cutting lubricant and cleaning solution, while synthetics use water as a lubricant and soap and water to clean up. The natural stones are dug out of quarries. The best stones here in

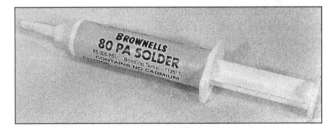

Silver solder has a higher strength than lead solder, but requires more heat to flow. The syringe from Brownells contains a paste of solder and flux. By squeezing out a small amount right onto the surface to be soldered you can easily heat and bond the parts involved.

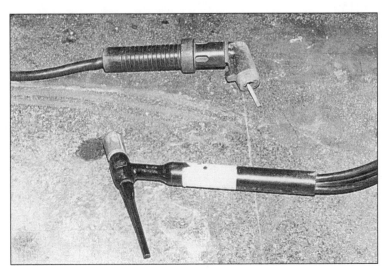

Different welding methods require different torches, and different techniques.

Soldering this extension onto the barrel at the temperatures required by law risks damaging the barrel. Welding is the preferred method.

Once everything is in place, and has been checked several times, only then can the welder drop his mask.....

And attach the extension.

the U.S. came from pits in the state of Arkansas. Coincidentally, they are called Arkansas stones, or hard Arkansas. Another grade of stone is found as a medium grit, and called the India stone. They are more useful for the professional, who is faced with a wide variety of gunsmithing problems.

For stoning parts you do not need a stone more coarse than your finest file. As a result, you should buy hand-held stones only in Fine or Extra Fine grit. If you will be inletting stocks you'll need to sharpen your chisels and scrapers. To sharpen the stock inletting tools you should buy larger stones in medium grit. Your minimum supply should include two stones, both synthetic. Buy the Brownells 6-inch ceramic stones that are already ground square. They are color-coded, with the medium-fine one being black and the extra-fine one white. For the inletting chisels, get a Medium Arkansas Bench stone. Once you have re-sharpened the cutting edge of your chisel or gouge with the bench stone, finish the job with the hand-held stone.

This welding machine is a TIG welder, and uses a tank of inert gas to protect the bead from atmospheric oxygen.

With the cover open we see the spool of welding wire which is automatically fed through the welding gun. A welding machine like this makes the job easy, but the cost is prohibitive for the home gunsmith.

The final polish on metal or wood is accomplished with sandpaper. The sandpaper can be paper backed or cloth backed. Once you have used a piece of sandpaper for either wood or metal, do not use it for the other. Switching from metal to wood will leave bits of metal in the wood. Going from wood to metal won't be a problem, at least not until you switch back. I keep my fresh paper in the drawer, and once a piece has been used on wood or steel I then drop it into a plastic storage box marked "steel" or "wood." A good basic grit that you should have a ready supply of is 200- or 220-grit paper. As a gunsmith working six days a week at a commercial location, I would go through a 50-yard roll of Brownells Metalite cloth-backed sandpaper in less than a year. I always kept a fresh roll on hand, and ordered a new one when I opened the last roll. I once went through a full roll just in the pre-hunting season rush.

For a finer finish you will need sheets or rolls of 320-, 400-, 500- and 600-grit paper or cloth. You will not need a 50-yard roll of each. Sanding is best done "wet." The solution keeps dust down, and also keeps the abrasive on the part being sanded. Without a wetting agent, the abrasive rubs off, falls away, and you are left with a non-abrasive polishing cloth in your hands. For sanding steel, I use mineral spirits. The mineral spirits are a common cleaning solvent, and easily obtained and used. For wood, you need to

A bare wood bench top will absorb spills. Some sort of sealant will protect the wood and make cleanup of spills easy.

use other solutions, depending on where you are in the stock finishing process. More on that in Chapter Ten.

If you plan to do any soldering at all, you will need a propane torch. Better yet, two of them. Some soldering jobs need large amounts of evenly-distributed heat. Switching back and forth from one side to another of a job is not enough heat, and not in an even enough distribution. The "Bernz-o-matic" torches available at your local hardware store are fine for most of the soldering you will be doing. If you need a higher temperature (unlikely) or a large volume of heat, then you'll need to look into a acetylene torch. Do not confuse this with an oxy-acetylene torch. The "oxy" means that you have two tanks, one of oxygen, and one of acetylene. The O-A torch is used for welding. The acetylene torch uses air as a source of oxygen to burn. It is not as hot as the O-A used for welding. The acetylene tank is usually larger than a propane torch and, combined with a larger nozzle, lets you put out more heat than the propane torch. If you are soldering large objects, you'll need the acetylene torch. Regular lead solder melts at temperatures of less than 500 degrees. It is very convenient to work with and the low temperature will not damage other parts, or even bluing if you are careful. However, lead solder has drawbacks. It has a low tensile strength, only around 4,000 pounds per square inch. That is, a properly soldered joint that is 1-inch square would require 4,000 pounds of force to pull apart. That may seem like a lot of force, but it is only a small fraction of the tensile strength of the steel which will withstand 150,000 to 180,000 pounds per square inch. Lead solder dissolves in the solutions used for bluing. If you drop a soft-soldered assembly into an acidic stripping tank or a caustic bluing tank, you will fish out a loose collection of parts. You will only encounter parts that are soft-soldered on in a few types of firearms. Old double-barrel shotguns are often soft-soldered assemblies. Older European rifles will have sights and ribs soldered on. If your father brought back a hunting rifle from Germany at the end of the war, don't let someone re-blue it without checking to see if the sights are soldered on.

To get more strength in solder you have to use solders composed of other metals. To get the highest strengths you need higher melting points. You need to use "silver solder," called such because of the high silver content. With silver solder you

Laminating sheets of plywood to your bench-top will improve it by making it heavier and stiffer.

can get tensile strengths up to 85,000 psi. Now you're up to half the strength of the steel itself. The low temperature silver solders such as Brownells Hi-Force 44 melt at 475 degrees, and have a tensile strength up to 28,000 psi. It does not dissolve in bluing tanks. The winner in strength is the 80PA Silver Braze from Brownells. Its tensile strength is 85,000 psi, but to get this you need a temperature of 1125 degrees. There are parts that you cannot subject to this temperature, and others that will require heat protection in order to solder.

Successful welding or the use of high-temperature solder can take more than a couple of propane torches, and a great deal of practice and experience. When we get to projects that require more than you can do, I suggest taking the job to a local welder with either firearms experience, or experience at welding small objects.

On welding: The oxy-acetylene torch uses a supply of pure oxygen in a separate tank to burn the acetylene. The torch generates a flame hot enough to melt steel. You should not be surprised at this, as welding is simply a controlled form of melting. In welding, the edges of the parts to be welded are pressed together, and then heated until they are at the melting point. A filler rod of similar material is fed

into the gap and melted to join the parts. The excess steel puddles on the top, forming a "bead" along the joint. To avoid undesired oxidation of the red-hot steel (called "scale") the rods are coated. As the coating is melted it forms a puddle of gas on the surface that protects the bead from atmospheric oxygen. Scale in the bead weakens the bond. Once cooled, the bead is ground flush with the rest of the part and then polished for re-blueing or plating. Without the bead the joint will be marred. As the welded joint cools it contracts. If you were somehow able to weld and leave the surface perfectly flush (a neat trick at 1300 degrees!) the contracting weld would leave the surface dished.

Welding requires a great deal of skill and practice. If you do not have the touch, you'll melt the parts you're trying to join. Even if you don't melt them, you might not get enough penetration on the joint, and only connect the parts at the surface. Welding must be done in a large, bare room to avoid starting a fire. The torch or electric arc is bright enough to blind, and cause sunburn. Welders wear goggles, a mask, apron, heavy shoes and long pants when working. The large bare room is cold in the winter, and the clothing is hot in the summer. The tanks themselves can be hazardous.

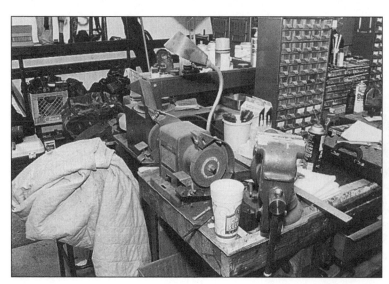

This bench grinder would be easier to use and more useful if it was not crowded by all the clutter. Keep your bench and its tools neat and free from clutter.

These two machines are an example of good machine layout. The belt sander on the left and the bench grinder on the right have plenty of light from the window and easy access. The light makes it easier for you to see the work, and the clear floor lets you stand at whatever angle you need to in order to use the machines.

The nearly-pure oxygen is kept at a high pressure, as much as 2,200 pounds per square inch. The threads in the fittings on the oxygen bottle must be kept clean of grease or oil. The oxygen is so pure and the pressure is so high that the grease or oil could spontaneously oxidize. Translation: The burning grease would quickly cause an explosion. The tanks have to be kept chained to a solid upright support. If the bottle should fall and the regulator gets broken off, the pressure would turn the bottle into a rocket. People have been seriously injured or killed by flying tanks. The acetylene must be treated carefully and its fittings maintained. Leaking acetylene can cause fires or explosions.

Electric welding rigs use a large electrical charge between the parts and the tip to heat the welded area. To avoid scale, electric welding uses an inert gas. Called "MIG or TIG", this method is preferred for rifle welding.

The flame of a welding torch or the arc from an electric welder creates a bright enough light that your eyesight can be damaged. You must wear goggles to weld. The arc of the electric welding rig creates enough ultraviolet light that you can become sunburned on exposed skin. Even in the summer time you must wear heavy clothing with long sleeves and long pants. Welders sweat buckets in the summer.

All of this is my way of saying you should not consider doing your own welding. Yes, introductory rigs can be cheap, and it may be fun to try your own welding, but.... you must practice on a regular basis to keep your skill, and you must practice on scrap or dedicated practice guns. And where will you find a large, bare concrete room devoted solely to your welding? If you think you want to do your own, then sign up at the local community college for a welding course and see if you like it.

When you need welding done to your firearms, call a few welders in town. Ask if they have welded on firearms, and if they do any work for gunsmiths in town. If not, then look for a welder who works on machine tools. He will be familiar with smaller parts, and hardened steels. If you have a choice, take the welder who does work on mills and lathes and their tools, rather than the one who welds on semi-trucks and trailers. They may both be good, but you want the guy who is practiced on small stuff, and is used to work that requires precision. Why the emphasis on smaller parts? To weld you have to pump a large amount of heat into a part, but no more than is needed. Excess heat fed into a small part can over-heat it and affect the temper. The fellow who welds onto a trailer is heating a "part" that weighs a ton

The three tap styles. The top one is a taper tap. The gentle angle of its tip allows easy starting in the hole. The middle is a bottoming tap, that taps right to the bottom of a blind (no exit) hole. The lower tap is a plug tap, and allows you to get the threading started when there isn't enough depth to let the tapered tap start biting.

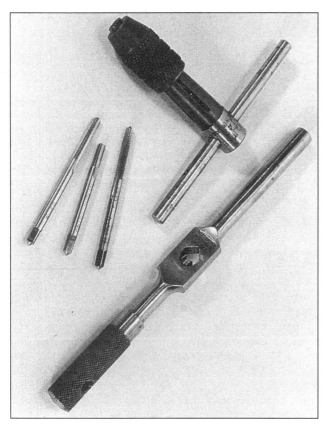

Taps require tap handles. Both styles work fine, and which you use is solely a matter of personal preference.

that were nearly large enough to act as a welcome mat for your front door. I picked up a few and used them as counter mats. Today the samples you are handed are no larger than your hand. No problem, Outers makes a synthetic pad that will keep your rifle off the benchtop. Get one and use it.

Two power tools that can be quite useful and not expensive to obtain are the bench grinder and drill press. While a bench grinder is heavy, noisy and dirty to operate, it does one thing well. It removes metal quickly. If you are going to have a bench grinder in your shop, you must have a shop larger than a broom closet. It must also be sound-proofed. Otherwise, when you are grinding on a screwdriver to shape it for a screw slot, you may not hear your housemate screaming at you to keep the noise down. If you track the metal grindings and the worn-off powder from the grinding wheel into the rest of the house you will find they are difficult to clean up. The drawbacks while using the bench grinder are heat and what I call the "oops" factor. If you grind too much, too fast, you will heat the part. This may draw the temper from it. If you are grinding a screwdriver tip and the tip changes color, turning bright blue, you have just drawn the hardness from the tip. The "oops" factor rears its ugly head when you decide to take one more pass to get the part just right, and then discover you have taken off too much. It is so easy to stop, measure and, if you have to, grind again, that it isn't worth it to forge on and find yourself muttering "oops." But if you want a tool that will remove metal fast, the bench grinder is for you.

The drill press is not nearly so noisy or messy as the bench grinder. If you want to drill holes for anything else besides sling swivels, you need a drill press. To drill properly you will need to equip the drill press with one or two machinists vises, and a couple of c-clamps large enough to hold the vise in place. If you are going to drill receivers and barrels, Forster makes a special fixture to hold a barrelled action. With this fixture you can drill all your holes in line with each other, on the centerline and straight up and down. B-Square makes a fixture just for drilling scope mount holes. If you will never drill a barrel for iron sights, the B-Square will suffice.

or more. Instead, go with the fellow who is used to heating the edge of a part that weighs a pound. Before I get accused of sexism, women can weld just as well as men, you just don't see as many of them in what is a hot, dirty job.

One last gadget to get is a guide for drilling stocks to install a sling swivel stud. The drilling itself is simple. The hard part is to get the holes in the right spot, and straight up and down. If you will be installing more than one set, do yourself a favor and get the B-Square swivel jig and drill set. I once drilled a stock without using my set. I was in a hurry, I couldn't find the set, so I just did it by eye. I came out darned close, but not perfect. Later, when I had some extra time I grabbed a broken stock from the scrap bin and drilled a dozen holes for practice and to test my eye. All of them were darned close, but not perfect. I grabbed another broken stock (professional gunsmiths collect a lot of that sort of thing) and used the jig for a dozen holes. They were all perfect. After that, I made sure I found the jig each time. Sure, you can do it by eye and probably get away with it. But if anything goes wrong, the time and cost you saved by not having the jig will not come close to repairing the mistake.

The bench top on which you work should be smooth and clean. Bare wood will absorb solvents, lubricants and other chemicals that are dropped or spilled. The minimum you should settle for is to paint the top. Better yet is to install some sort of countertop sheeting. In addition to the painted or laminated top, invest in a bench pad. The hard surface of your bench top will collect dust, dirt and grit, and should be wiped clean on a regular basis or you will scratch your rifle or stock. When I started gunsmithing, carpet stores provided samples

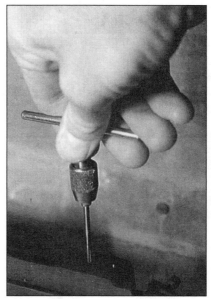

The rear scope mount holes pass through the receiver bridge. Use a taper or plug tap to clean these out. The front holes are blind holes, and you'll need the bottoming tap in order to do a proper scope mounting job.

A drill press needs drills to work. Eventually you'll need taps, too, but first the drills The drills you will need are the "number" drills. Drills come in four measuring patterns, Metric, fractional, letter and number. Metric and fractional are obvious. The letter and number drills use a letter or number designation to note the sometimes odd sizes that fall between the fractional sizes. For instance, a common drill for the gunsmith is a #31 drill. It measures .1200" in diameter. As a fraction, it would be an awkward designation of "5/40ths of an inch." Just call it #31.

Drills come in three materials, high-speed steel, TIN-coated (Titanium Nitride), and carbide. The cheapest are high speed steel. The HSS drill in a #31 size costs just under a dollar. The tin-coated one costs $3.50. I always spent the extra money. The carbide drill seems like the perfect all-around drill. It is super-hard and will go through anything. Save the carbide drills for special occasions. The cost for a #31 in carbide is $13.50, and if you abuse it you'll break it. Use the carbide drill only to punch through a case-hardened receiver. Then use a larger size for clearance or anneal the edge of the hole so you can tap it.

Speaking of taps, they come in three types, and the numbers that designate the taps do not correspond to the drills. The #31 drill we have been using as an example requires a 6-48 tap, pronounced "six-forty-eight". Taps come in taper, plug and bottoming shapes. The taper tap has a gentle start to the cutting threads, while the plug is more blunt. The bottoming tap has a single thread as its taper, so you can tap right to the bottom of a hole. If you are tapping a hole that goes through, such as a scope hole on the rear bridge, a taper tap will do. The scope hole on the front receiver must

As cool as a regular milling machine is, this gang-cut horizontal mill is really neat. But how often will you have to make the same milling cut on three rifles at the same time? However, note the coolant flowing over the cutters. Milling creates heat, and the heat can change the temper of small parts if you are not careful.

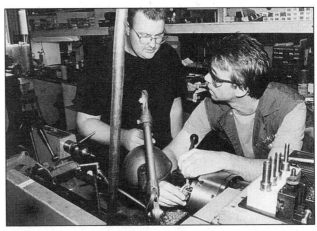

While a mill is a multi-purpose tool, lathes do one thing. What they do is precisely turn down the diameter of a cylindrical piece. They are not good at making the part larger. Measure your work frequently, and "sneak up" on the desired dimension.

have a plug and then bottoming tap. The taper tap won't reach to the bottom of the hole. Most pro gunsmiths do not buy bottoming taps. They make their bottoming taps from broken taper or plug taps. To make yours, grind slowly on the bench grinder, and do not let the tap overheat. If it gets too hot to hold you have over-heated it. Do not quench the heated tap, let it air-cool.

Tools that are less commonly used by the home gunsmith include the barrel vise and action wrench. Also in this category are free-standing power equipment such as a milling machine, lathe, belt sander and surface grinder. The barrel vise clamps a barrel so you can screw the action and barrel together or take them apart. The action wrench grabs the action to turn it. You can't just grab the action with a pair of pliers. Besides being inadequate for the job, pliers will mar the action. You only need these two items if you will be removing and replacing barrels. While you could get the tools to do one barrel, it is not cost effective. If you only want one barrel done, it will probably be cheaper to send it out. If you will be doing several barrels, then invest in the vise and wrench. Do not get the smallest ones available. False economy means additional expenses later on. Get a big, strong vise such as the Brownells, and bolt it to a solid bench. Or do as my friend Andy Manson did, and attach it to a steel post bolted to the concrete floor.

A milling machine is a cool machine. With the right attachments it replaces a drill press. It also takes floor space, power, and practice to use properly. You can drill precisely spaced holes, you can mill flats and dovetails and you can even re-contour military actions. What you can't do is get a good mill cheap. If you must have a mill, do your homework. Go to a machine tool store and look at mills. Check the specifications. You want a decent amount of horsepower, a precisely-moveable head and multiple speeds. The better the bearings you can afford, and the larger the table you can find room for, the happier you will be. You do not need a quick-change capability on cutting speed. You do not need quick-change capabilities on the cutting tools and you do not need power feed. Avoid hobbyist machines that do not offer micrometer-adjustable vertical travel. Trying to cut a

As with mills, small lathes are not useful for rifle work. This Clausing is 4 feet high, 7 feet long and weighs over a ton. Not only do you need floor space for it, the floor must be strong enough to hold it without adding vibrations.

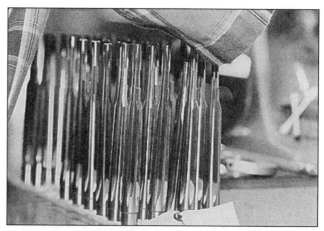

Not only does barrel-fitting require a lathe, it requires chambering reamers, too. Unless you are fitting a barrel from a blank, you'll only need a finishing reamer. These are a batch of .220 Swift reamers getting their final cutting edge at Loon Lake.

dovetail on a machine without micrometer adjustments is a real drag, and can eat up a whole afternoon on one dovetail. Heck, you could file it by hand faster. Once purchased, your mill will require cutting tools, vises to hold the parts being milled, and measuring tools. Do not spend all of your machine-shop budget on the mill itself, or you'll have a dull waiting period until you can afford the tools.

While a mill can replace a drill press, nothing can replace a lathe. While you have a number of uses for a mill, you will not have as many uses for a lathe. Lathes are used to turn

stock into cylindrical shapes. With a lathe and practice you can create a screw from bar or rod stock and you can modify a magazine tube for a lever-action rifle. With a sufficiently large lathe you can thread barrels or turn a barrel down to a smaller diameter, and do the rough and finish chambering. With a big lathe you can turn one barrel into another. One rifle I have in the rack is an 1896 Mauser with a Springfield barrel screwed into it. Someone with a lathe turned the threaded shank of the Springfield down from the 10 threads per inch square form and 1.040-inch diameter to the Mauser's 12 threads per inch "V" form and .980" diameter. (Unfortunately while he was good with a lathe he wasn't so good with headspace gauges, as the headspace is not correct. One of these days I'll have to adjust the headspace to make it right.)

How big a lathe do you need? Unless you are going to be installing barrels, a small one will do. If you are going to install barrels, then you cannot get one too big or too precise. A good lathe will cost you thousands of dollars, and for the cost of that lathe you can probably have someone else re-barrel every rifle you own. If you must have a large lathe, consider a used machinery auction. Cliff LaBounty bought his lathe at a used machinery auction, and got a good one. His purchase exemplifies the "no such thing as too big" philosophy. He bought a Dean, Smith & Grace lathe, made in England and considered to be the Rolls Royce of lathes. It has English and metric adjustments, a 16-inch swing and a 48-inch bed. It weighs 6,000 pounds, and if set on a rigid base the manufacturer promises accuracy to a 1/10,000 of an inch. A rigid base is a reinforced concrete block no smaller than six feet by ten feet by four feet thick. Cliff uses his to bore out barrels before re-rifling them. The last new price he saw on his model was many years ago, and then it was going for $125,000! He bought his used for a fraction of that, and re-built it.

Lathes require cutting tools, holding fixtures, and accessories of many kinds. All are expensive. Unless you are going to be using a large lathe as a full-time professional, you are better off spending your money on getting the work done for you, rather than on a lathe. You can, however, sign up at the local community college for a machine shop

What you get from a big, precise lathe are centered and beautifully-turned threads such as these for a muzzle brake.

A production shop will modify standard machine tools to fit their needs. You do not have this luxury, and should have a professional do the specialized jobs beyond your tools and experience.

One of the tools a professional shop has that you do not need is a bullet trap. The trap allows function-testing of a rifle without the need to take it to the range.

course, and learn how lathes work. The knowledge will come in handy when you are describing what you want done to the professional you are handing it to.

The belt sander is a compact machine in terms of the floor space it uses, but a big machine in the mess it makes. I used mine for stock length alterations and recoil pad installations. Even with a shop-vac attached to the belt sander to control the dust, everything, me, the benches, the other guns, the mail and the coffee pot, got covered by wood and rubber dust. The coffee pot got moved into another room right away. My only solution for the mess was to use the belt sander on only one day each week, and then clean up after that week's sanding was done. I was sorely tempted to get some dropcloths fitted to the benches to keep the parts and tools from getting dusted each week. If you will be using a belt sander for your pad installation, I suggest this routine: make sure the benches are clear of clutter before you start. Do your sanding. Once you are finished, stop the pad installation long enough to clean the shop. Vacuum the walls, the benches and yourself. Sweep the floor. Then get back to pad installation. More on this later. If you have a husky bench grinder you do not need a belt sander. Mount your bench grinder so one wheel projects to the side

over the edge of the bench and install a sanding drum. You won't avoid the mess, but it takes up less room than a belt sander, and costs less.

A surface grinder is a big, strong machine tool that offers capabilities beyond your needs. It is also expensive to buy, expensive to operate and requires a delicate touch. Lust if you must, but leave it to the pros.

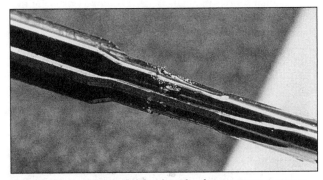

Cutting tools such as this chambering reamer remove metal. To prevent rust, always clean the chips off before you put the tool away.

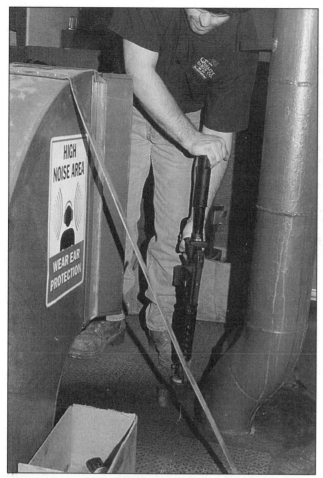

At Quality Parts they test-fire so many rifles that they built a special room, and shoot through the floor into it. Once the room fills up, they can then use a frontloader to clean up the lead and copper. (Photo courtesy Quality Parts/Bushmaster.)

When we talk about gunsmithing, many shooters focus on the glamourous tools, the screwdrivers and files, the fixtures and power machines. Keeping a rifle accurate and reliable in operation takes more than a snazzy set of screwdrivers or a sharp new file. You have to keep it clean. Firearms cleaning requires solvents, patches, brushes, and lubricants. Cleaning the action requires a different solvent than is used for cleaning the bore. The common solvent for cleaning actions in a professional shop is mineral spirits. The pro uses an automotive parts cleaning washer for the volume of solvent and for the elbow room to clean. Using a tank such as this, a really grungy rifle can be stripped, the parts placed in stainless steel pans, and the solvent left running over the parts. A few minutes or hours later, the grunge is softened by the flowing solvent. The drawbacks? Mess, cost and smell. I have never seen a parts cleaner that was not crusted with dried grease, oil and solvent stains. The floor and walls next to the tanks have all been dirty too. Whether this is an unavoidable result of the tank, or of the gunsmiths using them, I don't know. The parts tank can be expensive, costing more than a good rifle. The cheaper grades of mineral spirits have a kerosene odor to them. While this can be occasionally charming, if you spill solvent on your shoes and drag the odor through the house

A handy lathe accessory for accurizing rifles is this LaBounty bolt fixture. By clamping your bolt in the fixture you can use a lathe to true the locking lugs and bolt face. A must-have for building a beanfield rifle.

you will hear about it. Do not buy any reclaimed spirits, buy only the best grade.

One approach to cleaning that avoids the mess and smell is ultrasonic. L&R makes a line of ultrasonic tanks in various sizes, up to rifle size. The method is simple. Turn on the tanks, and if you have one with the optional heating elements, wait for the solution to heat up. Remove your rifle from the stock, and the scope from the rifle, and place it in the tank. Cycle the tank until the action is clean. Remove the rifle from the cleaning tank and place it in the water-displacing oil tank. Run this long enough to remove the water-based solvent. Oil, grease, powder residue will all be gone. Clean the bore with your usual method and then reassemble. One obvious drawback is removing the scope. With a good bore collimator you can get your scope reinstalled and within an inch of zero. The other drawback is cost. For the cost of a handgun-sized unit you can buy a really good rifle, complete with scope. The rifle-sized unit will set you back more than $5,000.

While they are popular with Police Departments, I do not expect ultrasonic units to be popping up in every other deer hunting camp.

The most important tool in cleaning your bore is the cleaning rod. Do not use the inexpensive aluminum rods

Nothing makes steel flat like a surface grinder. However, for the thousands of dollars it costs, can you live with slightly non-flat surfaces?

And if you thought a standard surface grinder was expensive, this computer-controlled grinder that Loon Lake uses is beyond the pale for home use.

Aerosol cleaners such as Crud-Cutter are great for use at the range, but are too expensive and messy for home use.

Unlike the shiny and clean parts cleaning tank shown earlier, this is a common example of the state of cleaning tanks. The floor is discolored around it, and the wall next to the doorway is splattered with oil from the compressed air used to dry the parts.

that screw together for your regular cleaning. Keep one in your range and hunting gear bag for use at the range or in your hunting camp. The once or twice a year use it may get will not harm your bore. For your weekly cleaning use a one-piece steel rod that is nylon coated. Many of my customers asked me how the soft aluminum of the rod could harm the steel of their barrel. It isn't the aluminum, it is the grit the aluminum picks up. Every sharp bit of dust, steel or grit that ends up embedded in the surface of the rod will get passed back-and-forth down your bore every time you clean it. The steel rod will not flex as much as the aluminum. Being one-piece there are no sharp edges from the joints to rub against the rifling. The plastic coating does not hold the grit. Every time you wipe the rod off, it wipes clean. This rod will not be cheap. It will cost twice as much for the one-piece rod alone than it will for the jointed rod in its complete kit. Buy both. With your coated rod also purchase a cleaning tip. Not the loop end to hold a patch, but a jag tip. You will wrap your patches around the jag to run them down the bore.

Improper cleaning can destroy accuracy. You should use a bore guide for your cleaning rod. The bore guide keeps the

rod centered in the bore. If you do not, pressure in the throat will wear the rifling unevenly. The throat is the beginning of the rifling, at the very front of the chamber and uneven wear here hurts accuracy. While it is best to clean the bore from the action end, this is not always possible. Some rifles just don't give you access through the action. For these rifles you will need a muzzle cap for your cleaning. The cap does for the crown what the bore guide does for the throat. Get a

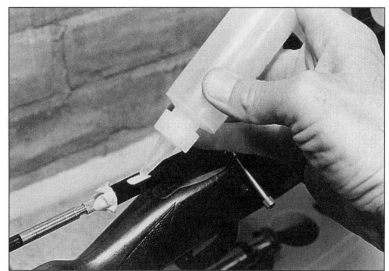

To clean your rifle you'll need rods, patches, solvents, and a rod guide. A small plastic bottle to apply solvent with is a nice addition to the set.

rifle cradle to hold the rifle while you clean the bore. Juggling the rifle and a cleaning rod with a wet patch on it while trying to avoid getting solvent on your clothes is not fun. Banging the rod or the rifle against the bench or the walls while doing this juggling will dampen the paint and your enthusiasm for cleaning. When using a cleaning cradle you can position a can under the muzzle. The can is where your used cleaning patches will drop, instead of on the floor.

Depending on the bullets you shoot, your bore will become fouled with either lead or copper. You will need a bore solvent appropriate for your bullets. The lead solvent doesn't do anything to remove copper and vice versa. Basic solvents do a good job of removing the powder residue, so use these first, then strip out the lead or copper with the specialized solvent.

Some shooters approach patches as if they were a terrible expense. They are tempted to buy the cheapest patches possible. Then these cheap shooters use them like a washcloth, scrubbing until the patch is too dirty to touch. This is the wrong method. A proper patch is a barrel life-extender. Buy the best patches, use them once, and throw them away.

A neat method of removing copper or lead from your bore is the Outers Foul-out. This uses an electro-plating method to remove the fouling. A sacrificial cleaning rod is placed in the bore. The bore is filled with the proper cleaning solution. Then an electrical charge is applied to the rod and rifle. The fouling is stripped off of the bore and plated onto the rod.

While elegant and fast, the Foul-out has to be supervised. When the rod is plated, the reaction stops. You have to remove the rod and sand the fouling off of it. If your bore is pitted, the reaction will be tainted. The electro-plating method will strip the rust out of the pits. When it runs out of rust, it will continue removing steel. If you don't change the solution as soon as the rust is gone, your bore will be eaten away. Each unit comes with complete instructions and all you have to do is follow them.

The cleaned rifle must be lubricated during assembly. For almost all lubrication I prefer a light synthetic lubricant such as Break Free or FP-10. There are a few rifles that need something heavier. When the M-1 Garand was in its final testing stages, the ordnance testers found that oil on the

Once it is clean and dry, you need to apply a lubricant to the working parts. A good synthetic lubricant like Break Free or FP-10 works in all temperature extremes.

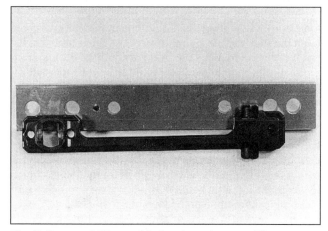

The B-Square drilling guide has bars for two different patterns. This pattern is for Mauser rifles, and you can see the holes line up perfectly for the Mauser base from Millett.

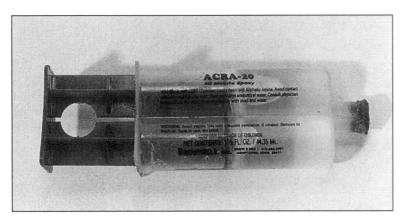

To secure screws and pins, use Loctite. To reattach broken wood, use Acra-glas. This syringe applies equal amounts of resin and hardener of Acra-20. It sets in 20 minutes, and the attached parts can be worked on in a few hours. Great stuff.

operating rod cam surfaces could be washed away by a heavy rain. The solution for the M-1 Garand was to issue a small vial of a grease called Lubriplate. It resisted washing away by rain, and kept the rifle working. When the M-1 Garand was improved into the M-14, the ordnance designers changed the right bolt extension from a round knob to a roller. Grease still helps it work correctly.

The Lubriplate is not just a rain-resistant lubricant, it also stays in place in all weather, hot or cold. It does not wear away under the pressure and heat of the bolt cycling back and forth. It is quite useful and I keep a tube of Lubriplate to lube other rifles besides the M-1 Garand. Every time I clean a rifle with a similar locking cam, the slot gets a dab of grease. The M-1 Garand, M1-A/M-14, the Ruger Mini-14 and Mini-30, M-1 Carbine, the Remington 740/742/7400 series are only a few that need this treatment. I would hesitate using it only if I were going to be headed to a very cold place for hunting. It may become too stiff once frozen in place overnight outside a hunting cabin in North Canada or Alaska. For those places, use the lighter oils.

The last vial or bottle to keep on hand is one filled with Loctite. You may find that even with the correct screw-tightening method some screw or another may not stay tight. Then you'll want to treat it to a small drop of Loctite to keep it in place. Use the blue goo, Loctite 242. You can still get the screw out later. If you use tougher stuff, you may have to heat the screw with a propane torch to remove it.

The most important shop tool you will need I have saved for last. You need some way to hold the rifle or parts you are working on. For the whole rifle you will need a cradle. For the action out of the stock you need a vise. A good cradle holds the rifle securely without marring the finish of the wood or metal. Once the rifle is in the cradle you can clean the bore, adjust or replace the scope, adjust the sights or install sling swivel hardware. Whether you buy or make it, you need a cradle. I learned to clean firearms from my father, and I never used a cradle as a kid. My father learned how to clean a rifle by stripping and cleaning an M-1 Garand. When he was finished with that, the Army taught him how to do the same thing to half a dozen other firearms. The Army didn't have cradles, and my dad never felt the need for one. The first time I used one it felt a little odd, but by the time I was done that day I was hooked. A cradle makes everything so much easier there is no point in not having one.

A bench vise serves the same purpose but for smaller parts. Buy a medium to large vise, one with a jaw width of at least 4 inches; 5 inches would be better. As with many things, the rule of "bigger is better" breaks down after you get too large. After all, working on rifles, how often will you need a vise large enough to clamp and hold an engine block? The rule of thumb I use on vises is simple: If I can pick it up with one hand, it is too light for anything but simple work. A good vise must be securely bolted to the bench. The bench must be heavy and stiff. As extra support you can fit a vertical post to your bench right underneath the vise.

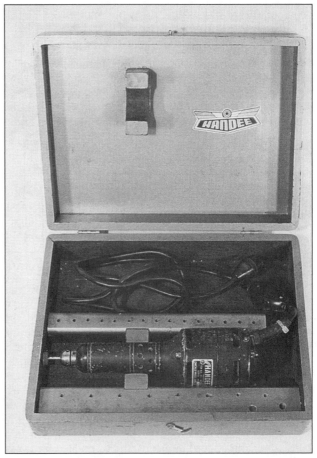

To cut small parts, grind or polish, a hand-held grinder can be just the ticket. It can overheat small parts if you aren't careful, so use a soft touch.

CHAPTER 4

Trigger Work

All rifles have a trigger. Indeed, all firearms have a trigger. The very idea of a trigger is so ingrained in our culture that there are many references to it. You have heard "He's quick on the trigger," and "You don't want to trigger anything," even in a situation where there is no physical trigger. The "trigger" is what initiates a process or starts an irreversible action. When you pull the trigger on your rifle and launch a bullet, there is no way to call it back. You must keep that in mind at all times when you are working on triggers and trigger pull. If you make a mistake you may be paying for it the rest of your life. That payment may mean a lengthy impoverishment, or a bright flash and then unending darkness. I don't mean to depress you, just to make sure we are starting with the same understanding.

If you are going to disassemble a rifle that is new to you, pull a disassembly manual off of your bookshelf and read up on how.

The trigger you see is just the operating lever for the trigger mechanism. The trigger mechanism exists solely to hold the firing mechanism in place. When the rifle is cocked, the striker or firing pin is held in place against the force of the compressed striker spring. Without some kind of trigger mechanism, you could only fire a rifle by grasping the cocking knob of the striker, pulling it back and then letting go. Or you could fire such a rifle by striking the back of the cocking knob with a hammer. If you think these methods sound silly, imagine trying to aim at the same time. Early firearms did not have a trigger. The shooter simply held a burning section of cord in one hand, and pointed the noisy end of the "gonne" in the general direction of the enemy. Triggers were a big advance for the time. The first triggers were simply the other end of the pivoting arm that held the

burning section of cord. Pulling the "trigger" pivoted the forward part of the arm down to the touch-hole, setting off the black powder. Trigger mechanisms have improved a great deal since then.

In order to hold back the striker, the trigger mechanism has to contact the striker. This contact area is often called the

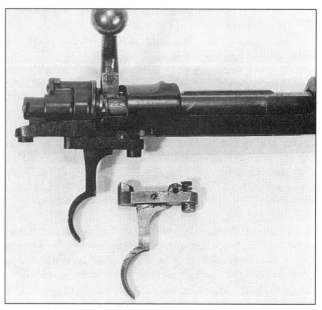

The trigger is merely the external lever that activates the mechanism. The sear (the upper left part of the detached trigger mechanism on this Mauser) holds the striker back in the cocked position.

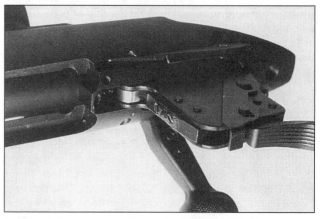

Modern trigger mechanisms like this Remington are sealed sub-assemblies that are attached to the receiver. They are easy to make, easy to adjust, and easy to assemble to the rifle.

European shooters either have to have the simplest or the most complex. Often, the simple Mauser trigger will be replaced with a set trigger. Instead of one trigger and five parts, the rifle now has two triggers and ten parts. By pulling the rear trigger, you can "set" the front trigger. Once set, the front trigger fires the rifle with a trigger pull of a few ounces. Unset, the front trigger fires the rifle with a pull of several pounds.

sear. In a simple trigger mechanism such as the Mauser 1898 the sear is attached to the trigger. Another approach is to make the sear part of a lever that at one end holds the striker and at its other end contacts the trigger. The Winchester Model 70 rifle uses this method. The modern approach is to construct the trigger mechanism as a complex and sealed unit, with the striker contact sticking up out of the box. Inside, the trigger contacts the sear and the activating springs out of view from prying eyes. The advantages of the simpler, older methods are cost and reliability. The advantages of the newer method are delicacy of adjustment and interchangeability.

Trigger pull as a shooting process

The classic trigger pull is described as something that cannot be anticipated. The best trigger gives no indication of the process going on inside the rifle. It simply waits for you to press it, and does not give you any feedback about when it will go off. If you can anticipate the moment of let-off, or the release of the striker, you will do bad things. You may clench the rifle, anticipating the recoil. If the sights are drifting you may try to snatch the rifle back to the center of the target. Anticipating the recoil, you may squint or close your eyes. Any of these things may cause you to miss. All of them together will cause you to miss badly.

A trigger that gives any indications about where it is in the process will encourage you to anticipate. The hardest thing to do in shooting is to not pick up bad habits from bad triggers.

Can a trigger be too good? No, but it can be too light. A light trigger does not make your flinching, grasping, clenching habits disappear.

Trigger pull as a mechanical process

Let us for the moment consider the trigger and how it works without worrying about the design that rests inside the stock. When it comes to triggers, the descriptive vocabulary of shooters rivals that of wine tasters. We need to get our language straight in order to be clear. We will start with the action cocked, the safety off and a target at which to fire. When your finger first contacts the trigger, the trigger moves freely. This is known as the "slack" or "take-up." At this point your finger pressure is not being applied to any other part than the trigger itself. Slack is a basic safety design that allows you to feel the trigger without working the trigger mechanism itself. Is too much slack a problem? Not unless the rattling of the loose trigger bothers you or scares your quarry. If it bothers you, you can either get used to it or put a dab of grease on the trigger to keep it from swinging freely. The game will

The Swiss Stgw 90 in action at Second Chance. Very accurate, very expensive and no longer importable.

never hear the trigger over your own movements. The act of pressing the trigger through this travel is called "taking up the slack."

At the end of the trigger's travel in the slack you will feel the trigger stop. To move it again will require more force. The force you apply will be used to move the parts of the trigger mechanism that hold the striker in place. Depending on how much force is required, and how much surface area there is between the parts, the trigger may or may not feel as if it is moving. In a mechanism that is well-designed and well-fitted the trigger does not seem to move. This is often referred to as a "glass rod" break. A glass rod does not flex before it breaks, and therefore does not move. The last time I broke a glass rod, I ended up stabbing the broken end of it into my left hand, and as a result I do not use this term. I just call such a trigger "crisp." Movement of the trigger during this part of the trigger pull is called "creep." Some movement is inevitable, but too much is seriously bad for accurate shooting. As an example, a creepy 3-pound trigger will be harder to shoot than a crisp 4-pound trigger. How much force should it take to release the striker? This is a question that does not have an absolute answer. Sometimes a very light trigger is appropriate. Sometimes a heavy trigger will not be a hindrance. For most shooters, for most shooting, the weight does not matter provided it is heavy enough to be safe and not so heavy it makes aiming difficult. A light trigger does not, by itself, improve your shooting.

There is a separate type of trigger pull known as "sponge." A spongy trigger does not have a clearly defined stop in the slack. A spongy trigger seems to get heavier, but not jump along as a creepy trigger can. I ran into an interesting example of a trigger designed to be spongy. I was at Second Chance, a shooting event in Michigan, on the back range taking a break from the rifle event. One of the other shooters offered me a chance to try his rifle. It was a Swiss Stgw 90, chambered in .223 Remington and issued to the Swiss Army, a group of known accuracy fanatics. They held off switching from their .30-caliber rifles to .223 for 25 years in part because the .223 was not accurate enough at 300 meters. Every adult male must do his National Service each year, and qualify annually. They were not about to adopt a rifle until they knew it worked and their scores would not suffer. The trigger on this rifle was all sponge. The slack blended right into the trigger pull, which got heavier but never stopped or jerked. Somewhere along the way the sear released the hammer, but I could never anticipate it. Without being able to anticipate firing, I just spent my time watching the front sight, and hit everything I fired at. It is a great rifle, and was staggeringly expensive then. Now, it would cost as much as a small used car to obtain one.

Once you have used enough force on the trigger to release the striker, the trigger moves to its rearward position. This is called "overtravel." The trigger comes to rest abruptly at the end of the overtravel. This jar occurs before the bullet has left the muzzle. Too much overtravel can have a detrimental effect on accuracy. However, the actual amount of accuracy loss is small. A competitive shooter may want a trigger mechanism adjusted for an absolute minimum of overtravel. As an example, an accurate rifle with the overtravel at a maximum may show an increase in group size of 1/4- or 1/2-half inch at 100 yards. Firing from the bench with sandbag supports, accurate ammunition and a good scope, you might be able to measure this amount. Offhand, you would never notice it. The competitive shooter sets overtravel to a minimum because he does not want to give up even one point in a match. That increase of 1/4-inch grows to 1-1/2 at 600 yards. Matches have been won or lost by less than that. What does he risk? Nothing, if he keeps his rifle clean and fires in good weather. A rifle with the overtravel set to an absolute minimum can be sensitive to cold, ice, dirt or bumping. I once worked on a rifle that refused to fire in the winter. The owner had adjusted the overtravel to the minimum. He tested it in his house, which was heated to 72 degrees. At the range, with the rifle cooled down to freezing, the trigger could not be pulled hard enough to fire the rifle. The parts had contracted in the cold, and the sear would no longer release the striker. Adjusting the overtravel to a larger amount solved the problem. Another customer dropped his rifle and when he picked it up he could not fire it. The trigger guard had been bent hitting a rock, and the trigger could not travel far enough to release the striker. Bending the trigger guard back to its original curve solved the problem. But if he had left a bit more overtravel in his trigger when he had adjusted it, he could have done more than just stare at the big buck he ran into during the walk back to his hunting cabin.

What should you expect from working on your trigger mechanism? You want a trigger that will not release the striker until you want it to. The trigger mechanism must hold the striker back until you press the trigger, regardless of any vibration, bump, jolt or drop. If the trigger mechanism is maladjusted, the striker could fall at an unexpected time. If the chamber has a round in it, the rifle will fire. You want a trig-

To check the security of the sear engagement, run the bolt forward briskly.....

and slap it closed in one smooth motion. The rifle must stay cocked. If it does not, you must go back and reverse the last adjustments you made until the rifle will pass this test. "Close enough" is not close enough. It must stay cocked every time you try this test.

ger pull heavy enough that you can feel it when your fingers are cold, or when you are wearing light gloves. Along with the trigger, all rifles come equipped with a safety lever or button. The trigger must not be adjusted, filed or stoned so the safety is difficult or impossible to engage. A rifle with an inoperative safety is a disaster waiting to happen.

For most shooters the lightest trigger pull that fits this description would be 3 to 4 pounds. I have fired rifles with

trigger pulls as heavy as 5 pounds where the trigger felt just fine. Trigger pull is more than just the weight of the pull. That rifle with the heavy trigger pull had a clean and crisp release with no creep. Most trigger mechanisms are designed to work in this range, at a low end of 3-1/2 pounds, and an upper end of not more than 6 pounds. What happens if you adjust a standard trigger mechanism out of this range? At the top end, the trigger pull becomes so great that accurate shooting becomes difficult. The force required to move the trigger also moves the rifle. At the lower limit, reducing the trigger pull below 3-1/2 pounds can be just as bad. Below the design limit, the tool marks on the engagement surfaces can affect the feeling of the trigger pull. A trigger that had been crisp can become creepy. With the lighter pull, you can feel the surfaces sliding against each other, jerking along or grinding away. This can be as distracting as a heavy trigger pull.

To get your trigger pull below 3-1/2 pounds you must replace the current trigger mechanism with one designed for a lighter trigger pull weight. When should you do this? Hardly ever. Competitive benchrest shooters, using single-shot rifles, use triggers upon which the pull is measured in ounces. Before you use that as a guide, consider that they do not have a safety on the rifle. They do not close the bolt until they are ready to fire. You cannot do that, sitting in a blind waiting for your big buck to show himself. Some varmint shooters use rifles with very light trigger pulls. They are sitting or lying in one spot, shooting at small critters out in front of them. They are not still hunting through brush looking to kick a deer up.

I cannot stress this too much or too strongly; good shooting is a matter of practice and good habits, not a light trigger pull. Do not be seduced by the dark side of the force and try to make your trigger pull lighter than 3-1/2 pounds. I've warned you.

Consider one thing before you begin the actual adjustment. Once you have done your setting and fussing, how do you check your work? Begin testing by making sure one more time that there is no live ammunition in the rifle. Check the chamber and magazine and make sure they are empty. During the first test, you will work the action vigorously and check between cycles to make sure the hammer or striker stayed cocked. Particular problems will be discussed with their rifles. To do this with a bolt-action rifle, run the

Pull the trigger with the safety on, and then release the trigger and push the safety to "Fire." The trigger pull must weigh the same as it did before this test. If not, reverse your last adjustments and try the test again.

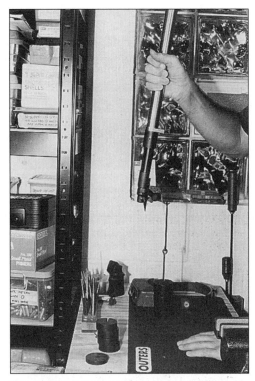

The most accurate method of checking trigger pull is by using weights. With the cocked and unloaded rifle pointing up, use the trigger to pick up a certain amount of weight. The trigger pull is the amount of weight that will cause the striker to fall.

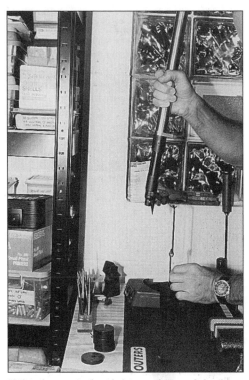

If the amount of weight you have picked up is not enough to dry-fire the rifle, add extra weights one at a time until the trigger does release the striker.

The final test is the "bump" test. With the unloaded rifle cocked and the safety off, gently rap the butt against a padded surface. If you can bump the rifle into dry-firing, you have made your trigger pull too light, or reduced the sear engagement. (Haven't I told you repeatedly not to reduce sear engagement?) Reverse your last adjustments and try the test again.

bolt forward as hard as you can and turn the handle down all in one motion. The fastest way is with your hand open, pushing with the palm. On a pump or lever-action, work the lever or forearm as hard as you can without breaking something. I used to advocate doing this just as hard as you could, until a 325-pound customer who was a power lifter bent the lever on his Marlin working it as hard as he could. If you weigh 165, don't worry about breaking something. If the hammer falls, or the striker fails to stay cocked during this test, your handiwork has failed.

Semi-automatics require a slightly different method. Unlike the manually-operated rifles, the semi-auto has additional parts in the trigger mechanism. These parts disengage the trigger mechanism from the rest of the rifle's action while it is cycling. The main part in this function is called the disconnector. Without a disconnector the rifle cannot re-cock while cycling. A faulty disconnector does not mean the rifle has been turned into a machine gun. Without a disconnector, or with a faulty one, the hammer usually rides the bolt forward and cannot strike the firing pin hard enough to set off the next round. When the action is manually cycled, the hammer can re-cock, and rifle will fire again. This "every other" firing mode is a classic symptom of disconnector problems.

I do not recommend trigger work on some semi-auto rifles. In particular, the Remington 742 series has the ham-

Rifles are not the only firearm requiring trigger testing. If you ever go to Camp Perry, your rifle and/or handgun will be tested for trigger pull. How much it must pick up depends on the category in which you are competing.

The Remington 721 receiver was not a forging, and was round on the bottom. Today, its successor the 700 is the standard that all other rifles are compared to.

mer and sear engagement designed so as to confound attempts at improving the trigger pull. This is not a problem, as most are quite suitable as they come out of the box. To test your trigger work on a semi-auto, first make sure the chamber and magazine are empty. If you can remove the magazine, do so. Dry fire the rifle and hold the trigger back. Draw the operating handle back and let it fly forward on its own. Do not ease it forward. Now gently release the trigger, and listen for the sound of it re-setting. If you do not hear the click, draw the operating handle back slowly, and gently ease it forward. If the hammer now cocks, your rifle has failed the test.

A passing grade at this point earns more testing. Next, cock the action and put the safety on. Pull the trigger hard, at least 10 pounds worth. Think of trying to win a hand-shaking contest. Release your grip and then push the safety off. The hammer or striker must stay cocked. The professional test then involves trigger pull weights. Test the weight of the pull 10 times without using the safety. Then, try 10 times after putting the safety on, squeezing the trigger, releasing the safety and then using the trigger weights. The average must be the same. If the trigger pull after each test is lighter than the average before, the safety is only partially blocking sear movement. The partially-moved sear then requires less force to release. You will have to adjust the safety engagement to fully block the sear.

The last test is the bump test. If your rifle's buttstock has a metal, plastic or horn buttplate, be sure and put some padding on the floor. I use sections of carpet samples as my pads. If your rifle has a rubber recoil pad, you don't need extra padding. With the rifle unloaded, the action cocked and the safety off, drop it straight down onto the butt. You do not have to drop it very far, only about 6 to 9 inches. The rifles with rub-

ber recoil pads will bounce. Keep one hand on the barrel to prevent the rifle from bouncing off in an odd direction and crashing to the floor. The hammer or striker must stay cocked.

If your rifle passes these tests, congratulations, your trigger job has passed muster.

Trigger work

For all rifles except the AR-15 you will have to remove the action from the stock. You will need extra screwdrivers, wrenches or drift pins depending on which rifle you are working on. For the AR-15, you will separate the upper and lower halves, and then press the hammer and trigger pins out of the lower. You may want to invest in a set of trigger pull weights or a pull gauge to check your work. While the actual weight does not matter, many shooters have a burning desire to know "how much does my trigger weigh?" Knowledge can be a dangerous thing. I have had shooters who were completely satisfied with the trigger pull of their rifle, until they found out it was a "heavy" 4-1/2 pounds. The rifle that had never failed them, and had bagged many deer, was now suspect. No one could rest until I had tuned it down to 3-1/2 pounds, and showed him with my trigger weights. Was his next deer any more dead? No.

The following general descriptions will be added to in greater detail in the chapter where that particular rifle is worked on.

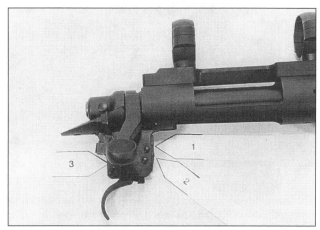

The Remington trigger. #1 is the over-travel screw. #2 is the weight of pull screw. #3 (Don't touch this one!) is the sear engagement screw.

The Remington Model 721 started the modern design revolution. Even though it has more old-style features than new, it outraged the purists.

Use a small-bladed screwdriver to adjust the weight of pull screw.

Have fun, but don't let some magical number consume your life.

Remington 700

Remington unveiled the Model 721 in 1948, and it made quite an impression. On the outside it did not have some features that were common and accepted on rifles of the day. On the outside it did not show an extractor. Instead of a large flat chunk of spring steel like the Mauser, Springfield or Winchester Model 70, the Remington had an extractor that was set into the bolt face. The safety was not on the cocking knob. Instead, it was a small button on the side of the tang. Inside, things got worse according to some shooters of the day. Instead of the receiver being made from a forging that was machined to shape, the Remington was a turned, bored and shaped piece of bar stock. Why, the bottom of the action was round! How could the action remain stable in the stock? The recoil lug was not an integral part of the receiver, but rather a plate that was clamped in place

by the barrel as it was screwed into the receiver. And the trigger mechanism? It was a sealed box with too many parts in it. Too many parts is bad, leading to breakage and failure. Despite all the grumbling the new Remington sold well. In 1962 Remington updated it and called the newer rifle the Model 700. The extractor is still small, the receiver still round, and the trigger mechanism is still a flat, sealed box with many parts in it. And the rifle has confounded all those critics by working superbly all these decades.

In all my years of gunsmithing, I have seen one Remington extractor that failed. The owner had allowed the chamber to rust, and had resorted to using a foot-long section of two by four to open his bolt and extract the fired cartridge. This failure was hardly the extractor's fault. I have seen one failure of a trigger mechanism. An overzealous gunsmith had used too much Loctite to reassemble the trigger mechanism. As a result it had been glued tight. I resorted to soaking the trigger mechanism in paint thinner to loosen the Loctite. After a week of soaking, I was ready to switch to

The sealing lacquer will be broken when you adjust the screw. Use paint or nail polish to re-seal it and to keep it from moving again until you want it to.

The Remington Model 720 was the last in the line derived from the Model 1917 Enfield of World War I. Try as they might, they just couldn't make it handsome.

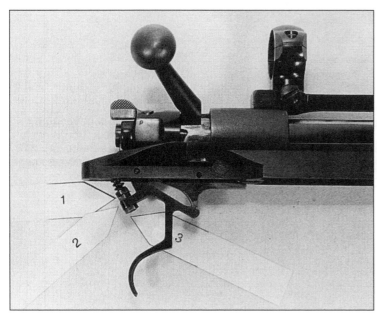

The Winchester Model 70 trigger mechanism. #1 & #2 are the weight of pull jam nuts. #3 is the overtravel lock nut. It rides on the overtravel shaft.

Acetone, but that was not necessary. And the round receiver? That turned out to be a godsend to gunsmiths who wanted to produced brilliantly accurate rifles. Because it is a simple tube, the action can be placed in a lathe and have all of the critical surfaces trued to the accuracy of the lathe. Doing this allows precise mating of bolt to receiver, barrel to receiver, and cartridge to the rifling.

And the trigger is still adjustable despite its complexity. To work on the Remington mechanism you will need a small flat-blade screwdriver and some sealing paint.

Remove the action from the stock and clamp the barrel in a padded vise. When you look at the muzzle end of the trigger mechanism you will see two screw heads sealed with paint or plastic. The upper one controls overtravel and the lower one controls trigger pull weight. On the rear of the unit is a screw head which controls sear engagement. Of these, the only one you need to adjust is weight, the lower front one. If you have weights or a scale, weigh and record your current trigger pull.

Open the bolt and leave it open. Scrape the paint or plastic off of the lower screw. Turn it one quarter of a turn counterclockwise. Weigh your trigger pull. Repeat this process until you have a pull of 3-1/2 pounds. Reassemble the rifle, check

again to make sure it is not loaded, and perform the safety checks by working the bolt and bumping the stock. If the trigger pull does not pass the test, remove the action and turn the screw a quarter turn clockwise until the test is passed.

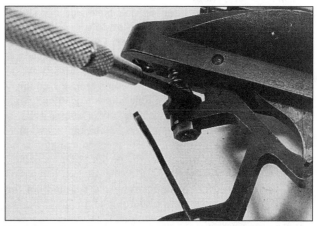

The side view gives you an idea of how thin the wrenches must be in order to not get in each others way.

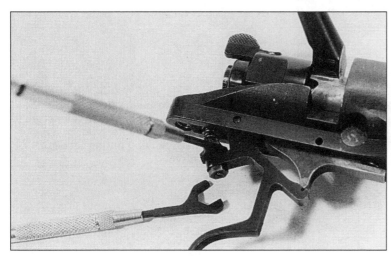

The lock nuts must be loosened, adjusted and tightened with special thin wrenches.

The Savage M-110 in its modern version. #1 is the sear engagement screw (Don't touch it!). #2 is the weight of pull adjustment. #3 & #4 are the overtravel and safety engagement screws.

When the trigger pull passes the test, remove the action from the stock and seal the screw with a dab of paint. The paint prevents the screw from rotating on its own during the vibrations of shooting or riding in a vehicle. It also assures you that the setting has not been changed if you should be so rash as to loan your rifle to someone.

The overtravel screw rarely needs adjustment. For shooters who are very picky, and are willing to run the risk of a bound trigger, you can adjust overtravel. Close the bolt on an empty chamber. Turn the overtravel screw clockwise a full turn and attempt to release the striker. It should not fall. While holding the trigger back, turn the overtravel screw counterclockwise until the striker falls. Release the trigger and work the bolt. Press the trigger again. The striker should fall. At this point your adjustment is right at the minimum, and anything can keep the trigger from traveling far enough to release the striker. I set the overtravel screw one third of a turn counterclockwise from this setting. For a rifle used on dangerous game, or in a cold or sandy environment, I would set the screw a half turn counterclockwise from the minimum point.

If you have adjusted overtravel, seal the screw with paint. The third screw should never be adjusted. Sear engagement as set by the factory does not need any adjustment by any user. Leave it alone. Any attempts to reduce sear engagement can lead to insufficient safety engagement, unsafe trigger pull or an inoperative rifle.

If you want a trigger pull lighter than 3-1/2 pounds, switch to a unit such as the Timney, which is designed to work at less than three point five.

Winchester Model 70

After The War to End All Wars (I can only conclude they were more optimistic about naming wars back then), the Doughboys were mustered out of service and went back home. While they all went back to work and family, many went back to rural homes. When the time came to go back to hunting, they choose their hunting rifles with new knowledge, the knowledge of bolt-action rifles. The lever-action hunting rifle had begun its slow descent. While not quite as quick on the follow-up shot, the bolt-action was fast enough. The bolt offered accuracy, power and as a result of the power and pointed bullets, flat trajectory. It was handy and more durable than a lever-action rifle. Except for the Savage, lever-action rifles used a tube magazine under the

The weight of pull adjustment screw (#2) rides on the side of the trigger assembly. Once set, it must be secured with Loctite, paint or nail polish to keep it from moving during recoil or repeated vibration.

barrel. The tube changed the rifle's balance as it emptied. It was prone to denting and rusting, which could hinder feeding. And it was attached to the barrel, decreasing accuracy.

After the war Remington offered its Model 30, 30S and 720. These were all sporterized versions of the 1917 Enfield rifle. While suitable for sporting use they were still a bit heavy and not very handsome. (Read: "ugly.") But the tooling was paid for, and the rifle sold well.

Winchester had also made Model 1914 and Model 1917 rifles during the great war, but they wanted more. That more came in 1925, with the Model 54. Compared to the Remington 30, it was sleek and good-looking. The design improvements that were to follow were delayed by the Depression, so it was not until 1936 that the Model 70 came out. Immediately dubbed "The Rifleman's Rifle," the Model 70 has had a devoted following ever since. One might even be unkind and call the collectors and shooters of these fine rifles rabid. The gun has been admired and even worshipped. Even gunwriters who are not automatically associated with rifles had to have one. Jeff Cooper, the father of the Modern Pistol Technique, bought a Model 70 just as soon as he could. It has a three-digit serial number and is chambered in .375 H&H. Why that one? "I already had several rifles in .30-06, and Winchester did not offer a larger caliber then. I was too fond of it to have it rebarreled when larger calibers became available."

The improvement that concerns us here is the new trigger mechanism. The improved design has persisted unchanged since 1936, even when the rest of the rifle was overhauled in 1964. It does not need to be changed now. It features one spring, two moving parts, and three hex nuts. It can be adjusted to a crisp 3-1/2 pounds, maintain full sear engagement, never need further adjustment, and stay that way for the rest of your life.

Remove the action from the stock and clamp the barrel in

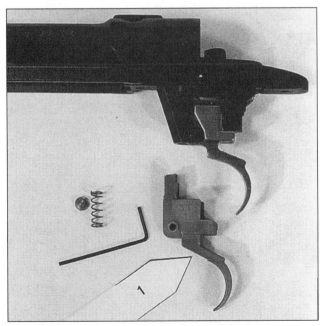

The only thing you can do with a current-production Ruger is to replace the trigger with another unit. This Spec-Tech trigger comes with a weight adjustment screw (#1) that lets you adjust the weight within a reasonable range.

a padded vise. To adjust the trigger of a Model 70 you will need two 1/4-inch open-end wrenches. If you use standard open-end wrenches you may have to dress the sides on a bench grinder to make them thin enough. If left too thick, the wrenches will not have clearance in the space between the receiver and the trigger. You can buy perfect wrenches from Brownells.

The Winchester allows only two adjustments, pull weight and overtravel. Since these are the only ones you need to make, the lack of sear engagement adjustment is not a problem. The upper pair of nuts adjust weight. They are jammed together to keep them from loosening. Open the bolt. Loosen the lower from the upper, and rotate it clockwise (down from the barrel) away from the upper nut. To reduce the pull weight, rotate the upper nut clockwise a quarter turn. Close the bolt and check trigger pull. Repeat until you get down to 3-1/2 pounds, then rotate the lower nut counterclockwise (up) until it is firmly locked to the upper nut. Do this firmly, but do not add leverage to the small open-end wrench to make the nuts as tight as possible.

Return the action to the stock and perform your safety checks. If the striker falls on any test, increase the trigger pull weight.

You probably will not have to adjust overtravel. The Winchester assemblers do a good job of getting the overtravel short enough without the risk of binding in cold or dusty climates.

If you feel the need, here is how: Open the bolt and make sure the rifle is empty. Turn the lower nut clockwise to loosen it. Use a small screwdriver on the threaded shaft the nuts ride on. Turning clockwise decreases overtravel and counterclockwise increases it. Turn the shaft a full turn clockwise. Close the bolt and pull the trigger. While holding the trigger back, slowly turn the shaft counterclockwise. When the striker falls, release the trigger and turn the shaft another quarter of a turn. If you will be in a very cold climate, a dusty one or hunting dangerous game, turn the shaft a half of a turn counterclockwise instead of the quarter. Tighten the overtravel nut. Perform your safety checks.

Savage Model 110

Savage introduced the Model 110 in 1958, the same year Ford Motor Company introduced the Edsel. Unlike the Edsel, the Savage was something the buying public wanted. The rifles Savage had to offer for the previous 60 years had been nice little inexpensive rifles for hunting in the woods. A fellow who couldn't afford a Winchester, and who wanted something other than a cut-down military rifle could get a Savage. The top of the line was the Savage Model 99, a lever-action rifle with a rotary magazine. What the would-be hunter couldn't get from Savage was a rifle in a larger caliber.

The 110 changed that. Offered first in .30-06 and .270, Savage upped the ante a few years later by offering the rifle in a host of calibers. As a trump to other makers, Savage also offered both right and left-hand versions. Left-handed shooters could finally use a rifle without reaching over the top to work the bolt.

The Savage 110 is similar to the Remington 700 in the design and assembly. The Savage receiver is machined from seamless tubing, with the recoil lug locked between the barrel and receiver. Unlike the Remington, the Savage uses a separate locking nut to clamp the receiver, barrel and recoil lug together. The trigger mechanism was yet another sheet metal box full of parts. The Savage did not have a hard time gaining public acceptance. The Remington rifles had proven that the old ways did not have to be the only ways, the cost was right, and every left-hander could have a bolt-action rifle.

Savage has continued manufacturing the Model 110, and while calibers come and go, and the choices for a southpaw vary from year to year, it remains a durable and accurate rifle.

Remove the barreled action from the stock by unscrewing the action screws. These are in front of and behind the magazine. The rear screw in the trigger guard only holds the trigger guard in place. Do not remove it. The trigger mechanism is the same sort of sealed box as found on the Remington rifles. Clamp the barrel in a padded vise.

At the front of the trigger mechanism is a large screw. This is the sear adjustment screw, and as with all the other rifles you should leave this screw alone. Directly behind the trigger pivot is the trigger stop screw. Next in line is the plunger for the trigger pull weight screw. The trigger weight screw itself is above, behind the rear opening in the receiver. The last screw behind the trigger is the safety stop screw.

Work the bolt and leave the action cocked. Push the safety to the "On" position. Observe the function of the safety stop. It should rest against the tail of the trigger without allowing it to move when you pull on the trigger. It must still do this after you have adjusted the trigger.

Open the bolt. Hold the trigger back and depress the lever on the right rear of the action. Remove the bolt from the action. Push the safety rearward. On front of the safety is a sheet metal cover that conceals the trigger pull adjustment screw. Pry this out with a small screwdriver or knife. Turning the screw counterclockwise reduces the weight of pull. If you turn the screw out too much it will interfere with the safety. Do not worry about this for the moment. Rotate the screw until you have your trigger pull to a suitable weight. If

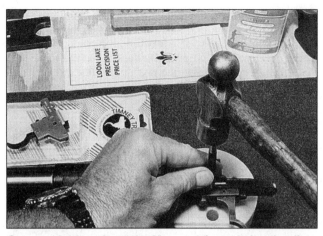

One good thing about the Mauser trigger is its simplicity. One pin holds the trigger on, and removing this pin lets you install the Timney.

the screw protrudes too high for the safety to function, use your dial calipers to measure just how much is too much. Then remove the screw, shorten it by that amount, and replace it. Once your trigger pull weighs what you want, reassemble the rifle and perform your safety checks. Even if the trigger passes the safety checks, remove it from the stock again. Work the bolt and leave the action cocked. Push the safety to the "On" position. Observe closely the function of the safety stop. Is it functioning as before? If not, you have to adjust it. The trigger must not have any movement when the safety is "On." The safety must not be hard to press "On." If the safety is too hard to press, you may push on the button and think the safety is "On" when it is not.

If the safety stop functions as it did before you adjusted weight, then the job is done. Replace the trigger adjustment screw cover and return the action to the stock.

Ruger Model 77

The Sturm, Ruger bolt-action rifle first saw the light of day in 1968. As with his other firearm designs, Bill Ruger incorporated the best of what he found in competitors rifles, while making the Model 77 hell for tough. It is also inexpensive. For Ruger, inexpensive does not mean a cheap

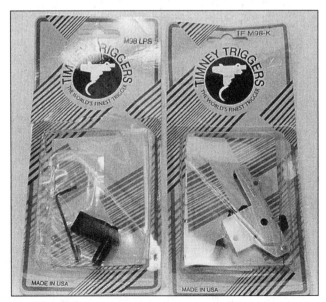

The Mauser is hell for tough, but the only thing you can do to improve the trigger pull is to replace the Mauser unit with a newer one. This Timney trigger is just the ticket.

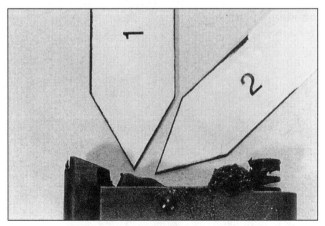

The two lumps on top of the Mauser trigger are the two cam surfaces that produce the two-stage trigger pull. The spring end is the forward end of the assembly.

At rest, the forward lump rides against the bottom of the receiver.

design or shortcuts in manufacturing. What it means is innovative design and fabrication. In the case of the Model 77 it meant an investment cast receiver. The receiver has gotten one change since the early days, when the scope mounting screws were deleted, to be replaced by integral dovetails for Ruger's own rings. Later, the trigger mechanism was overhauled.

There is one thing you must be aware of concerning Ruger firearms. Sturm, Ruger is the only family-owned fire-

arms company that makes a full line of guns. All of the other big handgun firms have been owned by various holding companies. Colt, in particular, was milked as a cash cow for decades. Sturm, Ruger has always been a private concern, and has always made a profit. As a result, Ruger has suffered a disproportionate share of liability lawsuits. No trial lawyer will sue a company that has no money or assets to claim. And a company with assets and profits will be sued even when they are not to blame. As a result of this, I would

Once the second lump bears against the receiver, the trigger can cam the sear away from the striker and fire the rifle.

not be surprised to find that somewhere in the design studios of Sturm, Ruger there is a committee that meets on a regular basis. The purpose of this committee is to make sure Ruger triggers are difficult to fiddle with.

The early rifles had adjustment screws for trigger pull weight, overtravel and sear engagement. The Ruger Model 77 Mk II does not have any of these.

If you wish to adjust the trigger weight on an early rifle, first remove it from the stock and clamp the barrel in a padded vise. Look closely at the assembly of the safety. You will not adjust it, but the parts are held in place by the stock. They may become dislodged or fall out during your trigger pull work. One method of keeping them in place is to slip a rubber band over the tang until you want to replace the action in the stock. At the front of the trigger housing is the overtravel adjustment screw. In the rear of the housing is the sear engagement screw. Neither screw will have to be adjusted. At the rear of the housing you will see a coil spring. Directly underneath that spring, in the trigger itself, is the weight adjustment screw. Use a small allen wrench to turn it. Turning the screw counter-clockwise reduces weight of pull. Turn the screw a quarter of a turn and check the trigger pull weight. Once you have gotten the pull down to 3-1/2 pounds, remove the rubber band and re-install the action in the stock. Perform your safety checks to be sure the striker remains cocked during brisk operation and bumping.

Seal the screw with a dab of paint to make sure it does not move from the vibrations of firing, or riding in a vehicle.

Those with Model 77 MkII (or the Model 77/22) rifles can adjust your trigger only after you replace it. You will have to invest in a Timney, Dayton Traister or Spec-Tech trigger. Once you have removed the factory trigger and replaced it with one of these, you can then use the adjustment screws to set your trigger up the way you want it.

Ruger 10/22

The Ruger 10/22 is another in the line of fabulously successful designs from the fertile mind of Bill Ruger. The niche of a .22 rimfire rifle is a difficult one to design for. It has to be light yet durable. It has to be handy yet accurate. It has to be inexpensive yet a possession to be proud of. Not all designers have done nearly as well in this balancing act.

The Ruger 10/22 is a blowback semi-auto rifle. The cartridge case is held in the chamber at the moment of firing by only two things: the weight of the bolt, and the power of the recoil spring. Unlike the bolt-action rifles we have discussed, the Ruger trigger mechanism has a disconnector. This removes the trigger from the linkage as the bolt cycles, keeping the rifle from firing more than one round per trigger pull.

Unlike the Sturm, Ruger bolt-action rifles, the 10/22 never left the factory with trigger adjustments. To improve the trigger pull of the 10/22 you have two choices. You can either invest in a stoning jig to stone the factory parts, or replace them with pre-stoned match parts. Of the two methods, the replacement one is faster, cheaper, easier and commonly done by competition shooters. Jim Clark, Volquartsen and John Power all make complete kits for your 10/22 trigger housing. Once you remove the factory parts and replace them with the match parts, your trigger will be a joy to shoot. Since there is no point in working with the factory parts, we will cover trigger work via the replacement method in Chapter Fifteen, Building the 10/22.

98 Mauser

Very few bolt-action rifles exist or are built today that do not borrow something from Peter Paul Mausers design. The precipitating cause of Mauser radically improving the design of bolt-action rifles was his losing a government contract. Instead of building the rifle designed by commit-

As you take up the slack, the second lump rises up to the bottom of the receiver.

The weight of the trigger pull doesn't make any difference to the Lahti rest. However, without the rest, the Spec-Tech trigger made a difference in accuracy. Shooter performance depends on a good trigger.

tee, he had to keep his company afloat by being a parts subcontractor. To avoid another such embarrassing episode in the future he had to design a rifle so perfect for the job that no committee could turn it down or modify it. His first patents were filed just in time to take advantage of the new smokeless powder. The first modern Mauser rifle, the 1889 Belgian was so superior to other designs that the effect on military rifle procurement was electric. Even while perfecting the design, the Mauser company had sales agents spread over the globe selling huge numbers of rifles to anxious War Departments. The advantages were so obvious that no army wanted to be without a Mauser, especially if their competitors had one. The design culminated in the adoption of the Model 1898 rifle by the German Army on April 5, 1898.

For those clients who insisted, Mauser would build a plant to produce rifles in their own country. The estimates of production of Mauser 98 rifles or their direct copies can only be general, but have exceeded 50 million! Not bad for a design that is over 100 years old.

Why was/is the 98 so popular? Strength, durability, safety to the user, versatility and looks. The 98 design is strong enough to contain any cartridge a brave shooter is willing to fire from the shoulder. The basic design has been modified and chambered for calibers up to .458 Winchester. A special oversized model built in WWI as an anti-tank rifle in 13 millimeter can be easily re-barreled to the .50 Browning Machinegun cartridge. As to durability, the Mauser may have peers but it has no master. An example would be rifles shipped to China. All of these rifles exceed half a century in age. The level of maintenance these rifles have seen varies from benign neglect to utter indifference. The bore may be worn, or rusted out and no longer have rifling. The stock may be held together with baling wire. If you put a cartridge in the chamber and pull the trigger, the rifle will fire. Not that you or I would do such a thing, but if you were a warlord issuing rifles to trusted peasants, these would be the ones you would want.

When it comes to safety for the user (especially with the Chinese rifle we just fired) the Mauser shines. Vent holes in both the bolt and receiver will allow gases from a ruptured case to spill away from the shooter. The clip-feed thumb slot

vents even more gas. Little gas will continue the length of the bolt. A shoulder on the bolt shroud diverts those gases away from the shooters eye. The extractor is designed to capture the rim of the cartridge as it feeds from the magazine. Called "controlled feeding" it ensures the cartridge will find the chamber despite how the rifle is held. It also prevents "double-feeding." With many rifles, pushing the bolt forward pushes the cartridge ahead of it, out of the magazine. The extractor does not snap over the cartridge rim until the bolt is turned down. If, in the excitement of a hunt (or the near-panic of dangerous game turning into a dangerous situation) the shooter does not turn the bolt handle down, the extractor will not snap over the rim on those rifles. When he pulls the bolt back the cartridge will stay in the chamber. Pushing the bolt forward will push another cartridge into the base of the chambered round. This situation is relatively easy to correct, except when you have to correct it in the next few moments.

The Mauser cannot be made to double-feed. As the bolt goes forward and the round feeds out of the magazine, it is corralled by the extractor before it finishes leaving the magazine. You can push the Mauser bolt forward and back without turning it down, and feed and extract one round after another.

The Mauser has been chambered in cartridges from rimfires to elephant busters, and even shotgun gauges. After WWI, the only thing Germany had a surplus of was rifles. With some modifications and a new barrel, they were sold overseas as two-shot shotguns.

As far as looks are concerned, few rifles can be turned into as classy-looking a sporter as the Mauser.

So, after all this, what is the drawback? After all, there has to be one, right?

There is one. It is the trigger. The trigger is tough, durable, and as adjustable as a brick. The Mauser 98 trigger has five parts of which only two move. The trigger has two bumps on its upper surface that act as the pivot points for the trigger's drawing of the sear. The two bumps intentionally create the "two-stage" or military trigger. The first pivot point creates the "slack" and the second pulls the sear out of contact with the striker. There are no built-in adjustments. For all of this complaining, the original Mauser trigger pull is quite good enough for the majority of shooting applica-

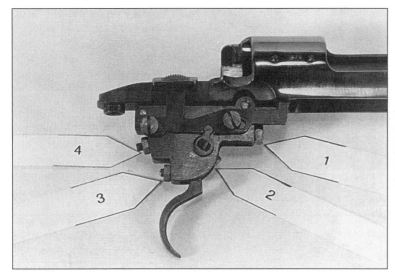

The trigger mechanism of the Mauser MkX. #1 is the weight of pull adjustment screw. #2 is the safety adjustment screw. #3 is the over-travel adjustment screw. #4 is the sear engagement adjustment screw (don't touch this one!).

tions. For precise applications the trigger must be improved. The traditional methods of improving the Mauser trigger pull involved stoning the engagement between the sear and striker. The small improvement that can be had from the original parts (the military original) is not worth the effort. Sit down with the Brownells catalog and select a replacement trigger that has the adjustments built in. Modify your stock if necessary to fit the new trigger.

Mauser Mark X

Pronounced "Mauser Mark Ten," the Ten is now an orphan. Made in a country that no longer exists (Yugoslavia) and imported by a company struggling to survive after the death of its founder, (Interarms) the Ten is nonetheless a great rifle to own and build on. Yugoslavia adopted the Mauser starting with the FN Model 1924. After WWII the government arms factory was in the business of making rifles for themselves. Importing rifles to the United States seemed like a good way to make money, so they improved the rifle for sportsmen and shipped them here.

The Ten differs from the military Mauser in several ways. There is no thumb cutout on the left receiver wall, the rear bridge does not have a slot for stripper clips, and the receiver is drilled and tapped for a scope mount. The big change is in the trigger and safety. The safety is not on the bolt shroud. It is a lever attached to the trigger mechanism, that sticks out of the stock on the right side.

The trigger is adjustable. To change the trigger pull remove the barreled action from the stock and clamp it in a padded vise. Make sure it is empty. On the front of the trigger mechanism is the weight of pull adjustment screw. Beneath it is the safety adjustment screw. Behind the trigger itself is the overtravel adjustment. In the upper rear is the sear engagement screw. The three main ones have lock nuts on them. You only need to adjust two of them, the weight and overtravel. You might have to adjust the safety screw after setting weight and overtravel.

Loosen the lock nut on the trigger weight screw. Turn the screw counterclockwise. Weigh the trigger pull after each turn until the weight is 3-1/2 pounds. Tighten the lock nut. To adjust overtravel loosen the lock nut. Turn the screw clockwise until it stops, then back it out 1/8 of a turn. My rifle is a .458, and just in case it ever goes someplace where it may be used on dangerous game, I have the overtravel

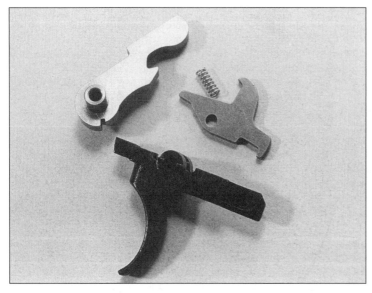

Unless you have bins of parts to select from and use the Armorers method of trigger improvement on the AR, you need to replace the military parts. The precision-machined hammer, sear and disconnector from Accuracy Speaks are a distinct improvement over the military parts.

screw turned out 1/4 turn. The extra overtravel is a small price to pay to make sure it never fails to work.

The safety blocks the trigger. If the mechanism shows wear, or has been adjusted down from a much higher trigger pull, the trigger may show movement when the safety is on. To tighten the safety bar and prevent trigger movement, cock the rifle and put the safety on. Turn the safety adjustment 1/8 of a turn clockwise and try the trigger. If it still shows movement, turn the screw in again. Continue until the trigger does not move when the safety is on. Check the safety to make sure you have not made it too tight. If the safety binds, loosen the adjustment screw just a fraction of a turn. You want the safety to block the trigger, but you don't want the trigger mechanism to be so tight the safety is a bear to push on and off.

AR-15

Unlike the Mauser, when the AR-15/M-16 was adopted it was not universally loved. It quickly gained an undeserved reputation as a rifle that jammed often and one that didn't have what it needed to get the job done. As the passions of that era have faded, the AR has had a chance to show what it is made of. Given the proper care that any rifle should get, it will continue working for as long as the user needs it. It can be tuned or built to be as accurate, heavy, light, unwieldy or handy as you want. What it won't do is respond to the usual trigger-improving methods. The factory trigger mechanism does not have any provision for adjustment.

The trigger parts are surface-hardened for durability. If you stone the engagement surfaces you can and will break through the hard skin and expose the relatively softer steel underneath. If you stone, the trigger job you sweated over will not last long. Do not polish or stone your AR hammer or trigger in an attempt to improve your trigger pull. Even apparent success can be soon followed by disappointment.

There are two methods of gaining an improved trigger pull in your AR-15. The first is the Armorer Method. Military armorers have many rifles to select from, and a vast number of replacement parts. To gain an improved trigger pull, the military armorer will sit down at his bench with a candidate AR (or M-16) and a couple dozen hammers and triggers. He will patiently install one pair after another and weigh the trigger pull each time. Eventually he will get the trigger pull he wants. When I used this method I often got positive results with as few as three or four hammers and triggers.

The drawbacks of this method are obvious. You have to invest in a bunch of hammers and triggers, and be willing to install each of them for testing. If you do not find a suitable pair within your selection, your investment is a bust.

As a result, enterprising manufacturers have fabricated match trigger parts. JP Enterprises, Armalite and Accuracy Speaks are companies that make match hammer and trigger sets. With one of these installed in your AR-15 and tuned according to the instructions, a 3-1/2-pound trigger is a cinch. We will be installing just such a match hammer and trigger in Chapter Eighteen, Building the AR-15.

Remington 742 Series rifles

The Remington 740 made its appearance after the Korean War. Before WWII, Remington had the Model 8 and Model 81 rifles in their lineup. Designed by John Browning, they were durable to a fault. Among their other faults were that they were too heavy, lacked accuracy except as a woods rifle, and were not capable of handling the .30-06 cartridge. In the design changes after the war the prominent "hump" on the rear of the receiver that had been on all Remingtons except the pump rifles, was done away with. Starting with the 11-48 shotgun and continuing from there, all Remington shotguns and rifles were brought into the modern age.

The 740 was improved to the 742, then the 7400. These internal changes from one model number to the next had to do with durability and accuracy. The basic trigger mechanism was not changed. Is there any way to improve the trigger pull of the Remington 74-series? Not by stoning the existing parts. Unlike many other rifles, the sear notch of the hammer on the Remington is on top of the hammer. When the rifle cycles, the hammer swings back and brushes past the sear. The sear, released from the trigger by the disconnector, is pressed forward by its spring. When the hammer swings forward, the sear must catch it and keep it. The sear is small, the hammer large. The sear does not have a lot of leverage, and the hammer has a powerful spring pushing on it. To ensure that the sear always captures the hammer, the notch on the hammer is angled inwards. If you reduce the depth of the notch, or alter the angle, the hammer will not stay cocked.

This will not turn the rifle into a machinegun. Each time you fire the rifle, the hammer will follow the bolt forward. If you pull the trigger then, nothing will happen. When you let go of the trigger and work the operating handle, the sear will probably be able to hold onto the hammer, letting you fire again. The symptom of firing every other round is a classic in the Remington. At the merest mention of it, any gunsmith can immediately dive into fixing the problem.

It is not a matter of admitting defeat to say that the Remington trigger cannot be improved, but a matter of facing facts. The trigger is good enough as it is, and the geometry is so much against us, that there is no point in trying to improve it.

CHAPTER 5

Scope Mounting

"They couldn't hit an elephant at this dist..."

General John Sedgewick in the opening moments of the Battle of
Spotsylvania, May 8th, 1864.

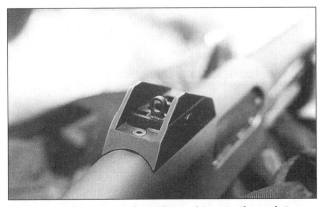

Centuries of progress have brought us to the point where current shotguns have better sights than the first rifles. While it is on a shotgun, this Gunsite-installed MMC receiver sight could easily be installed on a Remington 7400. The sight is so tough, I'm not sure you could hurt it with a hammer.

The current rear sight on the M16A2 is a very good sight, but nothing is too good for a dedicated target shooter. This sight has been updated with a hooded aperture and a quarter-inch click adjustment wheel. (Remember, a quarter-inch click at 100 yards is an inch and a half at 600.)

The whole purpose of a rifle is hitting a particular point on a target. Aiming is the only way to accomplish that end. When muskets were the most common individual military weapon, sights were a factory option most armies did without. Many muskets did not have sights, while those that did would feature only a front sight. After all, in the tactics of the time the volley was followed by a bayonet charge. The charge and resulting combat were what mattered. Why bother with sights?

The sights on rifles of the period were often mechanical marvels. While commanding officers wanted to win battles and wars, shooting competitors wanted to win matches. Then as now, no competitor wanted to be left behind if, by getting better equipment, he could keep up.

The main problem with iron sights (non-optical sights) is a matter of focus. Optical focus, not mental focus. In order to aim, you have to line up three things; the rear sight, the front sight, and the target. Depending on the design of the sights, you will have to shift your focus several times between at least two of them and sometimes all three. This

The problem with iron sights such as this is that your eye must constantly shift focus from this small blade and its notch...

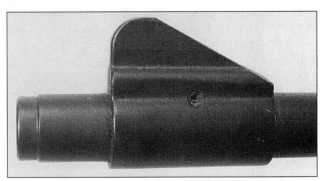

to the front blade, the target and back again. As your eyes (and you) age, the speed at which they can shift focus slows down, making aiming more difficult.

An aperture or receiver sight (such as this GG&G on a flat-top AR) make sighting easier. The trick to an aperture or "ghost ring" sight is to look THROUGH it and not at it. If you let your eye do its thing it will automatically center in the ring.

This German scope is not sealed very well, although they did their best back in the early 1940s. Still, it is bright, clear and as good as a common import scope. It is better than many "bargain" scopes, and features a range-drop compensator dial! What it really lacks are internal adjustments. This scope must be zeroed by moving the mounts. That's a big headache.

takes time and effort. As you get older, it becomes increasingly difficult. A telescopic sight greatly eases this process. Optically the crosshairs (the "reticle") and the target are the same distance from your eye. You only have to focus your eye on one thing, the aiming point of the reticle.

As with so many technologies, optical scopes for rifles got a big boost during a war. The war was the Civil War, and the scopes were used by sharpshooters. In later wars the name for the job would be changed to "sniper." The job of the sharpshooter was to use accurate rifle fire to make the enemy's job even more difficult than it would otherwise be. With the scope it was easier to identify and select officers, messengers and other sharpshooters. The scopes of the time were crude. Extending the length of the barrel and offering a dark view of the world, they still made the job of sharpshooter more efficient than it would be with iron sights. No doubt the General, sitting on his horse surveying the battlefield, made himself an obvious target. By staying in one spot for a few seconds, he made himself a target. His last comment made him quotable.

For a long time the drawbacks to scopes were fragility, adjustment, loss of zero, field of view and lack of a backup sight when the scope inevitably failed. For a long time scopes were fragile. A bump or jolt could dislodge or break the optics. Many scope mounts were designed with quick removal in mind. A shooter could remove the scope and

The European method of mounting scopes did not start out by drilling and tapping. With their customers favoring quick-detachable scopes, European gunsmiths fitted the front base into a dovetail on the front ring. On this Model 1903 M-S, the scope, base and rings are long gone, and the dovetail is filled with a blank.

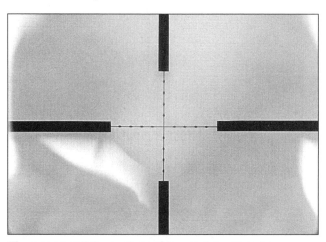

The scope reticle, such as this mil-dot reticle by Leupold, is the single object that competes with the target for your eyes attention. Focusing from the reticle to the target and back again is relatively simple.

The split bridge on the M-S meant the rear scope base could only be held in place with a single screw. The reason for all this effort was to allow quick removal of the scope and thus use of the iron sights. In an era of fragile and unreliable scopes, a prudent course of action.

Modern rifles are now almost all shipped already drilled and tapped for scope mounts on the rear......

keep it in a separate storage box during the trip to the hunting camp or target range. Or, if the scope broke, a replacement could be quickly slid into place. Scopes were not sealed. Moisture would get into them, fogging the optics. Early scopes did not have adjustments. The adjustments had to be made by adjusting the mount. The early scopes had narrow fields of view and did not gather light well. The images they presented were dim. Field of view is commonly measured as the width, in feet, of what you see through the scope at 100 yards. Early scopes sometimes would show you only a 10-foot slice of the world. And this with a 2-power scope.

The design of early rifles and stocks often made the scope-mounting methods awkward and fragile. Rifles were not designed with scope-mounting in mind. Since scopes were not popular with shooters, the gun designers were not going to make changes for a minority of shooters. These awkward mounts either blocked the iron sights or even took the mounting dovetails the irons used.

By "early" scopes I mean almost everything made prior to WWII. Again, the demands of war improved the technol-ogy. Leading the way in many regards were the Germans. I have a WWII sniper scope from Germany in my collection. Compared to a scope of today it is a plain bit of optical design. The glass is not coated and the tube is sealed poorly by today's standards. The only adjustment it has is a range adjustment, with no windage adjustment. Yet compared to an American scope of the period, the German scope is bright, clear, sharp and a marvel to use. It compares favorably with the economy scopes you could buy right now.

The latest reviews are in, and scopes have won the struggle. Scopes have won the struggle so convincingly that almost every rifle is already factory drilled-and-tapped for a scope, and many rifles now leave the factory with no iron sights at all. Nor is there any provision for mounting them. I can recall more than one customer of mine asking what the little holes were for, on the side of their rifle? "That is where you mount a receiver sight." I would reply. After a puzzled pause they would ask "What's a receiver sight?" Scopes have changed more than the fortunes of iron sight manufacturers, they have changed stock design. The line of sight for the use of a scope rests higher above the barrel than the line of sight for iron sights would. If the stock is proportioned such that your shooting eye is in line with the iron sights, the scope is too high. This stock proportion is called "drop."

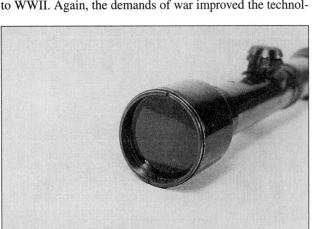

The glass of the German sniper scope I own is not coated. It is not as bright as it would be if it were coated, but it is so well made that it is still a bright and clear optical instrument.

And front of the receiver. The factory can be counted on to get the holes correctly spaced, straight up and down, and on the centerline of the receiver. If you have a rifle that was drilled and tapped after it left the factory, you might not be able to count on all of these.

If you shoot a rifle with a large drop in the stock, correct for iron sights, using iron sights, you will shoot comfortably. If you mount a scope, you must lift your face above the stock. This does two things. One, your face is not supported and can move behind the scope. This makes your aiming difficult. Secondly, the stock has running room before it strikes your face in recoil. This causes you discomfort. Many modern stocks are designed with so little drop that using iron sights would be difficult. I have shouldered rifles with so little drop that I could not scrunch my face down far enough to use the iron sights.

And the modern scope mounts are not at all like the fragile and awkward mounts of the past.

What should you look for in a scope? You will be hard-pressed in today's market to find a scope that is not multi-coated, sealed, guaranteed and inexpensive. The coating on a scope handles the pesky problem of reflection. Most of the light striking a piece of glass passes through it. Some is reflected. This is death to good viewing through a scope. Each surface reflects some light. If the reflected light is only five percent, and a scope only has three pieces of glass (six surfaces) your scope would reflect and lose 27 percent of the light entering it. The coating reduces reflections and increases the efficiency of the elements. Since an individual coating can only correct for reflections in a narrow section of the light spectrum, manufacturers use multiple coatings to handle reflections across the spectrum of visible light. When coatings first appeared, they were only on the outside, and only of one type. Modern scopes are coated inside and out, with multiple coatings.

Early scopes were not sealed against the elements. Rain, snow or high humidity could fog the glass. Mildew could grow inside a scope, etching the glass. The lenses would then have to be polished. By manufacturing to tighter tolerances and using internal rubber rings and gaskets, modern scopes are watertight. Leupold even tests their seals by placing each scope in boiling water. If a bubble comes out, the scope wasn't sealed, and it goes back to the line. The warranty on modern scopes is fabulous. In many scopes, if anything goes wrong you will get it fixed free. Even if you can't find the receipt, or remember when you bought it.

And cost? Before WWII, it was not unheard of for a

The collimator is a very useful tool. It spares you the headaches of sighting in a rifle that has a scope pointed way off, or of using your neighbor's deck awning as an aiming point for bore-sighting. This Simmons set has extra-long rods for use on rifles equipped with the Browning BOSS.

scope to cost more than the rifle it went on. Even an expensive rifle would be less costly than the cheapest scope. Now, you can buy a first-class scope for half the price of an ordinary rifle.

With all the advantages a scope has to offer, now is the time to put one on your rifle. Here we will cover how to mount a scope to a rifle that is already drilled and tapped. We will cover drilling and tapping later in this chapter, and in Chapter Twenty. To install a scope you will need your rifle, already drilled and tapped. You need a scope mounting system and a scope. You will need either a rifle cradle or a padded vise. The rifle cradle can be the same one you use to hold the rifle while you clean it. You will need some method to check the alignment of the scope once it is on the rifle. This can either be a distant object through a window, or a bore collimator. Pointing a rifle out of the window can get you in trouble in many places. Investing in a bore collimator can save you many headaches. You will need screwdrivers that fit the plug screws of your rifle, and the screws or Allen nuts on the scope mounting system.

Scope mounting systems come as two sets of components: bases and rings. The bases bolt to the rifle itself. The rings clamp around the scope, and then fasten to the bases. The scope mount world is divided into three camps: the Weaver system, the Redfield system, and the see-through rings.

In addition to the rifle and scope, you'll need a few other things to marry the two. A cradle to hold the rifle, bases and rings for the scope, a screwdriver set, a bore collimator, and a ring alignment/lapping tool like the Kokopelli, complete the ensemble.

The scope base for this Springfield M1A clamps into the single hole drilled and tapped into the receiver. The rings and scope then clamp to the base.

Not all bases are separate from the scope. This Colt scope has its base attached directly to the scope tube, and does not need rings. Why aren't more scopes made this way? Because no scope maker could afford to make a different scope for each model rifle, and no store could afford to stock them all.

When you order or buy your scope rings and base or bases, you have to plan where the scope will sit on your rifle. Each scope has a certain designed distance for your eye to rest behind it. There is some leeway for each scope. This distance is called "eye relief." You want your scope to rest about 3 inches from your eye. A rifle with very heavy recoil may require more eye relief to keep you from getting bitten by your scope when you shoot.

You will need your rifle, your scope, a ruler, some masking tape and a notepad. Take a piece of tape about two inches long. Shoulder the rifle and place the tape across the comb of the stock under your eye. Now place your rifle on its side on your bench. Place the scope on the bench, above the action, with the rear of the scope three inches from the tape. Note the location of the scope mount screw holes on your receiver. Check their locations against the front and

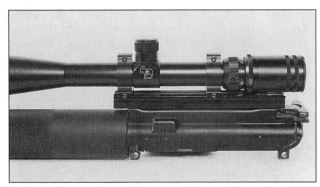

Before AR15s were available with factory flat-tops, gunsmiths had to mill the handle off and attach a base. This base had to be epoxied on before it would stay tight. If you want a flat-top, it is easier to buy one and switch the parts than to cut the handle off.

This flat-top from JP Enterprize is a first-class way to put a scope on an AR15. You can also have it anodized many other colors besides black!

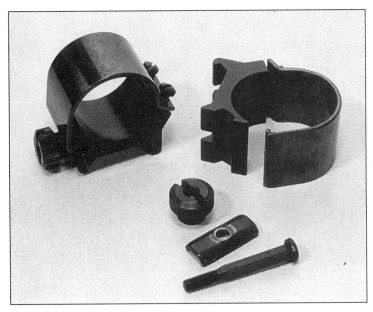

The Weaver rings come as an aluminum base, and steel screws, top ring, clamping plate and nut and screw. Light and durable, their only fault in some eyes is their lack of elegance.

rear bells of the scope. Also look at the center boss where the adjustment knobs are. If your bells or boss ride right over the screw holes, you may need an offset ring. An offset ring clamps around the scope but angles to the base rather than attaching vertically. You will not have a problem with full-sized scopes. The problem usually comes up when you go to put a compact scope on a rifle.

Weaver Scope Rings

The Weaver system is durable, cheap, light but somewhat bulky. Most of the parts are made of aluminum. The bases are flat sections of aluminum bar stock. The bottom of each base is contoured to match the front or rear of the rifle receiver it fits onto. The rings clamp to the bases by means of a large knurled nut which squeezes an angled plate against the bevel of the base. The top of the rings are steel. One end hooks over the bottom of the ring and the other end is secured with two screws. Once installed the Weaver is very durable. Being constructed of aluminum it is possible for you to break the rings if you install them improperly.

To install the Weaver rings you will need three screwdrivers, a small one, a medium one and a large one. You might have to grind a clearance notch in the middle of the blade of the large one. Secure your rifle in the cradle. Use a small screwdriver to remove the plug screws. Take a bottoming tap and run it into each hole to clean out the grease. Most rifles will have the scope mount holes tapped 6-48. Some, like the Remington 7400, will use 8-40 screws. Place the bases on the receiver and insert one screw. Turn the screw until the base is snug but not tight. Use a straightedge to check alignment of the bases. They should be level and parallel to each other. If they are not, check to make sure you have the right bases, and have them correctly installed front and back. If they are the right bases and correctly installed and they do not line up, you have a problem. If it is a new rifle, send it back to the manufacturer or take it back to the gun shop where you bought it. If the rifle pre dates standardized scope mounts, the tops of the receiver may have been heavily polished and thus lowered. You will have to use shims to get the bases lined up.

If the rifle predates scope mounts, and someone drilled and tapped the holes incorrectly, you have a big headache. To check you will need four taps. Remove the bases and

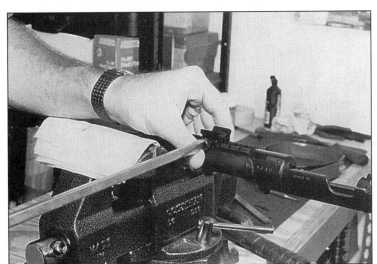

The ring bottom clamps onto the base. Start by securing the bases only finger-tight until you have established the correct scope location for proper eye relief.

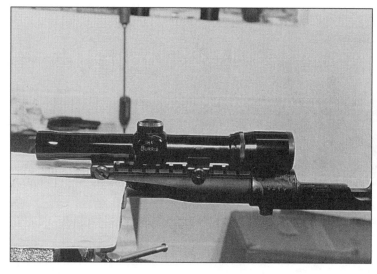

The proper eye relief on this Ashley scout scope base installation is with the rear bell clearing the receiver opening. Now tighten the ring bottom clamping screw.

screw a tap into each hole. Use the straightedge to check alignment of the taps. If they do not line up you will have to take the rifle to a professional to have the hole or holes welded, dressed down and re-drilled and tapped.

If only one hole is out of line, you can immediately switch to a Redfield one-piece base and not install the out-of-line screw.

With the bases in line, install the other screws and snug them down. Take the ring bottoms and place them on the bases, and check alignment again. Why all this emphasis on alignment? If the bases or rings are out of line the scope will be stressed. When you fully tighten everything you will at least mar, and maybe even damage the scope. If the ring bottoms line up, remove them and tighten the base rings. To do this, use a correctly-fitting screwdriver and press down with the palm of one hand while tightening the screw with the other. Go through the four screws in turn, and repeat. Many shooters ask the question "should you use Loctite?" I've installed scopes on rifles for nearly two decades, and used Loctite only on the really big calibers. I have seen too many cases where Loctite was used excessively, and gummed up the action. If you must use it, use it sparingly, one drop at a time.

With the bases secured, assemble the ring bottoms. Slip the clamping plate over the screw and turn the knurled nut onto the threads. Place the tip of the screw into the recess on the shouldered side of the ring bottom. Place the ring bottom onto the base with the knurled nut on the left side of the rifle. Doing this keeps the nuts out of the path of ejecting brass, and away from your hand when you work the bolt or operating handle. When you tighten the knurled nut the base will be clamped between the ring shoulder and the clamping plate. Make sure the plate rests against the base and snug the nut down by hand. Use the large screwdriver to tighten the nut.

The Weaver ring tops are steel, with both ends folded. One end is folded inwards, while the other is folded outwards and has two screw holes through the lip. If you press the ring over the tube by pushing both ends, the inward-folded end will scratch the scope tube. Place the ring tops over the scope tube by holding the bent end stationary against the tube and pressing the end with the screw holes down. Push the ring tops to opposite ends of the scope. Place the scope in the ring bottoms. Slide the ring tops to the bottoms, catching the folded inward lip of the tops under the ledge on the bottoms.

The tightened clamping screw holds the ring bottom to the scope base. Tighten this screw, and on a hard-kicking caliber, dab dark nail polish to mark the screw head location. If the nail polish mark is broken, the screw has moved.

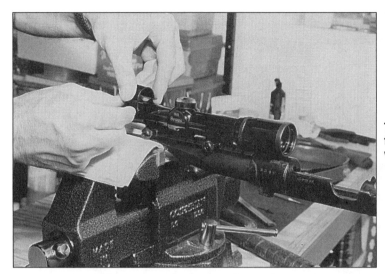

To snap the ring tops over the scope, hold the folded end against the scope and slide the end with the screw holes in it down over the scope.

Now the fussing begins. It is possible for you to over-tighten these screws and strip the threads out of the aluminum. Once stripped there is no easy way to repair the ring. The ring walls are thin and will not stand up to re-tapping to a larger thread. If you over-tighten and strip the threads you will have to buy new rings. Rings come only in pairs. Your excessive zeal means you will have to buy two new ones to replace the single one you damaged. The good news is that with extra rings you can use the damaged one to improve your control. Deliberately tighten the remaining undamaged screw a bit at a time. Continue until you have stripped that screw hole. Fix firmly in your mind just how much effort it took. Tighten less than that in the future. Since the screws should not be over-tightened, how can you make sure the scope will not slip under recoil? Degrease the rings and scope, and place a small drop of Loctite 242 on the ring bottom. It will keep the scope from slipping, but not interfere with scope removal if you want to change scopes later.

The locking screws are both on one side. As you tighten them, they will pull the ring top and the scope towards them, slightly tilting the scope. If you start with your scope reticle straight, the tightening will tilt it. To end up straight, you have to start with the reticle tilted slightly away from the locking screws. Then, as you tighten them, they will pull the scope up straight. Even after doing it for years, I would occasionally have to tighten a set of rings on a rifle two or three times until it was just right. If you tighten yours and the scope looks off, loosen the screws and do it again.

How to check reticle straightness? The easy answer is "if it looks straight, it is." However, there are many rifles that look straight to their owners, which are not straight.

Once the top is on the scope, slide the lip of the top under the notch on the bottom, and press the ring top into place over the bottom.

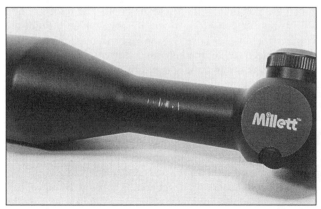

If you slide the folded end instead of the screw-hole end, you may scratch the scope body, as on this Millet.

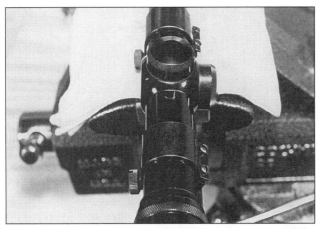

You can see here that both tightening screws for the ring top are on the same side. As you tighten them, the scope will tilt towards them, in this case clockwise. You must start with the crosshairs slightly "before noon" so the tightening will pull them up straight.

If your crosshairs are slightly "past noon" you'll have to loosen the ring screws, tilt the scope and tighten again.

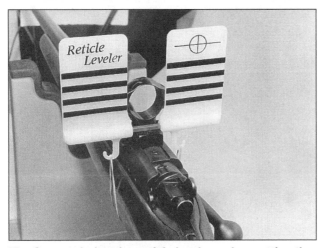

The Segway Industries reticle leveler makes getting the crosshairs level a lot easier. In this photo the scope has been removed so you can see the leveler. The crossbar rests on the base, and the rubber band pulls it tight. Let your eyes follow the lines across, and level the reticle as you go.

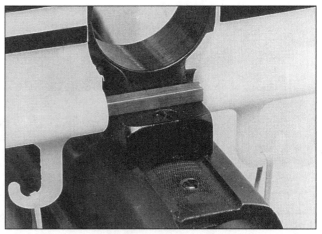

You can see that the leveler brings the scope level with the base. If your base is on the rifle crooked, you'll have to use the Eyeball, MkI as a leveling device.

One method that I used to good effect was to follow the vertical of the reticle down through the action of the rifle. If that imaginary line did not run through the center of the action, the scope was tilted. Getting the knack for seeing this alignment took quite a few rifles. Since you will not be mounting scopes on 100 rifles, there has to be another way. For bolt-action rifles an alignment scale that fits into the action will give you a guide. For other rifles, a guide that slips over the scope itself will help you level your scope. B-Square makes a clear plastic guide that slides into the rear of your action after you have removed the bolt. Segway Industries makes a unit that can be used on rifles that are not open in the rear, such as a Ruger 10/22 or a Remington 7400. The Segway leveler has two hooks on the bottom. By looping a rubber band over the hooks and around the rifle, the leveler is pulled flush to the scope base. The base is assumed to be square to the receiver, and level to the bore. If your rifle has had the holes drilled other than vertical, the Segway might lead you astray. More likely, the Segway reticle leveler will alert you to the fact that your scope is not mounted straight. Unless you have the experience of mounting hundreds of rifles, the reticle leveler will be a great aid.

Check scope alignment with the bore. Called "bore-sighting," this is a quick method of checking that the bore and the scope are pointing in the same direction. The basic method still works for bolt-action rifles. Remove the bolt. Point the cradled rifle towards a window and look through the bore at a distant object. Center the bore on the object. Without moving the rifle, look through the scope. If necessary, adjust the reticle until it is centered on the distant object.

The newer method, and one that does not require a window, is to use a bore collimator. The collimator unit consists of a mandrel that fits in your bore and an optical body. The body contains a set of lenses and a grid. When you place the mandrel in your bore and look through the scope you will see the grid. Adjust the scope until the reticle is centered on the grid.

While both methods will get you on paper at the range, neither will ensure you are in the x-ring. You still have to go to the range and shoot for yourself. Every year I would be faced with a steady stream of hunters who wanted their rifles "bore-

The scope on regular AR's sits too high to use a standard collimator. You have to use an offset tool to get the collimator up high enough to be in the scope's field of vision.

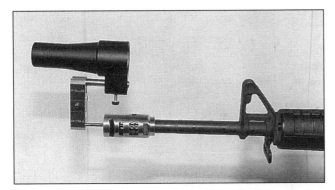

Here is the Simmons collimator in the B-Square offset spud, high enough to be seen in the scope.

sighted for 100 yards." Or 50 yards. Or 200 yards. After the first couple of years I gave up trying to explain about bore-sighting, and just centered their scopes on the grid. I suppose I shouldn't have been too critical, as many would come back with stories and photos of their successful hunt.

One additional use for the collimator is as a check when you go hunting. Once you have sighted your rifle in and it is hitting exactly where you want it to, check it on the collimator. Do not be alarmed if the reticle is not centered on the

Adjust the crosshairs to the center of the grid, and then go to the range and sight in your rifle. With the rifle zeroed, record the actual collimator settings for that rifle and ammunition. On a trip, you can check your zero without shooting by using the collimator.

grid. Just make a note of where it is. A small card to go in your gun case will do nicely. Note where on the grid you are such as "two squares left and three down, 100-yard zero with 180-grain Whamblaster ammo." When you get to the hunting camp, you can check your scope by installing the collimator and looking. If the scope has been jarred, the reticle will not be in the same location of the grid as it was when you left the range. A really careful hunter will zero his rifle with several acceptable factory loads and note the locations on the grid. If you get to the hunting camp and find out you haven't any ammo, you can buy any of the two or three loads you have checked. Crank the reticle to the location on the grid noted for that ammo, and you are zeroed and ready to go. It may seem like a bit of work, but if you've spent thousands of dollars to get there, spending an afternoon making sure your rifle is zeroed is small insurance.

The Redfield system

The Redfield base and scope ring system was developed back when scopes were fragile and uncertain. All steel, the bases come in two flavors, one-piece or two-piece. The front ring is secured in the base by a dovetail that slides into the base and is then rotated ninety degrees. The rear rings are held on by opposing screws that clamp to the rings bottom half.

The Redfield system is nearly indestructible in the field. The rotating front and screw-retained rear rings allow a scope to be centered on the bore even before you have to use the scope's internal adjustments. This was a definite plus in the old days when scopes had a limited or non-existant adjustment range. Now it just makes things easier in difficult cases.

When mounting scopes on hundreds of rifles a year, I occasionally saw strange things. An example of the Redfield system coming to the rescue involved a rifle that would hit the next target to the left. Yes, several feet to the side of where the scope was pointing. I checked the base and the base holes in the receiver. The holes were straight in line, and the base was straight to the receiver. Then I noticed the barrel. It must have been threaded at an angle to the bore. Or maybe the front of the receiver was dressed at an angle, because the barrel pointed off to the left. (I will not mention the maker because it was a single experience. I'm sure the

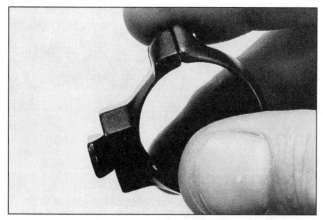

The Redfield system (this is a Millet ring) uses a rotary dovetail to secure the front ring. The mushroom-like extension has been cut flat on two sides, so it will.....

The rear ring has two semi-circular cuts on the bottom, where the locking screws nestle into place and lock the rear ring down.

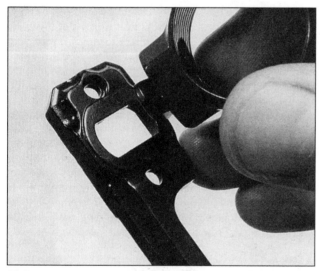

Fit into the front base hole. By turning the ring 90 degrees once it is in the hole, the front ring will be......

The locking screws clamp the rear ring, but also allow you to adjust the rear ring location for windage. Also note that most one-piece rings only use one of the rear screw holes to hold the base in place.

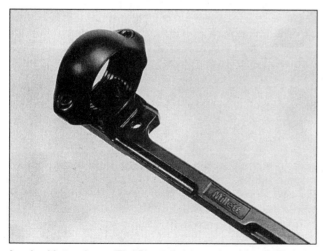

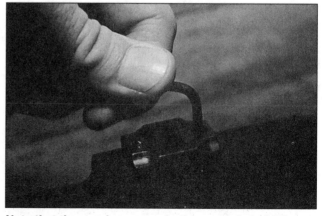

Locked into place. The front right can be turned slightly to adjust for windage, and let you get the scope centered before you start using any of the scopes internal adjustments.

Note that the rear base uses both screws to hold the base in place. Very few one-piece bases use all four screws to hold the base.

This is the rear of the Badger Ordnance scope base, available from the Chandler brothers at Iron Brigade Armory. It uses all four scope base screw holes, and also uses Torx screws for greater holding power.

manufacturer would correct it if the owner wanted to, but he did not. That rifle had been his father's, it was then his, and would be his son's. He would not allow changes to the rifle.) By changing to a Redfield mount I was able to angle the scope to the left enough to allow me to get the reticle on the grid. He got a deer with that rifle that season, and has gotten one every year since I've known him.

Both the Leupold bases and rings and the Millett bases and rings are made to the same ring-and-base interface dimensions as the Redfield. A set of rings for one will fit the base of another. Leupold now ships their bases and rings with Torx screws. At first the screws seem a little funny, not being a single slot or Allen head. The multiple shoulders, and the heat-treating of the screws allows you to tighten the screws more than slotted screws or Allen head screws. You can easily keep your scope on without Loctite.

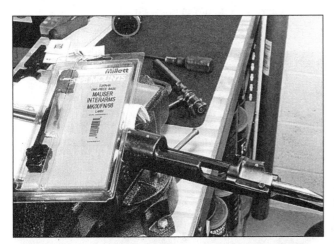

You need the correct base for your model rifle. While some rifles share receiver/scope base dimensions, there are a host that don't. If it turns out you've gotten the wrong base, don't hesitate to send or take it back for the right one.

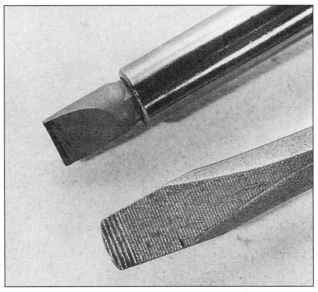

The standard screwdriver on the bottom has been modified. The blade has been ground to a curve to match the slot of the rear ring screws on a Redfield system ring. Don't be afraid to make a special-purpose screwdriver, but be sure to mark it and stash it with the rest of the tools for that particular job.

To install the Redfield or the Leupold you need a small screwdriver for the plug screws. For the base and ring screws you need either a slotted screwdriver or an allen wrench or Torx wrench. Redfield and Leupold include such a wrench with your rings and base. You'll need a ring wrench or 1-inch diameter rod at least a foot long. You will also need a large screwdriver with a fat blade. You have just found the sole case where the blade width of a standard screwdriver for home or shop use will be too narrow for gun work. If you do not have such a screwdriver, then a large bull-nosed pair of pliers and a couple of quarters will do. Do not expect the quarters to fit into a vending machine after you have abused them.

Remove the plug screws and clean out the threads in the receiver. Remove the base from the package and wipe off the protective oil. Place the base on the receiver and check for hole alignment and base alignment. For hole alignment, simply look through the holes in the base. For base align-

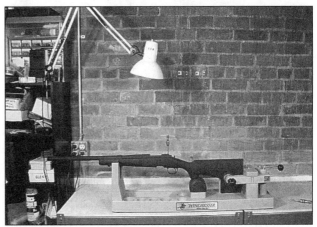

Before you try to tighten the base screws, clean the threads out.

You can sometimes clean an impressive amount of gunk out of the threads. All of this "stuff" would have made it difficult to properly tighten the base screws, possibly decreasing the security of the scope installation.

Torx screws can be tightened down effectively enough with the supplied wrench that you probably won't need a thread-locking compound.

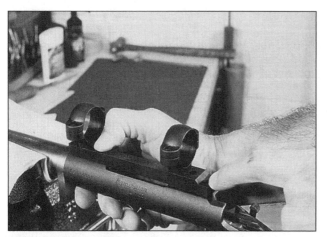

Place the base on the receiver and press the front and rear down, attempting to rock the base. More than a small amount (a few thousandths) must be shimmed for stability. On this Badger Ordnance/Chandler Co. base, no play at all could be felt.

ment, first press down on the base between the front screw holes. Then press down on the rear of the base. The base should not wobble on the receiver during this test. A small amount of movement is fine, but if the base clanks back and forth during this test you have a problem. Either you have the wrong base for your rifle, or the receiver has been polished or machined on its top. The base problem is easy, swap the base you have for the base you need. A polished or machined receiver is harder to deal with. If the difference is small, you can use base shims. If the difference is large you may have to have a base custom-machined for your rifle.

Install the screws and tighten them.

Take the rings out and make sure the front ring is securely screwed together. Place your rod through the ring and slide the ring down into the base slot on the front. Do not use the scope as a wrench to turn the front ring. You will damage or break the scope. Turn the ring 90 degrees, until the rod is parallel to the bore. If you have a ring wrench, you can use it instead of the rod for this. Remove the rod, and the top of the front ring. Remove the top of the rear ring and place the bottom of the rear ring onto the base. Install your bore collimator. Place the scope in the ring bottoms and look at the

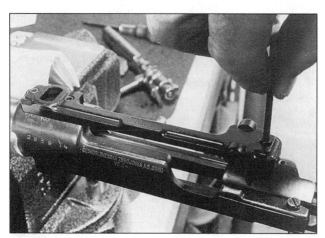

This Czech Brno receiver had not been polished, so the base fit in place with very little wobble. Tighten up the screws and pull out the rings.

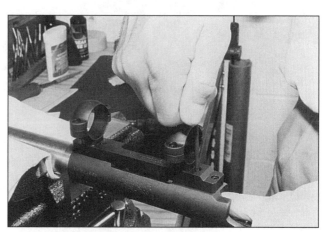

Gradually tighten each screw in turn and then work through them again, rather than fully tightening one and then doing the next.

Use a rod, bar or pipe (or better yet, the specific tool for the job, like the Kokopelli) to turn the front ring. Never use the scope!

Put a drop of oil on the dovetail, and be sure it is fully seated in the base before you turn.

Big differences will be readily apparent. An offset this large could be enough to damage a scope.

With alignment rods (these are the Kokopelli) you can get the front and rear rings aligned within a few thousandths. The scope will never notice such a difference.

This poor little Simmons scope was used by the customer as the lever to turn his front scope ring into place. The customer then wondered why it had a wandering zero, and fogged up in wet weather!

Once the rings are lined up, remove the tops and then lock the scope in place. Only finger-tighten the tops until you've checked eye relief and bolt handle clearance.

With the eye relief set, rings tight and the reticle level, now insert the collimator and grid-zero the scope.

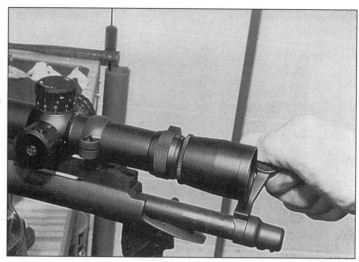

Be sure to check the bolt handle for clearance. If the bolt will not clear the scope, your choices are two; start over with higher rings, or alter the bolt handle. Higher rings are far simpler and less costly than altering the bolt handle.

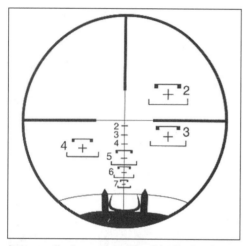

A range-finder reticle like this Springfield Armory is particularly sensitive to being level. If it is not, the cant induced in the rifle will mean you could miss your target at long range. The two posts at the bottom are centering posts for the bubble level. In addition to range-finding, you can keep the rifle level while shooting!

collimator through the scope. If the reticle is not centered on the grid you must adjust the front ring. Remove the scope and the rear ring and use your ring wrench to move the front ring a small amount. If you do not have a ring wrench you must re-install the front ring top half and use the rod again. Do not use a hammer to tap the ring bottom. You may bend the ring, or peen an edge onto its inner radius. Either will damage the scope when you tighten things down later.

Once the reticle is centered in the grid, snug the front ring top in place. Line the rear ring base up with the windage screw holes. Install the rear ring top and snug those screws down. Install the base windage screws finger tight on both sides. Tighten the windage screws by alternating on each side and tightening a small amount. You want to tighten them while leaving the scope centered in the grid. If you tighten first one screw and then the other, you will be flexing the scope as you tighten the first one. It is not a good thing for the scope. The stress of being flexed may cause the seals to leak, or the reticle to break or come loose.

At this point your reticle is probably not straight up and down. Loosen but do not remove the ring screws and turn the scope until the reticle is straight. If you cannot turn the scope in the rings then you have flexed the scope while tightening the rear windage screws. Loosen them. Set your reticle to vertical

Not all scopes are built the same. The Nikon on this Ruger just clears the rear sight. The Millett must ride slightly forward in the rings, and would not clear the rear sight. Simple solution, remove the rear sight, store it in a safe place and use plug screws on the holes left behind.

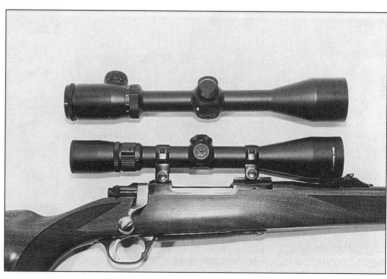

You can see how little clearance there is. If you wanted to install scope covers you'd have to remove the rear sight.

and tighten the ring screws. Then re-tighten the windage screws.

How strong is a well-designed and mounted scope mount? The rifle or the scope will break before the mount does. One of my customers was hunting out West when his horse took a spill off the trail. Luckily, the customer was not aboard. Falling down the mountain is not common, but it happens. This customer, like all the rest who lost a horse this way, clambered down to retrieve the rifle and saddle. The horse was a goner. As with all the other such cases I had seen, his stock was broken at the wrist and his scope was busted. His mount was unharmed, and we used it after re-stocking and re-scoping his rifle. None of the scope mounts have broken off of any of the rifles so involved. The stocks and scopes were batting zero, while the mounts all survived. Curiously, the barrels all survived as well. You would think the barrel would be bent sideways or at least off the target, and yet none have. Granted, the sample size is small, but encouraging.

The exception to the good news are see-through mounts. Many hunters want to still have their iron sights available even when using a scope. Back when scopes were fragile

Here is the Leupold installed on a tactical rifle. Careful readers will note the earlier use of the Redfield base, before the Badger Ordnance/Chandler unit showed up. The rifle shot well before, but the BO/C base is definitely stiffer and sturdier, and will improve accuracy.

This Leupold scope has additional features to make the shooter's job easier. The 30mm tube is stronger and makes for a brighter scope. It also means you need to use 30mm rings. The three knobs are external (no need to remove the caps to make adjustments!) and sealed for windage, elevation and focus. These are all things tactical and beanfield marksman require. They do add weight and cost, so be prepared.

this made sense. Mount makers developed tip-off and detachable scope mounts to keep hunters hunting even after their scopes had failed.

Today few hunters are worried about scopes failing. The typical user of see-through mounts wants to have a high-power scope, or a variable set at the high end, and still have iron sights for close-range shooting.

While this is a laudable goal, the see-through mounts have a weakness. All of the mounts I have seen are made of aluminum. They are probably extruded, that is forced through a die at high pressure. They are not forged or machined. The extruded aluminum can be soft. See-through mounts will not withstand the bumps and jolts that their non see-through brethren shrug off. If you take your rifle to your hunting camp with see-through mounts in a soft rifle case, you may not keep your zero. A bump, a jolt, or even setting a heavy suitcase on your rifle case could bend the mounts and change your zero.

Treat a rifle with see-through mounts gently.

To mount the scope is simple. Remove the plug screws and clean the holes. Attach the bottoms of the mounts with the provided screws. Place the scope in the mount bottoms and tighten the tops in place. You may experience an unsettling phenomenon. The surfaces of the ring bottoms that the scope rests in may not be parallel to each other. When you rest the scope in them, it may not sit straight, or rest in the bottom of the curve. When you tighten the tops down, the whole assembly will "squish" together. Do not be alarmed. A good scope is not disturbed by this. You may find your reticle is not straight. Loosen the top screws, set the scope straight and tighten again. You may have to do this a couple of times.

Bore-sight and range check the same way you would with any other rifle.

Drilling and tapping for scope mounts

What if your rifle is not drilled and tapped for a scope? Can you get a scope onto it? Yes, but...

There are many shooters who want to build up a custom rifle from a surplus action. Unless you can get the starting-point rifle dirt-cheap, the costs are not in your favor. After drilling and tapping, you have to alter the bolt handle and change the safety, which are additional costs. When "sur-plus" rifles were expensive ($200 for a Mauser!) the costs did not add up as they had in the '50s and '60s. Now that Mausers are under $100, the costs can work out, but you will still end up with a rifle costing you as much as a new Remington, Winchester, Ruger or others. The big difference is that it will be yours.

To drill your rifle for a scope mount, you must have a drill press and a drilling fixture. I suppose in an emergency you could do without one or the other, but you can't do it without both.

Any drill press will do. As a drilling fixture, you have two choices. One is the Forster fixture, which holds the barreled action. The two "V" blocks hold the barrel, and the rear support keeps the receiver from flexing away from you under the drilling load. The drill guide locating arm slides front to back on the fixture, allowing you to locate the holes where you want to. The best way to drill your receiver with the Forster tool is to use a one-piece base as your hole-spacing guide. If you "eyeball" the location of the holes on the rear bridge, you may end up with a rifle that can only have a scope mounted with a two-piece base.

Make sure the rifle is unloaded. Remove the bolt, and take the barreled action out of the stock. Place your base on the receiver and mark the hole locations with a china pencil or felt-tip marker. The location of the front holes are restricted by one important consideration: The location of the locking lug recesses in the front ring. Stick your little finger into the ejection port opening and you can feel the edge of the locking lug recess. The rear hole of the front pair must be in the recess, and not into the locking lug itself. Worse yet, you must not drill your hole so it is right at the shoulder of the rear of the recess. If you drill into the locking lug you will be drilling into heat-treated and hard metal. You will dull your drill, and you could break your tap trying to tap the hole. You also will weaken the locking lug. If your hole location is right on the edge of the recess, you'll break your drill when it comes through into the recess. You could end up with an oval hole, and even if you don't oval it, and somehow get the broken drill out, you'll have a tough time tapping the hole. Measure the locking lug thickness and mark the top of the receiver. Make sure your screw hole is

Here Andy Manson of Mountain Dog drills a Mauser receiver. The Forster fixture is clamped to the table of the drill press, and the fixture guides the drill straight and centered on its path.

It helps if you have small boxes to keep the parts and accessories of your tools together. This box used to hold the ribbons from teletype machines. (Never mind what they were, they're obsolete now.) It is the perfect size to hold the parts of the drilling jig in one location.

forward of the rear recess surface.

Place the rifle in the fixture and use the trigger as an aid to getting the receiver level. The receiver support is a help in leveling with flat-bottomed receivers. Line the front drill guide up with the first line of your scope base markings. (Hold the base up against the drill guide arm to make sure you've got the correct hole spacing selected.)

Lock the drill guide arm in place. Use the drill guide bushing as a drill stop. You cannot drill your front holes through the receiver and into the barrel. Measure the front ring diameter, and subtract from the measurement the thread diameter of your rifle. Divide by two, and that is your hole depth. Slide your #31 drill bit into the guide until it protrudes the calculated hole depth, and then slide the drill into the drill press chuck until it stops. Tighten the chuck. Your guide will now act as a drill stop, keeping you from drilling into the barrel. (This would be a lot easier if the barrel were

not installed, except how would you hold the receiver? That's where the B-Square fixture shines.)

Drill the front holes. Remove the drill guide and replace it with one that just allows a 6-48 tap to pass through. On a magnum caliber rifle, you could use a #28 drill and an 8-40 tap. However, you will have to drill the scope base holes larger to accommodate the larger screws.

Slide the drill guide arm out of the way and fasten the base using the front screws. Use the rear screw holes to locate your holes to be drilled. Slide the arm back and line the guides up with the located rear screw holes. These holes must be drilled through, so there is no need to use a stop. Once drilled and tapped, use a half-round file to deburr the inside of the receiver bridge. Your rifle is now ready for mounting and bore sighting.

The B-Square fixture works on rifles with and without barrels. With the barrel out you don't have to drill and tap a blind

With the location determined, the fixture keeps the drill from wandering or flexing, and drilling a crooked hole.

By switching the drill guide to a larger size to accommodate the tap, you can use the fixture to tap the threads straight through the hole.

Gentle downward pressure is all that is needed to let the tap "bite" the steel and start cutting. Without the fixture you'd have to press harder to make the tap bite and to keep it straight up and down.

hole, you can drill through the threads of the front ring (not the locking lug if the second hole happens to be located there). With the rifle apart for barrel installation, face truing, lug lapping and other work, it is a handier package to get onto your drill press.

The B-Square fixture has two drill guide bars, the "S" bar and the "M" bar. Unlike the Forster, where you have to move the guide arm, the B-Square has all four holes positioned for you.

To drill and tap with the B-Square tool, take your action and slide the bore align arbor in place. Place both "V" bushings with their "V" over the arbor holes. Place the bar counterbores on the "V" bushing. Put the base block against the bottom flat of the action and insert the screws. Slide the assembly forward until the stop pin is against the rear of the front ring. Tighten the screws. Place the assembly in your

drill press vise and clamp it with the guide holes vertical. An aid to getting things vertical is to put a 6-inch section of .120-inch rod into the guide. The extra length will let you easily set things up square and vertical. Place the drill guide into each of the holes in turn, and drill your scope mount holes.

Some military actions will be case-hardened. Case-hardening is an older method of getting hard and tough parts out of low-carbon steel. Instead of using alloy steels as we do today, the manufacturers in the first half of the century would use low-carbon steel, design the thickness to be enough for the job, and then harden the surface. The surface was hardened by forcing carbon into the skin of the finished part, heating and quenching it. The case-hardened part would have a soft and tough core, with a hard skin. The Springfield '03 rifle was made that way until increased pro-

The B-Square drilling guide works on receivers with or without barrels, while the Forster requires a barrel.

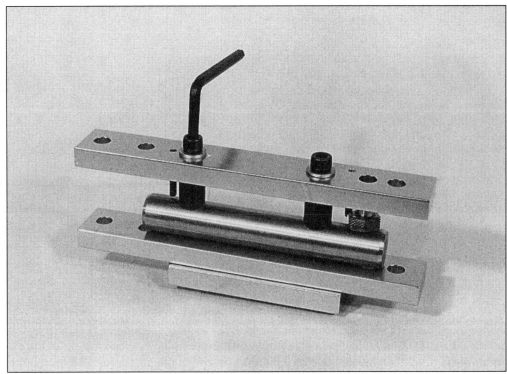

duction during WWI uncovered a problem. If the receiver was over-heated or quenched, or had too much carbon driven into it, it could be hardened all the way through. If an overly-hard receiver were over-stressed, it would shatter. A properly-hardened receiver did not shatter, but bent, stretched and twisted. To avoid blown-up rifles, the Ordnance Department changed the alloy and heat-treatment the rifles received. Known as the "double heat-treat" rifles, the new Springfields were tougher than the old. Later, the alloy was changed again, and the receivers became even tougher. Even though the new rifles were safer, some lamented the old ones being pulled out of production, as the hard skin made for an action that was beautifully smooth. Once broken-in, an old Springfield bolt worked like oiled glass. Unfortunately, it broke like it too. The old receivers can be identified by serial number. The cut-off serial number for Springfield production rifles is listed as approximately 800,000. For Rock Island Armory, the number is exactly 285,507. Do not use a rifle with serial numbers lower than these. The action may be too hard, and could shatter if stressed. The hardness cannot be reversed by annealing and re-heat treating. I would not use or fire, nor work on, a Springfield below these numbers. Are there many rifles that have been safely fired all these years, with serial numbers below the cut-off? Yes, but there have been millions more made since then that are all perfectly safe. If you have a family hunting rifle that is a low-number Springfield, retire it and build a new tradition. The only way to find out if your low-number Springfield is too hard is by breaking it. There is no reliable non-destructive test.

Also, I would refrain from working on a Mauser that was made during German production in 1944 or 1945. The war was not going well, and production short-cuts were a daily occurrence. A rifle could get out of the factory with indifferent heat-treating, and who would care? Certainly not the slave laborers who might be assembling them.

However, there are many safe rifles that have a hard skin. While you can drill a rifle with a hard skin, you can't tap it. To drill and tap it you must first spot-anneal the surface. The best way is one that came to me from B-Square, and involves a large steel rod. Locate the scope mount holes on your receiver using the drilling fixture. Mark the spots with a felt tip pen, and remove the receiver from the fixture. Then scrape the ink marks with a stone to mar the blueing just enough to permanently mark the locations. Take a 1-inch steel rod that is 2 inches in length. Turn or grind one end so it has a blunt taper down to a .250" tip. Heat the rod to red or orange hot and then hold (in a pair of pliers, obviously!) the rod against the receiver at each spot you wish to anneal. Leave it there until both parts are cool. Annealing is the SLOW cooling of a heated part. If you grab a torch, heat the spot and then turn off the torch, the spot will cool too quickly for proper annealing. Depending on the hardness or its depth, you may have to apply heat a couple of times.

Once annealed you can drill and tap without breaking tools.

The properly-attached scope mount will not shoot loose and will not come apart from vibrations. The temptation of many shooters is to squirt some sort of thread-locking compound into the screws to "keep them tight." While it is a common feeling, it is not necessary. McBride, in his book "A Rifleman Went to War" talks about using broken razor blades as wedges and carefully applying salt water to the scope mount screws on sniper rifles in WWI. The mounts stayed in place so tightly that "the ordnance workers complained about not being able to remove the mounts for maintenance" when he came out of the trenches.

You do not need Loctite for any but the most arduous uses. If you were going to Africa with a scoped rifle in .458 Lott, you might want to use Loctite. After the plane trip, and hundreds of miles of bad roads, no roads, Jeeps, Land Rovers, buses and walking, you want to be sure the scope is tight. Walking from the truck to the hunting blind in the woods of Pennsylvania, you don't need Loctite, just proper screw tightening procedures.

What scope?

The trend is to ever-higher magnifications. The battle between fixed-power and variables has been settled for some time, and in the favor of the variables. The modern variable is bright, clear, sealed and dependable. It also allows many hunters to select a scope with more magnification than they need, partly because it is there, and partly because they still have the lower powers to use.

Here in Michigan, most of the deer hunting is in thick woods, with narrow openings and small fields as "open" terri-

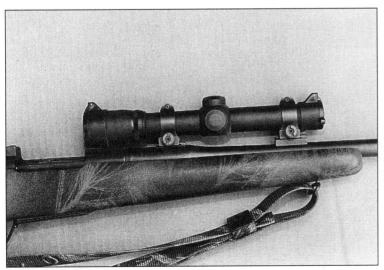

Some scope installations do not use bases drilled and tapped to the rifle. The scope bases on this Gunsite Scout Rifle were machined from the full-diameter barrel blank, and are an integral part of the barrel.

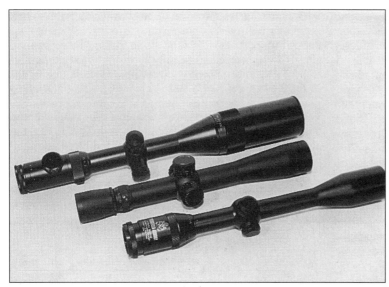

The trend is towards bigger scopes with greater magnification. While the Leupold in the middle is a straight 10-power, the Springfield on the bottom is a four to 14 power variable and the Nightforce on the top is a 2.5 to 10 variable. The Nightforce in particular is a large and impressive chunk of glass.

The Nightforce reticle. Not only is it a mil-dot reticle (the circles) but the open bars can be used for range estimation. The reticle lights up at night, but remains black when the battery is off. If you know how tall or wide an object is, the dots act as a scale to calculate range. They also act as known hold-over points if you do not have time to adjust your elevation knob.

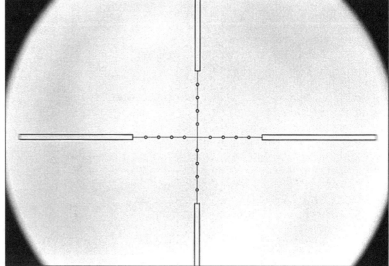

The Millett Buck Lightening has a lighted reticle in different colors, but when the battery is off the reticle is black. If the battery fails the scope stills works, unlike red-dot scopes.

tory. In the southern half of the state where much of the agriculture is, deer hunting is limited to shotguns, no rifles allowed.

For years the trend in our scope sales was to ever-higher magnifications. When I started in the late 1970s many hunters still stuck with fixed 4-power scopes, and rarely did someone select a 3- to 9-power. By the time I quit in the late 1990s, the most-commonly selected scope was the 3- to 9-power variable, with a significant percentage of buyers opting for a 4-12. In the woods at dawn, peering across a 40-yard bean field, a 12-power scope is a handicap. If you must have a high-power variable for those "power line shots", keep the scope turned down to the lowest power except when you are actually looking over that power line right of way cut through the woods.

As for which scope, I have never been dissatisfied by spending my money on quality. For a long time I stuck with Leupold and Burris, because one of our wholesalers made weekly deliveries, and they could bring whatever scope we wanted, sometimes just to look at it. Now that I am writing and have a chance to get a broader look at scopes, I am equally impressed by Pentax, Nikon, Lightforce and the scopes from Springfield Armory.

On a hunting rifle I would shy away from one of the new "red dot" scopes. The illuminated reticle in a regular scope such as the Millett Buck Lightening can be useful, but a scope that is totally dependent on battery power can let you down. Batteries are notorious for failing in the cold and damp, and if a deer blind is anything, it has great potential for being cold and damp. I use red-dot scopes on my competition guns, but for hunting I would stick with tubes full of glass. On the Millett scope, even if the battery goes dead the reticle is still there. For some competition applications a lighted reticle could come in useful. I'll have to take the Millett off of my hunting rifle and try it on a competition rifle.

CHAPTER 6

Barrels: Cleaning, Selection and Installation

"Why spend so much time on proper barrel cleaning in a book on gunsmithing?"

Your barrel is the heart of your rifle, and it leads a hard life. Think of each cartridge as a miniature welding torch. Every time you fire a round, that little torch gets turned on for a fraction of a second. Your bullet is forced down the bore and out of the muzzle by a raging pillar of hot gases and abrasive powder residue. The beginning of your bore, called the throat, gets it worst of all. At the very start of the rifling the pressure is the greatest, the gases are their hottest and the powder residue is at its hottest and most abrasive. If

Target shooters can be brutal on a barrel, and heartless, too. Nick Till will shoot this barrel until it starts to show a drop in accuracy, then sell it to someone who is less picky about accuracy. The new one will perform, or be scrapped or sold.

Barrels lead a hard life, and rifle makers and barrel makers make a lot of them. These are barrel blanks at Quality Parts/Bushmaster waiting to be turned (literally) into barrels. (Photo courtesy Quality Parts/Bushmaster.)

The copper fouling just visible in the muzzle of this rifle may have an effect on accuracy, and it may not. If it doesn't, the owner may not care it exists. But sooner or later, it will have to be cleaned out.

you are using ammunition loaded with a large dollop of slow-burning powder, there may even be unburned powder granules rushing through the throat.

The heat of the gases raises the temperature of the throat alarmingly, and quite quickly. The heat erodes the throat and the beginning of the rifling, called the leade. The steel crazes and cracks, like mud drying on a hot summer day. The relatively hot powder residue, meeting the relatively cool steel of the bore, collects on the bore in front of the chamber. This carbon forms a hard crusty deposit.

The force of the bullet striking the leade and the friction of the bullet passing down the bore rub jacket material from the bullet. The bullet wear will be made worse if your bore has miniature rough spots or machine marks. Each of these will tear bits of jacket from the bullet. The built-up lumps of jacket material deform the next bullet and the next, until the buildup breaks loose and races down the bore. Then the build-up starts over again.

The powder residue and jacket material affect accuracy and decrease useable barrel life. Considering how little care most shooters give their rifle's bore, it's a wonder that rifles shoot as well as they do for as long as they do.

Things were not so bad back in the black powder era. The bullets were lead or lead alloy. Lead is soft compared to the copper and brass of current jacket material. Black powder burns relatively slowly and at a low pressure. Properly

treated and not allowed to rust, a barrel subjected to black powder could last almost indefinitely.

The first smokeless powders were quite a shock to barrels and shooters alike. The British ran into difficult problems as they changed their Lee-Metford rifles over to smokeless. The first .303 British cartridges were loaded with a compressed charge of black powder. The first and, for a long time, the only British smokeless powder was Cordite. Cordite started out as 58 percent Nitroglycerine, 37 percent gun cotton and 5 percent mineral jelly. It burned hot and abrasively. The introduction of a Cordite-loaded cartridge into British military service came in March of 1891. It did not take long for problems to surface. Cordite was produced in long strands that were cut to length for the cartridge used. Think of a cartridge case loaded with strands of dry spaghetti. The rifling used by the British in the service Lee of the time was Metford rifling. In cross section the lands and grooves of the rifling were composed of shallow curves. The design was meant to improve accuracy and reduce fouling with black powder. Subjected to Cordite, the Metford rifling just melted away. A decrease in accuracy could be seen within a few thousand rounds. By the time a barrel had seen 6,000 rounds, it was completely unsafe to fire.

The new rifling, Enfield rifling, used lands and grooves that were rectangular in cross-section. The new rifling was approved and the rifle re-designated the Lee-Enfield in November of 1895. The square shoulders of the lands and grooves proved better able to stand up to the corrosive Cordite, and useful service life of the barrels more than doubled. The formula of Cordite was gradually adjusted and tested until it was as easy on the bore as possible. But the British never really replaced it due to its ease of manufacture and its stability under varieties of climate.

Lest you think that it was only a British problem, the United States Army ran into much the same problem a decade later. The Springfield rifle had just been adopted, and a nasty surprise was sprung upon the Ordnance Department, namely spitzer bullets. Instead of the 220-grain round-nose bullets that had just been adopted in

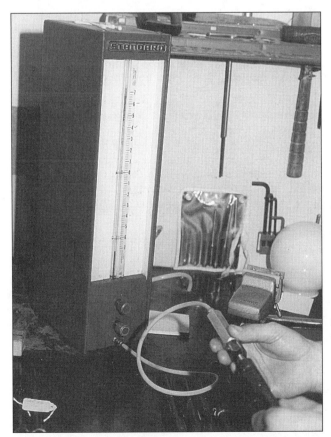

Barrel makers use an air gauge to check barrel consistency and quality. If the "bubble" strays out of a pre-determined range, the barrel is scrapped or sent back to the original maker. (Photo courtesy Quality Parts/Bushmaster.)

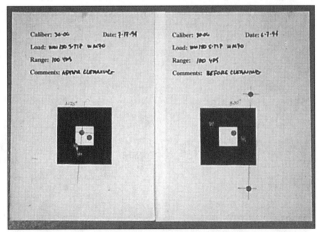

How often should a barrel be cleaned? Often enough to keep it shooting accurately. I bought a Winchester Model 70 because the accuracy was going, and I figured I'd install a new barrel when it gave up. Then I thoroughly cleaned the barrel and gave up any idea of buying a new barrel for it.

1903, the Ordnance department found itself scrambling to get 150-grain sharp-pointed bullets into their new cartridge. The hot powder they used, combined with the higher velocity of the new bullets, eroded rifling even faster than Cordite. Until DuPont developed a cooler-burning powder, the Army was in a fix. The new powder was quickly developed, and the cartridge re-designed and re-named the .30-06.

More than a century after the British experience, the powder manufacturers have learned many more tricks to ease the wear on your bore. Various additives cool the burning temperature, ease powder flow, decrease muzzle flash and soften the abrasive residue. How long will a properly-treated bore last? That is a question with many answers and many routes to get to the answers. The question is made difficult by your expectations.

Let me give you two examples that can give you an idea of the range of answers. The first is an ultra-long range rifle meant for competition. Let us chamber it for a large case such as the .300 Winchester Magnum, or even the .30-.378 Weatherby. Then we stuff the case full of a slow-burning powder and insert a heavy match bullet. A top-ranked competitor using such a combination will start to see his group enlarge enough to drop good shots out of the "X" ring in less than 2,000 rounds. Of course, this competitor expects his rifle to deliver groups well under 1 inch at 100 yards.

The second rifle is one of my own. An AR-15 with a 20-inch Eagle Arms (now Armalite) match barrel. I fired 15,000 rounds through that barrel before I retired it. When I sold the barrel it would still deliver groups just over an inch at 100 yards. The fellow who bought it was happy to get it, as he did not expect to ever shoot as well as the barrel could. I installed an Olympic Arms match barrel (it was handy and I needed a new barrel right away), and after I broke in the barrel, the rifle delivers groups well under 1 inch at 100 yards.

That original AR barrel lasted longer than the long-range one did for three reasons. First, I did not expect accuracy better than an inch at 100 yards. The targets I was firing at were generous in size and a lot closer than long-range rifle targets often are. Secondly, I did not load my ammunition to the maximum velocity and pressure. Once I had an accurate load that met the

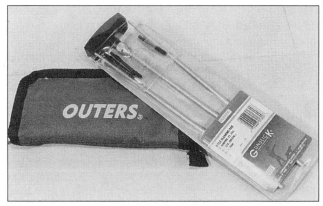

Save the jointed rods in your bag or hunting camp as emergency-use only rods. The bare aluminum can collect grit, and the non-flush ends can scrape the bore.

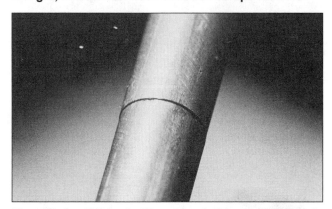

Magnified until it looks like a barrel, this .22 caliber rod shows the non-flush ends of the sections. You do not want this scraping down your bore if you can avoid it.

power threshold I had to meet, I stopped increasing the powder charge. My ammunition burnt slightly cooler with the loads I used than a maximum load would have. Finally, I took care of my barrel. If I was involved in a match that required rapid-fire shooting or large amounts of ammunition, I would clean my bore at every opportunity. A clean bore is a happy bore, and better yet a bore that will keep you happy longer.

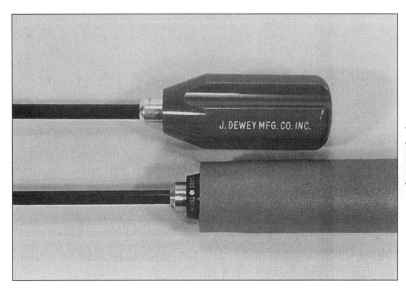

The best rods are one-piece rods such as these Dewey and Bore Tech rods. Both have bearings in the handle so the rod rotates with the rifling, instead of dragging the brush across the lands and grooves.

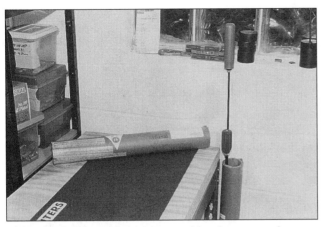

A bent rod defeats the purpose of buying a premium rod. Keep your rods straight by storing them where they cannot be bent or flexed. Cut the shipping tube down and secure it to your wall or bench.

You can see the difficulty in trying to clean a rifle in my original room designed for handgun use. Building a bigger space solved this problem.

So how do you clean a bore properly? How can you clean a bore without spending your whole life at the job? And just what are you cleaning out of it?

First you get the right equipment. Buy a one-piece cleaning rod. The segmented ones are perfect for your range bag or for a trip to the hunting cabin. The sections are easier to store and less likely to get bent in transit. You should not use them for bore cleaning at home. They are not the best thing for your bore. The mass-produced sections do not line up perfectly. As a result, the off-centered ends each have a square shoulder that sticks up past the other. The ends are not bored perfectly straight. The ends butt up at slight angles to each other, pressing the square shoulders against your bore. Don't believe me? Assemble your segmented rod and look at it from the end. You'll see what I mean. If your rod is steel, then you have sharp steel edges rubbing against the rifling. If your rod is aluminum, then the edges quickly pick up grit, grit that is then imbedded into the surface of the soft aluminum. This grit bears on and wears against your rifling.

A one-piece rod does not have shoulders to scrape your bore. Even if it is naked steel it will not get grit embedded into its surface. The best single-piece rods are nylon-coated to reduce the steel-on-steel wear. The nylon will not hold grit. When you wipe the rod clean, the residue comes off.

The best rods are the Dewey rods. Not all of their rods are nylon coated. Some shooters do not want nylon on their rods, so Dewey makes a hardened stainless steel rod. All of their rods have a ball-bearing handle attachment. With the rod free to turn as you push and pull the handle, the patch or brush follows the rifling as it turns. Your rod should be shipped to you in a heavy-duty shipping tube. Use it to store your rod so the rod will not get easily bent. One method I have used for rod storage is to cut the tube down so only an inch or so of the handle sticks out of it. I then used a wood screw to attach the tube vertically to my bench. Located at the end of the bench where it meets the wall, the tube is not likely to get kicked or bumped. The handle does not stick out of the tube far enough to let something bumping the handle bend the rod. As I added rods of different calibers I bolted the new tubes next to the old ones.

Yes, you should have several rods if you have several calibers. While you don't need a rod for each caliber, you do not want to have a rod too small for your bore. For example, using a .22 caliber rod to clean a .30 caliber bore is asking to bend the rod. If you run into a sticky spot in the bore you could flex and bend the rod trying to push it through. The

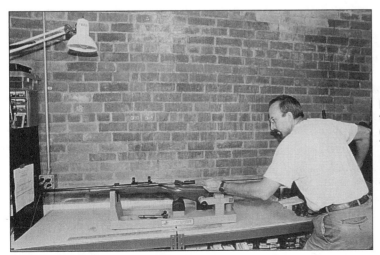

It takes a lot of space to use a cleaning rod. In this Winchester with a 24-inch barrel, the Dewey (35-inch) rod takes up 92 inches of floor space. The longer (44-inch) Bore Tech and its longer rod guide takes up 112 inches. Add the Patch Hog (9 inches) and you need 10 feet to clean your rifle!

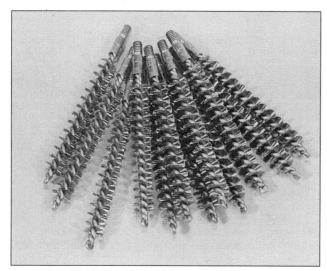

Use only brass brushes, and don't be stingy. If a brush starts to wear, replace it. Without sufficient scrubbing action, it can't remove the fouling that you want gone.

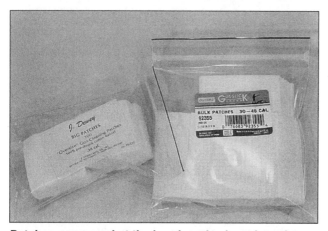

Patches remove what the brush and solvent have loosened. Buy lots of patches, and use them freely. Don't try to be stingy and re-use a patch two or three times. Over the life of a barrel you're saving a few dollars at the cost of a lot of hassle.

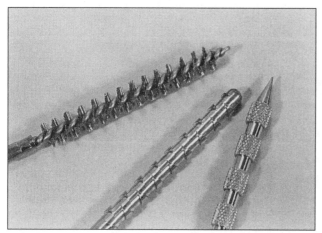

Along with the brush, you need some way to hold the patches. For a long time I used the jag (center) but then I found a better way to use the spear point. I now favor the spear over the jag.

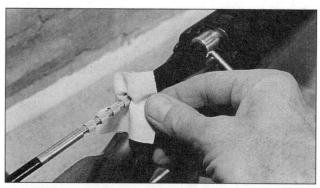

On the Dewey rod guide, spear the patch and push it forward....

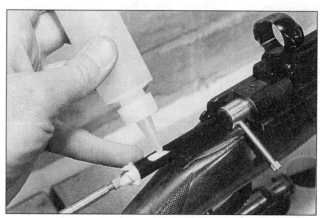

And then apply the bore solvent through the window.

The Bore Tech rod guide and its patch tray. Neater than sliced bread, and a snap to use.

The Bore Tech rod guide locks into the receiver after you have removed the bolt (like other rod guides) but the tray is the big difference. The tray does add length to the guide, length you must account for in your cleaning space.

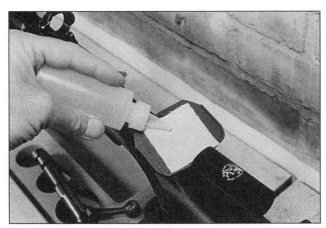

Here the patch is being treated to bore solvent....

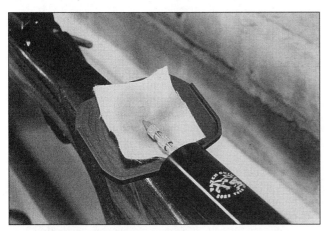

And the spear point tip collects the patch on its way through the rod guide.

The Bore Tech Patch Hog is a way to collect used patches without picking them up off the floor, or in a can. The Hog also cuts down on solvent smell by keeping the patches in a sealed bottle.

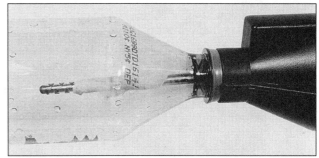

Screw the bottle into the Hog, and slide the assembly over the muzzle.

When the rod pokes through, the patch can fall off into the bottle. Despite the jag I'm showing here, the spear point works better.

flexed rod rubs against the rifling. I make sure I use a rod no more than two caliber "steps" smaller than the bore. For that .30 caliber bore I would not use a rod smaller than one intended for .25 caliber.

Get a rod long enough to pass completely through your bore from the action end, and still leave you knuckle room over the stock. For a bolt-action rifle with a 24-inch barrel, this means a rod at least 36-inches long.

Rods need tips. One tip is a brush. The purpose of the brush is to loosen the powder residue, called fouling. You loosen the fouling with a brush, but you don't remove it. The best brushes are made with a brass or bronze core with brass or bronze bristles. The plastic brushes will not work as well as brass. Do not use a stainless brush in your rifle unless your rifle is an AR-15 with a chrome-lined bore. The hard chrome lining will protect your bore from the brush. A chrome-moly alloy barrel will be scratched by the stainless

The rod guide you use should lock into place on the rifle, as this Bore Tech and the Dewey guides do. The rod guide will protect your leade and throat from rod wear.

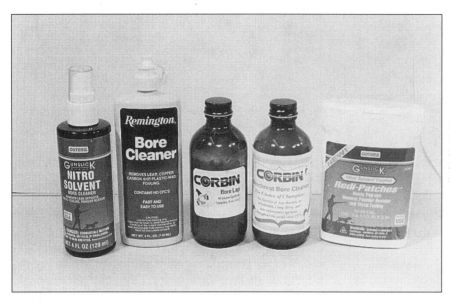

Brushes and patches are not enough by themselves. You also need bore solvents, and some rifles may need abrasive cleaners to cut through the accumulated fouling.

brush. A stainless brush in a stainless bore may gall. Galling is a problem of stainless-on-stainless wear. The two surfaces do not rub against each other, they tear at each other. This was a big problem when handgun manufacturers first tried to use stainless in their guns. They ended up making the major parts out of stainless alloys that were just enough different from each other to prevent galling. Avoid stainless brushes, you don't need them and they can harm your bore.

To remove what remains after brushing you need to use patches. The patch is your solvent delivery system and your residue removal system. Patch-holding tips come in three types, the loop, the spear and the jag. The loop is just that, a tip with a hole through it. You thread the patch through the loop and then press the patch down your bore. The problem with the loop is that the patch is all bunched up. If you try to use a patch that is the least bit too thick, it will wedge in the throat and stay there. The surface area of the patch actually used in a loop tip to swab your bore is small. The spear uses

a sharpened tip to spear the center of the patch and press it down the bore. Upon my introduction to the pointed tip, I thought "someday I will meet the sadist who designed this, and thank him for it." I had to get the patch wet before spearing it, getting solvent on my hands. The act of spearing the patch sometimes involved spearing my fingertip. And the patch did not always stay on long enough to enter the bore. My attitudes on the spear-point cleaning tip have recently undergone a change due to improvements in rod guide design. For years I used an old rod guide, and when I looked at the Dewey rod guide I found that there was a small window for solvent. How long has this been going on? The spearpoint is now much easier to use. Place the patch over the end of the guide. Run the spearpoint into the center of the patch and into the guide to the window. Place a few drops of solvent on the patch and then run the patch through the bore. Not to be out-done, Bore Tech makes a cleaning rod guide that has a patch tray built into it. Instead of spear-

Keep cleaning so long as your patches come out with any color to them. Copper residue may be blue or green, while powder fouling will be black.

The problem with cleaning an AR-15 is the lack of an opening without breaking the rifle open. How to keep it open?

By removing the bolt and op handle, and using the Sinclair cleaning link, the AR stays open and the muzzle is level or slightly downwards.

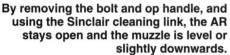

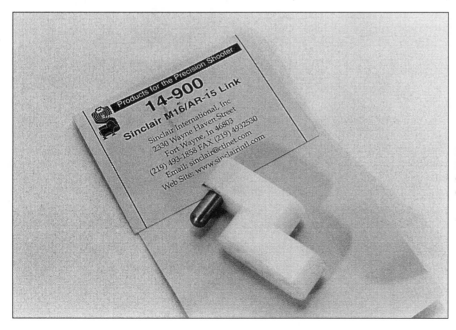

It's just a little plastic gizmo, but it's one of those "why didn't I think of that?" gadgets you have to have once you've tried it.

ing a wet patch, you place the patch on the tray and dribble a few drops of solvent onto it. When you run your rod through the guide, it spears the patch and then pushes it through the forward part of the guide. No handling messy solvent-soaked patches, and no stabbing your fingertips. As icing on the cake, they also make what they call the "Patch Hog." The threaded adapter fits on your muzzle, and you then screw a plastic soda bottle on the end. When you push the patch through, it falls off the tip and stays in the bottle. The only drawback is the difficulty of inspecting the patch to see how your cleaning progress is going.

Until the Bore Tech guide rod was introduced, I thought the jag was the best method. It still has much to recommend it. The jag is a tip that has a series of grooves turned into it. The Parker-Hale style uses a wood-screw thread ridge running along its length. The grooves or ridge hold the patch when it is wrapped around the jag. Using a jag, all of the surface area of the patch is used to deliver solvent and scrub your bore.

Buy a rod guide for more than a means of handling wet patches. Remember the throat of your bore? The part that gets scorched the most from shooting? Something has to keep the rod centered in your bore, and rather than make the throat do it you should use a bore guide. If you do not use a bore guide when cleaning, then in addition to the scorching it gets from firing, your bore's throat will get the most rubbing or scraping from the rod. In talking to barrel makers, I found that many of the barrels that are "shot out" that they replace are actually worn in the throat from improper cleaning. Only Chris Dichter of Pac-Nor Barreling reported more barrels replaced due to other causes. The single greatest reason for barrel replacement he sees is rust and pitting. Based in the pacific Northwest, his customers have to deal with a damp climate. A moist climate? OK, they basically shoot while standing in a shower stall with the water running. Chris sees many barrels pitted from end to end, and wishes shooters would do more cleaning, not less.

The rod guide takes the place of your rifle's bolt and keeps the rod centered in the chamber and throat. Remove the bolt and slide the rod guide into the receiver. The good ones have a small handle to lock the guide in place. The rod guide serves an additional purpose. It keeps bore solvent out of your action and off of the stock. Many bore solvents can soften wood and attack the epoxy of your glass bedding. The most aggressive ones can attack the finish of your rifle. Even if your rifle is impervious to solvents, if you drip them into the action you will end up with bore solvent over your hands and ammunition. Use a guide and avoid the mess. Rod guides were thought of by benchrest shooters. These shooters spend inordinate amounts of time fussing over tiny details, and their groups show it. A benchrest shooter may decide it is time to get a new barrel when his rifle starts shooting groups larger than .2 inches (that's point 2 inches) at 100 yards. To keep that rifle accurate requires proper cleaning, and proper cleaning requires a rod guide.

Buy good patches. Don't worry about getting cotton patches that cost another nickel a package more than synthetics or blended patches. Consider the total cost of your shooting. In using up a box of patches that costs a few dollars, you have fired ammunition that costs several hundred dollars. If you need to economize, shaving one percent off the cost of the ammunition will save enough extra money to buy the best patches ever made.

Buy solvent made for each job. You'll need two solvents and one paste. You need a general bore solvent to remove the powder residue. You need a copper solvent to remove the jacket fouling left behind by the bullets passage. You need J-B bore paste to scrub the last of the jacket fouling out of the microscopic pits and toolmarks in your bore.

What are we cleaning out of the bore? The short answer is, anything that is not steel. You need to remove the powder fouling, and you want to remove the jacket fouling. The powder fouling that is easy to remove is the soft residue that settles out after the bullet has left the muzzle. A patch removes this. The hard, crusty powder deposits adhere to the bore at high temperature and are difficult to remove. It takes a brush or abrasive to remove this stuff. The jacket fouling is formed by rubbed-off jacket material that either lies on the surface of the bore, or is scraped off into pits or tooling marks left behind by rifling.

Ideally, you want to start cleaning your bore before you have left the range. As soon as you are done shooting and will be heading home, run a patch of bore solvent through your barrel. Put the rifle in your case and take it home with the solvent still in the bore. This gives your solvent up to several hours to work on the powder residue. As useful as this is in giving you a head start, the drawbacks to this are obvious. You need to take your one-piece rod to the range with you, along with solvent and patches. The solvent will get into your gun case, adding solvent odor and perhaps stain to the case. The solvent may wick out, even if you plug the bore, getting into the action and on the stock.

If you forget about it the solvent may be working on your rifle and the case for days before you can get to it. Swab your bore at the range, for the trip home, only if you have all these problems covered.

As long as you are using the proper tools and methods, do not be afraid to clean your bore. I once loaned a rifle (what can I say, I was young, foolish, and thought I was doing him a favor) that came back looking as good on the outside as when it left. I should have looked through the bore right away, but I was in a hurry and just stuck it back in the rack. When I pulled it down later and looked through the bore, I almost had a heart attack. The bore looked like a section of coal mine shaft. I yanked the bore scope off of the shelf and had a look. What I saw were small flakes of reddish material that clung to the chamber and bore. Yikes, my barrel was rusted! Then I noticed that one of the small flakes I had bumped moved. Rust doesn't move, so I pulled the bore scope out and ran a dry patch through the bore. What came out of the muzzle was a puff of leather dust! The fellow kept the gun in a leather case, and flecks of the leather had gotten into the bore. Was I lucky? You bet. Did I learn a lesson? Actually two. Don't loan rifles, and run a patch down the bore of every rifle to keep dust from settling in the bore.

When it comes to determining the "proper" method of cleaning a rifle bore, shooters are more inventive than any other group I have run into. I once heard two shooters earnestly discuss the proper number of times an individual patch should be pushed through a bore. One held that the patch should only go once, and in one direction, while the other felt that three times back and forth was the correct procedure!

The Outers Foul Out (yes it is an old model, but it works just fine) is a reverse electro-chemical deposition process. The fouling is plated off the barrel and onto the center rod.

And they each had a sample target in their wallets to prove it!

The customary cleaning method used by many shooters begins when arriving home, and goes something like this:

Remove the bolt, clamp the rifle in the cleaning cradle, and install a brush on the cleaning rod. Brush vigorously back and forth for a few strokes, then remove the brush and install a patch-holder. Install a patch, dip it in bore solvent and scrub the bore with it. Clean the bore out with a dry patch. Alternate the wet and dry patches until the dry patch does not change color during its trip down the barrel.

Using this procedure will get your barrel clean. But there is a more efficient way.

Through the years I have swung from one extreme to another on the subject of bore cleaning. I started out with the mindset of "I'll shoot this rifle without cleaning until it either jams, or I notice a drop-off in accuracy."

My rifles in that period were rimfires and military-surplus Lee-Enfields and Mausers. They probably deserved better treatment. When I bought a match-conditioned Garand and a Ruger No. 1 in .22-250, I swung to the other extreme. I would use each patch once, and pull it off the rod at the end of the stroke, never pulling it back through the bore. For a while, I even discarded the use of brushes. I have one match AR-15 that has never seen a bore brush, only cleaning patches. Does it shoot well? It sure does. Does it shoot better than its identical twin that has been brushed at each cleaning? No.

I have two methods of cleaning, each differing slightly from the usual method and neither so persnickety as my cleaning extreme. I do not claim either is THE best way, but as a professional gunsmith and professional writer, I don't have a lot of time to spare waiting for solvent to work. The first method is for rifles that have premium-grade hand-lapped barrels. The second method is for factory barrels.

For the first method set your rifle in the cradle and remove the bolt. Get out your patch and solvent catching can and set it under the muzzle. When you lock the cradle to hold the rifle, make sure the muzzle is pointing slightly down. Doing this will ensure that any excess solvent will run out of the muzzle into the can you have left out front. If you don't tilt the rifle, the excess solvent will run back into the action and the stock. Insert your rod guide in the action.

Install a clean bore brush on your rod and drop some bore solvent on it. Run it through the bore and out of the muzzle. The purpose of the brush is to loosen the powder residue. Pull the brush back through the bore. I clean the brush between each push and pull stroke through the bore. Other shooters are not so picky. Dan Lilja, the custom barrel maker, scrubs his barrels back-and-forth without such a cleaning.

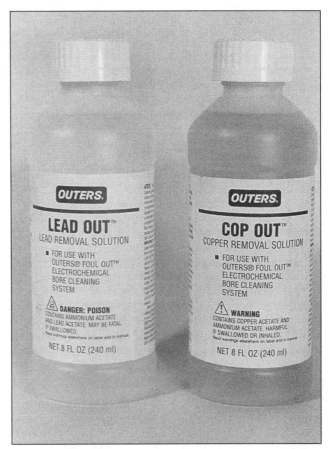

Copper and lead require different solvents to use the Foul Out. Using the wrong chemical will be frustrating, as the fouling will not budge.

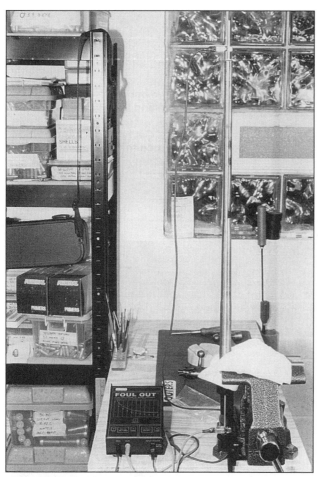

Once the "clean" light goes on, you can unclamp your barreled action and plan for more shooting!

barrel the dry patch will come out tinged blue or green. This is the solvent reacting to the copper and dissolving it. The particular color depends on the solvent you used and the bullets you were shooting. You may see some streaks of black on this first patch. This is powder residue that was not fully removed by the first solvent. Repeat using the copper solvent until the dry patch comes out without blue or green on it. With a premium barrel, you may see only traces of blue or green on this first patch. This is a good thing, it means you have little copper fouling present.

Using this procedure, it is possible to clean a barrel in about 15 minutes. I use this method at the range to clean and cool a barrel when testing for accuracy. As an aside, if you run a brass or bronze brush down your bore along with the copper solvent, you will have blue or green patches until you have dissolved the brush! You are picking up a false positive reaction from the brush itself. Stop that! Remember, only patches with copper solvent, never a brush.

The second method starts as with the first, with the rifle at a downward angle in the cradle. Brush the bore out as before. Wrap a patch around your jag and then rub the paste on the patch. Run the rod back and forth the length of the bore four or five times, then remove it. Wipe the rod clean, and put a fresh patch on the jag. Wet the patch with copper solvent and run it through the bore. Wait a couple of minutes and then run a dry patch down the bore. If it comes out

Remove the brush and install the Parker Hale jag. Wrap a dry patch on it. Run the patch down the bore and remove the patch after it comes out the muzzle. You will remove an impressive amount of black gunk with this patch. Pull the rod out. Wrap another patch around the jag and then dip the tip of the jag into your solvent. You will see the solvent wick up the patch. You do not have to immerse the patch, that will only load it up with more solvent than you need. Run the patch back and forth through your bore. Pull the patch off and replace with a dry patch. Wait a couple of minutes and then run the dry patch through the bore.

Repeat this process with solvent and dry patches until the dry patch comes out of the muzzle clean. With a premium barrel you may only need three or four patches.

If you are using a spearpoint tip, then a small eyedropper is useful in getting solvent on the patch. Once the patch shows through the window on your Dewey guide, or while it is laying on the tray of the Bore Tech guide, use the eye-dropper to place a couple of drops right where you need them. Properly applied with either tip, a bottle of solvent will last you a long time. If you use the solvent incorrectly, by swishing the brush into the bottle, your solvent supply will only last you a couple of cleaning sessions.

Now switch to your copper solvent. Run a patch wetted with copper solvent down your bore and then wait a couple of minutes. Run a dry patch down the bore. On a factory

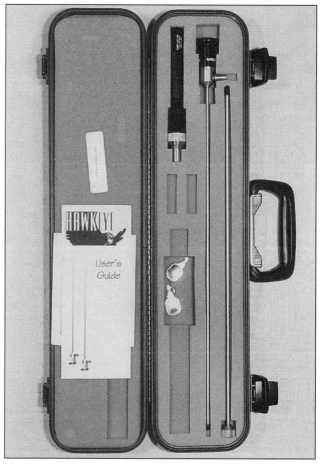

This Hawkeye bore-scope is just the thing to peer closely at your bore, but remember that the true test is performance, not appearance.

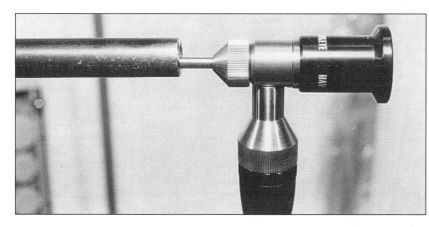

The Hawkeye bore-scope is a long tube with mirrors and lenses, the eyepiece, and sticking out of the bottom is the light adapter. The right-angle viewing mirror is a tube that slides over the regular scope.

Here I'm viewing the Marlin barrel after it has come back from Cliff LaBounty for re-boring from .30-30 to .38-55. The bore looked really bad before, and now it looks really good. But the true test is shooting it.

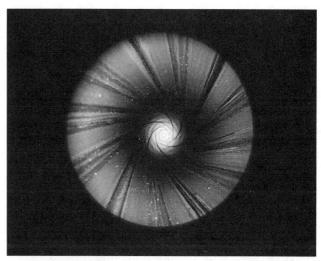

As you move the bore-scope through the barrel you will see the rifling flow by in a smooth stream. At least, it is supposed to be smooth. (Photo courtesy Gradient Lens Corp.)

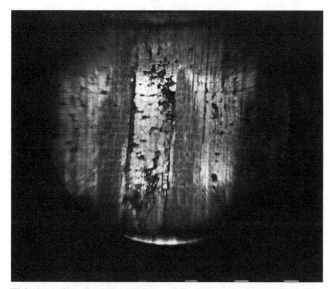

This heavily-shot barrel in an AR-15 is starting to lose its chrome plating. Continuing to shoot a hot barrel as in varmint shooting or competition can be very hard on a barrel. (Photo courtesy Gradient Lens Corp.)

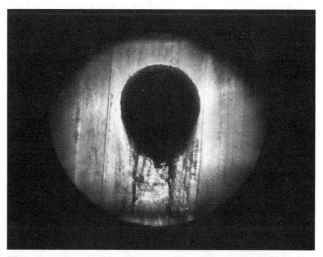

The gas port on this AR-15 is showing wear from the bullets' passage. However, such wear is not detrimental to accuracy. As soon as I saw this photo, I slid the Hawkeye borescope into each of my AR-15s. They all showed the same signs of wear, yet all are accurate rifles. Don't sweat this evil-looking phenomenon. (Photo courtesy Gradient Lens Corp.)

clean there is no copper fouling left. The hand-lapping that premium barrels receive leaves the bore very smooth. Other, later abrasive cleaning compounds may change the surface texture of the bore. It may seem picky to worry about the surface texture of polished steel. Remember that your bullet is accelerating down the bore pushed by a column of hot gases. The surface texture can make a big difference. I asked Dan Lilja about his lapping. "We experimented with a number of different compounds and methods, test-firing each barrel afterwards. Our hand-lapping improved accuracy until we actually made the bores too smooth. Don't use abrasives on our barrels."

If your off-the-rack rifle had a bore as highly-polished as Dan's barrels are, I would agree. His barrels are so smooth that there are no tooling marks in which jacket fouling or powder fouling may hide. Solvents and a patch will remove fouling in such a barrel. The standard hammer-forged barrel from the big rifle makers are not so smooth and they will not be harmed by using abrasive cleaners.

The Outers Foul Out is an electro-chemical method of removing fouling. The process is a reverse-electroplating method. Using an electrical charge and the proper chemicals, you plate the copper off of the bore and onto a sacrificial rod. Once the rod is plated you can scrape the copper off without worrying about harming the rod. While it is slower than an abrasive, you cannot harm your bore using the Foul Out properly.

I use the Outers Foul Out as an additional cleaning process for my rifles and handguns. Once a year I look through my shooting logs and see which firearms have been shot the previous year.

I learned a long time ago to keep accurate logs. Memory can only take you so far in keeping track of which rifles were used, and how many rounds they each got. All the rifles that have not been fired get a standard cleaning to remove dust and dried oil residue. All those that have been fired get a standard cleaning followed by a trip to the Foul Out stand. With the Outers Foul Out, I can be sure that each bore does not retain traces of fouling that can be starting points for corrosion.

How often should you clean? And how clean is "clean?" These depend on how often you shoot it, what your accuracy standards are, how forgiving your rifle is, and the shooting you have to do. To take the last pair first, you must define how critical your shooting is, and how forgiving your rifle is. Some rifles will shoot the first round from a clean and cold bore to a different spot than the following rounds. Many benchrest shooters will shoot a "fouling" round after they clean, to bring the bore back to the condition it was when they were shooting for groups. Why clean, then? They want to remove the powder fouling. Their premium barrels are so smooth that the copper fouling is removed along with the powder fouling. Unless you have the same quality barrel, you will have to go to greater lengths to get your barrel clean.

A Police sniper must know if his rifle shoots the first shot from a clean, cold bore to the same point as the rest of the shots. If it does not, he does not clean his rifle after he is done shooting, but during. His practice session ends by cleaning the rifle and then shooting another group to "condition" the bore. He must do this every time he shoots for practice or record.

A hunter who has fired his rifle enough to know that it will shoot under 2 inches at 100 yards hot or cold, clean or fouled, does not have to clean as often. He can clean his rifle just before hunting season.

Do you have to strip your bore down to bare steel every time you clean it? The heretical answer is no. To strip every trace of copper out of a slightly pitted bore can take hours of cleaning. The first shot will load the pits up with copper, sort of like filling the potholes in a road.

Your cleaning standards should be based on performance, not aesthetics. Does your rifle shoot accurately with a 15-minute cleaning job? Does it shoot any better if you spend three hours? If the respective answers are "yes" and "no", then any more than 15 minutes spent cleaning is a waste of time. If the answers are "yes" and "yes", then you have to figure out for yourself if the extra time spent cleaning is worth the extra accuracy.

If the answer to the first question is "no" then you need to either work longer or more efficiently in cleaning your bore.

And when should you clean? I cannot give you a hard and fast answer, only an upper and lower limit. At the lower limit, if you feel like cleaning, and you do it properly, you cannot harm your rifle. Do it as often as you like. Benchrest shooters may clean a rifle every 20 rounds. To find the upper limit, you have to do some testing. How many rounds can you fire through your rifle before you see a decrease in accuracy? And how long before the decrease becomes too great? As an example, if your hunting rifle delivers groups just over an inch wide at 100 yards when it is clean, but the groups have opened up to an 1-1/2 inches 50 rounds later, do you clean? If you are going to hunt the swamps where a long shot will be 60 yards, no. If you are going to Africa, yes.

Done the right way, cleaning is easy, relaxing and cannot harm your rifle. Do it as often as you feel like it.

The top High Power shooters favor non-chromed barrels. Many don't feel a chrome-lined barrel is as accurate. And when a barrel starts to show wear they don't want to worry about the chrome stripping off and further harming accuracy. My experience has shown that many chrome-lined bores are very accurate and do not give problems. (Photo courtesy Gradient Lens Corp.)

Looking at bores

Peering through a bore scope at your rifle can be a depressing experience. Many gun shops and gunsmiths that have bore scopes keep them a secret from all but trusted customers. Why? Because a barrel that delivers good or even excellent performance may look rough and ugly when magnified. A comparison may be in order. Think of your favorite super-model. Some of you may not have one in mind, so look at the next attractive lady you happen to meet. Now, think of what the tip of her nose would look like under a magnifying glass. Judge a rifle by its performance on the range, and a lady by her manners.

That said, what can you learn from looking through a bore scope? Let's work our way from the chamber to the muzzle and catalog what to look for on the trip. The view of the chamber will show you if there is any pitting. A pitted chamber can cause malfunctions and shorten brass life. A pitted chamber can be polished out, but again, brass life

Nick Till uses Blackstar barrels in his Bushmaster AR-15 and has shot to High Master using a Service Rifle. (Think of it as winning the next-faster class of cars in drag racing!) Sharp eyesight, steady nerves and a father who is a mean High Power shooter don't hurt. If you want to do well in competition, you need a reliable rifle and an accurate barrel.

will suffer. Moving up the throat, you can tell a lot about how a rifle was fired and treated by how the throat and leade looks. A heavily-shot rifle will have a pitted, cracked and eroded throat that looks like a section of bad road. A rifle vigorously cleaned without a guide rod will show washed-out areas of the throat. You can spot these by holding the borescope at the right spot to view the throat and then rotating the viewing shaft. If one or more of the lands are worn more than the others, you are probably looking at a rifle cleaned without a rod guide.

As you move forward of the leade, you will travel through the section of the bore where the carbon deposits settle. A rifle with only casual cleaning will have a darker surface look from the carbon deposits that have not been removed. Once you've cleared the carbon fields, the bore is pretty much the same out to the muzzle. Along the way you will see occasional patches of jacket fouling, tool marks and even some pitting. A semi-automatic rifle with a gas port may give you a start when you reach it. Appearing out of nowhere, the hole looks big enough to fall into. Look closely at the front edge of the hole. You will see that the bore is eroded. The more you have shot the rifle, the greater the erosion. The erosion is caused by gas jetting past the base of the bullet, and by the bullet flexing into the hole. While the erosion appears serious, it isn't.

To look closely at the rifling at the muzzle, you will probably have to swap ends with the bore-scope. At 17 inches, the viewing tube of the scope isn't long enough to reach from the breach to the muzzle. At the muzzle end you can look closely to see if the crown is nicked or worn from cleaning without a bore guide.

Lapped barrels

Once a cylinder of steel has been bored-through to make a tube, the rifling must be formed inside to make it a barrel blank. The steel can be shaped one of four ways, although only the first three are used in rifles. The first, and original method was to cut the grooves out of the tube. The simplest method involves a cutter that removes steel on one groove at a time in a method similar to planing a piece of wood. Not surprisingly it is called a "scrape cutter."

The scrape cutter is very slow, removing a thousandth of an inch of steel on each pass, requiring eight passes per groove. The industrial advance for mass-production involves a "broach" which looks like a gold-plated drill with sections missing. The broach is a stepped shaft with each step a specified larger diameter than the previous step. A broach only has to be pulled through the barrel once to fully form the rifling.

The second method is button rifling. Once the tube is bored, then a carbide button that is the contour of the rifling is pushed or pulled through the tube. The hard carbide irons the steel into the shape of the rifling. Button rifling also only needs a single pass to form the rifling.

The third method is hammer-forging. Once the tube has been bored, it goes into the hammer-forging machine. A hardened mandril in the shape of the chamber and rifling slides into the tube and then the machine cold-hammers the tube down around the mandril. Once done, the finished barrel is removed and ready to be threaded and installed in a rifle.

The fourth method, Electronic Discharge Machining, is used mostly on handgun barrels, but may be used in rifle barrels in

Caliber: 223   Date: 19 MAR 99

Load: HORNADY MATCH w/SIERRA 65 GR BTHP

Range: 100 YDS

Comments: QUALITY PARTS CO/BUSHMASTER CHROME-LINED BARREL

You have to be a very picky shooter to turn down accuracy like this. Any barrel that delivers sub-inch groups is not something to treat like a red-headed stepchild, even a chromed one.

the future. EDM uses a huge electrical charge to precisely erode metal by the spark that jumps the gap. In EDM rifling, a rifling head is pulled down the tube. On the head are tips shaped like the desired rifling. The electric charge sparking to the steel erodes the grooves as the head is slowly drawn down the tube.

All of these methods leave the steel ragged and stressed. Stress-relief by heat or cryogenic methods can lessen the stress, but the surface of the steel is still somewhat rough. To polish the surface of the bore, premium barrel makers lap it.

Premium barrels are expensive to make. To ensure correct headspace and locking lug engagement, those who make premium barrels for AR-15's will often fit a bolt to the barrel. When you install your new barrel, use the new, already headspaced, bolt that came with it. If you are buying a chrome-lined barrel, a new bolt already headspaced is a must. (Photo courtesy Quality Parts/Bushmaster.)

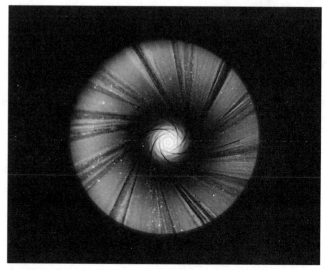

As you slide the bore-scope forward or back, you will notice that the rifling twists around your field of view. Straight "rifling" would not stabilize a bullet. (Photo courtesy Gradient Lens Corp.)

This Shilen barrel blank that will go into the Tactical Rifle in Chapter 17, is marked with all relevant data. It is a double-x blank (the best), .308 bore, 1.200 inches in diameter, with a 1 turn in 10-inch twist. Not surprisingly, it turned into a very accurate barrel.

Lapping involves casting a plug into the bore and then placing an abrasive compound on the surface of the plug. The barrel maker then cycles the plug back and forth along the length of the bore until the surface is polished. Once each grade of abrasive has done its work, the barrel is cleaned, a new plug cast, and the next-finer grade of abrasive is applied

Compared to the machine work of turning, reaming and broaching (or other rifling methods), lapping is labor-intensive, slow and requires much experience. The finest hand-lapped barrels are produced in few numbers, and sometimes require patience to obtain. I would not be surprised if the best lapper at a premium barrel maker like Shilen has a ritual he follows, and superstitions galore. For the results he produces, I have no complaints if he has to take the day off because the ritual was interrupted.

Is one method of barrel manufacture more accurate than another? That is a question that can start a fist fight. You can find superbly-accurate barrels of each kind, and it would take more than a few paragraphs just to lay out the reasons each of the three sides give for their method of manufacture. If you want a superbly-accurate barrel, go with a well-respected name and get the highest-grade barrel or barrel

You can go to extreme lengths to ensure accurate shooting, but if the twist is wrong for the bullet, your efforts will be for naught. This Lahti rest, as good as it is, will not make a M-855 ball shoot well in a 12-inch twist barrel.

The bullet length, not its weight determines the correct twist. The M193 bullets are short, and can be stabilized by a 1 turn in 12-inch twist. The M856 tracers are long, and require a 9-inch or faster twist.

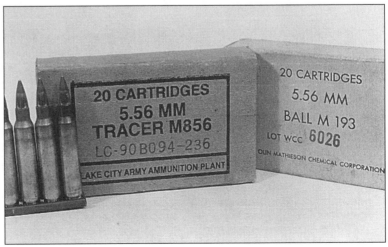

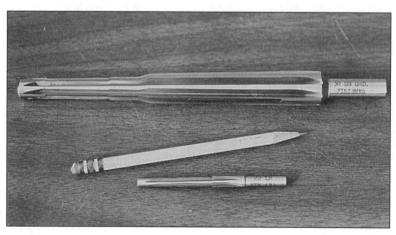

Date: 27 MAR 95   .223 Remington/5.56X45 test

Load: M856

Range: 25 YDS

Rifle Brand: AR·15

Barrel length: 20" Twist: 12' Brand: MIL·SPEC

Sighting Equipment: COLT 3X

TIPPING @ 25 YDS!

The M-855 at 62 grains, is not stabilized by the 12-inch twist. (The target info is wrong. The M-856 Tracers were completely hopeless, and I switched to the M-855s.) Notice that this group was fired at 25 yards, not 100, and the bullets are already tipping.

blank you can afford. Then have it installed by an experienced professional. Then you'll have an accurate rifle.

I have heard some shooters and barrel makers say bad things about chrome-plated barrels. Used only for the AR-15/ M-16, the chrome-plating increases durability and barrel longevity. For some uses, a chrome-plated barrel can be a minor hindrance. At extreme range, like NRA High Power matches

Colt marks their barrels clearly, once you know the code. C means it is chromed, MP means it has been magnetic particle inspected to detect flaws, the 5.56 NATO indicates the chamber meets NATO spec dimensions, not commercial .223 Remington dimensions, and the HBAR indicates that it is a heavyweight contour. This barrel, and any so-marked, are very accurate barrels. You could not do better without spending several hundred dollars for a premium barrel and more for its fitting.

(600 yards or greater) for a top-rated shooter, a chrome-plated barrel might not be accurate enough. But remember, such a shooter will complain about details that cost him only a point or two. For the rest of us, chrome-plating is plenty accurate. My Colt H-Bar delivers sub-inch groups with a dozen different loads. The Quality Parts hard-chromed barrel does nearly as well, but it isn't broken in yet, and I haven't fussed over it enough to find the loads that really make it shine. If that isn't accurate enough for you, then you'll have to spend a lot of money on a premium barrel.

The one drawback I have found to a chrome-plated barrel is the inability to use chambering reamers to adjust headspace. The chrome will dull and ruin a chambering reamer. If you are going to get a new chrome-plated barrel for your AR, order a bolt head along with it, and have the head space set by the barrel maker.

Barrel twist

The mere fact that a rifle barrel has grooves with a twist does not mean it will be accurate. In addition to the precision of its machining and the quality of its surface finish, a barrel must have the correct twist to be accurate. Twist is the rate of rotation of the rifling, and hence the bullet, through the barrel. Twist is referred to as the distance the bullet travels through the barrel while rotating once. A bullet in a barrel that has spun once in 10 inches is referred to as a "10-inch twist."

To chamber a barrel you need chambering reamers. The top reamer is for the .50 Browning machine gun, and is big and heavy enough to be used as a crowbar. The bottom one is for the .22 long rifle, and is so light it wouldn't make a very good paperweight. Somewhere in between is the reamer for your rifle.

How do you calculate twist? The method listed in the 1929 book *British Textbook of Small Arms* gives a formula plenty good enough even today. "The length of the bullet in calibers, multiplied by the twist rate in calibers per turn, is 150."

Known as the Greenhill rule after Sir Alfred George Greenhill, Professor of Mathematics at Woolrich, England, this formula gives a twist that produces a gyroscopic stability between 1.5 and 2.0. Gyroscopic stability less than 1.0 means a serious loss of accuracy, while 1.3 is a marginal level of stability. The "sweet spot" for most-accurate stability is right in the 1.5 to 2.0 area, although the useful range goes from 1.3 up to 4.0 or 5.0. The higher GS figures do not begin to affect accuracy until it gets larger than 5.0. An AR-15 with a 1-in-7 barrel using 55-grain full metal jacket bullets has a GS of 4.1. Many such rifles are quite accurate.

A 9mm carbine with a 1-in-10 barrel has a GS of 9.0. A slower twist would make for a potentially more-accurate rifle. It is easier to use the formula backwards. The U.S. military developed the .30-40 Krag cartridge to use a 220-grain bullet. The bullet is 1.35 inches long, or 4.5 calibers. 150/4.5 equals 33.3 calibers for the twist. So then, 33.3 times .308 equals 10.26 inches. The U.S. adopted the Krag with a 1-in-10 twist. When we went to the .30-03 with its 220-grain bullet, we kept the twist. When we updated it to the .30-06, the twist rate was not changed. After all, that would mean replacing barrels, not just setting the shoulders back and re-chambering them. The shorter 150-grain flat-base bullet used in the ".30 M2 Ball" doesn't need the twist the Krag did, but the US kept the 1-in-10 twist for the Springfield and later the Garand. The 150-grain flat-point of WWII only needs a twist of 1-in-12 or 1-in-13 to be stable in flight. The 1-in-10 twist over-stabilized it, but did not hurt accuracy.

Rather than calculate every example (you can if you want to) I have re-printed the following chart with the kind permission of Doug Shilen. The references to "VLD" bullets are for target shooters. The Very Low Drag bullets are designed to be very long for their weights. The low drag reduces velocity losses and wind deflection when shooting competitive matches. The bullets are not made for hunting, only competition. For the

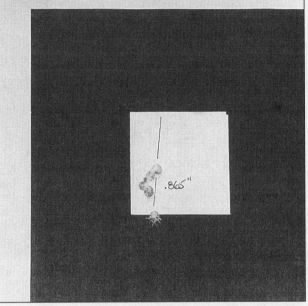

Date: 5 MAR 99   .223 Remington/5.56X45 test
Load: WW 63 Gr SP
Range: 100 yds
Rifle Brand: ETA Co
Barrel length: 20   Twist: 12"   Brand: MIL-SPEC
Sighting Equipment: LEUPOLD VXII 3.5-10

Remember, it is the ratio of twist to bullet length, and not its weight that is the determining factor of stability and accuracy. This hard-chromed 12-inch twist military barrel should not be accurate with 63-grain bullets, but it is. That is, with Winchester soft-points. The WW bullets are short for their weight, and thus are sufficiently stable to be accurate.

top-ranked competitive shooter the extra cost in bullets and barrels means a few more points. For the rest of us, it means extra cost.

Caliber

Twist rate

.224 Centerfire

1 twist in:
8 inches for bullets heavier than 70 gr
9 inches for bullets up to 70 gr
12 inches for bullets up to 63 gr (see text)
14 inches for bullets up to 55 gr
15 inches for bullets up to 55 gr driven to 4,100 fps or more
16 inches for bullets up to 55 gr driven to 4,300 fps or more

6mm/.243

1 twist in:
8 inches Special for VLD bullets over 100 gr

10 inches for bullets up to 120 gr and VLD under 100 gr
12 inches for bullets up to 85 gr
13 inches for bullets up to 75 gr
14 inches for bullets up to 70 gr

.257

1 twist in:
9 inches for bullets heavier than 100 gr
10 inches for bullets up to 100 gr
12 inches for bullets up to 90 gr
13 inches for bullets up to 80 gr
14 inches for bullets up to 70 gr

6.5mm/.264

1 twist in:
8 inches for bullets heavier than 130 gr
9 inches for bullets up to 130 gr

.270

1 twist in:
10 inches for all bullets

7mm/.284

1 twist in:
9 inches for bullets heavier than 140 gr

.308

1 twist in:
8 inches for bullets heavier than 220 gr
10 inches for bullets up to 220 gr
12 inches for bullets up to 170 gr
14 inches for bullets up to 168 gr
15 inches for bullets up to 150 gr

7.65mm/.311 inches

1 twist in:
10 inches for all bullets

8mm/.323

1 twist in:
10 inches for all bullets

.338

1 twist in:
10 inches for all bullets

9mm/.355

1 twist in:
14 inches for low-velocity wadcutters
16 inches for all other bullets

.38/.357

1 twist in:
14 inches for low-velocity wadcutters
16 inches for all other bullets

.358

1 twist in:
14 inches for all bullets

.375

1 twist in:
12 inches for all bullets

10mm/.400

1 twist in:
16 inches for all bullets

.411

1 twist in:
14 inches for all bullets

.416

1 twist in:
14 inches for all bullets

.44

1 twist in:
20 inches for all bullets
16 inches for low-velocity wadcutters

.451

1 twist in:
16 inches for all bullets

.458

1 twist in:
14 inches for all bullets

Why so few twist rates in some calibers? It's because of the bullet choices upon which shooters have settled. In the .224 category, varmint shooters use bullets as light as 45 grains, while target shooters use match bullets as heavy as 80 or 85 grains. While a shooter with a .30-06 might find a use for a 110-grain bullet or a 220-grain bullet, most of his shooting needs would be satisfied by bullets from 150 to 180 grains.

The hunter with a .338 Magnum is not interested in launching 130-grain bullets. He wants 200- to 250-grain bullets for big game hunting. If no one shoots 130-grain .338 bullets, why make a barrel with a twist other than 1-in-10? The same logic follows with the other calibers above .30. A rifle with a bore of .416 is probably a .416 Rigby or .416 Taylor. Launching only bullets from 350 to 400 grains, why have a twist other than 1-in-14?

Can you special-order a twist rate? Yes, but be prepared for a staggering cost, as you will have to pay for the creation of a new broach or button to form the new twist.

Andy Manson loosening an action with a wrench of his own design. Instead of trying to wrestle the action free with all 140 pounds of his weight, he lets Mr. Hammer loosen the action. Not one problem in 20 years of barrel fitting.

The correct twist rate of a barrel for a particular bullet relates to the length of the bullet, not its weight. However, bullet makers list their bullets by weight (and loading manuals, too) so we commonly compare twist rate to bullet weight. However, a bullet sufficiently longer for its weight than the "standard" may require a different twist. Generally in any given caliber, the heavier the bullet the faster (or "tighter") the minimum twist needed to stabilize it. Once the

When you are clamping the barrel, get the barrel vise around it as close to the receiver as possible.

The Brownells action wrench fits a number of rifles, and is sturdy enough to give years of trouble-free service.

The LaBounty action wrench is much faster to use than the Brownells, as it uses wedging to secure the wrench to the action, not large cap screws. Start with the channel resting in place over the receiver.

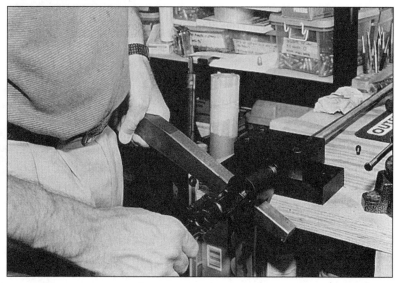

Then slide the wedge/lever into place through the holes in the wrench head. Tap with a hammer to seat the lever, and....

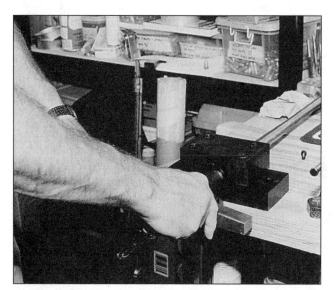

Turn the action loose. A piece of cake.

minimum has been met, a faster twist does not offer more accuracy, but it can offer greater penetration in the target. Minor variables that add complexity to selecting twist rates are velocity, air temperature and air density. Unlike bullet weight, which can be varied by selecting different bullets, once a barrel is rifled, its twist rate is fixed. Look at the sidebar on rifling twist and compare the 14-inch twist .224" barrel with the one with a 15-inch twist. For a 55-grain bullet, you have to up the velocity from approximately 3,200 fps to 4,100 fps, in order to regain the stability lost from switching from a 14-inch twist barrel to a 15-inch twist barrel. In the .223 Remington cartridge, this velocity gain is not possible.

The original M-16 (then called the "Armalite AR-15") had a twist of one turn in 14 inches. To reduce the cumbersome "one turn in X inches" I'll simply use the numerical designation for the twist. The 1-in-14-inch barrels were just fast enough to stabilize the 50- and 52-grains bullets being used. When the Army tested the AR-15/M-16 they found that as the barrels became worn accuracy suffered. The twist was too slow to maintain bullet stability as the rifling eroded from use. Also, in Arctic conditions the extreme cold and

Here is one of the lugs with Dykem applied, ready to be lapped.

Once the lapping removes all of the layout dye, your lapping is done.

At the end of this locking lug nearest the camera you can see the camming ramp. You do not want to lift the bolt handle in lapping far enough to be lapping this angled surface.

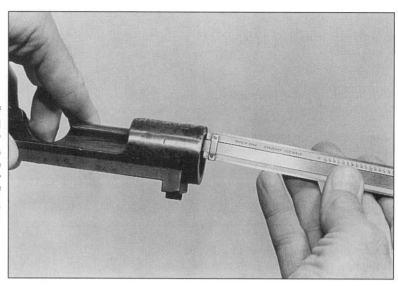

Measure the distance from the front face of the receiver to the inner collar. The best tool is a depth micrometer, but since I already had dial calipers I've used them for years rather than buy the mic. When using the dial calipers, measure the distance at four or five points along the circumference of the face and average them.

dense air caused accuracy problems. Having spent several winters on the Korean peninsula shooting at moving targets, the testers knew that accuracy losses in cold weather could have detrimental effects.

The twist was changed to 1-in-12, and the rifle became sufficiently accurate. The earlier twist had left bullets marginally stable. Upon striking a target the bullets would lose stability and dump their energy into the target at a greater rate. Why would a bullet lose stability? The twist rate sufficient to stabilize a bullet depends on the medium the bullet passes through. Water (the main composition of tissue) is denser than air, and requires a faster twist for the bullet to remain stable. The new 12-inch twist lessened the severity of the energy dump, and some felt the new twist was less effective for combat.

Benchrest shooters use the slowest-possible twist that stabilizes the bullets they use. They select the twist rate not to increase severity of the energy dump (they're shooting paper targets, after all) but because they want the least amount of stress on the bullet jacket. Stress degrades accuracy. For most of us the accuracy losses caused by bullet jacket stress are insignificant. For benchrest shooters, everything is important if it has an effect on accuracy.

When the military desired a heavier bullet for greater accuracy at longer ranges, and greater penetration of inciden-

tal objects, they found the 1-in-12-inch twist was too slow. As an example, if you take an AR with a 1-in-12 barrel and feed it ball M193 (55 grains) ammo it likes, you can get a group of an inch or 2 at 100 yards with no problem. Some ARs and many bolt-action rifles will do better. Give the same rifle ball M855 (62 grains) and your group can be a foot in diameter. Sometimes much more. I have an AR-15 that is a tack-driver with M193 ball. It will shoot sub-inch groups with 55-grain bullets. Feed it M855 62-grain boat-tail bullets and you will be lucky to get one-foot groups at 50 yards. The barrel is a military-production hard-chromed 1-in-12 M16A1 barrel. However, not all bullets that weigh the same have the same length. The Winchester 63-grain softpoint is a short bullet, with only lead and copper in it. The M855 bullet is a boat-tail (it makes the bullet longer) and has a steel penetrator in its tip (also making the bullet longer.) That particular rifle will stabilize the Winchester bullet but not the M855. The length difference is just enough for my rifle to deal with the Winchester and not the M855.

Calculating the twist for the M855 would have given the correct answer as a 1-in-9 twist for the M-16A2, but instead a 1-in-7 twist was selected. I have heard a number of explanations as to why. One is that the military required the M856 tracer bullet to be fully-stabilized to the full

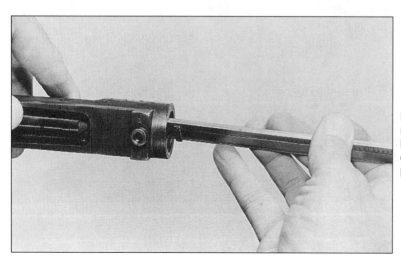

Here I'm measuring the distance from the receiver face to the bolt face, to calculate the headspace for the new barrel. As with the collar measurements, when using a dial caliper measure several times and average.

Looking inside the Mauser receiver, you can see the inner collar that the rear of the barrel should rest against when your replacement is torqued into place.

When the bolt turns down to lock in place, the extractor does not turn. Notice that the face of this bolt has been turned on the lathe just enough to clean it up, even though not all of the marks have been removed. It doesn't have to be completely clean, just clean of pits and tool marks.

The professional, and powered method of fitting headspace. Using the lathe to power and advance the reamer, the chamber depth can be controlled to a thousandth of an inch. The depth micrometer is used to check progress. The lathe can be used to correct the shoulder and inner collar locations as well as ream the chamber.

length of its burn. The tracer looks like a small brass copy of a #2 pencil. It took me a while to put my finger on just what was wrong with that one. A bullet becomes more stable, not less, the farther it travels. The bullet is forced down the bore, and must rotate around its center. Once it pops out of the muzzle it wobbles about a bit as its center of rotation shifts from the center of form to the center of mass. From the moment it leaves the muzzle the forward velocity is decreasing because of the drag of air. The rotation does not decrease as quickly as the velocity, so the ratio of its rate of rotation to its velocity increases. It becomes slightly more stable until its velocity passes through the speed of sound, which degrades accuracy. The tracer does not need to be over-stabilized in the beginning, in order to remain stable at the end.

Another explanation put forward was that after being accused of using an inhumane caliber in Vietnam, the US military wanted to make the new rifle shoot over-stabilized bullets. The Armed Forces are concerned with many things, but I don't think that was one of them.

When the bolt goes forward, it comes up to the inner collar.

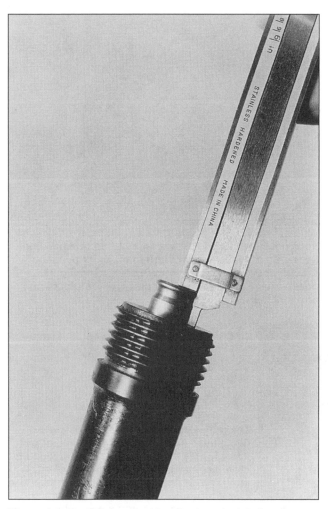

Measuring the GO gauge extrusion to calculate headspace.

Measuring the distance between front and inner collar bearing surfaces. Ideally, this distance will be the same as the depth to the inner collar of your rifle, plus .002" crush. This distance plus the gauge extrusion must be the same or slightly more than the distance from face to bolt on your rifle. If the total is less, you are faced with lathe work to make your barrel fit and headspace properly.

A full chamber gauge set is a "GO", a "NO-GO" and a "FIELD" gauge. While the GO and NO-GO are used to check headspace to see if it is within normal limits, the field gauge is used to check a chamber for safety. If a rifle swallows a FIELD gauge, immediately cease shooting it and have it checked out.

Headspace gauges have to correspond to the cartridges and chambers they purport to measure. The .50 BMG gauges look like steel bananas. The tiny little gauges in the left middle are for the .22 long rifle, while the slightly larger ones right center are for the .221 Remington Fireball, the smallest rimless centerfire case.

The most likely explanation was one put forth by Mark Westrom of Armalite. He figures that the Belgians in their ballistic testing of the .223 calculated the heaviest bullet they could ever make, and then made their test barrels with that fast a twist so every bullet could be tested without making special runs in different twist rates. A 7-inch twist will stabilize a bullet as heavy as 90 grains.

When the US military decided to go to a faster twist, they simply adopted the Belgian twist rate and utilized the already-produced ballistic data, or so Mark feels. Is there any chance of changing the M-16 over to a 1-in-9? Not really. Government testing and procurement procedures being as cumbersome as they are, it would be cheaper to simply re-barrel every rifle in the inventory to 1-in-9 twist, than prove that the new twist is better through sufficient testing.

Installing a barrel

Barrels are not like light bulbs. You can't simply unscrew the old one and screw in the new one, and then go about your business. For one thing, light bulbs don't have to be torqued in enough to withstand the chamber pressure of a rifle cartridge. Secondly, light bulbs don't have to be set up with correct headspace.

Replacing a barrel is not too difficult, and can be managed by the home gunsmith with a few caveats. First, you simply must have a correctly-fitting action wrench for the rifle you will be working on. You will also need a depth micrometer, headspace gauges, a finish chambering reamer in your caliber and a pre-threaded barrel. If you do not have a pre-threaded barrel, then you need a large and precise lathe that will probably not be found in most hobbyist's basements or garages. If you want to increase the potential precision of your rifle, get a bolt lug lapping kit in order to lap the lugs to full engagement.

I will go through the method for installing a new barrel on a Mauser action. The methods are the same for other rifles, with only a few details being different. In the follow-

ing description, your gunsmith who is installing a barrel that he has threaded from a blank will have stopped part-way through to turn, thread and short-chamber the barrel blank.

Start by removing the old barrel from the receiver. To do so, make sure the rifle is unloaded. Remove it from the stock. Remove the scope, scope bases, trigger and bolt. Closely inspect the front receiver ring. A common method of filling old scope mount screws is to tighten a screw in place, then file the head off and polish the action before bluing. A screw that bears against the barrel threads will lock the barrel in place and make removing it impossible. You will ruin the action trying to get it apart. Check the ring all the way around. Yes, we mount scope bases on top today, but in the old days side-mounts were popular. If you find a screw-filled hole ground flush, you'll probably have to take it to a professional to get the thing out.

To begin the barrel removal, clamp the barrel in the barrel vise as close to the receiver as possible. Orient the receiver so the front action screw, if it were installed, would be pointing at 4 o'clock. The Brownells action wrench is milled as a two-piece unit. The base fits all actions, while each head is machined to a particular action. The base opening has a milled recess on one side. It is the clearance gap for the recoil lug on Mauser-type rifles. Place the base of the wrench against the bottom of the receiver with the recoil lug inside the clearance gap. Place brass or steel shim stock between the action wrench and the top ring of the receiver to prevent marring the finish. Tighten the locking bolts evenly, so the gap on each side is the same. Despite the fact that everything involved is made of steel, you should be careful from this point on. The front of the receiver is immovably locked in place. You only need to apply a small amount of force to the rear of the receiver in order to bend it. A bent receiver may still work, but it will not shoot accurately. With the wrench handle pointing at 4 o'clock, you can now lift the handle straight up to unscrew the receiver. I find that lifting the handle in this manner lets me use my legs, back and biceps. It also keeps me from twisting the wrench as I

Here we see why pre-threaded and chambered Mauser barrels are common, while others are not. The Mauser barrel (on the left) has a flat face without an extractor cut. The barrel on the right (an FN/FAL) requires a slot for the extractor. To fit a new barrel to it you would have to thread, fit and headspace the barrel blank, then unscrew it and mill the extractor slot. Then screw it back in.

rotate it. Gradually increase pressure until the receiver comes loose. Do not jerk the wrench. If the receiver does not come loose with hand pressure on the wrench, slide a length of pipe onto the wrench to gain more leverage.

If you are removing an original barrel from a surplus Mauser, there is a small chance you will crack the receiver. A cracked receiver is not your fault, nor the wholesaler's or dealer's. A cracked receiver cannot be repaired. Jerry Kuhnhausen, in his book on Mausers, surmises that cracked receivers on barrel removal are due to slightly oval-shaped barrels caused by excessive factory proof-testing ammunition. I have heard of similar problems with 1917 Enfield rifles produced during World War I by the Eddystone arsenal. Although I have not cracked any Mauser or Enfield receivers, I warn everyone whose barrel I remove. If you are taking your barrel out, or removing the barrel for a buddy, be aware that someone may have to buy a replacement.

Once the receiver is loose, take the action wrench off and finish unscrewing the receiver by hand.

The instructions with the Brownells wrench come with additional notes about specific rifles, and with their kind permission I have paraphrased a few of them here.

Large-ring Mausers have been made in numerous places, they've been shipped around the world and been worked on for a century. Check the receiver with a straight edge to make sure it hasn't been bent before it got to you. Some barrels may be screwed in so tightly that they require great force to remove. (Strangely, I have encountered some military Mausers where the barrel was only slightly tighter than hand-tight.) Variations in front ring diameter mandate shim stock to avoid marring the finish.

Small-ring Mausers have a reputation for being slightly softer than the Large ring, and can be easily bent. The front ring can easily be marred by the typical "V" type action wrench.

Springfield 03 & 03A3 rifles have a projection on the right side of the front ring. Place the action wrench head with its milled clearance cut over this projection.

The Winchester Model 70 is treated the same as the large-ring Mauser.

The Remington 700 has a recoil lug that is a separate piece. The Brownells wrench encloses the front ring and correctly locates the recoil lug at the same time.

If you are going to work on only one rifle or type of rifle, then the Brownells wrench will do the job. As you add rifles to your collection you have to add wrench heads in the Brownells system. The LaBounty U-Turn action wrench is designed to fit a number of actions without additional parts. It works on 98 Mauser and Mauser-type rifles like the Winchester Model 54 and 70, the Springfield 03 and the 03A3, Ruger Model 77, Enfield P-14 & P-17, Remington Model 30 and most Sako rifles. Not only does it work on Remington 700's, it locates the recoil lug when re-installing the barrel. Additionally, the U-Turn wrench doesn't use clamping bolts. For the professional interested in reducing time spent at the work bench, the speed of the LaBounty is an asset.

To use the LaBounty wrench, clamp your barrel in the barrel vise. Place shim stock over the top of the receiver ring, and slide the "U" clamp down over the ring. Slide the handle/wedge through the square windows of the "U" clamp. Place a ball-peen hammer against the outside of the far side of the "U" clamp and then tap the end of the handle/wedge with a mallet to seat it firmly. Grasp the end of the handle/wedge and unscrew the action. As with the Brownells wrench, if the receiver resists unscrewing slide an extension pipe over the handle/wedge for more leverage.

To finish any barrel removal, remove the action wrench and unscrew the action by hand. Take the old barrel out of the barrel vise and stash it on the shelf.

Look at the locking lug recesses of the receiver. On the Mauser you'll have to peer past the front collar. A rifle subjected to overly high pressures can have the surfaces set back by the excessive bolt thrust. A receiver with set-back lugs cannot be repaired and must be replaced. (Cracked receivers, set-back lugs and bent rails are all hazards of buying surplus Mausers to build

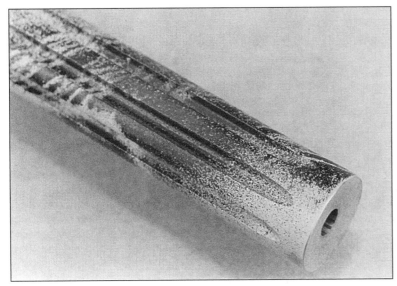

The muzzle of this barrel has been crowned with an 11-degree target crown. The recess protects the muzzle from the ravages of a harsh world, and evenly releases the bullet when it is fired. The 11-degree crown offers more protection in a bull barrel than a sporter. On a thinner barrel the muzzle might not be back far enough from the edges to be protected, which is why rifle makers offer lathe-turned rounded crowns on lightweight barrels.

on. All the more reason to buy one with a shot-out barrel, at a dirt cheap price, and minimize the potential loss.) Strip the bolt and remove the extractor if it has an external one.

Get out your bolt lug lapping tool. On the Brownells tool take the adapter sleeve for a Mauser rifle (because we are working on a Mauser) and loosen the set screw on the side. Slide the tool shaft through the threaded adapter and lock it in place with the set screw. Scrub the receiver clean and apply Dykem to the locking lug recesses and the bolt lugs. Screw the sleeve into the front of the receiver until it bottoms out. You do not have to tighten it firmly. Insert the bolt and close it. Then lift it 45 degrees and close it several times. Remove the bolt and the fixture. Inspect the bolt lugs and the locking recesses of the receiver. The surfaces should be in full contact. Don't settle for less than 90 to 95 percent.

If your lugs fail to make contact, then open up a vial of fine grit lapping compound, 600 or 800 grit. Place a small amount on the locking lug recesses of the receiver. Screw the fixture back into the receiver. When you push the bolt forward, push it all the way forward before you turn it down. To lap the surfaces, lift the bolt handle 45 degrees and then turn it down forty or fifty times. (If the engagement is already very close to perfect, you may only need to lift and close ten or twenty times.) Do not lift the bolt more than halfway while lapping. If you lift too far you will be lapping metal on the sloped "lead-in" part of the locking recesses. The manufacturer has gone to great trouble to give you a gentle taper on this lead-in, to make it easier to close the bolt. If you lap the lead-in, you can make operating the bolt more difficult. Once you have finished, remove the bolt and the fixture and thoroughly clean the bolt lugs and locking lug recesses.

Re-apply Dykem and repeat the first test for bolt lug contact. If you do not have 95 percent contact on both lugs, repeat the lapping. It never took more than the single lapping session to lap in any rifle have I worked on.

The abrasive compound will continue to do its work unless you remove all traces of it before you fit your new barrel. Scrub thoroughly!

Locking lug lapping increases headspace. You cannot remove your barrel, lap the lugs, and then screw the old barrel back into place. To do so may be unsafe. However, when installing a new barrel you'll be setting the new headspace AFTER you lap the lugs, and not before.

You're now ready to start the measuring to install your new barrel. On the Mauser, you have two sets of dimensions to keep track of. The first is the distance from the barrel shoulder to butt end of the barrel in comparison to the front edge of the receiver to the inner collar (the thread shank). The other dimension is the headspace, the distance from the front of the bolt to the front of the chamber.

To measure the thread shank length you need the new barrel, the receiver and a depth micrometer. On the Mauser rifle, the barrel bears against both the front shoulder of the receiver ring and the inner collar. With the depth micrometer, measure into the receiver from the front ring to the collar. When the barrel is torqued into place, the threads will be stressed slightly and the steel will be very minimally squeezed. However, it will be squeezed on both shoulders, provided they both come in contact as the barrel is tightened. The desired situation is for both measurements to come out the same. Indeed, the whole reason your local professional has a big, accurate lathe is so he can turn the shoulder of the barrel to make it the same as the rifle. If your pre-threaded barrel does not measure the same distance on the barrel thread shank as the depth of the receiver to inner collar length, what to do? First, don't panic. Gunsmiths have great pride in their abilities, and go to lengths to make things correct that probably aren't needed. Does the Mauser have to bear on both surfaces? Not really. The Springfield doesn't, nor do the Winchester Model 70, Remington or a whole host of other rifles. Provided it bears tightly enough to lock the barrel in place, either will do. Brownells sells many pre-threaded barrels, and I asked my contact in the gunsmithing Q&A department, Reid Coffield, about barrel fit. "Ideally, both should bear. If only one bears, I'd rather it was the inner shoulder. If it is the front face, the only problem you might have is if the thread shank is so short that headspace or unsupported case problems result." How short would the inner shank have to be, to cause problems? "Five or 10 thousandths would be no problem. By the time you get to 20 thousandths, you should have a pro set the shoulder back."

If your barrel comes within 10 thousandths of matching the receiver depth, you're in like Flynn. Remember, Mausers have been made by the tens of millions for a century, in dozens of countries and sometimes in a dozen plants in one or two countries. They are not absolutely identical.

The critical measurement is headspace. To measure headspace you need to add a set of headspace gauges to your tool kit. Take the depth micrometer and measure from the face of the receiver to the face of the bolt. If your initial measurements indicate that your barrel will bear on both shoulders or on the front ring, this is your front ring headspace measurement. If your measurements indicate your new barrel will bear on the inner ring, subtract the depth to the inner ring from the depth to the bolt face. The result is your inner ring headspace measurement.

To check headspace for a front ring or dual-surface bearing rifle, place the "Go" gauge in the chamber of the barrel and measure from the base of the gauge to the barrel shoulder. For an inner ring bearing rifle, measure from the rear of the headspace gauge to the rear of the barrel. Wherever your rifle barrel rests when it screws into the receiver, this second headspace-gauge measurement MUST be greater than the measurement of the receiver. That is, the headspace gauge sticks out of the rear of the barrel a greater distance than there is room for it in the receiver. If the barrel measurement is equal to or lesser than the receiver measurement, you will be screwing into place a barrel with excess headspace. In the case of excess headspace you should box the parts up and take them to a professional gunsmith with a lathe. He can then set the barrel shoulder and thread shank back to the correct minimum length for proper headspace.

If the headspace measurements on the barrel come to greater than the receiver measurements, you can proceed without outside help. Hand-reaming the headspace to the correct dimension is easier with the barrel off than on the rifle. On a notepad, write the barrel measurement at the top. Write the receiver measurement at the bottom. Clamp your barrel vertically in a padded vise. (Clamp it forward of the chamber to avoid slightly squeezing the chamber and reaming it oval.) Clamp the chambering reamer in a large tap handle and brush cutting oil on the reamer. Gently lower it into the chamber and rotate the reamer one turn. Pull the reamer out and swab the chamber clean. Insert the headspace gauge and measure the barrel headspace. How much did it change from the previous measurement? Write the new measurement below your barrel figure, and calculate how many times you will have to repeat this step to hit the receiver number exactly.

Remember when we discussed the "crush factor"? When the barrel is torqued into the receiver the parts will be squeezed together tighter by .002 inches than your measurements. As a result, you must cut your chamber .002 deeper (.002 LESS) than the receiver measurement. Proper headspace is not a figure, but a range. The full distance of this range is .006 inches. You MUST be careful in cutting headspace, as your crush factor is one-third the allowable range.

With the chamber cut to the proper headspace, all that is left is installing the barrel. Scrub the barrel and receiver threads clean. Clamp the barrel in the barrel vise as close to the threads as possible. Spread thread paste on the threads. The thread paste acts as an anti-seize agent. Yes, the barrel may stay on there for the rest of your life. Then again, you may want to take it off in a couple of years. The thread paste will make removal a lot easier without otherwise loosening the fit. Start the receiver onto the threads by hand, and screw it all the way forward. Install your action wrench. Tighten the action back onto the barrel firmly but not forcefully. The leverage of the action wrench gives you power enough to tighten the action properly without having to lean on the end of the handle.

To cap off a first-class job, mark the caliber on the barrel at the chamber. Again, you may have this rifle your whole life, but then again you may sell it. Or, you may leave it to your heirs. Save them the cost and hassle of having a gunsmith measure the caliber, and mark it. I still have a rifle left behind by a customer. It is a Spanish '95 Mauser that had been re-barreled. When he bought it, the owner knew enough about rifles to recognize that it had a Springfield military barrel screwed into it. He bought it, thinking it was a .30-06. When it didn't work, he brought it to me. Whoever had threaded the barrel to the Mauser threads did not have a working grasp of headspace. It won't even come close to closing on a .30-06 cartridge. I told him the only solution would be to re-cut the threads on the lathe and shorten it to .308 Winchester. He didn't want a .308, didn't want to spend more money, and would get back to me. That was five years ago.

To mark the caliber, get a roll of masking tape, a straightedge and a ball point pen. Roll out a foot of tape and stick it to a clean surface. Strike a straight line on the tape with the straightedge and pen. Now apply the tape to the barrel, on the left side above the stock line. Take your metal stamps and stamp the caliber on the line, going from right to left. If you are right handed, starting on the right lets you see the previous letters and numbers as you strike each in order. Lefties, go the other way. If you don't have metal stamps, again, the local 'smith can stamp them for you. When you take the barreled action, bring the bolt. He will probably want to check the headspace just for his own peace of mind.

Other rifles will have peculiarities in installing a barrel, some that require power tools to deal with. As a result, you will see Mauser barrels most often as pre-threaded barrels ready to install. One example of a problem needing power tools is the Springfield. The Springfield has a coned-shaped butt end of the barrel. This "cone-shaped breech" was intended as an aid to feeding when the Springfield was designed. Does it need it? Not really. Can you install a barrel without it? No. Once designed-in, you have to go with it. The problem with the coned-breech is that the cone goes back where the extractor would be. Once the barrel is installed and the head space properly set, then the barrel has to be marked, removed, and the extractor cut milled through the cone.

Another rifle that can pose problems is the Remington 700. The forward rim of the bolt encircles the cartridge for safety. The bolt rim fits into a recess in the rear of the chamber. If you do not have a lathe and the correct reamer for this recess you cannot fit a new barrel to your Remington.

With a new barrel on your Mauser, you're ready to install sights, a scope mount and drop the package into a stock.

Muzzle Crowning

The crown is the last part of your barrel that the bullet sees on its flight to the target. The condition of the crown can have an adverse effect on accuracy. If the muzzle has been cut off-square, then your accuracy can be decreased. A dent can score the side of the bullet, and nudge it off-course. If the muzzle is nicked or worn, then the powder gases can "jet" on the side of the bullet where they first escape. The eddies may jostle the bullet, or the gas may cut the edge of the base, harming accuracy.

Crowns, as they are cut on many factory rifles, are lathe-turned concentric to the bore with a curved cutter. The recessed crown protects the ends of the lands and grooves from impact. Imagine a barrel where the muzzle is cut perfectly perpendicular to the bore. The flat edge offers no protection to the rifling. If the end of the rifling is recessed, then something that hits the muzzle cannot harm the rifling. After much experimentation, target shooters uncovered the 11-degree crown. At an 11-degree recess, the rifling is protected from harm, while releasing the bullet in the most uniform manner possible. If the 11-degree angle is the best, why do the factories use the radius-style crown? Looks and tradition. The radius works, it is what many shooters and rifle buyers expect to see, and the factories have years of experience at getting it just right.

If your muzzle is dented, the rifling worn, or the crown has been abused in the past, you can re-cut it for better accuracy. If you want to re-create the radius-style crown, you will have to unscrew the barrel, center the bore in a lathe, and turn the muzzle with a curved cutter.

Brownells makes a crowning tool with interchangeable pilots that does not require a lathe, only your hand power. To use it, make sure your rifle is unloaded. Clean the bore and leave it well-oiled. Take the 11-degree cutter and insert the pilot that corresponds to your caliber. The Brownells tool comes with a small aluminum "T" handle that screws onto the back of the cutter. On hard rifle steels I have found it difficult to keep the cutter from chattering when using this small handle. My solution was to use a carpenters brace to turn the cutter. The risk of using a brace is in damaging the rifling with the pilot, or breaking the pilot. The pilot is hard, and can score the bore if you are not careful. I use a coating of high-pressure grease on the pilot to cushion its force against the bore, and keep it straight to the bore.

In use, grease the pilot and apply some cutting oil to the edges of the reamer. Slide the pilot in and begin rotating the reamer when it touches the muzzle. Stop after a few turns to clean the chips off of the reamer. While the reamer is out being cleaned, inspect the bore closely with your binocular visor. Stop reaming when the damaged portion of the bore has been reamed away.

Some rifles leave the factory with a muzzle rougher than you would like, and simply cleaning the crown with the reamer brings errant shots back into the group.

If you are shortening a barrel, you need to square it before you can cut the crown. To shorten a barrel, mark the new length with a china pencil or felt-tip marker. Take a fine-tooth hacksaw and cut the barrel as square as you can get it. (Remember, the legal minimum length for a barrel is "greater than 16 inches." The measurement is taken from the face of the closed bolt to the perpendicular of the crown.) Once it is shortened, clamp the barrel vertically in your padded vise and use a fine-cut file to remove the hacksaw marks. Also use the file to level the cut, filing down any high spots.

Mark the muzzle with Dykem. Turn the barrel back to horizontal. Insert your pilot in the 90-degree cutter, and make a pass at the muzzle. If you are not cutting more than half the surface, go back to the file and get the muzzle closer to perpendicular. Once the squaring cutter is taking a clean cut around the entire muzzle, then switch to the 11-degree cutter to do the crown. The recess the 11-degree cutter makes does not count against you in measuring the barrel, but if you need that raised lip you are literally cutting it close. Maybe too close.

Headspace. What is it? How to get it?

Headspace is the technical term for the size of the chamber. Something has to keep the cartridge from dropping out of the muzzle. In the days of muzzleloaders, a patch or wad served that purpose. Later, it served a dual purpose and engaged the rifling to spin the bullet. With cartridges, the problem is not so much keeping the round from falling out, as keeping it in place for the firing pin to strike it. Reloaders also have the problem of keeping their brass from wearing out prematurely.

Manufacturers like Remington go to a lot of trouble to make sure their rifles are properly headspaced and properly marked. If you buy a used rifle, a previous owner may have altered the chamber dimensions. Measure to be certain of caliber.

Headspace is the gap between the face of the bolt and whatever stops the cartridge. There are three ways to stop the cartridge. The first is a rim. The .30-30 is an example of a rimmed cartridge. The rim stops the forward progress of the cartridge, and serves as a place for the

Something must keep the cartridge from sliding forward and out of the muzzle. On the "rimless" cartridge on the left, the shoulder stops it. In the center the belt stops it. The rimmed cartridge on the right uses the rim as a positive stop.

extractor to hold on to and pull it out. Even when the cartridge has a shoulder, as the .30-30 does, the rim is the critical part of the headspace.

That headspace is critical and the shoulder is not so critical comes into play when American shooters use the British SMLE. The British set the headspace correctly for their rifles on the rim. I have checked perhaps 100 SMLEs, and they all checked out within the correct range for headspace. However, the British left the shoulder farther forward in the chamber than on the cartridge sometimes by a large margin. The Army doesn't care about reloading, and British target shooters don't reload (Berdan primers were and are tough to extract and replace). What the military did care about was continued reliable function under the worst of conditions.

So, the new American owner fires his Lee-Enfield, and carefully saves the brass. He reloads the brass, and finds that the next time he shoots them the cases separate just above the rim. What happened? When he fired them the first time, the case expanded into the larger chamber, with the shoulder well forward. That expansion had to come at the expense of some part of the case. The loss was around the base, at the point where the case wall thickness dropped off and the pressure was still high. The American reloader re-sized the cases, and shoved the shoulder of each back to where it was supposed to be. The next time he fired it, each case stretched again. The stretching occurred at the same place, and the brass ran out of stretch capacity and separated.

Look closely and you'll see the shoulder of the left case has moved forward. The .303 British headspaces on the rim. Unless this shoulder is sized back during the reloading process, it will not chamber in the rifle that produced the empty on the right. Continued stretching and setting-back will weaken and then break the case. The only solution is a new barrel that headspaces on both rim and shoulder. Expensive and uneconomical.

The solution should be simple. Start with new brass and expand the neck past .311" inner diameter. Then resize the neck in your .303 die until the new shoulder will just chamber. In doing so you form a new shoulder for the cartridge to rest on in the chamber and prevent stretching. I tried it, and it does work for one additional loading. Instead of separating on the third firing, they separated on the fourth firing. The only long-term solution is to have the chamber properly reamed for American brass, setting the headspace on both the rim and the shoulder, and that means more money. Spending several hundred dollars more to properly headspace a rifle that cost $100 is not good economic sense. Instead, shooters who use the SMLE should view their brass as disposable after one firing, and not spend any more for ammunition than they have to.

The second method of setting headspace is on the cartridge shoulder. The tapered part of the cartridge strikes the tapered part of the chamber, and the round is held in place. The shoulder is the common method of setting headspace, found on all non-rimmed cartridges. Provided the shoulder is large or sharp enough, this method works well.

The third method is a belt. The expanded rim of the cartridge acts just like the rim of the .30-30 to keep the round in place. If it works the same, why did belts get started? Because bolt-action rifles are not happy about feeding rimmed cartridges. The belt came about because British gunsmiths could not get rimmed cartridges to feed reliably in bolt-action rifles. Yes, the SMLE is awesomely reliable, but it cannot be chambered for cartridges with more power than the .303. To get real power, the British gunsmiths had to go to Mauser actions, and the Mauser actions did not like rims.

Do not confuse the rim with the extractor groove. The "rimless" case on the left still has an extractor groove. On the belted case, center, the headspacing rim is close to but not used as the extractor groove. On the rimmed cartridge, right, the rim is both headspacing shoulder and extractor groove.

So the belt was invented. Some cynics say that the belt was more marketing than ballistic necessity, but a century ago brass was not as strong or as dependable as it is today.

The drawback to the belt is the same as that of the rim. The belt holds the cartridge in place, not the shoulder. A chamber-brass mismatch between the rim headspace and the shoulder headspace usually means one thing: short brass life. A custom gunsmith can ream your chamber with separate shoulder and belt reamers, or use a reamer with a minimum shoulder dimension, and you will have less problems with premature brass separation.

These are Soviet-bloc M43 cartridges, otherwise known as "AK ammo". The taper to the case is to ease extraction. The cartridges headspace on the shoulder. The extractor groove is deep and the rim sturdy because the Soviets expected to use lacquer-coated steel cases most of the time. (The one on the left is steel.) Despite being made of steel, the case works like any other, except it cannot be reloaded.

How much headspace is too much? The Small Arms and Ammunition Manufacturers Institute (SAAMI) publishes the min./max. dimensions for commercially-accepted cartridges. The minimum is the smallest size a chamber can be. The maximum is the largest size the cartridge can be. The two dimensions meet, but do not overlap. They obviously cannot, as it would be a big problem if the largest cartridge was allowed to be larger than the smallest chamber.

The chamber maximum is only .006 larger than the minimum. The distance from the bolt face and the headspace location is defined within .006 inches. More than that is considered unsafe. However, just because your rifle has .007 inches of headspace (.007 inches over the minimum, .001 inches past the maximum allowable dimension), does not mean it is a potential bomb. What excess headspace means is that your rifle is potentially harder on its brass and less accurate than it could be.

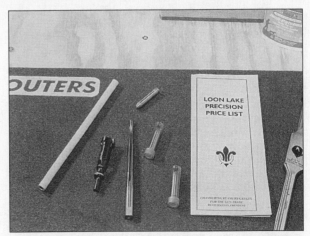

Adjusting the headspace on a non chrome-lined AR barrel is easier than on a bolt-action rifle. You need the barrel, a bolt minus its extractor and ejector, the gauges and a chambering reamer and a tap wrench with which to turn it.

Slide the GO gauge in place....

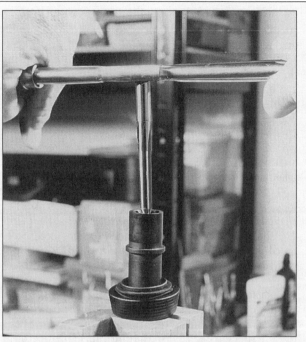

Slight downward pressure is all you need to ream. Let the reamer do the cutting. Pull it out after each turn, brush the chips off, swab out the chamber and measure headspace.

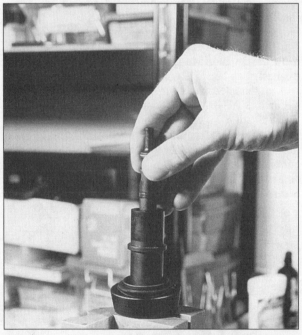

And try to lock the bolt in place behind it. If it will lock, you might be home free. Remove it and replace the GO with the NO-GO. If the bolt won't lock, your barrel and bolt fit correctly. You are done. If the bolt will not close on the GO gauge you need to ream the chamber. If it will close on the NO-GO you must try another bolt, until you find one that works. Failing that, send the barrel back.

How do we measure headspace? With precision-ground gauges. The gauges come in three sizes, GO, NO-GO and FIELD, The sets I have used in this book come from Dave Manson of Loon Lake Precision, and with proper care his gauges will last a lifetime. A correctly-headspaced rifle will accept a GO gauge and not accept a NO-GO gauge. A rifle that accepts a NO-GO gauge has excess headspace. A rifle that accepts a "FIELD" gauge is past the safe point. To test your rifle, clean the chamber and bolt. If possible remove the extractor and ejector from the bolt. Slide a GO gauge into the chamber and attempt to close the bolt with your fingertips. The bolt should close easily. Remove the GO gauge and insert a NO-GO gauge. Again, attempt to close the bolt with your fingertips. The bolt should stop before it moves to the closed position. Do not use force to close the bolt, you can damage the rifle or the gauge. The gauge is very hard, and closing the bolt after resistance is felt can swage the locking lug recesses, or crack the gauge.

Cartridges that are based on the same case can use the same headspace gauge. The .270 Winchester is a necked-down .30-06, and uses the exact same gauges. While rims differ between rimmed cartridges, the belt on a Magnum case is the same for all of them. You would use the same gauges for all of the belted Magnums, from the old .375 H&H or .300 H&H to the newest one based on their belts. Keep your gauges clean and well-oiled. Store them in the plastic tubes they were in when they were shipped to you. Do not let them rattle around in the drawers with other tools or parts, or you might damage them.

If your rifle has too much headspace, should you correct it? You bet. The only solution is to remove the barrel, turn the shoulder on a lathe, and then ream the headspace to its correct dimension before reinstalling the barrel.

Just as a matter of curiosity, Major General Julian Hatcher looked into the matter of excess headspace in rifles. He was the Head of Ordnance of the US Army for many years, and detailed his years of experience in his

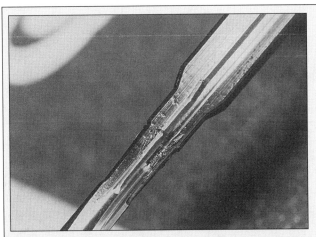

If you do not clean the chips out, you risk dulling the cutter and creating chatter, or cutting marks, on the surface of the chamber.

book "Hatchers Notebook". While it doesn't give much information about gunsmithing, it has a wealth of fascinating information about things you might not have heard or thought about. One 1917 Enfield he tested for headspace did not have case separations on the first firing even when he had reamed the chamber out to .025 inches over the minimum. (I imagine that the brass was so stretched that it would not have survived a second firing, even in another rifle with correct headspace.)

Gen. Hatcher writes about Lt. Robert Wyckoff, U.S.N.R. in 1943, conducting excess headspace tests with a test barrel and a chronograph at the ordnance plant at which he was working. He found that velocity increased and then dropped off as he reamed the headspace past the accepted limits! The highest velocity came when he was .035 inches over the minimum, and did not drop back down to the average at the start until the headspace was .060 inches over the minimum! And even then the cases did not separate on the first firing.

None of this means you can go ahead and ignore excess headspace. What it does mean is that both the rifle and ammunition manufacturers have built large safety margins into their products, safety margins you would be smart to maintain by keeping your headspace within accepted limits. Both experiments were considered only as curiosities of what might be acceptable in war-time production. After all, in a war who cares if the brass can't be reloaded? Most of the time it is simply lost to the soil or the sea. Only we hunters and target shooters who reload ammunition care about how our brass is treated. If your rifle is .007 inches over the minimum, get your headspace corrected. Your brass will thank you.

CHAPTER 7

Cleaning the Action

While the bore gets most of the attention, the action deserves its share. A spanking clean bore does you little good if the action is so gunked up that you can't work the bolt.

You will need a cleaning solvent, more than just the small amount that you get in a bottle of bore cleaner. A professional shop almost certainly uses a parts cleaning tank that has a multi-gallon supply of mineral spirits. Just like the ones used for auto parts cleaning, the tank your local gunsmith uses has an electric pump and some sort of filtration system. By holding the receiver under the stream of solvent he can quickly brush it clean. Then, with compressed air, he will blow the mineral spirits off and then lubricate the now dry and clean action.

If this system is so good, then why shouldn't you have one? You should, provided you are willing to put up with the cost, mess and hassle. Parts tanks are not cheap, even if bought at the local discount auto parts store. A compressor for blowing the parts dry costs more than the parts tank does. Buying these two items can run you more than a rifle. If you buy quality tools they will cost more than a good rifle. As for the mess, every parts tank I have ever seen used for cleaning firearms was a crusty black mess. The floor and walls for a foot or two around them were splattered with blown-off dirt, oil, grease and powder residue.

As for the hassle, the odor of mineral spirits is a persistent one. Even buying the good stuff, not the reclaimed spirits, I would smell of the solvent. After a day at work cleaning guns, and driving home for 45 minutes with the windows open (no mean trick in the winter) my girlfriend would remark "You smell like a gunsmith."

Some people remarked upon walking into the shop "What is that odor?" They did not find it disagreeable, but it was noticeable. Do you want your home smelling like a machine shop? The compressor would kick on when the pressure got too low, and if you were on the phone when that happened you would have to holler "Hold on!" to the person on the other end, and wait for the compressor to stop.

No, there are easier ways to clean your rifle without turning your house into a production facility. The first step is to get a solvent without getting the mess and odor. Brownells makes a cleaning solvent that comes as a concentrate. It's called "d'Solve" and you mix it with water to make your cleaning solution. I know that at least one reader at this point will sit up straight and remark something to the effect that "water ain't gettin near my rifle!" Calm down, we have ways of dealing with water. While you are waiting for the truck to show up with the latest delivery from Brownells, go down to the store and buy some non-stick cookware. You will not be using it for cooking, so buy the stuff that is on sale. Buy a couple of pans that will hold small parts. Buy a plastic half-gallon jar or jug that is tall and skinny. The mouth must be large enough to let you place your receiver in it with the trigger mechanism and scope base still in place.

In addition to these items, you'll need the things you normally associate with guncleaning, scrub brushes, dental picks, a hemostat or two, cleaning patches and 0000 steel wool. To finish cleaning you'll need a set of lubricants. The lightest, and what you use to deal with the water, are synthetic lubricants like Break Free or Rem Oil. Left on a

A sturdy bench and a few hand tools are all you need to keep your rifle clean.

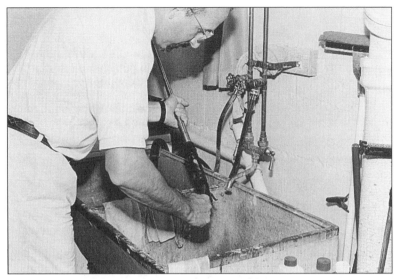

One advantage of the water-based Brownells d'Solve is that you can scrub your rifle in the laundry sink. Use dedicated cleaning pans (not from the kitchen!) to hold parts. A blow dryer or heat gun will evaporate the water, and then you can lubricate for protection.

dry and degreased surface, a drop of these will spread to cover many times the initial area. Use the dental picks to gently loosen packed-in crud, and the brushes to scrub the receiver clean.

Action cleaning is two parts, one easy but fussy, and the other not so easy and fussy.

The easy but fussy part is getting the action clean. Except for the semi-autos like the Remington 7400 and the Browning BAR, or the lever-action rifle, you can see into the action. Remove the bolt and you can easily get a cloth, cotton swabs or a cleaning brush in there to scrub stuff out. Darrell Holland makes a couple of tools that make the easy part of cleaning easier still. They are both short cleaning rods that are too large in diameter to fit down the bore of most rifles. The first one is a chamber cleaning rod. The rod is long enough to reach the chamber, and the mop on the end will swab all the gunk out of your chamber. Use solvent to clean the mop and let it dry. When the mop gets too worn or disgusting, unscrew it and replace it. The second one is

the really neat one. Darrell calls it the "Lug Raceway Tool" and it has a rectangular piece of felt secured to the end of it by an allen-headed set screw. Use the felt to swab the raceways clean, and to reach into the locking lug recesses and wipe the gunk out of them. Once I got one, I couldn't imagine cleaning a rifle without it. If the felt gets too chewed up or becomes too grubby to clean, loosen the screw and replace it with a new piece of felt.

Now, to deal with the pesky water. The cleaning solvent will wash away whatever you scrub loose. Left alone, the parts will dry, but you might find some rust later. To avoid the problem of unwanted rust (Is there such a thing as wanted rust? Yes.) use a blow dryer to heat and dry the receiver. Have you ever scrubbed the bottom of a copper-clad cooking pot? If you leave it wet the drying water will form oxidation. You'll be left with dark spots. To avoid a similar problem with your rifle, heat the water off. As soon as the receiver is dry and still hot to the touch, apply the lubricant. Reach inside the action, or onto the bolt rails, with

Knowledge is power, and also the means of keeping your rifle clean and in good repair. If you aren't sure on how to take it apart, look it up. If you try to force something that is not supposed to move, you could hurt yourself and damage your rifle.

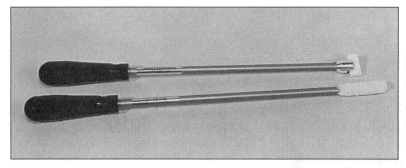

Daryl Holland makes two neat cleaning accessories. The lug cleaner on top reaches into the locking lug recesses. The chamber cleaner on the bottom is just long enough to reach the chamber, and too thick (and short) to be used as a bore rod.

The cotton swab for the chamber cleaner is threaded, and can be replaced when it gets worn. The felt of the lug cleaner is held in with a set screw. By loosening the screw you can replace the felt.

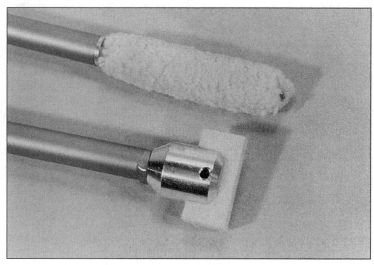

a lubricant-soaked patch held by a hemostat. Also reach up into the locking lug recesses, and the rear of the chamber. The Holland tools are useful in getting the locking lug recesses and chamber oiled after drying.

Once the interior is clean and oiled, you can wipe the exterior down with an oily cloth. The gunsmith who taught me the trade, Dan McDonald, told me "Oil is cheap, and rust is expensive. You can always wipe off excess oil. If you don't use enough, there will be trouble."

The 0000 steel wool is used to clean the exterior. If you have crusty deposits, or light oxidation, you can scrub the surface clean without stripping off your finish. Put a few drops of lubricant on the area, and rub with the steel wool. The oil floats the particles you have cleaned off of the sur-

face and keeps them from scratching. If you don't use oil and rub the area with steel wool, you'll dull the bluing and scratch it. With the oil, you can do a better job with less risk and less wear to the bluing. If the rust has eaten its way through the bluing, when you clean the rust off you will be left with white spots. There is no way to avoid this problem (besides not letting it happen in the first place) or to put the bluing back. If you don't scrub the rust off, the problem will get worse.

Cleaning the trigger mechanism is also a simple procedure. First of all, you do not have to disassemble the trigger mechanism in order to clean it. The ones that are simple enough to take apart are so durable they don't need disassembly for cleaning. The complicated ones that might "ben-

This Mauser has been stored in a slightly damp environment, and the front receiver ring has a red coating of surface rust.

efit" from a strip-and-clean are a royal pain in the butt to get back together. To clean your trigger mechanism, soak it (still attached to the receiver) in a pan of cleaning solvent. If you have a solvent tank with mineral spirits in it, then leave the pump running over the mechanism. If you are using Brownells water-based cleaning solution, then soak the trigger mechanism for a few minutes, then scrub it with a brush. Heat dry it along with the rest of the receiver, and then spray

The barrel is speckled slightly.

You start the cleaning by applying a light lubricant.

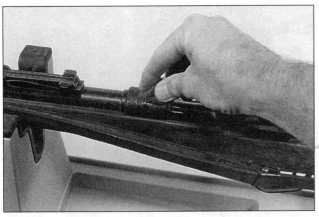

Then rub with 0000 steel wool, the finest readily available. The steel wool will scrub the rust off, and the oil will keep the rust particles in suspension so they won't scratch the remaining blue finish.

it with an aerosol de-greaser to strip the water out of it. Then apply a synthetic lubricant like Break Free or Rem Oil to lubricate it.

The fussy and not so easy part is cleaning the bolt. Simply wiping off the exterior may be enough. Most of the time it isn't enough. You have to strip the bolt. To do this you will often need tools.

While the instructions for taking bolts apart have been optimistic in the past, I will not be optimistic now. While disassembly instructions on a bolt may say "use a coin in the retaining slot to hold the cocking piece back" I will offer a better way. Please take my advice and use the proper tools. The striker spring on a rifle is very strong, and you can easily shoot a firing pin across the room like a spear. When launched this way, the firing pin will stick into wallboard. You do not want to be in the way.

General bolt cleaning

Bolt cleaning requires some different tools than does cleaning the rest of the rifle. To scrub inside the bolt, use a plastic-bristle cleaning brush like the one for cleaning barrels. Use a different-sized one to scrub the interior of the coils of the mainspring. Once you have the bolt apart, you want to focus on the important things. Scrub the striker clean and make sure that there is no hardened grease or scale from rust on it. A Scotchbrite pad works well for cleaning the striker. Scrub the mainspring clean. Scrub the interior of the bolt clean.

Once the parts are clean, heat dry them and lubricate them. The bolt body has an angled slot on the rear of the opening. It is the camming surface that cocks the rifle when you open it. One of the improvements that Mauser added going from the 1896 to the 1898 Mauser was the cock-on-opening feature. Previous Mausers (and other rifles) cocked the mainspring as the bolt was closed. The cam slot requires a different lubricant than the lighter synthetics you use elsewhere. A good gun grease such as Lubriplate will stand up to the pressure and friction of camming the sear to the cocked position. Dab a light coating along the length of the camming surface.

Bolts may look similar, but they are not interchangeable. Even in the same caliber and the same model from the same manufacturer, do not "mix and match" bolts as you do clothes. The Remington bolt on the left uses a push-feed extractor and spring-loaded ejector, while the Ruger, Mauser and Winchester (left to right) are controlled-feed with stationary ejectors.

98 Mauser

The easiest bolt to disassemble is the 98 Mauser in its original military form. You do not need tools to take it apart, but some tools will make the job easier. Any time you are working with compressed springs or parts activated by compressed springs, wear safety glasses. The safety is located on the cocking piece and has three positions. The position turned to the right is "Safe" and locks the bolt. Turned upwards so it blocks the sights, the rifle is on "Safe" but the bolt will work. The middle position serves two purposes. First, it was a handier safe position for the soldier, and by blocking his sights let him know the rifle couldn't be fired. Secondly, with the safety preventing firing but not preventing operation of the bolt, the rifle could be safely unloaded. If you push the safety over to the left you can fire the rifle.

Disassembly starts with the rifle unloaded and the bolt cocked. Place the safety lever in the upright position. Work the bolt and pull it to the rear. Pull out on the bolt catch on the left side of the receiver and remove the bolt. On the left side of the bolt shroud is a small plunger. Press this plunger back into the bolt shroud and unscrew the shroud. On the first turn you may have to press the plunger back in again to let it clear the bolt handle. Unscrew the shroud and pull it out of the bolt body. The removed assembly contains the shroud, sear, firing pin and firing pin spring. To disassemble it you need to compress the firing pin spring. Military rifles have a steel disk inlet into the stock for this purpose. To compress the spring, slide the front of the firing pin into the hole and press the shroud towards the stock. As the shroud moves forward it uncovers the tip of the sear. Once the sear is clear of the shroud, turn the sear one-quarter of a turn and lift it off of the rear of the firing pin. Ease the shroud away from the stock and slide it off of the firing pin.

If your rifle has a stock missing the disassembly disk, then you need to use a wooden block with a hole in it, or open the jaws of your vise just enough to clear the forward end of the firing pin. In a pinch, other objects will do. I once used a phone book as the support for the firing pin. The tip was driven deeply enough into the soft paper that it could not slip away. Even being careful, the tip went through the cover and dented the pages 35 deep. The spring is powerful, and you can be injured if the firing pin slips.

Scrub the firing pin and spring. Remove any hardened grease, rust or scale you find. To reassemble, place the firing pin in the disassembly disk or bench block to hold it in place. Slide the firing pin spring over it. Place the safety lever in the middle position and slide it over the rear of the firing pin. The rear of the firing pin has two flats ground on it, and the clearance hole in the shroud is a flattened oval. The shroud will only fit in two positions, and either one will work. Press the shroud forward, compressing the spring. Slide the sear over the rear of the firing pin, and turn it one-quarter of a turn to lock it in place. Turn it so the bottom extension of the sear is lined up with the slot cut on the bottom of the shroud.

You will rarely need to remove the extractor. To remove the extractor, turn it away from the bolt handle as far as it will go. With a padded pair of pliers, compress the rear of the extractor at the large opening. Some extractors will flex enough by hand that you can disassemble them. The compression at this point flexes the extractor and bows the front out of its slot. Rotate the extractor further until it is between the locking lugs of the bolt. Release the pressure of the pliers or your hand. Tap the rear of the extractor against your bench to slide it forward. It will spring free with some vigor, do not let it fall to the floor.

Check the extractor collar. It should rotate freely in its slot in the bolt body. If it does not, you must carefully spread the tips of the collar enough to slide the collar up onto the body of the bolt. Don't try to remove it from the bolt entirely, as you may weaken it by over-spreading it.

With the collar sitting on the bolt body, use wet-or-dry cloth to polish the slot. Use some 220 to clean the slot, and

The original safety on the Model 1898 Mauser. The safety lever does not merely block the triggers movement, it cams the striker away from the sear. This is the Fire position.

With the safety all the way to the right, the striker is cammed back and the bolt is locked shut.

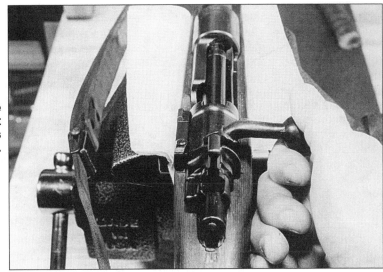

In the middle position, the safety cams the striker back but does not lock the bolt. The bolt can be worked to unload the rifle, and this is the start position for bolt disassembly.

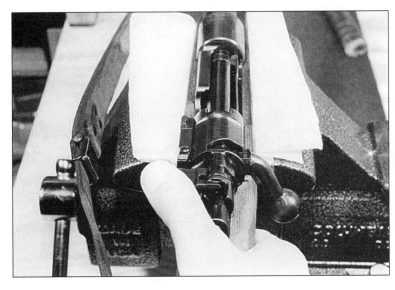

With the safety to the left, the rifle will fire. Even if the bolt handle was not a big clue, the direction the safety works shows us the Mauser was designed for right-handed shooters.

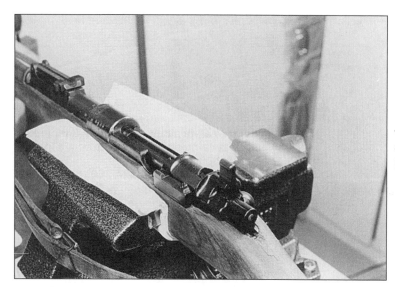

To start disassembly, unload the rifle and close the bolt. Place the safety in the middle position.

Open the bolt and as you pull it back swing the bolt retainer out from the receiver. The bolt will slide out of the rear of the receiver.

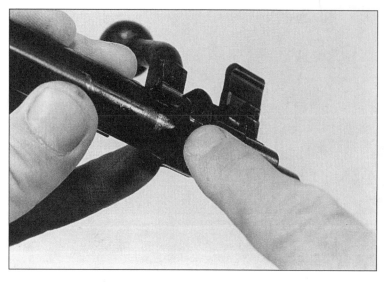

On the side of the bolt shroud you will see a plunger. Press this in while unscrewing the shroud and striker assembly.

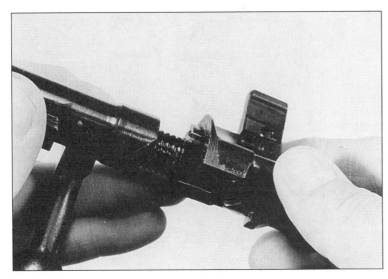

After a couple of turns you won't have to keep the plunger pressed in, and can simply unscrew the bolt.

The striker assembly of the Mauser. It looks similar to many other rifles for the simple reason it has proven so well-designed and durable that it only seems prudent for modern designers to "borrow" elements of it. On the striker in front of the striker spring are the safety shoulders. When the bolt is fully closed they slide into recesses in the bolt, and can reach the primer. If the bolt is not fully closed then these shoulders catch inside the bolt and prevent the rifle from firing.

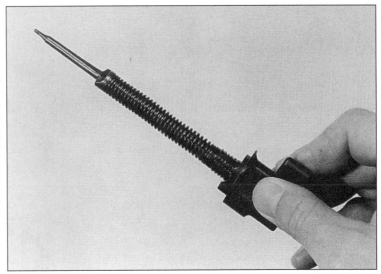

Mauser military rifles have some means of disassembling the bolt. On earlier rifles a hollow tube with sturdy shoulders was inlet into the stock. Late in WWII, the cup buttplate with its disassembly hole appeared.

Place the tip of the firing pin into the hole in the butt-plate and press the safety lever and bolt shroud towards the butt-plate.

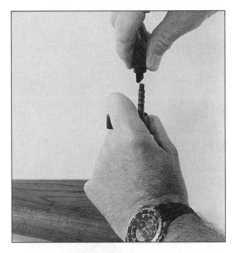

And lift it off the striker shaft.

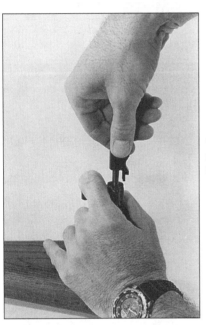

With the shroud clear, grasp the cocking knob....

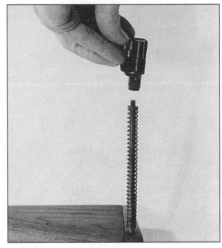

Ease the shroud off the shaft, and you may now scrub to your heart's content.

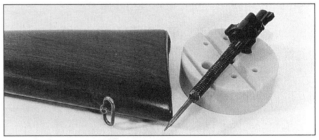

If your Mauser has been restocked and lacks the disassembly hole, use a gunsmiths block or piece of narrow pipe held in a vise.

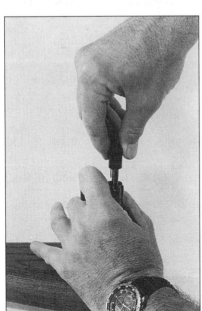

Rotate it a quarter turn.....

The extractor must rotate smoothly around the bolt body. If it does not (due to dust, rust or hardened oil or grease) remove the extractor and scrub the collar and its slot.

remove any rust, scale or hardened grease. Then switch to 400 grit to polish the surface. Clean the grit off, lubricate the slot and slide the collar back into place.

To replace the extractor, turn the collar tips to line up with the extractor between the locking lugs. Press the tips towards each other and slide the extractor over them. Flex the tip of the extractor outwards to clear the front of the bolt. Once the front bearing of the extractor lines up with its slot, turn the extractor towards and into the slot.

With the extractor back on, and the firing pin assembly together, slide the firing pin assembly into the rear of the bolt body and screw it until it locks in place. The plunger may stop against the bolt handle one turn before it is fully locked. Press the plunger into the shroud and continue turning until the edge of the shroud rests against the base of the bolt handle.

To screw the bolt body back on, you must press the shroud towards the bolt, compressing the mainspring. Once the threads catch, maintain pressure back with the bolt to keep the spring compressed until you can screw the bolt body fully home.

Mauser Mark X and others

The Interarms Mauser Mk X, and many sporting conversions of the Mauser, were faced with one large problem with the safety design: it wouldn't fit underneath a scope. The Mk X solution, and that of many other manufacturers was to move the safety off of the bolt and attach it to the trigger mechanism. The solution of many sportsmen was to alter the regular safety to a side lever. With the Mk X the safety no longer connected to the striker, and could not be used to hold the striker back while the bolt was disassembled. The side-lever conversions had only two settings; safe and fire. When on safe, the bolt could not be opened, again making disassembly difficult.

The solution to the problem involves some work.

With the bolt out of the rifle, clamp the edges of the sear in your vise. Press the bolt shroud plunger in and rotate the bolt. The front end of the cocking knob will snap down into the clearance notch in the bolt. Grasp the bolt body and pull it away from the vise, cocking the striker, and continue to rotate the bolt. The cocking knob will want to snap into the notch each time it comes around, so you will have to either pull it out or maintain steady pressure until the bolt is unscrewed.

When the bolt body comes free the striker will snap back to its uncocked position.

To strip the bolt of the Mk X, clamp the sides of the sear in your vise. Pull the bolt body to compress the striker spring.

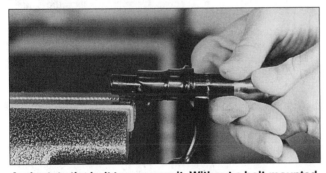

And rotate the bolt to unscrew it. Without a bolt-mounted safety to keep it cocked, the striker will try to uncock as you unscrew the bolt. Maintain steady pressure.

When you try to screw the bolt body back onto the striker, it will be uncocked. The bolt threads will not reach the shroud threads.

This Mauser has had the bolt shroud and safety replaced with a three-position safety similar to the Winchester. As with the military Mauser or Winchester M-70, place the lever in the middle position to disassemble the bolt.

To disassemble the Mk X striker is the same as the standard one. You have to compress the mainspring with the shroud and turn the cocking knob off the striker.

To reassemble, clamp the sides of the sear in your vise. In the uncocked position the bolt body cannot reach the threads on the shroud. With your left hand, press the shroud towards the bolt body and turn the body to catch the threads on the shroud. Once the threads catch, you'll have to maintain steady pressure to keep the cocking knob in the cocked position until the bolt is fully screwed into place. You may have to depress the plunger for clearance, although on many bolts the shroud will cam the plunger out of the way as you screw the bolt on.

Winchester M-70

The "Riflemans' Rifle" remains a popular choice. While Winchester has had some problems with the '70 in years past, its popularity has not waned with many shooters. The problems Winchester had stemmed not from use, durability, looks or function, but how to economically manufacture a product designed in the 1920s. How can this be a problem? When competitors have designs intended for ease of machining and assembly, then their labor costs go down dramatically. The actual cost of the steel that goes into a rifle is less than $10. The rest is labor, and its easier to cut the big costs than the small ones.

The first solution Winchester tried on their cost problem was to change the rifle from the controlled-feed extractor to the push-feed extractor. It did not go over well, starting the demand for "Pre-64 Winchesters." The second solution, and a better long-term solution, was to invest in computer-controlled machining equipment.

Disassembly of the Model 70 bolt rivals the Mauser in ease. Start with an unloaded and cocked rifle. The safety is again a three-position lever riding on the bolt shroud. Place the safety in the middle position and pull the bolt out, pressing the bolt release lever on the left side down.

Once the bolt is out of the rifle, press the breech bolt sleeve lock inwards and rotate the assembly out of the bolt.

Unlike the Mauser where the shroud and spring come off of the firing pin to the rear, with the Winchester they are to the forward. At the front of the firing pin spring you will see a collar with grooves turned in it. It is the firing pin sleeve. Brace the rear of the assembly against your bench. Grasp the sleeve and pull it down to compress the firing pin spring. The sleeve is small, and you will not have as much leverage as you did on the Mauser shroud. Be careful as you wrestle with the sleeve. Turn the sleeve a quarter turn (in either direction) and ease it forward. The sleeve and the spring then slide forward off of the firing pin. If you need to remove the shroud, first remove the firing pin stop screw. Then turn the safety to the "fire" position and slide the shroud forward off of the firing pin.

To remove the extractor, rotate it until it is on the bottom of the bolt, covering the gas escape holes, and then press it forward and off of the bolt.

The extractor collar of the Winchester serves the same purpose as the one on the Mauser, and must rotate freely.

To reassemble, if you have removed the shroud slide it back into place. Install the firing pin stop screw. Turn the safety to the middle position. Slide the firing pin spring over the firing pin, and use the firing pin sleeve to com-

To strip the Remington bolt, start by clamping the sear extension in your vise.

press the spring. Once the sleeve has cleared the safety lugs on the firing pin, turn the sleeve a quarter turn in either direction. Ease the sleeve forward. Keep your face out of the path of the sleeve. If you miss the locking slots the sleeve will be pushed off of the firing pin by the spring. When you have correctly installed the sleeve it will be held in place and will not turn without being pressed back.

Insert the assembly into the rear of the bolt and turn until the sleeve lock snaps into place.

Remington M-700

The Remington is the first action we will cover where the safety does not block the firing pin itself, but instead blocks the trigger mechanism. By moving the safety off the bolt shroud, the shroud can be made smaller, slimmer and more attractive. Personally, I don't find the Mauser bolt shroud ugly. The real advantage to production is that with the safety as part of the trigger mechanism, the safety can be adjusted as the trigger mechanism is being assembled. Once the unit is assembled and the settings locked into place, the unit is simply bolted or pinned to the receiver.

With a safety on the bolt shroud, the rifle must be assembled, the trigger pull settings made and then the safety must be adjusted to the finished assembly. The Remington design (or others of its type) using the safety-on-the-trigger design are faster and less expensive to make.

To strip the Remington bolt you'll need a coin (a dime will do) and a bolt disassembly tool. Remington makes one, but the one you will probably find on a professional gunsmiths bench is the Menck tool. The Menck tool is fast, easy and it works on both Remington and Ruger rifles.

Make sure the rifle is unloaded, and cock the action. Remove the bolt. On the rear of the bolt you'll see the bolt shroud and the sear. The sear has two notches, the forward one is the hold notch and the rear one is the disassembly notch. Hook the rear notch on your bench (or clamp the sear piece on your vise) and pull on the bolt. When you uncover the notch on the side of the sear piece, stick the dime into the notch and release your pressure. You can now unscrew the striker assembly from the bolt body.

To disassemble the striker assembly you'll need the Remington or Menck tool. You do not have to disassemble the striker for cleaning, only to polish it for smoother function or replace the striker and/or spring for better performance. Competitive shooters replace the striker with a Titanium one that is much lighter, and the factory spring for a stronger one, to reduce lock time. The faster your striker falls, the smaller your groups can be. I prefer the Menck

Grab the bolt and pull, exposing the disassembly slot.

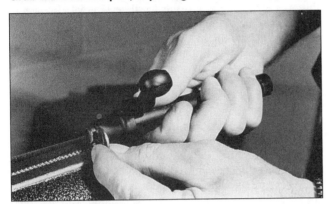

Place a coin in the slot.

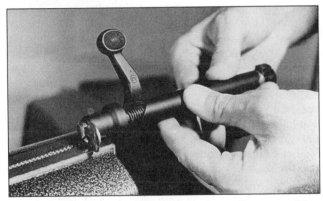

You may now unscrew the bolt from the striker assembly.

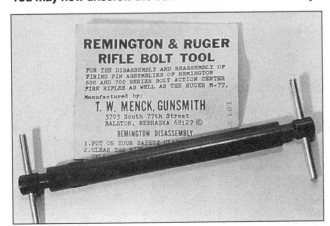

To strip the striker assembly you need a tool like the Menck. As a bonus, it works on both Remingtons and Rugers.

For the Remington, remove the handle on the non-knurled end. Screw this end onto the striker.

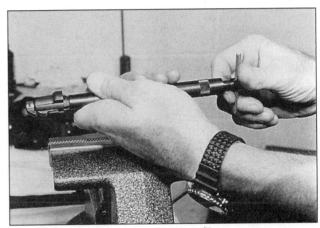

Use the other handle to compress the striker spring.

Once the cocking knob pin is uncovered you can drive it out. Then use the Menck tool to ease the shaft off the spring. The only reason to go through this is to replace the striker or spring with a speed-lock striker and/or spring.

tool, simply because I've had it for years and have become accustomed to its works. The Menck has two ends. For the Remington unscrew the handle from the un-knurled end. Screw this end over the Remington striker assembly. If the other end is screwed in too far you may have to loosen the other handle to ensure you get several threads onto the Remington striker at a minimum. Once the Menck is screwed on, tighten the other handle. You will be over-cocking the mainspring, and when you get far enough you will uncover the pin that holds the cocking piece onto the striker.

To replace the striker with a speed unit, drive the pin out and unscrew the Menck handle to ease the striker and spring out. Slide the new spring and striker into the Menck, screw the handle on to compress the spring and expose the pin hole. Replace the pin and then place your coin back in the slot as you loosen the Menck tool.

Replace the clean and lubricated striker assembly into the bolt body.

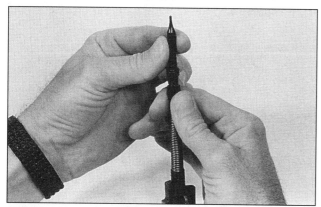

With the striker assembly out of the bolt, push the safety to the fire position and let the striker go forward. Then brace the back of the cocking knob against your bench and compress the spring using the front collar.

With the firing pin tip uncovered you can remove it.

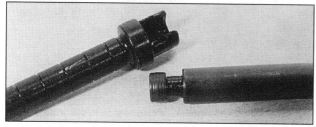

Yes, the tip is easier to replace, but the more fragile tip breaks more often than a Mauser firing pin would.

'03 Springfield

At the turn of the 20th Century, the United States military had to have a new service rifle. The Krag had serious shortcomings that had been quite apparent in the war with Spain. While the Krag was fast in operation it was slow to reload and limited in power. The Army spent several years developing an improved military rifle and ended up paying license fees to Mauser for utilizing some of his patents.

One "improvement" that the Army designed into the Springfield was a two-piece firing pin. The logic went something like this: if the firing pin breaks, it breaks at the tip. A broken firing pin makes a rifle inoperative. To make it easier to replace a broken firing pin, the Army designed a striker with a replaceable tip. There were two problems with this approach. One, firing pins hardly ever break. In over 20 years of buying, selling, trading, shooting and fixing Mauser and Mauser-type rifles I have never seen a broken firing pin. Two, the connecting collar of the front piece of the striker ended up being more fragile than the one-piece strikers were. Easy to replace? Yes. And, as a result of the design, more likely to need it, too. Despite this minor flaw, the Springfield was made in the millions, and issued for two wars, a police action, and used by hunters and target shooters for most of the 20th Century and into the 21st.

The Springfield disassembly is very similar to the Mauser and Winchester Model 70 process.

Make sure the rifle is unloaded and cock the action. Place the safety lever in the middle, upright position. Turn the magazine selector on the left side of the receiver to the middle position and remove the bolt. On the left side of the bolt sleeve is the bolt sleeve lock. Press this into the sleeve and unscrew the striker assembly. At the front of the firing pin spring is the spring retainer. Brace the rear of the striker assembly against the bench and press the retainer back towards the sleeve, compressing the spring. When the retainer moves back far enough, the forward part of the striker can be removed from the retainer to the side. Ease the spring forward. Pull the spring off of the rear half of the striker, and pull the rear half of the striker backwards out of the bolt sleeve.

The extractor is removed the same way as on the Winchester Model 70: Turn the extractor to the right until it is forced out of its retaining groove, and then press it forward and off of the bolt.

To reassemble, slide the rear half of the striker through the bolt sleeve. Slide the spring onto the striker. Use the firing spring retainer to compress the spring until you can slip the forward half of the striker onto the shaft, and capture it with the spring retainer.

Ruger Model 77

The Ruger bolt is quite easy to strip and clean. You'll need a drift punch with a nominal .100-inch diameter, your vise and the Menck tool. Remove the bolt and look at the sear bar under the bolt shroud. You'll see a hole drilled through the bar. On the side away from the bolt handle the hole is partly covered by the shroud. Clamp the sear bar in your vise and pull the bolt body to compress the striker spring. Press the drift punch through the now-uncovered disassembly hole. You may unscrew the striker assembly. If you simply want to clean and lubricate the striker, you do not have to go any far-

On the bolt handle side you can see the disassembly hole of the Ruger.

On the far side the hole is partly covered by the bolt shroud. You will have to over-cock the striker to gain clearance for disassembly.

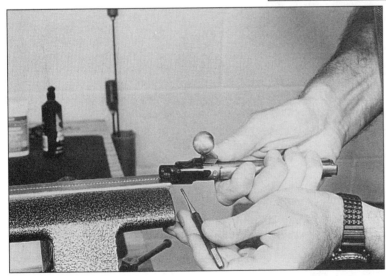

Clamp the sear in your vise and pull the bolt towards you.

ther in disassembly. If you are replacing the striker and/or spring with a speed-lock unit, insert the Ruger striker into the knurled end of the Menck tool. From there the process is the same as the Remington. By compressing the striker spring you uncover the pin that holds the striker to the cocking knob.

The Ruger, like the Mauser it is derived from, has a large and heavy striker propelled by a strong spring. It will not fail to fire. By trading some of the excessive force for faster lock-time you can improve your groups. Many long-range competition shooters view an installed speed-lock unit as a very close third "must have" right after a match barrel and a clean and crisp trigger pull.

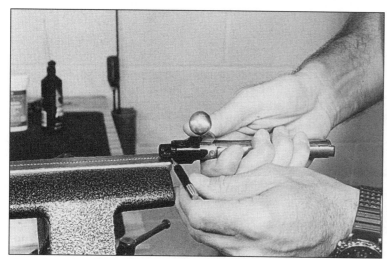

Slide a drift pin or steel rod into the disassembly hole.

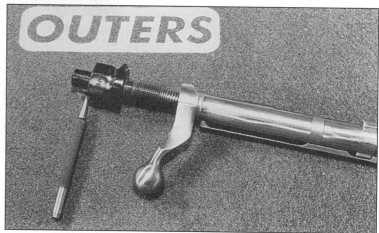

You may now unscrew the assembly. To remove the striker, use the Menck tool but screw the knurled end onto the Ruger bolt.

If cost was no object...

The easiest way to clean the action and bolt is to drop them into an ultrasonic cleaning tank such as the one made by L&R. The ultrasonic vibrations will loosen and float off most of the gunk, leaving the hardest stuff for you. But what was the hardest stuff is now made easier. The hard part is the cost. A rig large enough to immerse your entire rifle runs many thousands of dollars. But the handgun tanks can be made to work.

What you'll have to do with the smaller tank is set the cleaning tanks at a slightly lower level than a padded vise. Clamp the barrel in the vise with the receiver in the cleaning solution but not touching the tank. Unfortunately you won't

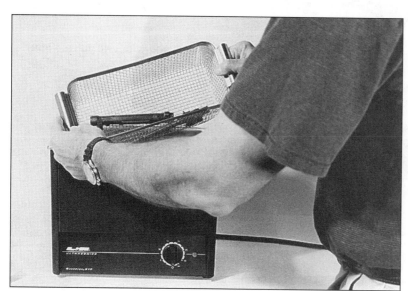

Ultrasonic cleaning is fast, efficient, and painless once you have the equipment. Place the parts in the basket.

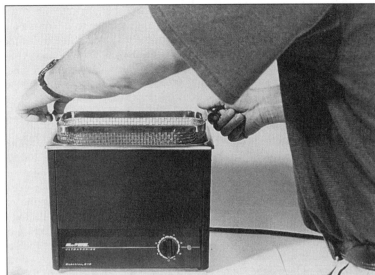

Slide the basket into the cleaning unit with enough cleaning solvent to cover the parts completely, set the timer, and

be able to use the lid, but draping a cloth over the cleaning tank will reduce spillage and evaporation.

The ultrasonic cleaners are fast and efficient at getting powder residue and petrified oil out of bolts and actions, if you can swing the cost.

Action smoothing

While modern rifle actions are smooth in the bolt throw, many surplus rifles can be a tad rough. After all, a Mauser (the one we'll be working on) was probably made as a military rifle; and ease of production and certainty of function were more important than a smooth bolt throw.

The trick is polishing the insides of the action after you make sure the action is the cause. What else can it be besides the action? To find out, strip the rifle and take the striker assembly out of the bolt. Check the bolt travel. Is the bolt travel now more smooth? Then one of the parts taken off was the problem. What parts might cause bolt binding? It could be a rough follower, an overly-long rear action screw, or a bent ejector. If the bolt is still rough with these parts out, check the extractor. If it is bent, bowed, rough or

nicked, it could be rubbing. The extractor collar can cause friction. If these parts are rubbing, they will have bright areas from the friction. The bolt shroud could be rubbing, especially if your rifle has been assembled from surplus parts at an arsenal sometime in the past. If you'll be replacing the shroud with a new one with a new safety, don't worry about the old one. If you'll be retaining the old, one, track down the friction point and file or stone it smooth.

Brownells makes an action polishing tool I call the tuning fork. The operation is simple. The polishing grit will get everywhere, so remove the trigger mechanism. On Mausers and other rifles with mechanical ejectors, take the ejector out, too. You'll be thoroughly scrubbing the action once you are done, so take the scope off, unless you think it will do better being dunked in cleaning solvent. (Use your collimator to check the bore sighting, and take the scope off!) Scrub the receiver clean. Any leftover grease or powder residue will clog the abrasive cloth and reduce the cutting action. Take a piece of abrasive cloth and wrap it around the tines of the fork. Clamp your barreled action in a padded vise, or if the barrel is off, then hold the fixture in a receiver holding fixture. Use the fork as a sanding block to smooth the action

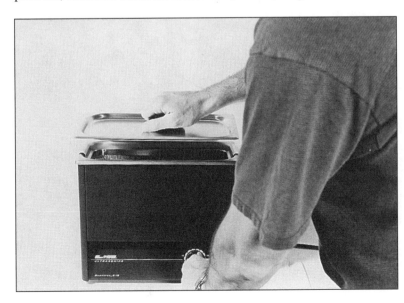

close the lid. Once the time is up, repeat the process in the tank filled with water-displacing oil. A handgun tank such as this one costs more than a rifle. A rifle tank costs as much as five good, plain rifles would. Convenient, but expensive.

rails. Keep the abrasive cloth wet with light oil (the lighter the better) or mineral spirits. You do not want to remove any more metal than you have to in order to smooth the surfaces. You would probably start with 320 cloth, unless you have a very rough war-time rifle, and then start with 220. The easy way to tell is to do a test-scrubbing on the inside left rail, where you can see it through the ejection port. Is the sanding you are doing rougher or finer than the surface texture that is already there? Your test spot should be the same or finer than the original surface. Progress to finer grits, ending in 400. Yes, you could go to 600, but the bolt itself is rougher than that, and you'd simply be roughing up your polish job every time you worked the bolt.

The purpose of polishing is to make the sliding surface smoother, not to eliminate contact between them. You do not want to sand until the bolt is loose in the receiver. The Mauser is loose enough at the rear end of its travel, you do not have to add clearance.

If you've polished the action and eliminated the bolt parts as the cause, and the bolt is still rough, then you'll have to polish the bolt. Coat the bolt body with Dykem and work it back and forth. Once you have located the friction points, use 320 and 400 abrasive cloth to smooth the affected areas. Once the bolt moves smoothly, clean up the surface of the bolt. You don't want to leave the bolt with each area sanded in a different direction, it looks bad. We are definitely going into cosmetic territory here, as the smooth-working bolt obviously doesn't depend on good looks. In the past, shooters tastes sometimes leaned towards "jeweling" or "engine-turning" of the bolt. Using an abrasive tip not unlike a pencil eraser, the bolt would be polished into a pattern of overlapping half-circles. Few shooters opt for this look today. Instead, use the 400 grit cloth to sand the bolt body in a "shoe-shine" manner. With care you can avoid showing the edges between each strip of sanded bolt body.

Another option is to take the bolt body to a sand-blaster or your bluer, and have them blast the bolt with either the finest sand they have, or a coarse to medium glass bead. A fine glass beading might not be enough to remove the traces of the sanding or stoning you did to reduce friction. The blasting will very slightly increase friction, but not enough to be a problem. Be sure to thoroughly scrub the bolt clean of the blasting media before re-assembly.

All the sanding and abrasive cloth leaves residue behind in the action, which you'll have to clean out thoroughly to avoid problems. Do not depend on cleaning cloths and patches, but proceed right to the "dunk and brush" method of cleaning. Scrub the action, locking lugs and chamber while liberally applying cleaning solution to them. Air-dry then lubricate to avoid rust, and then swab the bore out. Any grit left behind will seriously wear, and can even damage, your rifle

CHAPTER 8

Break-in, Cryo and Fire-lapping

Any brand-new mechanism must be properly broken in to ensure long life and worry-free operation. Auto makers suggest you drive your car gently for the first few hundred miles and then change the oil. At least they used to. Newer cars apparently do not all have that advice in the glove compartment. Failure to go easy that first month usually meant an otherwise good car was turned into a borderline lemon. After a while I began to wonder if the failure to break in a car and its subsequent spotty service record was a function of the failure on the owner's part to follow advice on breaking-in or a continual failure to follow common sense. The people I saw who didn't break their cars in were also the ones who failed to provide good service. They would drive hard, accelerating and braking aggressively. They failed to get their oil changed at regular intervals, or at all. After driving hard on rough roads they wouldn't get their alignment checked. Their car, or truck, was never washed.

Little wonder that these people can't get a car to last very long. Back when I owned a Ford Escort, I gave it regular maintenance and had it looked after as soon as I noticed anything going wrong. I traded that car for a rifle after getting 135,000 miles out of it. Nine years later the rifle still works fine. The car is long since gone, due mostly to a lack of maintenance.

What does this have to do with rifles? By treating my high-volume AR barrel the same way I treated that Escort, I got 15,000 rounds out of it. Proper break-in and proper treatment of a rifle (or a car) pays off.

You should properly break-in your rifle for long life and good accuracy. At the end of its manufacturing process the bore of your rifle is in one of two states, rough or smooth.

Whether hammer-forged, cut-rifled or button-rifled, there will be tool marks on the surface. The hammer-forged and buttoned bores will be a bit smoother than the cut-rifling bores. The cut rifling will have microscopic wire edges on the top corners of the lands. To remove these microscopic tool marks, the makers of premium barrels hand-lap the bore after rifling.

To break-in a barrel, you start the shooting life of your rifle by cleaning as frequently as you shoot. As soon as the powder or copper fouling builds up (even from one shot) the break-in process slows down or stops. The break-in process uses bullets to smooth down the tool marks and strip the wire edges from the bore. In order to do this, the bore has to be clean. Even a hand-lapped bore benefits from a proper break-in. Once broken-in any barrel will shoot more accurately, foul less and have a longer life than if you had not followed the breaking-in ritual.

Does this work, or is it just a conspiracy concocted by the bullet makers and the barrel makers to get you to do more shooting? When I first heard about breaking-in a barrel I was sceptical. I shouldn't have been, considering my experience with that Escort. In order to test the idea I selected one of my AR-15's as a test bed. I had worn out the original barrel, and it was in need of a new barrel. At the time I was shooting many, many rounds of .223 through AR's, and I would find out in short order if there was anything to this breaking-in talk.

The old and new barrels were both Eagle Arms match barrels. Eagle has since changed their name to Armalite, but the quality of their barrels has not changed. It is top-notch. I had abused the first barrel, firing many rounds through it,

To properly break-in your barrel you have to take your cleaning equipment to the range. Scrub the bore out between shots or groups until the bullets themselves have burnished the bore.

A wise shooter takes care of his equipment. These two bowling pin shooters will travel many miles for practice and competition, and expect their trucks and their rifles to perform reliably. They protect and maintain both.

almost always in rapid fire, and hardly ever cleaning it. More than once I'd gotten the barrel hot enough to create smoke from the oil on the outside of the barrel. As an example, I fired the rifle in one match called "Mad Minute." This contest had two targets, one at 50 yards and one at 100 yards. The course of fire required me to alternate between the targets, firing one round at each. The total time allowed was 60 seconds, and all hits would be scored. I fired on that course five times in an afternoon. My record was 60 shots in 60 seconds, for 59 hits. To cool the barrel between runs, I poured water through the holes in the handguard.

That barrel lasted about 5,000 rounds. Even though it was a match barrel, I did not properly break it in, and at its best it delivered groups just over an inch in diameter.

I gave the replacement barrel much better treatment. After a proper break-in, the new barrel delivered half-inch groups, and would do that no matter how much I shot it in a day. That barrel lasted 15,000 rounds, and delivered better accuracy when I traded it than the barrel before it did on a good day.

One barrel treated in each manner is not statistically significant. However, I cannot afford the cost or time of testing a dozen barrels in each method in order to satisfy statistical rigor. I know what I have seen, and what other shooters who have tried this have seen. I believe in proper barrel break-in.

Breaking-in a barrel requires that it be cleaned thoroughly before starting the operation. You must clean before you shoot, and then clean between each shot. Some experts advocate cleaning between two, three or five shots right from the start. I figure if you are going to be cleaning the barrel of your new rifle a dozen times in an afternoon, you might as well get it done. How can you do this without spending your whole precious day off of work at the range cleaning your barrel?

As with cleaning, I have two break-in plans, one for premium barrels and one for factory. Both take 60 rounds and a little less than two hours. Before you put the first round downrange, brush the bore and run wet and then dry patches

through it. You do this to clean out any preservative oil and dust that may be in the bore. This also cleans out any copper left behind by the factory test-firing. Check your scope to make sure it is securely mounted. Put up a target to shoot at. I know some shooters who simply bang away at the backstop when breaking-in a barrel. Why not check the zero while you are at it?

Fire the first 10 rounds, cleaning the bore to bare steel between each shot. If you are careful in your shooting, you can also have the scope zeroed in these 10 shots. The next 50 rounds should be fired in five shot groups, cleaning between each group. Each group should be on a separate target. Record the group size and group center and save the information for future reference. If your bore will be broken-in by shooting, this method will do it.

The cleaning method for premium barrels uses brush, bore solvent and patches. The factory barrels get cleaned by brushes and J-B or Corbin paste.

You do not have to use your expensive-bullet hunting ammo for break-in. Instead of a premium bullet designed for controlled expansion, go to the local gun shop and get three boxes (or more if it is on sale) of generic ammo. Use this ammo for your break-in and save the brass. Then use the brass to reload your premium-bullet hunting loads.

Once your barrel is broken-in, you should record the results of your practice sessions. The records will let you determine such questions as how long will your rifle remain accurate between cleanings? If you will not be going to the range on a regular basis, this can be determined by testing in an afternoon of range shooting. Bring several hundred rounds, targets for five shot groups of all the ammo, and your cleaning equipment. For this test you must use the ammunition you will be using for hunting or competition. Substitutes will not give you meaningful data. Swab the bore out and shoot a group. Let the barrel cool off. On a hot summer day this might take more time than you wish to wait. If you want to cool your barrel off faster you can use ice cubes. Store them in a small cooler. To cool the barrel, turn the rifle upside down and rub a cube back and forth the length of the barrel. If, and only if, you have a stainless barreled rifle in a synthetic stock, can you leave the rifle right side up. Water flowing between the barrel and the stock can rust a blued barrel, and warp a wood stock. Cool your barrel upside down and prevent rust and warping.

Once the barrel is cool, shoot another group. Plot the group size. Once the groups are larger than you feel is appropriate, clean the bore and repeat the process. For hunting, you want to know what kind of accuracy your rifle will deliver when it starts cool. If you are a competitive shooter you may not have time during a match to let your rifle cool off. In that case you should check accuracy under match conditions. One of the matches I compete in with a rifle is Second Chance. The rifle competition calls for rapid-fire offhand shooting until 15 steel targets are knocked down. Competitors may re-enter and shoot again for score. The fastest single time wins, and shooters may shoot the course a dozen times in a day trying to put together their best run. Barrels get hot doing this. To test a rifle for these conditions takes work. I start with a cold group. Then I fire 20 rounds rapid-fire offhand for practice. Then I sit down and carefully shoot a group for accuracy. Then I shoot another 20 rounds rapid-fire practice, and follow that with a benchrest slow-fire group. Some rifles will maintain their group size and zero under this torture test. Others will not. Unless you commonly hunt herds of deer, this sort of test is totally unnecessary for your hunting rifle. To compete at Second Chance and have a chance at winning, you must use a rifle that passes this test.

Competitors who shoot in Department of Civilian Marksmanship courses, also known as NRA High Power, have to use a different method. They will shoot their slow-fire and rapid fire stages starting with a clean bore. Then, when they go back to 600 yards, they will have to start firing with a now-cool but fouled bore. To add complexity, they may not be using the same bullet or powder for the 600 yard stages that they used for the closer ones. Hunters do not have this problem. Switching from one bullet and powder to another in competition can change the size of the group. The top competitors do not want to give up any points they do not have to. Serious High Power competitors go so far as to find pairs of powder that do not alter group size or zero. They will use a medium burning rate powder with 68-grain match bullets for the 200- and 300-yard relays, and then switch to an 80-grain bullet with a slower burning powder. By testing powder combinations they can find powders that do not cause a change in zero or group size when switching from medium to slow. Is this picky, bordering on obsessive? Yes. Does it gain them a few more points in a match? It can, if their shooting skills are up to it.

There is one heated test I would perform for a hunting rifle, and that would be on a rifle taken on an African safari. Instead of heating the rifle by shooting it, I would heat a rifle in the summer by leaving it in the sun. You and your rifle will be in the sun all day on such a trek, and the rifle will get almost too hot to handle. You should find out at home if being baked changes your zero. If you live in the south or southwest, you won't have any problem conducting this test. First fire a group from the bench. Then leave your rifle out in the direct sunlight for an hour. Fire another group. If the group changes size or zero, you must find and fix the problem. Those of us who live in northern climes must resort to aluminum-foil reflectors to get enough sunlight on a rifle in order to perform this test.

If you have a rifle with a bore that is too rough or pitted, then you cannot break it in by shooting. You have four choices: Live with the rough bore. Fire lap the bore. Replace the barrel. Re-bore the barrel.

Right off the bat, if your rifle is a brand new one and the bore is rough and pitted, send it back. The manufacturer will replace a barrel if you have not done anything to it. Enclose a target, and describe the specifics of what you see in the bore. Insist on a new barrel. The gunsmith from whom I learned my trade, Dan McDonald, had just such a problem. He had bought a new Smith & Wesson Model 29 with a 10-inch barrel for silhouette shooting. It proved to be a quickly-fouling shooter, with group size rapidly increasing. A look

The NECO fire-lapping kit contains everything you need to fire-lap eight or ten rifles, including complete instructions.

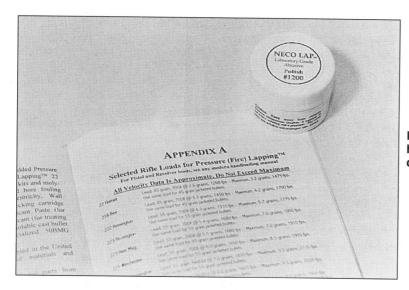

Fire-lapping take special loads, and NECO has found suitable loads for all the common calibers.

down the bore showed that the finish reaming of the bore had been skipped or done poorly. The tops of the lands showed heavy chattering from the tooling used to ream the bore before the rifling had been broached. He sent it back and S&W returned it quickly, with apologies, a new barrel and a test target. You can expect much the same response to a rifle arriving from the factory with a rough bore.

What about an older rifle, a used rifle, an heirloom or a recent import? Can you live with a rough bore? A rough bore may shoot quite accurately. I have an SMLE of World War I vintage that has a bore pitted enough to be gray in appearance. Dated 1915, its exterior has held up better than the bore. It shoots groups under 2 inches with iron sights until the bore fouls. Then groups open up. I will not change the barrel, I simply clean it after shooting. I also have a pre-war Winchester Model 70 in .30-06. The throat and leade show signs of heat cracking and crazing. A close inspection of the bore with my Hawkeye bore scope shows fine pitting in the corners of the grooves the length of the barrel. Some previous owners obviously used it quite a bit, despite its solid original bluing.

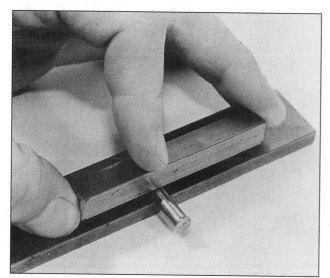

Roll the bullet between two plates that have the appropriate lapping compound on them.

When I feed it Winchester Silvertips it shoots groups of just about an inch. There is no point in changing the barrel of either rifle. They work well for what I ask of them.

Premium rifle barrels are hand-lapped by the manufacturer to polish the surface and remove toolmarks. A lapped barrel fouls less and is easier to clean than one that is not lapped bore. Can you hand-lap your barrel to remove roughness and pitting? Not without precise equipment, the right lapping media, and a lot of experience. You need a slug that fits the bore exactly. If it does not you will not be lapping all of the interior. You also need a fixture to hold your lapping rod on the centerline of the bore. If you try to hold it straight without a fixture you will sometimes be pushing slightly from the left, and sometimes slightly from the right. The uneven pressure will mean uneven lapping of the bore. And what media to use? Too fine and you won't cut the roughness. Too coarse and you'll prematurely wear the bore and decrease the barrel's life.

What to do? Unless you have just bought a hand-lapped barrel from a maker of premium barrels, then you let the bullet do the job. In breaking-in a barrel the bare bullet does the job of knocking down the burrs and tool marks. In fire lapping the bullet carries a film of abrasive in its surface, and the abrasive cleans off the interior of the barrel. The abrasive does the lapping for you. The bullet fits the bore exactly. The bullet stays centered in the bore. And the correct lapping media has been discovered for you. There is one advantage to fire-lapping that regular hand-lapping does not provide. The bullet starts out its trip with a full film of unused abrasive. The abrasive is used up during the trip down the bore, and laps less towards the muzzle than it does near the chamber. The lapping ends up very gently tapering your bore towards the muzzle. The effect is very small, and could only be determined by before and after measurements with an air-gauge, but it exists and it is beneficial to accuracy.

NECO makes a fire-lapping kit with complete instructions to treat your bore. You can either follow the full procedure or do the quick-and-easy method. The full procedure involves measuring your bore and checking for tight spots with the pure lead slugs included in the kit. Clean the bore thoroughly, and then run an oiled patch down the bore. Start

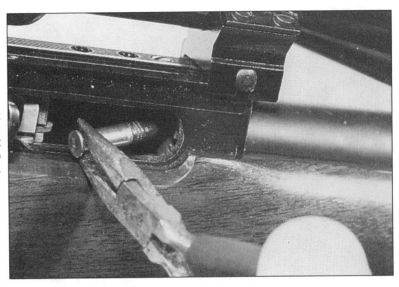

Carefully load the cartridge so it does not get the abrasive on the rest of the rifle. With the .22 long rifle you may have to work at it to get the cartridge in without getting goop all over everything else.

one of the slugs into the breech end of the bore with a dowel that is near-bore size and a mallet. Then with a one-piece cleaning rod, press the slug the length of the bore. As you get to a tight spot the rod will become difficult to push. If you encounter a loose spot the rod will jump forward. Record the distances of each, and make a note about how hard or easy it was to push through each of them.

You can even measure the muzzle and breech ends to see if they are larger or smaller than the full-bore measurement.

You are now ready to start loading ammo. You need to create a lapping load, and not use your full-power hunting load.

You want a medium-pressure load, around 30,000 psi peak pressure, and with a clean-burning load. Do not, repeat DO NOT, simply load back your medium-rate powders until you get an estimated pressure of 30K. While the exact mechanism is still a matter for discussion, loading down from the standard pressure and velocity has been implicated in a number of destroyed rifles.

Instead, look up cast-bullet loads. A cast-bullet load using a clean-burning powder would be perfect for the job of fire-lapping.

The task breaks down into three sections; treating the bullets with the correct abrasive, loading the ammunition, and firing the ammo through the rifle.

The NECO instructions are detailed and exacting. If you want to know the exact state of your bore at every stage of the process, follow their instructions to the letter. You will be shooting, cleaning, and then checking the condition of the bore with a pure lead test-slug pushed through the bore, at every step of the process. I have followed the process exactly, and to do it takes at least two or three trips to the range with all the gear. It can take longer if you do not have a full day to devote to each trip. The simpler method is as follows:

Load 10 rounds of fire-lapping ammunition with the 400-grit, 10 rounds with the 600-grit, 10-rounds with the 800-grit and 10-rounds with the 1,200-grit. Keep each batch separate. Take the ammo, rifle, cleaning gear and regular ammunition to the range.

Fire five rounds of the 400-grit ammo and clean the bore. Repeat with the second set of five, and clean again. Fire the 600-grit fire-lapping rounds in the same pattern. Ditto the 800- and 1200-grit ammo. Do not hurry through the procedure. If at any time the barrel begins to become warm to the touch, wait for it to cool. Once you have used all the ammo, throw the brass away. The abrasive will be embedded in the case necks, and will wear the brass, bullets and bore if you try to be cheap and re-use them.

Once lapped, clean the bore again, and begin your standard barrel break-in process. Do the break-in even if you are fire-lapping a used barrel that has already been broken in.

The Eley Match Extra groups hardly changed at all. The Before group in the Butler Creek barrel was .525 inches, and the after was .540. Statistically, nothing. The real test would have been 10, 10-shot groups before, and 10, 10-shot groups after. Sounds like fun, but you have to go to work sometime.

The CCI Green Tag definitely liked the fire-lapped barrel. Before it was .475 inches, while after it delivered a .325-inch group.

Once broken-in, you can test your barrel for accuracy.

Rimfire rifles are only slightly different. You are obviously not going to be loading special fire-lapping ammunition. Instead of treating the bullets and loading them as per the center-fire rifle, you will dip just the nose of a cartridge in the lapping compound, then carefully place it in the chamber. Lapping compound rubbed on the sides of the chamber can wear it, so be careful. I use curved hemostats to handle the cartridge, and swab the chamber out with a cleaning patch between each round fired.

What kind of results can you get with fire-lapping?

While results will vary depending on the rifle involved, I have had positive results with the rifles tested. The Ruger 10/22 was treated with both the factory barrel and with a Butler Creek barrel installed. The best groups with the factory barrel went just over an inch at 50 yards before, and turned in 1/2-inch groups after. The Butler Creek barrel started out just under an inch and, after fire-lapping came in at just over 1/2-inch. The Volquartsen barrel? Since the worst groups it has shot have

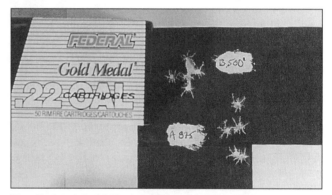

The Federal Gold Medal also didn't like going through a fire-lapped barrel, as the group opened up .375 inches. As expected, some ammunitions shot better, some worse, some stayed the same. The very next Butler Creek barrel off the line could have reverse results by ammo brand than this one.

On the other hand, the Remington Target did not like the fire-lapped barrel. The test groups went from .580 inches before to .810 after.

only barely been over 1/2-inch, I really didn't feel there was much point in fire-lapping it.

The Utility Scout in .308 turned in 2-inch groups with any match factory load before I fire-lapped the bore. The improvement was significant, as afterwards it began to turn in groups just under an inch in size with Federal match ammo, and just over an inch with Remington.

Some contend that fire-lapping simply wears out the throat and leade of a rifle prematurely. For a competition shooter operating at the top end of his sport, this may be true. The top shooter is likely to invest in a premium barrel, load perfect ammo, and views a 10,000 round service life of a barrel as a single season of practice and competition. For him, cutting a couple thousand rounds off of the life of the barrel is poor planning. For the hunter who will put 2,000 rounds through a rifle in his whole life, taking a couple thousand rounds off of the potential life of the barrel (rounds he will never fire or see fired) is no loss at all. There are rifles you cannot fire-lap. Any gas-operated self loading rifle cannot be fire-lapped. The abrasives will get into the gas system, and either wear the piston or seize it. The only way I could see fire-lapping a gas-gun would be to remove the gas system from the barrel so the gas port simply vents pressure into the air. Once the rifle was fire-lapped and cleaned, then you should re-install the gas system.

You cannot fire-lap chrome-plated bores! The abrasives will strip the chrome off of the bore unevenly, ruining the barrel and creating a safety hazard.

Testing the cryo treatment from Pacific Cryo

The test rifle is a Ruger Model 77 International in .308 Winchester. To test the accuracy, I mounted a Nikon scope on it in the factory-supplied rings. Before cryo treatment, it turned in entirely respectable groups from just over an inch to just under 2 inches. The 1-inch groups were with various match target and premium hunting ammunition, while the two-inch groups came from surplus .308 I use as practice ammo.

To prepare your rifle for cryogenic treatment, remove it from the stock and strip all parts off of it except for the barrel. The scope, scope mounts, trigger, ejector, you want all of them off when you ship it. The bolt will not be treated, so keep it, too.

After getting the rifle back from pacific Cryo, I re-installed the scope and tried again. The top-grade ammunition showed a slight improvement, with some of the groups dipping under 1-inch. The surplus ammunition showed almost no improvement. Neither situation surprised me. The Ruger barrel is obviously well-made and straight, so the amount of stress available to be relieved was small. The good ammo could shoot better than the barrel, so when the barrel was improved, the groups improved. The barrel is obviously better than the surplus ammo, so improving the barrel could do nothing about the group sizes of the surplus ammo.

Re-boring an existing barrel

Replacing the barrel can be expensive, but worth it if you want greater accuracy. We have discussed how to change a barrel in Chapter Six, and in Chapters Sixteen, Seventeen, Eighteen, Nineteen and Twenty we will discuss different rifles and the results of installing a new barrel. But what if the rifle is a cherished heirloom, and changing the barrel removes an irreplaceable feature?

In that case, the barrel can be bored out and re-rifled. The limits of reboring are strict, and you cannot always turn your rifle into one chambered in another common cartridge, but when re-boring works out, it can perform near-miracles. Cliff LaBounty bores out many rifle barrels, and can offer suggestions as to caliber conversions for your rifle.

The basic limits of reboring are simple: One, you have to increase the bore diameter to the point where the tops of the lands of the new bore are larger in diameter than the depths of the grooves of the old bore. You might be able to bump up one caliber size, but usually you must go up two. As an example, you can easily go up from a .224 bore to a .243. But, a particular barrel may not allow you to go from a .257" bore to a .264" one. Two, you have to either keep the same chamber size, or slightly increase the chamber. So, you can go from a .22-250 chamber to a .308 Winchester chamber, but not the reverse. You can go to a slightly smaller chamber size only if the barrel has enough steel that you can set the shoulder back and re-cut a smaller chamber. Third, you have to maintain enough wall thickness at the muzzle. The new barrel wall cannot go below .100 thickness at the muzzle. As an example, if you have a lightweight .270 Winchester, the muzzle diameter cannot be less than .508 in order for you to be able to bore it out to .30-06. Fourth, you cannot change to a cartridge that the rifle's action cannot handle. If you have a short-action Remington 700 in .243, you can't have it re-bored for .30-06 as the action is not long enough to handle it.

Some rifles have certain peculiarities. Lever-action rifles depend on the length of the cartridge for proper feeding. If you are going to have your .30-30 bored out, the new cartridge will have to be the same overall length. Are there bullets available that will properly seat in the case and come out to the correct overall length?

The best candidates for re-boring are the Ruger #1's. By changing the extractor, you can open a barrel out to anything the outer diameter of the barrel can stand. If you have had a burning desire to shoot a .500 Nitro Express, but can't stand the cost of a British double (the last relatively cheap one I saw was offered at $35,000) you can have Cliff bore out a Ruger and beat your shoulder all you want. With the $34,700 you save, you can make a down payment on a nice little house, and build both a reloading room and a massage bench for your chiropractor. Why a chiropractor? Have you ever fired a .500 Nitro Express?

Cliff is familiar with the big-bore rifles. Every year he re-bores a number of single-shot and even double rifles to different calibers. Some of them are done to get the rifle into a caliber where ammunition is available. Others, the original caliber is not very popular, and the owners wants it re-bored to something more common.

Blackstar

A different approach to smoothing the bore is to avoid the use of abrasives. Any abrasive has to ride on a solid carrier, and the fit of the carrier to the bore determines the quality of the lapping. While the barrel makers who do hand-lap their bores go to great lengths to get things right, (do they ever!) the mechanical limitations still exist. Blackstar gets around the mechanical limitations by using an electrochemical polishing method.

The process is a closely-guarded secret, but basically it avoids the need for a form-fitting slug. To add icing to the cake, Blackstar not only offers the treatment to your barrel, but they make their own barrels and treat them before shipping.

Does it work? Yes. And it works well. One of the shooters at our club, Nick Till, shot his way to High Master in NRA High Power competition using a Blackstar-barreled AR that meets Service Rifle specs.

The Blackstar treatment will not resurrect a used or abused barrel, and works best on a new or nearly-new barrel. Like the fire-lapping, it creates a slight taper to the muzzle

Moly Treatments

Moly-treated bullets are becoming all the rage for accurate shooting. However, they do not offer any advantage in a rifle with a rough bore. The Moly works best with a bore that has been produced with a smooth surface, or has been either hand- or fire-lapped. Save your Moly bullets and treatment equipment until after you have the rifle firing accurately with standard bullets. Then add Moly to your preparations. Once your bore is smoothed out, then the Moly will make it shoot like crazy.

Cryogenic treatment

Steel is a form of iron with specific carbon content. Steel that has other metals included in the mixture of the steel, called an alloy. The carbon improves the hardness of the iron, while the other metals alter certain characteristics of the steel. They might improve its machining qualities, rust-resistance and resistance to abrasion.

Steel alloys are created to alter the reaction of the steel to heat-treatment. Heat-treatment involves heating the

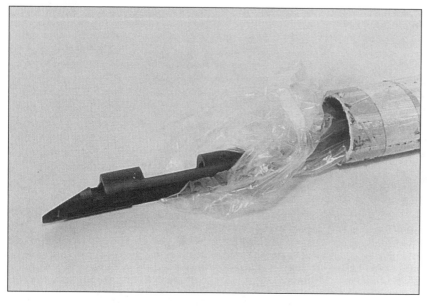

To have your barrel Blackstar treated, send the barreled receiver and nothing else. (Well, a letter of instructions and a return address would be prudent!) No scope, stock, sights or trigger assembly. You'll get it back the same way, but more accurate.

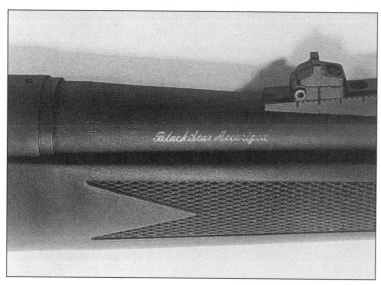

It will also come back engraved, so all your shooting buddies will be green with envy. Now get out there and practice so that accurate rifle can live up to its potential.

Don't use Moly-treated bullets to break-in your rifle. Save this Midway Moly tumbler for after the rifle is broken in.

steel above a certain temperature and then quenching the heated piece of steel in water or oil. The sudden drop of temperature, called "quenching," cools the steel faster than the crystalline structure can change. Some alloys are too hard when heat-treated with a single quench and would be too brittle to use. To prevent cracking, the steel is heated up near, but not past, the previous temperature used as the quenching starting point. The "draw" reduces the brittleness of the steel while keeping some or most of the hardness and toughness.

As you can imagine, the steel does not cool evenly, and stresses can be created during the quenching. The drawing does not entirely remove these stresses. In the case of a rifle barrel, the stresses trapped in the cylinder can shift as the exterior is machined down to the barrel profile, or as the bore is drilled, reamed and rifled. In a serious case, a previously straight cylinder can become slightly bent as the cylinder is turned into a barrel. Factory-produced barrels used to be regularly checked for straightness, and bent straight if they needed to be. Modern production methods reduce the need for barrel straightening.

Cryogenic treatment reduces stress and improves abrasion resistance of certain steel alloys. The machine-tool industry has used cryogenically-treated machine tools for years now, and the documented improvements in wear and tool life seemed the perfect thing for rifle barrels.

Cryogenic treatment involves slowly cooling the barrel or parts down to 300 degrees below zero, then slowly warming them. Each cryo treatment operator has his or her own schedule of cooling and heating. Some will cool to 300 below, then warm up to 300 above, down again and up.

How does this help you? By relieving the stresses in a barrel you improve accuracy. Remember that factory barrel that had been straightened? What do you think happens to it when the barrel heats up from shooting? The stresses will adjust themselves to the warmer state and the barrel will bend again. Some barrels will shoot fine cold, but when you warm them up the zero shifts or the group size opens up. A cryogenically-treated barrel will do less of that.

The increased abrasion resistance of the steel after cryo increases the longevity of the barrel. The throat of a cryogenically-treated barrel shows less erosion and heat crazing than a non-treated barrel.

Custom barrel makers use cryo to stress-relieve their barrels several times during the manufacturing process. By relieving the stress in a barrel blank during each step of the manufacturing process, any hidden stresses will be eased, and any stresses produced by the manufacturing process itself will be eased.

Should you or shouldn't you? The firmest answer is "it depends." The rifles that are likely to show the largest benefit are rifles that are new or nearly new and have a potential for being accurate. A new factory barrel can show a large improvement after cryo treatment. An old, or heavily-used rifle cannot be helped much. If the limiting factor of the potential accuracy of your rifle is the fact that the throat is burned out from too much shooting, cryo treatment won't help. If your rifle has a heavy trigger and is not glass-bedded into the stock, you could have an accuracy improvement from cryo, but one that is hidden by the trigger and bedding problems.

At the other end, sending a custom match barrel out for cryo treatment is gilding the lily. A barrel from Shilen, Lilja or Pac-Nor is likely to have already been cryogenically treated. Doing it again will probably show little if any improvement.

But for the dedicated competitor, to whom "every advantage, real or imagined" is not just a motto, but a lifestyle, cryo is a must. For the varmint shooter, who puts many bullets downrange in each session, the increase in useable life of a barrel is worth the extra cost.

CHAPTER 9

Stocks

While many parts of rifles have not undergone change in the last century, stock designs have. A shooter from before World War I would instantly recognize a Mauser bolt-action rifle. He could easily understand the Winchester Model 70, and with a minute or two of fiddling he would know his way around a Remington Model 700 or a Weatherby Mark IV.

What would puzzle him would be the stock.

At the beginning of the 20th Century stock design was still heavily influenced by the legacy of flintlocks and percussion caps. When the flint on a flintlock rifle struck the frizzen and ignited the powder on the flashpan, that powder went up with vigor. A smart shooter wanted to keep his face far way from that flash. To keep their faces away from that burning flash, shooters kept their heads up. The erect posture inflicted certain design restrictions on the rifle stock. Rifle sights back then were low to the barrel for greater durability. With the barrel close to the shooter's line of sight, the stock had to have a large angle down

When shooting a flintlock, it is prudent to keep your face away from the commotion going on in the flashpan. Flintlock shooters keep their heads up, requiring a stock with a lot of drop.

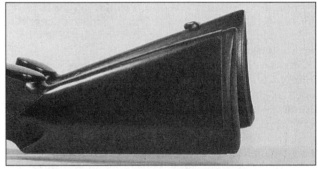

The closer stock is a Remington Mountain Rifle stock, with very little drop to it. The stock behind it is a Winchester Model 70 from 1942. Even though the Remington weighs almost two pounds less as an assembled rifle, it is more comfortable to shoot than the Winchester.

Drop is the distance down from the centerline of the bore to the heel of the stock. Modern rifles have much less drop than rifles from before WWII.

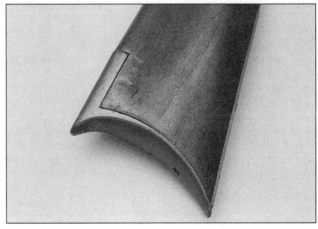

Crescent buttplates were all the rage until rifles started getting the power of the .30-06. Then, those narrow and sharp buttplates hurt too much to shoot.

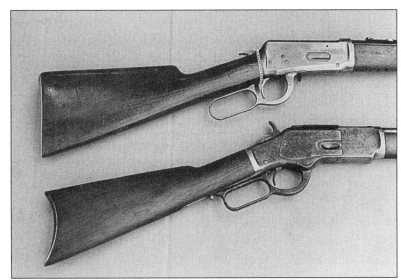

The Winchester 1894 on top has less drop, a shotgun-style buttplate and a slightly longer pull than the M-1873 on the bottom. The recoil of the .30-30 (M-1894) is a whole lot more than the .44-40 (M-1873) can drum up. What was fine in a sedate pistol cartridge was uncomfortable in the new rifle cartridge. Stock designs have been getting straighter ever since.

from the barrel. This angle is known as drop. In order for a right-handed shooter to keep his left arm from reaching all the way across the body, he would "blade" his body into the rifle. That is, rather than stand with his shoulders on a line at a right angle to the line of fire, the shooter would bring his left shoulder much closer to the muzzle than his right shoulder.

To keep the rifle from sliding off the shoulder, many stocks had a crescent buttplate. The top edge of the stock, on the centerline, is known as the comb. In the heavily-bladed shooting position, and with an erect head, the shape of the top edge of the comb has little mechanical importance. By the fashion of the time a sharp-edged comb looked good.

All this stock design worked well for shooters back then. There were stocks designed differently, and for different reasons. Stocks on British double shotguns had less drop, wider combs and flatter buttplates. The British style of shotgun shooting calls for a consistent body position and for the use of the aiming eye as the rear sight. It also makes the shooter's life easier under recoil. The British shotgun shooter favors a lighter shotgun than American tastes customarily call for. A day of driven pheasant shooting could require several hundred shots. The effects of recoil could tire a shooter, resulting in missed birds.

The German military Mauser, the U.S. Springfield and the British Lee Enfield rifle had straighter stocks than American sporting rifles at the turn of the century. American sporting stocks would not begin to straighten out for another 30 years.

Two things caused American stocks to straighten. The first was a combination of the acceptance of the bolt-action rifle starting with the '03 Springfield, and the power of the .30-06 cartridge it was chambered in. The recoil you would feel in shooting a rifle with a dropped stock, crescent butt-

plate and narrow comb is acceptable with a medium-power cartridge like the .30 Remington or .30-30 Winchester. With a sedate number such as the .44-40 or the .25 Remington you won't notice the recoil.

Take the same stock design and marry it to a rifle in .30-06 and you will quit trying to sight it in before you finish a box of ammo. The experience hurts, and can lead to bad shooting habits. It hurts even more if you try to use the modern technique with the old-style stock. If you do, you'll find the curve of the crescent buttplate does not match your shoulder. The now-excessive drop in the stock drives the rifle upwards on recoil. The sharp comb, resting under your cheekbone instead of next to it, will drive right into your face. The result of each shot will be painful, and can even be bloody.

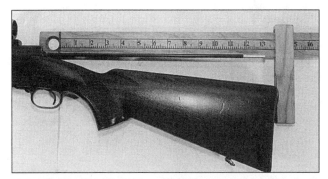

This Winchester M-70 from 1942 has almost 2 inches of drop. Fired offhand and with iron sights it is comfortable. Put a scope on it or shoot it prone or from the bench and it kicks you. Stocks can't be bent to reduce drop, they can only be replaced.

This Remington M-30 was a factory-sporterized 1917 Enfield. While the stock has less drop than rifles commonly had a generation before it, it still had plenty of drop by today's standards because it used iron sights close to the bore. There had to be room to get the shooter's face behind the sights.

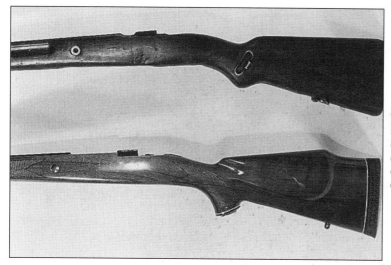

The military stock on top was designed for iron sights, and has more drop and pitch than the commercial stock on the bottom. The commercial stock (both are meant for '98 Mausers) was designed for a rifle using a scope, and the lack of drop also requires less pitch.

The second cause for change was the acceptance of scopes as a viable shooting aid. A scope rides higher over the barrel than iron sights do. If you mount a scope on a stock with lots of drop, you may find that your face does not touch the stock at all while you are sighting through the scope. Aiming such a rifle is difficult, and the stock has a running start on recoil before it strikes your face.

The changes in stock design made it possible to satisfy the American shooter's taste for more power. If the .30-06 generated too much recoil for comfortable shooting with the old-style stocks, just imagine what it would be like touching off a round of .300 or .338 Magnum.

At the transition from the 20th century to the 21st, American shooters have stock designs that closely mirror the design of British stocks a century ago. If any of them still had rifles or shotguns, our British cousins would be asking what took us so long.

What is a stock supposed to do for us? As a general description, a stock holds the rifle action, barrel and trigger. By containing the parts, the stock protects them from the elements. No trigger mechanism is rugged enough to exist outside of a stock. The action mechanism, if not protected, could get tangled up in branches, clothing or you. The stock protects you from the rifle. A hot barrel cannot be held for shooting except in a dire emergency. The stock gives you a place to hold, and a surface to rest against your body and face. By stabilizing the stock in three locations, you can aim to a finer degree than you would with a handgun.

A stock that fits comfortably is easier to shoot and allows you to comfortably absorb recoil without tiring or building bad habits.

To make comfortable shooting possible on a scoped AR-15, you can clamp on a cheekpiece. With it in place, using the iron sights is impossible.

The AR-15 stock has a negative drop. The top of the comb is higher than the centerline of the bore. Recoil is nil, but the iron sights have to be 3 inches from the bore to do this. A mounted scope is even higher, and a shooter's face might not touch the stock while trying to look through the scope.

The stock gives you a place to hold, protects your hands from the hot barrel, and provides a solid rest for your face to aid aiming. What you can't see in black and white is that the plastic furniture on this AR-15 is hot pink. Accuracy and style.

This Remington 721 has a stock designed in the transition from irons to scopes. With a low-mounted scope it is comfortable to shoot. If you were to put a large-diameter scope on it, requiring high rings, it would be much less comfortable to shoot. (Especially since it is chambered in .300 H&H.)

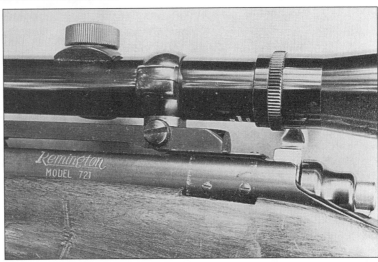

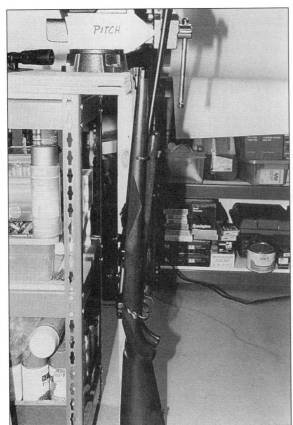

Pitch is the angle of the buttplate to the line of the bore. A stock with more drop requires more pitch in order to keep the butt-plate on the shoulder during firing. More pitch means more upward recoil into your face. With their combs aligned you can see the Ruger stock (ca. 1999) has much less pitch than the Winchester (ca. 1942).

The stock on this Winchester rifle, while appearing the same as those on a Model '94 of a century ago, is quite different. It is straighter, has less pitch and a wider butt-plate than the originals. And all are improvements. (Photo courtesy U.S. Repeating Arms.)

Last but not least, a stock should look good. A handsome stock builds pride and acceptance in an owner. These intangibles improve confidence and help improve shooting ability. After all, how much are you going to practice with a rifle that is so ugly you can't stand the other shooters in your club seeing it?

Stock Materials

The first wood of choice is walnut. Walnut has many virtues, but the primary one is that it looks good. In addition to looking good, walnut is soft enough to shape and hard enough to keep its shape. It is dense enough to create a stock that balances the weight of the rifle, without making it too heavy. Walnut is strong enough to withstand the shock of recoil (within limits) without distorting, chipping, splitting or expiring under the load. It takes any number of finishes without complaint, unlike some woods that are so oily they reject stock finishes. And it looks good. You might think I'm prejudiced in favor of wood and of walnut and you'd be right.

Are other woods useable? Certainly. But for most shooters, other woods are chosen for a particular "look" or just to be different. Maple is a hardwood that stands up well to the rigors of being a gunstock, but maple is a light-colored wood. Bird's-eye maple has figure, and maple can be dyed, but if you dye maple, why select it to begin with? I have heard some shooters exclaim that "Maple is for floors and bowling alleys." I would not go that far, having seen some fine examples of stock work in maple. Oak is a hard wood with figure and color, but oak is both too heavy and too brittle to be suitable gunstock wood. Screwbean mesquite is a popular choice among shooters who want a two-tone effect of dark bands and swirls in a light wood.

While it is suitable as a gunstock, mesquite can be expensive. The trees grow slowly (for gunstock quality wood, not charcoal wood), not very large, and a tree may produce only one stock.

Back when military rifles used wood, walnut was always the first choice. In peacetime, walnut was easy to get. Once the war (any war) started, any suitable wood was pressed into service. Woods that are suitably hard and found in surplus rifles, are birch, beech and elm. All three have the unforgivable sin of being bare white with no figure. Military stock makers solved that problem by dying the stocks. If you go to re-shape and sporterize a military stock, be prepared to stain or dye the wood once you have stripped off the old finish and sanded it to the new contours.

Walnut comes in an array of names. Claro, English, American, Circassian, French, the list goes on. The only two real differences between any of these as far as stock-making is concerned is price and looks. Some stockmakers can wax rhapsodic about the harness of this or that, its ability to take super-fine checkering, and small pores that don't need stock filler. The truth is, the older the tree and the slower it grew, the tighter the pores and the denser the wood. The more figure a stock has, the more it costs. Base your choice of walnut on what looks good to you, and what you can afford. Don't let your selection be swayed by snooty comparisons of "American" to "Circassian" walnut. Do you like it? Can you afford it? Then buy it.

For those who want to keep up with the Joneses, and know which wood is which, I offer the following for your consideration;

American Black Walnut

Found in the East, out to the Great Plains and south almost to the Gulf Coast, American Walnut is the choice of

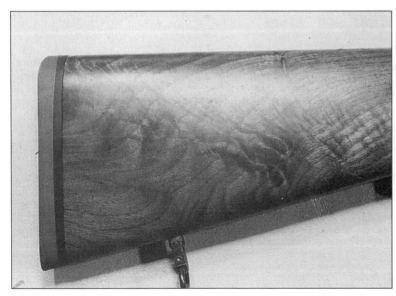

Walnut has been the choice for stock wood for centuries, and for good reason. It is strong, durable, and it looks good.

From left to right, a Maple stock in Extra Fancy grade and three stocks in Special Selection English Walnut. Notice that the three English Walnut stocks have different patterns to the wood's figure. That is why you buy wood, because no two are alike. (Stocks by Wenig Custom Gunstocks, Photo by Hutchinson Studios.)

rifle stocks. Hard, tough and medium in density (around 38 pounds per cubic foot). It can be found in highly figured pieces, and takes checkering and finishes well.

Claro Walnut

A California native (unlike most of the inhabitants of that sunny state) Claro is not as hard as Black Walnut, has a contrasting figure color and is usually darker than its Eastern counterpart.

European Walnut

A tree native to Western and Central Asia, it is grown commercially in a band of countries from France to Turkey. The grain tends to be wavier than American Black Walnut, and the color difference between the light and dark bands is greater. Density is a bit more than Black Walnut, but not enough to prevent its use as a stock wood.

Circassian Walnut

Native to the Black Sea area in Russia, the Circassian stock you look at has been grown here in the U.S. Circassian tends towards shades of brown. It has all the desirable qualities of the other walnuts.

English Walnut

A slightly lighter version of Black Walnut, it also tends to be lighter in color.

From left to right, two Special Selection English Walnut stocks, a Medium Fancy Claro Walnut, and a red and gray laminate. (Stocks by Wenig Custom Gunstocks, Photo by Hutchinson Studios.)

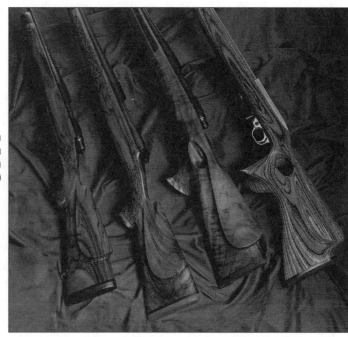

Left to right, a Special Selection American Walnut, two Special Selection English Walnut stocks, and an Extra Fancy American Walnut. (Stocks by Wenig Custom Gunstocks, Photo by Hutchinson Studios.)

Bastogne Walnut

A cross between English and Claro, Bastogne is very strong and stable. It features the figure of Claro with the color of English, and works well.

Laminates

In World War II, the German production base could not keep up to the demands of wartime consumption. The Mauser rifle plant was producing 50,000 rifles each month, and they were just one of many plants. That many rifles needed a lot of trees as stocks. To stretch the supply of wood, the Germans experimented with laminated stocks. Shaving the wood into thin sheets and then gluing the sheets together eliminated much of the scrap wood lost in standard stockmaking. As a military solution, it had a lot of virtues. It was cheap, durable and recyclable. For many decades after the war, a laminated stock was viewed as either ugly or an affectation. In the 1980s, public tastes changed. Lured by the weather-resistant stability of a laminate, competitors started using them. Soon, laminated stocks were all the rage.

Working a laminated stock is the same as any other, with the exception that the wood and the glue in a laminated stock will be harder than a stick wood stock. You'll spend more time sharpening your tools when working on a laminate than you will on non-laminate stocks.

Even laminated wood wasn't enough for the Germans to keep up (not starting things in the first place would have been a better choice, but not one considered for very long) so the next step was to use synthetics. At the end of the war a few rifles were made with molded stocks, cast out of plastic. The Germans were not concerned with stock stability as we are today when considering synthetics. They wanted fast production. Once the mold was made, stocks could be produced as quickly as the mold could be injected, cooled and opened.

If the best choice for stock wood is walnut, why are so many stocks made of other woods? Why laminates and synthetics? Cost. A plain walnut stock will not have looks any better than a stained birch, beech or elm stock, but it will cost more. It takes a long time to grow a walnut tree to gunstock size, and we have been cutting walnut trees for stocks for a long time. Once dropped, a tree is sawn into slabs, and the slabs are cut into blanks, each one suitable for a single gunstock. It takes a careful and practiced eye to cut blanks so the grain of the wood runs straight through the wrist of the potential stock, and shows its figure when finished. A walnut tree that produces blanks of the best quality is a tree that has essentially been tortured. A blank that has figure and color is a tree that grew in poor soil, with sparse water and harsh growing conditions. The wildly swirling figure called marblecake or feathering

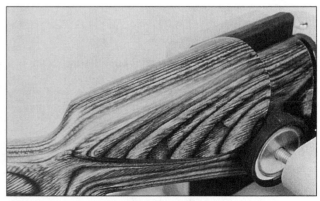

The laminated stock (this one a Volquartsen 10/22 stock) is formed by bonding sheets of wood together with tough glue. By alternating grain direction, warping is all but eliminated.

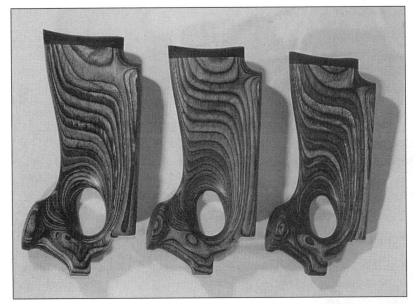

The color and pattern of laminates is created by alternating sheets of wood dyed different colors. Red, green, blue, black, brown and tan are common. These stocks are intended for AR-15's. (Photo courtesy JP Enterprize.)

Laminates can be cut, drilled and sanded just like wood, only tougher.

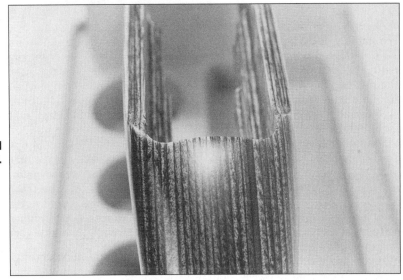

comes from the section of the trunk just at and above ground level. I have read of tree growers who wrapped the trunks of trees at the base with chains to promote the formation of wild and colorful figure in the grain.

In a grove of walnut trees, each tree might produce five, 10 or 20 stocks. Of all those stocks, a handful will be very attractive, a couple will be striking, and one, maybe one, will be drop-dead gorgeous. That stock will belong to the shooter who wants it the most, and who is willing to pay for it. That is why walnut is expensive.

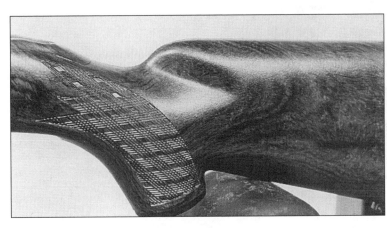

Tougher even than laminates or synthetics, this Ram-Line Syn Techr stock has the checkering already molded in place. It even has a wood pattern in the resin.

The advantage to any molded synthetic is that as fast as you can cool and prep the mold, you can make the next stock.

Once it is cut from the tree, stock wood must be dried. The stability of the eventual stock depends on the moisture left in the wood when you turn it into a stock. Too much, and the stock will continue to shift as it dries. Too little moisture, and the stock could shift as it sucks up more moisture. The best stock wood is air-dried, which takes two to five years. Kiln-dried wood is good enough for lumber, but not stocks. Once the tree has been cut into the slabs of stock blanks, the ends are sealed with shellac or paraffin. If left to dry without the end sealant, the wood might crack as it dries. By slowing the drying rate, the wood can adjust to the new and lower level of moisture without cracking. You do not have to bid on an aged blank that has the promise of great beauty in order to have an attractive stock. Besides, making a stock from a blank is a graduate exercise in wood-working, not the starting point.

If you want a new stock, get a pre-machined and pre-inletted stock that is ready to be fit to your rifle with a little finish inletting. I have heard shooters describe pre-inlet stocks as "stocks with 90 percent of the easy work done." Easy, if you have the machine tools to inlet stocks quickly. Or, plenty of time on your hands. For a stock with the inletting and outside contours already cut for you, order a pre-inlet stock from Wenig Custom Gunstocks. If you only want to do the exterior work yourself, you can send your barreled action in and they will fit the stock and send both back with the stock ready for sanding and finishing. Fred knows wood, and he makes really nice stocks. Using the price guide for wood quality and your wallet as a guide, get the nicest piece of wood available. You will never regret spending a little more money to get the next-better grade of wood. Once the stock arrives, admire it and set it aside. Then proceed to practice and improve your skills on a used stock bought at the local gun show for less than $50. Once you have gained the skills and confidence you need to work on your "pretty stock" then start fitting it to your rifle.

Custom Stocks

A custom stock maker is an artisan in wood. Once he (or she) is done, your rifle's inletting will look as if the stock has grown around it. The wood will have a beautiful and

The synthetic stock on this Savage Scout does not need to be air-dried, and changing ambient humidity will not warp it. The magazine button (bottom right) is held in place by the stock itself, a method not possible using wood.

The Savage stock is pillar-bedded. The sleeves are molded in place when the stock is formed, and provide a non-compressible surface for the receiver and bottom metal to ride on.

Laminates have become so accepted that this little Winchester 9422 comes with a laminated stock. (Photo courtesy U.S. Repeating Arms Co.)

understated satin sheen to it, with no marks left from any tool or sanding apparatus. The checkering will be perfect in every one of its little diamonds, and the pattern will match on both sides and over the top of the wrist. The stock will be a thing of beauty. It will also take a year or two to be finished, and the change left over from your pair of $1,000 bills might, just might, buy your family a dinner at the local restaurant.

As beautiful as a custom stock is, it is frightfully expensive. So expensive that the stockmaker himself may only have one or two sample stocks to show you. After all, he invests a huge amount of time in each one and can't afford to keep a large number of them on hand just to show off his (or her) work. He has a family, too.

Can you make your stock look that good? In time, yes. The more practice you take, the closer you can get. Is the stockmaker someone who walks on water? No. As a matter of fact, modern techniques have made his job easier and faster, but not less expensive for you.

Machines make his job easier. In the old days a stockmaker would carve a stock from a blank with hand tools.

The modern stockmaker quite often uses machines to rough out the stock. By using a pantograph cutting machine, he can copy a sample stock close enough that he then does the final shaping and sanding by hand. Buying such a machine is not an option for you. It can cost tens of thousands of dollars and you'd have to make quite a few stocks to pay for the machine.

Stock dimensions

The first dimension to consider is length of pull. Pull is the distance from the trigger to the center of the buttplate. The old test of stock pull was to grasp the wrist in your shooting hand and see if the buttplate came to the crook of your elbow. As a rule of thumb, it works reasonably well. Where it falls down is for shooters who are not average in shape. A tall, rangy shooter may need a longer stock than his "elbow" measurement calls for and a short, barrel-chested individual may need one shorter. Most factory stocks measure about 13 inches in pull, with some variation plus or minus. I'm 6-feet, 4-inches tall and 200 pounds. I can comfortably shoot a rifle with a pull out to 14.5 inches. I have one shotgun that I shoot slugs and buckshot with that has a pull of 15 inches. It is not meant to be a wing-shooting shotgun, so quick mounting is not essential. What I must be is comfortable, and the 1.2-inch thick Sorbothane pad from Kick-Eeze easily soaks up the hundreds of slugs and buckshot I shoot through that shotgun in a couple of days at a match.

Melvin Smart, the owner of Artistry in Wood, who makes the acra-bond stocks, once made a stock that had a 17.5 inch pull for an NBA player. The trick was not in finding a stock blank big enough or making the stock, but in making it look good and not like an oar. "When I first opened my door, I couldn't see his face above the lintel, he is that tall." Mel did such a good job that he's made several more stocks for this fellow.

A closer rule of thumb than the "elbow" test is to start with the "elbow" test, then subtract an eighth of an inch from this length pull for each inch shorter than 5-feet, 10-inches you are, or add an eighth of an inch for each inch taller. I am six-four, and the stock on my Clifton Scout rifle is 14.5 inches. It is a smidgen too long for use in cold weather with heavy clothing. Otherwise the pull is just right.

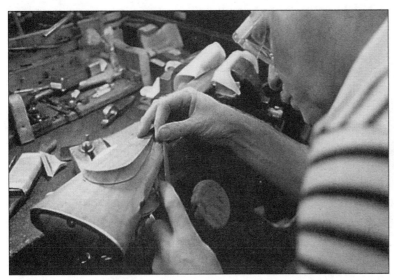

The custom stock maker works long and hard to turn out a thing of beauty. You can do it too, but it will require practice and patience. (Photo courtesy Remington Arms Co.)

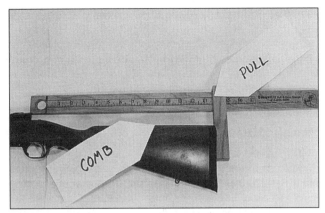

Pull is the length from the trigger to the buttplate.

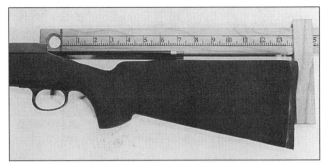

This H-S Precision stock has almost no drop. It is meant to be used on a rifle with a scope only, and usually from prone.

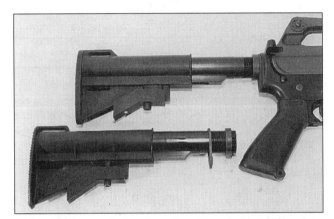

Once advantage to the "shorty" AR-15 is the adjustable pull. By stopping the stock lock in one of the intermediate positions, you can have a rifle with three or four different pulls.

The next critical dimension on stocks is the comb height. How high is enough? Your face determines the answer. Can you comfortably get your face down to the stock and use the sights? Then the stock is the correct height. Is your face floating above the stock? Then you need more height. Unfortunately, there is no way to put wood back. For a higher comb, you must go to a new stock.

The wrist of the stock is more than just a resting place for your shooting hand. A stock with a thick wrist will feel clumsy and awkward in handling, and slow down your shooting. A stock with a tight curve to the wrist, on a large-caliber rifle, will cause the trigger guard to rap the knuckle of your middle finger. Unfortunately, changing the curve of the wrist is not as easy as changing the thickness of the wrist. If you alter the curve, you leave a partial bit of the pistol gripcap to deal with. If you have a tight-curve grip and a hard-kicking caliber, then you need to install a curved, shotgun-style trigger guard to protect your knuckle. You can slim the wrist, provided you are willing to eliminate or replace the checkering.

The last stock dimension to consider is the length and shape of the forearm. Benchrest shooters use forearms that are flat on the bottom. Their rifles spend all of their time resting on sandbags. A flat forearm prevents canting or tipping of the rifle. Target shooters who shoot from different positions prefer a round or oval forearm of generous dimensions. The large diameter of the forearm fits the curve of the forward hand or hand and glove, keeping the rifle stable in the shooter's grasp. Hunters who will be faced with snap shots or the need for a shot on running game favor smaller forearms, with the forward hand closer to the barrel. As far as looks go, what looks good can dictate other hardware decisions. A narrow and short forearm, as found on British-style rifles, requires a barrel-band forward sling swivel. If you install the sling swivel on the forearm on a short, narrow forearm, the rifle sticks too far above your shoul-

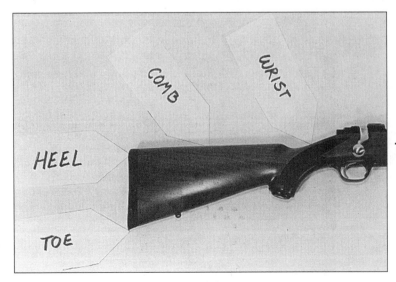

The stock and its basic nomenclature

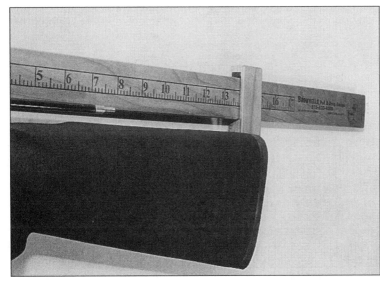

Looking closely, we might say it has all of 3/8 inches of drop.

The cheekpiece is a means of getting support for the face when using a scope, without turning the stock into something that looks like an oar. Some stocks, like this one, feature a comb that drops towards the action (forward). As the rifle recoils, it slides out from under the face, decreasing felt recoil.

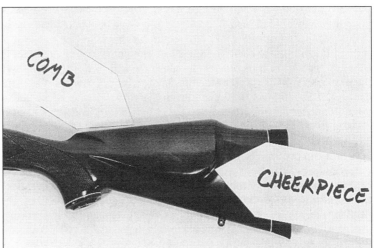

This elegant Mannlicher-Schoenauer has a grip cap and a curved trigger guard. As elegant as the trigger guard is, it certainly isn't needed against the sedate recoil of the 6.5 M-S cartridge.

The forearm of this Ruger International is sleek and sexy to some eyes. To the benchrest shooter it is too skinny and not flat enough.

der when you carry it. In open country the extra height may not be a problem, but the first branch you walk under could knock the rifle off your shoulder.

Stock Alterations

The greatest resource to modifying your rifle's stock is your local gun show. Go to the show and pick up a used stock of the kind that is on your rifle. Even buy a cracked one, and

practice by repairing the crack. The newly-acquired stock is your practice stock. It would be best if the stock fits your rifle. It does not have to, but if it does you can try any modifications at the range. Mistakes made on the practice stock do not have to see the light of day unless you want them to.

For our practice stock, let us take a portly factory stock and slim it down to a trim sporter stock. We will install an ebony forend tip. The recoil pad installation will be covered in Chapter Thirteen, on recoil reduction.

To slim down the stock you need a patternmaker's cabinet rasp, sandpaper, and a stock finishing kit. If you want your

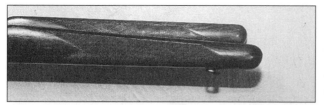

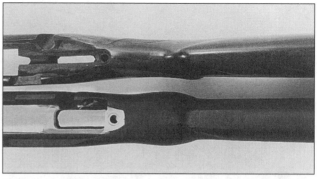

Stock modifications have an effect in other places than where the wood has been altered. The rear Winchester stock was shortened and had its steel buttplate replaced with a rubber recoil pad. The change in pitch has brought the forearm tip up. The drop of the stock hasn't been changed, but it has been made more comfortable to shoot.

While a military stock won't be as clubby through the wrist as this H-S Precision stock is, it would be thick. To make it as slim as the Model 70 stock on top is simply a matter of patience with a cabinetmaker's rasp.

modified stock to be checkered, you will need checkering cutters and a checkering cradle. As insurance on a slim-wristed stock I install a reinforcing rod through the wrist, epoxied in place. For the re-rod you will need a variable-speed drill, Brownells stock repair pin kit and a hand-held grinder.

Place the stock in a padded vise. Install the drill bit into your drill and drill through the wrist, from the rear of the action relief area of the stock. Clamp the brass rod in the drill and degrease the rod. Apply a small amount of epoxy to the threads of the rod. At a low rpm, use the drill to screw the rod into the stock. If your stock had a pistol gripcap, you can install another rod from underneath the wrist. Remove the drill and let the epoxy set. Once the epoxy has set, use a carbide cutter in the hand-held grinder to remove the end of the rod and the excess epoxy. Use small cuts and let the rod cool between cuts. If you cut too much and overheat the rod, you will degrade the epoxy.

Now you are ready to slim the wrist. Use the patternmaker's rasp to take wood off the wrist evenly around its middle. The patternmaker's rasp is designed to remove wood without gouging the surface, and without filling the teeth with wood. To get the cleanest cut, clean the wood out of the rasp's teeth on a regular basis with a stiff-bristle brush. Check frequently to grasp the wrist and feel your progress. Avoid the edges of the comb, action inletting and trigger guard recess, and work on the area that you grab when shooting. Once you have a wrist that feels comfortable, it is time to test it at the range. To protect the wood, take a can of spray clear finish and spray the bare wood with it. I use Krylon satin clear. If you do not seal the wood, you will get dirt in the pores of the wood from handling and firing. The dirt will not come out, and you will have to sand the surface clean again. The Krylon protects the wood, and can be sanded off when you re-finish the stock.

Slimming the forearm takes more time unless you have power tools. The danger with power tools is the ability to exceed your desires. You can take off too much wood. I used a belt sander on some stocks and to avoid a costly mistake you should follow the same method I did. Do not let the sander touch the wood for more than a few seconds. Check the forearm thickness each time you have removed wood. Once the forearm is close to the thickness you want then switch to the patternmaker's rasp.

With the wrist and forearm slimmed down to the dimensions you like, it is time to install the ebony forend tip. With a miter box and a sharp saw, shorten the forearm by the length you want your forend tip to be, about 3 inches. Sand the cut edge smooth and keep it square to the barrel channel. Drill the stock and tip for a guide rod. I used clipped-off stubs of the Brownells repair rods, and filed the rods slightly undersized. Mix your epoxy and put black dye into it. Clamp the stock in a padded vise with the forend up, install the guide pin and put epoxy over the end of the forearm. Slide the tip down over the guide pin and place a sandbag on it as a compression weight. An old shot bag with a few pounds of sand in it will do nicely. Let the epoxy cure overnight.

Rough-contour the tip with a belt sander if you have one. If not, then use the patternmaker's rasp. Once the tip is close to the contour of the forearm, you can begin blending the cut surfaces with the rest of the stock. At this stage your stock (practice or real) is in a sorry-looking condition. Some sections are in the original finish, others are rasped-down, and the forend tip is still slightly over-

This forearm tip was installed with a white line spacer, a cosmetic touch that has diminished greatly in use in the last couple of decades.

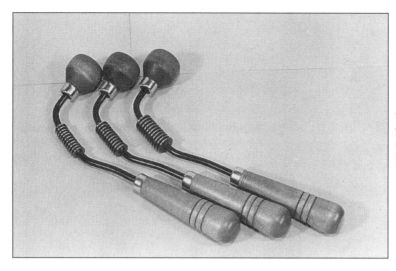

These barrel channel rasps are used to scrape the barrel channel smooth and remove binding spots. You can easily use them to free-float a barrel before sealing the channel.

sized. If your stock had checkering, the checkering is mostly gone, but some section may still remain. Now is the time to start making it look good. Use the rasp to blend the newly-cut surfaces to the old, uncut ones. Remove all of the old checkering. You want a smoothly-flowing contour. Trying to re-contour the stock surfaces and then re-cut the checkering to match the remnants of the old pattern is not possible. Once the lines flow the way you want them, making your stock sleek and elegant, you switch to sanding the surface. Skip ahead to Chapter Ten for sanding and refinishing.

Inletting

At its simplest and ugliest, inletting consists of gouging a channel for the action and barrel to rest in. No one wants to be seen with a "chainsaw job" so a certain level of detail is called for when removing wood. Whenever you are going to shave off some wood, only take off the smallest amount possible. If you take off more, you can't put it back.

To inlet a stock, you usually need a replacement stock. The one that is on the rifle (assuming it is a factory stock) has already been inletted. The new stock will have all of the important dimensions closely machined, but it will not be a "drop-in" fit. No stock can be. The dimensions of your rifle may vary slightly from the pattern rifle the stock-maker's used to cut your new stock. The wood of the stock

may have shifted slightly while on the shelf, or in transit to you. A "drop-in" fit is probably a loose fit. The stock on your rifle can be checked for proper fit. An action that is loose or binding in its stock can have accuracy problems. A barrel that rubs the forend can also have accuracy problems. Even if your rifle shoots well you can practice (without scraping the stock for clearance) on your existing stock.

With the rifle and new stock on hand, you'll need action and barrel channel scrapers, inletting guide screws and inletting blue or black. The scrapers are used to remove wood where it binds as the action is pressed into the stock. In order to reach the areas that will be binding, you need scrapers with an angle to them. The "hook" or bend gives you clearance to scrape the stock without the cutting action of the edge getting away from you. The barrel channel will require a special cutter. The barrel channel cutter is built from a series of hardened disks fastened to a shaft. The shaft has both ends bent for easy holding. Inletting is not the place for hand-held power tools. Resist the temptation to "speed things up" by putting a sanding drum into a hand-held grinder and reaching in to remove wood in a pesky spot. You will regret it. Maybe not now, or tomor-

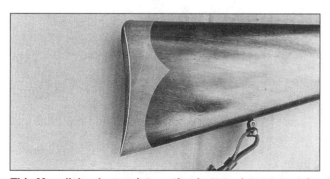

This Mannlicher has an interesting buttstock treatment. I can only surmise that the stock had been shortened in the past. In order to get it back to its original length, a subsequent owner had this extension installed of a contrasting wood. It is expertly done and kind of interesting.

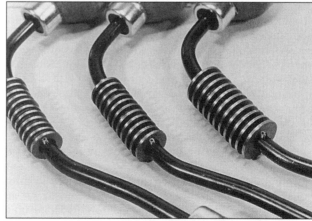

The cutting edges are hardened steel disks separated by rubber or plastic washers. Available in different diameters, they make short work of the task of opening a barrel channel.

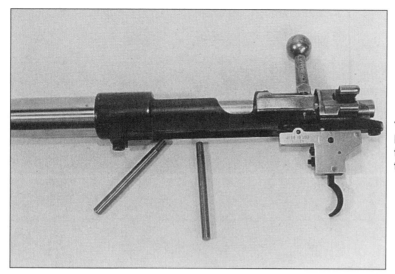

To properly fit a barreled action to a stock you have to have inletting screws. By installing them on the action you can slide the steel into the wood straight and vertically.

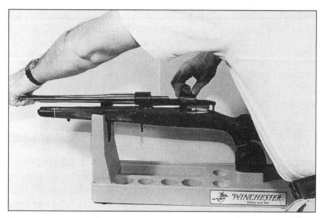

Here you see the barreled action being lowered into the stock. Where the inletting blue rubs off, the wood will have to be rasped, filed, chiseled or sanded away.

row, but soon, and every time you look at that stock. The inletting guide screws are not like regular action screws. They are longer and do not have heads, slots or other means of holding things fast. To use them, you take the barreled action out of the old stock, and screw the guide screws into the action. When you lower the rifle into its new stock, the guide screws keep the action lined up with the action screw holes that the stockmaker has drilled for you. The guide screws are cheap, and do not try to inlet a stock without them. The inletting blue goes on the rifle. If you do not have inletting blue, you can use carbon deposits from a candle, or even lipstick. When the rifle is pressed into the stock, any place the rifle binds the blue is rubbed off and left behind on the wood.

Inletting a pre-cut stock is easy. Take the rifle out of its old stock. Remove the scope and magazine box and clean all dirt and grease off of the action and barrel. Place the new stock in your cradle. Tighten the inletting guide screws into the action, and coat the underside of the action and barrel with inletting blue. Holding the rifle by the action (the scope rings work well as a handle) and the barrel forward of the forearm, lower it straight down into the stock. Be careful as you lower the stock. It is easy to bump the messy inletting blue against

edges of the action opening. Once it has stopped, press down on the action only. Or, use a rubber or rawhide mallet to tap the action down into the stock. Grabbing the barrel again, lift the action straight up. Set the rifle aside and look at the stock. Wherever the inletting blue has rubbed off, you must shave that wood out. Remember the admonition to be careful in lowering the action? A steady hand early on means you won't be doing much sorting out of the real high spots from the inadvertent bumps. Don't take off much wood because as you shave wood off other high spots will appear. You want to sneak up on proper bedding, not try to do it all at once. A very dark walnut stock benefits from the use of a light-colored lipstick, otherwise you might have a hard time seeing the dark carbon or inletting blue against the dark wood.

Look at the bottom of the receiver cutout. Is the receiver bearing evenly on the bottom of the cutout? Remember, you are seeing the image of the high spots pressed against the blued receiver. If the receiver cutout is evenly covered by inletting blue, then your rifle is resting evenly. If the blue is spotty, then you have to shave off the spots.

Early in gunsmithing, everyone has the impulse to briskly clear away all the wood that binds, because "after

Once the stock is properly inletted, the layout dye will be deposited across the width of the recoil lug and receiver base. You'll notice that the top of the receiver channel is still slightly binding, as there is a bit of layout dye left on the edges.

The rear of the receiver is resting solidly on the stock, as the continuous ring of layout dye left behind shows.

all, we're glass bedding it, right?" Sure, if you want the glass bedding to show around the edges, go right ahead. Patience is its own reward in gunsmithing. That, and a job you are proud to show off.

Once the barreled action is resting evenly in the action cut-out, and the barrel does not bind in the forearm, you are ready to start on the magazine box. A rifle like the Remington ADL, with a blind magazine, takes less work than other rifles. The blind magazine does not go through the stock. Instead of a magazine plate on the bottom of the stock, there is wood. Inletting the ADL and others of its type simply requires fitting the trigger guard. For the rest, you have to fit the bottom metal.

Again, you need the inletting guide screws. You also need straight chisels, which may not have been necessary on the action bedding. Place the barreled action upside down in your cradle, with the inletting guide screws installed. Place the stock over the barreled action, with the guide screws sticking out. Slide the bottom metal down over the guide screws. If it binds, pull it off and apply the inletting blue. You have a particular problem ahead of you. When you were inletting the barreled action, you had places to hold it that were not covered with inletting blue. The trigger guard does not offer you many such places. Keep a roll of paper towels handy. Any time you get inletting blue on your hands, wipe them off. If you get inletting blue on the outside of the stock, you'll have a devil of a time cleaning it off before you finish the stock.

Follow the same procedure for inletting the magazine box as you did for the action. Gently slide the inletting-blued

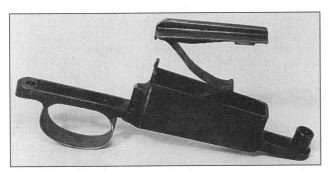

Once the barreled action is fitted, then you have to fit the bottom metal to the stock.

magazine down over the guide screws and press it into the stock. Pull it out, and then remove the stock from the action. Where the inletting blue has rubbed off the bottom metal and onto the wood, your metal is binding. Use the chisel to slice a thin layer of wood at the high spots. Once the bottom metal slides into the stock, leaves an even line of blue, and comes out without binding, your inletting is done.

Stock furniture

No, not an easy chair or a La-Z-Boy, but the stuff that is attached to the stock. Basically we have the recoil pad or buttplate, the gripcap if any, and sling swivels.

The buttplate or recoil pad covers the rear of the stock. Not only is that area the main interface between you and the rifle, it is a location prone to wear, tear and moisture entry. At the very least it should be sealed with the same stock sealer you use on the rest of the wood. While some expensive shotgun stocks are made without a pad or plate of any kind, rifles rarely get that kind of treatment. Today, most recoil pads are rubber, and ground to the contour of the stock. In the old days, rubber was viewed as something for sissies or shooters who really needed it, like big bores. Bigger than .30 caliber. When my dad first took me to the range, someone who showed up at the range with a rubber recoil pad on a .30-06 was viewed as a wimp, and to put a recoil pad on a .30-30 was the mark of a "Nancy boy." The British wanted to have things both ways, so after installing a rubber recoil pad, a British gunsmith would fit it with a leather cover. It is classy, expensive, and reduces the softness of the rubber.

Today's shooters do not have the same regard towards recoil. Partly because many are shooting big magnums and do not want to walk around work like Quasimodo, and partly because it is hard to buy a rifle that doesn't have rubber on the back end.

In the old days, buttplates were steel or plastic, and were looked at more with the idea of "does it slip on my shoulder" than "does it soften the kick?"

Many custom stockmakers prefer to install a steel buttplate in the softer-kicking rifles for several reasons. It is harder to do than a rubber pad, and done right shows off the workman's skill. The steel can be engraved, color case-hardened, or both. The ultimate expression of the steel buttplate is

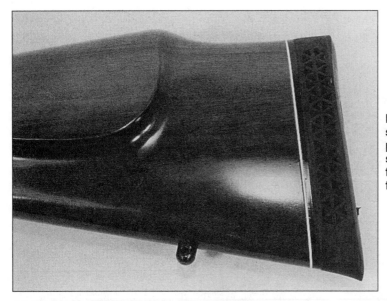

Rifles usually have a buttplate or recoil pad of some kind. This big magnum has a soft waffle pad to soak up recoil. The Uncle Mike's QD sling swivel stud has been installed 3 inches from the end of the wood. It should be safe from chipping.

In the old days they didn't have rubber recoil pads, so your choice was iron, brass or German Silver (an alloy of three parts copper, one part zinc and one part nickel, usually used for ornamentation.)

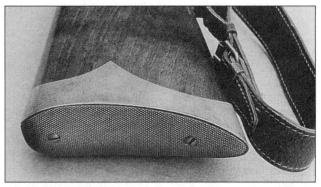

This steel buttplate is elegant and useful, provided it is on a relatively soft-kicking caliber. On anything bigger than a .270, it can make a grown man wince.

to install a skeleton buttplate, engrave and color case-harden it, and then checker the wood exposed inside the perimeter of the steel. Regardless of the rest of the work done to the stock, such a buttplate can easily set you back $400.

The gripcap is another cover, and goes on the end of the stock wrist. It serves no function other than cosmetic, although gripcaps are available that have a small trapdoor. A spare front sight blade can be stored there, although you have to have a front sight with quick-change capabilities or the cap is an affectation. Custom builders also spend large amounts of time on the gripcap, and follow the same pattern that they did with the buttplate on the stock. A skeleton buttplate will almost always have a skeleton gripcap.

Sling swivel installation

Last are the sling swivels, and you would think such a prosaic item would have to be simple, right? Not really. While picking a rifle up and carrying it for short distances is easy enough to do with your hands, sometimes you need more. Hiking through rough terrain is easier work if you can use your hands. If your hands are full of rifle, you might slip and fall. If you are carrying a pack, or packing out quarters of your game, you need your arms for balance. Cradling a rifle is work, and a sling can ease that work.

On the other hand, there are times a sling is a hindrance and can cause problems. Stalking through thick brush on an

This elegant Mannlicher-Schoenauer has a gripcap and a curved trigger guard. As elegant as the trigger guard is, it certainly isn't needed against the sedate recoil of the 6.5 M-S cartridge.

African Safari, looking for the wounded game animal is made difficult with a sling. (Yes, the pinnacle of hunting is a clean kill, but sometimes things happen. Your bullet can be deflected by an unseen branch, the animal may move to a slightly different angle just as you fire, many things may lead to a wounded animal that has to be followed-up.) Packing the quarters of your game through bear territory, you might have to keep your rifle handy "just in case."

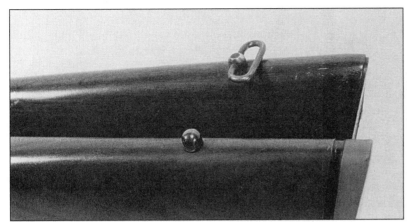

The older style sling swivel in the rear is not detachable, and the only way you can get the sling off is to disassemble it. By using an Uncle Mike's QD sling swivel kit, you can have a sling on your rifle that comes off at a moment's notice, but stays on until you want it off.

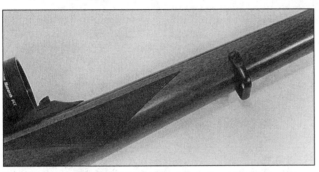

The forward sling swivel arrangement on the Mannlicher-style stock precludes the use of a QD sling swivel stud. If you must have a full-length forearm you'll just have to live with the non-detachable front.

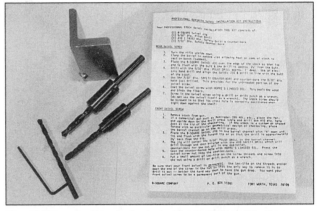

The B-Square sling swivel stud installation kit. Everything but the power, rifle and sling hardware.

In typical European fashion, this M-S front sling swivel and its non-detachable design have been dealt with by incorporating a buckle in the sling.

The drill guide ensures that your sling swivel stud holes will be drilled straight up and down and on the centerline of the stock.

So a sling must be quickly detachable to be useful on a hunting rifle.

Rather than simply knotting a section of manila rope around your rifle, install sling swivel studs and use quick-detachable sling swivels.

First, set out the tools you'll need. The sling swivel stud set. The B-Square alignment tool. A sling swivel thread tap, and a small bar of soap. Some woods will not need both the soap and the tap, but the hardest ones will. The simple and elegant method is to go with the Uncle Mike's system. The studs come in a paired set for your particular rifle. In almost

every case the rear stud is a simple affair that has wood-screw threads on its shaft. To install it, use the B-Square installation guide. Proper use of the guide ensures a straight installation. Take the rifle and clamp it in your cleaning cradle upside down. You might have to take the stock off of some rifles with large-diameter scopes or see-through scope mounts in order to clamp the stock securely. Place the angled guide on the bottom of the buttstock, with the drill in the guide hole. Slide the guide front to back until your

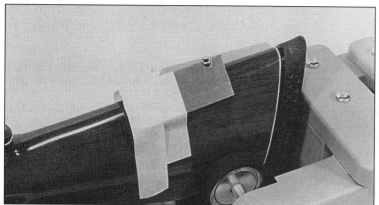

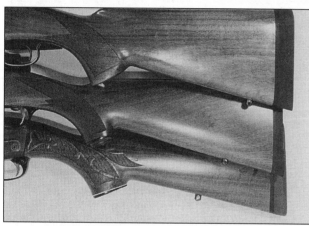

The B-Square sling swivel drilling guide taped to the stock, ready for the first hole to be drilled.

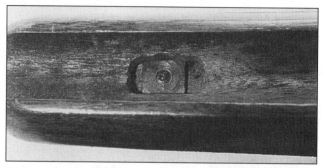

Here is the front sling swivel recess as routed by the factory. The hardware for the stud must not stick up high enough to touch the barrel.

Three sling swivel stud locations. The top one is too close to the end of the wood. It was probably installed before the stock was shortened and the pad was added. The center one is 3 inches from the end of the wood, a good distance for strength and looks. The bottom one is more than 4 inches up. It looks odd, but it is there to keep the muzzle out of the dirt when it is carried slung muzzle down.

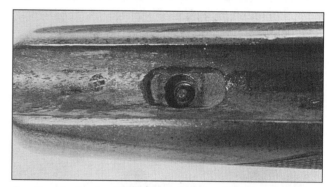

Another factory routing job, with an additional drilled hole for the Uncle Mike's QD stud nut.

drilled hole will be four inches from the wood end of the buttstock. Do not count the recoil pad in the four inches. If you drill the hole too close to the rear of the stock you risk chipping the stock toe on the line of the grain that runs to the hole. Marlin owners: the "Bull's-eye" plastic insert is the Marlin logo, and does not indicate "drill here."

Now move the guide side to side until the drill bit in the guide indicates that your hole will be vertical to the rest of the stock. Once it is in place, use masking tape to keep it there. Take the drill bit out and lock it into your variable-speed drill. Drill the hole a quarter of an inch longer than the threaded shaft of the stud. Remove the guide and replace the plain drill bit with the drill bit that has the rear stud counterbore installed. Run the drill with the counterbore on it into the existing hole until the counterbore has just made a complete circular cut into the stock. Without the counter-bored cut, when you screw the stud into the stock the wood will be chipped by the shoulder of the stud, marring the look. On a stock with soft wood and a polyurethane finish, you could even chip part of the stock off by screwing the stud in without a counterbore.

Take the swivel stud tap and tap the wood for the stud threads. It may seem like extra work to tap wood when you

are going to be screwing into it a wood-screw threaded stud, but it is worth the effort. If you do not have a threading tool, rub bar soap onto the threads of the stud to make screwing it in easier.

Use some of your stock finish to seal the wood where you have cut the counterbore flat. If you do not seal the wood, moisture can enter the stock in the cut area and migrate under the finish, lifting it, especially the varnish or lacquer finishes.

Front swivels come in a variety of installations. The simple one is for bolt-action rifles. The bolt-action front swivel has machine threads instead of wood threads on it. The front stud comes with a knurled nut that screws onto the shaft. The stud and nut clamp the forearm between them to stay in place. As with the buttstock, find the centerline of the fore-arm and a location that is away from checkering. Drill the hole through, and then use the front counterbore drill to cut

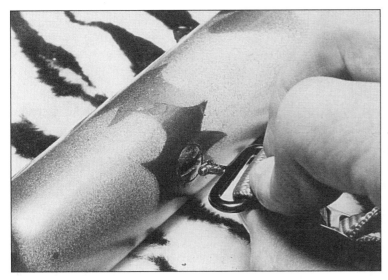

The Pachmayr/Millett flush-mount quick detachable sling swivel. The stud attached to the sling goes into the slot of the stock hardware.

a flat on the exterior of the forearm. Turn the forearm over and use the counterbore to drill a recess in the barrel channel. The recess must be deep enough to fully contain the nut, and keep it from touching the barrel.

Seal the drilled hole and both ends. Press the nut down into the counterbored hole. Thread the stud into the nut and screw it tight. Inspect the stud to make sure it does not stick up high enough to touch the barrel. If it does, unscrew it and shorten it with a file. Once it is the correct length, put a drop of Loctite on the end threads to keep the stud in place.

Lever-action rifles do not have enough wood in the forearm to hold a sling swivel in place. Instead, they use a band that fits around the magazine. Magazine tubes come in different diameters, and you must measure the diameter of your magazine tube before ordering your band kit. The bands come in two types, the two-piece and the one piece. The two-piece ones are easier to install, and look quite good. If you insist on the one-piece band you will have to install it by removing the front fasteners of the magazine tube. In some cases you will not have enough clearance to slide the band down the tube without scratching either the tube or barrel, and you'll have to remove the tube or even the forearm. Partly assemble the two-piece band by screw-

ing the large adjustment screw into one side. Hold the band halves against the tube and use a screwdriver to adjust the screw until the gap between halves is even. Then install the locking screw and draw the band halves up tight around the tube. Before you do your final tightening, check the alignment of the band to be sure your swivel will be vertical to the magazine tube and barrel.

Not all sling swivels are simple studs screwed into the stock. The Millett system differs from the Uncle Mike's in that when the sling is removed, the remaining studs are flush with the wood. One of the reasons rifles built for dangerous game have the front sling swivel on the barrel is to avoid the front stud hitting the left hand on recoil, and bruising the shooter.

Installation of the Millett system starts out the same as the Uncle Mike's, with the drill guide. The Millett swivels use a different counterbore. The Millett stud assemblies have two methods of fastening to the stock: the glue-in and the screw-in. The glue-in is just that, the studs are a press-fit to the counterbore, and then you use epoxy to hold them in place. I am a belt-and-suspenders kind of guy, and prefer to glue-in the screw-in studs, especially on a dangerous game rifle. Once the counterbores have been drilled, use a large-bladed screwdriver to turn the studs into the stock. Once the

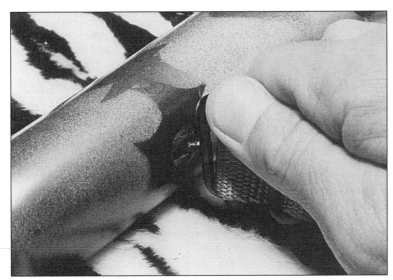

Turn it a quarter-turn to seat it.

Press it against the spring inside the hardware.

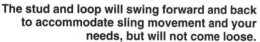

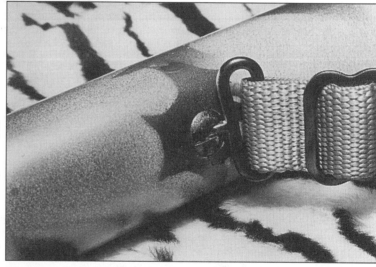

The stud and loop will swing forward and back to accommodate sling movement and your needs, but will not come loose.

Instead of a threaded shaft that screws into the wood, this QD sling swivel stud is a machined block that you have to inlet into the stock. Once inletted, then (and only then) do you drill for the screws. Elegant, and ten times the work (or more) of the Uncle Mike's system.

fit is correct, remove them, degrease them and apply a small amount of epoxy or Acraglas to them. Screw them in and let them set overnight.

The top custom-made rifle makers or stockmakers would not consider using something so prosaic as an Uncle Mike's or Milletts sling swivel system. Personally, I'm not so snooty, but some shooters and gunsmiths cannot stand the thought of having something on their rifles that anyone else would find easy to do.

The Dakota or Dave Talley swivel studs are fastened to the stock with a pair of screws, and must be inletted into the wood. Remember how we inletted the barrel and action into the stock? The sling swivels go into the wood in the same manner, except they are a lot smaller. Do not start by drilling your screw holes. First, determine the sling swivel location. Then, with the swivel in place, draw a line on the stock where the swivel will go. If you have a steady hand, you can rough nearly to the line with a carbide cutter and a hand-

The AR shorty stock does not have standard sling swivels. What it has are two slots to hold the nylon carrying strap called a sling. There are no convenient ways to thread a sling through them.

The GG&G Sling Thing clamps onto the stock through the lower slot, and has a sling swivel attached to it.

On the front, the GG&G Sling and Light Combo clamps to the front sight assembly. The right plate nestles into the triangle hole...

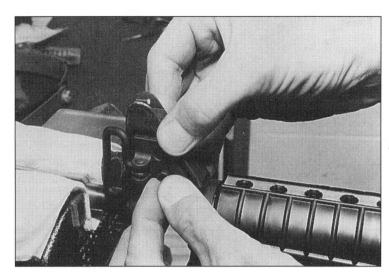

And then the left plate fits in.

Tighten the plate-holding screw first....

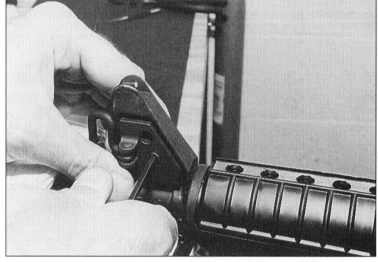

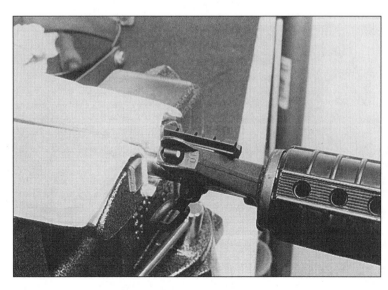

And when you tighten the second screw, it clamps the light plate to the sight assembly. The light plate is a Weaver/Picatinny rail that you can clamp a light to, for low-light identification.

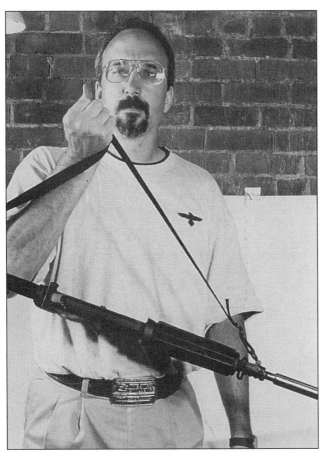

With the GG&G hardware in place, the rifle now has a side sling that doesn't obscure the front sight, or require a 7-foot strap to wrap and knot in place.

held grinder. Then, it is a matter of using layout blue and sharp, small chisels to remove the wood until the swivel sinks deeper into the wood each time you try the fit. You level the bottom of the recess with small scrapers and flat-ended rasps. Only when the swivel is completely fitted to the stock do you then drill the holes for the fastening screws. Why drill last, instead of first? If you drill the holes and get them the slightest bit misaligned, you cannot adjust the fit of the swivel to the stock as it "sinks" into the stock. Stocks are not symmetric, and you may have to adjust the fit of the swivel to the wood as the job progresses.

The sling swivel that is identified with British and African Safari rifles is the barrel-mounted swivel. While many are barrel bands, some have been made as "buttons" soldered to the bottom of the barrel. After all, even weak soft solder has a tensile strength of 4,000 pounds per square inch. Even a small button can be close to an inch in size, giving it more than enough strength.

The barrel band installation is easy to do, but tough to get looking right. First, measure the diameter of your barrel at the location you desire the band to be. You may have to compromise a little bit, to accommodate the available band sizes to your barrel taper. A barrel with no taper is easy, provided it is close to the diameter of available bands. London Guns makes barrel bands that have taper built-in. Brownells carries them, and ordering one is simple. With the band on hand, remove the front sight and ramp from your barrel. Slide the band on and see how close it comes to your desired location. If you need to open the band up, you can use abrasive cloth with a round backer to open the band a few thousandths.

Once the band settles to the right place, your choice is solder or epoxy? In both installations you must polish the barrel down to bare steel where the band will be. If you are careful you may not have to re-blue. However, since the band comes "in the white" and must be blued, don't worry about your current bluing job. Epoxy is easy. Degrease the barrel and band. Apply a thin layer of epoxy to the barrel, covering the entire area of the band installation. Slide the band in place and tap it with a plastic or rawhide mallet to seat it tightly. Before you set it aside, make sure it is straight. Solder is not difficult. Select a solder that will withstand hot bluing, and you will not have to depend on a rust-blue job to keep from dissolving your solder when you blue the rifle after installing the band. Rather than use the old "tinning" method of solder, take advantage of the wicking ability of flux. In tinning, you would apply flux to both parts, and apply solder to their joining surfaces while they are separate. Once cooled, you would then press them together and then apply heat. The problem with tinning and a tapered installation is that the tinned surfaces take up more space than the untinned ones. Your barrel band will end up installed closer to the muzzle than intended because of the extra metal.

Rather than tinning, slide the band in place and mark the barrel at the front and back edge of the band. Remove the band and degrease the barrel and band. Apply soldering talc to the barrel behind the line indicating the back of the barrel band. The talc will keep the solder from flowing down the barrel. Apply flux to the barrel between the lines. Apply flux to the inside of the band. Slide the band in place, tap it with a plastic mallet to seat it and stand by with your solder. Clamp the barreled action in a padded vise with the muzzle up. Heat the barrel and band until they are up to the solder's melting temperature. Bring the tip of your flame to the rear of the band. Apply the edge of the solder wire to the forward edge of the band/barrel joint, and let the heat and flux suck the solder through the joint. When you see solder bubbling out of the bottom of the joint, it has flowed through and coated the barrel/band surfaces.

Remove the heat and let it cool. Clean off the talc, excess solder and flux, and prepare for bluing.

AR slings

Not all sling swivel installations are meant to be unobtrusive and elegant. Some are meant to do a job and be out of the way. The AR-15 and M-16 started out with the standard kind of sling swivels, one in front and back, on the bottom of the rifle, for carry. In some situations, over the shoulder carry is slow or awkward. Earlier military rifles also had this problem, and the solution was to install sling swivels on the left side of the rifle. On a rifle with a wood stock and barrel bands, installing an extra set of sling loops is easy. On the AR, the buttstock is a plastic shell, and the front attachment of the sling is the gas block/front sight assembly.

How to attach a side sling? One method involves about 5 feet of sling material, and looping the sling around the buttstock and through the front sight assembly. The big problem is that it often blocks the front sight when you attempt to aim. GG&G has a better solution, called the "Sling Thing." The Sling Thing works on the rear only for the shorty rifles with a telescoping stock. The rear swivel has a mounting plate with two holes through it, a clamping plate, and a pair of screws. The rear swivel clamps through the lower sling hole of the sliding part of the buttstock. The front sling swivel clamps through the opening of the front sight assembly. With the two sling swivels in place, the rifle does not hang upside-down when it is slung in front. As an added bonus, the front sling swivel keeps the front of the sling from bunching up in front of the front sight.

CHAPTER 10

Wood Repair and Refinishing

Wood is a fragile substance to depend on for some of the things we ask of it. Stocks will crack and chip if mistreated. Left exposed to the elements, wood will warp, twist, crack and rot. Although it is dead, wood will react to the weather like your great uncle's knees, which are not dead. Wood is heavy, and easily scratched, dented and nicked.

If wood is so bad, then why do we use it? For the longest time it was the only game in town. Prior to modern chemistry, there were no synthetics, no marvelous plastics from which to choose. Is wood really as bad as its detractors claim? No. While traveling in Turkey I stopped in at the Anatolian Civilizations Museum in Ankara (which was a 1997 recipient of "European Museum of the Year" award) and saw a remarkable sight. They had on display a wooden box that had been made during the Phrygian period, the 8th Century B.C. It is almost 3,000 years old. I guess that counts as being durable enough. As for all the bad events that can befall a stock, proper treatment and a proper finish can go a long way towards keeping the wood looking good. And that is the main reason to use wood, for looks. Yes, a synthetic stock is wonderfully tough and durable. It can withstand more abuse than you can, and won't care about rain, snow, humidity or brothers-in-law. After 3,000 years in the ground it will look just as good as it did when it was made. But for all that it still looks like, well, a hunk of plastic. If you want good looks you have to go to wood. Nothing compares to the patterns of light and dark wood in a well-figured stock.

And a damaged wooden stock can be repaired and still look good.

Plastic works well as a wood substitute, but as good as it is, it still looks like plastic. Left buried, long after the steel rusted and even the aluminum eroded from oxidation, the plastic in this AR would be a recognizable man-made object.

What a home workshop this would be! This is the Remington Custom Shop where, among other things, chunks of wood are turned into beautiful stocks. (Photo courtesy Remington Arms Co.)

Before we go further into stock repair and then finishing, let's cover what a stock finish is and does. The finish seals the wood away from the elements, away from you, brings out the color, and hardens the surface. It can do these one of two ways. It can sit on the surface and seal the wood in, or it can soak into the wood and protect the wood by rebuffing the elements. A sealed stock will not warp, twist or crack. It may shift its dimensions slightly, but only a little. Rain, snow and sweat will not affect it. The finish keeps dirt and bodily oils from penetrating the wood. Without a finish, bare wood will collect dust in its pores. Sweat and grime from your hands and face will soak into the wood, discoloring it. A sealed stock can be wiped clean. Bare wood with body oils in it must be cleaned by chemically extracting the oils, a traumatic event for the wood. A finish brings out the color of the grain.

Wood is an amazing substance, but there are limits to what it can withstand. This laminated stock finally chipped behind the tang after 50 years of occasional use. Repairing it with Acra-20 will be easy.

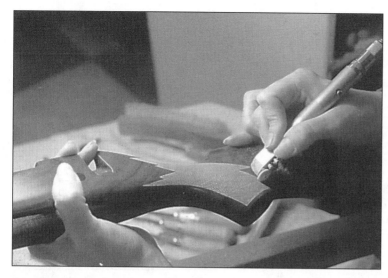

To cut checkering in a fast and efficient manner, pros use power checkering tools. If you expect to checker through a polyurethane finish, you'd better be using a carbide cutter in that power tool. (Photo courtesy Remington Arms Co.)

A rather plain-looking piece of wood can come alive with color and figure once a finish is applied. A bare piece of wood that looks like it has some figure can be turned into a spectacular stock with some finish. The finish offers a small amount of protection against bumps and dings, but not much. The best-protecting finishes are the hard plastic ones.

Stock finishes that sit on the surface include all of these plastic ones. To see this type of finish pick up a Browning with a glossy stock. You are looking at a catalyst finish. The sprayed-on plastic is similar in function to the epoxy you will use later to repair the stock. The common name for such a finish is polyurethane. The two components of the finish, resin and hardener, are mixed and then sprayed onto the wood. Upon mixing they react to each other and create a new form, one that is hard, durable and transparent. The Browning finish is very tough. So durable, in fact, that Brownells sells a specific stripping agent to remove Browning finishes. If you go to re-finish a Browning, use this stripper. If you try to sand or scrape the finish off you will work hard, create large piles of dust, and might damage the stock in the process. A side note, if you plan to checker your stock the hard, glossy surface of the polyurethanes is so tough that checkering through the finish is a waste of time. If you plan to use one of these finishes and want your stock checkered, checker first, then spray on the finish. Professional stockmakers and checkerers who deal with these finishes either checker first, or use a power checkering cutter with carbide blades.

If this finish is so tough and so good, why use anything else? First, the finish is hard, but not hard enough to protect the wood completely. If you ding the surface hard enough you will dent the finish and the wood, with no convenient way of raising the dent. The irony of epoxy resin finishes and durability is that on the hardest woods they offer the most protection. The hardest walnut doesn't need the protection. The softest woods are protected least. The stock that needs protection, doesn't get it. The hard, glittery surface shows scratches. The scratches can be rubbed out, but they will reappear faster than other finishes. The main fault is cosmetic. The stock looks shiny and plastic, and many shooters do not like the looks. For someone who hunts hard and has to have wood, the epoxy resin finishes will give good protection to their stocks.

Varnish and lacquer have been used to protect gunstocks for as long as there have been firearms that were not artillery. And even some artillery had their carriages lacquered or varnished. Many older rifles will have a varnish or lacquer finish, which are essentially clear paints. For a factory, the spray-on and fast-drying characteristics of lacquer and varnish made them an attractive choice. They are not as shiny as the polyurethane, they are cheaper, and if a stock sprayer forgot his respirator he wouldn't keel over dead. A scratched or dented stock with a varnish or lacquer finish can be repaired and touched-up. The hardest part of repairing a stock with a lacquer or varnish finish is getting the blended-in new area to match the old finish. If you use a spray with a slightly different composition than what is on the stock, the edges of the new and old finishes might react and the surface may mist or end up with an "orange peel" look.

The second type of finishes, the soak-in ones, are oil finishes. An oil finish is soaked up by the wood of the stock, the same way a sponge soaks up water. To keep from having to soak the entire piece of wood through, you treat the stock to fill the pores. An additional advantage of filling the pores is that this helps to smooth the surface. Without filling the pores of the wood, a magnified view of the surface would take on the appearance of a section of pot-holed road. You

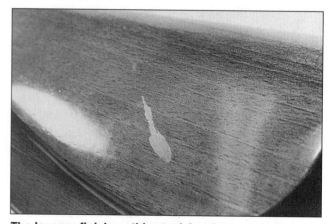

The lacquer finish on this stock has been scratched on the cheekpiece. It will be a simple matter to sand it smooth and spot-finish the area.

This Gunslick kit by Outers contains the essentials to re-finish a stock. The "Natural Oils" indicate that this is a sanded-in finish.

also have to fill the wood when you use the other finishes we mentioned. With the earlier finishes you use a separate solution to fill the wood. With an oil finish you use the oil and the sanded wood itself as a filler.

The oil exposed on the surface of the wood oxidizes and turns into a harder compound, sealing the wood. Unlike the standing finishes you can't scrape the oil finish off of the stock. A dented stock can be raised, and a scratched one sanded to repair it. Once the surface has been smoothed, an application of the oil blends the appearance of the surface over the repaired area, and the stock looks like new.

Stock finishing

Once a stock is properly inletted and any furniture is installed and checkering done then the only things left are to glass bed the action (go to Chapter Fifteen for that) and to seal and finish the stock. Many shooters seem so eager to get on with things that they apply the finish, and then go back and install the sling swivels, recoil pad, checker the forearm and wrist or install a forend tip. Tsk, tsk. All of these things should be done before the finish is applied. A minor slip while installing a sling swivel before the finish is one that is easy to repair. That same slip after the finish is on can take hours of fussing to correct.

The key to a good finish is proper sanding. The only finish that will cover a rough surface is a sprayed-on resin finish, and even then it won't help much. What is left behind on a rough surface? File marks, sanding scratches from a coarse-grit paper, uneven edges around the comb or maga-

zine box, these are all signs of incomplete sanding. A correctly sanded stock looks as if the application of an oil finish isn't needed.

Stock sanding is done dry. The traditional method is to use a sanding block, a rubber block that you secure the sandpaper to. The block keeps the sandpaper flat and prevents you from sanding dips and waves into your stock.

Stock repair with epoxy

The first item to obtain, is Brownells Acra-glas. With AC, you can repair just about anything. The liquid, runny consistency of AC enables you to get it into deep cracks, and to form a tight bond with a thin line at the old break. On a stock that is dark enough, the repair may not be visible.

Keep in mind the triumvirate of bonding: clean, dry and clamped. You cannot get any epoxy, even Acra-glas, to adhere to a surface that is wet, oily or covered with debris. The surfaces you are going to bond must be clean. Degrease the surfaces, even if the degreaser strips stock finish off the wood. You can spot-finish the exterior, but your stock may not survive a poorly-bonded repair. Brush dirt, dust, lint, and flecks of wood and stock finish off of the bonding areas. Sometimes doing this is tough, if you have a cracked stock with the broken piece still attached.

The tighter the physical match, the tighter the epoxy bond. The more pressure you can place on the part being bonded, the stronger the attachment. For many jobs, I use the surgical rubber tubing that Brownells offers. Epoxy will not stick to it, and the rubber will pull away. Just don't get so messy with epoxy that you encase the rubber in the overflow. I had to rescue a home experimenter who heard about the "magic" of surgical tubing, but was too free with epoxy. I ended up using a belt sander on the mass of tubing and epoxy on his stock. It was not fun, and I charged him accordingly.

For some repairs, I use a special product from Brownells, Acra-20. It has the same runny consistency, but it sets up to handling strength in 20 minutes. I use it with dowels to plug screw holes in buttstocks when installing a recoil pad. The fast-setting time meant I could drill and plug the holes

The cracked sidewall of this stock is another easy repair. Mix Acra-20 and use a needle to place it in the crack while it is flexed open like this. Press the sidewall back in place and use masking tape to hold it until the epoxy has set. Clean off the excess epoxy and spot-finish if necessary.

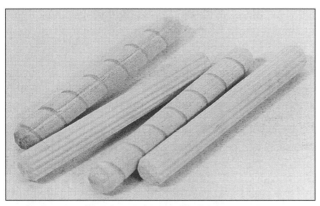

These are repair dowels, found at any hardware store. When I was selling lots of Mossbergs, the wooden dowel duck plugs served the same purpose. For filling pad screw holes when installing a recoil pad, drill the old hole out with a quarter-inch drill. Apply epoxy and tap the dowel into the hole. Let it set and then sand smooth. You'll now have a free hand in locating your new pad screws.

The buttplate is supposed to protect the stock. The designers of this laminated stock for a military Mauser went farther and designed the buttplate to cup around the stock and contain it to preclude damage to the lamination.

before lunch, then install the pad after lunch. Trust me, you do not want to install a pad before lunch. Even wearing a respirator to grind the pad, your lunch will taste like a rubber recoil pad.

As our first project, let us look at a stock with a chipped toe. A hard plastic or steel buttplate can only do so much to protect the stock. If you set it down sharply enough on a hard surface, you can crack the stock. The main reason I

Of these three sling swivel locations, the one on the right is too close to the end of the wood. If not for the rubber recoil pad, the toe would chip on a line where the grain meets the stud hole.

saw stocks with the toe chipped out came from the sling swivel being installed too close to the buttplate. The ones I saw were chipped along the grain right to the sling swivel hole. It was because of seeing so many stocks chipped that I changed my sling swivel installation to put the rear sling swivel not closer than 4 inches from the end of the wood.

To repair the stock you need the chipped-out piece of wood, Acra-glas, surgical rubber tubing, a degreasing agent, plastic food wrap and a locator plate. You will have to make the plate. You need a piece of steel plate, an inch wide by 2 inches long by an eighth-inch thick. A quarter-inch from one end, drill a clearance hole for a wood screw. The plate will keep the chip in place while the 'glas sets. Once the Acra-glas has set, you will need a smooth cut file, sandpaper and stock finish to touch up the repaired area. Remove the buttplate from the stock. If it is steel and bent, straighten it. If it is plastic and cracked, you will have to replace it. Place the stock in a padded vise. Place your locator plate against the stock, with the end away from the hole sticking a quarter-inch past the edge of the crack. Locate the center of the hole, and drill a hole for the wood screw. Remove the sling swivel stud. Brush both surfaces clean, and degrease them. Allow the degreasing agent to fully evaporate. A stock that has a surface finish will be easy to degrease. An oil finish will be more difficult. The oil has soaked into the wood, and at the edges of the chip may prevent the epoxy from adhering. With care you can degrease the broken surfaces without stripping the finish off of the exterior of the stock. You will have to touch up the surface anyway, so err on the side of getting the broken surfaces degreased.

Place a piece of plastic wrap against the butt of the stock, and screw the locating plate into place. Check the fit of the chip on the stock. You may have to adjust the fit of the locator plate against the butt until the chip is held correctly.

Mix the Acra-glas and spread it onto both surfaces. Place the chip onto the stock and press into place. Use a card to clean the excess off the stock. Next, wrap the surgical tubing over the repair. You will need the entire length. Tie the tubing around the stock right behind the pistol grip. Now begin wrapping the stock all the way back to the butt. Run each wrap of tubing right against the previous one. Pull the tubing gently as you wrap it, to get tension on the wrap. Once you get to the butt, you can wrap back towards the pistol grip, placing each wrap in the joint between the lower rows. Why wrap the whole length? The buttstock is shaped like a wedge. If you only wrap the repaired area, you may come back the next day to find that your tubing has rolled and squeezed itself down the stock towards the pistol grip. Once the epoxy sets, you have a real mess on your hands. The fully-wrapped stock prevents the tubing from shifting on you.

To finish the wrap, run the free end of the tubing under the last row or two of wrapped tubing. Check your locator plate to be sure the chip has not shifted. You have plenty of time to adjust before the epoxy sets. Leave the stock overnight.

The next morning, unwrap the rubber tubing and remove the locator plate from the buttstock. The over-runs of epoxy will have oozed in between the wrappings of rubber tubing. There will be choppy, saw-tooth edges of epoxy, and a smooth layer clinging to the outside of the stock. Clamp the stock upside down in a padded vise.

Practice for your next step by working first on the butt-plate surface. Use a small curved file to clean the over-run epoxy off of the buttplate area. Sand the repair smooth. Use your stock finish to seal any places where you filed through the original finish.

Switch to the outside of the buttstock, where the repair can be seen. With your smooth-cut file remove most of the surface deposits of Acra-glas. The finish of the exterior depends on the stock finish, oil, lacquer/varnish or epoxy. An oil finish is easy. When you have filed almost all the way down to the wood, the remaining 'glas can often be peeled off of the exterior of the stock. For final filing, do not follow the contour of the stock and file parallel to the joint. You will be able to fill the epoxy repair flush to the wood. Once the epoxy repair is flush, use wet-or-dry sandpaper and your stock finish oil as a lubricant and wet-sand the repair. Then follow the regular stock finishing procedure for your finish.

The lacquer/varnish surface presents a slight problem. If you try to peel the over-runs off of the stock once you have filed the high spots down, the epoxy over-runs will lift the lacquer or varnish. If you file or sand the epoxy off, the existing finish will get sanded off. Either way you will have a larger area to re-touch than the oil finished stock would present. Once the repaired area is sanded smooth and clean, then wipe the dust off with a tack rag and apply your replacement finish.

The epoxy repair can be very easy, or very difficult. With luck and proper care in aligning the chipped stock, all you have to do is file the epoxy over-runs down to flush with the finish. Wipe the surface clean and use a 600 grit wet-or-dry paper and water as a lubricant. Once the surface is smooth, switch to 1200 paper and continue wet-sanding the surface. As your final step use rubbing compound to blend the stock finish appearance across the repaired area.

The difficult repair occurs when the chip alignment was not perfect. When you file the repair flush you cut through the finish into wood. Once the repair is smoothly filed, switch to 320 wet-or-dry paper and sand the repair smooth. Once smooth, work your way through the grades of paper until you have sanded with 600 grit. Dry the surface and wipe with a tack rag. Finish with the standard epoxy finish application procedure. Apply your epoxy finish in light coats, letting each coat dry before applying the next.

Reinforcing the repair

A rifle with a steel buttplate may crack again. You can make sure the stock won't chip again on a different line of the grain. Or, if you have a rifle with a steel or plastic butt-plate that you want to prevent cracking, you can reinforce the toe. You will need a variable speed hand drill, epoxy, narrow masking tape, side cutters, a hand-held grinder with a sanding drum and Brownells brass pin stock repair kit. Remove the action from the stock, the rear sling swivel and the buttplate. Clamp the stock upside down in a padded vise. Mark the centerline of the buttstock an inch down from the toe. You will start drilling here. Take your tape and run a six-inch section of it from this mark. Line the top edge of the tape to the mark, and run the tape at an angle past the sling swivel stud hole. The hole you drill must pass under the stud hole, or you won't be able to get the sling swivel stud back into the stock.

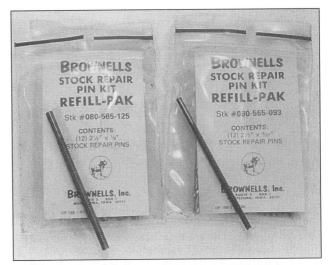

Brownells threaded brass rod is perfect for stock repairs and/or reinforcements. You can drill into or through the stock, or inlet it into the recoil shoulder on the stock as reinforcement.

Stocks chip in the toe along the grain leading to the sling swivel stud hole. The repair is easy.

With the included drill bit, drill down the centerline of the stock, following the tape edge. Remove the drill and take the drill bit out. Take a brass rod and with your file sharpen the tip to a point similar to the drill bit point. Use a wire brush to clean the brass rod. Clamp the rod into the drill and then degrease the rod. Mix your epoxy and spread a light and even coating on the rod as you rotate it at low

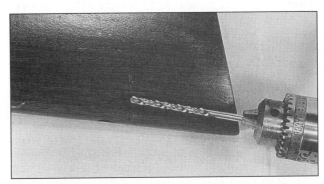

Once repaired, the stock can chip again unless reinforced. Drill on the centerline of the stock, starting from the flat of the butt. Do not drill through the stud hole, or you will not be able to re-install the sling swivel stud. The drilled hole and subsequent brass reinforcing rod must pass through the repaired surface of the chip in order to support it.

This is the sole external evidence of a stock repair to this No. 1 Lee-Enfield. The forestock split from the front screw (visible under the brass dot) back to the rear. As you would expect, accuracy went to hell. Repaired, it shoots as good as ever.

rpm. Place the tip of the rod into the drilled hole, and again at low rpm, drill the rod into the hole. The threads on the rod will grab the wood and pull into the stock, so you will only need light pressure to help it. Once the tip of the chuck contacts the wood, stop the drill. Loosen the chuck and pull the drill off the rod. Wipe excess epoxy off of the chuck. Take the stock out of the vise and re-clamp it with the buttstock pointing up. Doing this allows the epoxy to puddle around the rod, rather than running off onto your finish.

Let the epoxy set overnight. The next day, use a pair of sidecutters to clip off as much of the protruding rod as you can. With the sanding drum in the hand-held grinder, dress the rod and epoxy bubble down flush with the surface of the wood. Go slowly, or you will heat up the rod. The rod will conduct the heat and damage the epoxy.

Epoxy reinforcement

Working in a commercial gunsmithing operation you can always count on a really interesting job coming through the door. I had a fellow show up with his Safari Grade Winchester Pre-'64 Model 70 in .375 Holland & Holland. At the time it was $2,500 dollars worth of rifle. He was due to head off to a trip to Africa, and the rifle had suddenly stopped shooting accurately. I checked the bore and found nothing, so I pulled the action from the stock. To no great surprise, the stock was cracked between the front action screw and the rear one. Not a problem to fix; I would reinforce the action, glass bed it and test-fire it. I gave him a time and cost estimate, and then found out what the real problem was. He was leaving in three weeks for Africa and none of the repairs could show on the outside. While he was willing to decrease the value of a collectors item by taking it to Africa and hunting with it, he wasn't going to decrease the value of the rifle with an ugly repair. I had two weeks to repair and test it, follow-up the repair if needed and test-fire again, and get it into his hands so he could check the sights and adjust them if needed.

Whew! We agreed to a time and cost. I assured him the repair would not show (I had not planned on letting the repairs show in any case, so the assurance was easy to do) and ordered a couple of boxes of .375 H&H for test-firing.

The procedure was simple and would not have been necessary if the rifle had been glass-bedded prior to cracking. For the complete method of glass-bedding, go to Chapter Fifteen. In order to reinforce your rifle this way, you will need the following in addition to the regular glass-bedding equipment: your handy-dandy surgical tubing, a wedge of some kind and small sections of threaded steel or brass rod. The rod can be cut-off sections of screws. First, repair the crack. Wrap the surgical tubing around the stock in front of the recoil lug recess and around the wrist. The crack will spread if you do not protect the stock for the next step. With the Acraglas mixed, gently wedge the magazine opening of the stock open wider. Folded sections of cardboard can be used as a wedge. Be gentle or you will make the crack worse. Drip the Acraglas into the opened crack. To repair the crack you have to get the 'glas down into it. Simply slathering the 'glas over the top won't fix it. Prepare the action and bottom metal for glass bedding. Remove the wedge and spray the action and guards with release agent. Place the action into the stock, finger-tighten the action screws and then gently compress the action area of the stock in a padded vise. Step one is done.

The next day, remove the action from the stock. With your hand-held grinder rout two troughs. The first one should be behind the front action screw. The second should be in the thickest part of the stock in the immediate area of the rear action screw. Make each trough as wide side-to-side as possible. Make them deeper than the thickness of the threaded rod you are using. If you are using Brownells brass repair rods, make the trough wide enough front-to-back to hold two of them. Mix epoxy, degrease the repair rods, place epoxy in the troughs and push the rods in place.

Heavy kicking calibers might need more strength. In that .375, I used a small nut-and-bolt and routed the trough in a dumb-bell shape to hold the head and nut. Another approach is to use Steel-bed with a dumb-bell shape. A real belt and suspenders type would go the full route: nut and bolt, dumbbell trough and Steel-bed.

Spray release agent on the action and re-install the action into the stock.

The third step is to glass bed the rifle in the normal fashion. Could you repair the stock and not glass-bed it? Sure,

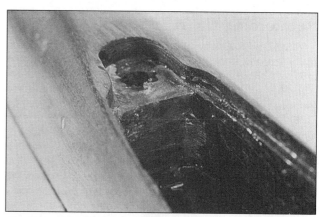

The No. 1 forestock with the bottom metal removed. The shoulder behind the front screw was replaced and epoxied together, then reinforced by the Brownells repair screw.

You can reinforce the wrist of a stock so that the support doesn't show by installing the rod through the tang. Before or after glass bedding doesn't matter. Drill the stock, apply epoxy and install the brass rod. Once the epoxy has set, use a carbide cutter in a hand-held grinder to dress the rod flush.

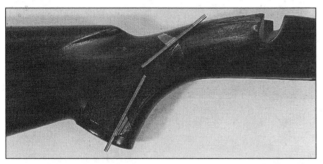

The rods taped to the exterior of this stock show how to reinforce the wrist. Without a grip cap, the bottom rod would show as a brass dot. With a grip cap, it would never show.

but why would you? You have the 'glas, the tools and practice, and you just repaired it. Any collector who comes across the stock will understand the need for the repair. A glass bedding job that doesn't show on the outside will not detract from the value of the rifle. Go to Chapter Fifteen and finish the job.

The hunter? His rifle worked just fine the first time around. It did not need any more work than the first repair. After the repair I took it to the range and test-fired it. After 40 rounds of .375 H&H 300-grain solids I was whipped. I checked the stock to make sure it was not cracked (it wasn't) and then took four aspirin and a nap, and then spent the rest of the day doing paperwork. He went off to Africa and hit everything he shot at. That rifle was accurate, even if it kicked hard.

Military stocks

A military stock was designed to protect the rifle from the elements and protect the soldier from the rifle. In the classic design, the forend goes up to the bayonet attachment, and the top of the barrel has a handguard in front of the receiver ring. The wood is intended to protect the soldier's hand from a hot barrel. Remember, in combat (combat with bolt-action rifles, it seems almost quaint, doesn't it?), there is no stopping to cool a barrel. As long as there is ammunition and targets left, the soldier is expected to keep shooting.

On this Mauser stock you can see the top handguard, the barrel band with its sling swivel attached, and the rear part of the bayonet lug. These all protect the soldier from his rifle, and add weight.

Without the full-length handguards, a soldier could burn himself on his own barrel.

The barrel bands keep the handguards in place, and also provide another curious device, the stacking swivel. In the old days, soldiers were expected to stack their rifles against each other in pyramids of three or four rifles. The "stacks" kept the rifles out of the dirt or mud while the soldiers went on to other soldierly tasks like digging trenches, washing laundry or listening to sergeants' complaints of inactivity and laziness.

All of this adds weight while providing no benefit to the hunter or target shooter. The first thing to do in sporterizing a military rifle is to make the excess weight go away.

Cutting off the excess wood and casting off the useless furniture only goes part of the way to making the rifle look presentable. The next step is to shape the wood, as we did with the bulky factory stock earlier. But not all of the wood is shaved down, and some areas retain the old oiled finish. Do not sand the wood to remove the oil, the oil is too deep in the wood to do any good. Besides, the removal of the oil will raise the grain of the wood, requiring sanding. There is no point in sanding twice. How to get the oil, finish and petroleum, out of the wood? In the old days, the "solution" was to mix a powder call "whiting" with a solvent. All of the solvents that worked the best are now known to be unhealthy and even possibly carcinogenic. The solvents that we commonly used with whiting were acetone, toluene, methanol or Tri-Chlorethane. Back when I was in Chem lab, we used to use acetone to scrub the stains off of our hands. It turned out to have been such an unhealthy practice I shudder to think about that today. In addition to being bad for your health, all of these solvents are flammable.

Rather than mix your own, I have a solution from a can. Go to the store and buy Easy-Off oven cleaner. I'm not kidding. To scrub the oil out of your stock, find a place where you can work outdoors. Buy some rubber gloves and a roll of paper towels, and a plastic garbage bag. To get the oil out of your stock, first heat it gently by placing it in the sun. Once it is warm to the touch, spray the oven cleaner on one side. Let it sit for a few minutes, then wipe it off with the paper towels. Repeat the application as necessary on the most heavily-oiled sections of the stock. If you find a section that continues to expire oil, apply the cleaner and scrub the wood with a plastic-bristled brush. Once one side is dry, turn the stock over and do the other side.

While the oven cleaner will suck the oil out of the wood, the passage of the oil through the stock surface will have raised the grain of the wood. With the stock shaped and the oil removed, you must closely inspect the stock for cracks. Repair any cracks you find.

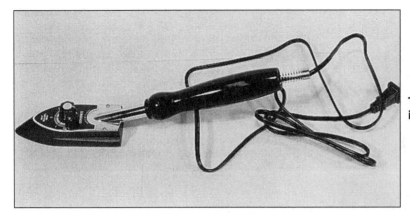

To lift dents from stocks, you'll need a stock iron such as this one and a damp cloth.

The business end of the stock iron has a variable heat control.

Spot finishing

Some rifles do not need to have the whole stock refinished. A scratch that breaks the finish or a dent or an old bubbled finish can sometimes be repaired just in the affected area.

One problem you'll see in stocks are scratches. In an oiled finish, a scratch is no big deal. Use the 600-grit paper to sand the scratch out (with a sanding block backing the cloth!), then re-oil and sand the area until the finish blends in with its surrounding area.

The oil finish may seem more difficult than a lacquered or varnished finish, but it is easier. The sprayed-on finish takes a bit more work to blend the edges of the new and old. Start by sanding the damaged area with 600 cloth to remove the scratch and the lifted finish. Around the scratch you'll see parts of the old finish that have been flaked and lifted. If you simply spray your new finish over the old damaged sections, they'll pull the new finish off when they decide to finally leave the stock. Sand the scratch and the damaged finish until you have feathered the edge into the undamaged area.

If your stock is a light-colored wood that has been stained, the sanding may have removed enough stained wood to alter the color. You will have to match a stain to your stock, and blend the sanded portion to the color to the rest of the stock. Any stock finish darkens the color of the wood being treated, so mix your stain with water to lighten

it, and apply several coats until the newly-stained wood matches the old stock. The color of the stained wood when wet with stain is the color it will be with finish on it. As the stain dries it will lighten, but it will darken again (and stay dark) when you apply the finish.

For many stock finishes, I have found a clear Krylon spray works well as a spot-refinish. For the high-gloss finishes I use the clear gloss, and for the duller finishes the clear matte blends in well. Wipe the area you will be spraying with a tack cloth to remove dust, lint and residual oils. Spray on light coats, letting each coat dry between applications. Once you have the sanded area sealed with several coats, use 1200-grit cloth with water to blend the edges and smooth the newly-sprayed surface with the old. Getting your stock looking good is now a matter of fussing over the patched area until it disappears and looks like the rest of the stock.

If you have a polyurethane finish, the job is easier. Like the lacquer or varnish, you sand the scratch down and then spray light coats of your new finish on, letting each coat dry before applying the next one. The "plastic" finishes are more sensitive to a heavy application and will sag or run if you spray on too much. If you have a sag or run, wipe off what you can. Once it hardens, sand what is left of the sag or run until it is flush with the finish and continue your applications.

Once you get a smooth surface, apply the final surface finish with a super-fine rubbing compound to blend the patched area with the existing surface.

Dent Raising

Dents are the warts of rifle stocks. Unlike a wart you can't remove a dent by cutting it off. You have to raise it, a task sometimes doomed from the start. To successfully raise a dent, the dented wood must not be cut. If your dent is cut or crushed you will only be partially successful at best. Dents are particularly difficult to deal with on a stock with a polyurethane finish, as the finish can sometimes keep the wood from expanding under the steam.

Clamp your stock in a padded vise or cleaning cradle with the dented section up and horizontal. You'll need a stock iron and some clean cloth. Plug the stock iron in and let it heat up. Dampen the cloth and lay a section of it over the dent, and place the iron on the cloth. Lift after a few seconds and inspect the dent. If you leave the iron on too long you can dry the cloth out and scorch the wood. Dampen the cloth between heating sessions as needed, and apply the iron repeatedly.

The heat and steam will raise the wood in the dent, and some dents can be completely removed. However, the steam will also raise the grain of the surrounding wood. You may have to do a little finish sanding before you apply your stock finish to blend the repaired area to the rest of the stock.

Applying finish to a ready-made stock.

The pre-inlet stock we finished fitting to the rifle in Chapter Nine now needs some sort of finish applied to it. Before we can apply the finish we have to sand it. Without sanding, the rough exterior of the stock will simply be sealed in the finish, as rough as it is now. In the old days, sanding was a laborious task that could take days. Old texts even talk of using a section of broken glass as a scraping tool to get the finish as smooth as possible. The thought of advising my readers to handle pieces of broken glass does not thrill me, and I'm sure my editor would agree.

Luckily, we have power. As an aid to all but the final sanding, consider buying a palm-sized high speed orbital sander. The first time I heard of it, I thought "You'd have to be crazy to use a sander on a rifle stock." You can persist if you have the time, but if you want to do a good job and not spend the rest of your life sanding, get one.

Install some 220-grit paper or cloth in your sanding tool, power or hand. If you will be sanding by hand use a sanding block to back the paper and avoid waves and dips in your surface. If you are refinishing a stock that had finish on it, go over the whole stock to remove the last of the old finish. If you are sanding a pre-inletted stock, sand the exterior to remove the marks left by the profiling machine. In either case you have to bring the entire surface to an equally-sanded finish. Once the stock is smooth, switch to the 300-grit paper or cloth. The block or orbital sander must be used with delicacy, as their flat surfaces will flatten curves on your stock. Keep the orbital sander constantly moving or you will sand flats into your stock. With the sanding block, constantly adjust the line you are sanding to avoid sanding a flat into the stock.

The power sanding and finish is done dry. The finish sanding is done by hand and can either be done with the 300-grit, or on a really hard stock, 400-grit. Keep a pump spray bottle of water handy. Once the surface appears to be sanded smooth, it still needs some work. If you were to see the surface magnified greatly, you would see small fibers of wood that had not been sanded off, but sanded down flush with the surface. These whiskers of wood will pop up at the slightest hint of moisture. If you do not remove them, when you apply the stock finish they will spring up and make your surface rough to the touch. Mist the surface of the wood in an area. Do not spray the surface damp, or you will have to wait until it dries. Use a hairdryer to gently heat the wood. The damp wood fibers will stand up straight. Take your finish-grit sanding block and sand against the grain of the wood, cutting off the whiskers that have popped up.

Once the whole stock has been de-whiskered, you are ready to apply the finish.

A pre-cut or semi-finished stock will come to you ready for the final sanding or you can re-contour it, sand it and then go to the stock finishing steps. A semi-finished stock will have to be inletted, where your factory-made practice stock does not.

To apply your stock finish, treat the whole stock as a repair stock being spot-finished. If you are going to be installing a recoil pad or buttplate that covers the butt, screw an eyelet into the butt and hang the stock from the ceiling. Spray on light coats of any spray-on finish and let them dry. Once each coat has dried, wet sand with 600 or 1,200 paper or cloth, let dry, wipe with a tack cloth and let dry, then spray again.

The virtue of a spray-on finish is that it does not require a large number of coats to be finished.

Oil finishes

The oil finish not only takes more coats, but gets better the more coats you use. With a spray-on finish each coat sits on the previous layer. With an oil finish each coat soaks into the wood, extending the finish deeper and deeper.

Oil finishes used to be individually mixed, and many custom stock makers still mix their own. The old texts were written when the usual oils were linseed oil and tung oil. The old mixes did not have drying agents and so it was common for a freshly-oiled stock to take days to dry. Modern mixes have improved the oils so they dry in as few as an hour or two, letting you apply several coats a day if you want to. Mel Smart of *Artistry in Wood* makes his by mixing two different solutions. The first one is to seal the wood, the second is the finish that he sands in. The first formula is one part tung oil, one part spar varnish or marine polyurethane, one part Flecto varathane, and three parts mineral spirits. He brushes this mix on as heavy as the stock will take. He has even gone so far as to dip stocks into this solution to speed the process up. Once the stock has soaked up as much of this solution as he can get it to, he sets it aside to dry.

The second solution is much the same, omitting the varathane and only using two parts mineral spirits. He then brushes the second solution on and sands the stock with 320 or 400 cloth. As the solution and the sanding residue build up as a thick paste, he continues sanding, using the paste as an abrasive and filler. If it gets too thick to move, he adds a little more solution. Once sanded, he lets it dry. The sanding is done solely to work the finish into the wood, not to change the shape of the stock. All sanding is done by hand, with a sanding block behind the cloth.

Once dry he wipes off the excess, applies more of the second solution and sands again. The fineness of the sandpaper determines the gloss of the finish. Depending on how matte or satin you want your stock to be, work up to 400-, 600- or 800-grit cloth. Work up to it by the 10th coat, because the best finishes built-in this way will take 20 or 30 applications of sanded-in finish.

Once the final coat is sanded in, wiped off and dried, Mel uses some paste wax to protect the finish and get more of a gleam to the surface. If you want an understated look, you might omit the wax.

If you do not want to mix your own solutions, then you can simply purchase pre-mixed finishes ready to be applied. Brownells has a number of solutions, from the Chem-Pak Pro-Custom to the Birchwood Casey. To apply them, you simply follow the process that Mel does, sanding your finish into the wood.

Applying an oil finish to a stock is a messy and time-consuming operation, but one that turns out a classy-looking stock that can easily be repaired or updated as it wears. An oil finish also brings out the grain and figure of a stock, so if you've spent extra money on good wood, you might consider an oil finish in order to show it off to best advantage.

CHAPTER 11

Metal Finishes

With some exceptions, we make rifles out of steel. Oh, the AR-15 has large amounts of aluminum and plastic. Remington makes a light-weight barrel that is a steel liner wrapped in a synthetic stiffening sleeve. Synthetic stocks are found almost everywhere, and at least one custom gunmaker fabricates the receivers of bolt-action rifles from blocks of titanium.

But for now, steel rules the roost. While it is heavy, steel is durable, cheap, and easy to form and shape into the desired design. By mixing it with small amounts of other metals or elements, steel can be produced in a range of alloys that can greatly improve its basic strength and durability. One thing steel cannot do is resist rust. While many

Professional refinishers have a chemistry lab on premises so they can check their solutions. Once a tank-full has been exhausted, it must be replenished or replaced.

Some treatments require strong chemicals. Do you really want to keep five gallons of 20 percent Muriatic Acid on hand to strip off old finishes?

of the modern characteristics of steel have changed how steel is used, steel has always rusted. Before steel there was iron, which rusted even faster. Bronze was the preferred metal of the ancients not because they were lazy, but because they did not have huge mills to produce steel. When a foundry could only produce several tons of metal a year, the best metal to make was one that would not melt in the rain. Bronze statues in Europe survived for centuries when subjected to nothing more corrosive than rainwater and pigeon poop. When the pollution of power plants and automobiles became high enough, the bronze (and stone, too) statues started eroding at an increasing rate.

The bronze survived until this century because the film of oxidation formed on it sealed the surface from further corrosion. This is a trick that iron oxide has not learned. The rust on the surface only offers small protection to the underlying steel.

For a long time, iron and steel was protected one of two ways. Either it was left bright and continually scrubbed clean, or it was carefully corroded by chemicals that left a film that was mildly corrosion-resistant. The military approach was to scour the rifles bright. Water and campfire ashes seemed to be the preferred paste. Many Civil War muskets with an "original patina" have nothing of the sort. When it was in the field looking for trouble, its owner kept it bright and clean. The lovely brown coloring it has was gained in the century and a half since then. In the civilian market, rust-blued and later caustic solutions for bluing were used to give rifles a measure of protection. None were really satisfactory, as they offered hardly any protection at all.

Early in the 20th century a chemical process was created that offered the military a better alternative. Called Parkeriz-

Collectors looking for pristine specimens are sometimes frustrated by military procedures. This Springfield has two shades of Parkerizing and three shades of bluing on its various parts, and is all original.

This M1 Garand has a beautiful dark green Parkerized finish. The color depends on the dyes used during Parkerizing, and the treatment it has received since then.

ing, it involved placing the parts to be treated in a tank of boiling phosphoric acid. Dissolved in the phosphoric acid are filings of steel, zinc or manganese. The parts react to the acid and the dissolved metals to form a tough coating that resists rusting much better than bluing does. The downside is that Parkerizing is ugly. While ugly does not matter to the military, many sportsmen do not like ugly rifles.

Despite this aversion, many rifle manufacturers now use Parkerizing as a means of controlling cost. The Parkerizing process roughens the surface of the steel. In so doing, minor tooling marks can be hidden. Rather than spend money polishing the parts, manufacturers will Parkerize the parts and save those polishing costs and the cost of bluing. Do not buy a Parkerized rifle with the idea of polishing it and getting it high-gloss blued. If you have a Parkerized rifle, the effort of polishing out the Parkerizing and tool marks, and then re-bluing the rifle can be more than you bargained for.

All surface treatments are highly dependent on the surface finish of the parts being treated. Except for Parkerizing and some of the bake-on finishes, none will hide tool marks, pitting or rust marks. Do not expect a blemish to go away as a result of any of these treatments.

What do we expect from a metal finish? The first thing is attractiveness. As with so many things in life, beauty is in the eyes of the beholder. One avid hunter I know views a rifle sprayed down with several dark shades of bake-on engine paint as the most beautiful thing he owns. He spends more time scouting out potential hunting sites than I do at the range. His success rate is nearly 100 percent, and the bucks he has bagged are huge. For him, what the rest of us would view as an ugly rifle is handsome, indeed.

The finish should protect the steel from the elements. A beautiful finish that doesn't protect a rifle from the rain won't be viewed with much favor. It should also be durable enough to survive normal use. A finish that protects the steel from rust but is rubbed off by your hands is stupid.

In his book "*Modern Gunsmith*" (modern at the time of WWII) James Howe had nearly 50 formulas for metal finishes of various kinds. Each of them listed a recipe for the prospective gunsmith to mix on his own and then apply as needed. Now, Brownells can supply you with everything you need already pre-mixed and complete with instructions.

Metal preparation

Even if you are going to have someone else do the chemical work of finishing your rifle, you can do the metal work. The purpose of polishing is to remove nicks, scratches, pits or tool marks and leave a smooth surface that your finisher can deal with. After you are done, the finisher will treat the rifle to an acid bath to remove old finish and surface oxidation. Once

Buying a Parkerized rifle because it is cheap, with the intention of polishing it later is a waste of time. Unless you consider the time and effort spent getting it smooth and even as practice.

Bob Cogan of Accurate Plating, showing off the plating tanks.

stripped, the finisher will either bead blast the surface to give it an even texture, or buff it to give it a mirror shine. Which way he goes is your choice. Getting to where he can deal with it is your option. Polishing out the scratches, gouges, pits and other cosmetic metal failings of your rifle yourself can save you a lot of money on a metal refinishing job. The last time I was down in Florida visiting Bob Cogan of Accurate Plating, he remarked that some guns show up for plating that are really rough. "We have to charge them more for the polishing and metal prep than we do for the plating, 'cause we won't plate an ugly gun."

To polish metal you need fine files, emery cloth, stones and a hand-held grinder with felt polishing bobs.

The metal polishing comes after you have done all of the other metal work. The receiver must be held securely. In order to hold it you must either clamp the barrel in a padded vise or secure the receiver to a holding fixture. An action with the barrel still in it is easy. An action by itself can only be cleaned up for refinishing by securing it to the holding fixture. Obviously the barreled action will work in the holding fixture.

With the action secured, start by cleaning off the old finish with an abrasive cloth. If you will be removing pits and scratches, start with the 220 cloth. If you simply want to even out the surface texture (from spotted bluing or a screwdriver scratch) you can start with the 320 or 400 cloth. To reach into curves, use a round backer such as a section of rod. Once the surface is uniform in texture with the grit you are using, switch to a finer grit. Your last application of cloth is the one that determines how much work the bluer will have to do. If you have sanded each surface in a different direction, the edges of each sanded area will not blend smoothly with the next. Your last grit, whether it is 400, 600

Professional metal finishers polish barrels by holding it at an angle and sweeping down the barrel in a smooth stroke. Stopping means the barrel is getting more buffing at that point, and dishes the finish.

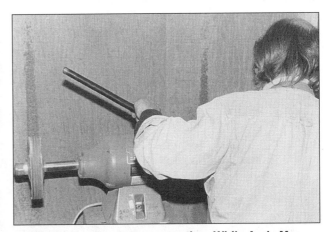

Buffing is another messy operation. While Andy Manson buffs this barrel (notice the angle at which he is working) you can see the wall behind the buffing wheels has a stripe of the buffing compound.

The simplest bluing setup available from Brownells runs $460 (in 1999) and contains everything you need to get started.

The bluing setup complete with stands, gas heaters, instructions and chemicals runs three times the bare-bones set-up.

or 800, must have the grain all running in the same direction.

Polishing barrels is not always easy. The bluer will polish with power, and draw the barrel down the polishing wheel or belt as it polishes across the barrel. By moving the barrel this way he avoids lines between sections of polishing. What you will have to do to avoid these lines is to polish a barrel its length, not side to side as if you're polishing shoes.

The purpose of polishing your rifle is not to turn it over to the bluer or refinisher "ready to go" but to save him time and you money by turning your rifle over to him ready for the final strip and dip. He can then easily apply the final polish or bead-blast that you want, strip and degrease the rifle, and proceed to apply the finish.

Bluing

The time-honored finish. In the 19th and into the 20th century, bluing was sometimes heat-bluing, and occasionally rust-bluing. In heat-bluing (sometimes called "fire-blue") the parts are placed in a furnace and carefully brought up to the oxidation temperature of steel, around 600 degrees Fahrenheit. The parts are soaked in the furnace until the surface has entirely reacted to atmospheric oxygen. Colt did this with their handguns, and many rifle makers did it to smaller parts. The process produces a beautiful blue that does not look anything like a chemical blue. Heat blue does not offer much protection. If you have modified a small part

by filing and stoning it, you can blue the file surface by heat-bluing it using a propane torch.

Small parts on European pistols used to be "strawed" which is a similar process but a different desire. The straw color was a result of slightly annealing an otherwise hard part.

Hot-dip bluing involves heated tanks of caustic salt solutions. It is fast, efficient and reasonably durable. However, you cannot set up the bluing tanks in your laundry room or a corner of the garage. The drawbacks to hot-dip bluing, while many, are not insurmountable. You must have a bare

If you do not have gas available, you can go with electrically-heated bluing tanks, for $2,000. That is the cost of a lot of guns blued by someone else.

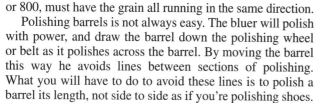

As you can see, production tanks are even more elaborate than the Brownells tanks. The extra hardware allows many guns an hour to be blued, with several in each tank at once.

The bluing salts seeping out from this banded front sight are only unsightly, and not a cause for alarm. Wipe them off and apply some penetrating oil.

room to blue in. No other steel parts can be in the room, or they will be vapor-blued. Hot-dip bluing requires large amounts of fresh air. In the winter those doing the bluing get cold, and in the summer they swelter. A separate room from your gun room in the basement, with a forced-air ventilation system would be just the ticket. The initial cost of a set of tanks that can handle a rifle, and the chemicals to go with them can exceed the cost of a new rifle. A set of tanks to handle multiple rifles in a professional manner not only exceeds the cost of several rifles, but requires a hookup to your gas company. No gas? Then an electric system runs twice the cost of a gas-burner set up.

The solutions are hot, and you can burn yourself. Spilled chemicals will dissolve your clothes.

The process is involved, but reasonably quick. The finished rifle is dipped in a degreasing bath to remove all oils, petroleum, synthetic or perspiration. Next it goes to the pickling bath, which lightly etches the surface and strips off any surface oxidation that might have happened since it was given its final polish or bead-blasting. Next are the bluing solutions, caustic salt solutions that create the actual bluing. Depending on the alloys of steel involved, the particular chemicals, how fresh they are and how pure the water is, the bluer will adjust the heat of the solution and the time of exposure. Once the proper blue is reached, the rifle is then dipped into clean water to remove the bluing solution, and then into a water-displacing oil to prevent rusting.

If you sometimes pull a rifle out of the box and find a crusty white deposit leaking out if joints, that is residual bluing salts leaking out. They don't harm anything, just wipe them off and apply some oil.

Cold blue is a chemical that reacts to the steel and forms a dark deposit on the surface. All cold blues I have tried involve some variation of a sulfur reaction to the steel. This is fine for touch-up of worn or scratched areas, a whole rifle can't be cold blued successfully. While you could cold-blue

a rifle, the finish would quickly wear off, and the rifle will smell of rotten eggs.

Use cold blue as a touch-up. To prep the surface, use a small ball of 0000 steel wool to scrub the area, removing dirt, powder residue and surface oxidation. To apply cold blue, degrease the area you will be bluing. Apply some cold blue, such as from the Outers Blue-stick and its three-applicator set. Once the blue dries, rub it with some clean cloth, degrease again and apply more. With a couple of applications you should be able to blend the worn surface into the color of the rest of the finish.

Rust bluing

Rust-bluing involves controlled rusting of the surface with chemical solutions and humid rooms. Back when rifles were rust-blued from the factory each rifle would be rubbed with the rusting solution and then stored in a steam room. The next day the resulting rust would be "carded" or buffed down to blued steel and given the chemical treatment again. This would be repeated for days or weeks until the parts were deemed "blued." The process offers more protection than fire-bluing but is labor- and time-intensive. In the really old days, labor was cheap and steel was expensive. Today the steel in a rifle is the cheapest part of it. Out of favor as a manufacturing process, it is widely used by custom gunsmiths. The finish is a very attractive satin blue when the parts are properly polished and the blue applied.

To do rust-bluing at home you will have to have a dedicated rusting closet or cabinet. In that cabinet you have to have the one thing you try so hard to keep out of all the other areas you store rifles: humidity.

Some advances have been made in the rust-bluing front, as they have in other gunsmithing areas. With the Pilkington Classic solution, you don't need a humidity-controlled closet or cabinet. However, you do need a tank of boiling water large enough to immerse the rifle in. To use the Pilkington Classic solution, start with the metal-prepped and degreased rifle. Plug the muzzle and chamber (you don't want rust on the inside, only the outside!)

Swab the solution on, wait a few minutes and swab on another coat. Hang the rifle up for a few hours to let it rust. Dip it into the boiling water, remove and let dry. Once dry, card the rust down to blue. Repeat as many times as you want to, or until the finish is a deep, rich blue.

One advantage rust-blue has over hot-dip blue is that it does not attack soft solder or epoxy. You can rust-blue a rifle with sights, sling swivels, scope mounts and ribs held in place by soft solder or epoxy. Hot-dipping a rifle with a soft-soldered front sight ramp on the barrel is a sure way to remove it, and a mistake you'll only make once.

Stainless steel

Obviously, this isn't an applied finish, but an alloy of steel. Stainless isn't. Stainless steel is formed by alloying nickel and chromium with the steel. If you add enough nickel and chromium to the steel to make it completely rust-proof, the steel cannot be hardened. If the percentages of alloying metals are kept low enough that the steel can be hardened, then it will rust.

While it does rust, stainless rusts slowly. Stainless steel is also more resistant to abrasion and heat than carbon steel. Many barrel makers only make their top-grade barrels out of stainless in order to increase durability and longevity.

Stainless cannot be blued. To make an otherwise white rifle dark, you have to use some sort of bake-on finish. Many shooters do not care if the barrel or the whole rifle is bright metal, and leave the barrel alone. Others insist on covering the stainless.

Stainless used to be an exotic steel for rifles. While the handgun market was being taken over by stainless, rifle shooters resisted. Then almost overnight it became fashionable to have a stainless rifle, and now the manufacturers make more of some models of rifles in stainless than they do in blue steel.

Hard Chrome

Hard chrome is an electrochemical deposition of chromium onto the surface of ferrous alloys. Consider your rifle

Hard chrome can be very attractive, if you like that sort of look. Hard chrome is not applied internally, so remember that your bore can still rust even when the rest is protected.

to be "cast in stone" when it goes off to be plated. Any change in the rifle will require removing chrome. The repair/change/replacement cannot be patched over. To repair a busted chrome job requires stripping the whole rifle and re-plating it. Hard chrome plating is durable and rust-resistant. Harder than the steel it protects, hard chrome resists abrasion very well. It is a stark white in appearance, not like stainless steel which can have a slight yellow or gray look to it. A very popular finish on handguns, hard chrome is not often applied to rifles. The main reason is the cost of the application. A rifle might require two or three times as much chromium as a handgun, and bigger tanks to hold the solution. While a dedicated handgunner would be willing to pop $125 to plate his sidearm, spending two or three times as much for a rifle may not be so appealing. A plater basing the bulk of his business on handguns will not buy tanks any larger than he needs to. The large tanks would be used for racks of handguns, but would only hold one or two rifles. His unit cost for labor would increase.

Despite the cost and the looks, hard chrome is the most protective finish you can apply to a rifle.

As a finish for a rifle sure to see hard use or a harsh climate, a hard chrome finish has a lot to recommend it. If you will be carrying your rifle around Alaska, call platers

Stainless is not a finish, but an alloy. And it isn't stainless, but much slower to rust. The popularity of stainless steel in rifles has not slowed down in the last couple of decades.

This Teflon/Kevlar finish from Ram-Bear Enterprises is tough as nails, impervious to solvents, and a shiny black. It faithfully reproduces all the markings on this slide.

and see if they do rifles. Not all do. Once plated, I would then use a flat-black paint to hide the whiteness of the rifle and hide it from the sharp eyes of game. Unless I was using it in the winter, in which I'd leave it "in the white" so to speak.

Teflon

Not to be confused with your frying pan, although the approach is similar. The Teflon is bonded to the steel and protects it. Teflon can be applied to both stainless and carbon steel. While Teflon does not have the abrasion resistance that hard chrome does, it will shrug off everything but direct abrasion. Teflon will not be rubbed off by sliding in

and out of a gun case, as bluing does. Teflon has to be applied by aerosol spray and then baked onto the surface. Just as with chromium, Teflon is not as popular with rifle shooters as it is with handgun shooters.

Teflon finishes do have a segment of the shooting public where it is popular. Many owners of tactical rifles like the looks of a camouflage pattern. Since the Teflon is applied with an airbrush, different colors can be used. Once baked on, the finish protects while it hides.

Ram-Bear Enterprises has a Teflon/Kevlar mixture that is tough in the extreme and resists abrasion better than standard Teflon mixes. Called Bearskin, it can be plated on a piece of sheet metal, and then the metal is continually bent until it breaks, the Bearskin does not lift off of the metal at the edges.

NP3

Offered by Robar, NP3 is a Teflon/electroless nickel mixture that plates onto the surface and offers protection and increased lubricity. The electroless nickel has Teflon particles suspended in it, and if you wear down the nickel, it simply exposes new nickel and Teflon. If you wear through the surface (hard to do!) the exposed steel still has some protection, as any resulting rust will not work its way under the NP3 edges. Unlike hard chrome it is a dark gray in appearance.

Bake-on

The bake-on finishes are variations of either epoxy resins or baked-on paints. Some combine both approaches. The bake-on finishes can hide some blemishes. One advantage to the bake-on finishes are color variations. If you want to, you can paint your rifle in a camouflage scheme. For the varmint hunter, serious big-game hunter or the precision marksman, a camouflage pattern may be just the ticket.

A bake-on finish can be patched-up when it shows wear, unlike the various platings.

Bake-on finishes can be applied by commercial companies like Robar and their Roguard and Accurate Plating and their Enduracoat. The commercial applications will go on in a coating only .001 of an inch thick, preserving the markings and look of your rifle.

You can spray on a finish yourself. Brownells offers bake-on lacquers and Teflon/Moly. The two drawbacks to

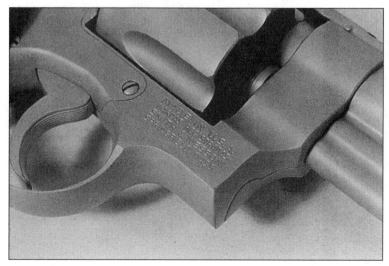

The Robar NP3 finish has a darker gray appearance than hard chrome. The Teflon particles in the plating increase lubricity and reduce friction.

When they were in business, Essential Arms Co. made good rifles. However, they made them with a light gray anodized finish. A bake-on finish can turn gray into black. To show the difference, the upper has been refinished while the lower remains its original color.

Anodizing can be any color you want. This JP Enterprize rifle has a silver-gray lower and a dark green upper. (Photo courtesy JP Enterprize)

ing anything. Strip all the parts off of the barreled action and suspend it on your rifle rotisserie. Clean and degrease the rifle. Gently heat it with a blow dryer or heat gun, until it is warm to your hand without having to touch it. If you touch it, the oils in your perspiration will prevent the finish from adhering to the surface.

Spray light, even coats onto the surface. Two or three passes, depending on the particular product. Pre-heat the oven to 350 degrees while the rifle dries for 30 minutes. Once dry, bake for 30 minutes.

The resulting finish will be reasonably durable, impervious to oils, and smooth to the touch. If it wears, sand the worn area to provide a clean surface for the new finish, and apply the patch as you did the previous coat.

One particularly useful application of the baked-on finishes is on the AR-15. If you have several uppers for a lower, as many shooters in our club do, the finishes may not all match. Or if you have an AR that is particularly hard-used and showing its wear, the steel and aluminum may be showing through the black. The cousin of one of the fellows at the gun shop enlisted in the Marine Corps a year before Desert Storm. He recounted his experiences in Boot Camp and qualifying with an M-16. "Those rifles had been cleaned so thoroughly by so many Boots that they were practically all-white." Even with a rifle worn down to bare metal in many spots, he still qualified the first time through the course for record.

The finish on AR's is "hard anodizing," and is a finish applied only to aluminum. The anodizing is an electrochemical treatment that creates a hard skin of treated aluminum on

baking on your own finish are the smell and the need to have an oven large enough to hold the barreled action. If your oven is large enough, (and the smell doesn't bother you) then the process is simple. First fabricate some sort of holding device that will keep the rifle suspended without touch-

To further show off anodizing, JP Enterprize has done this rifle in electric blue and medium green. (Photo courtesy JP Enterprize)

When it comes to proper ventilation, nothing beats a warm climate and fresh air. Provided the chemical exposure of your neighbors doesn't bring the EPA down on you. If you plan to do your own bluing, you cannot have too much ventilation.

the outside of the treated part. The color of the anodizing depends on the dye used in the treatment. It is possible to treat aluminum to be one of many different colors, but the part must be the same color, no camouflage patterns. Can you get your parts re-anodized? Yes, but not easily. Steel contaminates the chemicals, so you must remove every steel part from the aluminum being treated. On the AR this is not a problem. However, the anodizer you approach will probably be a production shop, turning out hundreds or thousands of identical parts for a manufacturer. The shop will not want to risk ruining a parts batch from their regular supplier by including your part in the batch. As a result, your part or parts will run by themselves, and you will have to pay the flat rate to treat a vat of parts. Depending on the size of their smallest vat, it could run $50 to $100 to re-anodize your AR.

Instead, use a baked-on finish. One AR manufacturer that decided to get out of the business, Essential Arms, made good rifles. However, the finish they applied (or had applied for them) was a gray anodizing. The aluminum sometimes showed up almost silver in color. To get it closer in color to the rest of the AR's out there, I used Brownells Teflon/Moly bake-on. The hard work is in getting the lower completely stripped. Once stripped, it is easy to degrease, warm, spray and bake the new finish onto the lower. If your AR has an odd color to the finish, or your upper and lower do not match, you can easily spray them to match. Or to blend in, using the baking lacquers in different colors and applying your own camouflage pattern.

If the Brownells route seems too complicated, you can always fall back on good old flat-black engine paint. However, paint tends to chip under use, and I have found that the Brownells coatings do not.

Rifle Interiors

Except for the hot-dip bluing, none of the other finishes treat the interior of your rifle. The Parkerizing is so rough the bore and chamber must be plugged to keep them from being roughened to the point of being useless. Plating, with such metals as hard chrome, electroless nickel, NP3 and Armaloy, does not migrate into holes well. Even if they did, your bore and chamber have already been manufactured to the correct dimensions. The chrome-plated bore of an AR barrel was made slightly oversized and then plated to its correct dimension. Without the over-sized start, the .0004 inches thickness of the plating would greatly increase pressures.

The spray-on finishes, like the Roguard, Enduraguard, Bearskin, other Teflon finishes and the bake-on finishes from Brownells are only applied to the exterior of your rifle.

If you want the interior to be protected, you have two choices: settle for hot-dip bluing or start with a stainless steel rifle.

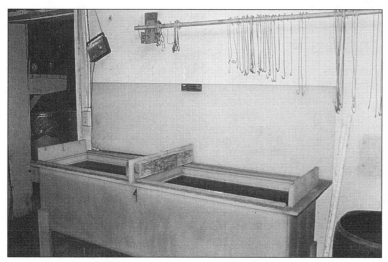

Everywhere you turn in a commercial refinishing shop you find tanks of solutions. Some hot, some cold, some acidic, others oil. There are even tanks of clean and filtered water for rinsing the rifles.

CHAPTER 12

Accuracy Testing

You go to the range for one of two reasons: you either want to test yourself, or test the rifle.

If you are testing yourself, then you would shoot from whatever positions your competition requires or hunting experiences have called for. You shoot at a target that is the same size as the acceptable target you are shooting at in a match or during a hunt. To practice for many rifle matches you stand up and shoot offhand. One of the favorite activities of the members at my gun club is offhand shooting at the gongs on the rifle range. We compete against each other for shortest time to the first hit, number of hits in a row, or fastest string. The scoring is simple: hit or miss.

To properly test the rifle, you obviously need the rifle and ammunition. You also need a stable shooting platform, targets, protection for yourself, and some way to store and sort through the information you are generating. You also need a consistent technique to generate consistent results. If you are testing the rifle there is only one position to shoot from. Sitting at a bench. Preferably a solid bench, with solid, padded rests on which to place the rifle. To precisely test the rifle, you want to eliminate all of the variables and errors that you, the shooter, would introduce. The only way to really do that is with a machine rest. However, you can come quite close to the level of accuracy a machine rest would get out of a rifle, using the proper equipment and technique. The target you should shoot at would not be a hit-or-miss target like a gong, but a paper target that measures the rifle's performance. Testing two rifles, or two brands of ammunition, and determining that any combination would shoot a group smaller than the heart/lung area of a deer doesn't tell you much. Hitting the gong 10 times in 10 shots doesn't tell you if one group of five

To shoot well, you need a stable bench, a solid rest and patience. This is only a demo, the actual shooting line is too dark to take photos properly. Notice the elbow pad, and the fact that the bench is too low for me. Your bench should be high enough that you can sit upright to shoot.

shots was significantly smaller than the other. Only paper will do that for you.

If your club has solid benches, resting on a concrete slab, then you are a lucky shooter. Do whatever you have to in order to stay a member of that club. Offer to maintain the benches and shooting line if you have to. What if your club does not have such amenities? Offer to build a good bench. Construct it out of 4-by-4 posts and a double thickness of plywood. Use pressure-treated lumber if you can. If not, then give the bench several coats of outdoor porch and deck

While ringing the gongs is fun, it doesn't tell you as much about the rifle and ammo as it does about you. These are our club's 100-yard practice gongs, which we work over with handguns, shotgun slugs and rifles. For a match, the club uses falling plates a quarter the size of these.

The Bald Eagle front rest is engineered better and built better than some firearms I've had to test-fire. Solid, adjustable and built for the ages, it is perfect for accurate shooting. The white-tipped rod is the front stop. The forearm on the Remington is a little small, and the stop bears against the barrel if I try to use it.

Here the jaws of the Bald Eagle front rest have been adjusted to fit snugly on the handguards of this AR-15.

The top of the Bald Eagle rest has a padded rest with an adjustable opening. You can move the jaws back and forth for an even fit on the forearm of your rifle. Do not rest the barrel against the rest, as here, or any other obstacle. Doing so will change both group size and group location.

Supporting the buttstock is a Bald Eagle rear bag. The angle of the stock and the pad allows you to adjust point of impact by sliding the rifle slightly forward or backward on the bag.

paint. When it comes to benches, heavier is better. A bench that is heavy enough does not need a concrete slab. To keep the mud down, spread wood chips or gravel.

Sitting down to shoot and resting your elbows on the bench is more accurate than standing, but just barely. And just barely comfortable. The rifle should rest firmly without you having to hold it. Invest in or build shooting bags or a shooting rest. You can make a rest out of scrap lumber. Design your rest to take some padding. Resting the rifle on a hard object can alter group size or location. It can also dent or mar the forearm of your stock. A fabricated bench rest is only a compromise, done to save money. I'm all for saving money, but sometimes money saved by making things yourself is false economy. You save money by building a rest. What it costs you is extra time fiddling and adjusting the rifle and rest until you are on the target. The time lost and the effort spent adjusting and re-adjusting the rifle means less time spent shooting and less information garnered.

The best rest for your rifle is an adjustable rest. As a professional gunsmith, I found that a top-grade shooting rest made a big difference in comfort and ease of range testing. The Bald Eagle rest is top-of-the-line. Made of aircraft aluminum and fine grain cast iron, it is solid, adjustable and comfortable to use. I don't have to squirm around on the bench to get the crosshairs right where I want them. Having said that, I have to admit to using a front rest made of plastic. Why? The plastic one can ride in my truck 365 days a year and not rust. If I need to do a quick zero check, I can drag it out of the truck and use it. Would I subject the Bald Eagle rest to the same ill-treatment? No. Would I try to sort out which rifle, or which load, is the most accurate without it? Again, no.

To squeeze the last bit of accuracy from your rifle tests, you need several shooting bags or pads. The front rest needs a bag for the forearm to rest on. The butt of the rifle needs another bag, called a "rabbit ear" bag. The rear bag is angled. The angle lets you slide the rifle back and forth to roughly adjust the elevation of the sights on the target. Some front rests have a forward stop. The stop gives you a reference point. With the tip of the forearm up against the stop, the rifle is always in the same position on the shooting rest. You are always sitting in the same posture and position. To use a front rest with a stop, press the rifle forward to the stop. Then move the rear bag around until the sights are on

This AR is set up in the bags and rest for comfortable, accurate shooting for a right-hander. In the left of the photo is the elbow pad, and on the far side of the rifle is a towel for the left arm.

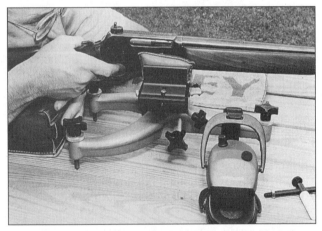

Some lever-action rifles shoot best from a rest when the receiver is supported, not the forearm. Apparently, such rifles are sensitive to the upward pressure from the rest that does not exist when you are shooting offhand. Also on the bench are the Ridgeline "Pro Ears" that I have found so useful. Wear protection, save your hearing!

the target. For fine elevation adjustments, you use your left hand (for right-handed shooters) to squeeze the rear bag. After the recoil from shooting, push the rifle forward until it touches the stop. Check your sights and squeeze the rear bag to get the crosshairs in the center again, and repeat.

You need two elbow pads. You can use folded-up towels, or sections of firm rubber padding. These pads protect your elbows from the tabletop. These pads are for comfort and to fight fatigue, not recoil. Unless you are shooting a large caliber rifle, the recoil won't drag your elbows across the table. If your elbows hurt, or your arms are tired from resting on the hard wood, you are not going to be able to concentrate on your shooting. Not everyone feels the need for the next-to-last pad that I use. Some rifles, especially large-caliber ones, do not shoot their best with your left hand at the rear bag. In order to control the recoil, you must grasp the forearm. I designed a block and pad to sit under my left hand when grasping the forearm.

The last pad does not go on the bench, it goes on you. Yes, I know we are all tough guys (and gals) and recoil

doesn't hurt us. Like heck it doesn't. Even if you don't think it does, recoil tires you and makes good shooting increasingly difficult. If you want to see what large amounts of heavy recoil do to shooting skills, plan a trip to a bowling pin match with shotgun side events. To knock the pins off the table takes buckshot and to down the falling steel plates takes slugs. The fastest shooter wins, with many entries allowed. Even the best shooters pace themselves. After 50 or 60 factory 12-gauge loads, even a big tough shooter looks whipped. If all you do is fold a towel and put it between the butt of the rifle and your shoulder when you sit down to test your rifle, you increase the number of shots you can take before your shooting skills suffer. I have had great success with PAST recoil pads. Made of a space-age synthetic, the PAST pad will take the sting out of the recoil of many calibers.

You need paper targets to shoot at. Target design can be a personal thing. I know successful hunters who view the expense of using anything other than a paper plate as a target as frippery. The plates are cheap (even cheaper used!) and are the same size as the vitals of a deer. The thing I've noticed about such hunters is that they are much better hunters than shooters. After all, if the farthest deer they have ever shot has been 35 yards away, how much accuracy do they need?

We are interested in a more precise view of things.

I use two types of targets, aiming-point and grids. I spent some time developing them on my computer, and printing out test targets to try at the range. The aiming-point targets come in two sizes. The first is a scope target. It has a one-inch white square in the center, with a black square border one inch thick. At 10 power on a target scope I can place the crosshairs right in the white center square. With the center square and border each being 1 inch, I have a quick gauge by which to measure my groups. The second aiming-point target is for iron sights. It has a 2-inch white square center with a 2-inch black border. It is large enough to see in broad daylight, but not so large I can let the sights "wander" around the bull. The grid target is a checkerboard of 1-inch squares. I use it when testing handguns in the Ransom rest and rifles in the machine rest. Since the mechanism does the aiming I don't need an aiming point, and the one-inch squares quickly tell me group size.

I print each from the computer onto regular paper, and then take them to the copy shop and make a bunch of copies. The master print includes spaces for all the information I need to keep. I used to keep the targets, but after I had several hundred on hand storage became a problem. Now I simply measure the group size and record those measurements in my shooting log. These targets are cheap and easily made. If you don't have a computer, you can sit down with ruled paper, a straightedge and a felt-tip marker. The size is convenient, and you can staple as many as you need to a target holder without feeling like you are pasting up a billboard. And you will need a bunch of them. One target per group, to be exact. To see the groups after you have fired them, use a spotting scope. Mine is an old Freeland scope that was once used for small-bore rifle shooting. A spotting scope gives you a better view of the target. You can have more magnification in a spotting scope than in a rifle scope, aiding your view of the target you just fired. Rather than straining your eyes through the rifle scope, or walking down to the targets and back, get more glass.

Protection of your eyes and ears is vital. I recall one instance of going to the range with my father when I was just a kid. We were shooting .22 rifles, and even back then we had glasses and muffs on. A fellow club member showed up to sight in his deer rifle. After he had touched off a few rounds of the .300 Savage, my father went over and offered the fellow some ear plugs. "No, that's all right," he said "After a while you get used to it." As we walked back, I heard my father remark "Yea, you get used to it by going deaf." The noise of shooting will damage your hearing if you do not wear proper protection. Puffs of cotton, wadded-up cleaning patches or empty pistol cases do not protect your hearing. Wear muffs or foam plugs. If you shoot on a covered firing line as I do, you may want to wear plugs and muffs. One drawback to hearing protection is that you cannot hear people talking to you. Invariably, when you peel back the muff to listen, someone else on the line will touch off a 7mm Magnum. I avoid that problem with Ridgelines "Pro-Ears." The Pro-Ears have electronic circuitry and external microphones built into them. The mics pick up outside noise and transmit the noise to the speakers in the muffs. If a noise occurs that is too loud for your hearing, the circuitry protects your hearing. Most electronic muffs either clip off the extra volume, or shut down for a split second. The Pro-Ears compress the noise down to an acceptable volume. You still hear what happened, but it is prevented from being too loud.

As your last piece of equipment, you need a shooting log. A loose-leaf binder with standard notebook paper in it will do. If you have a home computer you can experiment with designs of columns and boxes for the information you need. You should make entries into your log each time you go to the range. Include the day and time, the weather, which rifle you are using and what ammunition. Note how much ammunition you fire, and the results you obtain. If you are testing for accuracy, then be sure to save the targets long enough to measure the groups, and enter the measurements into the log. If you are testing ammunition over a chronograph, be sure to list the velocities along with the lot

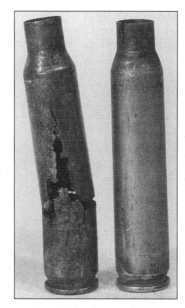

Tired, old brass, reloads and borrowed ammo will not tell you how well your rifle performs.

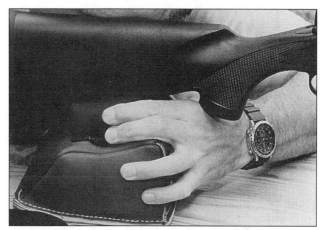

With the rifle adjusted so the crosshairs are on the target, gentle pressure on the rear bag adjusts the crosshairs dead center on your aiming point.

To get good results, you need to use good ammo. While the military surplus on the right is good for plinking and practice, you need to use the match ammo, or your actual hunting ammo, to determine just how accurate a rifle is or isn't.

While the left hand adjusts the rear bag, your right hand exerts gentle, even pressure on the wrist of the stock as you slowly take up the slack and then fire the rifle.

numbers of the ammo tested. Why go to all this trouble? A rifle can be a lifetime investment, if you treat it properly. By keeping track of your practice and testing sessions, you can tell how your rifle is shooting. Is it shooting as well as it did before? Has the accuracy dropped off or improved? Don't just rely on your memory. Keep a log.

So there you are, at the range with 100 pounds of rifle, bags, pads, ammunition, spotting scope and assorted other gear. That doesn't include the weight of the bench. How do you test the rifle? To sit at the bench and shoot you must be comfortable. Take your time and get in a good position. Sit upright. You don't want to be in a "sitting prone" position. You've seen it, where the shooter is sitting down but his upper body is practically resting on the benchtop. Breathing is difficult in this position, and your neck gets tired quickly. Plant your feet on the ground or concrete. Changing your foot position can shift the point of impact. Do not rest your body against the edge of the bench. Rest the butt of the rifle against your shoulder, and move the front rest under the rifle's forearm. Look through the scope and move the rest on the bench until the target is in the crosshairs. Slide the rear rest under the butt of the stock until the rifle is supported by both rests. Fine-tune your adjustments until the crosshairs are on your aiming point. Snuggle up to the rifle and aim at the target. Set

your elbow pads down to keep your elbows off the table. With a solid rest and a high-powered scope you should be able to see the effects of your heartbeat in the crosshairs.

Sit in the same position at the bench for each shot. Practice by dry-firing. Make sure the rifle is empty, and close the bolt. Snuggle up behind the rifle and place the butt solidly into the pocket of your shoulder. Grasp the wrist of the stock and place your finger on the trigger. Line the crosshairs up on the target. Reach under the stock with your left hand and squeeze the rear bag until the crosshairs are centered on the target. Let your breath out and continue pressing the trigger until the striker falls. The press should only take a few seconds. Work the bolt, take a couple of breaths, and then repeat. With practice you can "call" your shots. Calling a shot means you can tell exactly where in the target your crosshairs were when the striker fell. Once you can call your shots dry-firing, it is time to go to live ammo.

I am leaving out any talk of dealing with the wind or mirage. I do this not because wind drift is trivial (it isn't!) but because it is outside the scope of a book on gunsmithing. If at all possible, do your test-firing on a calm day or early in the morning when the wind is likely to be down. My range is completely ringed by tall berms, and the wind is not at all predictable. Not a problem, as the wind is not often

The left round is an M-856 Tracer, not known for its accuracy. The center round was the one chambered after a case separation, and the right one has had the bullet set back into the case. None of these will shoot accurately, and the use of reloads to determine accuracy of a rifle should be considered suspect.

Does your rifle change its point of impact or group size with the muzzle brake off? It shouldn't, but you must test to be sure.

More suspect ammo. I had a customer complain about the accuracy of his Remington 7400 while using just such a mix. Two different lots of 1918 production ammo, and a 1934 surplus round, and the last one liable to pierced primers! Fed current sporting ammo, his gun shot very well, and he later bagged a buck with it.

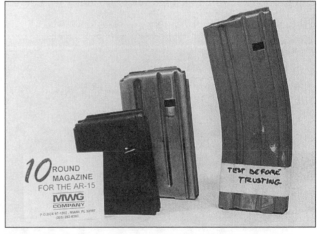

For a competition rifle, you should check group size and point of impact not only when the barrel is clean, but after it has fired several magazines of ammunition. Otherwise, you may get halfway through a match and find your accuracy is deteriorating.

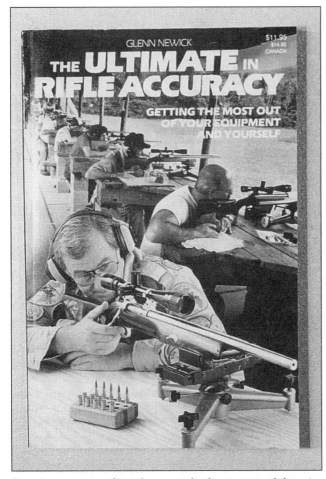

Benchrest competitors have worked out many elaborate tricks to wring the last bit of accuracy out of a rifle. However, some of the things they do don't help the hunter. One Benchrest technique, demonstrated on the cover of Glenn Newick's useful book, is to only touch the trigger when firing. This is fine on a .222 Remington or .22 PPC, but imagine the results of doing this with a .300 Magnum!

The Lahti shooting rest. By holding the rifle consistently and mechanically, you can remove the shooter as a variable. Well, almost, as you still have to adjust the scope and press the trigger.

strong enough to drift bullets during their 100-yard journey.

How much shooting is enough? Tailor the amount of shooting you do to the information you need to know. If you are checking your rifle to see if the zero has changed since the last hunting session, a single three-shot group will do. If you are final-testing a rifle and ammunition combination to see if it is accurate enough for competition, then you should shoot five, 10-shot groups. For general testing in between those two conditions, I fire three, six-shot groups. Why three? Because I can't get more than that out of a box of ammo. It isn't a matter of division, but fouling.

When I was doing accuracy testing for handguns some years ago, I found out that many handguns had sudden increases in group size switching from one ammunition to another. I was using a Ransom rest, and the accuracy would settle down after a couple of groups were fired of the new brand. I only had to see this a couple of times to realize that the fouling for each brand was different. Until the new brand had blown out or overlaid the old fouling, accuracy suffered. I had read about fouling shifting group size when reading about benchrest shooting, but had not seen it until then.

When switching brands or ammo lots in testing rifles, I first clean the barrel. Once the barrel is clean and cool, I fire

The rear of the Lahti rest has a socket for the buttstock, and a velcro-secured strap to hold the rifle down. Unless you are going to be using a .577 Nitro Mag, you do not have to install the extra recoil buffer.

With the front arm of the Lahti hooked over the shooting bench, adjust the control knobs until the scope is perfectly on your aiming point. Do not touch the stock with your face.

a fouling shot. One round out of a box of 20 leaves 19 rounds. Three, six-shot groups take 18 rounds, leaving one round as a spare. I could shoot five-shot groups, but that leaves four spares.

Testing for competition purposes is more rigorous. To test for accuracy in a USPSA/IPSC rifle competition, I will fire at least 10, six-shot groups. If the last group is the same size as the first, then I don't test slow-fire any more. If the last group is larger, then I continue testing until group size is unacceptable for competition. I then plot group size and point of impact changes for future match use. I have only had to do this for one rifle, and I replaced the barrel soon after going to all this work.

If the group size has not changed (which is usually the case with a good barrel) then I test it for changes from heat. Practical rifle competition is a rapid-fire sport. I test a potential rifle by firing three, six-shot groups from the bench. Without cleaning or cooling it, I then fire a magazine in rapid-fire practice on other targets or on the gongs. I then sit down and fire another set of three, six-shot groups. A good barrel will have a minor change of zero and group size on the second set of targets. A great barrel will show no change.

How much accuracy is enough? That depends on the rifle, ammo, and your needs and ability. An expensive rifle with a guarantee of accuracy must deliver as promised. A hand-me-down hunting rifle may be doing well if it does three or four inches. Be sure of the ammunition and yourself before starting to blame the rifle. One day, when I went to the gun club, one of the other members was there with an expensive rifle. It was a purpose-built, imported and expen-

sive sniper rifle. He was not having fun, because his thousands of dollars worth of rifle had not shot a group under an inch yet. (As I recall, the rifle ran him right around $5,000, without the scope. The scope added another $1,200. You can imagine his distress at its lackluster performance.) I asked him if he had broken-in the bore, and his reply was "yes." What ammo? He showed me a box of Federal Match .308 Winchester. Hmm. The rifle and ammo should be capable of much better than an inch. I sat down at the bench, adjusted the rests a bit, dry-fired the rifle a few times, and then fired a five-shot group that measured .695 inches.

Happy as a kid on Christmas, he sat down to try it himself. Later, he showed me several targets, including one that was three shots under half an inch. The rifle was up to it, but the shooter wasn't sure he was. If he had been using a lever-action with a four-power scope on it, chambered in .30-30, his expectations of a group under an inch would have been completely out of line.

So how much is "enough"? Most out of the box bolt-action hunting rifles should do under two inches with factory ammo. Some will do an inch, but you have to search for the ammo they like. Hunting levers, pumps and autos will probably shoot larger groups than 2 inches, with some exceptions. Browning BARs tend to shoot better than 2 inches, as do Remington pumps.

A trued-action rifle with lapped bolt surfaces should do under an inch. The same rifle with a premium barrel had better do under an inch, or someone somewhere forgot an important step. It should easily do under half an inch, with the right shooter sitting behind it.

If you want to truly test the rifle/ammunition combination without the variable of the shooter, you need to use a machine rest. The Lahti company makes such a rest. The Lahti rest sits on a shooting bench and you fire the rifle by remote control. The hydraulics of the standard unit are good until you get to .577 Nitro, and then you need to install the extra cylinder.

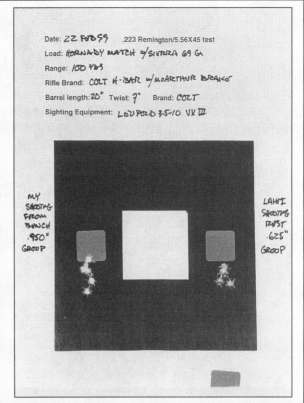

Date: 22 FEB 99   .223 Remington/5.56X45 test
Load: HORNADY MATCH w/SIERRA 69 Gr
Range: 100 yds
Rifle Brand: COLT H-BAR w/McARTHUR BRAKE
Barrel length: 20" Twist: 7° Brand: COLT
Sighting Equipment: LEUPOLD 3.5-10 VX III

MY SHOOTING FROM BENCH .950" GROUP

LAHTI SHOOTING REST .625" GROOP

Without touching the stock, press the trigger. Lahti makes a remote trigger actuator, but I found reaching around to press the trigger easier and faster. Once the round is fired, work the bolt and use the knobs to tweak the reticle into perfect alignment. Fire again.

Using my Colt H-Bar and Hornady ammo, I tested the Lahti shooting rest. Off the bags, I printed a .950-inch group, respectable but not the best this rifle has done. With the Lahti, I fired a .625-inch group. If you must know the absolute truth about a rifle, use the Lahti rest.

CHAPTER 13

Recoil Reduction

"That wasn't so bad, let me try it again."

Me at 14, trying a 12-gauge shotgun with duck loads for the first time. Two shots gave me a flinch so bad that I couldn't hit anything the rest of the day with my 20-gauge.

The first thing you have to realize is that recoil hurts. Oh, we all know shooters who say recoil doesn't bother them, but they are kidding themselves. When I started shooting seriously (not just plinking, but practicing with the idea of improving my skills), I had already spent years reading writers such as Elmer Keith, who proclaimed that with diligent practice recoil could be overcome.

As a skinny kid reading about his large caliber cannons, and shooting my "lowly" .30-06, I could not imagine getting used to recoil. Later, I found that after a while working at a gun shop and test-firing rifles and shotguns I had gotten to the point where recoil was no longer a big deal. But, I found there were subtle ways recoil hurts.

Even though each shot did not hurt by then, my ability to shoot tight groups decreased during the progress of each range day. Oh, I would start out shooting well, but after a few hours my groups were average at best. Recoil was wearing me down, even though it didn't hurt anymore.

Recoil can hurt your shooting, too. If you don't reduce it, you may never know that the best rifle/ammo combination you ever tried was the last one you shot that day, when you were tired and couldn't shoot well. The fatiguing effects of recoil can build a bad habit like flinching. Or, it may dampen your enthusiasm for shooting your expensive new mountain rifle that is so delightfully light to carry.

Don't let anyone tell you that recoil doesn't hurt, because it does. If they want to kid themselves, fine. But don't let someone talk you into more caliber, or a lighter rifle than you want because "you'll get used to the recoil." In this regard recoil is like muzzle blast. You may never notice the muzzle blast when you are focused on a big game animal, and you may tell anyone who asks "I never heard the shot." But that does not mean the noise never happened. Your hearing is damaged even by the shots you don't notice. Likewise, your ability to concentrate on your shooting is worn down even when the recoil doesn't hurt for each shot.

All other things being equal, the steel buttplate will hurt more to shoot than the rubber pad will. Recoil hurts, and it hurts your shooting skills even when you think it doesn't.

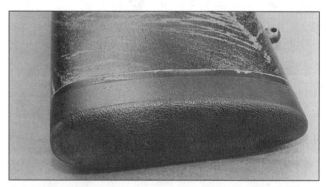

A thick pad like the one on this 10-pound tactical rifle will make recoil no big deal.

One approach to reducing recoil is to go to a smaller caliber. This Winchester 9422 would make a great practice companion to a .30-30 '94. It would also be a great way to introduce a new shooter to the sport, at low cost and no recoil. (Photo courtesy U.S. Repeating Arms Co.)

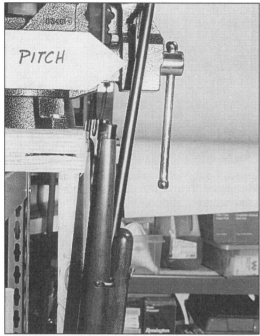

The pitch of the buttplate effects how the stock moves under recoil. The greater the pitch, the more likely the stock is to rise during recoil and hit your face. The Ruger (ca. 1999) nearer the camera, has less pitch than the Winchester (ca. 1942) and will be "softer" to shoot.

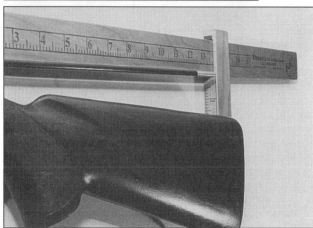

Drop also increases the pivot of the stock under recoil. The Winchester has almost 1-1/2 inches of drop. Designed for iron sights, the drop becomes worse if you install a scope, as your face has to sit over the stock to see through the scope. The room the stock has to get a running start before it hits your face can lead to painful recoil in a large caliber.

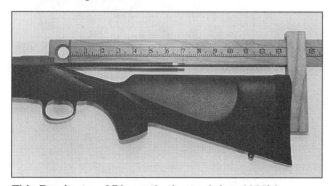

This Remington ADL synthetic stock (ca. 1999) has about 5/8 inches of drop. Designed for scope use, the recoil your face feels is negligible for calibers less than .308/.30-06.

What can you do to lessen the effects of recoil? First of all, there are some things you cannot change, and the laws of physics rank right up there with death and taxes. A light rifle is going to kick more than a heavy one, and a large caliber is likewise going to kick more than a small one. If you combine the two, you can have a real problem. Stock design can magnify recoil. The aspects of stock design that magnify felt recoil are: large drop in the stock, a narrow buttplate, a buttplate made of a hard material, a narrow comb, and a short stock.

Of these, only the hard buttplate and short stock can be corrected without buying a new stock. Too much drop pivots the rifle around your shoulder and into your face. A narrow comb focuses the recoil into your face. A narrow buttplate focuses the recoil into your shoulder. A hard buttplate does not give against your shoulder. Obviously, the opposites of these factors reduce felt recoil.

A short stock and a hard buttplate can be corrected with a rubber recoil pad. The other faults can only be corrected by replacing the stock, unless you are a competitive shooter who does not care what his stock looks like. I have seen stocks built up by the shooter with fiberglass, epoxy and plastic wood until they fit comfortably. Some shooters then take the custom-modified stock and get a good-looking one built on the identical pattern. Others shoot the rifle just as ugly as it is. I guess the latter shooters are looking to gain a competitive advantage by turning the stomachs of their competition.

Recoil pads come in a variety of styles and colors, and several materials. The oldest style, and one that many shooters like, is the "waffle" pattern. Viewed from the side, the recoil pad appears to be composed of crossed rubber strips bonded together and to a hard plastic plate. The honeycomb of openings allows the rubber to flex under recoil, dampening the thump to your shoulder. The waffle pattern commonly comes with a white layer of rubber or plastic in it, called the "white line." Many shooters like it. Many do not. The most expensive of custom rifles never have it. Whether to "white line" or not is purely a personal choice in looks. It has nothing to do with performance.

Solid pads have always had a following. Some prefer the solid pad to avoid the need to clean dirt, mud and gunk out of the voids of the waffle pad. Others prefer the solid pad for larger calibers, to avoid the prospect of the pad bottoming out against their shoulder under recoil. Many "solid" pads have a hollow inside them, for the look of a solid pad but the softness of a waffle pad.

Pachmayr Decelerators have a hollow and high-tech wizardry. The Decelerator is made of a special synthetic that

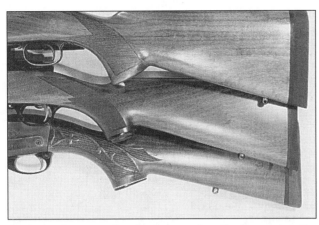

Of these three stocks, the top one has the longest pull and the thickest pad. All other things being equal, it will kick less than the other two. Not by much, but every little bit helps.

You can get recoil pads in a variety of materials, construction and colors. The waffle pad has a white-line spacer, a feature that is apparently diminishing in popularity. The solid pad is a Kick-Eeze pad made of Sorbothane, and very good on heavy-kicking rifles.

looks like rubber but is softer. It has the softness of a waffle pad but does not bottom out like waffle pads do.

Another synthetic pad is the Kick-Eeze, made of Sorbothane. It is somewhat firmer than the Pachmayr Decelerator, and I have used Kick-Eeze pads on my hardest-kicking and high-volume guns.

Installing a pad is simple in theory and a mess in the execution. Recoil pads come oversized, and you grind away the excess rubber. You, the stock, the grinder and the room will all become a mess. When I was installing pads as a full-time gunsmith, I would only do pads one day a week. I would save up all the pad jobs for the week and grind them on a single day. Then I would sweep and vacuum, and use compressed air, to clean up the mess.

To install a recoil pad you will need a straightedge, pencil, belt or disc sander, breathing mask and protective glasses (preferably with side shields), hearing protection, masking tape, a felt-tip marker and the pad. You may need a quarter-inch drill, dowels and epoxy. Afterwards you will need a vacuum cleaner or Shop-Vac, a shower and a change of clothes. A shop apron will not do much to keep you clean. Drops cloths over everything in the

room might help in clean-up. If you still want to do it, here is the process.

Measure the width of the buttstock of your rifle at the buttplate. Order a pad just larger than this dimension. If you order a pad that is too large you will have to grind off too much rubber. If you order one too small you will not cover the buttplate surface. Remove the action from the stock. Remove the rear sling swivel stud. Remove your old pad or buttplate. If the original buttplate was curved, you must straighten the butt of the rifle. Stand the buttstock up against a wall, with the comb towards the wall. Measure the distance from the wall to the tip of the forend. Use the belt sander to sand the buttplate surface of the stock straight. Stand the stock against the wall to check your progress. Measure the distance from the wall to the forend tip. When the butt is correctly flat this distance should not change from its previous measurement. Also, view the stock from its bottom and make sure the new flat surface isn't tipped side-to-side.

Seal the sanded surface with a stock sealer. Once dry, clamp the stock in a padded vise with the butt towards you and the comb up. Take your straightedge and strike two horizontal lines across the buttplate surface. Measure across

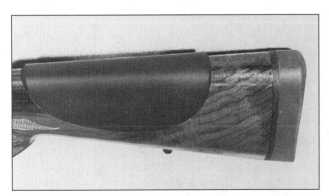

On a really hard-kicking rifle (I draw the "hard-kicking" line at .375 H&H. More than that and I won't shoot it if it doesn't have rubber on the back.) you might want to add protection for your face with a comb pad. This "Cheekeeze" (from Brownells, who else?) takes the sting out of the big guns.

Given a choice I will install a solid pad, such as the Pachmayr Decelerators on the middle and rear stock. But, a waffle pad still works well, so I haven't changed the one the front stock came with.

To fit a pad you need a belt sander, or a belt and disk sander combo like this one. The sanding is incredibly messy. You'll need eye, ear and breathing protection, and a way to clean up the mess when you are done.

these lines, divide the distance, and mark the centers. Draw a vertical line through the centers. This is your centerline. On the back of the package you will find the pad screwhole dimensions. Take the top one, from the top hole to the top of the pad and subtract .200 inches. Mark your centerline down this distance. Then take the between-holes distance and mark down from the first hole.

At this point you may need the drill and dowels. If your new holes come closer to the old holes than a screw-shaft diameter, you will have to plug the old holes. Take a moment and see if you can cheat. Will the new pad work in the old holes? No? It didn't work very often for me, either, but I check every time just in case. If the old holes work out you can skip the next step.

To plug the old holes, drill them their full depth with a quarter-inch drill. Mix your epoxy and place some in the holes. Take a dowel just under a quarter-inch in diameter. I found that Mossberg shotgun duck plug dowels worked perfectly for this job. Without the duck plugs, get a dowel from the local hardware store. Scrape the dowel with a knife to create room for the epoxy, and tap the dowel into place with a hammer. Let the epoxy set. Trim the dowel off and sand it flush.

Drill your new holes in the marked locations. To place the screws in the pad, press a drift punch in from the rear of

the pad, raising a bubble on the pad surface. Slit this bubble with a razor blade. Rub the threads of the screw on a bar of soap to lubricate them. Place a drop of synthetic oil on the slit in the pad, and press the screw through the hole. The oil lubricates the screw and screwdriver and keeps them from tearing the rubber of the pad. Tighten the screws into the wood. Your pad should now be flush and vertical.

Place strips of tape on the stock, butting up against the overhang of the new recoil pad. Use three layers of masking tape, pressed smoothly into place. Use the felt-tip marker to darken the surface of the masking tape.

Now comes the messy part. Put on your mask, muffs and glasses. Turn on the belt sander. Stand to the side of the belt sander, close enough to look directly down on the area of the pad being ground. If you have one, direct a strong light into the belt to see the pad and belt. Hold the stock firmly and with the side of the buttstock parallel to the belt. Press the recoil pad against the moving belt. Do not press hard, let the belt do the work. Move the pad away from the belt and

The left pad is a waffle pad factory-installed on a .458 Winchester Magnum. It isn't enough, and I will soon switch the .458 to another stock and put a Kick-Eeze Sorbothane pad on it like the one on the right.

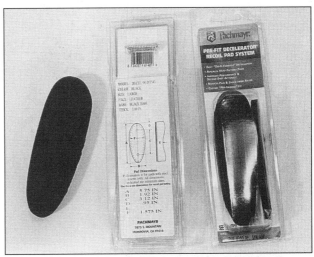

To save the hassle of fitting a pad, Pachmayr makes a pre-fit pad you can install on some rifles. Instead of being oversized, the pre-fit pad is already contoured and has the screw holes on the factory-stock hole spacing. Just take off the old and put on the new.

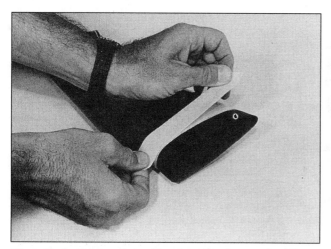

Place three layers of masking tape on the stock, adjacent to the new recoil pad but not overlapping it.

Mag-na-port has been in the recoil reduction business for more than 20 years. If you send them your rifle you can be sure it will be well cared for and shipped back pronto.

look at the ground area. It will be a flattened section of the pad edge. You do not want to leave your pad flat, so now you have to make the edge curved. Turn the stock at a slight angle and press it against the belt. As the belt cuts the rubber, slowly rotate the stock so the ground edge matches the contour of the stock.

Stop frequently to inspect the edge of the pad. You must keep the belt parallel to the surface of the stock, including the heel and toe of the stock. If you tilt the stock you will either cut the pad at an angle away from the wood, or you will "kiss" the stock with the belt and mar the finish. Continue grinding the rubber until you begin hitting the masking tape. The ink from the felt-tip marker will get ground away by the belt. If you have ground away more in one area than another, the ink will not be evenly removed.

Once the ink is ground off evenly all the way around, stop the belt sander. Remove the tape, and re-apply a single layer. Ink it with the felt-tip marker. Now begins the delicate part of the job. With only a single layer of masking tape as your margin of error, grind the recoil pad down until you have removed the ink from the tape. The real daredevils will take this one step further and use a single

strip of cellophane tape. Brave men (or women) and steady hands prevail in this step!

I never tried to prove my manhood this way, preferring to chicken out and go to the file. The relatively coarse belt sander has left its marks in the hard plastic base of the recoil pad. Take a medium file and remove them. Place your left hand on the stock with your thumb sticking towards the pad. Place the file on the pad with its safe edge towards your thumb. Move your left hand until your thumb acts as a stop on the file, not allowing it to touch the wood. Gently file the belt sander marks out of the plastic.

If you are working on a stock that is finished except for the application of a stock sealer, then you can use sandpaper instead of the file. Do not use your thumb as a guide and stop. Sand the pad and stock at the same time, for a perfect fit.

Pachmayr has recently saved us all a great deal of trouble in pad fitting. They now make pads available already cut to the dimensions of the stock. If you have a modern production rifle that matches the list available from Pachmayr, you can simply remove your old recoil pad and replace it with a Pachmayr Decelerator pad. The pre-fits are not available for

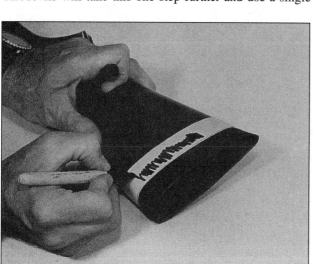

Mark the tape with a magic marker so you can see when the belt begins scuffing the tape as you grind down the stock.

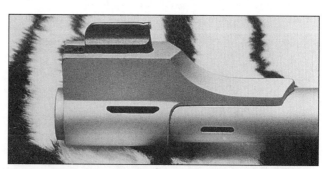

The original Mag-na-porting used EDM to burn slots through the barrel. There is no discoloration, no burrs and no change in velocity or accuracy. If your rifle is a Ruger with a barrel-band front sight, MNP will port it. Other bands may be rejected. If the band is not properly installed, the gases can force their way between the band and barrel, and blow the band off. MNP doesn't want disappointed customers, and will send back a barrel they are not confident in.

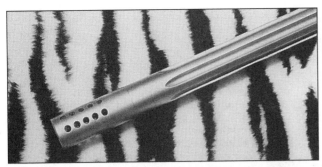

The newest in recoil reduction from MNP is the Mag-na-brake. It is more efficient than their original porting, but at the expense of noise and muzzle blast.

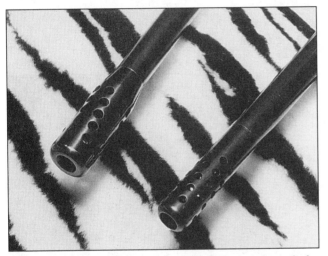

While they used to offer two sizes, MNP now does their brakes in a barrel-diameter profile. The marginal increase in effectiveness did not warrant the larger number of product inventory. Besides, most shooters wanted the smaller diameter ones.

Just in case you were wondering, brakes do work on Ruger Mini-14s. Every other AR has a brake, while hardly any Minis do. The basic reason is that most ARs come with barrels already threaded, while the Ruger has to be threaded to install the brake. This Mini-14 shoots as if it were a really loud .22 rimfire.

rifles that come from the factory with a plastic buttplate, only those that have factory recoil pads.

As good as the best pads are, you can do more to reduce felt recoil. The oldest method of reducing felt recoil is to stuff a wadded-up shirt or towel between the stock and your shoulder. The oldest effective method of reducing actual recoil is to send your rifle off to Mag-na-port. Using Electrical Discharge Machining, they will cut slots through your barrel to vent the powder gases. EDM was developed by Larry Kelly to machine the tough alloys used in rocket engines. EDM uses what amounts to a huge sparkplug to burn a hole through your barrel. At an extremely high electrical charge, a spark will jump from the carbon electrode to your barrel. The spark erodes the tough steel of a rifle barrel, but slowly without heat or stress. The spark can only jump a few thousandths of an inch, so the shape of the electrode will be faithfully reproduced through your barrel. There are no burrs kicked up, no change in bluing, no increase in noise, no loss of velocity and no change in accuracy. Without a close inspection, no one will be able to tell your rifle has been changed.

The drawback? The small nozzles (for they are rocket nozzles) cannot compensate for all the recoil you feel. They are effective, but if you want more recoil reduction you need to get a more efficient method. To avoid large, multi-ported comps I have used multiple slots of Mag-na-porting on pistols and revolvers. While effective, it is easier and more cost effective on a rifle to go to a muzzle brake.

To cause more reduction of recoil you need to vent more gas, and for that you need something besides just more ports. You need a muzzle brake. A properly-designed and installed muzzle brake can make an impressive difference in felt recoil. As a rough guide, think of reducing your recoil caliber steps. If you Mag-na-port your .30-06, it will feel more like a .270. If you put a brake on it, that rifle will feel like a .25-06, or softer. Can you go even farther? Yes, I have seen muzzle brakes so efficient that you can (and I did) fire a .375 H&H one-handed. I can see someone in the back getting antsy about getting something for nothing. Sir, you are correct, you cannot get something for nothing. What the muzzle brake costs you is a busier muzzle, more noise and lots of vented gases streaming by. Sometimes lots of noise and gas. The most effective brakes can peel paint off of a shooting bench. You will not be a popular companion on the firing line using an effective muzzle brake. That's because the more noise and gas they divert, the better they work.

Mag-na-port makes a muzzle brake called the Mag-na-brake. Some shooters want recoil reduction while practicing, but don't want their hat blown off while hunting. MNP also supplies a knurled nut to replace the brake and protect the threads. If you are going to practice with the brake, and then hunt without it to protect your hearing, make sure you check the rifle zero both with the brake and with the nut installed. It would be a shame to spend time and money on a big-game hunt and find out the hard way your rifle hits to a different point of impact with the nut on than it does with the brake on. To fit a muzzle brake, Mag-na-port (and other brake makers) turn threads on your barrel at the muzzle. To accurately turn threads in a barrel concentric to the bore takes a large and precise lathe. The muzzle brake must also be threaded concentric to the bore, and bored out concentric as well.

If you visit Mag-na-port you'll also get a chance to see the Handgun Hunters Hall of Fame. Every one of these animals was brought down by a handgun, in some cases a handgun with more energy and recoil than your deer rifle. To shoot a handgun like that you need an efficient muzzle brake. The same brake on your rifle can make a big difference for you.

Can you do either the EDM slot burning or the threading for a muzzle brake yourself? Only if you have either an EDM machine (and want to violate the patents) for the slots, or a large lathe for the threads. A large and precise lathe. You cannot use a hand thread tap to thread your muzzle as you cannot get the threads concentric to the bore. You cannot make a brake with a tap and drill press. If you thread your barrel, and fabricate your own muzzle brake without a lathe, you run the risk of getting your brake on crooked. If the bullet even so much as rubs the brake on its passage through, your accuracy will suffer. A severe enough misalignment can be hazardous, even blowing the brake off the muzzle. If you open the holes through the baffles to allow clearance, you lose efficiency and reduce the effectiveness of the brake. When it comes to making muzzle brakes there is no substitute for precise power machinery.

But the people who have the precise power machinery make sleek and elegant muzzle brakes, and efficient ones too. At least within the limits of the technology.

There are muzzle brakes that make no pretense of being sleek units suitable for mounting on a hunting rifle. These are units for competition. One such type is available from Bruce McArthur of Flint'n Frizzen Gun Shop. Don't let the

The Mag-na-brake is threaded on, and the brake can be removed and replaced with a knurled nut. Use the brake for sighting-in and practice, then install the nut for hunting.

name fool you, Bruce is an avid bowling pin shooter who also dabbles in machine gun shooting. To counter the recoil of full-auto fire he developed a muzzle brake that is perhaps the most effective I have ever seen. If you see someone shooting very quickly with what looks like a silver pop can

To properly install a brake and not harm accuracy requires a large and precise lathe. Large enough to hold the barreled action, and precise enough to ensure concentric clearance of the bullet through the brake.

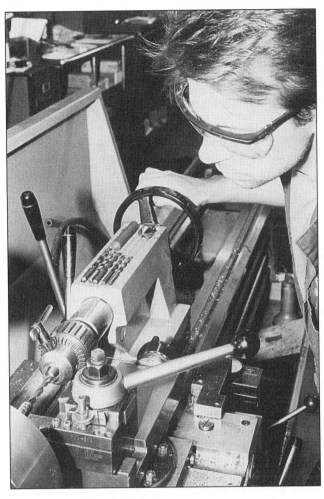

It doesn't hurt to have a skilled and experienced operator working on a brake. After installing thousands of them, this gunsmith knows all the ins and outs of installing a muzzle brake.

on their muzzle, you are probably looking at a Bruce's PGRS-1. The brake works so well that when firing at bowling pins I can see the impact of the bullet on the steel pin through the scope. The PGRS-1 scavenges so much of the gas from the muzzle that I have seen the painted surface of a plywood shooting divider blasted clean of paint by a competitor who was practicing for his turn at the pins. He was shooting a .223. The .375 H&H I shot that had a PGRS-1 on it diverted so much gas to the sides that empty cardboard boxes would be blown off the shooting table.

Another super-effective brake that takes a different mechanical approach is the JP Enterprize brake. Compared

The muzzle brake on this rifle is unobtrusive enough that you might not notice it at first glance. It is good enough to be a viable choice in the heated competition of Second Chance.

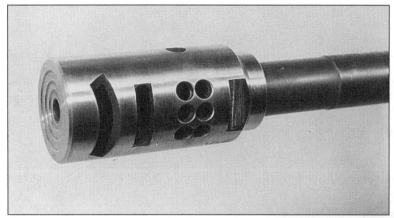

This McArthur PGRS-1 is the most efficient compensator/muzzle brake I have ever seen or shot. It redirects so much gas to the sides and back that it will literally strip paint off a wall, or blow the hat off a bystander, in .223. In a larger caliber, you must be careful where you shoot to avoid giving other shooters a flinch from your rifle's blast.

Facing an array of targets such as the pins at Second Chance, scored solely by the time it takes to knock them down, you want to have every advantage on your side. A good muzzle brake is worth its weight in loot and glory.

to the McArthur brake the JP may seem kind of Spartan. Don't be deceived. The JP works just as well as the Bruce Brake in semi-auto shooting. Bruce's works a bit better in full-auto fire, and they are both a real hoot to test that way!

If you do not want a brake that looks like a piece of industrial equipment on your rifle (competitors don't mind, but some hunters really object) then you can get a Mag-na-brake in either the standard or the slim-line version.

Another compact brake that works well is the Hollands Gunsmithing brake. The AR version is not large, an inch and a half long, but the multiple ports dampen recoil quite nicely. On a pre-ban rifle it is easy to use. Clamp the barrel in a set of barrel blocks and use a wrench to turn the old flash-hider off. Screw the brake on and tighten it. You're ready to go. Hollands does not make their brake for post-ban rifles. If you want to use a threaded brake on your post-

This Ruger Mini-14 has had three things done to reduce felt recoil. It has a rubber recoil pad. The barrel has been replaced with a heavier one. It has a McArthur PGRS-1 on it. As a competition and varmint gun, it is a hard one to beat.

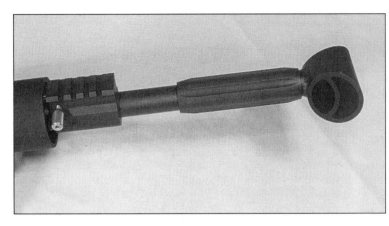

The JP Enterprize muzzle brake is not as racy-looking as the PGRS-1, but it is very effective. I have used both for competition, and found both satisfactory.

ban AR you'll have to get the barrel threaded, and then have the brake pinned, soldered or welded in place. Chapter Eighteen has more information.

The best way to mount a brake on any rifle is to thread the barrel. If you are going to mount a brake on a non-threaded barrel, you must have clearance "dimples" or a ring for the set-screws to lock into. The non-threaded brake is an option that only AR owners go for, as there is no regulation against threading the muzzle of a bolt-action rifle.

What is the cost of recoil reduction with some sort of muzzle brake or ports? The smallest cost would be borne by an AR owner of a pre-ban rifle. Simply buying a threaded comp or brake and screwing it on in place of the flash-hider could cost as little as $50. When you consider going with a Mag-na-port job, then the cost comes in just under $100, and the Mag-na-brake runs in the mid $100's. The most-efficient comps cost more. If you are going to get a McArthur PGRS-1 then the comp costs close to $200. To install it on a post-ban AR would entail threading the barrel and then welding, silver-soldering or pinning the comp in

Take the upper and lower apart, and clamp the upper in a pair of barrel blocks. Use a wrench to remove the flash hider, and screw the Holland muzzle brake in place. If you have a "closed bottom" (no ports on the bottom to reduce dust in prone shooting) peel off layers of the split washer that held on the flash hider until the brake tightens up with the closed portion down. Use Loctite!

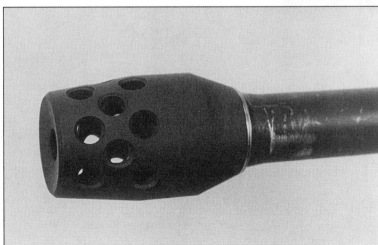

The Holland muzzle brake is an elegant and effective muzzle brake. Installing it on a pre-ban AR is a piece of cake.

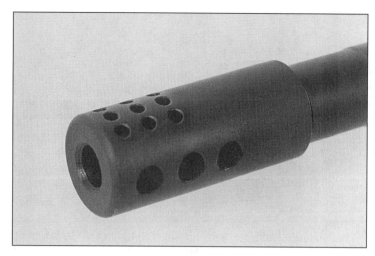

Many AR barrels are available with a muzzle brake already installed. This American Spirit Arms barrel comes with a brake silver-soldered on, so it is an allowable barrel on post-ban rifles.

place. A bolt-action rifle would be the same, minus the need to permanently attach the comp over the threads. Threading, attaching and securing could run another $50-75.

If you are going to be building a lightweight mountain rifle in a Magnum caliber, then the extra cost of low-recoil practice is worth the investment in a muzzle brake.

Stock design is an expensive solution to recoil control, but not a solution you should overlook. If you are going to replace your stock anyway, then getting a stock that also helps dampen felt recoil is only smart. The things to look for when ordering a stock are: as little drop as possible, a wide buttplate with a recoil pad on it, a wide comb with little or no drop to the comb, and a shallow curve to the wrist.

Most stock makers know what shooters are looking for in a recoil-countering stock. A few minutes spent reading their catalogs, and voicing your concerns over on the phone can gain much information. One avenue to approach is to consider stocks designed for dangerous game. A stock intended for a rifle going to Alaska for big bears or Africa for dangerous game is a stock that will go on a hard-kicking rifle. The stockmaker will use all his skill to design the stock as recoil-friendly as possible.

CHAPTER 14

Buying a Used Rifle

"I wonder often what the vintners buy one half so precious as the stuff they sell" Omar Khayyam, the Rubaiyat.

New rifles are expensive. Always have been, and always will be. A used rifle can be a great bargain, provided you don't buy one that has been used up.

The old phrase of "Lock, stock and barrel" came about from black-powder gunsmiths. Those were the three components of a muzzle-loading musket or rifle. While some gunsmiths would specialize and make one of this trio, some gunsmiths made all three. Thus, "lock, stock and barrel" meant the complete package came from one source. What you should do is consider that you need all three to buy a used rifle, and all three need to be on the same rifle. Otherwise, your "bargain" will simply drive you to additional expenditures.

The best thing you can do to ensure you don't buy a lemon rifle is to buy it from a gun shop that offers a guarantee. Do they have a gunsmith there who inspects all incoming rifles? Can you return a rifle that doesn't work right? If so, you are probably shopping at a place where the staff does all the following tests before you get a look at the rifle.

The first thing to do when considering a used rifle is to give it a quick look-over and get a general impression of its condition. Is the stock finish all scratched-up and battered? Is the bluing worn? Are there dents and dings in the stock, barrel, action and scope? Look through the scope if it has one. Is the view clear, or foggy, with scratched lenses? From this first look try to determine if the wear you see is from use or abuse.

Buying a new rifle is like buying a new car. As soon as you walk out the door you've lost a large percentage of its value. Buying a used rifle can be a cost-effective and prudent decision.

If you buy a used rifle from a shop that has a good reputation, and offers a guarantee, you can greatly cut the chances of being stuck with a lemon.

One problem rifle makers have that vintners do not is that rifles are durable. Once you drink it, wine is gone. You could use this brand-new Winchester the rest of your life and not use it up. If you take care of it, this rifle could be traded in for another many years from now. (Photo courtesy U.S. Repeating Arms Co.)

The first thing to do when considering a used rifle is to give it a quick once-over. Has it been modified? Does it show wear? Is it worn from use, or dinged and dented from abuse?

A battered rifle is not necessarily a rifle you want to pass by. If the marks are all from carrying but not from shooting, then you could have a gem in your hands. The classic evidence of carry in a lever-action rifle is worn bluing on the bottom and sides of the receiver near the front. The front of the receiver is the balance point, and the long-gone bluing is removed by perspiration. After all, if a rifle was carried out every November for one day to shoot a deer for 30 years in a row, it is hardly used up. Well-treated and left in the gun cabinet the rest of the time, that rifle would have several lifetimes of use left in it. The big thing to watch out for in a rifle that has been carried a lot is rust. Not just the minor darkening of the bluing, or white flecks from the bluing being lifted off, but red, scaly rust. A rifle with rust on the outside probably has rust on the inside, and certainly has rust on the barrel and action under the stock. Rust usually means a pitted barrel. After all, if the outside, which is easy to wipe off and keep dry, is rusted, how much treatment could the bore have gotten?

Unless you are looking for a rifle to re-build with a new barrel, pass on one that is rusted and pitted. A rifle with patches of bluing gone, but no pits, is worth a closer look.

Check the screw slots for the action and the scope mount. If the screw slots are all chewed up from an improperly-fitting screwdriver, be wary. While the screws may be chewed up from disassembly and cleaning, they could indicate that a previous owner was a ham-handed tester and experimenter. Keep the chewed-up screw slots in mind when you check the trigger and safety. Problems there, in combination with chewed-up screws here, usually means a rifle that has been experimented on, and it may be one big headache in the future.

A big turn-off to many shooters are extra holes in the receiver. Before the factories offered rifles already drilled and tapped for scopes, shooters had to either get the work done or do it themselves. Some were not as successful at drilling holes in the correct locations as others. After drilling one set of scope mount holes, some shooters would change their minds and their scope mounts. I have seen rifles with as many as three separate sets of scope mount holes in them. While they are ugly, the extra holes do not weaken a receiver. If you are looking at a rifle that has too many holes, do not consider buying it to have the holes welded up. The results will not be pleasing. The problem

Most hunting rifles get carried a lot more than they get shot. If the bluing wear corresponds to carrying, look to see if there is a gem in there.

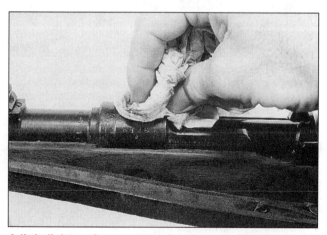

A little light surface rust can be cleaned off with steel wool, light oil and a shop cloth. An established store that cares about their image has probably already scrubbed the "crusties" off.

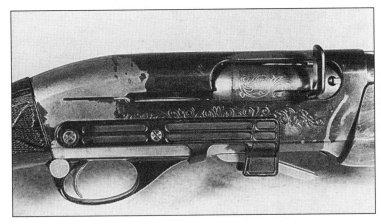

Some guns can look a lot worse than they really are. This Remington has lost the bluing from of all things, soda pop! While it is a very popular brand, I hesitate to name it. The bluing here was stripped off within a couple of minutes after a spill. It shoots fine and could be re-blued in a snap, but is such a jarring example that I leave it as-is.

with welding the holes up and refinishing the rifle is spot-changing of the temper of the steel. Even if the welding rod is the same alloy as the receiver, the heat generated by welding will change the steel around the welded hole. When polished and blued, the steel would show the welded spot as a different texture and color of steel. If a rifle has too many holes but is otherwise sound, buy it as an "ugly" rifle to use as a spare or a loaner. Don't try to make it pretty.

As with any rule, there are exceptions. If someone offered me a Magnum Mauser action that had been drilled in two or

three scope mount patterns, I would snap it up. I would then have the holes welded up and dressed down. To prevent the color changes from appearing on bluing, I would then send the receiver out to have it re-heat treated. Would I do this with any other rifle? No, the alloys of other rifles do not lend themselves to re-heat treating, and are not valuable enough to warrant the cost. Not even a pre-64 Winchester.

The last thing to look at in your general inspection takes a great deal of experience to master, but is worth the effort. Besides, it can be fun. Look at the wood and metal finish to see if it matches factory-new finishes. To get an "eye" for the original look of bluing and stock finish requires looking at hundreds or even thousands of rifles. To look at this many rifles may require repeated trips to your local gun shop or gun shows. It's a dirty job, but someone has to do it. The limitations of photography make it difficult to use photographs as a guide to learning the "look" that is proper. Bluing is harder to sort out than stock finish. After you have looked at a bunch of rifles you can get an eye for the proper color of a blued finish. The big giveaway is surface texture of the steel. If you are looking at a rifle that usually leaves the factory with a high gloss, and the rifle you are looking at has been glass-beaded, ask why. Another big tip-off of a re-blued rifle are the roll-markings. It takes a master bluer to polish the roll markings on a rifle and not make them appear "pulled," "smudged" or "blurry." Pulled marks are usually found with "dished" screw holes. The buffing wheel used to polish rifles and other firearms is made of circular pieces of cloth loosely stitched together. In buffing, the cloth can get

Not having a really rusty rifle on hand to show an extreme case of cleanup (the horror!) I went with the next best thing, a rusty magazine. This Beretta magazine had an almost-furry red crust on it.

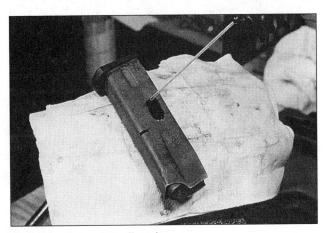

By spreading some oil on it...

And rubbing vigorously with 0000 steel wool...

When I wiped the oil/rust slurry off...

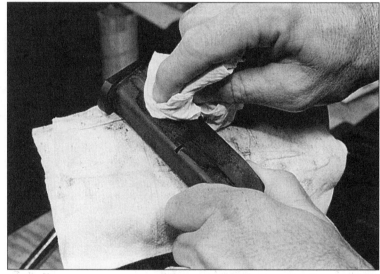

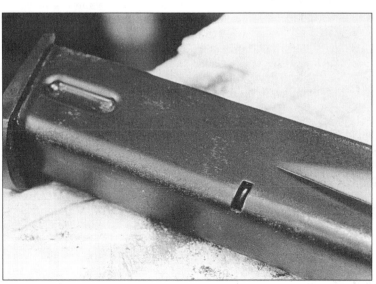

The magazine had cleaned up almost like new. There are a few spots where the bluing is a bit thin, but no rust left behind, and no rough patches. If you like a rifle in the rack, but it seems a bit "crusty," suggest it be scrubbed with steel wool and oil.

This rifle was drilled and tapped for a side-mount ages ago. As a shooter it is not worth much. It is useful as a practice rifle for your gunsmithing endeavors.

down into the markings or screw-hole, and wear the far edge as it pulls out. The letters look as if they have been pulled across the steel. The screw hole looks oval. Smudged and blurry letters are an indication that the polisher went across the roll marks in several directions, not just one.

If someone is telling you a rifle is brand-new, and you are looking at an obvious re-blue, then hand it back and keep going.

Stock finish is easier to acquire the eye for. If someone has touched-up a finish with something different, the gloss of the surface will be noticeable. A hastily-refinished stock will show runs, drips and sagging. One particularly bad example of hasty work that I saw was a stock that had bristles from the brush sealed in the finish.

With a thorough look at the outside and a rifle that passes the visual test, check the action. Does the bolt move smoothly? If the bolt binds in its travel, pass. While the cause may be simply a patch of rust that momentarily slows the bolt, it may be from a dented or bent receiver. A dropped rifle can twist its receiver, binding the bolt. I once inspected a rifle that had been in the trunk of a car during a rear-end automobile accident. It was a very nice BSA in .30-06, built on a Mauser-type action. While at first glance the rifle did not appear to have been harmed by the accident except for a minor crack in the wrist of the stock, the bolt only moved half-way back in its stroke. The action had twisted enough to keep the bolt from going all the way back.

The muzzle of this rifle is a demonstration of a condition anomaly. The bluing has gone gray, there is light pitting and the front sight is missing. But the muzzle has been recently recrowned. Why? Find out, and you could have a diamond in the rough. (In this case, the barrel has just been re-bored and a new chamber cut.)

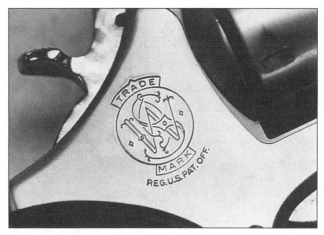

The roll marks should be crisp, clear and even. This S&W is unaltered.

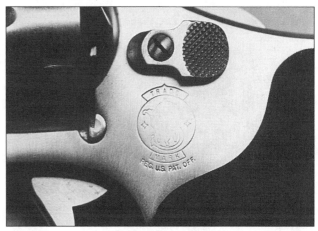

This S&W has been buffed by someone with a heavy touch on the buffing wheel.

Next check the action in its stock. Does the action sit solidly, or does it wiggle in the stock? A wood stock that has been subjected to rains and desert can shrink, changing the bedding. A rifle that is loose in its stock must either be glass-bedded or have the stock changed.

Then check the safety. Ask if you may dry-fire the rifle before starting. Most rifles are not harmed by dry-firing, but some owners object. Testing the safety involves dry-firing, and if the owner will not let you do it, you cannot properly check the safety functions of the rifle. Make absolutely sure the rifle is not loaded. Work the bolt, then push the safety on. Try to pull the trigger. The striker must not fall. Let go of the trigger and then push the safety off. If the striker falls as the safety goes off, someone has been fiddling with the trigger. Bargain for a lower price, or to have the problem corrected before you purchase. If the striker does not fall when the safety is pushed off, dry fire it. Is the trigger pull lighter than before? Work the bolt and dry fire it to get a feel for the regular pull, then work the bolt, push the safety on, pull the trigger, push the safety off and dry fire. If the trigger pull is lighter, the safety is only partially blocking the trigger function, and the sear is being partly pushed off. Again, either bargain for a lower price (you will have to correct the problem after you buy the rifle) or have it corrected before you will buy it.

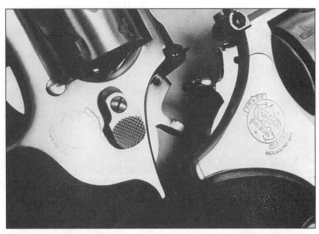

Here you can easily see the difference between the two logos. Rebluing does not harm a gun, but a bad buffing job does decrease the value.

Remington 740's and 760's suffer a unique malady; rail peening. The locking lugs on the bolt are small and hard, and when they bang into the guide slots in the receiver they can peen the receiver. Peened enough, the slot allows the lugs to jump the slot. There is no way to fix a peened slot.

To check for peening, open the bolt and look at the rail. On this rifle you can see that the rail is peened to the point of being bent out of line. Pass on a rifle with this much damage.

Check the forearm for dents, dings and cracks. These are Winchester Model 70 stocks, dating from when Winchester installed front screws that attached to the barrel. Collectors want the screw, shooters remove them for better accuracy. The permanent sling swivel is correct for the collector, the Uncle Mikes QD is better for a hunter. Are you a hunter or collector?

Pull the bolt out of the rifle. At a gun show it is only common courtesy to ask if you can pull the bolt out before you do so. The operator may be leery of having several rifles apart, and not getting the correct bolts back into their respective rifles. Look at the face of the bolt. Is there a dark ring around the firing pin hole? Is it crusty, pitted and corroded? It should not be. A dark ring indicates that the rifle has had a few rounds fired that were too much for the primer to keep sealed. Crusty, corroded and pitted bolts are caused by corrosive primers and gas leaks. Even if they properly clean the bore for corrosive ammo, many shooters forget the bolt face. While a rusted barrel can be replaced, the pitted ring on the bolt face can't be replaced or removed. Re-facing the bolt of a rifle is a delicate operation, and only a few thousandths of metal can be removed safely. Remove any more and you can run into extraction problems. On Mauser rifles with surface-hardened bolts, if you take off too much you'll break through to soft metal underneath. Not all crusty stuff is bad. I once bought an M-1 Garand for a song because the owner had "shot-out" the bore. Sure enough, there was a bright red ring around the firing pin hole, and the bore was dark. What he didn't realize was that the red ring was lacquer residue from the primer sealer on military ball ammo. The dark bore? He had only cleaned the bore with oily patches, and never used bore solvent. Once I cleaned the bore it sparkled like a new dime, and shot just fine. I should have kept it, but I traded it for something or other that I needed at the time. I have no idea what it was.

If the design permits, strip the bolt and look at the striker. Is the oil or grease old, dirty and packed with powder residue? Then the bolt hasn't been cleaned in years. Check the tip of the striker to see if it is smooth and rounded. A chipped, rusty or eroded striker tip indicates neglect or blown primers. Blown primers are a sign that a previous owner used ammunition loaded to too high a pressure. The bolt locking lug seats may be set back, something you cannot check without unscrewing the barrel. Remember the eroded ring around the firing pin hole? Erosion combined with gas-cut striker tip means high pressure loads. If you see that combination, pass on that rifle.

One advantage of shopping at an established store is the availability of accessories. If you don't like the scope on a rifle, you can bargain for another, and maybe even have them mount and boresight it for you. Or get the correct rings for the new scope and do it yourself.

If you are going to replace the stock, then do not pay any more attention to it than you need to in order to get a feel for how the rifle has been treated. If you are going to keep the stock, look at it again. Has the stock been repaired? Some stocks will crack on top of the wrist, right behind the action. The crack is not a problem and can easily be fixed. If a previous owners "fixed" the crack in an ugly or ineffective manner, it can be a headache repairing both the stock and the previous repair. Another location stocks are occasionally cracked is at the toe. When a wood stock with a hard plastic or steel buttplate is set down on a hard surface in a brisk manner, the toe can crack. The crack is usually right in line with the rear sling swivel stud. If the stud is placed too close to the toe, the crack can extend enough to chip a piece of wood off.

If poorly repaired, you may have to refinish the stock once you repair it correctly. A crack can be easily repaired if the previous owner has not messed with it. If the chipped wood is held in place with duct tape, you can epoxy the chip back in place yourself. The worst-case is a chipped stock with the wood missing. Then you must find a piece of wood that matches the stock color, and epoxy the replacement piece on.

Then you have to contour the replacement to match the stock and then you must re-finish that area of the stock. Take all this work into account when you bargain for the rifle.

A serious crack that you cannot see without taking the action out of the stock is one that extends through the action area of the stock from the front action screw to the rear one. Found on large caliber rifles, this crack has a serious negative effect on accuracy. If you continue to shoot a rifle with this crack, the stock can split right through the wrist. Repaired early, the crack is not a problem. Left until the wrist cracks such a crack may not be repairable.

Press your thumbnail into the stock right behind the tang. Well-oiled and left standing in the rack for years, a rifle can have the oil drip into the stock. Petroleum oil degrades wood over time. Oil-soaked wood becomes spongy and soft. An oil-soaked stock is difficult to repair, and after the repair will sometimes require re-finishing.

The last thing to look for are buttstock alterations. Has the stock been cut to install a pad? Is the pad straight, centered, and properly fitted? Has the stock been shortened, perhaps for a child? A short stock may not be a problem, but a poorly-fitted pad is. If the angle of the pad has been

Pull the bolt out and look at the lugs. Has it been lapped or lathe-turned for full lug engagement? If so, ask for a headspace check. You don't want a rifle, even an accurate one, that has excess headspace.

Look at the face of the bolt. If it has been fired, there will be a dark ring around the firing pin hole. Dark is OK, but pitted isn't. Pitting can indicate corrosive ammo, or excessively hot handloads.

Cracked or modified stocks can be repaired. This stock was relieved for a receiver sight installation. Fitting a new piece of walnut, epoxying it in place and refinishing the stock is delicate work. It is also good practice.

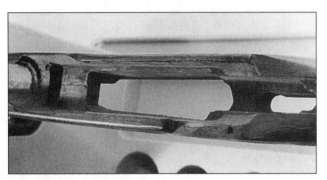

This stock is cracked between the recoil lug recess and the magazine opening. Before this rifle will shoot accurately the crack will have to be repaired and reinforced.

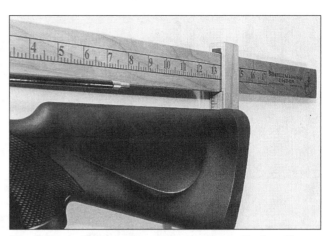

Check the buttstock for pad alterations. Is the length correct? Has the stock been shortened? When the stock was cut for a pad (or shortened) was the pitch changed? A well-stocked gun shop will have unaltered rifles of many models against which to make your comparison.

changed the rifle may be harsher in recoil than it was before the pad had been installed. I recall one very painful rifle to shoot that had the recoil pad screws sticking up. The previous owner had shortened the stock and installed a pad. He had not drilled the pad screw holes deeper. The shortened pad screw holes did not allow the new pad screws to pull flush. Instead of deepening the holes or shortening the screws, he tightened the screws as much as he could and only fired the rifle with a wool overcoat on. The new owner had tried to sight the rifle in at the range while wearing a t-shirt. In three shots he had tears in his eyes. He brought it to me to ask why did it kick so hard? The repair was minor, but the memory was long-lasting.

The barrel completes your inspection. Without placing the rifle to your shoulder, point it at a light and look down the side of the barrel. By slowly turning the rifle you can determine if the barrel is bent. A bent barrel is a bad thing, unless you plan to change the barrel anyway. Then it is a good thing, as it give you some real bargaining leverage.

Remove the bolt if you can and look down the bore. It should be clean and straight. The second test of straightness is to look at reflections from light fixtures down the bore. At the bent point, the shadows will be broken. If it is available, a bore scope can do wonders at this point. With a bore scope you can inspect every inch of a bore and determine if it meets your standards. Do not let the bore scope scare you away from a good bargain. If you think any barrel will look as good through a scope as it does to the naked eye, you are fooling

Your external inspection should include the barrel. Has it been bent? Has it been buffed? In both cases the pattern of reflections off the barrel will be visibly changed.

Run a brush and patch down the bore. Inspect the color of the patch. Green or blue is copper residue, black is powder, and brown or red is rust.

yourself. A brand-new match barrel will look clean and shiny. Any regular-production barrel will look rougher. Any regular production barrel that has been shot will look dark and rough. The first time I looked at my rifle barrels through a bore scope it was almost frightening. If I hadn't know for certain that many of them were tack-drivers, I would have sold the lot and replaced them. Yes, they looked that ugly.

Look at the muzzle. Inspect the crown to see if it has any dings, dents or creases in it. A dinged muzzle is relatively easy to re-crown. Look at the bore at the muzzle. Are all of the lands and grooves of the rifling even? If a previous owner had not used a bore guide, or cleaned from the muzzle, the lands can be unevenly worn. Cleaning rod wear at the muzzle can have a serious effect on accuracy.

Somewhere along the way be sure to check the caliber. For some choices, the caliber doesn't matter. If you are looking for a rifle to build on, then the barrel that is there will be coming off. Bent, rusted, used as a prybar, the old one hardly matters. Just be sure the caliber is compatible with your desired new one. Changing a .30-06 over to a .270 is a piece of cake. Changing that same .30-06 over to a .300 Win Mag is not. If you are looking at a fine rifle at a good price, do you have any need or use of the caliber? Or desire?

Look at the muzzle. Has the crown been altered? Is it nicked or dented? If the rifle has been fired and not cleaned, is the powder residue pattern even around the circumference of the muzzle?

I once passed on a custom Springfield that had been re-done to .270 Ackley Improved. While it was a nice rifle, I had no use for the caliber. Converting it to some other caliber

Has the caliber of the rifle been changed? If so, is it properly marked? If the caliber is not as marked, will the store let you return it? If not, then don't buy a rifle there.

The .300 H&H is a neat old cartridge. However, many .300 H&H rifles have been re-chambered to .300 Winchester Magnum. Again, ask to have the chamber checked, and if it has been altered, can you bring the rifle back?

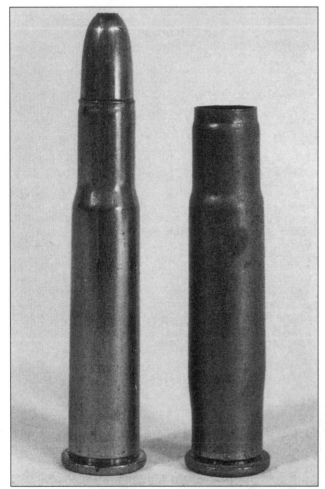

Sometimes using the wrong ammunition is just embarrassing, most of the time it can be dangerous. The owner of a Marlin in .35 Remington tried shooting this .30-30 ammunition through it. He equated "lever-action" with .30-30. Luckily, neither he nor the rifle were harmed, but not all combinations are so benign. He brought it to me because the accuracy was poor. No kidding.

would have turned a nicely-priced rifle into an expensive project. Today, I would probably pick up that rifle (if it were offered again) and send if off to Cliff LaBounty to have it rebored to something larger, but in a standard case. I'm sure I could find a caliber better-suited to my reloading and shooting tastes than the .270 AO, but I might have to spend some time mulling it over.

Part of the fun of buying a used rifle as a project to build is the anticipation. Surveying a table full of rifles, you can't help but wonder "Which one of these is a diamond in the rough?" The weighing of calibers, action types and features can be entertaining at the show. At home, you can continue the thought flow, even if you haven't bought anything yet. I view gun shows and gun shops with used rifles on the rack as entertainment, much like a lottery ticket when the prize is a whopping sum. I don't think my particular ticket will be the winner, but the dollar spent on the ticket is a cheap price for the entertaining thoughts of what I would do with the money if I won.

Similarly, looking over a battered rifle in .458 Winchester Magnum, with a beaten and cracked stock brings forth thoughts of wading through streams in Alaska trying to spot bears before the bears see you. Or, traveling

While most Lee-Enfield rifles will suffer case separation when the cases are reloaded, this one suffered it on the first firing of factory ammo. If you've purchased a rifle that does this, take it back immediately for a refund or exchange!

If the shop has a guarantee, you have less chance of ending up with a problem rifle.

to Africa and looking for a Cape Buffalo that is up for a game of tag. A lightweight carbine in need of a home brings up thoughts of going south to the hills and hollows of Tennessee looking for a wild boar with an attitude and pluck.

Dreams are what keep us going in this hectic, workaday world, and even if you never make that trip, building the rifle for it could be all the entertainment you need to keep you upright and moving forward after one of life's tricks get played on you.

Who hasn't succumbed to the lure of an exotic caliber, a rare rifle, or a "project" rifle that offers dreams of trips to faraway places? "A man's reach should exceed his grasp, or what are dreams for?"

CHAPTER 15

Glass Bedding

In the beginning, there was wood.

Because that was all there was, shooters and gunsmiths resigned themselves to the fact that wood is a dead, but still reactive, material. Despite extensive experimentation to find just the right oil, shellac, varnish or paint, earlier shooters and gunsmiths could not keep wood from reacting to the elements. Anyone who lives in an old house can tell you about it. If you fit a door so it closes tightly in the winter, it will wedge in place during the heat and humidity of summer. So it is with rifle stocks. A stock carefully inletted to be a tight fit in the dryness of the winter air can bind on the action and barrel in the summer.

What did they do about it back then? They fit stocks loosely, and accepted accuracy we would deem only average today. And yet, it worked. I have a Smith-Corona '03-A3 Springfield in its original configuration. It spent the decades after the war as a drill rifle at a VFW post. When the post closed, I managed to snap up the rifle for a small sum. It had not been fired, even with blanks, in the time it spent going to parades. That rifle with iron sights and my eyes, will do two inches or less. Winter, summer, hot, dry, the rifle doesn't care. Would it do better if I glass-bedded it? Almost certainly. Will I glass-bed it? Probably not. So many Springfield rifles have been altered that this one in its original condition is practically a rarity; and I think I'll leave it as-is for now.

The change in bedding techniques of rifles was gradual, and involved synthetics. First came synthetic finishes that did a better job of sealing the wood. Well-sealed wood was less responsive to changes in climate or weather conditions. Then came epoxy-bedding. A "glass-bedded" rifle was effectively insulated from the wood. The wood could change in response to the

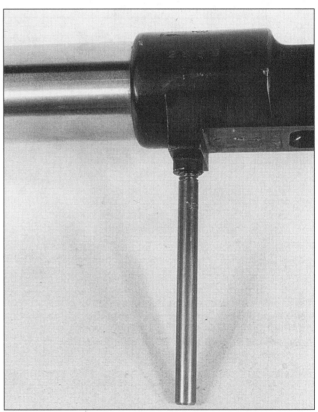

To check the fit of receiver to wood, you need layout dye and inletting screws such as this. The screw slides through the screw holes and keep the receiver properly aligned as you check the fit.

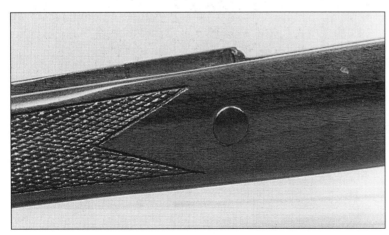

Before there was epoxy, Mauser used a cross-bolt through the stock to spread the force of recoil. The cross bolt also acted as the recoil shoulder for the recoil lug of the receiver.

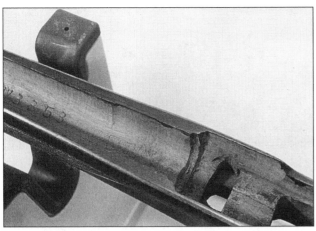

The unsealed wood of this stock will absorb and release moisture like a sponge. Also like a sponge it will change shape as it does so. The changes will likely harm accuracy.

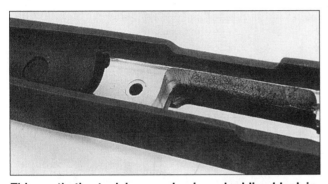

This synthetic stock has an aluminum bedding block in it. The synthetic stock will not warp during climate changes, and the bedding block provides a solid clamping surface for the receiver.

weather, but the rigid epoxy bedding kept the rifle from being effected. Last came synthetic stocks. The kind of climate changes that would make a synthetic stock respond would be far more than you or I could stand. An added benefit of epoxy bonding advances was the improved ability to repair damaged stocks. In the old days a cracked stock could sometimes be repaired, but because the glues in use were only so-so in strength, some stocks could not be repaired at all. A crack in the forearm or bedding area meant a stock had to be replaced. A cracked buttstock could be glued, but would eventually crack again. A chipped stock would have to have a new piece spliced in, not just glued on. If it were simply glued on, the glue would eventually fail and the new piece fall off. Now, we can repair the crack stronger than the original wood.

Improved stock finishes were discussed in Chapter Nine, as were synthetic stocks. "Glass bedding" refers to the use of epoxy compounds to create a perfect fit between the action and the stock. Whether wood or synthetic, a stock has to be epoxy-fitted to the action in order for you to realize the full potential of that rifles accuracy. Glass bedding is a general term that covers a number of methods. All utilize epoxy or "glass" to create a skin-tight fit between the metal and stock. The two most important things to remember about epoxy is that it sticks to everything except the release agent, and it goes even where it isn't wanted if you let it. When

you are going to glass-bed a stock, preparation is everything. Gooping the epoxy in and tightening the action takes a minute. Getting there takes an hour or more. Benchrest shooters do not use a release agent, and glue the action and stock together. Why not take this approach and save the hassle? Aside from the fact that Benchrest shooters are a strange group, they have decided to accept other compromises that make a glued-in action attractive. BR shooters use single-shot rifles with no ejector or bolt stop. Their rifles do not have to have action cuts for the bolt stop or release, no magazine and no magazine cutout in the stock. As a result the action is stiffer, and there is more surface area between the action and stock. BR shooters use Remington actions or copies of the Remington action. The trigger mechanism can be removed by drifting the two pins out. The action does not have to be removed from the stock if you are willing to live with two holes in the stock. If you glue-in an action that is not stainless steel, it may corrode under the stock. BR shooters are also fanatical about keeping bore solvent out of the action. Bore solvent can soften glass bedding compounds and if the rifle is not properly cared for, the action could inadvertently release itself from its bondage to the stock. Unless you are using a benchrest action, you do not want your action and stock glued together. Invest in a release agent and use it.

All glass-bedding methods reinforce the recoil lug seat of the stock. At first this was the only use for glass-bedding. Later, other areas of the action and even barrel were seated in epoxy. The simplest form of glass bedding is called "two-point" bedding. In two-point bedding the action rests on a pair of epoxy pads located around the front and rear action screws. The pads take the force of the compression of the action screws, and isolate the action from the wood. Simple glass bedding is good, but only a start. The next step up is pillar-bedding. Some early rifles had a form of pillar bedding. The Mauser and Springfield had steel action screw liners inserted into the stock. The liner took the compression of the action screws and kept the wood from being crushed. Without an epoxy the liners could loosen. If loose, they can still prevent wood crush but do not prevent unwanted vibra-

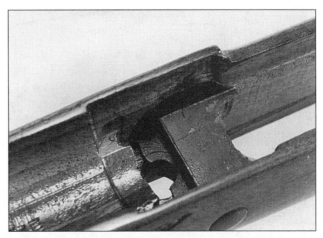

Glass bedding as it is used to reinforce and stabilize the recoil shoulder of the stock. Note that forward of the recoil lug recess, the barrel channel has not been glass bedded for three-point support. But, the channel has been sealed to keep it from warping.

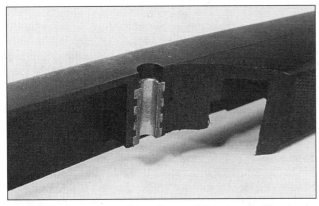

This synthetic stock (from Savage) has been pillar-bedded. The pillar acts as a support for the action screw and receiver, and precludes compression in the stock from tightening the action screw.

Various pillars and the clearance drill to drill out the stock. On the left are banded pillars that provide more surface for the epoxy to hold. Next are smooth pillars. The threaded ones are Brownells adjustable pillars, and the right-hand ones are the small-diameter pillars that Mauser actions require.

tion of the action in the stock; vibration that can harm accuracy. In modern pillar bedding you epoxy metal sleeves into the action screw holes. These sleeves are much thicker than the older liners. Like the earlier liners the sleeves rest against the bottom of the action and the tops of the trigger guard and/or magazine box metal. The sleeves take the compressive force of the tightened action screws. Over time wood can compress or shrink. Action screws in a wood stock may become a loose fit. The pillars do not compress under any load.

Last is a full-action bed. Used mostly on Remington receivers where the round action makes full-bedding easy, the epoxy is a continuous sheet between the wood and the action along the action's full length. Doing a full action bed to a Mauser takes more work than it is worth. An additional step to any bedding is to bed the first inch or two of barrel for support and vibration damping. Called "three-point" bedding, the extra epoxy supports the weight of a heavy varmint barrel or dampens the vibrations of a ultra-light barrel. The third point of epoxy bedding should not extend farther forward than the beginning of the taper of the barrel. If your barrel tapers quickly from the receiver ring then you must shorten the distance your front pad of epoxy extends. If your barrel has a long cylindrical section before it tapers down, you can extend the front epoxy pad out to as much as 2

inches. Contrary to what you might think or have heard, custom gunsmiths do use glass bedding. They fit the action and stock so well before bedding that they need very little epoxy. Some custom 'smiths use a particular combination of bedding techniques: they pillar bed, support the first inch or two of barrel, and then use a thin coat of epoxy to seal the action recess and barrel channel. A well-seasoned wood stock that has been bedded in this manner is almost as impervious to the climate as a synthetic stock.

Our demonstration rifle will get this combination, pillar bedding three-point glass with a sealed barrel channel. To glass-bed and pillar bed the rifle, you will need an epoxy compound such as Acraglas Gel by Brownells. The original Acraglas is a thinner and runnier composition. If it is not dammed-in completely it will run to other places. Acraglas Gel is of a buttery consistency and will not run. For jobs that require wicking such as crack repairs, I use the original. For bedding I use the Gel. An epoxy compound that is used by shooters and gunsmiths with more access to industrial supplies is DevCon. An epoxy mixed with titanium powder, this is very hard, very durable and resistant to solvents. It is also more difficult to work with. If you are bedding a large-caliber rifle, like .338 Magnum or larger, you may want to use Steel-Bed. Brownells Steel-Bed is an epoxy compound with finely-ground stainless steel mixed into it. It is immensely strong,

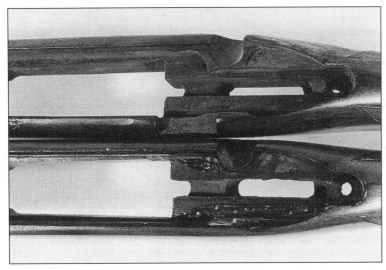

Of these two Winchester stocks, the lower one has been glass bedded. In this case, the bedding is full-length bedding. Rather than only bedding around the action screws, the receiver is fitted and supported from front to back by epoxy.

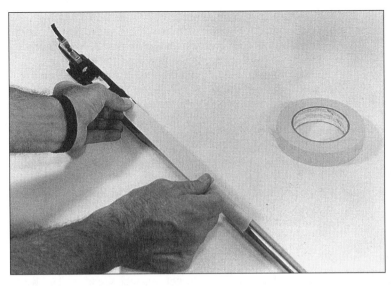

Place two layers of masking tape on the bottom of the barrel. Unless you want a "masking tape bedded" barrel, spray release agent on the tape before you insert the barreled action into the freshly-epoxied stock.

impervious to the elements, and non-rusting. It does not take dye well, so if it will show on the edges of your bedding job, you will have a bright line.

You will need to coat the action with a release agent, and the handiest I have found is Brownells aerosol. To pillar-bed you will need the pillars, a variable-speed drill or drill press, and a piloted bit. To open the barrel channel you need 120-grit sandpaper or an inletting tool. Your hand-held grinder with a selection of small carbide bits, dial calipers, a china pencil, masking tape and modeling clay fill out the list.

Glass-bedding a rifle is usually a multi-step process. If you are going to glass-bed a rifle and not pillar-bed it, you could do all of the epoxy work at once. I have known shooters and gunsmiths who would do a rifle in one fell swoop. I prefer to do the job in stages.

Both wood and synthetic stocks are treated the same and glass bedded the same. The only stocks that you would not bed are stocks that have a bedding block installed or inletted into them. The bedding block is a piece of metal, usually aluminum, that acts as the clamping surfaces between the action and the bottom metal. The bedding block is precisely machined for a particular action. When the appropriate action is bolted in place, the action cannot shift in the stock and the stock cannot influence the action.

The starting point for your bedding job is the barrel channel. With the action tightened into the stock, slide a thin piece of paper under the barrel and see if you can slide the paper from action ring to muzzle. If you cannot, use the china pencil to mark the forend at the binding points and remove the action from the stock. Use the sandpaper or inletting tool to clean the binding wood away from the barrel. You need to start your glass-bedding project with a free-floated barrel, or all your bedding will be for naught. A glass-bedded action with a forend that binds the barrel still won't shoot accurately. You will find that many factory stocks are bedded with a pressure pad near the forend tip. The pad exerts an upward pressure on the barrel, dampening barrel vibrations during firing. As a production method it serves to keep all rifles shooting "well enough." But what happens if your stock shifts slightly due to temperature or humidity? The amount of upwards pressure changes, and so does your accuracy. Once the barrel is free its full length,

then apply the tape. The masking tape creates the stand-off to maintain your barrel free-floating after the bedding is done. Apply a smooth layer or two of tape to your barrel from the recoil lug out to the full length of the forearm. One layer is enough for a tight-fitted look and stock finish to seal the barrel channel. Two layers are needed if you plan to epoxy-seal your barrel channel. Assemble the rifle and tighten the action screws to their correct torque. The front screw on most rifles should be hard-tight by hand, while the rear screw should just be snugged up. Use your pencil, a china marking pencil or fingernail polish to mark the alignment of the screws and the guards they rest in. Measure from the top of the receiver to the top of the front action screw. Write this on your notepad. Measure from the receiver to the rear screw head and write this distance down. Remove the action from the stock. Reinstall the action screws through their guards. Tighten the screws until the pencil or nail polish marks line up and the length from top to bottom is the same as your previous measurements. Once the screws are back to their previous length, measure the gap between the guards and the bottom of the action. You now have the respective lengths of your pillars.

The easiest way to shorten pillars is on a lathe. If you do not have a lathe then you can carefully file the pillars shorter. The pillars must not be shorter than your noted dimensions, and may be as much as .020 inches longer.

With the stock in a padded vise, drill the action screw holes out with the piloted drill.

To avoid filing or lathe-turning the pillars to length, Brownells makes adjustable pillars. The top section of the adjustable pillars has two ends. One is flat and the other curved. To switch, unscrew reverse and re-thread the top onto the shaft. The adjustable pillars are not suited for use on Mauser, Springfield or Ruger rifles. They work well on Remington and Winchester rifles. Fit the adjustable pillars after you have free-floated the barrel and drilled the action screw holes out. To adjust the pillars, remove the rifle from the stock and set the rifle upside down in your cradle or padded vise. Remove the magazine box. Place the stock over the action. Press the pillars into the holes and turn the slotted inner sleeve until the pillar is just below flush with the inletting for the trigger guard.

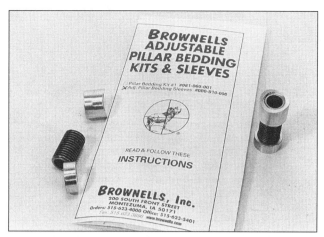

The Brownells adjustable pillars do two things. They offer you a means of adjusting pillar length without a lathe, and the threaded portion gives plenty of surface area for the epoxy.

Once the pillar looks correct, try fitting the trigger guard into the stock and tightening the screws. The pillar should be short enough that the trigger guard tightens up without stock wobble. If the pillars are too long the stock will still move slightly even when the guard screws are tight. Once the trigger guard and stock are tight, remove the screws, install the magazine box and check the fit again. Once the pillars are adjusted properly, disassemble the rifle and pull the pillars out. With the pillars removed, a small dab of Loctite, paint, superglue or fingernail polish will keep them from shifting from their proper length while you handle them during glass-bedding.

If you are glass-bedding a Remington 700 or other rifle where the tang rests on the top of the stock, trace the outline of the tang with your pencil. Remove the action from the stock. Follow the traced line about a sixteenth of an inch inside the edge of the tang. The line is your routing limit. You want the stock to hold the action in place while the epoxy is setting. With your hand-held grinder and carbide cutters, rout one-eighth to one-quarter of an inch deeper the bottom channel of the front action area all around the front action screw. Do not do anything to the recoil lug area yet. Leave small islands of unrouted wood to support the stock. Rout the tang area up to your inner line. If you are fully-bedding the action then your routing will extend from the front to the rear action screw holes, around both sides of the magazine opening.

Measure your recoil lug. The sides must taper from the section directly underneath the action to the bottom. If the lug is straight, or even expands downward, you can end up mechanically locking the action into the stock. In such a case no matter how thoroughly you have used release agent you won't get the stock out. If the lug does not have any taper, file the sides to gain the taper. The recoil lug should be .020 inches narrower at the bottom than at the top. Look at the rear face of the recoil lug to see if there are any tool marks that might lock the action in place. If you find any, polish them out.

Apply masking tape to the recoil lug. On rifles with a flat bottom, such as the Winchester Model 70 or the Mauser, apply the tape to the sides, front and bottom of the lug. You want the epoxy to support the recoil shoulder without making it difficult to remove the rifle from the stock. A rifle tough to take apart doesn't get cleaned as often as it should, and the bedding gets chewed up during your struggles. The Remington is different, a not unusual situation. The Remington recoil lug should be taped on the front and bottom, but not on the sides. The flat-bottomed receivers resist the torque of firing by being flat. The round Remington receiver cannot resist torque, so the recoil lug takes the job. The tapered lug allows easy disassembly, while the tight fit of the taper in the epoxy resists torque. The tape on the bottom of the lug gives enough clearance for the action screw to pull the receiver tightly to the bedding behind the recoil lug. If you have replaced the factory barrel with a custom barrel you have probably also changed the factory recoil lug with a heavier custom one. The custom lug will not need polishing or tapering, just the masking tape.

Remove the trigger assembly from the action. Use the modeling clay to fill any holes, slots or gaps that are anywhere near the action screws. Fill holes or gaps in the trigger guard and floorplate. Do not be cheap with the clay. It is much easier to clean clay out of a hole in the action than it is to clean hardened epoxy out of that same hole. Spray release agent on the action, the guards and the action screws. Spray release agent onto a cotton-tipped applicator and rub release agent inside the pillars. Be absolutely certain that everything that may come in contact with bedding compound that is NOT going to be permanently wedded has a thorough coating of release agent on it.

Install the trigger guard and magazine well in the stock and hold them in place with masking tape. Place the stock in

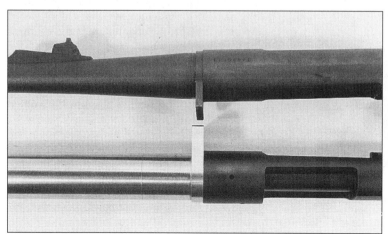

Check the recoil lug for machine marks and burrs. Measure it to ensure it has a taper. Without a taper you might mechanically lock the rifle into the stock, despite the use of release agent. The Chandler lug on the bottom is much thicker than the factory lug, and you might have to open up the recoil lug slot in the stock for clearance.

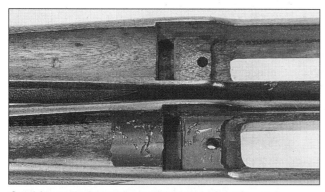

On this preliminary three-point glass bedding job, you can see that the surface of the epoxy has voids in it. Degrease the surface, grind the voids rough, re-apply epoxy (and release agent to the receiver) and tighten it up again. The stock above is original and untouched.

your cradle. Mix your epoxy and coat the pillars with 'glas and press them through the holes. Fill the routed areas with it. Avoid pushing the bedding compound into the guard screw holes of the pillars. Tighten the front action screw until it is snug. The rear screw should be tightened only enough to pull the tang down to the stock. You do not have to tighten the screws any more than is needed to keep the parts from shifting. If the action recess of the stock has been routed or molded slightly incorrectly, tightening the action screws will flex the receiver. By only tightening the screws enough to hold the receiver in place you allow the epoxy to establish new, dimensionally correct surfaces. Use a card to scrape excess epoxy off the rifle. Leave the rifle in the cradle and let the epoxy cure overnight.

The next day, remove the action screws and lift the action out of the stock. Check the bedding for bubbles and voids. Small ones do not matter, but anything larger than a quarter of an inch should be ground out and recast. Degrease the epoxy and use a hand-held grinder with a carbide cutter to open up the void. While you are dealing with potential voids in the upper bedding, you can glass bed the trigger guard and floorplate. Use your grinder to rout the wood out from around the pillars. Apply release agent to the rifle, trigger

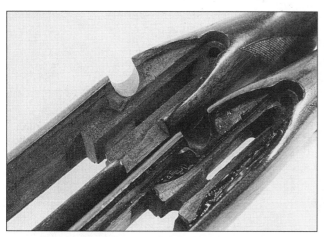

The glass-bedded stock (bottom) has also had the interior sealed with stock finish. It isn't often needed, but doesn't hurt and only takes a little extra work to do.

guard and floorplate, place new epoxy in the void and in the lower bedding areas you just routed and tighten the action screws. Set overnight. The next day remove the trigger guard. If the floorplate is a hinged one, check to see that the floorplate pivots as intended. If it does not, use the hand-held grinder and a carbide tip to cut a clearance path for the hinge through the epoxy.

Next you will bed the recoil lug. Remove the action from the stock. Degrease the new epoxy surfaces. Use your hand-held grinder to rout the recoil lug shoulder back a quarter of an inch, leaving the ends alone as support. To do a three-point bedding job, remove the masking tape from the barrel forward of the recoil lug and reapply release agent to the bare metal. Remember, do not epoxy-bed the barrel forward of the beginning of the taper down from the chamber diameter. Rout the barrel channel forward of the recoil lug. Mix your epoxy and apply release agent to the action, recoil lug, barrel, action screws and guards. Spray the release agent right over the masking tape. Apply epoxy to the routed area in the front of the recoil lug recess. For a three-point bedding job, apply epoxy to the routed area of the barrel channel in front of the recoil lug opening. To ensure a crisp corner between the receiver and recoil lug, apply epoxy directly to the receiver at that corner. Tighten the action screws and let the rifle set overnight. The next day remove the action and check for bubbles or voids. Treat them as before.

The last epoxy treatment is to seal the barrel channel. Some prefer to take the easier way of sealing the channel with the same finish they used on the exterior of the stock. For many this is a reasonable compromise. Hunters in wet environments and competition shooters use epoxy. Some, like Tim LaFrance of LaFrance Specialties, glass-bed the barrel the full length of the stock. He does it on rifles that are threaded for silencers, and finds the extra weight of the "can" does not alter zero on rifles so bedded. Is there an advantage for the rest of us? A very, very small one. Most shooters prefer a free-floated barrel that can vibrate on its own. Rarely will a barrel that does not shoot well free-floated improve in accuracy by being full-length bedded. One application for a full-length bedding job does not involve improving accuracy, but reinforcing the forearm. A very slender forearm or a Mannlicher forearm can be strengthened by full-length glassing the barrel.

Strip both layers of the masking tape off of your barrel and degrease it so the reapplied tape will stick. Apply a single layer of masking tape the length of the forearm and into the area of the third point of bedding under the chamber. Take your 120-grit sandpaper and sand the stock finish out of the barrel channel. If the stock has been sealed with a finish that sits on the surface, then when you hit bare wood you are done sanding. With a finish that has soaked into the wood, like a rubbed oil finish, you will have to be content with roughing the surface enough for the epoxy to get a good grip. Mix Brownells Acraglas without any dye. The thinness and runny characteristics of the Acraglas now will work in your favor. Take a small brush and apply the Acraglas to the barrel channel in a thin coat all the way from the barrel support epoxy out to the tip. I use disposable brushes for the simple reason there is no way to clean the brush after you are done. Spray the barrel and tape with release agent all the way out to the muzzle, and tighten the barreled action into the stock. Use a card to scrape off any excess epoxy. Use an extra piece of tape to create a dam just in front of the forearm. The dam will catch any epoxy that runs out from the barrel channel. Set the rifle in your cradle with the buttstock propped up slightly and let it set overnight. The epoxy will run, and resting the rifle muzzle downwards controls the direction of that running. If you place the rifle horizontally in the cradle the epoxy may run back into the action. If you stand it muzzle-up in a rack the epoxy is sure to run into the action. Cradle it upside down and the epoxy can dribble out around the barrel. Storing it muzzle down leaves you the easiest clean-up job. Once the epoxy is hardened, remove the barreled action from the stock and clean up any excess epoxy with a file. Acraglas will dry with a slightly honey color to it. Without dye the clearness of the epoxy will go unnoticed with the rifle out of the stock. You also don't have to worry about the 'glas showing its presence at the edges of the barrel channel.

What about using the same method to seal the action surfaces around the magazine? Unnecessary. Instead, sand the unglassed surfaces. Mask the exterior of the stock and the glass-bedded surfaces. Spray the action opening with a polyurethane stock finish. If you brushed 'glas onto those surfaces as you did with the barrel channel you could end up binding the action on reassembly. The polyurethane will go on thin enough that you don't have to worry about that.

To finish up, strip the tape from the barrel. Scrub the release agent from the action and scrape the modeling clay out of the recesses. Save the clay, you can use it repeatedly. Reinstall the trigger mechanism. To check for proper function, slide the barreled action with the trigger mechanism into the stock. While holding it in place, check the function of the trigger and safety. If it is binding, find the spot and file until the binding goes away. Once the trigger works correctly, install the bottom metal and tighten the action screws. Check the trigger and safety again.

Your rifle is now ready to go to the range for testing.

Laminated stocks

Synthetic stocks are a war-time solution to the problem of getting enough wood. The German Army had more than one arsenal producing as many as 50,000 rifles per factory per month. It takes a lot of trees to make that many stocks. As a production expedient the R&D sections tried to apply plywood technology to rifle stocks. By laminating thin sheets of wood together into a block, the available wood could produce more stocks. The early problems encountered were what you would expect; the glue has to be tougher than the wood, or the stock comes apart. Germany had by then been a pre-eminent country for research in chemistry. In fact, the standard encyclopedia of chemical reactions was gathered and published by a German chemist of the latter 19th Century, Bilstein. Finding the right glue was easy.

Overcoming consumer resistance was more difficult. As there was a war on, it didn't take long for the rifle purists to decide "this new stuff works OK."

By the 1980s, the cost of wood had gotten pretty high for rifle makers in the United States. Laminated stocks were one solution, but one that took some getting used to. I still remember overhearing a conversation at a gun show at that time, where one shooter remarked that he would rather engage in any of a host of unnatural activities before he would buy a laminated stock.

I don't know if he's come around by now, but many other shooters have. The primary wood used in laminated stocks is birch. Birch is a hard wood with great strength and ease of machining. What it lacks is color. As a plain stock, a birch stock is a light gold or honey color. Stained it can approach walnut in color, but not figure. The lack of color is an asset for lamination. The white wood is easy to dye any color the customer desires.

Synthetic stocks

The bedding compounds commonly in use will bond to synthetic stocks. To ensure a good bond you must clean any residual release agent from the stock surface. The molding or fitting required the use of release agents to ensure the stock would come out of the fitting blocks. Unless you degrease the surface, the stock will have some release agent still on the surface, and your bedding compound will not adhere. If the stock is painted, scrape the paint off of the surface where you will be bedding. While the bedding compound will stick to the paint, the paint won't stick to the stock. Once the surface is clean, treat the synthetic stock as you would the wooden one, except for sealing the barrel channel.

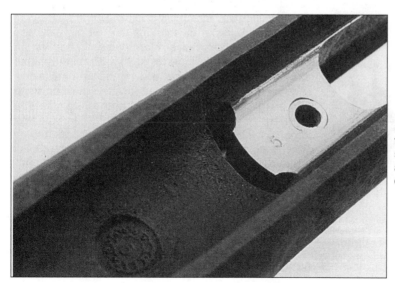

Before you go to the work of glass-bedding this synthetic stock, take it to the range and see how it shoots. If you get the kind of accuracy you expect, pass on the time and effort of glass bedding it.

The Ruger bolt-action rifle differs from other bolt-action rifles in some significant regards. For one, the receiver is an investment casting. Rather than machining from a forging or a piece of bar stock, the receiver is cast pretty much as-is, with a little polishing and machining before the bluing.

The big difference we are concerned with is the recoil lug and the safety. While the bottom of the receiver is flat like the Mauser, the recoil lug of the Ruger is not perpendicular. It is angled. The front action screw is threaded right into the center of the recoil lug surface, so as you tighten the front screw you are clamping the recoil lug harder and directly to its recoil surface. The front screw does more of the work of holding the action in the stock than the front screw on rifles with perpendicular recoil lugs.

Bedding the Ruger is a different multi-step process. First you prepare the barrel support surface in front of the receiver. Instead of removing wood under the receiver in one step and then on the recoil lug in another as with the Mauser (as one example) you remove wood only from the recoil shoulder on the Ruger. With the wood relieved, apply masking tape to the forward portion of the barrel. Apply release agent to the barrel and action, and mix your Acraglas Gel. Apply the gel to the barrel support and the recoil lug. Keep the gel away from the front action screw hole. Slide the action down into the stock. Apply release

You can see that the stock of the Ruger has an angled surface for the angled front action screw to bear on.

agent to the action screw and slide it into the stock. Tighten the action screw finger tight.

Once your 'glas has set, remove the action and look for voids. If you find any, treat them as you did with the other rifles, by grinding them out and re-casting the 'glas.

Now for the tang. The Ruger safety is on the tang of the rifle, and connects to the trigger mechanism. To keep the bedding epoxy from binding the safety, you have to encase the safety in modeling clay. Skim the clay close to the safety bar, but do not let any parts poke through. Use the carbide cutter on your hand-held grinder to relieve the wood around the rear action screw hole. Spray release agent on the tang and the modeling clay, and apply Acraglas Gel to the stock around the tang screw hole. Do not get epoxy in the hole or you will have to grind or file it out. Lower the action into the stock and tighten the front screw finger tight. Do not install the rear screw. By leaving the rear screw out, and supporting the action on the pads of epoxy on the recoil lug and barrel support, you prevent stressing the Ruger action as the epoxy sets. Once the epoxy sets, it will support the action without bending the action when you tighten the rear screw.

With the action bedded in three points, you can go on to full-length bed the action if you want.

To finish the job, strip the masking tape off the barrel, clean the modeling clay off of the safety, and file the rough edges of the bedding smooth. Check the barrel channel to see that the barrel is free-floated. If not, relieve the channel and reseal it.

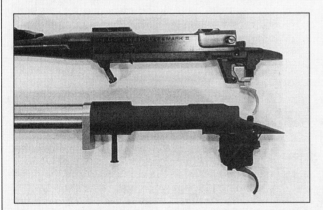

The Ruger action (top) has an angled front action screw. The screw not only pulls the action down into the stock, it pulls the recoil lug back against the stock shoulder. It is a bit more work to glass bed, but worth the effort.

Additional bedding for Magnums

Many African safari rifles were built by British and German factories and gunsmiths. The bolt-action rifles were almost all made on 98 Mauser actions. While the Mauser action is strong, tough and reliable, the recoil lug is not very tall. The brunt of the recoil is borne by a small shelf of wood. When a Mauser was barreled in a large, hard-kicking caliber, the stock could crack after a small amount of shooting. Mauser and the custom gunsmiths quickly determined

that a reinforcement bolt placed through the stock could lessen the chances of a stock cracking. On the largest calibers even the extra bolt was not enough. To reinforce the recoil lug on the action, custom gun makers would place an extra recoil lug on the barrel. The extra lug spread the force of the recoil out over a larger area of wood, and decreased the chances of splitting a stock.

To glass-bed the second recoil lug, first you three-point glass bed the action. Then, treat the front recoil lug to the same process that the action recoil lug received.

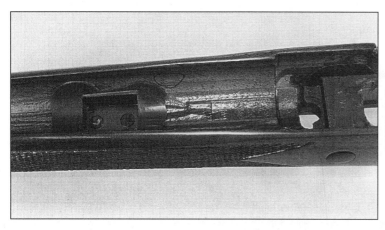

On large-bore rifles it is customary to add a recoil lug to the barrel. To be effective, the lug must bear against the stock. If you are glass bedding the action, you must finish by glass bedding the front lug.

Surplus rifle bedding and repairs

With the large number of rifles being brought into the country, you can be sure that some of them need work. The Mauser rifles have been floating around interesting parts of the world, or sitting in an unheated and uncooled warehouse for more than 50 years. Ditto for the truckloads of Enfields.

The wood on many of these rifles has dried, and shrunk away from the steel. Almost every Mauser will benefit from a proper glass-bedding job. The Enfields do not respond to glass bedding, but there is one repair that crops up from time to time. The front magazine housing screw is also the action screw. It clamps the stock between the magazine ring and the action. The wood between this screw and the magazine opening is thin. When it dries out, it can crack under recoil. The Enfield has a two-piece stock, and the buttstock cannot offer any support to the forend. My first Enfield cracked between the magazine and front action screw. The first attempt at repair did not hold, and soon the wood had cracked out completely. Also, the rear end of the front stock had cracked from moving when the first crack turned into a missing chunk.

To repair it I used a patternmakers rasp to clean the edges where the wood was missing and squared them off. Then I fitted a piece of hardwood to fill the gap. Once it was epoxied into place, it was treated to the same cross-pin and epoxy method the Winchester Model 70 mentioned before received. Then the rear of the forend received the same treatment, inset crosspins epoxied in place. If your Enfield has not cracked yet, it may. You can forestall the crack and get practice in epoxy repairs by reinforcing it ahead of time.

The forestock of this Lee Enfield cracked after 60 years. With a replacement piece of wood epoxied between the screw hole and magazine opening (the old wood was oil-soaked and deteriorated) and a reinforcing pin crossways through it, the stock will not crack there again.

CHAPTER 16

Building a Ruger 10/22

The Ruger 10/22 is a wonderful bit of engineering. It first saw the light of day in 1964, and almost every aspect of it differed from the standards of the day.

Many .22 rimfire rifles of the time had receivers made of tubular steel. Only a few besides the Ruger used lightweight alloy die castings as the receiver. One problem with a die casting is how to attach the barrel? The receiver has to be thick in order to support a threaded barrel. Most other rimfire rifles had (and still have) their barrels held in place by pressing the barrel into the receiver and drilling through the receiver and barrel shank for a cross pin. While this is an acceptable manufacturing process for .22 rifles that are going to be "cheap and easy plinkers" it is not at all sufficient for a rifle that is expected to be accurate.

The Ruger uses a dovetail cut on the barrel, and the fastening clamp is drawn tight by a pair of bolts. An extension of the receiver provides the thickness needed to hold the bolt. The extension is out of sight and inside the stock. Unlike many rifles of the time, the Ruger barrel increased in diameter near the receiver seat. This allows a heavy barrel to be installed. Putting a heavier barrel on other rimfire rifles can't be done because the barrel seat diameter is too small to support the extra weight. On the Ruger, barrels close to 1 inch in diameter are now standard for target rifles.

Instead of a tube magazine, the Ruger uses a rotary magazine. Tubular magazines must be attached to the barrel to

The broad and flat top of the Ruger receiver is a convenient place to mount a scope. For a small game hunting rifle, the receiver scope mount and this Redfield four-power scope are plenty good enough. For match shooting, the scope mount should be attached to the barrel.

The Ruger receiver is a die cast lightweight alloy. Unlike so many other rifles of its period (designed in the early 1960's) it has room to be built past its design performance.

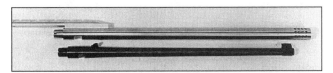

The Ruger barrel is easily switched from the standard lightweight sporting barrel to a bull-barrel match tube like this Volquartsen.

keep them from being easily damaged. Even a securely attached tube can become dented. Securely attached to the barrel, a tubular magazine can have a negative effect on accuracy, changing vibration as the number of rounds changes and stressing the barrel as it heats up. The Ruger magazine is held in place by the receiver. The magazine cannot have any effect on the barrel. As a nearly cubical plastic, aluminum and steel assembly, it would be difficult to damage a Ruger magazine short of running it over with a truck.

The broad and relatively flat receiver of the Ruger is already drilled and tapped for a scope mount. The common rimfire in the mid-sixties used two grooves milled into the top of the receiver as a place to "secure" a scope.

The Ruger offered many design advantages, the Ruger reputation for reliability and durability, and a good price. No wonder it sold like hotcakes.

As a result of all the above, the Ruger was too good a canvas not to be experimented on. With a match-grade barrel installed and a scope on top, the Ruger started shooting groups too good to ignore. As gunsmiths and competitors egged each other on, special matches began to form. Now, 35 years later, the lowly 10/22 has evolved into a rifle so accurate some shooters refuse to believe it. Faced with a target featuring one ragged hole as a group, many shooters will name expensive, or steeply expensive and imported, target rifles as the likely culprit.

No, the Ruger did it. What the Ruger has done is to carve out a niche all to itself; the semi-auto target rifle. How accu-

The Chevy Truck Team Sportsmen's Challenge has been the main driving force for high-performance auto-loading .22 rimfire target rifles. If your rifle won't do under an inch at 50 yards, you are working with a serious handicap in this match.

rate is it? And what uses has it been put to? The 10/22 venue most familiar to many shooters would be the Chevy Truck Team Sportsmen's Challenge. A combined rifle, shotgun and handgun team match, the "Chevy Truck" rifle stage features falling steel plates out to 90 yards. These are, I might add, small targets. The best shooters would not try the course with anything less than brilliantly accurate rifles, and they fire the course with match-tuned Rugers.

Second Chance has a match for rimfires, the Very Light Rifle, and the targets are just as difficult as in the Chevy Truck. The farthest ones are "only" 50 yards away, but the smallest of them is the size of your thumb.

The most demanding course is the BR-50 course. It features bench-rest shooting with a rimfire rifle at 50 yards. The BR-50 targets make the thumb-sized bowling pins of Second Chance look like a billboard.

Competitors are not the only shooters to take note of the capabilities of an accurate rifle. While a bull-barrel Ruger may be a bit heavy to carry, it is certainly up to the task of knocking squirrels out of trees. Or tagging that bunny trying to hide in the brush. The dedicated hunter who wants superb accuracy without the weight of a bull barrel can cast an admiring glance at the new epoxy-wrapped match barrels. As accurate as a bull barrel while being as light as a slender sporter barrel.

As a final note, there are SWAT teams that include a Ruger in the gear they pack into their van. If they wish to sneak up on a dope den without being seen, a subsonic round of .22 rimfire can be just the thing to turn off a particular floodlight or spotlight. The combination is quiet, offers pinpoint accuracy, and is reliable to a fault.

While some .22 rifles will continue to work even without cleaning, for best reliability and accuracy you want to clean any rifle now and then. Cleaning the Ruger action is easy. Make sure the rifle isn't loaded. Remove the action from the stock. Press the two action pins out and remove the trigger mechanism from the barreled action. Press the bolt-limiter pin out of the receiver. Clamp the barreled action upside down in a padded vise. Pull the operating handle all of the way back and hold it in place. With your other hand reach into the action and lift out the bolt. Ease the handle forward and remove the action spring. Scrub the bolt clean. Use a

solvent to clean the gunk off of the recoil spring and its guide rod. You should soak the trigger mechanism in a cleaning solvent and then air-dry or blow dry with compressed-air. Wipe the inside of the receiver with a solvent-soaked patch, and then wipe the solvent-loosened gunk out with a paper towel. You should use a cotton-tipped swab to scrub the packed-on gunk from the rear of the barrel extension. Take a small eyeglass screwdriver and scrape the extractor slot clean. Lubricate the bearing points of the trigger mechanism, the recoil spring, the bolt and extractor. Reassemble and have fun.

What goes into making a Ruger a tack-driving little funstick? At a minimum you need a good trigger, a good scope and an accurate barrel. You can even improve the accuracy of the factory barrel if it isn't good enough. For a top-end Ruger you would replace everything but the receiver, bolt and mechanism, and replace some or all of the trigger parts. The top end Ruger will shoot better than almost anyone who is shooting it.

Let's start with a basic Ruger and improve its performance at the least cost possible. To do this you will need screwdrivers, a scope and mount, a glass-bedding kit and a replacement trigger and hammer for the trigger mechanism. Later on, we'll start making a larger investment in parts for a greater return in performance.

Remove the barreled action from the stock. Remove the trigger mechanism from the receiver. On the side of the trigger assembly you will see the ends of several pins. The trigger parts are held in the housing by the pins, with internal springs keeping things in place. Look in from the top and you'll see that the hammer pivot pin also holds the bolt lock spring in place. The ejector pin keeps it under tension. You should memorize their positions so you can get them back correctly when you put the new parts in place.

Push the ejector pin out and remove the ejector. Push the safety off, and use your thumb to ease the hammer forward when you pull the trigger. Reach in with needle-nose pliers or a hemostat and pull the hammer spring strut assembly out. Press the hammer pin out and lift the hammer out. The hammer has two bushings it pivots on. Place these in the new hammer when you install it.

For quick reloads and bolt manipulation, the factory magazine catch and bolt catch should be replaced. The lever in this rifle is the Alfaro unit, made of Delrin. The bolt catch has been replaced with a Clark catch.

Just above the trigger is the trigger pivot pin. Press it out and let the trigger plunger push the trigger out of place. Remove the sear from the trigger.

With the rest of the parts out of the trigger housing, you can install the Alfaro magazine catch and the Clark bolt release. The Ruger magazine catch is flush under the receiver, and can be tough to activate. The bolt catch/release requires finger pressure to engage and release. For competitions like the Chevy Truck Challenge, where the rifle sits open at the start, and reloading is required, both designs are awkward. With the Alfaro magazine catch you can quickly drop an empty magazine and replace it. With the Clark bolt release, once the bolt is locked open, pulling the bolt handle back and releasing it closes the rifle and chambers a round.

Press the magazine catch pin out and pull the mag catch and bolt stop out. The magazine catch plunger will move

The best way to get a top-notch trigger in your Ruger is to replace the internals with a match kit. This Volquartsen unit has all the parts you need to make your Ruger's trigger crisp and clean.

forward, and as you put the new magazine catch in place be sure it engages the rear collar of the plunger. With the release and catch in place, press the pin through.

To install the Volquartsen parts, first apply a lubricant such as McCormick's Trigger Slick to the engagement surfaces. For the trigger assembly, a "slave pin" makes assembly easier. The slave pin is a small steel or aluminum pin that fits through the pivot pin hole, but does not extend outside of the trigger. The slave pin keeps the sear and disconnector in place until you can press the trigger pivot pin through. Put the Volquartsen sear and disconnector in the trigger and insert the slave pin. Place the trigger plunger and spring in the rear of the trigger guard. Use a hemostat to hold the trigger assembly in the housing and press the pivot pin through.

Place the trigger housing on the bench on its right side or in a padded vise. Grasp the hammer with your left hand and place the bushings on it. Place the bolt lock spring over the right bushing, and slide the parts assembly into the housing. Press the hammer pivot pin in through the left side. Once it is in place, look inside the housing to see that the bolt lock spring is resting on its notch in the bolt lock. If not, adjust it. Insert the ejector pin, and catch the hole in the ejector over the pin. Swing the ejector down into place, and press the pin to the right until it is almost in the right-hand wall. Press the bolt lock spring down until the pin can pass over it, and press the pin into place.

The hammer strut assembly has a rear plate that keeps the spring in place. Clamp the head of the strut in your vise and compress the spring. Slide the retainer off the strut and ease the spring off. Use a fine-cut file to knock the sharp edges off of the strut where the spring rides. Install the Volquartsen spring, compress it and slide the retainer into place.

With the pliers or hemostat, slide the strut into place behind the hammer. Cock the hammer. Use your thumb placed in front of the hammer as a cushion, and check the trigger pull for weight. It should be about three and a half pounds.

On the Volquartsen trigger there is a small screw sticking out of the back of it. It is your over-travel adjustment screw. You want to set the screw so the trigger moves the smallest amount possible once the hammer has been released. If you adjust the screw with too little overtravel, the trigger might not travel far enough to release the hammer. While it can be frustrating squirrel hunting, it can be particularly disap-

If you try to improve the original parts, you'll be forced into an ugly compromise. This Ruger has had an external trigger stop screw installed to control overtravel in the factory trigger. It works, if you can stand the looks of it.

pointing in a match. Check your trigger over-travel settings thoroughly before you lock them in place with Loctite.

Unlike other rifles, the Ruger 10/22 receiver is not the part that the rest of the parts depend on. The receiver does not have the mass or strength to secure the rifle in the stock. Match rifles do not glass-bed the Ruger receiver and free-float the barrel, instead they do the opposite. Bedding the match Ruger involves using the barrel-support part of a glass-bedding job, and then leaving the receiver to float in the stock without resting against the stock. The barrel is glass-bedded for several inches at the rear, and free-floats to the end of the forearm.

Fire-lapping the Ruger is simple, with a twist. You obviously cannot load your own ammunition, so instead use subsonic or target ammunition. Dip the tip of the bullet into the lapping medium. The inertia of the medium when the bullet is fired will spread the lapping compound onto the driving bands of the bullet. Lapping medium on the chamber walls can abrade them, increasing extraction forces and potentially increasing the chamber size. Use curved hemostats to individually insert each treated cartridge into the chamber. Also, be sure to thoroughly scrub the chamber clean each time you clean the bore.

Unlike centerfire rifles, where you might have to start with the most coarse compound, with the .22 you start with the 600 only for a rough bore, and for most you'll start with the 800. On a barrel like the Volquartsen I wouldn't fire lap at all.

To get more performance out of your Ruger than you have gotten so far, you need to make an investment in better parts. The first to consider is the barrel, then the stock.

You can obtain the barrel and stock as a matched pair if you wish. Almost everyone who makes barrels for the Ruger also offers a stock that fits their barrel.

One such combination is the Butler Creek barrel and stock combo. The barrel is a .920-inch blued or stainless barrel that plugs right into your Ruger receiver. The stocks are synthetic and come in two styles.

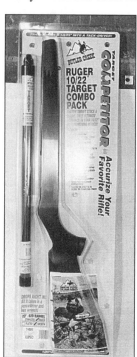

Rather than opening up the barrel channel of your existing stock for a target barrel, you can get a complete kit. This Butler Creek kit has a match barrel and synthetic stock that fits the barrel. Installing these will greatly improve your rifle's performance.

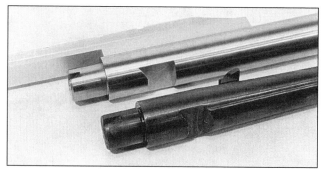

Every replacement barrel for the Ruger will have the barrel-clamping dovetail already milled into place. Thus it is a simple matter to switch barrels.

Replacing the barrel is simple, and the same regardless of the make of the new one. Remove the barreled action from the stock and clamp it in a padded vise with the barrel vertical. Use an Allen wrench to loosen and remove the two bolts holding the barrel clamp in place. Remove the receiver from the vise and then pull the barrel out of the receiver. Remove the bolt. Wipe the new barrel's extension clean, and brush clean the barrel seat in the receiver. Take your new barrel and try to press it into the receiver. It should be a snug, but sliding fit. If not, you will have to polish the barrel extension down with 400-grit emery cloth. Use Dykem to see where the extension is binding, and polish there. In replacing several dozen barrels on Ruger 10/22s, I have had to polish the barrel extension once.

Remove the receiver and install the bolt. Hold the bolt back from its forward travel and slide the receiver back onto the new barrel. Put on your binocular magnifiers to get a close-up view. Adjust the receiver by tilting it until the extractor slides into the extractor cut of the new barrel without binding. Tighten the two clamping bolts. Look at the extractor slot and extractor to make sure the latter is still not binding. If it is, loosen the bolt, adjust the barrel and tighten again.

Remove the receiver from the vise and place it in the Butler Creek stock. Tighten the stock bolt and head off to the range to test-fire. If the rifle does not reliably extract, the extractor is binding. Adjust the barrel to keep the extractor moving cleanly.

If the extractor is binding or rubbing in its slot in the rear of the barrel, you will have malfunctions. The extractor alignment is the first and main reason for malfunctions on a replacement barrel. Do not look into any other alteration until you are sure there is no contact.

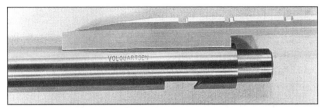

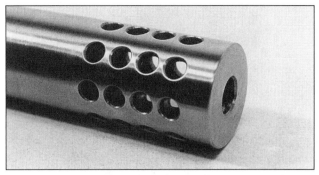

This Volquartsen barrel has the scope mount attached to the barrel for the absolute minimum of play in scope/barrel alignment. To see why this is necessary for top-grade accuracy, attach a high-power scope to a mount on the receiver. Then dry-fire over sandbags. You will see the reticle move against the target when the hammer falls. Switch to a barrel-mount and the problem goes away.

It may seem silly to put a muzzle brake on a .22. After all, how bad can the recoil be? The brake is for accuracy, not recoil. By stripping the muzzle gases away from the bullet as quickly as possible, accuracy-harming turbulence is diminished.

Is it possible to just replace the barrel and not the stock, saving the cost of the stock? Yes it is, but you probably don't want to be that cheap. The new barrel is considerably larger than the old one, and will not fit into the barrel channel. You will have to rout out the barrel channel to 1 inch in diameter, which is a lot of work. When you are done you will have an odd-looking stock with a smooth plastic buttplate and too much drop in the butt. I have a Ruger Sporter stock that has the barrel channel opened up for a heavy match barrel. My hat is off to whomever did the work, because they had to take a lot of wood out. The Ruger Sporter stock is the only one I would consider for such work, and then only because of its looks and fit. Oh, and because of the rubber recoil pad the factory installed. Replacement stocks will be proportioned for use with a scope, and will almost always come with a rubber recoil pad installed. The Butler Creek stocks start for under $100, a bargain that's hard to beat.

For more performance you have to step up in cost. But what performance you get! The Volquartsen Custom shop has been in business for more than a couple of decades, and they make rimfire barrels that are superbly accurate. A Volquartsen barrel is designed and crafted to deliver the best performance possible. Building your Ruger on Volquartsen parts is easy. Once you have selected the barrel and stock you desire, look into a couple of extra touches that will improve the performance of your rifle.

The first is the barrel mount scope mount. While the Ruger receiver is firmly attached to the barrel, there is room for microscopic "wiggle". Attaching a scope to the receiver works for almost every application. But when you want the absolute best accuracy, the scope must be attached to the barrel. While the Volquartsen mount is attached to the barrel, it extends back over the receiver to mount the scope.

The second is the Volquartsen trigger improvement kit. The kit is a hammer, sear, disconnector and trigger, all with a special industrial coating for smoothness and wear. To replace your standard springs, Volquartsen includes a trigger plunger spring and hammer spring. The HP Action Kit, as Volquartsen calls it, gives you a clean, light, crisp trigger pull that you have to try to believe.

The re-barreled Ruger now shoots like a dream. And you want to keep it that way.

Cleaning the action is easy, use solvents on the bolt, action spring and trigger mechanism. To clean the bore is tougher. Remember in Chapter Six where we discovered that much of the wear of a bore came from improper cleaning? This holds true for rimfire rifles, too. For some rimfires it is even more important. A cheap rimfire may lose its accu-

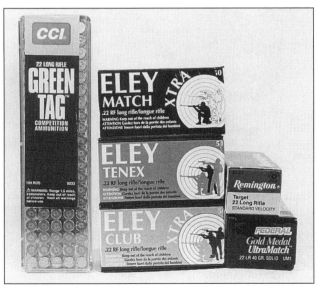

Match barrels need match ammunition to perform well. Try your barrel with everything. Most .22s can be very particular about what they like. Once you find what your rifle likes, stick with it. The Volquartsen barrel on my Ruger is inordinately fond of two different loads, a lucky break for me. If I can't get one, then I can switch to the other.

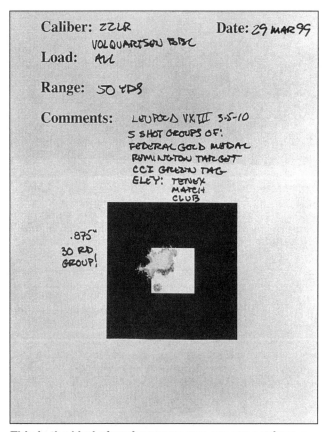

Caliber: 22LR   Date: 29 MAR 99

Load: VOLQUARTSEN BBL
ALL

Range: 50 YDS

Comments: LEUPOLD VXIII 3.5-10
5 SHOT GROUPS OF:
FEDERAL GOLD MEDAL
REMINGTON TARGET
CCI GREEN TAG
ELEY: TENEX
MATCH
CLUB

.875"
30 RD
GROUP!

This is the kind of performance you can expect from a Volquartsen barrel. Six, five-shot groups from six different match rimfire ammunitions! A 50-yard group less than an inch across. If you want this performance, you'll have to go buy your own Volquartsen, as this barrel is in my will, to my heirs.

racy even faster as the softer steel it is made of wears away faster under the abuse of improper cleaning.

Use a bore guide. One kind of bore guide slips over the muzzle. Slide your rod through the guide, and then install brush or patch. To run the rod down the bore, hold the guide to the front of the rod and slide the guide on the barrel as you slide the rod into the bore. Do this each time you insert the rod.

Another way to prevent rod wear on the bore is to make the receiver the rod guide. You can drill the rear surface of the receiver. To drill the receiver, use a Brownells receiver drilling jig. You'll need an electric hand drill, the jig, aluminum cutting oil such as Do-Drill or Tap Magic, a size "F" (.257-inch diameter) drill bit, and a countersink or de-burring tool.

Remove the rifle from the stock, and take the trigger group off and the bolt out. Clamp the rifle in a padded vise, right side up. Place a layer of masking tape on the right side of the receiver to protect the finish. Place the jig on the right side of the receiver with the receiver trigger pin holes lined up with the holes in the jig. Hold the front spacer tube in place and slide the clamping screw through. Be sure the fiber washer is between the screw head and the receiver left wall. Hand tighten. Slide the rear screw through and hand-tighten it. With both screws in place use an Allen wrench to snug the screws down. Turn the barreled action upside down. Cut some cardboard so the pieces will fit into the receiver at the breech. Install the drill bit and lube it with the Do-Drill or Tap Magic, and drill through the rear of the receiver using the jig as a guide. The cardboard is there to protect the breech in case you push too hard in drilling and the bit goes forward from the rear receiver wall. Use the countersink or de-burring tool to clean up the edges of the hole. Use a file to clean any burrs off the inside of the receiver wall.

The new hole now acts as your cleaning rod guide.

CHAPTER 17

Building a Precision/Beanfield Rifle

There is something about an accurate rifle that brings out the competitive aspect of some shooters. Oh, there are shooters who don't know how accurate their rifles are and don't care. Poor guys. While accuracy has always been a serious subject, once a high level of accuracy could be taken for granted in rifles, some shooters wanted to stretch the limits. Some did this by expanding the benchrest format. Instead of shooting for group size at 100 or 200 yards, these fellows insisted on doing it at 1,000 yards. With what success? The match-winning group size at a 1,000-yard benchrest match might be less than 6 inches. Don't brag about your rifle or shooting skills to these fellows if you can't bring in a group under 7 inches at 1,000 yards.

But some shooters want more than just a concrete bench and a paper target. As the nature of agriculture changed, so did hunting. Deer aren't dumb. They don't have to walk out into a field to eat, they will nibble at the edges. If you are on one side of a 40-acre field and the deer is on the other, he won't see you. But if you are armed with a trusty .30-30 lever gun, you can't hit him. Depending on the proportions

This 200-yard group is just over an inch and a half, and is only average for this rifle.

An accurate rifle should be cared for. This tactical/beanfield rifle has a scope pad, an inner bag, and an external waterproof bag. All of this can then go into a hard case for protection from baggage handlers and other demolition experts.

of the field, that deer can easily be 400 yards away. In Texas, much deer hunting is done from stands positioned along paths bulldozed through the brush. If a deer steps out onto the path, you do not have the option of stalking closer. Whatever the shot is, you must take it or leave it.

Such hunting requires superbly accurate rifles. Usually these rifles are chambered for flat-shooting calibers, to minimize the mental calculations of bullet drop and aiming holdover. After all, that deer isn't going to stand there for very long.

Another approach to accurate rifles is to forego the flat-shooting hot Magnums for an accurate standard caliber with a known trajectory. If you know your caliber, and the distance, you can adjust the scope for a hit. Such marksmen depend on stalking and camouflage. We used to call them snipers, but the word has taken on such bad connotations lately that some other word will have to do. The current vogue is "precision" rifle and marksman, or "tactical" rifle and marksman. The overwhelming standard for such rifles is .308 Winchester. Why? The territory is heavily trod by police and military specialists. They cannot handload their ammunition. If you want to buy the most accurate ammunition over the counter that you possibly can, it will be in .308.

This Winchester .30-30 is a great deer rifle for many times and places, but reaching across a beanfield with it is not prudent. (Photo courtesy U.S. Repeating Arms Co.)

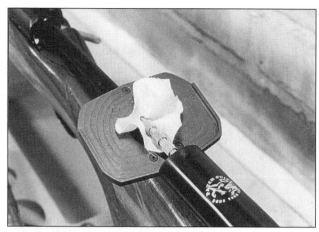

An accurate rifle should be cleaned properly. If you skipped the chapter on proper cleaning, again I offer the strong suggestion to always use a rod guide when cleaning the bore.

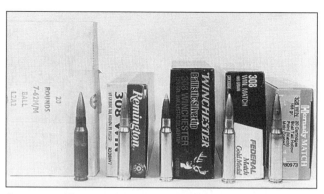

Accurate rifles need accurate ammunition. While the British surplus on the left is fine for breaking-in the bore, and plinking with less capable rifles, for gilt-edged performance you need top-notch ammo. I have had spectacular results with each of these four.

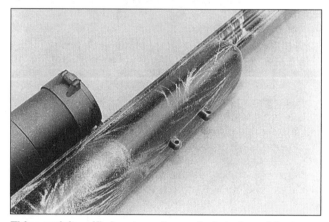

This precision rifle has two sling swivel studs, not for two slings, but for sling and bipod attachments. Many tactical marksmen use a bipod, as do many long-range hunters.

While you can make a beanfield or precision rifle light, not many shooters opt for one. After all, the beanfield hunter is sitting in a tree blind. The precision marksman is not still-hunting, and will almost always shoot from prone. If not prone, then some other supported position. The priority is a not a rifle that is light to carry, but a rifle that never changes its zero. The beanfield and tactical rifles have small differences, but these differences are not absolute. Beanfield rifles tend to have longer barrels, often fluted. The beanfield hunter wants more velocity and the tactical marksman wants a compact package. But some hunters don't feel the extra length is worth the extra velocity, and some tactical shooters don't mind the extra length. Tactical rifles often have a paint job. While basic black is good enough for many beanfield hunters, others will insist on some sort of camo job, just to keep the odds in their favor as much as possible. Off the shelf tactical rifles such as the Remington PSS come in black, and many owners do not change.

To save a bit of typing, ink and confusion, I will condense the two categories into one, and call our project rifle a long-range rifle. Not capitalized, as a Long-range rifle would be something used out to a thousand yards. Not that you couldn't use our rifle out that far, but there are rifles more suited to shooting into "the next zip code."

Much of the work that goes into a super-accurate long-range rifle is beyond the abilities of the home, hobbyist, or casual gunsmith. Much of it requires large, precise machine tools. However, you can farm the work out to non-gunsmith machinists and do the hand-work yourself. To describe the

For long-range deer hunting, or tactical shooting, nothing beats an accurate rifle. The laser range-finding binoculars make scope adjustments for range a snap.

While free-floating the barrel is mandatory for top performance, a fluted barrel and a paint job are matters of personal taste. If you like it, do it. If not, don't.

operation to him, I will describe the basics to you. For those who are not prepared to hunt up a machinist and are shipping your rifle off to a gunsmith, you may want to know what he is doing with your new toy.

The almost universal action selected as the starting point for an accurate long-range rifle is the Remington 700. Since many are built up in .308 Winchester we will use a short action. Why the Remington? For the simple reason it is very easy to square and true its working surfaces. Remington designed the 700 with the idea of ease of production in mind. The receiver is a tube. The recoil shoulder is a flat plate caught between the front of the receiver and the rear shoulder of the barrel. While Remington makes a very accurate rifle, they cannot be persnickety in manufacturing. The front of the receiver is turned square to the tube, but not perfectly. To increase accuracy we have to get closer to perfection.

Conjure up in your mind the image of the receiver and the barrel as two cylinders floating in space. The centerline of each of them must be concentric to the other. If there is any tilt in the marriage, then the rifle will not be as accurate as it could be. The threads of each must be concentric to the centerline. In order to get the most out of the potential accuracy of a barrel, the barrel must be screwed into a squared receiver shoulder, perpendicular to the axis of the bore. If

The Remington 700 action is the most-often selected action upon which to build a precision or long-range rifle.

Here is a precision rifle ready to head out to the fields. The scope cover protects the scope until you get to the blind or ridge line. The sling makes it easy to carry, and the bipod aids in aiming.

You can see at the top of the photo that not all of the tool marks have been removed on this first pass at squaring up the receiver face. The next pass will remove a few thousandths more, and clean the face square.

the bolt lugs are not square to the bore the bolt will flex under the load of firing, and the flex will introduce variables that harm accuracy.

The chamber must be reamed on the centerline and straight.

To true an action takes quite a bit of equipment. First off, you will need a lathe, and not a small one. A hobbyist lathe will not be large enough to hold the receiver or accurate enough to improve the front shoulder squareness. The basic work is a simple machine-shop operation, and you can find either a gunsmith or a machinist in your area who has the lathe and is willing to do the work. You will need a barrel vise and action wrench, and a locking lug lapping kit from Brownells. If you are not going to lap the lugs, but turn them square instead, then you'll need a fixture to hold the bolt while the locking lugs are machined, such as the fixture from LaBounty. You will need a recoil lug indexing plate. You will also need the usual assortment of basic tools to disassemble the rifle.

First square the receiver. The Remington receiver is a tube. Remove the barreled action from the stock and remove the bolt and trigger mechanism. Clamp the barrel in a barrel vise and with an action wrench unscrew the action. With the barrel unscrewed and the recoil lug removed, the receiver is chucked into the lathe. With a dial indicator, center the receiver in the chuck. Centering won't change facing the front, but it is a must in order to chase the threads. The face of the receiver is dressed off with a cross-cut until the cut surface is clean, with no irregularities or tool marks. Then the threads are chased with a threading bit and the power feed of the lathe. The receiver now has a front shoulder and threads that are square and concentric to the bore axis respectively. If you are simply truing the action and barrel shoulder, and then reinstalling the old barrel, do not chase the receiver or barrel threads. You will be making the fit looser, which is worse than being slightly misaligned. If you are installing a new, but pre-threaded barrel, again, don't

The cylindrical construction of the Remington receiver makes it a snap to center in a lathe. Once centered, the face and threads can be turned square and concentric, respectively.

To start the accuracy improvements, clamp the barrel and remove the action.

Square the face of the receiver.

If you are threading a barrel blank to install, chase the threads to clean them up and make them concentric. If you are reinstalling the old barrel, do not chase the threads as you will only make the fit loose.

Here the new barrel is threaded to fit the receiver.

chase the threads. Chasing is done ONLY when installing a new barrel threaded from a barrel blank, where the thread diameter of the barrel can be adjusted to fit the chased threads of the receiver. Gunsmiths who frequently true Remington actions will invest in a tap for the threads, a 1-1/16-inch X 16 tap, to clean up the threads without increasing their diameter. While convenient, a tap is not quite as good as a single-point for precision, but the convenience is worth the small percentage of potential performance. Worth it for many, but some shooters insist on every advantage and will want the more precise method.

The last operation is to reach into the front of the receiver and kiss the locking surfaces of the receiver to even them up. The amount of metal removed is the absolute minimum to get the shoulders square to the axis of the receiver, and even with each other. Some rifles require less than a thousandth of an inch of steel be removed, hardly enough to measure.

When the receiver comes out of the lathe each surface on it will be perpendicular to the centerline except for the threads, which will be centered on and co-axial with the centerline. Not that all these surfaces were not close as the rifle came from the factory. But when you want to improve accuracy, close is not as good as closer, and closer is not as good as perfect.

Now the locking lugs. To lap the locking lugs, strip the bolt to remove the striker, striker spring and cocking piece. Insert the bolt into the receiver and turn the handle down to the closed position. Screw the lapping fixture into the front of the receiver until you feel the tension spring being compressed. Mark the lapping tool and receiver with a felt-tip pen so you can return them to the same position. Turn the bolt and remove it, and apply a small amount of lapping compound to the rear face of the locking lugs. Insert the bolt and open and close it a few times. Remove the bolt and lapping fixture. Clean the lapping compound off of the bolt and receiver. Apply Dykem to the locking lugs. Reinstall the lapping fixture and once the Dykem is dry, close the bolt. Remove the bolt and see how much of the Dykem has been rubbed off. Repeat as necessary to get complete engagement between the locking lugs and their seat in the receiver.

A drawback to lapping is that while it polishes the surfaces into full contact with each other, lapping cannot correct a dimensional imbalance. Suppose, for instance, that one of the bolt lugs is shorter than the other by a thousandth or two. The longer lug will take all of the force of the cartridge on firing. The bolt will flex under the load until the second lug bears enough to take up some of the load. The flex harms accuracy. If you lap the lug, the higher one will get ground down until the other one begins to bear, and then they will grind evenly. The lugs will both bear, but they will be offset to each other. The offset harms accuracy, but not as much as the flex does. Lapping improves accuracy, but not as much as lathe-turning does.

The simple method of lathe-turning uses the tailstock of the lathe and the chuck to hold the bolt. The stripped bolt has the bolt sleeve screwed back on. The firing pin hole of the bolt face is placed on the tip of the tailstock. The bolt sleeve is clamped in the chuck. Using a dial indicator, you adjust the chuck until the bolt is centered and running true along its length. With a High Speed Steel tool, the rear of the locking lugs are faced off, removing the smallest amount

To square the locking lugs without the LaBounty fixture you have to adjust the lathe until the bolt body is running true and centered.

Once the bolt is centered, either bare or in the LaBounty fixture, then you can dress the lugs until they are square and fully engaging in the receiver.

of steel that will clean up both lugs. There are drawbacks to using the simple method. The firing pinhole takes the load and wear of bearing on the tip of the tailstock. With the bolt centered on the tailstock, it isn't possible to turn the face of the bolt. If you true the lugs, but leave the bolt face untouched (and it is slightly tilted or rough) you have not trued every surface that has an effect on accuracy.

Cliff LaBounty decided, after trying various methods,

The LaBounty fixture clamps the bolt and holds it centered.

The big advantage to using the LaBounty fixture is that with the bolt face exposed, it is easy to dress the bolt face square in the same setup as the locking lug dressing.

that there had to be a better way. So he designed a fixture to hold the bolt for turning. Using the fixture is simple. Clamp the stripped bolt into the fixture with enough of the bolt sticking out to provide clearance for the cutting tool between the rear of the lugs and the front of the fixture. The fixture has a "V" groove running down the center, and the groove and clamps hold the bolt parallel to the outside of the fixture. Place the fixture in the lathe chuck and adjust the jaws until the bolt is running true. Once the bolt is centered, it is an easy machine operation to true the bolt face and square the locking lugs.

Once turned, the lugs should be lapped. Since the tool trued and smoothed the surfaces involved, you can lap the lugs with medium and fine grit using the tip of a finger as pressure to keep the lugs in engagement to the locking shoulders. A spring-loaded tool to keep them pressed together is overkill.

At this point it is possible to gain much of the performance improvement of the tactical rifle without going to a premium barrel. Chuck the original barrel into the lathe and center it. With a squaring tool, turn the shoulder of the barrel until it is square. If you have iron sights on the rifle and want to use them, then set the shoulder back by one thread, minus the amount removed from the face of the receiver.

Here you see the locking lugs turned square to the bolt body. Lapping the lugs at this point is simply a means of removing tool marks.

With the new barrel threaded and the shoulder length set, the chamber is now reamed.

The Remington barrel requires a recess in which the nose of the bolt will fit. The recess has to be turned, and the best way is with a special reamer.

The threaded, headspaced and recess-reamed barrel is now ready to go onto the receiver.

Once you reinstall the old barrel and adjust the headspace, your rifle will be more accurate than it was before. The headspace has to be adjusted because the front face of the receiver and the rear of the barrel shoulder were both dressed back on the lathe, shortening the chamber. Your machinist will have to shorten the rear of the barrel (not the shoulder) by the combined amount that he took off of the

receiver and the shoulder. He will have to deepen the bolt nose recess by this amount, too. A rifle with a trued and squared receiver, glass bedded in its stock, can approach the accuracy of a top-notch long-range rifle. You are, of course, limited by the quality of the factory-produced barrel. If the barrel on your rifle was one that was just "good enough," while the receiver surfaces were already close to perfect, then your accuracy improvements will be small. If your receiver surfaces were machined badly, but the factory barrel was the best one made that year, your accuracy improvements gained by truing the action surfaces can be startling.

But we aren't stopping there, or depending on the factory barrel. The old recoil lug, while adequate for the job Remington asked of it, is not enough for the top-end long-range rifle. The old plate was blanked out of heavy sheet steel. It is not thick enough or flat enough. A thicker plate, surface ground on both sides, provides a flat surface between the barrel and receiver. The thicker plate flexes less under recoil, improving accuracy. The thicker plate also complicates the arithmetic in machining the receiver and barrel. The barrel shoulder must be cut forward by the difference between the old recoil plate and the new recoil plate. Otherwise, you may end up not with a rifle with headspace under minimum (as you would have by cleaning up receiver and barrel, but not reaming the chamber) but with a rifle with

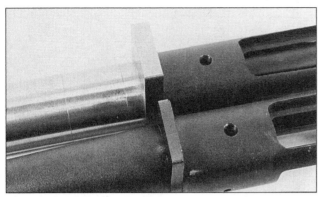

If you are replacing the factory recoil lug with a thicker one, you must adjust the location of the barrel shoulder to account for the extra thickness. If you are reinstalling the old barrel you must move the shoulder forward. If you are installing a new barrel you have to calculate the new shoulder location.

At .313 inches, it is twice the thickness of the factory lug.

excess headspace. If you square the receiver and barrel shoulders, then insert a thicker plate between them, you end up with MORE headspace than you need.

When it comes to recoil lugs, there are many good ones. I have used the recoil lug from Holland Gunsmithing and been happy. But for total thickness, you can't beat the lug from Iron Brigade Armory. Offered by Norm and Rocky Chandler, sniping experts with many years of military, shooting and gunsmithing experience between them, and also a host of books, the IBA recoil lug is .313 inches thick!

The lug is simply clamped between barrel and receiver. Without this guide fixture you'll have the devil's own time of tightening the barrel and keeping the lug straight. Buy it, use it and store it safely.

The Badger Ordnance lug, available from the Chandler Brothers at Iron Brigade Armory, is the thickest I've found. Thick, stiff and surface-ground to be flat, it will not flex under recoil.

When you install a barrel, use anti-seize paste. You may never have to take the barrel off, but if you do you'll be thankful you spent the couple of bucks for a near-lifetime supply.

The action wrench gives you plenty of leverage to tighten the barrel. You don't need to lean on it.

With the barrel clamped and the lug locator in place, now you can tighten the new barrel back into the receiver.

One method of bedding a precision rifle is the three-point, with glass bedding support at front and rear of the receiver, and the first inch or 2 of the barrel.

More than twice the thickness of the factory lug. No caliber you can fit into a Remington receiver is going to make that lug flex under recoil. Anything that comes close would hurt far too much to shoot more than once.

The recoil plate is clamped between the barrel and receiver. The plate must be absolutely flat, or the machining you have done to the receiver and barrel shoulder are for naught. Any good recoil lug is surface ground, and flatter than you can turn the receiver and barrel shoulder. In order to make sure it sits at the correct spot, you have to have an indexing plate. The indexing plate extends in front of the receiver and is held in place by a screw that goes into the front action screw hole. Lock the indexing plate in place and slide the recoil lug onto the front of the receiver. Clamp the barrel in the barrel vise and handturn the receiver onto the barrel threads. Tighten the receiver hand tight and then install the action wrench. Tighten the action and then remove the wrench and barrel vise.

The barreled action must now be bedded. The free-float with the first inch of barrel bedding method detailed in Chapter Fifteen is the method you want to use. One exception to the free-floating method that I discovered is the method used by Tim LaFrance of LaFrance Specialties. His tactical rifles are usually bedded by the one-inch rear of the barrel method. Some, however, are bedded the full length of

the forearm. Those are the rifles that have his suppressor installed. The extra weight of the suppressor can affect the hot and cold zero of the rifle if the standard glass-bedding method is used. Tim full-length beds his suppressed rifles to avoid zero shift as the rifle warms up.

You do not have to full-length bed your barrel unless you find that your zero shifts as the rifle warms up.

You can use a wood stock for a long-range rifle, but most shooters prefer a synthetic one. Whether wood or synthetic, it should be pillar-bedded and three-point bedded unless it has a bedding block in it. The stock for the project rifle is a Remington PSS stock with a cast-in-place bedding block. If the performance is not up to par, then the aluminum bedding block may be relieved slightly with a

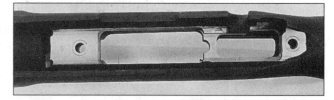

Another method to bed the barrel is to use a stock with a bedding block in it. By clamping the barreled action into this stock, you might not even need to bed under the barrel. If you do, the synthetic stock will not be a problem for the epoxy to adhere to.

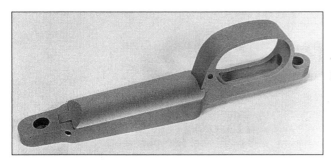

The Badger Ordnance trigger guard magazine plate assembly. A machined work of art, and as tough as a crowbar.

The floorplate release latch is machined so tightly that while you can see the joint, you can't feel it.

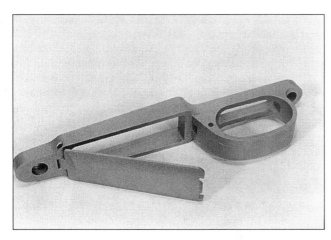

With the floorplate down you can see how thick the magazine walls are, and how thick the floorplate is.

The curve blending the magazine sidewall to the trigger guard does not show a machined line past the black button you see. This is beautifully precise machining.

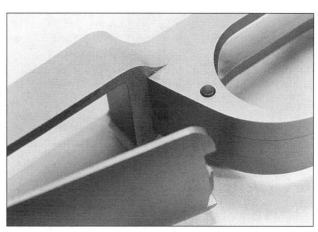

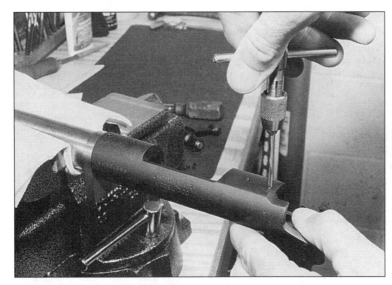

When installing a scope on any rifle it is important to clean the screw holes out. If you do not, the screws may not fully tighten, and/or the base might not be pulled completely flush to the receiver.

mill, and the rifle bedded to the block with Dev-Con. To replace the factory aluminum trigger guard and magazine floorplate, I went with the Iron Brigade Armory trigger guard. While the IBR recoil lug impressed me with its strength, the trigger guard impressed me with its attention to detail. While it is heavy and heavily-made, the exterior of the trigger guard does not show any tool marks. None. The release lever is so closely fitted to the trigger guard bow that it shows only as a line. The floorplate swings down smoothly without any play. The only tool marks to be seen are on the inside of the floorplate, and they are so regular and even that it almost appears as if the machinist was just showing off. "Engine turning? We don't need engine turning, I can do that with a pass of the end mill."

And the amazing part of this is, this is a part that is intended to be Parkerized, fastened to a synthetic stock, painted flat black, and then beaten to death by the issued Marine or police officer. And it starts out so pretty! It is almost too good-looking to be hidden in a rifle that looks like an industrial tool.

The long-range rifle is clamped in its stock with the trigger guard as the far-side anchor. With the Iron Brigade Armory trigger guard on the bottom, any rifle is well-anchored. Installing it is simple. With a sanding drum in the hand-held grinder and goggles and a facemask on, the contact points of the stock were dressed down until the trigger guard slipped into place. Once in place, it was glass-bedded.

The trigger of your long-range rifle can either be the factory mechanism lightened as per Chapter Four, or you can replace it with a new one from Timney, Canjar or others. In either case you will not need a pull less than three pounds.

The last thing to go onto the rifle is some sort of sighting system. For long-range work you want to use a scope. Yes, much long-range target shooting is done with iron sights, but the challenge is a different one than the precision rifle or beanfield rifle is called on for. In target competition the distance is fixed and known. You only have to account for wind

4-14x40 Tactical Government Model™
5.56mm Patented Reticle

To take advantage of the long-range accuracy of a precision rifle, you need a top quality scope. This Springfield scope has a range-finding and trajectory-compensating reticle, and a bubble level at the bottom to preclude scope cant.

You can see how much stuff came out of this brand-new receiver. Imagine how much is in a used one that hasn't been cleaned out, ever?

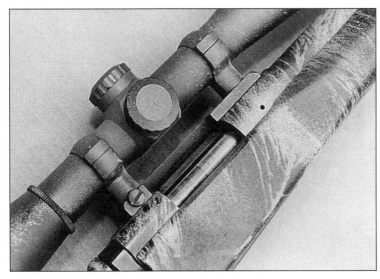

A standard one-piece scope mount has to be shimmed for long-range work. If you do not shim the base, you will run out of scope adjustments for range compensation soon after 500 yards. DO NOT! shim a two-piece scope base.

and light on the iron-sight matches. For a long-range rifle, you will also need to account for odd distances. How many clicks do you move your iron sights to deal with a target that is 527 yards away? And how can you know the distance? A scope offers both the means to estimate distance and the ability to adjust for it. One difficulty in using a scope at long range is the small range of adjustments in the scope. You can only crank the internals of the scope around so far, and then the knob stops. Think of a narrow cone extending out from the scope. The cone is the adjustment range the scope can "see" in. For long-range shooting the entire lower half of the cone is wasted. Once the rifle is zeroed, you will not need to adjust the scope below the centerline of the cone. Once you get to the greatest distance that your scope can "crank up" for, farther targets must either be dealt with using hold-over, or ignored.

In order to use all of the adjustments for upwards correction, you have to tilt the rear of the scope up. Properly accounted-for, the tilted-down scope now provides all of its vertical adjustments as upwards "clicks," allowing you to precisely dial the scope in to any distance you need to shoot. To do this requires either a single-piece base with a shim under it, or a base machined on a taper. DO NOT shim a two-piece scope base. The offset between the front and rear rings will not tilt the scope, and may damage it. The simplest way to tilt the scope base is to use a one-piece Leupold, Redfield or other scope base with a shim under the rear of the base. The shim should be .022-inches thick. Degrease and tighten the base down using a medium-grade Loctite to secure the screws.

While shimming the base started out as the only method, it is not the best method. As the need for long-range bases was voiced by more shooters, gunsmiths responded. If you take a one-piece base and machine the bottom of it so the base is tilted down, you have accomplished the same thing as shimming the base, but by a stronger method.

Several companies offer tapered bases for long-range shooting. After seeing the Iron Brigade recoil lug and magazine box,

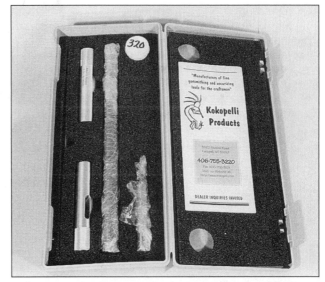

If you are going to lap your rings, the Kokopelli kit is just the thing. With it, you can get your rings centered, on line, and fully-bearing on your scope without damaging the scope.

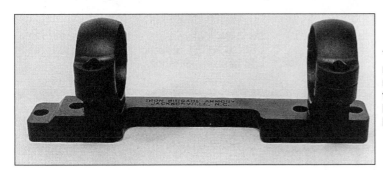

You do not have to shim the Iron Brigade scope mount for long-range shooting, as it is machined with a taper to the base to account for the needs of long-range rifles. You also don't have to lap the scope rings, that has already been done for you.

If your base wobbles on the receiver, you'll have to shim it. Or, send it back for one that fits. If the receiver is the fault, the new base may not fit any better. This Badger/IBA base fit perfectly.

Tighten the base screws in order, front to back or vice versa. You want the base to be pulled down evenly as the screws are tightened.

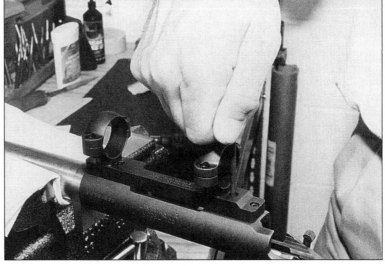

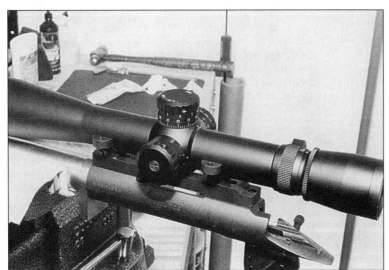

Set the scope in place and slide it forward or back to adjust eye relief. At this time, check bolt handle clearance.

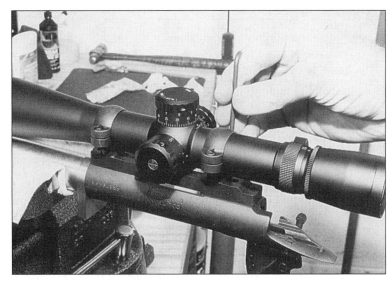

Tighten the scope ring screws in the same pattern you would the lug nuts on your car. Snug them down right rear, left front, right front, then left rear. Then go back in the same pattern and tighten them again. And again.

I thought I was prepared for the scope base. I was wrong. The base is a one-piece steel rail machined on a taper that provides 20 minutes of angle upward pitch to the axis of the bore. The heavy-duty rings are nickel-brazed to the rail, and then bored concentric. After looking at the base and rings, I'm convinced that the rifle could fall on the rings and not hurt them.

As an added measure of precision, after you align most rings, lap them for full concentricity. For other scope rings, I have the Kokopelli ring lapping kit. On the IBA rings, I didn't need it. Before you lap, you must check alignment, and adjust it if necessary. Start with the base installed. Align your rings as in Chapter Five, but instead of installing the scope, use the alignment bars in the lapping kit. The Kokopelli kit has one of the bars bored out in the front. Slide a quarter-inch rod into the bar, and when the bar is placed in your front ring, use the extended rod to tell when the ring is parallel to the barrel. Use the bars only as a test, not as a lever to adjust the rings. The bars are aluminum and will not take rough handling and still accurately measure alignment. Tighten the rings on the bars just enough to keep them from slipping, and check the fit of the smooth ends of the rods to each other. If the rings are off, the bars will be off.

Use the bar alignment to adjust the windage match of the front and rear rings on a Redfield-type scope system. Once the windage is set, check the fit of the bars vertically. On a two-piece base, you can shim one or the other base to adjust a vertical mismatch. On a one-piece base you will have to remove and reverse first the front and then the rear ring to try and get proper alignment. If switching rings does not solve your problem, then you have to see if the receiver is off. A poorly machined receiver bridge could cause the base to flex when tightened, and throw off ring alignment. Remove the rings and loosen the base screws. Does the base rock front to back when you press down on it? If so, you'll have to shim the base to remove the play. Once shimmed, start over on your ring alignment. If the base fits the receiver, but the rings don't line up send the base back and explain your problem. If it is the base, the manufacturer can replace it.

Once aligned as closely as possible, then you lap the rings to a perfect fit. You can only lap steel rings. Weaver rings with their aluminum bases cannot be lapped. The softer aluminum will be more-quickly eroded by the lapping compound, and the rings will lap to an oval and not circular.

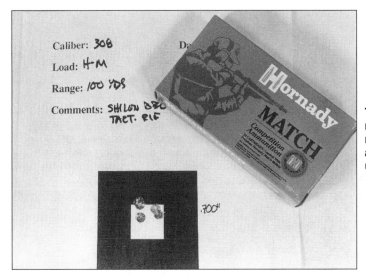

The project Tactical rifle shows promise with a number of match loads. The Shilen barrel and Hornady moly-Match ammo easily goes under an inch at the range. I wonder how well it would do if I gave up coffee?

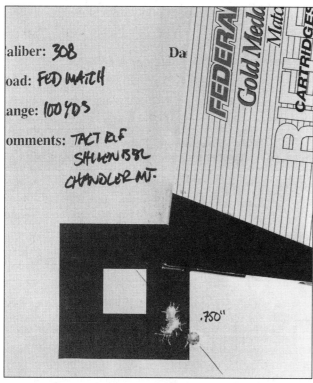

Caliber: 308   Da
Load: FED MATCH
Range: 100 YDS
Comments: TACT RLF
SHILEN BBL
CHANDLER MT.

.750"

With its Shilen barrel, Chandler scope mount and Night-force scope, Federal Match ammo turns in another sub-inch group.

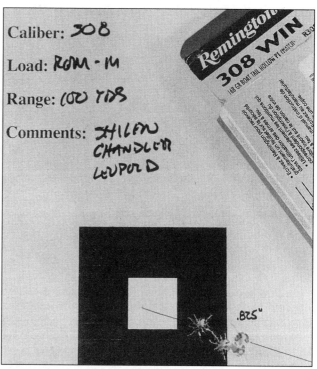

Caliber: 308
Load: RGM - 14
Range: 100 YDS
Comments: SHILEN
CHANDLER
LEUPOLD

.825"

The Remington Match .308 is a stellar performer in my match-conditioned Springfield M1A. In the project Tactical rifle it doesn't do as well. I will have to look into this, and see if I can find out why.

Also, the lapping compound will become embedded in the aluminum, scratching any scope you ever install in the rings. If you are going to be lapping stainless or nickel-plated rings, coat the insides with Dykem before you start lapping. Take the ring tops off of the scope bars and set them aside, taking care to keep the front and rear tops with the front and rear bottoms, and pointed the same way they were on the rings. It doesn't hurt to mark them with a per-manent-ink felt tip pen to keep things from getting jumbled. After all, there is no point to precisely-fitting all of these parts if you are going to assemble them at random. If you will be trying several different scopes in your rifle, then you

need a permanent marking method. I use a center punch. I mark the right rear of each ring and base. The front ring gets a single punch mark, while the rear gets two.

Lapping is simple. Wipe the lapping compound onto the lapping bar (not the aluminum measuring bars!) and place the bar in the ring lowers. Place the ring uppers onto the bar and tighten the rings no more than you need to in order to feel that the bar is dragging on the rings. Tighter is not better. Slide the bar back and forth, rotating it as you do, to evenly lap the rings. The lapping com-pound will migrate into the grooves, so apply more com-pound as needed. The lapping will loosen the fit of the

The Redfield-type single-piece bases only use three of the four base screws. Older ones use slotted screws like these, which are slightly more difficult to get tight than the new Torx screw.

The Badger/IBA base uses all four screws, and comes with Torx screws. You can easily tighten the screws past the need for Loctite.

rings on the bar, so you will have to gently tighten the rings as you proceed.

The first time the bar feels looser and smoother sliding through the rings, remove the bar and take the upper rings off. Clean the lapping compound out and look at the inside of the rings. The lapping you have done will have cut through the blued surface of the steel or the Dykem. If your rings were perfectly matched when you checked them with the aluminum bars, you may be done lapping. You want your rings to be lapped into 75 to 80 percent contact. If you do not have that much contact, apply Dykem and lap again. If you lap too much, you may make the rings loose on your scope. You can attempt to salvage the rings by filing the flat contact surfaces. The flats that the scope rings pass through to secure the tops to the bottoms act as the stopping shoulder on the rings. By removing a few thousandths of steel from the shoulders you may be able to

tighten the rings. If you go too far in lapping, you'll have to buy a new set of rings and start over again.

Remember, 75 percent contact is plenty. Be sure to scrub the rings clean after lapping and before installing the scope, or you'll scratch the scope tube with the residual lapping compound. I have heard some shooters (and even gunsmiths) suggest leaving some grit between the scope and rings to prevent slippage. Supposedly, this keeps scopes from slipping under the recoil of large calibers. A properly tightened scope will stay put without grit. I have kept scopes in place on .375 H&H's, .416 Remington Magnums and .458 Winchester Magnums without grit. Lap the rings and tighten the screws and your scope won't slip.

With the assembled rifle, the last piece of equipment is the scope itself. For a long-range scope you need a serious piece of glass. Two scopes I have on hand that fit this bill are the Leupold and the Lightforce.

The final step is to break-in the bore and zero the rifle.

CHAPTER 18

Working the AR-15

The AR-15 is a demonstration of the design genius of Eugene Stoner. But it had a rocky start in life. It was adopted by the U.S. Air Force as a replacement for the aging and unsatisfactory M-1 Carbines that Air Force base guards were then issued.

Before the build-up in Vietnam, the M-14 program had also been going through a rocky start-up. Despite the adoption of the M-14 in 1957, so few had been manufactured and issued that during the Berlin Crisis of 1961, the Berlin Brigade still used the M-1 Garand as their issue rifle. It was partly because of the low rate of manufacture TRW decided to get into the M-14 rifle business. They invested heavily in numerically-controlled, multiple-station milling machines, and designed the manufacturing process to remove bottlenecks and speed assembly. They succeeded so well that TRW made more money off of the early delivery bonuses and low reject bonuses than they did off of the basic profit on each rifle itself.

However, the U.S. was engaged in a police action where the average distance to the enemy was measured in feet. A powerful, long-range rifle was not needed. Secretary of Defense, Robert McNamara, came from a manufacturing background where everything could be measured and quantified. He determined that what was needed was a light rifle with relatively short range and low maintenance. He canceled the M-14 program and forced the adoption of the new and untested Armalite rifle.

The AR-15 was renamed the M-16 and adopted as a light, short-range rifle needing little maintenance. The M-16 had the same problems another light, short-range rifle needing little maintenance ran into 20 years earlier. The M-1 Carbine was rushed into production because there was a war on, and the military needed rifles. Ditto for the M-16. Rifles (M-16s) showed up in Vietnam with no cleaning kits, little instruction

What the military wanted in the M-16 was a light, handy, close-range rifle. What they got in the beginning were lots of headaches. Now, the rifle works well.

To work on the AR-15, you should be familiar with the layout and the parts. The Colt manual will explain the parts and show their assembly. "Black Magic" will give you a feel for the exotica of competition ARs.

and lots of promises. Those soldiers who believed the "sales pitch" (Light, Lots of Power, "buzzsaw bullets" that cut through brush, and never needs cleaning!!) ended up with rifles that jammed. Those who treated it like any other rifle they had ever been issued had no problems.

And ever since then, the AR-15/M-16 has had to live with the reputation as an inaccurate rifle that tends to jam.

This is an undeserved reputation, I might add. A properly assembled AR-15, fed good ammo, will continue to shoot even after it is so grubby that you don't want to touch it, let alone shoot it. To keep it going only requires brushing the chamber and bore. I do not recommend this as the preferred cleaning method, but mention it only to point out the rifle's reliability. Each one of mine get scrubbed after its range session. As for accuracy, the AR with a match barrel, fed match ammo, will easily do under an inch. Many will do half an inch.

When you go to work on your AR, you will find yourself working in one of five areas: Fit and Feel, Trigger, Barrel, Sights, and Function.

The AR has upper and lower receiver halves. The lower holds the trigger mechanism, magazine latch and buttstock

with recoil spring. The upper holds the barrel, bolt and bolt carrier. The two halves are held together by cross pins. The cross pins are held captive in the lower by spring-loaded plungers. The upper has two lugs, fore and aft, with holes through them. When the cross pins are pushed into the mated halves they pass through these holes in the upper. Fit and feel covers the tightness of the closed upper to the lower, the shape and length of the buttstock, the pistol grip and the forearm. The fit of upper to lower is not crucial to good operation. An upper that is loose on the lower will still function, but may not deliver tack-driving accuracy.

If you have a paired upper and lower that are a tight fit, congrats. If you want a pair that are a tight fit you can order them. Any of the companies I have dealt with are more than happy to make sure you have a tight-fitting upper and lower. If you already have an AR and the upper and lower are loose, you can tighten them up. The first avenue is the cheapest. Install an Accuwedge. It is a small plastic lump with a wedge-shaped extension on it. To install, push the

In its present incarnation, the AR can be a strikingly accurate rifle, even for long-range competition. Here Nick Till practices dry-firing with his Match Bushmaster AR.

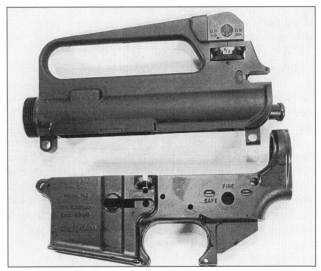

The best way to get an upper and lower that are a tight fit is to order them both from the manufacturer at the same time. Tell them you want a tight fit and will send it back otherwise, and you will not be let down.

The AR is comprised of two assemblies, the upper and the lower. By pushing two pins loose, you can separate the two and swap different uppers to your lower.

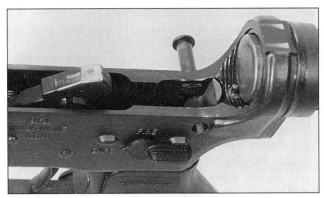

If you have a rifle already assembled and it is loose, you can install an Accu-wedge. The plastic of the Accu-wedge squeezes under the rear lug of the upper, and when the pin is pushed across the assembly stays tight. In some rifles it is so tight as to be difficult to strip the rifle for cleaning.

rear disassembly pin out and hinge up your upper. Press the Accuwedge in place in the rear of the lower, behind the rear disassembly pin and under the buffer tube. Close the upper and press the rear pin to the locked position.

Your upper and lower should now have less wobble. Some high-volume shooters do not like the Accuwedge, suspecting that it will weaken over time. None of mine have, but if you do not trust rubber than we can offer you steel. JP Enterprize makes a tensioning wedge rear pin to replace your current one. To install it you have to remove the rear pin. To do this, unscrew the upper screw on your buttstock. If you have a shorty with a telescoping stock, you have to loosen the buffer tube lock nut. Pull the buttstock away from the lower and remove the capture spring. Use a small wire to press the capture plunger away from the rear pin, and remove pin and plunger. Save all three, spring, plunger and pin in case you need them.

Reattach your buttstock. Close the upper and insert the JP tensioning pin. Rotate the pin so it will tighten back and down, and tighten the screwheads. Snug the screwheads, but do not force them. Your upper and lower now fit tightly.

The Army Marksmanship Training Unit takes a more permanent view towards tight fit. They use epoxy to fill the gaps between upper and lower. To do the same to your rifle

requires Brownells Acra-Glas Gel or Devcon epoxy, degreaser, release agent, dye, an Accuwedge and toothpicks. To epoxy your rifle, first remove all moving parts from the upper and lower. Thoroughly degrease the upper and lower. Apply release agent to the crosslugs of the upper, the pin holes and the delta ring. Coat the bottom edges of the upper where it meets the lower. Extend this coat up the sides of the upper, inside and out. Apply release agent to the disassembly holes of the lower, and the sides of the front hole slot. Apply release agent to the bolt catch and the slot it rides in. Apply release agent to the disassembly pins. The only places you want the epoxy to adhere are on the top edges of the lower, where it meets the upper.

Clamp your lower in your cradle. Mix the epoxy according to instructions, and include black dye. The dye will cause your epoxy to blend in with the rest of the rifle. If you do not have a black rifle, then use a dye color that corresponds to the

With a match barrel installed, tightly fitted upper and lower, a match trigger and A2 sights, the AR is a formidable match rifle. So much so that Nick used his to shoot into High Master with a Quality Parts/Bushmaster Service rifle.

For a super-accurate long-range rifle, you can use epoxy to fit the upper and lower tightly together. As with glass bedding, be sure to use a release agent, or you'll have a permanent assembly.

For shooters with long arms, Olympic makes a buttstock extender that can add up to an inch to the pull of the AR.

The black plastic part of the Olympic extender fits on the buffer tube at the rear of the lower. The aluminum parts fit inside the buttstock, out of sight.

lowers around until they find pairs that fit tightly. After all, they have many rifles to choose from. Every rifle in the Army inventory can't be loose?

The buttstock of the original M-16 was short. So short that tall recruits were exhorted to press their noses against the charging handle as a method of ensuring consistent cheekweld and eye position. When the M-16A1 was upgraded to the M-16A2 one change was to make the buttstock 5/8 inches longer. Even that is not long enough for some shooters. I have 37-inch sleeves and a long neck. Even the A2 buttstock comes up short on me. To extend the stock, install an Olympic Arms stock spacer. The package consists of a longer buttstock screw, an internal spacer and an external extension. You can get them in 5/8-inch or 1-inch lengths. To install, remove the upper screw from your buttstock and store it in a safe place. Slide the buttstock off and keep an eye on the rear disassembly pin capture spring. Slide the stock extension over the buffer tube and press it

color of your rifle. Use a toothpick to apply the epoxy to the edges of the lower where they meet the upper. You do not have to use much, but spread it evenly. Insert the Accuwedge in the rear of the lower, and then press the upper in place. The Accuwedge provides upwards tension on the disassembly pins. The tension removes slack from the fit. Without the Accuwedge, or something else to provide tension, you could epoxy your two halves and end up not removing the wobble. Press the pins in place. Use a stiff card such as an old business card to scrape the excess epoxy from the outside. Leave the rifle alone until the next day.

Once the epoxy has set, press the pins open and lift the upper straight up. Don't lever it open. Use a file to clean the excess epoxy from the inside. Until you use it and shoot it enough to wear the epoxy, your upper and lower will be a tight fit.

After doing this several times, I began to wonder why the Army Marksmanship Unit doesn't just swap uppers and

The collapsing stock of the AR has the advantage of intermediate steps. The standard is a three-position, while Olympic makes one that has four positions. The typical folding stock is either out or in.

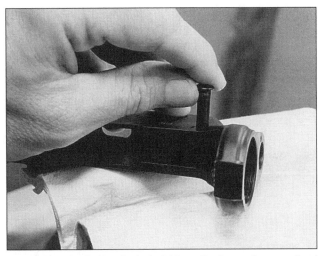

The rear takedown pin is held into the lower by a spring and plunger. Without a buttstock, the spring and plunger can become lost.

against the lower receiver. Doing this will press the capture spring back into place. Place the internal extension on the end of the buttstock. Slide the buttstock onto the buffer tube and tighten the new screw in place. If you later remove the extension, re-install the old buttstock screw. If you use the longer Olympic screw without the extensions in place, the screw will stick into your buffer tube and get hammered by the buffer weight on every shot you take.

A less-comfortable but racier-looking stock is the collapsing stock. Originally designed as an aid to airborne troops who had to have their equipment as compact as possible, it is one of the features prohibited on "post-ban" rifles. If you want to assemble one on a pre-ban rifle, the process is simple. Remove the upper buttstock screw on your present stock. Pull off the buttstock, and pull out and save the capture spring. Clamp the lower in a padded vise. Look in the lower receiver at the front of the buffer tube. You will see a plunger, which is the buffer weight retainer. With your thumb press the buffer into the buffer tube. Use a small screwdriver to depress the plunger, and ease the buffer

With the rear takedown pin in place, insert the plunger and spring.

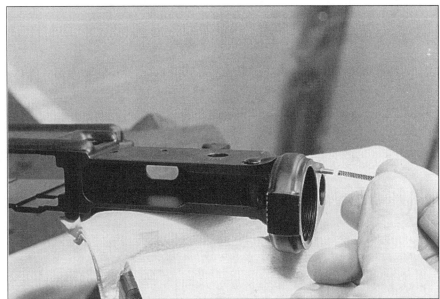

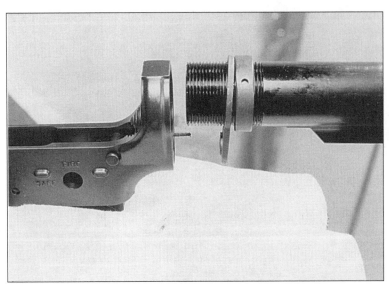

With the lower clamped in a padded vise, begin screwing the buffer tube in. Note that the retaining plate has its button forward, and the plate and locking nut are screwed to the back of the buffer tube threads.

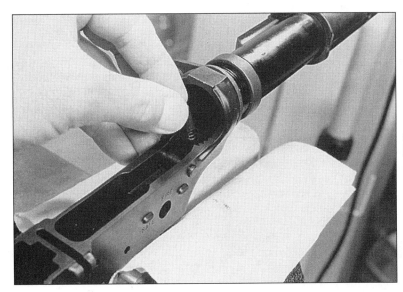

Once the buffer tube is started, insert the buffer retainer spring and plunger.

Screw the buffer tube into the lower until it binds against the retainer. Press the retainer down and continue to turn the buffer tube in.

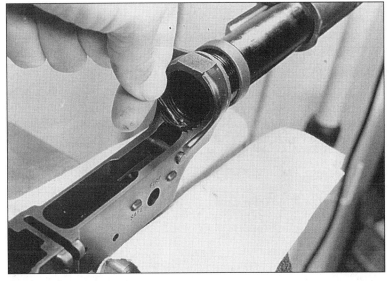

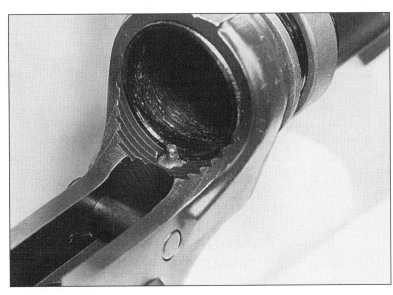

Once the buffer tube bears against the upper stud of the retaining plunger, turn the buffer tube back out only until the buttstock is vertical. If you turn the stock too much the retainer will pop out.

weight forward. Pull it and the buffer spring out of the buffer tube. At the rear of the buffer tube is a knob with two flats on it. This is where you grab the buffer tube to turn it. Use a wrench on these flats and turn the tube. Once it is loose you can turn the tube by hand. As you unscrew it you will uncover the buffer retainer plunger. Keep the thumb of your other hand over the plunger to keep it from launching itself across the room.

With the tube off, pick up your collapsing assembly. Take the buffer tube lock nut and screw it onto the buffer tube. Turn it on at least an inch. Slide the receiver plate onto the tube. This plate looks like a tennis racquet without strings and a little stub in the center of the hole. The stub slides in the slot cut through the threads on the bottom of the buffer tube. Slide the plate onto the tube with the "bump" in the handle towards the lower. Using both hands, screw the tube into the lower until it reaches the buffer weight retainer hole. At this point you will have to juggle three things: the tube as you thread it, the plate to keep it in position on the tube, and the buffer weight plunger depressed in its hole.

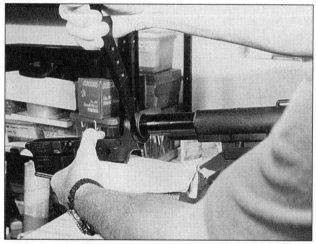

It takes a special wrench to tighten the locking nut without marring it. After breaking several regular wrenches, I found the wrench from American Spirit Arms to be up to the task.

Instead of growing a third hand, use a piece of masking tape to keep the plate in place. Screw the tube on until the front edge of it binds against the tip of the depressed plunger. Back the tube out only until the buttstock is vertical. Reinstall the capture spring. Press the retaining plate forward until it is against the lower. Tighten the lock nut against the retaining plate.

Before you use the wrench to tighten things, check looks and function. Does the buffer retainer move up and down? Does the rear disassembly pin move freely, and stay in the lower? Is the buttstock vertical? Does the stock open and close? If the answer is yes, then use the lock nut wrench to tighten the lock nut. I have broken many lock nut wrenches in the past, but not any more. American Spirit Arms makes a wrench that looks like you could break a rifle or two with it. It also doubles as a barrel wrench. If you work on AR's, this wrench is just the ticket.

Loosen the lock nut a turn or two and place several drops of low-strength Loctite in the gap. Tighten the lock nut firmly. The buffer tube is subjected to much vibration. Check your tube or lock nut after the first 200 rounds to make sure it is still tight. If it has loosened, use more Loctite and tighten the nut more than you did before.

Changing pistol grips on the AR is easier than falling off a log. Turn the unloaded rifle upside down. Reach into the pistol grip with a large screwdriver and turn out the screw attaching the pistol grip to the lower. When you lift the grip off you will see a small spring in a hole in the grip. The spring activates the safety plunger. Save the spring. Do not turn the rifle right side up until the new pistol grip is on or you will drop the plunger. Slide the screw into the new grip and wiggle it around until the screw slides through the hole. Doing this now saves fiddling with it once the grip is on the lower. Place the spring into the hole of the new grip and slide the new pistol grip onto the lower. Tighten the screw.

Easy, but why change grips? The original grip is a skinny affair. For shooters with large hands the original grip is too small and uncomfortable to hold. A larger grip such as the Lone Star Ordnance trapdoor grip fits larger hands comfortably. The Lone Star grip also gives you a place to store small extras that won't fit in the buttstock recess. For match shooters who are not restricted to service-equivalent pistol

The ASA wrench tightens both the locking nut on telescoping stocks and the barrel nut on all rifles. Forget the military wrench (in the foreground) it isn't worth using. If you are going to change barrels, you'll need the aluminum barrel blocks.

The standard pistol grip on AR's is a skinny, "one size fits all" part. For match use (does not pass muster on a Service rifle) the Sierra grip is much more comfortable, especially if you have large hands.

grips, then an ergonomically-shaped grip like the Sierra precision grip is just the ticket. While the original grip is a reasonable compromise, it is at an awkward angle for prone shooting. The Sierra grip makes lying in the hot sun shooting at far targets more fun.

The last areas for fit and function on the AR are the handguards. The original ARs had triangular handguards, like the M-16 and M16A1. These were comfortable and sat level on sandbags, but they were not very durable. They also came in lefts and rights, complicating military supply. With the upgrade to the M16A2 the handguards were changed. The new ones were designed circular in cross section instead of triangular. The two halves were made identical. While the front retaining plate was changed from triangular to round, the new handguards were designed to fit either round or circular plates. The new 'guards were made stronger and have a more effective heat shield in them.

While a vast improvement, they have one small problem and one large one for target shooters. The small problem is that round guards are harder to keep level on sandbags. This is a problem only with accuracy testing from the bench. If you have a scope with a bubble level in it like the Springfield Government scopes you do not have a problem. Keep the bubble level, and shoot away. Careful and fussy work with the sandbags can also keep your rifle level.

The big problem for target shooting is sling attachment. The sling swivel on the AR is secured to the front sight

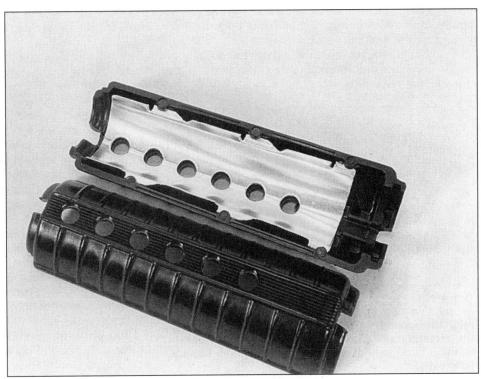

The original handguards were triangular and came in rights and lefts. The A2 style is round, interchangeable, and should come with heat shields installed.

When using the AR from the bench, you'll probably have to turn your front rest around. The Bald Eagle rest is very sturdy, but the rear leg (as usually used) interferes with the magazine. I turn mine around. The rifle doesn't notice, and the rest doesn't care.

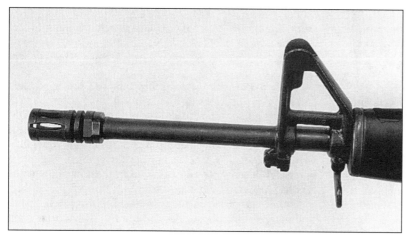

One problem for the match shooter is the front sling. It is attached to the front sight assembly, which is pinned directly to the barrel. Even with a heavy match barrel, sling tension can change the point of impact.

base. Tight sling tension on the AR can flex the barrel and change the point of impact. Greater barrel thickness only diminishes this flex but does not eliminate it. A rifle can show a change in its zero even with a heavy barrel. The only way to avoid this is to attach the sling swivel to something that does not touch the barrel.

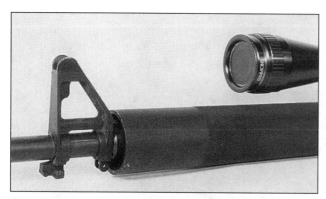

One solution to the sling problem is to change the hand guards to a tube. The tube is threaded to secure the barrel to the upper. By attaching the sling stud to the tube, the barrel is unaffected by sling tension. This approach is not allowed for those wanting to shoot in the Service Rifle category.

The simple solution is to use a tube handguard and attach the sling swivel to the tube. You will need the new handguard, barrel blocks or a Peace River upper fixture, an armorer's block, snap-ring pliers and a wrench. The wrench can be a pipe wrench with a PVC adapter, or a strap wrench. You will need drift punches for the front sight pins and a hammer.

To install the tube handguard, remove the upper from the lower and remove the bolt and carrier. Remove the handguards. Place the barrel on an armorer's block. The block supports the barrel while you drift the front sight pins out. If you do not have an armorer's block then you need to make one. Do not try to drift the pins out with the barrel held in your vise. You can damage the barrel and hurt yourself. Look closely at the pins in the bottom of the front sight base. On a properly manufactured barrel these pins are taper pins. The heads will be smaller on one side than on the other. If you are not sure which side is smaller use a dial calipers to measure the head diameter. Remove them from the sight base with a drift punch and hammer. Strike the sight pins on the smaller of the two heads. Once they break free, press them out by hand.

Use a plastic or brass mallet to tap the front sight off of the barrel. If you will be using the same front sight base leave the gas tube attached. If you will be changing bases,

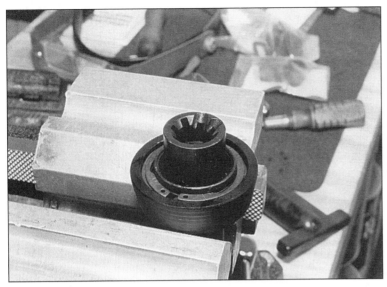

Unlike most other rifles, the locking lugs of the AR are not on the receiver, they are part of the barrel. Below the chamber opening is the delta ring assembly, which retains the rear of the handguards.

To clamp the upper without damaging it you need to use the Peace River AR block. The hinged halves clamp around the upper, supporting and holding it.

drift the small roll pin securing the gas tube from the sight base, and pull it out towards the rear of the sight base.

Clamp the barrel in your vise using aluminum adapter blocks, or the receiver using the Peace River fixture. With the barrel wrench unscrew the barrel nut. Pull the upper receiver and barrel apart. With a snap-ring pliers open the delta ring retainer and pull it off the barrel nut. Pull the delta ring and spring off of the barrel nut. Remove the barrel from the blocks and set it aside. Pull the barrel nut off the barrel. Take your tube handguard and check its fit to the upper receiver. It must screw completely and easily onto the upper. If not, clean the threads of tube and receiver of gunk and thread-locking compound. Take the tube off and slide it over the barrel. Press the barrel into the upper and screw the handguard on by hand. Once it is snug, either re-clamp the barrel in the vise blocks or the upper in the Peace River fixture. Here is where the fixture is worth the money you paid for it. Since you can only clamp the barrel forward of the handguard, you may bend the barrel while tightening the new handguard. The point you are tightening is a foot and a half away from the barrel blocks. With the fixture, you are

With the barrel nut loose, or the tubular handguard unscrewed, the upper slides on or off the barrel extension.

With the upper secured in the Peace River blocks, and clamped in the vise, you can work on the upper without risk of damaging it.

You have lots of elbow room to use the barrel nut wrench to tighten a standard barrel or a tube handguard.

The tubular handguard for Service rifles fits inside a modified set of plastic handguards.

With the sling swivel attached to the tube, sling tension will not affect the barrel.

One advantage of the ASA wrench is that it works with tubular handguards.....

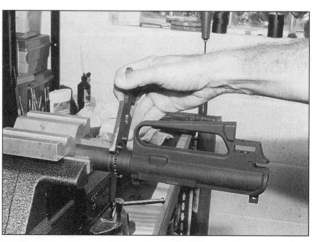

Where the mil-spec wrench will not.

The barrel nut must be tightened until its splines leave a slot for the gas tube. This nut should be tightened about a minute clockwise.

These are AR parts, not M-16 parts. Do not buy "surplus" M-16 parts if you can avoid it. All standard AR-15/M-16 parts are case-hardened, and if you try to stone them for a better trigger pull you may end up with an inoperative rifle.

tightening the handguard a fraction of an inch from the clamping point.

To tighten the new handguard (or a new barrel nut when replacing the barrel) grasp it with your hands and tighten it onto the receiver as tight as you can. Then loosen it and tighten it again. Loosen the handguard and then place your wrench on it. Tighten it the third time using the wrench. Do not be bashful about tightening it, turn the handguard until it bottoms out. Look through the handguard and see if one of the gas tube clearance holes lines up with the hole in the receiver. If it does, you are done tightening.

If not, you must do more work. The gas tube has to pass through the handguard into the upper. If the holes do not line up you cannot make the rifle work. If the handguard is almost turned far enough, then try tightening it more. If the handguard is just barely past lining up you can loosen it. If the holes are off enough that the clearance to the upper is blocked, you have to remove metal. To remove metal from the handguard or barrel would take a lathe. You are left with removing metal from the receiver. Unscrew the handguard and remove handguard and barrel. With a large clean file carefully file the front ring of the upper receiver. You do not have to remove much metal to allow the handguard to rotate. Take two passes and reassemble. Keep filing and checking until the gas tube holes line up.

Slide the front sight assembly onto the barrel and snake the tube through the holes. Press the front sight pins into place by hand. Place the front sight on the armorer's block and with a drift punch and hammer tap the pins back in place.

If you are using the old handguards but replacing the barrel with a new one, the procedure is the same. One advantage in using the old handguards is that the barrel nut is in plain sight. You do not have to peer down the tube handguard to see if the gas tube has clearance.

Trigger

The trigger on the AR-15 is simple and straightforward. There is no intermediate sear or linkage between the trigger and hammer. The front of the trigger rests in a notch in the hammer to keep it at full-cock. Riding inside the trigger is

the disconnector and its spring. At the rear of the trigger is the safety bar. On the rear of the hammer is the disconnector hook. When the safety is on "safe" it prevents the rear of the trigger from rising. When pressed, the trigger cannot move. By pushing the safety to "fire" you rotate a clearance slot into place. The rear of the trigger is now free to rise. When you press the trigger you, in effect, yank the trigger down out of the notch on the hammer.

The hammer swings forward, strikes the firing pin and fires the round. When the bolt carrier moves back it cams the hammer back towards the trigger. Your finger is still holding the trigger back. As the hammer comes back its disconnector hook catches on the disconnector. The hammer is held there until you release the trigger. As the trigger moves forward when you release it, its tip rises until it has gotten high enough to catch the hammer. At this point in a properly-timed AR the disconnector lets go of the hammer, and with an audible "click" the trigger mechanism is re-set.

The disconnector must sit in the trigger within a small range. If the disconnector tilts too far back it will release the hammer too soon in the re-set. The result is a rifle that fires twice: once when you pull the trigger and once when you release the trigger. Such a rifle is not only unsafe, it is illegal. If the disconnector tilts back too far it may not catch the hammer at all. The usual result is a rifle that fires every other time, not the "machine gun" you might expect. What happens is instead of the hammer striking the firing pin with the bolt closed, the hammer rides the bolt down, dampening the impact. When you manually work the action the trigger is free to catch the hammer, starting the frustrating cycle over again.

A disconnector that tilts too far forward will not release the hammer during the re-set phase.

The tilt of the disconnector is adjusted by filing the bottom, not the tip. Filing underneath the front tip of the disconnector where it rests on the trigger tips the disconnector forward. There is no need to tilt the disconnector back unless it will not release the hammer on re-set.

A drop-in hammer and trigger set like the one from Accuracy Speaks can solve many of your trigger problems. Unlike the mass-produced parts made for the government,

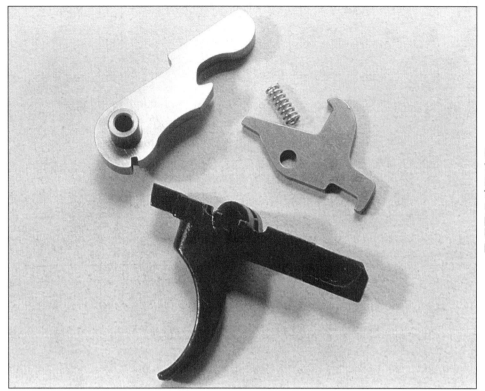

If you want a better trigger in your AR, switch the standard parts for match parts, like this trigger set from Accuracy Speaks. Instead of a 6-pound-plus trigger pull, you have just under 4 pounds of pull.

the Accuracy Speaks hammers and triggers are individually machined to correct engagement. Once you drop them in, all you might have to do is adjust the disconnector for proper hold and release.

Barrels

The AR has one huge advantage over other rifles for the home gunsmith: the barrel does not need threading to fit into the receiver. The AR barrel slides into the upper and is held in place by the barrel nut. The barrel nut screws onto threads cut into the upper receiver.

Fitting the barrel is the easy part. The hard part is selecting one. Not just a manufacturer, that is hard enough because there are many good barrel makers out there. No, picking the right length, weight or diameter, type of steel and rifling twist can make you dizzy. Add in pre-and-post ban and you may need to sit down for a while. Length first.

Your choices are, 16 inches, 20 inches and longer. Sixteen inches is the shortest barrel you can legally have unless you have a "papered" M-16. Then you can get silly with a 10-inch barrel if you want. For the rest of us, 16 is long enough to deliver accurate shots and not lose much velocity. The "shorty" as it is sometimes called, is a very handy package, especially if you couple the 16-inch barrel with a collapsing stock on a pre-ban rifle. The standard length barrel is 20 inches, and this gives you the full velocity of the .223 cartridge in a handy package. Long-range match shooters put longer barrels on their rifles not for added accuracy, but for greater velocity and a longer sight radius.

Twenty is handy, 16 is handier, both are accurate. As an aside, barrel makers offer barrels that are 10 or 11 inches of rifled barrel with a welded-on 6- or 5- inch flash-hider. They look neat, but suffer two problems. Velocity is decreased several hundred extra feet per second from the full 16-inch barrel. And as a reversal of the expected, such a barrel actually has more muzzle flash than a 16-inch barrel with a standard "bird-cage" flash-hider. If you want your rifle to have the look of an ultra-shorty with a large flash-hider like the XM-177 used in Vietnam, use a 16-inch barrel and get a Choate flash-hider. The Choate unit is threaded at the front. It slides over the barrel and gives the look of the XM-177.

For weight or diameter I pick the heaviest barrel I can get or fit to the rifle. I am not anticipating

The AR barrel extension is smooth, and the threaded barrel nut clamps the barrel into the upper receiver.

The barrel inserted into the upper. The threads of the upper match the threads of the barrel nut. Notice the locating pin. Do not file the pin or the slot in the upper to make it "easier to assemble". This pin keeps your front sight vertical, don't make it a loose fit!

carrying the rifle all day looking for trouble. If I do ever find myself in such a predicament I may regret the extra weight I have to lug around. I select a heavy barrel for balance and heat control. A heavier barrel balances out front, the way I like a rifle to feel. A heavy barrel takes more shots before it heats up. One compromise is to install a fluted barrel. Lighter than the heavy barrel, it dissipates heat even faster. Yes, a fluted barrel is a stiff barrel, but it is not stiffer than the full-diameter barrel, rather it is stiffer than the same-weight barrel.

For type of steel, there are only two choices in my book. One is stainless, the other is chrome-lined. A stainless barrel is easy to clean and resists corrosion better than a carbon-steel barrel does. For the ultimate in corrosion and wear-resistance you can't beat a chrome-lined barrel. The government insists on chrome-plating for all of its rifle barrels, and many other firearms as well. One knock on chrome-plating is that it is not as accurate as plain bore. I will have to take the word of the people who claim this, as I have not seen it myself. I have fired many chrome-lined

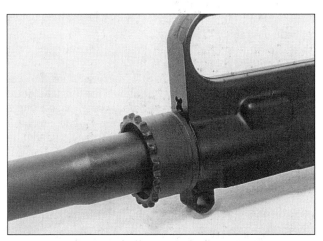

Here is the barrel nut screwed onto the upper without the delta ring and spring. On the front of the carrying handle is the gas tube hole. Tighten the barrel nut so the gas tube passes through, do not file the hole in the upper.

If you have a legally-owned M-16 or short-barreled AR-15 then you can install this barrel as-is. Otherwise, you must permanently attach an extension that makes it more than 16 inches. (As an aside, it is legal to own such a short barrel, provided you DO NOT assemble it to an upper. Once installed, it is a federal felony to own it.)

rifles that shot groups under an inch. Some have done spectacular work. My friend Jeffrey Chudwin who has won many events, including the Light Rifle at Second Chance, has such a rifle. It is a Colt with a chrome-lined bore, and I have seen it shoot five-shot groups that could each be covered with a single target paster a half-inch square. The observation I have noted is that the people who do not like chrome bores shoot slowly and at long range. For them, dropping a point at 600 yards is a big deal. For shooters involved in something faster, such as shooting bowling pins, the ease of cleaning, durability and longevity far outweigh a theoretical accuracy loss.

The big question is twist. How fast is enough? The original Armalite had a twist of one turn in 14 inches. This was not enough to stabilize bullets under Arctic conditions, or when the barrels began to wear. The twist rate was tightened to 12 inches. This is fine for bullets around 55 grains. To use a heavier (longer) bullet you need a faster twist. The government went to a twist of 7 inches on the M-16A2. Why? Ostensibly to fully stabilize the tracer bullets to the full distance of their burn, 700 meters. This twist is very close to the rate used in the German test in 1967 by IWK, and by the Belgians in their tests. My guess is that when the improved M-16 program got underway in the early 80s those involved jumped on the earlier tests to solidify their plans. Do you need a 7-inch twist? Probably not. Even the long and heavy 80-grain Very Low Drag bullets used by long-range competitors are stabilized by a twist of 8 inches. Is there any harm in a 7-inch twist? Again, probably not. Some argue that the 7-inch barrels "burn out" faster due to the fast twist. My experience has been that barrel life depends more on proper cleaning and the rate of fire than on the twist of the rifling.

Unless I am buying a barrel for long-range use with extra-heavy bullets, I buy a 9-inch twist. This will stabilize anything I load or buy as standard ammo. For long-range target shooting I buy barrels with an 8-inch twist.

A new barrel has to have the headspace checked before installation. One way to ensure proper headspace is to order a bolt head with the barrel. The manufacturer of the barrel will be happy to supply you with a new bolt with the proper headspace already set to your new barrel. If you want to use your old bolt, you will need headspace gauges and a finishing chambering reamer. You cannot adjust the headspace on a chrome-lined barrel. The chrome lining will eat your reamer for lunch. If you want a chrome-lined bore, buy a new bolt with the barrel. For the stainless barrel, remove the extractor and ejector from the bolt. The extractor pin will press out, but the ejector pin must be punched out with a 1/16-inch drift punch and a hammer.

Scrub the chamber clean. Place a "GO" headspace gauge in the chamber and attempt to insert and rotate the bolt. Either the bolt will turn or it won't. If it won't you need to ream the chamber. It will not take much. If the bolt does turn, jump to the next paragraph. To ream the chamber remove the bolt and headspace gauge. Take your chambering reamer and brush some cutting oil on it. Lower the reamer into the chamber and turn it one rotation clockwise. Do not reverse the reamer! Unlike tapping threads you do not need to break the chips. What reversing will do is prematurely dull your reamer. Pull the reamer out and swab the chamber clean. Once it is dry, insert the "GO" gauge and attempt to turn the bolt. Repeat the process until you can turn the bolt on the "GO" gauge. Do not attempt to ream the chamber in one step. If you go too far there is no way to put the metal back.

Once you can turn the bolt on the "GO" gauge switch to your "NO-GO" gauge. Insert the gauge and try to turn the bolt. It should not turn. A tightly-headspaced chamber will accept a "GO" gauge but not a "NO-GO" gauge. An AR with a chamber cut this tightly may begin to malfunction when it gets dirty. When I ran into this problem I used the rifle I was working on as an experimental subject. I had set the chamber up with minimum headspace. The bolt barely turned onto a "GO" gauge. The rifle would fire about 200 rounds then begin malfunctioning. I then reamed the chamber one turn, reassembled it and continued test firing. I found that when I had reamed the chamber to the point where I could just catch the corners of the bolt head and the locking lugs under each other, but not turn the bolt, on a "NO-GO" gauge, the rifle worked flawlessly. The chamber is not so large that brass life suffers from case stretching, but is large enough that powder residue does not make it choke.

Short barrels can be accurate. This ASA 16-inch barrel is not broken-in yet, and it is already shooting sub-inch groups. Now if the shooter will only do his part....

Whether you have reamed your chamber or not, if the bolt will turn and lock with the "no-go" gauge in place you have excessive headspace. If you have reamed your barrel you have gone too far. You should not use a rifle with excess headspace. While it may be safe in an emergency, your brass will stretch. Reloading stretched brass invites case separations. Cases that separate on firing are a headache to clear, and harmful to your rifle. They may even injure you. You must correct excess headspace. Your choices at this point are all headaches, headaches brought on by over-enthusiastic reaming. The first is to ship the barrel and bolt to someone to have the headspace set properly. The manufacturer will have to remove the barrel extension, re-cut the shoulder and re-install the barrel extension. Then, he'll ream the chamber again to headspace on your bolt. Or, ship the barrel back and ask for a bolt to fit. The manufacturer, if he has a bin full of bolts, will test these bolts until one fits. The last option is to try a bunch of bolts yourself. How many bolts will you have to buy to find one that fits? I don't know. Will the dealer take back the ones that don't fit? You had better ask him before you start.

My advice would be to send the barrel and bolt back and ask the manufacturer to do what he has to in order to make the headspace correct.

Once the headspace is properly set, fitting a barrel to the upper only requires a few tools and a little attention. You need barrel blocks or an upper fixture such as the Peace River fixture. You need a barrel wrench. You may need drift punches for the front sight pins, and will need a punch for the gas tube pin. Finally, you may need a long screwdriver to adjust the gas tube.

Follow the instructions for replacing the handguards on your AR with a free-floating handguard. Instead of installing the handguard, slide the new barrel into place and tighten the barrel nut. Use the same procedure to adjust the nut alignment if the barrel nut does not allow the gas tube to slide through. Install the gas tube and front sight. Clamp the barrel in a padded vise with a strong light shining into the ejection port. Remove the bolt from the carrier. Slide the carrier into the upper, and onto the gas tube. The tube should be straight and level, and the carrier should slide over it without needing extra force. If the gas tube is slightly out of line the carrier will rub on it. The gas tube carries the gas from the gas port in the barrel to the bolt carrier. If the tube and carrier are out of line the tube will wear on the side where it rubs. A few thousand rounds later you may not get a good gas seal, and the rifle may start short-stroking.

To align the gas tube, use your long screwdriver as a pry bar. Gently adjust the gas tube until the carrier slides over it without hesitation.

Sights

The original AR sights are adequate for combat, but are sorely lacking for target work. The adjustable sights on the new M-16A2, and other makers such as Armalite and Olympic, offer target shooters sights equal to the ones they used to use on the M-1 Garand and the M-14/M-1A. Yes, used to use. It seems now that the supposed accuracy and

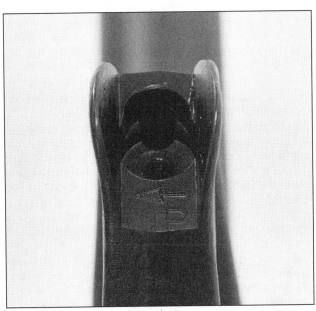

The front sight of the AR screws into the front sight assembly, and is held in place by a spring and plunger.

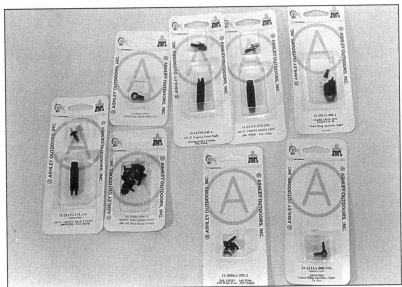

Emerson Ashley makes a full line of sights for rifles in general, and the AR in particular.

The standard four-stop square post. The original posts had five stops and were tapered cylinders. In a match the round sight could be hard to accurately align, so one of the A2 upgrades was to make the post square.

offers front posts with a difference. One style has a white line running up the center of the blade. The lined front sights come in .080-inch and .100-inch widths. At close range or in low light, your eye can hardly miss it. My favorite is his extra-wide front with a white dot and a tritium insert in it. The dot or the tritium insert center themselves in the rear aperture quickly for me, while I have to hunt for the top of the lined blades. (Perhaps I have spent too much time with a shotgun and bright bead sights to follow the blade?) Each comes with a front sight installation and adjustment tool.

The only drawback to the blade or the dot is front sight adjustments. The blade only offers two settings per turn, and the dot one, versus four or five on the standard sight. The worst-case would be where your rifle hits off the adjustments of the front sight. However, the error can only be an inch at 100 yards with the blade, and 2 inches with the dot, and these are intended to be close-range sights.

While the front sight is often adequate, the rear sight adjustment plate can be improved. The Rapidex sight replaces the rear sight plate. Instead of needing a sight tool you can use your fingers to adjust windage. To replace the old plate with a Rapidex you will need the new unit, a hammer, drift punch and needle-nose pliers.

functioning problems of the AR have been solved, competitors are flocking to the low recoil the AR offers.

The original sights were designed with simplicity and durability in mind. The front sight rotates up and down to adjust the point of impact vertically. The rear sight is windage only. The spring and plunger that keeps each sight in place was designed to be adjusted with the tip of a bullet. Soldiers may lose a sight-adjustment tool, but they will always have ammunition. While a bullet works, the brass rubbings can be unsightly. Use a sight adjustment tool.

Replacement front sights come in a variety of styles. The target competitors replace the round post with a wedge-shaped front that offers a flat face to their eye, and clearly-defined edges on each side and the top. For some shooters, who are planning on having their targets closer than 200, 330, 500 and 600 yards, Ashley Emerson of Ashley Outdoors

Competition shooters are so picky about details. Once the front sight has been adjusted they do not want it to wiggle. (What can it move, a thousandth of an inch? At 600 yards that thousandth becomes just over an inch!) This front sight is locked in place with a set screw.

The match front sight is machined to taper to the front, for a clean vertical line on each side.

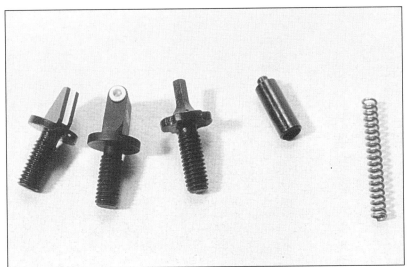

Left to right, the Ashley vertical line sight, the Ashley night sight, a standard A2 post and the plunger and spring that keep them in the sight assembly.

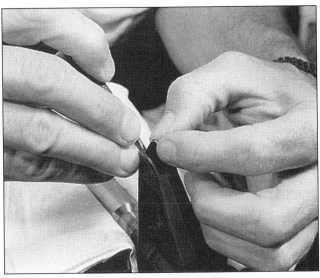

To install the Ashley sights (or any others) depress the front sight plunger and screw the sight in.

Some night sights for the AR are small lines. The Ashley is a large dot surrounded by a white circle.

Because the Ashley dot is only on one side of the four notches, you have to make a complete revolution for each adjustment. As the sight is meant for close-range use, this is not a problem.

If your previous sight was zeroed, measure down from the ears before you remove it, and then install the new sight to the same location. If you are assembling the upper from parts, start your sighting-in with the front sight base flush with the "UP" surface. Remember, screw the sight in to raise the bullets, out to lower the bullets.

The rear sight plate is held to the shaft by a roll pin. Turn your rear sight plate until the roll pin lines up towards the upper rear corner of the carrying handle. Remove the upper from the lower and remove the bolt and carrier from the upper. Lie the upper on your bench on its side. Take a drift punch and a hammer and tap the roll pin out. Remove the old sight plate. Line the Rapidex knob pin hole up with the pin hole on the shaft and press the knob down onto the shaft. Insert your drift punch from the ejection port side of the

knob. Press the drift punch through the shaft. The knob will now stay in place. Hold the new roll pin with the needle-nose pliers and tap it into the knob. Once the roll pin has gone in far enough to capture the shaft, pull out the drift punch. Use the punch to center the roll pin in the shaft. Click the rear knob back to its previous position and your rear sight is ready to go.

The A2 rear sight offers both windage and elevation adjustments. Target shooters improve their sights by replacing the assembly with one that has finer adjustments. To do this you will need a rear sight assembly like the one from Smith Industries. To remove your A2 assembly, remove the upper from the lower and take the bolt, carrier and charging handle out. With a drift punch tap out the rear sight spring pin, just under the rear sight assembly. The spring powering the sight is a strong one. Once you have the pin halfway out the spring will begin to press on the punch. Be careful not to

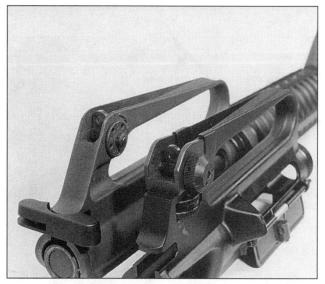

The A2 sights have windage and elevation knobs that you can adjust without a tool. While they are greatly favored by target shooters and the Marine Corps, many shooters find that the A1 sights work fine.

On the left the original small rear sight plate, that needed either a bullet tip or a special tool to adjust. On the right is the Rapidex knob, which allows you to adjust windage with your fingertips.

Working the AR-15 • 277

Available from Smith Industries, this A2 target sight assembly gives a target shooter quarter-minute clicks instead of the half-minute ones on the standard A2. The extra precision can mean more points in a match.

During a match, a competitor will be constantly evaluating the wind, and adjusting his sights for the differing distances. To make sure he (or she) knows just where their zero is, they use paint, white-out or nail polish.

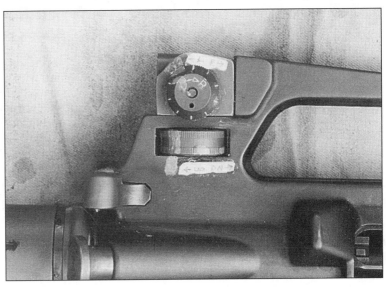

To set the elevation ring properly, bring the ring eight clicks up, and then adjust the upper and lower halves of the ring until the "3/8" mark is right over the roll pin. Then zero with the front sight.

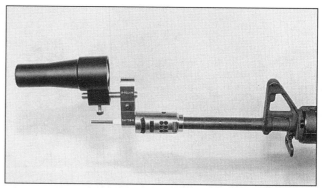

With the scope mounted in the handle, you have to use an adapter like this B-Square in order to see the collimator through the scope.

The iron sights are already high above the stock on an AR. If you mount a scope in the carrying handle, you'll have to use a bolt-on cheekpiece to give your face support while you aim.

strike the far side of the receiver with the punch. Pull the pin and spring out. Rotate the elevation knob of the rear sight and raise the sight assembly. You will have to keep track of two spring-loaded ball bearings. The first to appear will be the sight body tensioning bearing. It rests in the sight body and bears against the carrying handle. When you have turned the sight up far enough it will come out of the body. Set the bearing and spring aside. Lift the sight body and its threaded shaft clear from the elevation knob. The elevation bearing and spring will pop lose when you pull the knob out of its slot in the upper.

To install the new knob, insert it from the right side of the receiver. Place the bearing on its spring and use a small screwdriver, knife point or feeler gauge to depress it. Slide the elevation knob over the bearing, pushing the screwdriver out of the way. Hold the knob in place while you insert the new sight body. As you press the sight body shaft down into the upper, hold the rear sight ball bearing and spring in their hole with a fingertip.

Once the body is in the upper, turn the elevation knob to catch the sight threads. Rotate the knob until the sight is all the way to the bottom. Turn the receiver on its side and start the sight spring pin in its hole. Once it is in place, insert the sight spring. Hold the spring in place with a screwdriver blade and tap the spring pin in far enough to hold the spring. Pull the screwdriver out enough to release the spring, and then press the tip of the screwdriver against the spring pin. Use pressure with the screwdriver against the sight spring to keep the spring pin lined up. Tap the spring pin flush.

At this point your elevation knob probably does not line up with the appropriate yardage. If your knob is not marked, then you have to sight in your rifle and then use a dab of paint to record your zero. For a marked knob, bring your rear sight up eight clicks from bottomed out. You will have to take the rifle to the range and sight it in for elevation using the front sight. Once your rifle is zeroed, count the clicks as you turn the elevation knob so the "3/8" marking is on the left. You will see a small hole in front of your rear sight aperture. At the bottom of this hole is the Allen screw holding the two halves of the elevation knob together. With a 1/16-inch Allen wrench reach down and loosen the Allen screw. Do not remove it. Leave the Allen wrench in place. Now turn the lower half of the elevation knob the same number of clicks you counted, but in the OPPOSITE direc-

Springfield Armory makes a scope with a rangefinder reticle and bullet drop compensator just for the AR. Mounted on a flat-top it makes a particularly nice long-range AR.

tion. Tighten the Allen screw and remove the wrench. You now have the elevation knob set for your basic zero.

Some shooters do not feel the need for a new assembly, but would like to have a larger or smaller aperture rear sight. To change the aperture you do not have to remove the sight body from the rifle. Use the same procedure to remove the windage knob that you used before to install the Rapidex knob. With the knob off, set the knob, spring and bearing aside. The rear sight windage screw has a screw slot on the left side. Turn the screw counter-clockwise until it releases the rear sight aperture. Slide the new aperture onto the screw and turn the screw clockwise. Once the tip of the screw pokes through the other side of the aperture, press the aperture down against the flat spring. Continue turning the screw until it sticks through the right side of the sight body. Line up the retainer pin holes and re-install the knob as in the Rapidex procedure. Take your rifle to the range and test-fire to re-establish your windage zero.

Ashley Express offers a Ghost-ring rear aperture that you can use as a replacement for the standard rear aperture.

Match shooters do not miss a trick if they can avoid it. A serious competitor will use a hooded rear aperture to prevent changing light conditions from having an effect on his sight picture.

A flat-top AR without the carrying handle has no rear sight. If the scope breaks you could be out of luck. GG&G makes a rear sight that fastens to the rear of the upper. Folded down it is out of the way.

With the ASA scope mount and the GG&G fold-down rear sight, the only thing left to do is select a scope that will be up to the rest of the package.

The GG&G sight even has the flip-up short and long range apertures of the standard sight.

GG&G offers a sight that will be of interest to owners of flat-top rifles. The flat-top rifles came about as a means of getting a scope mounted on an AR without having the scope half a foot above the bore. By cutting off the carrying handle and installing a Weaver base or Picatinny rail, you can mount a scope lower to the bore. Or you can order an upper and swap your parts into it. But, with a scope in place, what do you do if you need iron sights? The GG&G A2 IRIS clamps onto the rail and offers an A2 sight picture. When you don't need it, the little thing just folds out of the way. If you select a scope with sufficient eye relief you don't have to remove the IRIS to have your scope in place. If the scope breaks, remove it, flip the IRIS up, and continue.

In addition to the IRIS, GG&G offers a fold-down front sight. Unlike the rear, which simply clamps on to the rail, the front replaces the front sight assembly.

A neat addition to the Sling Thing which allows you to put your sling on the side of the rifle is the Sling and Light

Raised, it sits at the same height as the standard rear sight.

The GG&G side sling gives you a side-mounted sling swivel....

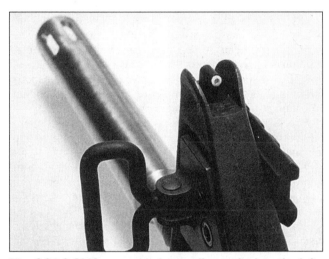

The GG&G SLIC assembly has a sling swivel on the left side, not the bottom....

And a light mount on the right side.

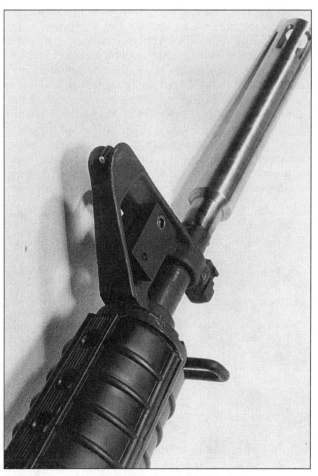

Without extra hardware on the right side.

Combo, or SLIC. The SLIC assembly uses a clamping plate that has a short section of a Weaver-type base on it. You can attach a scope ring or rings to the base and mount a 1-inch or 30mm-tubed flashlight. Rather than replacing your forearm with a bulky and dedicated unit, you can attach the SLIC and use a flashlight you already have.

Function testing the AR

In the early 1990s it seemed as if every other shooter in my metropolitan area was building an AR. The stream of non-working ARs that came through my shop seemed endless. Sometimes I would go to the range to test-fire three, four or five at a time. What I found out was that most of the problems could be traced to a few sources. And not one of those problems came about because of the gas port, except for the unfortunate few who thought their problems could be solved by drilling the gas port. DON'T drill the gas port!

A properly-functioning AR will toss its brass in one of two places. A full-sized AR will throw the empties to the right rear, at a 30- to 45-degree angle. Older rifles without the deflector lump rarely toss the empty as far "up" as 45 degrees, so the brass is usually behind the shooter. Shorty ARs, with 16-inch barrels, toss the empties forward at a 30- to 45-degree angle.

The two main problems that caused ARs to become inoperative were poor ammo and faulty magazines. If you want to know if your rifle is working properly, do not test it with reloads. Unless those reloads are as good as factory rounds, such as Black Hills reloaded ammo, you are working in the unknown. Test your rifle with factory ammo, and not imported surplus. I was recently teaching a class on the AR, and one of the students was having trouble with his rifle. It turned out that the imported surplus ammo he was using was the problem. I ended up testing a small batch of that ammo in seven different ARs and M-16s, and only one fed the stuff. The rest exhibited various malfunctions. Always do your definitive testing with a clean rifle and factory ammunition. The weak link in any magazine-fed rifle is the magazine. Only buy top-quality magazines in good shape. Despite the signing of the Crime Bill that prohibits the man-

ufacture of high-capacity magazines, AR-15/M-16 magazines are in plentiful supply.

Do not use tinny-sounding steel magazines, or surplus magazines that look like they have been dragged down a couple miles of bad road. Spend a few dollars more and buy magazines made by government contractors.

The main source of malfunctions not related to ammo or magazines came from improper headspace. A rifle with insufficient headspace may operate violently and not always eject the empty. It may eject the empty but not have enough bolt energy left to feed another round into the chamber. When the bolt closes on a cartridge trapped in the undersized chamber, the locking lugs are put under greater pressure than the rifle was designed for. When the round is fired, the already squeezed-shut bolt would be wedged against the locking lugs even harder. More of the force of the gas system than normal is needed to unlock the bolt. Often this does not leave enough force to work the action. The poor unfortunates who drilled their gas ports assumed that short-stroking the bolt meant not enough gas flow. What it really meant was the gas pressure had to be used to overcome the greater frictional forces of unlocking the bolt when headspace was too short. Having drilled the gas port, when the chamber was reamed to proper dimensions, his rifle would operate violently due to the now-excessive gas flow.

If you have a gas port that has been drilled out, there are two solutions, one expensive, the other experimental. The expensive solution is to buy a new barrel. The experimental solution is to crush the gas tube in a vise and restrict the gas flow. Buy a spare gas tube before you attempt the experimental method, because if you crush the tube too much you will stop the gas flow and the rifle will not function.

Excessive headspace does not keep the rifle from working, but reloaded brass starts separating at the base after a few loadings.

The second-largest cause of malfunctions came from improper cleaning. Cleaning kits for the M-16 include a strange looking brush. It appears to be a chamber brush, but has a stiff ring of brass bristles at its base. The "collar" scrubs the locking lugs. To properly clean your chamber, install this brush on a rod that has a "T" handle. Press the

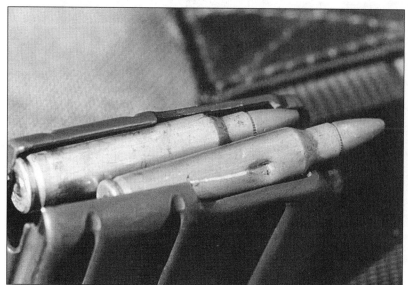

The two main causes of malfunctions in the AR are ammo and magazines. If this (called "bolt over base failure") happens with a single magazine, you have found the problem. If it happens with any magazine, it is an ammo fault. Probably.

brush into the chamber until it stops, turn it two rotations and then remove. Use a patch on the end of your rod to wipe the chamber clean. Then proceed to clean your bore in the normal fashion. Do this each time you clean your rifle and you will never have a malfunction caused by a dirty chamber.

Another source of malfunctions in the rifles I was testing came from improper buffer weights. These malfunctions usually showed up on ARs with a collapsible stock. One or more manufacturers of buffer weights uses a plastic container filled with lead shot. While it weighs the same as the mil-spec buffer, it does not always work the same. I have had such poor results from rifles with these "shot" buffers installed that the first thing I do when running into one is replace it. The proper buffers are turned from aluminum and have several steel weights in them. Once you see the difference you won't have any problem picking out the proper ones.

The extractor on the AR is weaker than the cartridge rim. In the situation of a case that is wedged tight and will not extract, the extractor will slide off of the case rim. A worn extractor can slide off even if the case is not wedged in place. If your extractor slips off the rim, disassemble the bolt and look at the extractor. The spring may be tired and shortened, or the buffer may be missing. There isn't much room in the extractor slot for a stronger spring, so the designers slipped a small plastic stump inside the spring. If your stump is missing, replace it. Replace a shortened spring. The plastic formula has been changed several times since the early 60s, so look at the color. Your buffer should be blue, green or black. I talked to Chris Burnham, the Assembly Supervisor at Quality Parts/Bushmaster about the plastic buffer predicament. "The buffer is mostly for full-auto fire," he said. "Under combat condi-

The AR extractor is a weak one, deliberately so. If you begin experiencing fired cases being left in the chamber, and you have a proper buffer, pull your extractor out and look at it.

If the plastic part is missing, replace it. If the plastic is there on your old one, replace the extractor.

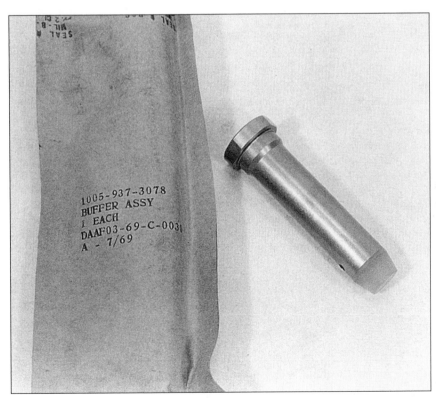

1005-937-3078
BUFFER ASSY
1 EACH
DAAF03-69-C-0030
A - 7/69

A common AR malfunction is caused by improper buffers. (The usual symptom is fired cases left in the chamber.) Only buy and use buffers that are machined aluminum cylinders filled with steel weight. Never use the plastic buffers filled with lead shot.

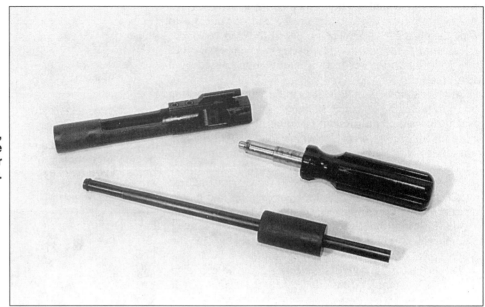

To keep your AR running, you'll need a bore guide (lower) and a Brown carrier scraper.

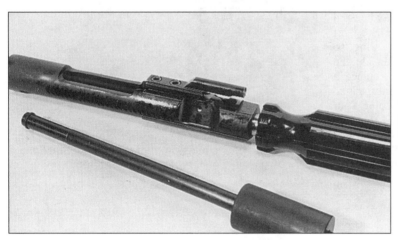

The scraper goes into the front of the carrier, and scrapes the carbon out of it without scoring the inside of the carrier.

tions and full-auto fire the buffer keeps the extractor from bouncing as the bolt cycles." As cheap as extractors are, buy and keep a spare.

Some shooters do not lubricate their rifles. For long-term storage or use in desert conditions the military shies away from oil. You should not. A dry rifle is an unhappy rifle. Don't lube it up until oil sprays out every time you shoot, but keep the internals slick with oil.

Dirty rifles are prone to malfunctioning. Clean the carbon off of the bolt and carrier. The AR-15/M-16 system is known as a "gas impingement" system. The gas from the port blows back through the tube to the carrier, and blows it open. The gas gets dumped into the carrier and the action. The gas vent hole from the carrier key goes directly into the bolt clearance hole. The carbon must be scraped from the bolt and out of the bottom of the bolt hole. The bolt can be cleaned with a brass brush, but cleaning the bolt hole in the carrier takes a special tool. Mark Brown makes a carrier scraper to ream the carbon out of the carrier. Brownells carries it. To use it, remove the bolt from the carrier. Insert the scraper and turn it several rotations clockwise. Pull the scraper out and tap the open end of the bolt hole against your bench. If you haven't cleaned your rifle in a while you will be surprised at how much gunk comes out. This tool is a must for high-volume shooters.

Pre- and post-ban parts; know the difference

What is this "pre-ban" and post-ban" stuff all about?

When the subject of AR-15s comes up, much time and effort is spent muttering about "pre-ban" and "post-ban" and how arbitrary, illogical and unfair it all is. Yes, it is. But it is the law, and as the old axiom holds true I cannot help but repeat it: "Ignorance of the law is no excuse."

When the bill was signed into law, semi-automatic rifles were judged to be "assault rifles" by a list of cosmetic features. A rifle fits the description if it would accept large-capacity magazines (greater than 10 rounds), and had two or more of the following features: A prominent pistol grip, a bayonet lug, a flash-hider or grenade launcher, a barrel threaded at the muzzle, a folding or collapsing stock. To avoid being an "assault rifle" a rifle could only have one feature. A newly assembled "assault rifle" could only be sold to law enforcement agencies or personnel. Rifles that fit the new description, but had been assembled before the law went into effect were grandfathered. Those older rifles can still be bought, sold, traded and re-built. You can install a threaded, bayonet-lugged barrel on a pre-ban rifle.

The AR-15 cannot be fired without a pistol grip of some kind. The ATF has not accepted any thumbhole stock as removing the "prominent pistol grip." That means everything else had to go. Luckily for shooters, none of the other stuff mattered.

As of Sept 13, 1994, there are two classes of ARs. (And other rifles, too.) If you have a post-ban rifle, you cannot install certain cosmetic flourishes on it. If you are uncertain of the law, write to the Bureau of Alcohol, Tobacco and Firearms and they will send you the info you need.

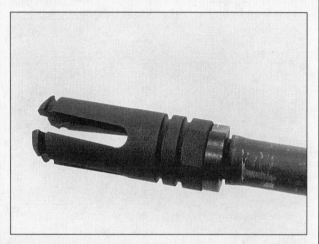

This barrel is threaded, and cannot be put on a post-ban lower. Even if you were to solder the Smith flash-hider on, the flashhider is a no-no in post-ban rifles. And that is a shame, because the Smith is the most effective flashhider I have seen or fired.

While they can be a blast to shoot, these M-4s from Quality Parts are not kosher for civilians for at least five different reasons. (Photo courtesy Quality Parts/Bushmaster.)

Even if this barrel was long enough, the threads and the bayonet lug would preclude it from being legally installed on a post-ban rifle.

If you want to know if your AR is a pre- or post-ban rifle, write the manufacturer and find out when they shipped it. Remember, Sept. 13, 1994, is the cut-off date.

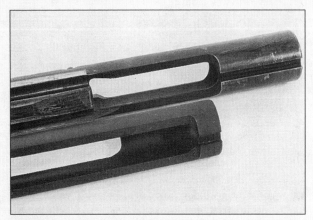

Colt installed the pinned blocks in their ARs to prevent the use of the M-16 carrier, seen on top. You should not have M-16 parts in your AR-15. Swap them or modify them, but don't keep them.

This is a box full of assembled bolts and carriers. Factory assembly of rifles requires lots of parts on hand. (Photo courtesy Quality Parts/Bushmaster.)

Since many rifles are assembled from parts, how can you tell if your rifle started life as a pre-ban or a post-ban? The simplest way is to call the manufacturer. They will be able to tell you if the rifle you have left the factory before the bill was signed. Even so, there are a lot of rifles in the inevitable gray area. You see, when the bill was signed many manufacturers had a shop floor of receivers, but not enough parts to assemble them. An unassembled receiver at that moment of the bill's signing became a "post-ban" rifle. Yes, yes, it had been made, serial-numbered and put in a box, but it hadn't been assembled. And the law was devoted to "assembly." For a while there was a brisk business in "pre-ban receivers" until the gun-buying public wised up.

If you are going to buy an AR that is held out to be a pre-ban rifle, I would suggest getting it in writing on the receipt, along with a guarantee that you can return it if it proves to be a post-ban. Then call the manufacturer and find out. Owning a post-ban rifle that has too many pre-ban features on it is a federal felony, and punishable under the law.

Some Colt rifles have modifications not related to the ban. Colt voluntarily took the bayonet lug off of their rifles several years before the ban came about. If you have a pre-ban Colt without the bayonet lug, you can install a new barrel with one. The rifle was in existence before the ban, and is not a new "assault rifle." Colt also installed a steel block in the rear of the lower. The block is designed to make it impossible to alter the lower in order to install an auto-sear. (Both of these modifications were done in a vain attempt to placate legislators. It had no effect on the law that followed.)

To prevent installation of M-16 length extensions on the lower part of the carrier, the rear of the Colt carrier was cut off on the bottom. An older AR-15 carrier will clear the block. An M-16 carrier will not. What if you want to install an upper with an M-16 carrier onto a Colt lower with the block? Both block and carrier are very hard. A file will not make an impression. A carbide end mill in a milling machine can cut the steel, but will take a beating. A surface grinder is the tool needed to make the alterations. My choice would be to alter the carrier. Functionally, cutting either or both will work. I prefer to avoid installing M-16 full-auto parts into a semi-auto rifle.

Gun shows are chock full of tables offering "surplus" parts for sale. Some may be surplus, some may be scrapped out by the government, and some may be deliberate contract over-runs by the manufacturer, making some extra money on the government set-up charges. All M-16 parts you buy as surplus parts to keep your AR running, should be modified to AR configuration. While it is unlikely, it is possible for you to be ground through the legal system on suspicion of illegal activities, of owning an AR and a bunch of "machine gun parts," your surplus spares.

A bench grinder will remove the offending features of the M-16 parts. And for goodness sake, under no circumstances should you hang on to the M-16 auto-sear, the one part essential to full-auto fire. You can argue convincingly about the other parts, but that one is an albatross.

Changing the barrel

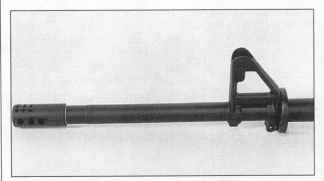

This barrel from American Spirit Arms has a soldered-on muzzle brake and lacks a bayonet lug. You can install it on either a Pre- or Post-ban rifle.

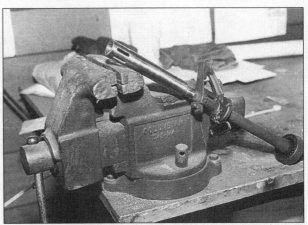

With the extension welded in place, this barrel is now long enough to be legal. However, it has slots like a flash hider, and has a bayonet lug, so it must go onto a pre-ban rifle. Were you to mount this on a post-ban you'd have to grind off the lug, and have welded on an extension without slots.

Changing barrels on an AR is a snap. Trouble arises when the temptation of a cheap "G.I. surplus" barrel proves too much for the owner of a post-ban rifle. There is no need for a bayonet lug, so no one misses it. Walk over to your bench grinder and grind it off. The threaded muzzle is a different matter. Flash-hider aside, threads are the easiest way to attach a muzzle brake or compensator. What if you want to install a comp on your post-ban? You can order a comp that will slip over the muzzle of your current barrel. By using locking screws or cross pins you can keep it on. Or, you can use that threaded barrel. At this point someone in the back is raising his hand to say "no threads!" Yes, but, if your comp is permanently attached to the threads then the ATF does not acknowledge their existence. The catch is that the standards are strict, and the ATF does not fool around.

To be permanently attached, the comp on a threaded muzzle must be secured one of several ways: You can silver-solder it on. You can weld it on. You can use a blind pin or a welded pin. You can use a non-standard thread pattern. While legal, these methods are not equally suitable. Soldering troubles me. You must use a high-temperature solder, 1100 degrees or more. You have to heat the barrel all the way around. Putting this much heat into a barrel can't be good for it. Without a controlled-atmosphere furnace the barrel may suffer. Welding can be a bit gentler on your barrel. The comp must be secured by four equally-spaced tack welds. You must get a good welder with a Mig or Tig welder to do this for you. Even with a delicate touch he may put too much heat into the barrel. A blind pin involves drilling a hole into the comp and barrel threads, a hole that does not come out the other side. Once the pin is driven in it cannot be removed. Or, drill the hole through the comp and threads (but not through the bore!) and weld one or both sides of the pin.

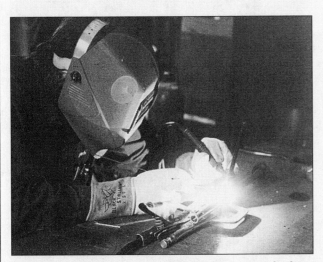

To cover the threads or make a barrel long enough, the cover/extension must be permanently attached. Welding is permanent enough for the ATF.

Here you see one of the four equally-spaced welds that hold the extension on the barrel.

I have barrels with attachments equipped by all of these methods, and they all shoot accurately. If I were putting a threaded barrel onto a post-ban rifle I would use the blind pin or welded pin method.

The trick with using a non-standard thread pattern involves the lack of flash-hiders in that thread pattern. If you have your barrel and comp threaded for a weird thread you'll be OK. That is until someone makes a flash-hider in that weird thread pitch. Then your barrel will not be kosher for a post-ban rifle.

As a last note, no industrial fastener liquid passes ATF muster. You cannot Loctite, epoxy or glue your comp in place.

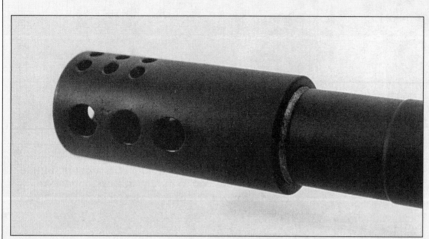

The silver ring at the back of the muzzle brake shows it has been soldered on.

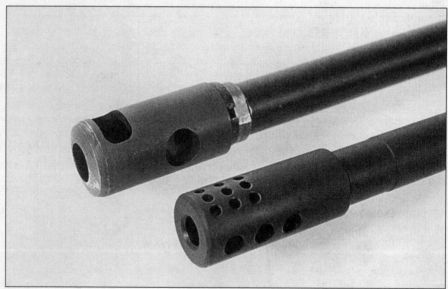

One disadvantage to the soldered or welded on brake is that you cannot remove it if you have to remove or change the front sight assembly. The upper, threaded barrel would not pose this problem. However, in years of working on ARs, the only time I "needed" to change front sight assemblies was when I wanted to.

Stocks on post-ban guns

A post-ban rifle cannot have a folding or collapsing stock. The only option is to install a stock that looks like it is a shorty stock, but does not move. Simply pinning a shorty stock is not a sufficient modification unless the pinning is permanent. The test of any modification would be this: do you have to essentially destroy the part in removing the altered section? Do you want your modified collapsing stock tested?

If you have a post-ban rifle but want the looks of the pre-ban collapsing stock, then American Spirit Arms has the buttstock for you. In looks and in length it appears to be an extended collapsing stock. In the metal, it is a solid stock that does not collapse or telescope. In addition to giving you the looks of a pre-ban shorty, it has two other advantages: It uses a standard buffer weight, and it does not wobble. Instead of the shorty buffer weight, which can make some rifles harsh in recoil, the ASA uses a standard-weight buffer. Combined with the travel of the standard length tube this takes the "jounce" out of recoil. Many collapsing or telescoping assemblies have so much play in them that the stock on the tube can wobble. When I had a beard, I found some would even pluck hairs from my beard under recoil. The solidity of the ASA assembly prevents both wobble and plucking.

For a post-ban rifle with pre-ban looks, this is just the ticket.

If you have a Post-ban rifle and want the look of a telescoping stock, then you are in luck. The ASA stock on the bottom looks like the shorty sock, but doesn't collapse. No movement of the stock, no problem with the ATF.

Not all AR pins are the same. The disassembly pins for Colts differ from ARs made by other makers and military M-16s. The military rifles and others are called "double push-pin" lowers. Front and rear pins are 1/4-inch in diameter and push out from left to right. Early in the AR-15 (1960s) production Colt modified the front pin to 5/16 inches in diameter. These pins had two screw-slotted heads. To remove the front pin on these Colts you have to have a pair of screwdrivers.

Is this a case of "never the twain shall meet?" Not at all.

Vendors make adapter pins to place Colt uppers on double push-pin lowers. You can make your own. The local hardware store probably has a supply of bronze sleeve bearings. You want one with a 1/4-inch inner and 5/16-inch outer diameter. It will cost a couple of dollars. When you get home, slide a quarter-inch drill in and clamp the bushing in your vise. File the bushing shorter until it passes between the front bosses of the lower. It will end up just under 1/2-inch in length. Slide the bushing into the upper before placing the upper on the lower.

To fit a double push-pin upper to a Colt lower requires an eccentric pin. The pin will have a slotted nut that screws onto one end. To use it, place the upper onto the lower and slide the pin through. You may have to hinge the upper up and down a few times on the lower to get the pin fully seated. Close the upper and press the rear pin in place. Screw the nut onto the front pin and tighten it in place.

In the mid-90s Colt changed their ARs to the double push-pin front pin. The new pins had two slotted heads of the smaller diameter. It is a snap to remove the double screw-head pin and install the proper push pin with its plunger and spring. Unfortunately on some of the early rifles the front pin did not have the plunger and plunger spring hole drilled in the side boss of the lower. You cannot drill this hole with a variable-speed drill. It is a task left to a professional machinist or gunsmith. If the drill wanders, you could have new holes appearing in your lower receiver.

The hammer and trigger pins on all AR type rifles have been a nominal .154 inches in diameter. In the mid-90s

Colt, in another attempt to prevent the use of military-surplus or full-auto parts, changed the diameter of their hammer and trigger pins to a nominal .173 inches. In order to obtain the correct hammer and trigger parts for your rifle you must know which diameter your pins are.

To mount an old Colt upper on a double push pin lower, buy a bronze bushing from the local hardware store, and shorten it to half an inch.

With the bronze sleeve slipped into your Colt upper, you can now install the Colt upper on your non-Colt lower.

Early Colt ARs used a double-screw head pin on the front to prevent the use of surplus uppers. Later, they switched to the double push pin lowers. You can put double push pin uppers on an old Colt by using an eccentric front pin.

Mil-spec and non-Colt ARs use hammer/trigger pins that are a nominal .154 inches in diameter. Old Colts have these pins. Newer Colts use .173-inch pins. If you have a Colt, measure your pin diameter before you order parts.

"Mil-spec" and the free exchange of parts

What is "mil-spec?" The government, in order to ensure that what they ask for is what they get, issues a set of specifications for each item they intend to buy. If you are going to supply the government with chocolate chip cookies, there is a specification for those cookies. (More likely, several pages of specifications!) The specifications list how much each cookie must weigh, its diameter, and the number of chips it must contain. (I'm not kidding, they really do this!)

A "mil-spec" rifle meets all of the specifications listed in the relevant Department of Defense regulations. The mil-spec comes as a two-part package; the verbal description and the reference documents governing production. You cannot buy an entirely mil-spec rifle. Why not? First of all, the specs call for a select-fire or burst-fire rifle. Second, the rifle must have a bayonet lug and flash-hider. Third, only those manufacturers who are engaged in making rifles for the government, or their sub-contractors, are making mil-spec rifles. Finally, a rifle has to be accepted by the government to earn true mil-spec status. Even though Colt makes rifles for the government, the Colt rifle you buy is not, and never has been a fully mil-spec rifle. It can't be. The only real mil-spec rifles out there must belong to the government, or they must be papered "retired" M-16s in the hands of machine gun collectors, or are black market rifles.

Mil-spec and non-Colt ARs use hammer/trigger pins that are a nominal .154 inches in diameter. Old Colts have these pins. Newer Colts use .173-inch pins. If you have a Colt, measure your pin diameter before you order parts.

Mil-spec is more than just the manufacturing dimensions. If these lowers are not meant for the government (And they aren't, being AR-15 lowers. The sharp-eyed reader can tell why.), then they can't be true mil-spec even if they come off the same assembly line.

This is a real mil-spec rifle, as it is going to be shipped to a storage depot after its fun run. What most dealers probably mean by "mil-spec" is: "Except for not being full-auto..." (Photo courtesy Quality Parts/Bushmaster.)

So what does a dealer mean when he offers you a "mil-spec" rifle? Probably that he doesn't know how stringent the mil-spec regulations are. Perhaps he does know that the manufacturer of that particular rifle makes parts or rifles that would meet mil-spec if they were tested. I have had good luck with, and been pleased with the rifles and products from a number of manufacturers. I do not claim that this is an exhaustive list, only what my experience has taught me. For a military-style AR-15 you can expect top quality from American Spirit Arms, Armalite, Colt, DPMS, Olympic Arms, and Quality Parts. For a non-military looking AR, then go to DPMS or JP Enterprises.

Not everyone wants a mil-spec rifle. Wyatt Taylor, at the USPSA 3-Gun Nationals in 1997, has exactly one mil-spec part on this rifle. The rest of it is shades of red, gold, black and blue.

I have interchanged uppers and lowers from all of these manufacturers with each other, and with M-16s. They have all worked. Does this mean you can interchange uppers and lowers willy-nilly? Pre- and post-ban considerations aside, no. In testing the fit of hundreds of AR-15s, I have found that some uppers will not fit on some lowers. There has not been a pattern, so I cannot predict if your lower will take any particular upper. If you want to build another upper on your existing lower, the best way to make sure the new upper fits is to try it.

This may mean going to a gun show and trying the fit of uppers until you find one you like. Or, you can order a new upper from the manufacturer of your lower. Lastly, you can ship your lower to the manufacturer and ask them to select an upper that fits snugly.

The AR is unique in its ability to interchange uppers and lowers. You can build several specialized rifles from uppers, all fitted to a single lower. For less than the cost of another rifle, you can have a new upper for another sport or hunting challenge.

Factory assemblers use parts in bins, to keep from inadvertently installing the wrong parts in a civilian-legal AR. When it is time to change production runs, the bins are swapped, not just the parts. (Photo courtesy Quality Parts/Bushmaster.)

A big advantage of the AR is the interchangeable uppers. After I used this Armalite rifle as-is at Gunsite in an AR-15 class, I then swapped a scoped upper onto it to shoot at Second Chance. Two rifles for the price of one and a half!

Among those who offer more than just "black rifles" is JP Enterprize. This flat-top match rifle is not only accurate and soft-shooting, it is red, blue, gold and black. (Photo courtesy JP Enterprize.)

And then, for varmint shooting out West, I built another upper with a flat-top and a Simmons 6.5-20X silhouette scope. Three rifles for the price of two!

CHAPTER 19

Building a Scout Rifle

Have you ever handled a rifle that was so light and responsive you hated to put it down? That almost seemed to find the target on its own? Many deer hunters will tell you their good old .30-30 is such a rifle. Have you ever shot that rifle to see if it delivered on its promise? Have you ever shot a rifle that was so accurate it seemed as if you couldn't miss? Any benchrest rifle shoots better than the casual shooter could believe. Is that benchrest rifle at all handy in the field? Can we get a rifle that covers both extremes, or at least comes close enough? Would you like a rifle that was light, handy, accurate and useful for a wide range of shooting experiences?

Who wouldn't? The problem is, what rifle does everything? Some come closer than others. The Winchester Model 94 is one early example, and the rifle that started the trend.

When the '94 was introduced, a rifle powerful enough for big game was large, heavy and chambered in a caliber that started with the number 4.

One example is the stablemate of the Model 94, the Winchester 1886. The '86 is a beautiful rifle, but light it isn't. Chambered in a black powder cartridge large enough for big game, the '86 is a heavy rifle with big bullets that generate heavy recoil. The '94 was as light and handy as the smaller, handgun-caliber rifles that Winchester offered, but was chambered in a caliber capable of bringing down anything in the Lower 48. Well, at that time it was the 46 States. But the power level of the '94 could not be stretched much more. The two-piece stock and tubular magazine limit the potential accuracy of the '94. An early competitor, and later winner of two wars and hunting-camp favorite was the Springfield in .30-06. Originally the caliber was .30-03 but the idea was the same, to make an accurate, flat-shooting rifle for general use. Earlier military rifles, in the U.S. and in other countries, had been made in rifle and carbine styles. The army infantry rifle commonly had a barrel up to 30 inches long! The cavalry carbine would be the same action and caliber, but with a 20-, 18- or 16-inch barrel. The U.S. decided, as did many other armies, to split the difference, and issue a rifle with a 24-inch barrel. Both cavalry and

The Winchester Model 94, especially in a carbine size, is very handy, but lacking in accuracy, durability and power for use as a Scout Rifle. (Photo courtesy U.S. Repeating Arms Co.)

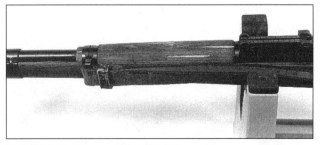

Until the M-16, even "light" military rifles were heavy. The weight of the hand guards, bayonet lug and other military necessities keep this Mauser (and others like it) heavy. But the military wants durability, then and now.

The Scout Rifle. Light, handy and convenient, fast in use and delivering enough power to be suitable on medium to large game.

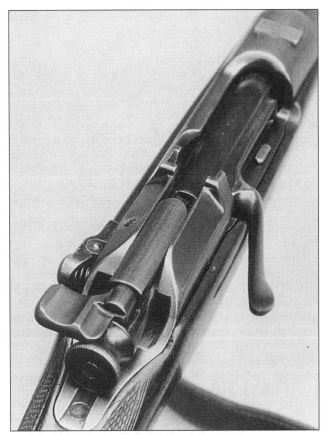

The Mannlicher-Schoenauers are light and handy rifles, but the split rear bridge makes scope mounting difficult. The striker assembly is also heavy far beyond the need to hit the primer, making a fast lock time only a dream.

The Springfield Scout is heavy by Jeff Cooper's standards, but a convenient and powerful rifle. With a five-round magazine it is suitable for hunting medium to large game. With a twenty round magazine it is a very capable defensive rifle.

starting point was the beautiful little Mannlicher-Shoenauer carbine. Developed in the same time period as the Winchester 1894 as a rifle for hunting in the mountains of Europe, they are light, handy little rifles with some major mechanical faults. The rear of the receiver is split to allow passage of the bolt handle, making it impossible to mount a sight close to the shooter. Iron sights on the M-S are either an open blade in front of the receiver or a spring-loaded aperture in the rear. The blade is durable and fast but coarse, while the aperture is slow and precise but fragile. A scope mount must be a side-mount with clearance for the bolt handle.

The bolt handle on the M-S is too far forward for fast manipulation. Even if it was farther back, the "butter knife" shape of the handle would make it hard to quickly work the bolt.

While it was a good starting point as a theoretical exercise, the M-S carbine did not offer the fast, accurate and durable package Jeff Cooper sought.

While the Mannlicher hinted at possibilities, it did not have a design that could be stretched to cover this new territory. The search went on to consider other bolt-actions. Why a bolt-action, and not other actions? Semi-automatics were either too heavy or not durable enough. Lever-action rifles use a tubular magazine, slow to load and fragile. The Savage lever-action uses either a rotary magazine or a box magazine, but it is heavier than desired. A single-shot rifle could easily be made light enough, but single-shots are too slow on a follow-up shot. Not that all of the previously-mentioned actions cannot work as Scout-like Rifles. Springfield Armory makes their M1A as a Scout Rifle. With the short, bush-rifle barrel and a scope mount on the barrel, it is

infantry units complained. The cavalry complained about having to carry a rifle with 2 extra inches of barrel. The infantry complained about having 6 inches less reach when charging an opponent with a bayonet. The next war would provide answers to both complaints.

But even the compromise Springfield was not the light, responsive, compact rifle we all want. Few rifles came close, and those that did had design problems.

So what rifle could cover a wide enough range of things to be useful as a general rifle? Jeff Cooper, Founder of Gunsite and the well-known advocate of the Modern Technique of shooting, puzzled over this problem for some time. His

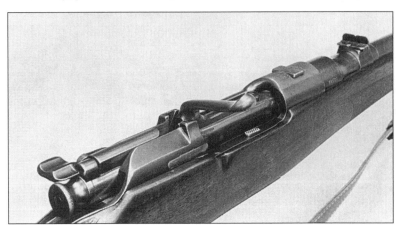

The "butterknife" bolt handle, and its location forward of the trigger, makes fast bolt manipulation difficult with the M-S rifles and carbines.

Firearms Instructor John Farnam is a firm advocate of the Scout Rifle in its self-loading form as an eminently suitable defensive rifle.

While this Winchester Guide Rifle would be very useful and comforting to have along with you in the Alaskan bush, it is not a Scout Rifle. Chambered in .444 Marlin and ported from the factory, it would be handy for many problems you might encounter. (Photo courtesy U.S. Repeating Arms Co.)

The Gunsite Gunsmithy feels that the Sako AII action is the best one on which to build a Scout. The Sako action will cost more than a Remington, and the rifle from Big Green will make a Scout that is just as good. Unless you get a Sako for a bargain, build on a Remington or a Mauser.

a very handy package, and one favored by the tactical firearms instructor John Farnam. John is not worried about the extra weight, since most of his students will not be carrying that, or any other rifle, long distances. Especially for a police officer who is working in and around automobiles, the power of the .308 is desirable, the squad car carries the weight, and the scope makes it fast and accurate. However, the Springfield isn't light enough to make Jeff Cooper's requirements. Jim Brockman makes scouts on leverguns, and for someone afoot in Alaska the larger calibers would be comforting indeed. As a compact unit, a take-down scout built on a heavy-caliber lever-action rifle stored in a light aircraft is a highly desirable commodity. Packed into a storage box not much larger than an attaché case, a Brockman takedown Scout is a comfort to have in the wilds. One bonus

of a takedown Scout is that the scope is on the barrel, and wearing of the assembly joint does not affect the point of impact. But the true Scout is intended to be a general-purpose rifle, and most of the calibers a lever-action rifle would be chambered in are too specialized. The lightest bolt-action receiver that accepts a medium caliber is the Sako. A good second and third choice would be the Remington short-action and the Mauser 98. The test-bed that Jeff Cooper used was a Remington M-600 in .308 Winchester.

While researching potential sighting systems, Mr. Cooper tested a pistol scope mounted in front of the receiver. The results were encouraging. The advantages of a medium eye relief scope mounted in front of the receiver are: it keeps the rifle balanced slightly forward, it keeps the shooter from becoming lost in the scope, and it allows much faster aiming. A small added bonus is that with the top of the receiver open, loading and unloading are much easier. A light rifle, with the scope on the receiver, balances closer to your rear hand than your forward one. As a result, ultra-light rifles can be difficult to shoot. With little weight forward, the rifle does not "settle down" in aiming. The Scout Rifle, even though it is light, has its balance forward, to dampen the rifles motion while aiming. A standard scope, close to the dominant eye, overwhelms your brains ability to keep track of your peripheral vision. You only see the world through the scope. Many shooters close or squint their off eye to aid in aiming through a regular scope, further cutting down peripheral vision. With a forward-mounted scope, your view of the scope does not overwhelm your peripheral vision. You can shoot with both eyes open. If something happens off to the side while you are focused on the target, you can still see it. What advantage could this give you? If you are aiming through a regular scope, you might never see that monster buck standing off to the side of the one you are aiming for. Or much worse, you might not see that other

With the scope so far forward, you are less likely to suffer tunnel vision. With the receiver opening clear, loading, unloading and malfunction clearance are easier.

member of your hunting party stepping around the timber to get a better look for himself.

Last is the ability to aim quickly. With both eyes open, you look at the target, and then shoulder the rifle. The crosshairs float across your field of view until they rest on the target, and then you fire. A standard scope requires you to transition from "the world" to "the scope" as you attempt to keep the target in sight. The Scout method is faster. How fast, and how precise? In the General Rifle class at Gunsite when Jeff Cooper was the owner, students would finish their rifle instruction by shooting at clay pigeons with their Scout Rifles. Thrown clay pigeons, on the straightaway. A score of five-for-five was not unheard of. Of course this was done on a range with two miles of safety zone downrange, but to hit a thrown clay pigeon with a rifle is both fast and accurate shooting!

So, with a sighting system settled upon, the Scout Rifle fell into place. As defined by Jeff Cooper, a Scout Rifle is a medium-caliber rifle with a forward-mounted scope, that weighs two kilograms and is one meter in length. With such a rifle you can go anywhere, hunt under any condition and take game up to half a ton in weight. With a properly-constructed bullet and a cool hunter who is a crack shot, the weight limit can be extended past the half-ton mark. Yes, some rifles will do better in some areas than a Scout will, but none will do as well in all of them. Some skeptics would point out that a scout scope is only 2-power, a little light for long-range shooting. If you define long-range as beyond 300 yards, I might agree. However, I have used my Scout rifle out to 400 yards on a 10-inch gong, and done quite well. My best runs were back-to-back five-shots for five hits. Even out west in the wide open spaces you can stalk to

Don't let someone tell you that Scout rifles are short-range rifles, or that they trade accuracy for speed. This plate is a piece of cake (or toast, judging from the hits) at 300 yards.

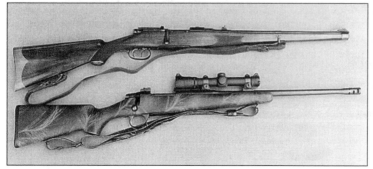

With a Gunsite Gunsmithy Scout Rifle as a guide, you can see how close the M-S carbine started out. Note the bolt handle and how far forward of the trigger it is.

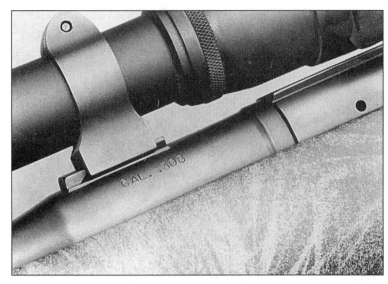

The best caliber for the Scout is .308. Larger calibers add weight to the rifle, for little extra use. Lighter calibers are of limited use on big game. The .308 is available in a bewildering variety of ammunition, from FMJ military surplus to Match.

within 200 yards of your quarry. Why not one of the ultra-light rifles to fill the bill? The sole advantage of the very light rifles over standard rifles is weight. Or the lack of weight. You buy an ultra-light rifle because it is easy to carry and not because it gives you any advantages in shooting. For close-range fast shooting, an ultra-light rifle does not give any more advantage than its standard-weight starting point.

What caliber is the Scout? Properly, the .308 Winchester. The .308 offers enough power to take medium to large, hoofed and non-dangerous game. It is common to the point of ubiquity. You can buy bullets or loaded ammunition in .308 that run the gamut from ultra-precise target ammunition to heavily-constructed hunting bullets that will not break apart if driven through a railroad tie sideways. The sole drawback is that some potential owners may live in countries that do not allow its citizens to own military-caliber firearms. Fine, then pick one of a half-dozen cartridges that fill the bill that are ballistic clones of the .308.

As icing on the cake, Jeff Cooper then used the basic design and extended it, building a Remington M-600 in .350 Remington Magnum into what he called his "Lion Scout."

A light, handy package that delivered power enough to get up to the one-ton hoof weight, and some dangerous game as well. My only qualm about a six-pound rifle chambered in .350 Mag would be how to attach a muzzle brake. Luckily, by the time you fit a .358 caliber barrel to the action, the weight slides up past 7 pounds.

So, now that you are intrigued, how do you go about getting a Scout Rifle? Two ways, buy or build. On both paths, you can go for the top of the line, or you can economize and have most of the performance for a fraction of the cost. Also, if you build it yourself you can select the caliber you want. If you buy one ready-made you are limited to the caliber or calibers the manufacturer offers.

To buy a Scout Rifle is easy. Steyr now makes a high-tech Scout Rifle that is everything you could wish for. Designed by the Steyr engineers under the guidance of Jeff Cooper, the Steyr is a Scout with the technological improvements of the last century of firearms development. The receiver is aluminum, and extends far enough forward to serve as the scope base. The bolt does not lock into the receiver. Instead, like the AR-15, the rear of the barrel has locking lugs machined into it. The locking lugs of the bolt

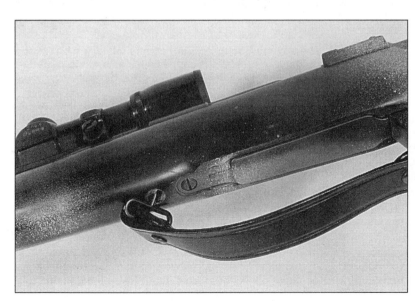

This Scout rifle (not a Steyr) shows the third sling swivel location, just forward of the magazine. With a Ching Sling, the rifle is easy to carry and fast to use.

Ted Yost, head Gunsmith at Gunsite Gunsmithy, in the fresh, thin air of Gunsite, Paulden, AZ.

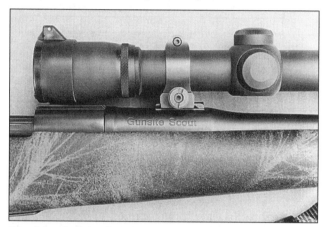

The barrel of the Gunsite Scout Rifle starts as an oversized blank. The scope mounts are machined from the blank, not attached later.

The Savage Scout is one of their lightweight rifles, but with a special mount and an aperture sight already attached.

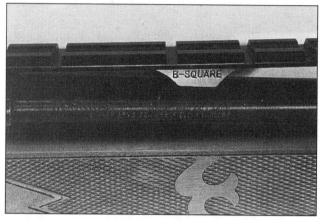

The mount is made by B-Square for Savage, and attaches to the front receiver ring and the barrel.

The Savage Scout (bottom) comes out of the box ready for its scope. While it isn't as slick as a custom-made Scout, it is up to the job, and a great bargain.

engage the barrel directly. The receiver doesn't take the stress of firing, so it can be light. Theoretically, you could make the receiver out of a durable, glass-filled polymer.

The stock is synthetic, and has a folding bipod that forms the forearm. Folded down, it can be used as an aiming rest. Folded up, it is not just out of the way, it is the forearm. The buttstock has a receptacle to hold a spare magazine. The magazines are synthetic, and hold five or 10 rounds. The magazine locking mechanism has two stops. The first one holds the magazine in place, but too low to feed. The magazine can be held in reserve while the rifle is single-loaded. Pressing the magazine up to the next click puts it high enough to feed when the bolt is worked.

The Steyr Scout has three sling swivel studs. While the original scouts were light and handy, getting a light and handy sling was not easy. A sling large enough to be fast off the shoulder was too loose to be an aid to aiming. A tight sling was not fast. Eric Ching, an Adjunct Instructor at Gunsite at the time, developed a three-point sling that was fast, handy and could be used as an aiming aid. The third sling swivel stud is in front of the magazine well.

The barrel is pencil-thin, short and fluted. The Scout is not intended as a high-volume shooting machine. It is designed to be carried all day without tiring you out, and still be accurate. A heavy barrel is not needed for accuracy.

Apparently some of the Cantons of Switzerland do not allow rifle barrels shorter than 20 inches. Curious. After all, the Swiss government issues select-fire rifles, and machine guns, that are stored in the soldiers' homes. But those some soldiers cannot buy a rifle with a barrel shorter than 20 inches? Oh well, Steyr solved the problem by making a model with a 20-inch barrel. The calibers are .308 Winchester, and a .375 short cartridge intended to deliver the same ballistics as the .350 Remington Magnum.

All this does not come cheap. The current suggested price of a Steyr Scout is $2,600. To a shooter used to scouting the gun shows and picking up a used lever-action rifle for under $300, that seems like a lot of money. But compared to other firearms the figure is not out of line. Right now, an accurate production rifle with scope can easily run $1,000, and if you insist on a Sako or a Weatherby, even more. A plain custom 1911 can run $1,500, and a top-of-the-line pistol goes for more than the Steyr Scout would cost. If you want the performance of that used lever-action, great. But if you want more, you have to look for more. The Steyr delivers.

You can also go to the original source and get a Scout from the Gunsite Gunsmithy. Built on a Sako or Remington action, the Gunsite Scout uses pedestal mounts for the scope instead of the aluminum extension of the Steyr. To craft the mounts, the Gunsmithy has to start with a barrel blank. The blank is lathe-turned down to the desired contour except for two rings, each at the location of a pedestal. The barrel is then threaded and screwed into the receiver and the chamber is reamed. The receiver is then placed in a mill, and the pedestal mounts for the scope rings are milled out of the rings left after the lathe-turning.

Then the action is glass bedded, tuned, the trigger adjusted and the rifle tested. Once it performs up to spec, then it is shipped to its new owner. Ordering a Gunsite Scout takes longer than ordering a Steyr Scout, but only by a bit. The cost is comparable to the Steyr. As an added bonus over the Steyr, you can specify the caliber you want.

What if you want a Scout, but can't swing the payments? Savage has an option for you. Starting with their synthetic-stocked lightweight .308, Savage designed a forward scope mount that uses the rear sight holes and the front receiver mount holes. What are the drawbacks of spending one-quarter of the amount for a Savage as for a Gunsite or Steyr? The Savage is heavier, but not by much. The Savage bolt action is not as smooth as the Gunsite or Steyr. Out of the box the Savage trigger will not be as nice as the other two, but you can adjust the Savage trigger to be good enough. If you find the Savage appealing but later want a more-refined rifle, you can order the Steyr or Gunsite Scouts, and then sell your Savage off to someone else in the gun club who is also thinking of a Scout. If the Savage serves your purpose, then the price difference pays for a lot of practice ammunition.

Building your own Scout Rifle is not difficult. You must select four things: action, barrel, mount and stock. I sort out the choices in three categories: utility, economy and select. The

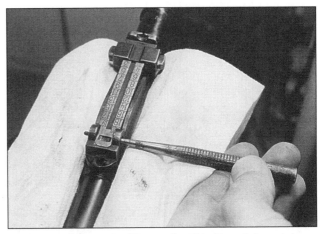

While working on the Mauser for this Scout, I ran into the exception to the Mauser sight rule. Instead of a spring-loaded and retained rear sight, this one has its blade held in with a cross pin. I guess every rule has its exception, and if you stick around long enough you'll see them all

Utility Scout is the least expensive, and also the ugliest. To build a Utility Scout, you need a surplus Mauser in .308, but .30-06 will do, The .308 Winchester offers a larger choice of factory ammunition in both hunting and match applications.

To work on the rifle you will need a dial caliper or micrometer, hacksaw and muzzle crowning tool, an Ashley Outdoors Scout Mount, drill press and epoxy. If you are going to use the standard stock you will need stock routing equipment and a re-finishing kit.

To obtain the Mauser, either go to a local gun show or order one through your local gun shop. You want a no-frills import Mauser in .308. Extras are not needed, so pass on bargains like thrown-in scope mounts, turned-down safeties or bent-down bolt handles. You already know which mount you need, and you can modify the safety or bolt handle later.

You have to remove the rear sight. You will need a pair of propane torches (one will do, but two make the job much easier), a ball peen hammer, screwdriver and a large drift punch. You will need one shop cloth to pad your hand with and another to act as a coolant for the receiver when you use the propane torches. The military Mauser rifles were

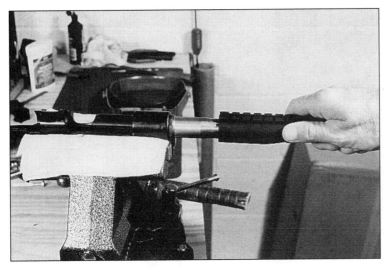

With the rear sight removed, the Ashley Scout Scope mount slides right into place.

With the barreled action in the Ram-Line/Ashley stock, move the mount until it is level......

And then mark the location of the screw holes.

Here are the screw hole locations. Slide the rifle into the Forster drilling fixture....

And lock it in place.

Line the drilling guide up with the locking screw locations. Be sure to adjust the drill bit in the chuck so the guide acts as a stop and keeps you from drilling into the chamber.

designed and built to be tough and survive the rigors of combat. The rear sight is not held on with a couple of screws, oh you aren't that lucky. The rear sight is part of a hollow tube that is soft-soldered onto the barrel.

Remove the barreled action from the stock. Clamp the barrel in a padded vise. Look closely at the front part of the rear sight. What looks like a cross-pin is not. To remove the rear sight adjustment bar you have to press down hard on the front of the bar, and then slide the bar towards the action. When it comes free you will see a flat spring held in place by a large screw. Remove the screw and spring. Remove the barreled action from

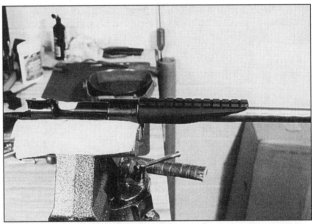

Here is the Ashley mount in place on the barreled action.

the vise and take the padding out. Clamp the rifle on the barrel, below the sight, muzzle down. Clamp the rifle high enough that the clearance between the front edge of the sight, and the top of the vise, is longer than the sight tube. Tightly knot a shop cloth around the receiver ring. Dampen the cloth and keep a jar of water handy to keep the cloth wet if you need to.

Use your propane torches to heat the rear sight tube until the solder is softened or melted. If the sight tube does not drop of its own weight, then use the ball peen hammer to tap it down until it falls free of the barrel. Once the barrel is cool, clean off the left-over solder.

Measure the barrel diameter just forward of the receiver ring. The Ashley mounts come in four different diameters. Order the mount with an interior diameter just larger than your barrel diameter.

Once your mount arrives, check it for fit on the barrel. To install it slide the mount over the barrel and adjust it until the mount is level. Mark the barrel through the locking screw holes. Remove the mount and drill the barrel at the marks. Use a #31 drill and tap the holes 6-48. The holes only have to be .100 inches deep, enough to let the locking screws hold fast. The screws hold the mount in place while the epoxy sets. Once hardened, the epoxy does the work of keeping the mount in place. Degrease the exterior of the barrel and the interior of the mount. Mix your epoxy and spread an even layer over the barrel. Slide the mount in place, and then tighten the locking

If you are using another barrel than the one that came on your Mauser, you'll have to have the barrel turned down to fit the Ashley Scout mount. With the barrel out of the rifle, this is a stone-simple turning operation for any machinist, even if he's never worked on a rifle before.

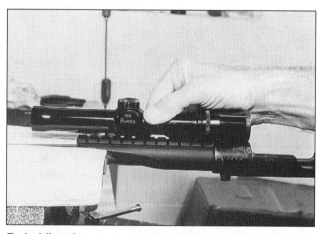

By holding the scope over the mount you can eyeball the ring locations. For this rifle (and other Mauser/Scouts), use the front base slot and the third from the rear.

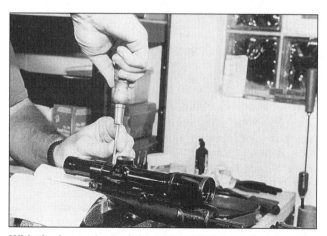

With the bases locked down, install the top rings and loosely install the ring screws.

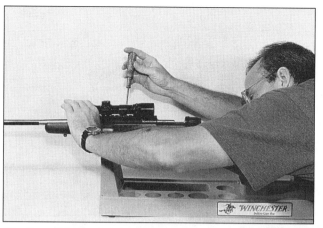

Starting with the reticle slightly tilted, tighten the rings....

And check the final location from the shoulder. If the reticle appears tilted, loosen the rings and try again.

screws to keep the mount steady. Let the epoxy set overnight.

What if you cannot get a surplus mauser in .308? Then get an even cheaper one in 8mm and change barrels as described in Chapter Six. Brownells has a selection of replacement barrels that are already threaded and short-chambered. To the added cost of the barrel you will also have to have the barrel turned on a lathe for the Ashley/Clifton scope mount. Even with the added expense, you will have an economical scout rifle.

Whether factory-original or Brownells replacement, the barrel should be shortened. You don't have to shorten it if you don't want to, but the whole idea of the scout is to be handy. Trimming the barrel back from 24 to 18 inches will do just that. Measure 18 inches forward from the receiver ring and mark the barrel with a felt-tip pen. With a hacksaw, cut the barrel at the mark. With the Brownells muzzle crowning kit, cut the muzzle flat, and then crown it with the 11-degree cutter. Use lots of cutting oil and even pressure to avoid chatter marks. The crowning will leave the outer edge of the muzzle with a sharp edge. Use a swiss pillar file to break the outside edge.

The last thing to take care of on your bare-bones scout is the stock. With the scope mount in place the action will not fit into the stock. Rest the barreled action in the stock. Mark the edges of the scope mount with a pencil. With your barrel inletting tools, relieve the barrel channel until the scope

The Ashley Scout Rifle Kit includes a Ram-Line stock that has been specially-modified to take a barrel that has the Ashley mount on it. It is light-weight and durable.

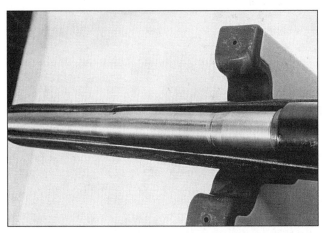

The barrel channel of the Ashley-modified Ram-Line stock is cleared for the scout mount. If you don't use the mount, you'll have a large gap just in front of the receiver.

mount clears the wood. Glass-bedding the scout does not differ from the standard glass-bedding procedure. Treat the bottom of the Ashley/Clifton scope mount as the third bedding point on a three-point glass bedding job.

With the scope mounted forward, you do not have to modify the safety to a low-mount or side-swing safety.

The bare-bones Scout may be too Spartan for some shooters. While it is perfect as a tool to rattle around in a pickup truck on the ranch, or as an emergency rifle in the trunk of your car or the cargo compartment of a light aircraft, it does not lack for ugly. The stock can be cleaned up as we described in Chapter Ten, but even with the oil sucked out and the excess wood trimmed away, a military stock may be too ugly for some people. To improve the looks (and performance) of your Scout at low cost, look into the Ash-

The customary location for a front sight on a Scout rifle is just in front of the scope, to preclude getting the front sight tangled up in brush. If you prefer, you can certainly attach the sight in the traditional location, at the muzzle.

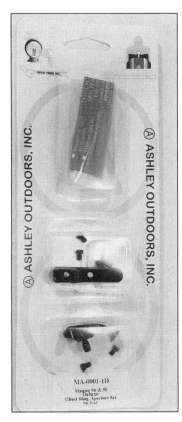

Included in the Scout Kit, or as a separate accessory, is a set of iron sights with a ghost ring rear.

The Gunsite ghost ring rear is low, solid and has the edges rounded off to take it easy on your hands.

The Gunsite Scout Rifle front mount. The front sight blade is part of the mount, protected by the scope. When you remove the scope, the sight is ready to go.

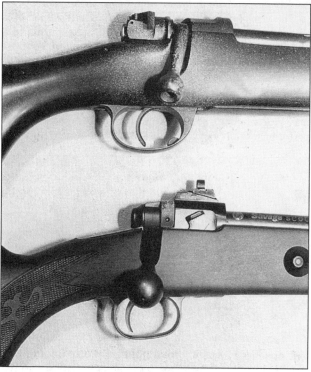

The Savage Scout on the bottom comes with a ghost ring sight.

ley Outdoors Scout kit. In addition to the scout scope mount, you get a Ram-Line stock already modified to take the mount, and a set of back-up iron sights. The only extra work is to install the iron sights.

The stock is a Ram-Line synthetic stock that has the barrel channel opened up to accept the Ashley Scout mount. I talked to Ashley about the stock, and he wishes there were a few improvements that could be made to it. "If we can do without the magazine floorplate we can save more weight. If we could get Ram-Line to pillar-bed the action screws and make the stock a blind-magazine design, we could save half a pound," he said. As it is, the stock is lighter than a similar-contour wood stock, so you're saving weight by going synthetic. And you don't have to worry about climate changing your bedding.

For the back-up sights, the procedure is simple. Back in Chapter Five we used the B-Square scope-mounting fixture to locate the screw holes for a scope mount. The Ashley aperture sight uses the rear scope mount holes. If you want to save the work of going back and doing the whole thing over again, drill and tap the front ones, too. After all, the rifle may not always be a scout, and you can install plug screws to fill the holes up front. The rear of the scope will cover the plug screws. For the front sight, you need a barrel-drilling fixture like the Forster. As described in the next chapter, center the barrel and get the front sight vertical.

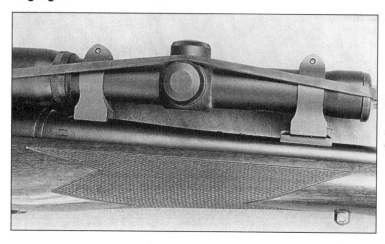

As an alternative to the cost of a custom-built Scout, the Gunsite Gunsmithy can modify a Remington Model Seven. The front mount is soldered to the barrel, and the rear mount grooves are milled from the barrel itself.

The rear mount of the Gunsite Seven Scout. For a fraction of the cost of a full-up Scout, they can turn your Seven into a fast, handy Scout.

Then drill and tap to install the front sight. You can install the front sight in one of two places. The customary location for a front sight is at the end of the barrel. On a Scout, it is customary to install the front sight just in front of the scope mount, underneath the objective of the scope. The iron sights are meant to be back-ups, and should be out of the way. You don't need them until you have removed the scope. The Gunsite Gunsmithy installs the front sight blade in the front scope mount base. By getting the front sight out of the way you reduce its tendency to get caught on things and possibly end up damaged.

One thing I would do before installing the front sight under the scope is to use the masking tape mohawk front sight to determine just how high the blade has to be. After all, you can't make your front sight blade any higher than the space between the barrel and the scope. Install the rear aperture, and put your masking tape in place with the scout scope base installed. If your required blade height comes out too tall, you have to figure out how to lower the rear. You have to leave the front and rear high enough to be seen

over the scope base. I have only seen one rifle where the irons could not be made to work, and that rifle had a bent barrel. It struck so low that neither the scope nor the irons could be adjusted to the point of impact. It was a good thing the customer had bought the rifle at such a bargain, as the first thing we did was to install a new barrel.

If you can luck onto a surplus Mauser in .308, the Ashley Scout Kit gets you a Scout Rifle for less than a quarter of the cost of a custom-made Scout Rifle. Even replacing the barrel gets you in for less than a third of the cost.

The economy Scout is an option that owners of the Remington Model Seven can take. The Seven is already a light, handy and short rifle. What it lacks is the forward-mounted scope. Burris makes a scope mount that uses the rear sight screw holes and the forward holes of the receiver as the scope mount holes.

Remove the Remington rear sight. Unless you are going to install an aperture rear as a back-up sight, then also remove the front sight.

The Burris mount does not come contoured to your barrel. You will have to file the base to fit. First install the rings on

Factory-original except for the Scout scope and mounts, this Remington Seven is a good start. Later, you could either fit the stock for a three-point sling, or switch the wood for synthetic.

Here is my Select Scout. With a Mauser action it is a bit heavier than Col. Cooper's criteria, but I don't mind. Note the Ching Sling. The spare scope will soon have its own rings, and be kept as a spare when going to classes or matches.

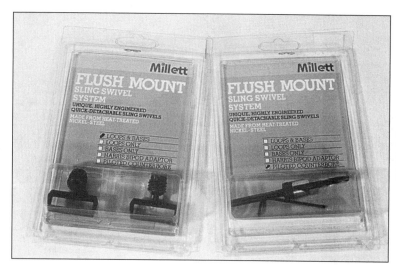

To install the best sling swivels, you need the swivels and installation tools. Unfortunately, you'll have to buy two pairs of swivels, and use three of the four. The fourth? Save it, you may need it later.

the base using alignment bars such as the Kokopelli bars. Once you have the rings lined up, mark the rings and bases so you can get them back to their proper mates. Remove the rifle from its stock and take the bolt out. Clamp the barrel in a padded vise, with the barrel pointing at a distant object. When I had a commercial shop, I would open the door and use the upstairs attic window of a house down the street as an aiming point. Bore sight the barrel on the distant object. If you do not have a luxury of windows, then use your scope collimator as a reference point. Place the base with the lower rings installed on the barrel, lined up with the rear sight screws. Place a scope in the rings and look through it. See that the scope does not point at the bore-sight object? It should be pointing high. You will have to file the front legs of the base to match the contour of the barrel, and bring the reticle down to the aiming point. Remember, all three legs must maintain contact. Once you are close, use Dykem on the bottom of the legs, and tighten the front screws. The pressure will rub through the Dykem and you will also see if your filing has angled the base, pulling the rear leg away from the barrel.

Once the legs have been filed and the reticle is on your aiming point, mark the rear mount screw hole for drilling and tapping. The rear screw goes in over the chamber, and you must not drill too deeply. Use the Forster tool to get your hole straight and centered, and use the drill guide as a stop to keep from drilling too far. The wall thickness of your barrel is around .350 inches (Barrel thickness minus cartridge base width, divided by two.) You should not drill a hole more than .100 inches deep. The Burris base uses 6-48 screws, so drill with a #31 drill and tap 6-48.

Installing the scope mount follows the same basic proce-

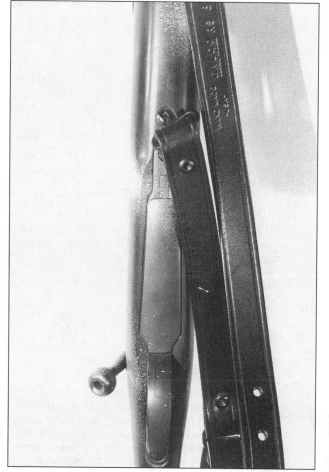

The middle mount on my Scout has been installed at a slight angle. For right-handed shooting the sling is pointed to my left forearm. It is a bit more secure, and a tad faster.

The standard Mauser safety was replaced on my Select Scout, with a three-position Winchester-style safety.

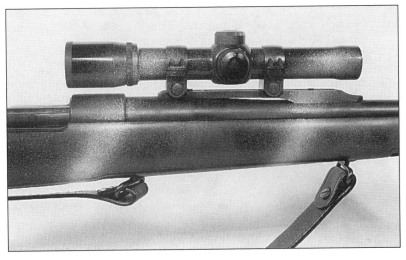

The Ruger Number 1 rib, with a Scout scope attached. A pedestal-mount barrel would get the scope 1/4-inch lower, for $1,000 of work. The Ruger will do fine for me.

dure as mounting a scope over the receiver would follow, with one extra step; once the scope is installed, and the rifle is zeroed, take it off to make it solid. Remove the ring tops and take the scope out. Without removing the ring bottoms, remove the base from the rifle. Degrease the base and rifle, and then use either an extra-strong grade of Loctite, or epoxy, to lock the base to the rifle. Apply the Loctite or epoxy, and tighten the base down. Wipe off any excess. Let the locking goop set. Re-install the scope and ring tops.

The Economy Scout suffers from the same malady that the Utility Scout does, excess weight, and you are limited to the calibers Remington offers in the Model Seven. The only way to get weight off either is to install a lighter stock. An ultra-light stock such as the Pound'r by Brown Precision, or a lightweight stock from McMillan or H-S Precision can cost as much as the Scout Scope did. But they will shave as much as a pound off a Pudgy Scout, and keep your total budget under $1,000 dollars. To change calibers, you have to get a new barrel and then install a Scout scope mount. Cost and weight go up, getting into Select Scout territory.

The Select Scout starts as a Sako, Remington or Mauser action, in increasing action weight. The first thing you do is select a barrel for it. One easy course of action is to pick a pre-threaded barrel from one of the many offered by Brownells.

While Brownells offers many choices, they can only give you barrels for the latter two action, Remington and Mauser. Do not worry about your choices being limited, as they offer barrels from Shilen and Douglas. You can also go with a caliber other than .308 if you want.

On my Select Scout I went with a Mauser action, and used a Douglas barrel in .308. (What can I say? I have the reloading dies, buckets of once-fired brass, and about 500 pounds of bullets to load. Why not a .308?) The pre-threaded barrel is also pre-chambered, but the chamber is deliberately left short. You can adjust the headspace one of two ways. The first is with the barrel installation method detailed in Chapter Six. The other method is once you tighten the barrel into your action, use a chambering reamer on an extension rod to cut the chamber. You just used that method in Chapter Eighteen when adjusting the headspace on an AR-15, and the procedure is the same here. Once installed, I shortened the barrel to 18 inches and crowned it with an 11-degree crown with the Brownells crowning tool.

The stock picked out for the Select Scout is a Clifton synthetic. I ordered the stock with the integral bipod that hides away in the forearm. I also ordered the stock with a longer pull. I am a tall fellow with long arms and a long neck. I was tired of getting my thumb up against my nose

The Ruger Number 1 mount uses four screw and two recoil pins to secure the rib to the barrel. Properly installed it will not come off inadvertently.

when firing regularly-stocked rifles, so I asked the folks at Clifton to make my stock longer. It showed up at a hair under 15 inches of pull. I haven't had any problems using it yet, even with full winter clothing on. The stock came with three sling swivel studs installed, with the third right in front of the front action screw. The three-sling swivel system is part of the Scout Rifle concept. A sling is both a carrying aid and a shooting aid. The problem with most slings is that if they are loose enough to act as a fast-into-action carry sling they offer no support in shooting. If they are fitted tightly enough to aid in aiming they are slow to get off the shoulder. The Ching Sling and the three-swivel setup solves both problems. The center swivel is attached to a sliding sling stub. In carry, the slider moves out of the way and keeps the sling open on the shoulder. When you swing the rifle into action, the slider comes back until it stops against the rubber limiting post, and then acts as an aiming aid. It seems strange at first, but once you get used to it, the system is fast, stable and accurate. My Ching Sling is from Galco and made of leather. The Galco sling is durable enough to use as a tow strap. If you want to save a little bit of weight, and don't feel the need for leather, the Spec-Tech makes a nylon Ching sling. It also costs a bit less, too.

The emphasis of the Scout Rifle for many is defensive. While a Scout makes a very good hunting rifle, it makes an exemplary defensive rifle.

The next step was glass bedding the action into the stock. I bedded the recoil lug and action, and the first inch of the barrel. The rest of the barrel is free-floating.

The trigger on the Mauser was everything you would want in a military rifle, durable, positive, creepy and heavy. I replaced it with a Timney Featherweight. Right out of the package and fastened to the rifle, it gave me a trigger pull of 3 pounds. Rather than fuss over it I left it alone except for applying Chip McCormick's Trigger Slick to the sear surfaces. Over time I expect it to smooth up and lighten to a perfect 3 pounds. Since the Timney F does not come with a safety, I had to replace the safety. When I was building this particular Scout I felt a bit flush with money, so I splurged on a Dakota safety. The Dakota replaces the Mauser bolt shroud with one that is streamlined and has a three-position safety built into it like the Winchester Model 70. Actually, it's like the post-war three-position safety. The pre-war safeties differed in that they went to "Fire" by pulling back from the left side, while the post-war ones went to "Fire" by pushing forward on the right side.

The only fitting required was to adjust the safety lever so it properly cammed the cocking piece back when the safety went "on." Once blued, it looked just like it was meant to be there.

The only thing left to do was install the Scout scope. I had to do some thinking on this one, as the Burris mount did not work with the barrel contour I had selected, and the Ashley Outdoors mount had not yet been invented. What I ended up doing was installing a Ruger quarter-rib from a Ruger No. 1 rifle. The Ruger quarter rib came about on the No. 1 for a number of reasons, one of which is that it looks good. Putting a scope on the No.1 posed a slight problem. While the rear scope base could have been put on the receiver, the compact size of it did not leave much room. Also, the short length of any dropping-block single shot rifle pulls the receiver and chamber back towards the shooter. A scope base or mount on the receiver puts the scope too close to the shooter's face. By putting both rings on a bar attached to the barrel, both of these problems and one more is solved. If the scope is attached to both receiver and the barrel (as it would have been with a base on the receiver) as the barrel heats up it can place stress on the scope. Ruger insists on accuracy, and the No. 1 had to be accurate. The quarter-rib gave the Ruger designers a place to put the scope and iron sights, and made the rifle "look" right.

It also gives us a place to mount a Scout scope. The only drawback is that there are only four sized ribs, and if your barrel does not match the contours you are out of luck.

The ribs have to be ordered by barrel designation, not by barrel diameter. I have assigned the diameters "A" and "B" with "A" being the diameter of the barrel under the center of the front pair of screws, while "B" is the diameter of the barrel at the chamber. The pairs of holes have their center-points 3 inches apart on all of the ribs. Measure your barrel at the chamber. If your barrel measures at or close to the two diameters Ruger uses, continue. If not, you can't use the Ruger quarter-rib. Next, measure 3 inches forward of the beginning of the barrel's taper down from the chamber diameter. If your barrel falls at or close to one of the three front diameters, you're in. You do have some leeway, as the rib location is not fixed. You can potentially slide the rib forward or back to get the front dimension just right. The designations and their diameters are:

Ruger barrel designation	A	B
1-A & 1-RSI	.900"	1.156"
1-B & 1-S	.900"	1.200"
1-H1	.165"	1.200"
1-V1	.070"	1.156"

One advantage of the Ruger rib as a scope mount is its great strength (and its good looks.) The thickness of the barrel gives you leeway to drill the holes you need, and the base contact gives a lot of surface area for Acra-glass, epoxy or Loctite to bond. The drawback is weight. The rib is heavy, and it requires a thick barrel. You will not have a scout with a pencil-thin barrel using a Ruger rib as your mounting method.

Personally I don't have a problem with it. I find a heavier rifle is easier in recoil, and hangs ands swings better for me on offhand shooting. If you view the rifle as a combat tool as some who follow the Scout rifle philosophy, then a heavier barrel is tougher under the knocks of hard use and its potential use as an impact weapon. If I am going to strike someone with the barrel of my rifle (a really big IF on that transaction, over!) I'd rather be doing it with a heavy barrel than a light one.

My custom Scout did not have iron sights on it for a long time, only because I had been too busy to get irons wrestled onto it. As soon as I saw the Ashley Express backup sights, I went ahead and did the drilling and tapping to get them installed.

Complete with its Ching Sling, my rifle is a pound and a half over the rule laid down by Jeff Cooper. At 6 feet, 4 inches and 210 pounds, I don't think an extra pound and a half is going to give me any problems.

All through the proper barrel break-in procedure I was ready to explode to know what kind of accuracy the rifle could deliver.

CHAPTER 20

Refreshing the Hunting Rifle

I don't know what it is like where you live, but here in Michigan it seems that no one ever retires a hunting rifle. I had some of the oldest rifles you could imagine come into my shop for cleaning and upgrading. Rifles that should have either been worked on a lot sooner, or retired by the time I saw them. Is there any reason a rifle can't go on forever? With proper care, no. With abuse, there are several.

The areas most needing improvement in a tired hunting rifle are, in the order you should address them: the bore, the sights, the recoil pad, the stock finish, the trigger and the bluing. Even a relatively new rifle can need work in one or two of these areas. As examples of what can be done to bring a rifle back to life, I've selected two rugged old models that look bad, but have plenty of future use left in them.

The first project rifle is a Marlin 336 before they were calling it that. It has difficulties in all of the areas listed. The bore is pitted in spots. While it shoots reasonably well for a .30-30, it fouls quickly, and accuracy declines. The sights

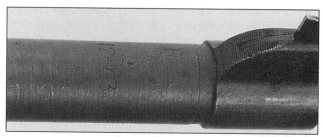

If you are going to turn a Springfield into a sporter, you will have just as good a base as a Mauser to start with. If the bore is in good shape, don't change barrels. Even military-production barrels are first-rate. This one was made by Remington in December of 1943, and it shoots great.

are the open sights that Marlin shipped the rifle with. It is not drilled and tapped for a scope. Sometime in the past the buttplate disappeared. The stocks are bare wood. The bluing has gone gray.

The second rifle is a surplus Mauser, a typical example of the many that are being imported to the United States. I found it at a local gun show. It was just one of many Czech VZ-24 carbines in a rack, with a sign that said "your choice, $59." I looked them over closely, checking to find one where the bolt face was clean and for signs of pitting underneath the stock. While many had mild pitting on the bolt face, none had pitting under the wood. Also, none of them had much of a bore. All were dark, pitted messes with only vague memories of rifling left in them. Perfect for our needs.

The third rifle getting a little improvement is a Ruger M-77 International. Many shooters complain about Ruger triggers, and while some are tough, most are livable. But,

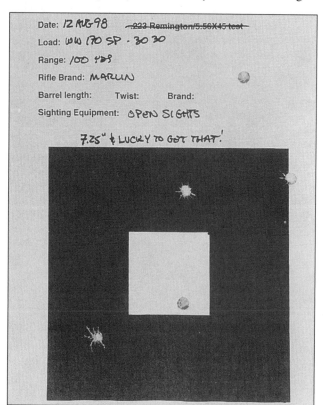

As you can see, the groups from the Marlin when it was a .30-30 were disappointing. It would be adequate but not confidence-inspiring out to 50 yards. Installing a scope would not help much, if at all.

Do not use a Springfield '03 with a serial number lower than 800,000. This Smith-Corona (yes, the typewriter company!) is well after the changes that made the 1903 Springfield receiver tougher and safer.

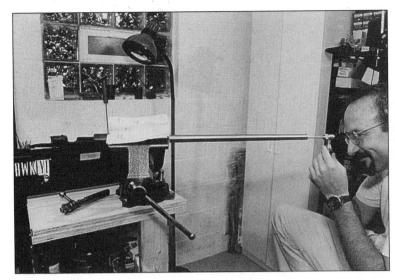

If a rifle is not shooting well, you need to know why. A quick look down the bore with the Hawkeye bore scope will tell if the problem is pitting, fouling, an eroded leade or a muzzle worn from cleaning rods.

mechanical devices exist to be improved, so we will be installing a Spec-Tech trigger in the Ruger.

Some places to hunt are worse than others. You could hunt many times in Texas and not get wet. In Michigan you can get soaked going from the cabin to the woodshed and back. The Northeast coast is even more damp. Chris Dichter of Pac-Nor Barreling tells me that the majority of the barrels he replaces are gone not from being shot out but from being rusted or pitted out. Even careful hunters can be victims of rust and pitting if they forget just once to swab the bore out after a day of hunting.

If your bore is shot, what can you do? The obvious solution is to replace the barrel. For the Mauser we'll be doing just that. For the Marlin, I was reluctant to invest in a new barrel. The problem with replacing the barrel on a lever action is not just a matter of turning a new barrel in place and adjusting the headspace, but fitting it for the dovetails for the magazine tube hanger and the forearm wedge. A better solution is to get the barrel re-bored. A re-bored barrel is one where the rifled section has been reamed out to a larger diameter, and then re-rifled. Re-boring works because most cartridges are built in "families." The .243 is a necked-down .308 Winchester. The .358 is a necked-up .308. If you have a rifle with a rusted, worn-out or abused bore, and you are willing to renew it in a larger caliber, then you can get it re-bored.

Re-boring lets you keep the original barrel exterior. If you have a classy old rifle with special sights fitted to it, or

are simply reluctant to alter its look, then re-boring can be just the ticket.

As with all things, there are limits. If you have a rusted-out .243 and you want to go to a larger caliber, you probably can't go to a .30-06. You certainly can't go to a .300 Win Mag. What stops a .243 to .30-06 conversion is the length of the magazine box and the feed lips. The .243 left the factory designed to feed a cartridge of a certain length. The longer .30-06 can be troublesome to feed, and correcting the dimensional problems might end up costing more than a new barrel. You also must keep sufficient barrel thickness for safety. The minimum diameter of your barrel at the muzzle is .200 inches larger than the new bore diameter. If you have an ultra-light rifle in a small caliber, you may not be able to bore it out very much larger. You need to go to a new diameter where the tops of the rifling are larger in diameter than the old grooves were. For a .243 bore, your smallest new caliber is .257. It would be better to go to a 6.5 mm, .264 inches, just in case there were pits extending deeper than the .257 rifling. In this case your barrel cannot be less than .464 inches at the muzzle to be re-bored.

How does Cliff re-bore your rifle? First, he unscrews the old barrel and sets it up in the reaming machine. After a few passes, with much noise and pumping of large amounts of cutting fluid, your barrel has been reamed out to its new diameter. The next step is the rifling machine. Since the rifling is cut new, you can specify any twist,

Cliff LaBounty bored out, rifled and re-marked the barrel of my Marlin. It is very important that your rifles be clearly marked as to their caliber. We all know people who can use the wrong end of a rake. In the event of an accident, who is responsible? You, the owner of the rifle.

within reason. If you want something too far from the ordinary, be prepared to defend your selection to Clifford. He wants you to be happy with the results, and asking for a 6-inch twist on your .338-06 will not gain you any benefit in accuracy.

Once reamed and rifled, then the bore is lapped to remove burrs and to bring the grain and texture of the new surface to a uniform direction. The last step is to cut the new chamber. In some situations, the new chamber is simply a cleaning-up of the old. For instance, converting a rifle from .243 to .308, the chambering reamer will simply cut the shoulder and neck dimensions. The body dimensions are the same between the two calibers, and the bore has just been reamed and rifled. Converting a .22-250 to .243, the new chamber removes just about all of the old.

If you plan to do much of the work yourself, you can unscrew your old barrel or buy a replacement. If you remove your barrel you know the torque shoulder or shoulders are in the correct locations. If you are buying a replacement to be re-bored, do the measurements listed a little later to be sure the torque shoulder or shoulders are correctly located. Then send it in for re-boring and rifling. When it comes back to you, all you have to do is properly ream the chamber for correct headspace and tighten the barrel back into the receiver.

On the Marlin, going up from .30-30 does not offer many choices. My first thought was to go up to the .348/30-30 cartridge, a wildcat of dubious benefit. Once I looked into bullet selection, and found only a single choice, I dropped the idea. I still like it, but I'll wait for a real .348 to come by to indulge myself in a .34 caliber levergun. The next step up was to a

The rims and bases are the same size. While ammo for it was hard to get only a few years ago, the explosion of interest in Cowboy Action shooting has brought many calibers back into use, including the .38-55.

After boring and rifling, Cliff re-crowned the muzzle. The bore looks beautiful, and the rifle shoots great.

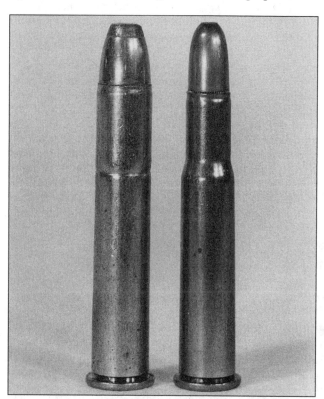

The .30-30 and the .38-55 are rimmed. They have the same overall length. A caliber conversion from the .308 bore to the .375 bore is a snap for Cliff LaBounty.

Out in the open, showing the proper technique (or one of them) for accuracy-testing a rifle. On rifles with two-piece stocks I prefer to either grasp the forearm (as shown) or rest the receiver on the front rest without using my left hand. This photo was not taken on the line (note the lack of hearing protection) only because of lighting. Taking photos on the covered firing line at my range is like taking snapshots in a coal mine.

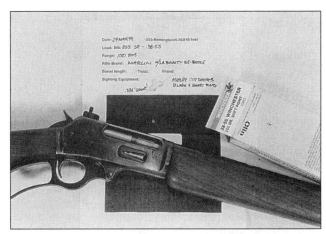

Once the bore was broken in and the sights roughly zeroed by shooting at the gong, I tried it on paper. These are the first three shots. .375 inches! Subsequent five-shot groups ran just over an inch, but this is the target I'm keeping.

.35/30-30. The bullet selection is large, and the power options are many. As a wildcat, the cartridge is popular with cast-bullet shooters, and in an improved-style case offers

plenty of power for a lever-action rifle. However, I have other rifles in .35 Remington and .35 Whelen, and didn't see a need to split the difference. The last step up is to .375. I wasn't keen on a .375 Winchester, as I can just get a new Winchester chambered for it. Cliff suggested the .38-55 cartridge, with a twist. The original bore diameter of many late 19th and early 20th century rifles chambered in .38-55 was .377 to .382. He would bore the Marlin to .375. I could use either the low-power factory ammunition in the tighter bore with no problem, or load my own ammunition using the common .375-inch diameter bullets intended for the .375 Winchester. As the Marlin is plenty strong, I can get as much power in the .38-55 as I could from the .375 Winchester, and still use .38-55 brass. The details settled, I sent the barreled receiver, bolt and locking block off for re-boring and re-chambering. When it came back, the bore was not at all its previous ugly self. It was also much larger. When I had looked through the bore scope before shipping it, the corners of the grooves had been finely pitted the length of the bore, with scattered patches creeping up over the lands. After Cliff was done with it, the bore looked, and was, brand new.

In order to hit with a rifle, you have to have sights. Current Marlin rifles all come drilled and tapped for scope mounts. The project Marlin left the factory years before drilling and tapping became standard, so we have to do the

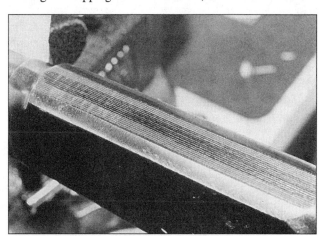

Start the scope mount drilling by running a stripe of Dykem down the middle of the receiver.

Measure the thickness of the receiver, and divide by half.

While a mill can be very useful as a drill press, and allows precise hole spacing, it isn't necessary. You can drill and tap with a drill press and drilling guide fixture.

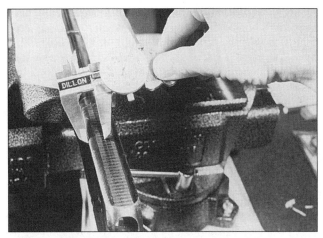

Use the dial calipers to mark the centerline of the receiver.

Use the scope mount holes to locate the spots to drill, and mark them with a center punch.

drilling and tapping. The flat-sided design of all lever action rifles is a big help. You'll need a drill press, #31 drill, 6-48 tap, dial calipers, Dykem, center punch and half-round file. A drilling fixture like the one from Forster is a big help. First, order a single-piece Weaver mount for the Marlin 336. If you are doing the drilling in a mill, then the dimensions

Set the barreled receiver in the Forster drilling guide and lock it in place over the hole locations. Drill through the receiver top.

Replace the drill guide bushing with one larger, and tap the hole without changing the guide bar location.

alone will be enough, but to do the job on a drill press the one-piece mount is a big help. Clamp the receiver in a padded vise. Take your Dykem and run a line down the center of the top of the receiver. Take your dial calipers and measure the thickness of the receiver. Divide this number in half, and adjust the dial calipers down to the half-thickness. Using the side of the receiver as a guide, draw a line down the center of the receiver through the Dykem with the tip of the calipers. Do this from both sides of the receiver. With the centerline marked, place the scope base on the receiver over the centerline and tape it in place. The standard location places the rear-most hole more forward than it should be if you are going to use the scope mount holes to install an Ashley Express aperture sight. If you use the standard locations, you should then drill a fifth hole behind them, as the rear screw location for the Ashley sight. Or, just shift the whole base back far enough that the rear hole is .500 inches from the rear of the receiver. Mark the hole locations in the Dykem by scratching a circle with a dental pick. Take your center punch and mark the first hole lightly. Mark each hole in turn. With the hole centers marked lightly with the center punch, look through the base to make sure each mark is centered in its base hole. If they are, mark each one heavily with the center punch. Remove the base and clamp the receiver in your drill vise. If you are using the Forster fixture, adjust the vertical until the top of the receiver is just under the drill guide holder. The fixture takes some fussing to get set up for each rifle, but it ensures your holes are parallel to each other. The hardened drill guides keep your drills from "walking," that is flexing away from where you want the hole to be drilled. A drill that walks will drill in the wrong spot, drill an oval hole, break or do all three.

Without the Forster fixture, you must use a C-clamp on the table of your drill press to keep the vise steady during drilling. Drill the holes through the receiver. To tap the holes, install your 6-48 tap into the tap handle. With the Forster fixture, remove the drill guide for the #31 drill and replace it with a guide that the tap just slips through. (Another reason to consider the fixture, it ensures your holes are tapped straight after they've been drilled straight.) Place a couple of drops of cutting oil on the tap threads. Grasp the body of the tap handle with your left hand and pull it towards the receiver. Grasp the handles with your

Here is the Ashley Ghost Ring sight in place, in the rear two holes of the scope mount base holes.

The easy way to remove it is with a sight pusher.

right hand, with your elbow pointing straight up. Pull down with the left while you rotate with the right hand. Using your elbow pointing up as an indicator, keep the tap vertical as you turn. If you do not press down, the tap cannot bite into the steel and begin tapping. Once the tap has gained sufficient purchase, you do not have to press down, as the tap will pull itself through the steel as you turn it.

Once the tap has cut through into the receiver body, reverse the rotation and remove it from the receiver. Repeat on the other holes. Once all of the holes have been tapped, unclamp the receiver and place it in your padded vise, upside down and clamped by the barrel. Use your half-round file to file off the drilling and tapping burrs kicked up on the inside. Finish by using the file as a backer to a piece of 300-grit emery cloth. Scrub the receiver clean of all filings, grit and chips.

With your holes drilled and tapped, you can now reassemble the rifle and mount and bore sight the scope.

If you are installing an aperture sight like the Ashley Express one, you have a small problem. How high should your front sight be? The traditional method was to calculate the height of the rear sight, and then use geometry to figure the theoretical height of the front sight. I place great emphasis on the word theoretical. I tried the accepted

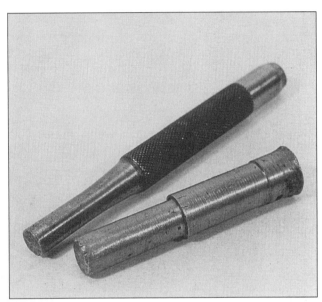

If you do not have a sight pusher, then use a drift punch or a brass drift (foreground) to tap the sight out of its dovetail.

With the Ashley Ghost Ring in place, the front sight is not the correct height. It must be removed.

The Ashley experimental sight is plastic, and presses into the dovetail. Take the rifle to the range and plink at the backstop.

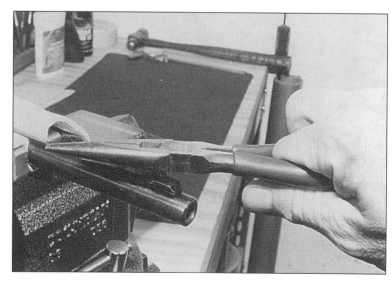

Your point of impact will be too low, so clip the sight with pliers or sidecutters until the sight....

is the correct height. Now it is a simple job to measure the height of the plastic insert, and order a steel blade the same height.

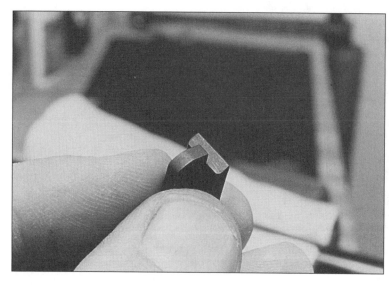

The replacement blade will be too thick to fit the dovetail.

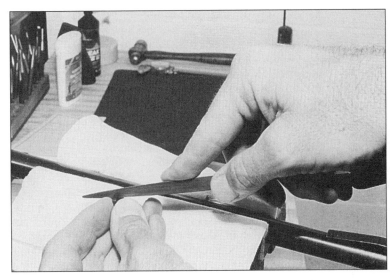

Take your three-sided file and file the face of the dovetail of the sight.

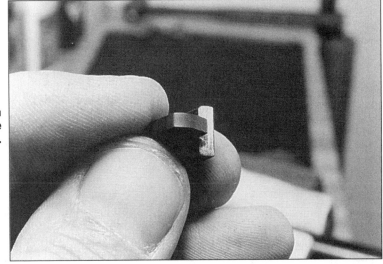

You can see the area where steel has been removed. Once the sight will start into the dovetail, your filing is done.

Use the sight pusher to insert the new blade into the dovetail of the base.

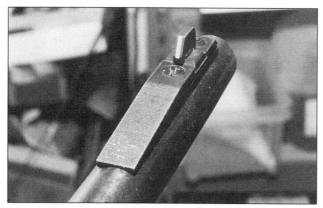

Once you are done, the only thing left is to take it to the range again, and finish sighting-in.

method several times when I began, and found my calculations off by large amounts. I wondered why. My conclusion was that almost immeasurable variations in the barrel to receiver assembly could have large effects on the point of impact. If the front of the receiver was machined so the top was off by .001 inches from the bottom, the barrel could be stressed enough to strike quite a distance from the calculated point of impact. My solution involved several strips of masking tape placed around the muzzle as a mohawk-like hairstyle. I would use a felt-tip pen to mark the back of the strip black, and then range-test it. The tape was fragile, but I could trim it with scissors until the rifle was hitting close to the point of impact. A quick measurement, and I knew how tall to make the new front sight. Emerson Ashley went a step farther. Since he was having all sorts of things

molded of plastic, he had his mold maker fabricate a mold for a plastic front sight. To find out how tall your new front sight should be, install the plastic one and take the rifle to the range with a pair of side cutters. Start at close range (25 yards will do) and shoot at a mark on the hill. A spot of spray paint in the dirt will do, but remember as the plastic sight is too tall, your bullet will strike low. Test-fire the rifle, and use the sidecutters to shorten the sight as needed. Once it is the correct height, either measure it or take the rifle back home to install a steel sight.

The old buttplate was plastic. Not unusual for a plastic buttplate, this one got cracked, pieces fell out, and eventually it was less hassle to shoot the stock bare than put up with the protruding plate screws. We will install a thin rubber pad. After all, even in its new caliber the recoil is not going to be harsh. A half-inch solid rubber pad should do the trick. Since the stock is going to be re-finished we don't have to be hyper-careful about kissing the stock while fitting the pad. Remove the buttstock from the action by unscrewing the action screw that goes through the wrist. As explained in the chapter on recoil reduction, plug the old screw holes with epoxied dowels. Once the epoxy has set dress the surface flat. Next measure and mark the centerline of the butt. Clamp the buttstock in a padded vise. Strike two straight lines parallel to the floor, each a third of the way from the top and bottom. Measure the length of the line from side to side and divide by two. Set your dial calipers to the half-width and mark the line at that distance. The straight vertical line through the marks on each horizontal line is your centerline. Measure down the vertical for your pad screw holes, then center punch and drill them. Install the new pad and grind flush with the edges of the buttstock.

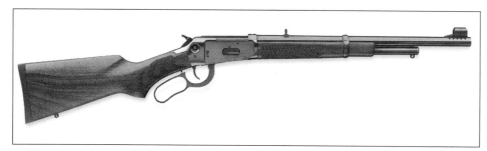

If I could have opened the Marlin up to .444, I would have. That option is not possible (there just isn't enough room!), so for a larger rifle I would have to go out and buy a new one, like this Winchester Guide Gun. (Photo courtesy U.S. Repeating Arms Co.)

If you take it outside, the weather will get to it. Your perspiration will take the bluing off the steel and finish off the wood. With proper care and maintenance, your rifle will last as long as you will, or longer.

The wood needs to be re-finished. While the buttstock is easy to remove, the forearm is harder. Start by removing the magazine tube. Unscrew the front screw and both side-screws holding the forearm nosepiece in place. Lift the forearm and magazine tube until the tube clears the stud on the magazine dovetail. Pull the magazine tube forward and out of the forearm. Now you can swing the forearm away from the barrel and receiver, and pull the nosepiece off. With the forearm and buttstock off, let the sanding begin. The stock originally had a lacquer or varnish finish, so there is no oil to extract from the wood. Multiple coats of the Pro-Custom stock oil from Brownells can be sanded into the wood until it glows with a satin sheen.

Hunting is not an indoor sport. The statement may be obvious, but from the reactions of some hunters to their bluing fading away, you would think it had never occurred to them that much of the activity takes place outside. There are several methods to keep the rifle going. The first and simplest is to use a spray-on finish now that the action has been separated from the wood. The spray-on finishes will not protect the interior of the rifle, but will protect the exterior.

The most protective but also most expensive method is to send the metal off to a plater for a hard-chrome job. While quite popular with handgunners, rifle shooters do not seem to be so hot on plating a rifle.

The good old standby is bluing. The bluing should be done after you have done the drilling and tapping for a scope mount, or other metal changes. You can either send your rifle out for bluing, or blue it yourself. Home bluing is not convenient at all, or cost-effective for one or two rifles. Bluers keep costs down by keeping the tanks hot all day, and rifles going into and out of those tanks. If you buy a bluing set-up just to do one or two rifles, you will not be realizing any cost savings.

The Mauser had served someone very well, and for a long time. By the time I bought it, the stock was dark and oil-soaked, the bore was shot and the bolt number did not match the receiver number. None of these mattered, as the stock would be replaced, and a new barrel took care of the dark bore and the potential headspace problems that an incorrectly number bolt indicated.

To upgrade a Mauser, first pull it from the old stock and clean the bolt, receiver and barrel. If you plan to re-use the

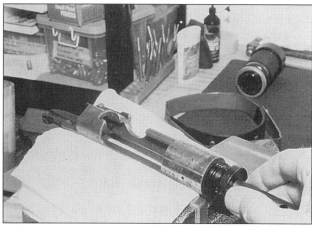

Screw the lapping tool into the receiver and adjust it for tension on the bolt.

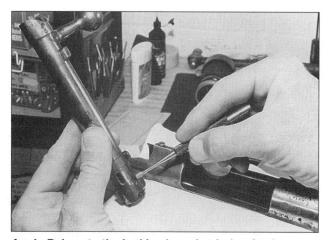

Apply Dykem to the locking lugs. Let it dry. Apply some lapping compound on the lugs and insert the bolt into the receiver.

Lapping the locking lugs on the Mauser is simple. You'll need the receiver, bolt, lapping tool and some fine grinding compound.

Lift and close the bolt. Pull it out and clean off the abrasive. Inspect the surface of the locking lugs to see how much engagement there is. Continue until you get more than 80 percent.

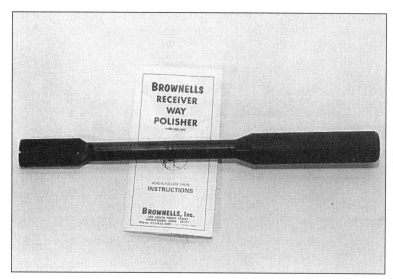

To polish the receiver for smoother function you need either a bunch of sticks or this way polisher from Brownells.

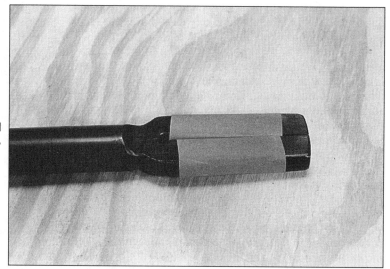

Here is the abrasive cloth wrapped around and tightened into the way polisher.

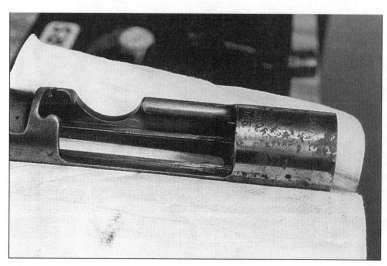

The unpolished receiver appears dark.

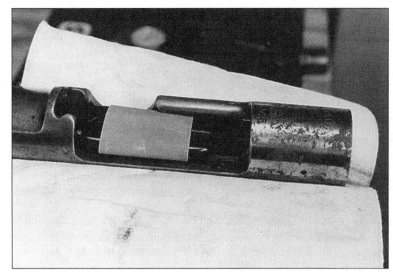

Using the cloth and some lubricant, polish the bearing surfaces of the receiver.

The bolt raceways of this Mauser are starting to look better.

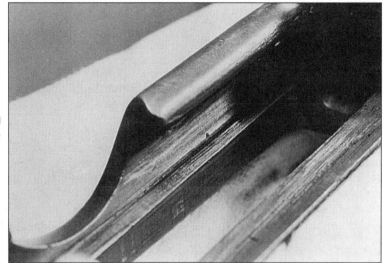

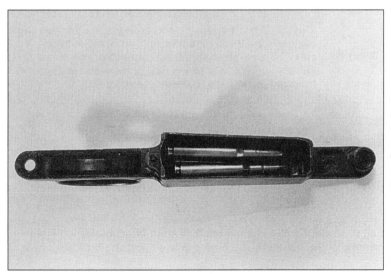

The magazine box of the Mauser is part of the feed system of the rifle. If you change calibers too radically, you'll have to change to another magazine box. Otherwise, your rifle may not feed well. Changing this rifle from 8mm Mauser to .35 Whelen was not a problem. The box is longer than the .35 needs.

The .35 Whelen came about in the early 1920s in an attempt to build a bigger-game rifle without having to go to imported (and expensive) rifles.

The case is simply a .30-06 necked up to take a .358 bullet. If you can't get Remington ammo or brass, you can make your own .35 Whelen brass from .30-06.

stock, then go through the oil-stripping and refinishing method described in Chapter Ten. On this rifle, the old stock was not at all what I wanted, so it ended up on the shelf. The barrel was unscrewed and the locking lugs lapped in as in Chapter Six, and the receiver drilled and tapped for a scope as in Chapter Five. Once apart, drilled and tapped, I polished the bolt ways as per Chapter Seven. Now, to install a new barrel. The original rifle was chambered for 8mm Mauser. For proper feeding, a cartridge whose dimensions were close to the 8X57 would be best. When Peter Paul Mauser was making rifles in dozens of calibers, and shipping them to clients all over the world, he used a different magazine box for each caliber. For best feeding, the box taper must mirror the cartridge taper. Today, the best custom gunsmiths fabricate their magazine boxes for Mauser rifles to the same dimensions that Mauser used, and different ones for each cartridge.

The bad news is that such a custom-made magazine box can cost several hundred dollars. The good news is that using the original box now does not preclude installing a custom one later if you feel the need.

My choice of a caliber for this rifle was .35 Whelen. The Whelen began life in the 1920s, as a means of getting larger calibers for American hunters. Back then, if you wanted something larger than the .30-06 your choices were sparse. You could either go with a lever-action rifle such as the Winchester 1886 in .45-70 or the Winchester 1895 in .405. Or you could buy an imported British or German Mauser built on the Magnum action (very expen-

sive!) chambered in British or European calibers (expensive ammunition to buy!). As an added "bonus" the imported ammunition would be Berdan-primed and difficult to reload. By using a .35 caliber barrel, basing the cartridge on the .30-06 and building it on a Springfield rifle or surplus Mauser, the American hunter could have a medium or large bore at a fraction of the cost of an imported rifle. Hunting the Canadian Rockies and Alaska was now possible without breaking the bank just for the rifle and ammo.

The .35 Whelen offers a good compromise for hunting big game in terrain like this section of the Rockies. If you trail an elk into this stand of timber, you might stumble on him at a few yards, or have a shot at several hundred as he tries to sneak around you.

For calibers bigger than .30-06, hunters early in the 20th century had to rely on lever action rifles like the Winchester 1886, or this Model 1895. They were chambered in straight-wall large-diameter calibers at relatively low pressures. The Whelen calibers offered more bullet weight, pointed bullets and high pressure performance. (Photo courtesy U.S. Repeating Arms Co.)

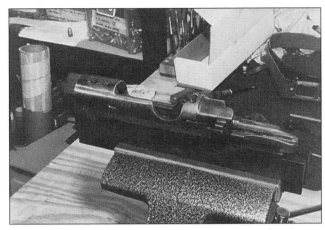

To work on the Mauser action without dropping it or marring it in the vise, you should consider the receiver holding fixture.

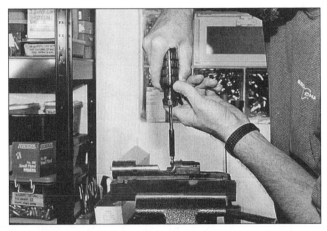

By tightening the locking block, you clamp the receiver in place. There is also a hole in front for the action screw.

With the locking plate in place, the receiver is firmly held, without having to clamp any part of it in the vise. The fixture is particularly useful if you are going to do any milling, drilling and tapping, or polishing of the receiver.

The late Elmer Keith did much the same with his .333 OKH, and the Whelen series of cartridges included .375 and .400 as well as .35.

For my tastes, the .333 (now .338) is too close to the .30-06 in performance to be a choice for now. Later, who knows. The .375 and .400 are too large a bore for the size of the case. The resulting lowered velocity and blunt bullets result in a cartridge with a trajectory too high. For a balance of bullet weight, recoil, trajectory and power, the .35 Whelen is an excellent choice for non-dangerous game larger than deer, such as moose and elk. It offers bullets of 200 to 275 grains with controlled expansion construction in spitzer shapes, for flat shooting and deep penetration. Using 300-grain round-nose bullets, a cool shot and experienced hunter could use it to good effect even against bear. The trajectory with Remington factory ammunition is flat enough for 250-yard shooting with the 200-grain bullet. Zeroed at 200 yards, the 200-grain Pointed Soft Point is 2.3 inches high at 100 yards, 2.0 high at 150, and only 4.0 inches low at 250 yards. The 250-grain PSP keeps its energy better, and with a 200-yard zero drops only a couple of inches more at 250 yards.

How does the .35 Whelen stack up against the big magnums? The vaunted .338 Magnum gives you about 20 percent more recoil for only a couple of inches less drop at 250 yards. The target doesn't know the difference in drop. As a

The flat breach end of the Mauser (on the left) lends itself to easy caliber conversions. The barrel on the right shows the extractor clearance slot that some rifle's barrels require.

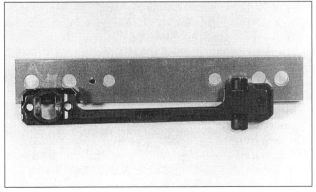

The B-Square drilling guide has bars for two different patterns. This pattern is for Mauser rifles, and you can see the holes line up perfectly for the Mauser base from Millett.

The B-Square drilling guide locates all of the holes at once.

The New England Custom Gunsmiths EAW quick detachable scope mount, with the auxiliary rear sight.

Here you see the B-Square drilling guide with a drill in place, ready to go into the front ring of the Mauser.

By removing the scope and rings (here I have simply removed the rear ring) you can clamp the rear sight in place.

matter of fact, if big-game animals were sentient enough to know the difference and object, we wouldn't be hunting them. (A number of Science Fiction stories have been written on the ramifications of finding out the game is smarter than the hunter.) But, we know the difference. For me, the few inches less drop is not worth the extra recoil I have to put up with. For you, the flatter trajectory may be worth it. My threshold of "too much gun" on non-dangerous game is in calibers with more recoil than the .35 Whelen. If the quarry can fight back, I'm willing to put up with more recoil. If it can't, I'll depend on stalking and marksmanship. Some days the threshold is a lot higher, other days it isn't. However, I know I can shoot the Whelen as accurately as lesser calibers and not get beaten up by the recoil.

I used a Pac-Nor barrel that Chris Dichter profiled and threaded for me, leaving the chamber short. It was a simple matter to install it by the method described in Chapter Six.

The receiver had already been drilled and tapped, so mounting the scope is a matter of installing a mount and rings. Much elk territory is what I call "pie-bald," that is either open spaces with sections of dense woods, or dense woods with small, medium and large openings. A hunter who has traveled a long distance to his hunting camp may find that his scope is unsuited for the climate or terrain, or that a ham-handed baggage handler has caused the demise of his scope. What to do? Remove the scope and buy one where? Use the iron sights (if any) for a 200 yard shot? A solid scope mount that returns to zero is

As with any scope mounts, you start by screwing the bases to the receiver.

always useful, especially if you have a spare scope along with you. For the Mauser/Whelen I selected New England Custom Gunsmiths EAW quick-detachable scope mounts and rings.

Installation is simple. As with any scope mounting, clean the top of the receiver and use a tap to clean out the mount holes. Install the mount bases on the receiver with the adjustment screws and locking lever on the right side. NECG recommends using Loctite on the base, but I don't use it unless I'm mounting a scope on a rifle .375 or larger. Loosen the leveling screws in the front ring and tension adjustment in the front base. Place the front ring in the base and lock the rear ring in its base. Loosen the rings and slide your scope alignment bars into place. If your rings do not line up, do not shim the bases. The rear ring has a replaceable elevation block available in .020-inch increments. You can exchange the block you have for the block you need. Center and tighten the windage screws on the rear ring in the same manner you would center and tighten the windage screws on a Redfield-style scope base.

Once the rings are aligned, you can install the scope. For the best possible installation, I use a beater scope to set the tension adjustments. Then, once the tension is set, I pull the beater scope off, lap the rings, and install the scope I intend to use.

To adjust tension, install your scope and tighten the rings around the scope. As with any scope mount it will take some

The front ring has locking screws. Tighten the right side...

and then the left side. In the base, below the ring-tightening screw is the rotation tensioning screw.

Once the rings are level and aligned, clamp the scope in place.

On the rear base you see the locking lever in its full-down position.

Once adjusted, the scope can be removed and replaced with no loss of zero.

Here is the rear sight in place after the scope has been removed.

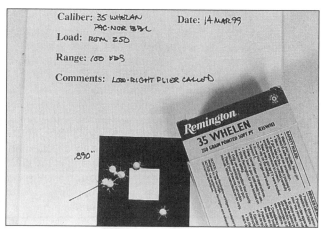

The Mauser with its Pac-Nor barrel and NECG scope mounts works great. The Nikon scope made shooting this group easy, except for my own twitchy finger that day.

fussing to get the reticle level and the ring gaps even on both sides. Now tighten the leveling screw on the RIGHT side as tightly as the included wrench allows. Then tighten the left side. Lift the locking lever and swing the scope back and forth. Gradually tighten the tensioning screw on the front base until the scope moves with tension but without excessive effort. Once the tension is set, tighten the front base tension locking screw.

Swing the scope into its locked position. Loosen the locking screw, the one on the left side of the rear base. Lift the locking lever up and turn the adjustment screw partway counterclockwise. Lower the lever. Does it return all the way down on its own? If it does then you need to adjust more. Repeat until the lever will not return all the way down on its own, and must be pushed the last fraction of movement. Tighten the locking screw. You have removed all of the play. As the rear lockup wears over time, you can adjust it to remove any play that the wear creates.

If you are fitting a second scope to the same mounts, do not adjust the bases. Use the tension adjustments of the front base and stone the engagement surfaces of the new rear ring to fit the pre-set bases.

As an added bonus, NECG offers an aperture sight that fits into the rear base. It is windage and elevation adjustable with screwdrivers at the range. Once your scope is installed and zeroed, remove it. Install the aperture sight. As with the rear ring, the aperture has replaceable elevation blocks. If you can't adjust the sight enough to get on paper, calculate the amount you are off by and exchange the current elevation block for one that is the right height.

To complete the scope package, I installed a Nikon 3-9X40 Monarch scope. Compact, light, bright and durable, it offers the performance needed to take advantage of the .35 Whelen's capabilities without being bulky on top of the rifle. With irons as a backup, you would be ready for any hunting situation, for deer, elk or moose. If I was to fit a backup scope in another pair of rings, I would probably go with something like the Leupold low-power compacts, the 1.5 to 5 or 1.75 to 6 variables. As mentioned before, I am not a fan of the trend towards high-power magnifications on hunting rifles. A deer offers a target of its vitals that is at least six inches across. An elk or moose has a vital area nearly the size of a basketball. You don't need a 12-power or 16-power scope to hit that target at 200 or 250 yards. A smaller scope is handier and less likely to get damaged than a large one.

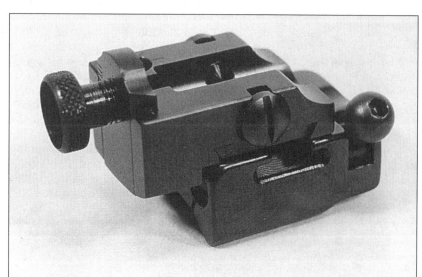

The rear sight is a nicely-machined little jewel that has windage and elevation adjustments. Not just a crude emergency sight, but a capable iron sight on its own!

The Brownells bolt body heat sink protects the threads and cocking cam on the rear of the bolt from the heat of welding.

The mass of the heat sink pulls heat away from the threads and cocking cam. If you do not use a heat sink, your threads or cocking cam could get covered with scale, or even annealed and soft from the heat of welding.

One small problem remains. The factory-original bolt handle and the three-position safety will not clear the scope. The solution for each is simple. Surplus Mauser bolt handles come in two styles, straight and bent. The bent ones are not bent enough to clear a scope, although I have seen some attempts to grind enough clearance. All the attempts left the bolt handle so thin I wasn't sure it would stand up to fast bolt manipulation, and I cannot recommend trying to just grind a path through the bolt handle. Of the two, the straight handles are a bit easier to alter. By changing the angle of the existing handle, you can get it to clear the scope. One method is to cut the handle off and then weld it back on at the correct angle. The drawback to this is the need for a bolt holding fixture. B-Square makes one, and I have used it for years. However, for the straight handles I hit on a method that is a bit easier.

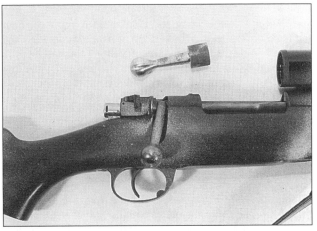

The bolt handle on the project Scout was cut off and replaced with a Dave Talley extension like the one above.

To replace the old safety with a Timney, you have to disassemble the old bolt and striker assembly, remove the safety, and then reassemble the striker and bolt.

You'll need a hand-held grinder, cut-off wheels (and a dust mask to go with them), a propane torch, ball peen hammer and a welder willing to weld your bolt when you're done. If the welder does not have a heat sink, invest in one from Brownells. The heat sink acts as a draw for the heat of welding, keeping the excess from soaking into the bolt body, the rear threads and the cam surface.

Remove the bolt from the rifle and strip it of all parts except the extractor collar. With your cut-off wheel, slice a wedge out of the bolt handle at its root and on the underside. Leave a connecting bridge of steel between the handle and the bolt body. This bridge should be a bit more than 1/8-inch thick. On the sides of the cut on the handle itself, bevel the edges. Once you have bent the handle down, the welder needs access to the interior of the joint so he can get good penetration of the weld. Without this clearance bevel the weld will only be around the border of the new joint, and be weaker than is really needed.

Clamp the bolt body in an unpadded vise, with the body parallel to the floor and the handle sticking up. The vise jaws will act as a heat sink, protecting the rear of the bolt body. With the propane torch heat the bridge of steel connecting the handle to the body. Once the bridge is a dull red, pick up your ball peen hammer and gently tap the handle to bend it over. The hotter you get the steel, the less tapping you'll need. Keep heating and tapping until you have bent the handle flush to the body in the previous wedge. Let the bolt cool. With the scope in place, try fitting the bolt into the action and working it up and down to open and close the action. You may have to grind a bit of steel from the "knuckle" of the joint to clear the scope. Don't do that until it is welded, or the handle might fall off!

By bending the handle this way you avoid the need for a holding fixture. There are two small drawbacks to bending and welding. One is that the bolt handle is still perpendicular to the bolt, and forward of the trigger. If you want to have your bolt handle swept back, or at an angle, like the Winchester Model 70, you must both have a bolt holding fixture to either hold the old or a replacement bolt, and you must account for the new bolt handle angle on your new stock. Mauser stocks are slotted for the bolt handle on the assumption that the bolt handle stays perpendicular. If you bend yours back, you must order a stock with the bolt slot uncut, so you can cut it after you have bent the bolt.

The second drawback is that the bolt handle can sometimes be a bit shorter than one designed to clear a scope. The bolt handle on the project Mauser bucks the odds, coming out 2.350 inches from the bolt body. It sticks out the same amount as my Winchester Model 70, and more

Without the safety to keep it cocked, you'll have to use your hands to keep the striker spring cocked as you screw the bolt body back on.

Once the bolt is back on, leave the bolt body in the cocked position....

Look closely at the bolt handle on the Mauser, top. Even though it has been swept back, it is still forward of the Enfield bolt handle. (Imagine where the knob would be if the handle had not been swept!) The Enfield is one of the fastest-to-work bolt-action rifles, partly because of the location of the bolt handle.

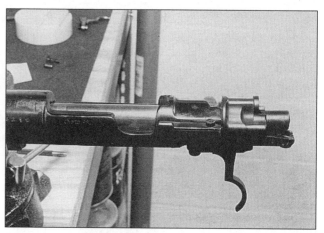

And insert it into the receiver.

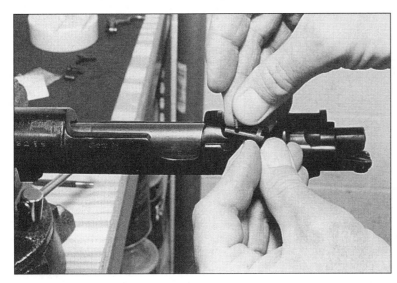

The new safety has a tensioning spring that fits into a hole in the safety shaft.

As you slide the new safety into place, press the spring flush with the shaft as it slides into the shroud.

Press the safety shaft until its shoulder comes flush with the end of the shroud.

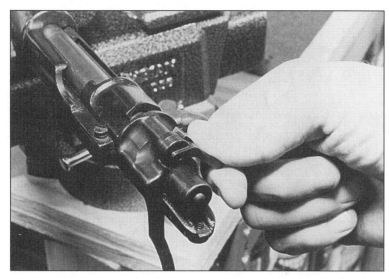

Place the safety lever into the recess on the end of the shaft....

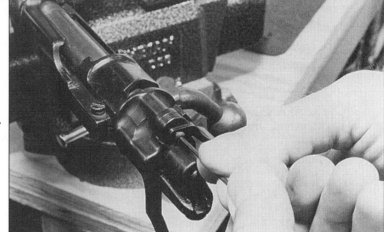

And tighten the holding screw.

The new safety has to cam the striker back away from the sear when you lift the lever. This one worked, first try.

The advantage to the Timney Featherweight is that you can use a bolt shroud mounted safety. If you do not want a safety on the shroud, or prefer a smaller bolt shroud, then go with the Featherweight Deluxe, with its own safety.

than the project Ruger, whose bolt handle length is 2.20 inches. The Mauser bolt handles that are already bent tend to end up short more often than those that started out straight. If you want your bolt handle longer, you have to replace it. On my Custom Scout, I replaced the bolt handle with a bolt knob from Dave Talley. I didn't mind a bolt handle that was perpendicular to the bolt, but if you want a handle that compares in looks and sweep to the Winchester Model 70 or the Ruger Model 77, then use a Lenard Brownell knob.

With the bolt handle welded, use your hand-held grinder and files to clean up the weld bead. If necessary, grind the final clearance for the scope on the bolt knuckle. Your final task is to ensure the bolt rotates to the fully-closed position. The extra steel underneath the joint of the handle and bolt body may keep the bolt handle from turning fully closed. The Mauser is designed with a safety shoulder on the striker. If the bolt is not fully closed, the striker cannot protrude through the face of the bolt to set off the cartridge. On the top of the handle/body joint there should be a small flat left over from the original bolt handle. Does this flat turn to horizontal? If not, the underside of the handle is striking the receiver before turning fully closed. Rather than relieve the bolt handle, and weaken the joint, we will cut clearance in the receiver. This part of the receiver is a non-critical area,

and removing a small area will not cause any problems. Use your hand-held grinder and carbide cutters to remove steel until the bolt closes completely.

Now the bolt clears the scope, but the old safety does not. Timney makes a two-position safety that replaces the old blade and clears any scope. Take the striker assembly and disassemble it. Remove the old safety. Reassemble the striker assembly and install it on the bolt. Install the bolt into the unloaded rifle. Remove the Timney safety lever from its shaft. Place the safety spring in the hole in the shaft, compress it flush and slide the shaft into the cocking piece. Reassemble the safety by sliding the lever onto the shaft and tightening the rear screw.

The new safety operates by camming the cocking piece back from its engagement with the sear. You can make the operation smoother by polishing the camming surface on the Timney safety shaft, and by stoning a bevel on the shoulder of the cocking piece engaging surface. The cocking piece can be quite hard, so use a stone and not one of your good files, or you might end up with a dull file. Do not do more than break the sometimes sharp edge of the cocking piece, adding the bevel reduces the rearward distance the safety cams the cocking piece when going on "safe."

If you fit your new safety and then install a new trigger unit you may have to re-fit the safety. Sometimes a new trig-

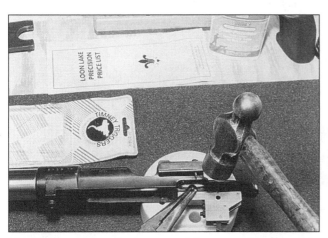

The Timney trigger is an easy replacement for the original Mauser. Drive out the old pin, place the Timney over the retaining stud, and drift the pin back into place.

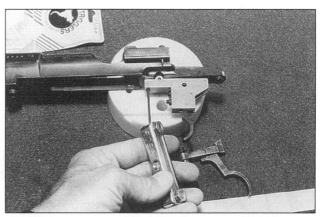

Tighten the locking screw to hold the Timney in place. Then use the adjustment screws to set the trigger, if needed. This trigger did not need to be adjusted, and most won't.

ger and the old safety requires re-fitting of the safety. Why is this? If the new trigger sear sits slightly forward in the receiver in relation to where the old one sat, the safety cannot cam the striker back. The striker rests at full cock too far forward for the safety cam to scoop it away from the sear. In this case the safety can't be engaged. Conversely, if the new trigger sear sits farther to the rear, the safety can't cam the striker back because the striker is already farther back than the safety. Here, the safety goes on, but it doesn't provide protection. If you have a rifle with this problem, and you put the safety on and pull the trigger, the striker might be released, only to be caught by the safety. When you push the safety off, you could fire the rifle, putting a hole through whatever you were pointing the rifle at.

Whenever you make changes in the safety or trigger, you must make double-damn sure that the safety and trigger work as they are supposed to, and no other way. The proper checking method involves an unloaded rifle. Cock the rifle, and pull the trigger. The striker should go forward. Cock the rifle, put the safety on and pull the trigger. The striker must not go forward. If you hear a click you may have a cocking piece alignment problem. Push the safety off. If the striker goes forward, you definitely have a problem. If it does not, pull the trigger. Does the trigger pull require less force than it did the first time? If so, you have an alignment problem.

How to adjust the rifle if you have a trigger/safety misalignment? In many cases you have to either replace the cocking piece, or cut it back and re-harden it, or weld it up and re-harden it. These are all jobs for the professional. Take all your parts, original and replacement, and the rifle to a pro and explain the situation to him. He will tell you what has to be done, and the time and cost. On matters of critical safety such as these, do not be embarrassed about letting the guy who does it for a living step in and make things right.

That said, how to install a better trigger?

For the project Mauser I selected the Timney Featherweight rather than the Featherweight Deluxe. The F-model uses the safety on the bolt, while the FD uses its own safety, and removes the need for a bolt-mounted safety. Some shooters prefer the FD, as they can replace the Mauser bolt sleeve with a streamlined unit. I prefer a safety on the bolt.

Measure the distance your current sear protrudes above the slot in the receiver. You will need to compare this with the amount the new sear sticks up. Some Mausers have a thick web at the seat slot, and the new sear may not stick up high enough. If it does not, you can send the trigger back to Timney and ask for a unit with a high sear. Include your measurements. Place your stripped receiver on a plastic gunsmith's block. Drift out the trigger retaining pin. Check the fit of the Timney over the trigger mounting lug. If the fit is too tight and you try to hammer the pin back in, you can damage the trigger or the mounting lug. With the trigger in place, tighten the installation screw. Check the movement of the sear through the sear slot. If it binds, remove the trigger and file the slot to provide clearance. Once the trigger is in place and the sear moves freely, turn the rifle over and install the bolt. Do your safety check. If the safety either cannot be applied, or goes on "safe" but does not sufficiently block the cocking piece as described above, again, take it to a professional. Grinding, stoning, welding or filing on the cocking piece to make it fit usually also entails re-hardening the cocking piece. Leave such delicate operations to the pros.

If you have decided to go with the Featherweight Deluxe and its integral safety, you have some extra steps once the trigger is in place and the sear moves freely. Install the bolt and check for proper safety function. Also, check the safety plate on the right side of the trigger. In some cases it may ride high enough to rub against the bolt sleeve, rear (safety) lug or the extractor. If it does, gently bend it out until it clears those parts in both the Safe and Fire positions. Also, you may have to relieve the stock inletting in the trigger area to gain clearance for the safety plate and safety button.

Once the trigger is installed and the safety works properly, then you can adjust the trigger weight. The minimum weight for good function, accurate shooting and safe operation is 3 pounds.

The .35 Whelen now has a scope and rear sight, but lacks a front sight. A quick-detachable scope mount is not a great asset without irons or another scope. Front sights can be attached in one of several methods. The dovetail method is used on inexpensive .22 rimfire rifles. The dovetail for the front blade is milled right out of the barrel. The dovetail method doesn't work well for centerfire rifle due to the need for a higher front sight than is usually found on rimfires. The

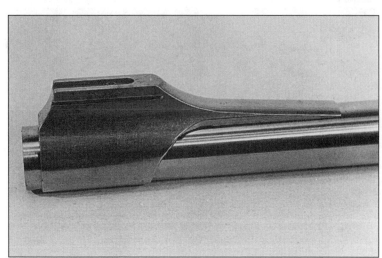

The barrel band front sight (and the barrel band sling swivel) are attached by soldering. Use flux and talc to control solder flow as you heat the barrel and sight.

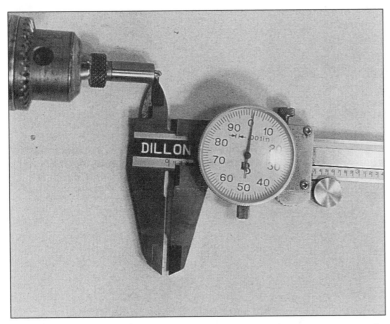

If you are going to drill and tap your barrel for a sight ramp, use the drill guide as a stop, and a shortened drill. By sliding the drill into the chuck, and using the guide as a stop, you can measure exactly how far into the barrel you drill. The guide must rest against the barrel when you start drilling. I have shown this out of the drill press and the Forster fixture only for clarity.

centerfire rifle receiver is thicker than the rimfire one, making the rear sight higher above the centerline of the bore. A sight that is high enough is easily knocked out of the dovetail. Centerfire front sights are commonly placed in a ramp that is attached to the barrel. The ramp is larger than the dovetail would be, and can be attached more securely. Commonly held on with screws or soft solder, a ramp can look good and serve well. The most elegant method of attaching a front sight is with a banded ramp. The ramp, instead of simply sitting on top of the barrel encircles it. Held on with screws, soft solder or epoxy, it is very difficult for the sight to be damaged or knocked off center by being dropped or knocked. As with so many things that are better, a banded front sight is more difficult to install than a simple ramp.

For the banded front sight, you have to measure the diameter of your muzzle, and determine how high the front sight must be. Dial calipers will tell you muzzle diameter. To determine front sight height, you have to have a rear sight installed, and use a masking tape mohawk as your aiming post. Once you know both dimensions, look in the

Brownells catalog and you will see banded front sights and front sight blades. You must have a combination of band that matches your barrel diameter, and band base height and sight height that total the height of your masking tape sighting post. Without a matching total, your only recourse is to change or modify the rear sight to correct your front dimensions. If the muzzle of your barrel does not measure at or just under the inner diameter of a commonly-available banded front sight, you have two choices. One, you can contact New England Custom Gunsmiths and see if they can custom-bore a front band to your dimension. Or, you can have the muzzle of your barrel turned down to just under a sight band diameter. As I mentioned, it can be expensive and a hassle to get a banded front sight on your rifle. With a matching barrel and sight band, slide the band on the barrel to check the fit. It should slide past the muzzle, leaving a quarter inch or so of barrel sticking forward of the band. With the unloaded rifle in the stock, shoulder it and look at the sights to make sure they are straight up and down. Adjust as needed. If the sight has a locking screw,

Many Mauser receivers have been ground, polished and otherwise altered through the years. Even after using a drilling guide to drill and tap for scope mounts, you must make sure your mounts fit properly. If they do not, use shim stock to remove wobble in the fit.

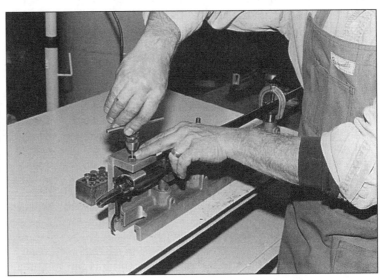

The weight of the trigger pull doesn't make any difference to the Lahti rest. However, without the rest, the Spec-Tech trigger made a difference in accuracy. Shooter performance depends on a good trigger.

tighten the screw enough to leave a mark on the barrel. If the sight does not, remove it from the barrel and drill and tap a hole down through the front sight dovetail. Use a #31 drill and tap the hole 6-48. Put a dab of Dykem on the top of the barrel under where the band will be. Once it is dry, slide the band on and use an overly-long 6-48 screw to mark the Dykem.

Drill a depression in the top of the barrel where the screw has marked it. The depression is the locking shoulder for the screw. The screw will not be the only thing holding the sight on. Clean and degrease the band and barrel. Mix a small batch of Brownells Acra-glas, and put some black dye in it. Spread an even coat of the Acra-glas on the inside of the band, and slide it onto the barrel. Tap the band back with a plastic mallet until it is as far back as it was when you first fitted it. Shoulder the rifle to make sure it is straight up and down. Tighten the locking screw into its dimple. Clean off the excess Acra-glas. The 'glas will keep the sight in place and even resist any bluing salts it may be exposed to, and the black dye will give a close match to the bluing. With a tightly-fitted band, the thin edge of 'glas will probably go unnoticed.

On the project Marlin, the front sight base was integral to the barrel itself. A common design earlier in the 20th century, the production costs caused it to be dropped after WWII. It was cheaper to turn or grind barrels cylindrical and then drill and tap them for a ramp, than retain the more-expensive integral ramp.

Drilling and tapping a hole for the front sight base is delicate work. On a lightweight rifle your available wall thickness may not allow drilling and tapping. You need at least .100 inches depth for the hole, and .100 inches as a safety margin. If your barrel wall isn't at least .200 inches thick, either consider a banded front sight or abandon the idea of iron sights. Calculating wall thickness is easy. Measure your barrel diameter. Subtract your caliber, and divide the result by two. On a .30-06 or .308, you need a muzzle diameter of at least .708 inches to install a ramped front sight.

If you will be installing a ramp, you must have the Forster fixture or something like it. Clamp the barreled action in the fixture with the drilling guide at the muzzle end. To set the drilling depth, adjust the height of the rifle in the fixture so the drill guide touches the barrel. If the barrel lifts the

drill guide slightly up in its guide, fine. Take the drill guide and your #31 drill to the drill press. Slide the drill into the guide until only .100 inches protrudes out of the bottom end. Then slide the drill into the chuck until the drill guide stops against the front of the chuck. Tighten the chuck. Check your measurement. The drill guide will now act as your stop, preventing the drill from going deeper into the barrel than .100 inches. When you drill, clean the chips out regularly, or they will lift the drill guide and make your hole shallower than you intended.

Once the hole is drilled, use the bottoming tap to cut the threads. The hole will not be deep enough to use a tap with any taper to it. Once the bottoming tap stops, pull it out and use a specially-ground tap. Remember what I said about professional gunsmiths using broken taps to make their own bottoming taps? Even a bottoming tap has some taper to the start of the cutting threads. The ground-down broken one can be made without any taper. Even with a modified tap without any taper, you will have two threads, maybe two and a half, to hold the front sight on. Once the ramp is fitted and test-fired, I prefer to remove it, degrease the barrel and ramp, and then re-install it using Brownells Acra-glas as an adhesive. Attached with epoxy, it won't come off until it either breaks loose (unlikely but possible) or I apply heat from a propane torch to burn out the epoxy.

Not everyone is convinced of the need or utility of a quick-detachable scope mount. For a standard mount, I have a one-piece Millett base and standard rings to put on the rifle. One small drawback to the project Mauser is the front bridge. Sometime in the past, the crest was ground off of the receiver. The top of the front ring was the common location to identify the rifle in some manner. During WWII the German production requirements called for the year of manufacture and the arsenal markings to go on the front ring. Soon after the war started, they began using a three-letter code to indicate which arsenal made the rifle.

Before the war, and in other countries, the markings included a national crest of the country purchasing or making it, or the manufacturer's logo. After the war, many rifles had the crest ground off to make it harder to identify where the country involved was getting its rifles. My rifle was so ground. As a result, the top of the front receiver is slightly lower than it should be. With two-piece bases this isn't a problem, as the rings would be lapped anyway. With a one-piece mount the base would be flexed as the screws are tightened. To prevent base flex (which places a heavy load on the base screws) I placed several shims under the front of the base until it stopped rocking when pressed down. With the base screws tightened, installation of the Millett rings followed the standard procedure of Chapter Five. Obviously, with a scope base that was not quick-detachable, the iron sight setup would have to be different. While the front sight could remain the same, the rear would have to be different.

I have always favored the quarter-rib as a location for a rear sight. (Classic stock style, banded front sight, quarter-rib rear sight, my tastes are easy to see. I also think the first two years of Thunderbird production are the best-looking cars ever made.) The easy way to mount a quarter-rib with sights is to order a Ruger No. 1 rear sight. The only catch is, your barrel has to correspond to one of the sets of barrel dimensions on the list in Chapter Nineteen. Otherwise, you have to go with a rear sight like the Williams style, or the Ruger rear on the Model 77 International.

The only thing left on the project Mauser is to drop it into a replacement stock. I have two stocks for it, one is a Ram-Line synthetic stock, and the other is a plain wood stock that I picked up years ago for just this sort of project. Using the inletting procedures in Chapter Nine and the glass-bedding from Chapter Fifteen, I have fitted both stocks to the barreled action. One is durable and impervious to the weather and hard knocks. The other looks like a stock, and gives me a canvas on which to practice future stock and rifle furniture projects.

The project Whelen turned out to be just the ticket. Once the Pac-Nor barrel was broken in, Remington factory ammunition turned in groups a fraction over an inch, using the Nikon Monarch. Iron sight groups were just under 2 inches, but I am not the best marksman around with iron sights. If I turned the rifle over to one of our club's high power shooters, they should be able to bring the iron sight groups down to the scope group sizes. Experimentation in handloads should be able to bring the scope-sighted groups down under an inch.

The third rifle is the Ruger M-77 International. Bill Ruger is a great firearms designer, and has made a lot of money designing and building rifles. (A lot more than I will ever make writing about them, but I'm not the jealous type.)

What success attracts, besides money, is lawsuits. Sturm, Ruger has been sued by stupid, negligent and uneducated people in many cases because Ruger had the money. I'm sure there were some lawsuits that did not fit the harsh description above, but without having read all of them, I'll stick to my description. Heck, I even like lawyers. As a result, Ruger firearms are designed without trigger adjustments. They leave the factory the way they were meant to, and do not have any means of adjusting the triggers. Not all of us fit the three categories I listed above. Many people find that a better trigger improves their shooting. As a result, replacement triggers for Ruger rifles, triggers that have adjustments in them, are available.

Not to sound callous, but when you install a replacement trigger, Ruger considers the warranty to be void. I can't say that I blame them. When you go to work on your own rifle, you have stepped outside of the umbrella of concern of the manufacturer. You're on your own.

That said, how to improve the trigger pull of your Ruger rifle? Not by doing anything with the factory trigger. Replace it with a new one, like the Spec-Tech trigger. Make sure the rifle is unloaded. Remove the rifle from the stock and clamp it in a padded vise. Open the bolt. Push the trigger pin out and remove the old trigger. The Spec-Tech trigger takes the place of the Ruger trigger, and must slide into the slot. If the trigger does not, stone the sides of the trigger pivot hole until it slides into the receiver. Once it slides into place, slide the pivot pin through. Close the bolt.

Push the safety on. If it will not go on, look closely at the shoulder where the safety engages the trigger. Stone the shoulder just enough to let the safety ride over it and block the trigger. If you go too far the safety will not block the trigger, so check frequently. If the safety goes "ON" the first time you try it, attempt to pull the trigger. Does the trigger move? It should not! If the trigger moves, you have a dimensional mismatch that will have to be attended to. Either the trigger or the safety are not large enough. First, look at the safety bar to see if it has been filed-on by a previous owner. If it has, then replace the safety bar and then fit the trigger. If it has not been altered, call Mark Garst at Spec-Tech to see if he can provide a slightly larger trigger. The last resort is to get one or the other welded, to build them up.

The project Ruger did not present any problems, and most don't. With a little stoning, the Spec-Tech trigger slid right into place. Once in the trigger and safety fitting is done, remove the trigger and place the spring seat and spring in place and re-install the trigger. The adjustment screw is on the bottom of the trigger body, just above your trigger finger. Use a little Chip McCormick Trigger Slick on the sears and adjust the pull to 3 pounds. Apply a little Loctite to keep the adjustment screw from loosening under the vibrations of shooting.

The Spec-Tech trigger brought the M-77 International trigger pull down from 4.75 pounds (light for a Ruger) to 3.5 pounds.

CHAPTER 21

A Century and a Half: The Lever-Action Rifle

The history of projectiles in the hands of man has shown progress on a number of fronts including the force at which they could be propelled, the range they could travel, and the frequency with which they could be hurled.

Spear, bow, or sling, there was always a perceived need to get more. I have read of Chinese designs of crossbows, mounted on the ramparts of castles, that used a magazine-feed system for faster firing. I have no doubt that the Roman Legions had standards of accuracy and rate of fire for archers and slingers. "Marcus Aurelius Lucilius, your qualification scores are down. Get them up or you'll be demoted to Princeps Posterior." Roman standards being what they were, strict, I'm sure lots of hot sweaty practice ensued. Practice will only get you so far, for more improvements you need a better design. Many design improvements came from the bench of John Moses Browning.

The story of the repeating lever-action rifle is to a large extent the story of John Moses Browning and Winchester. One of the first experimental rifles that John Browning built was a repeating rifle. He built the first one sometime between 1834 and 1842, and produced them for nearly 10 years after. It used a "magazine" that was an iron bar with holes in it for each charge of black powder and its ball. The bar slid partway through the rifle for each round. I'm sure some wag at the time called it a "harmonica rifle" as a put-down. Browning also built a revolving rifle in the same time period. He did not make either of them after he moved to Utah, building standard rifles of the time until the technology of cartridges improved.

The limiting factor for any repeating rifle is the cartridge. Until an efficient method of holding the powder, primer and bullet in a single case was worked out, repeating mechanisms were just eccentric toys. Once the tricks were worked out, look out! While Browning is the design genius remembered for lever-action rifles, cartridges and levers had been teamed up in a useful way during the Civil War. The Spencer rifle had been patented in 1860, and was superior to the muzzle-loading rifled muskets then in use in every respect except power. Offered a rifle with rapid-fire capabilities, magazine fed and already in production, did the War Department jump at the chance to buy wagon loads of them? No, and was anyone surprised? Only the inventor, Christopher Spencer. He finally talked his way into the office of President Lincoln. Once Lincoln had fired the rifle himself (and shot a respectable group, too) the War Department was instructed to purchase Spencer rifles. (How far we've come: from Lincoln test-firing military weapons to see if they live up to the manufacturers claims, to Teddy Roosevelt who was an avid hunter, to the current situation at the end of the 20th Century.) The combat experience of troops armed with Spencer repeating rifles was simple: with a suitable supply of ammunition they could out-fight units several times their size. With a seven-shot magazine in the rifle, and a box of ten more magazines on the belt, each soldier armed with a Spencer could put out a volume of aimed fire that was impossible to face.

Ogden, Utah was a long way from any of the fighting, and Browning spent his time building single-shot rifles as customers ordered them. The story of Winchester began right after the war, even though their main product was introduced before the war. The Winchester Repeating Arms

The lever action rifle has come a long way since the first Volcanic Repeaters, the predecessors to the Henry rifle. It now has performance that would astound riflemen back then, and optics that let the hunter take cleaner shots and cleaner kills for deer, bear, moose and elk. (Photo courtesy U.S. Repeating Arms Co.)

The beginning of the Browning legacy was not at the start of the Model 1894, but it was the start of the smokeless revolution. The Winchester Model 1894 has been in continuous production (except for War production) ever since. (Photo courtesy U.S. Repeating Arms Co.)

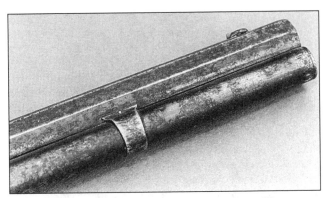

One of the big steps forward from the Henry rifle was the closed magazine tube. The open tube on the Henry had to be made with thick walls to make it strong enough. A closed cylinder is stronger, and could be made lighter.

Company charter went into effect in 1866, and the first rifle offered was called the Model of 1866, even though it was not available until 1867. The '66 was an improved Henry rifle. The Henry had seen action in the Civil War, and had been well-liked despite its shortcomings. The main source of those shortcomings centered around the magazine. On the Henry the magazine tube was slotted, and the muzzle end of it rotated to open the magazine for loading and unloading. The slot guided the magazine follower. To load the rifle, the tab sticking through the slot had to be drawn up to the muzzle, and the front end rotated. Cartridges were then dropped into the magazine, and then the front was turned and the spring eased into place. The slot allowed dirt, gunk and water into the magazine. To keep the tube from collapsing during hard use the walls had to be made thick, increasing the weight of the rifle. And the front sight sat on the rotating front band of the magazine tube. Accuracy suffered due to the moveable nature of the front sight.

The 1866 improved the Henry by using a closed tube for the magazine and a loading gate on the side of the receiver. One aspect of the Henry was not changed and that was the cartridge. The .44 rimfire cartridge was not even a powerful handgun cartridge. However, in the 1866 you could have as many as 17 of them in the rifle at once, and reloading was a fast affair. Under-

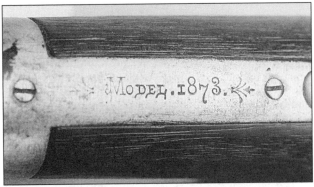

The Model 1873 was an improved '66, which was an improved Henry. But it wasn't good enough. Sure, it had lots of ammo and could deliver it quickly, but there wasn't enough power for really big game.

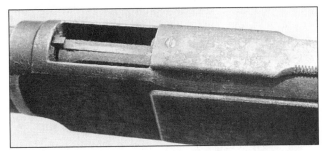

The 1873 had a sliding dust cover, and a bolt which was only as large in diameter as the cartridge it contained. The toggle-link locking mechanism was not particularly strong.

powered, yes, but there were plenty of bullets available. The "Yellow Boy" so-called because of its brass receiver, was quite popular, and Winchester sold many of them.

The under-powered cartridge as a feature of the lever-action rifle recurs through its history. Winchester improved the '66 and made it stronger. The new rifle was the Model of 1873, and it utilized the same centerfire cartridges then becoming popular in handguns. Within three years Winchester had increased the size of the receiver and its parts, and the Model 1876 entered the catalogs. It ended up being the last non-Browning designed lever-action rifle Winchester offered until the Model 88 in 1955.

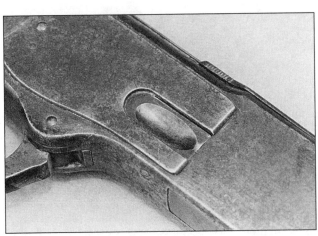

To go with the closed magazine tube, the loading gate was invented. By loading the rounds through the receiver, loading was made faster and safer.

The '73 had the receiver open on both sides, covered with plates. The plates made assembly, service and cleaning easy. The openings made the receiver weak and unable to support larger cartridges.

The big bad boy that started Browning to fame, and sealed the fate of Winchesters competitors, the Model 1886. A repeating rifle chambered in the then-current Government cartridge of .45-70. It had power, speed of action, accuracy and durability. Why buy anything else? (Photo courtesy U.S. Repeating Arms Co.)

The first cartridge repeater Browning invented was a tube-fed bolt-action rifle. Built in early 1882, its description is similar to the Mauser bolt rifle of the period. The next rifle in the Browning line was a lever-action that used the fewest number of parts to produce a repeating rifle. The hammer had to be manually cocked on each shot, probably as a safety feature.

The next rifle was a home run. Built in early 1883, it became the Winchester 1886. What distinguished the 1886 from other lever-action rifles was the strength of the locking mechanism. Previous Winchester designs, the models 1873 and 1876, used a toggle mechanism to move and lock the breechblock. Working the same way the human knee does, the toggle locks lacked the strength to handle cartridges more powerful than those of handgun power. The breech-block on Browning's 1886 was locked into the receiver by paired sliding locking bolts. Attached to the lever, the bolts

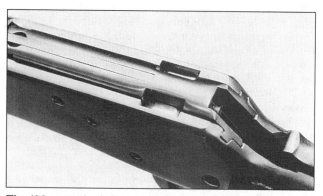

The '86 uses dual rising locking blocks that keep the bolt locked against the thrust of the cartridge. Here the bolts are coming up to their locked positions.

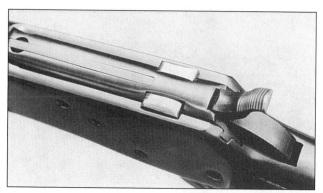

Up and locked, the bolt of the '86 would not move under the load of firing. Also notice that the bolt of the '86 is much larger in diameter than the cartridge it contains, unlike the '73.

slid vertically into place to lock the breechblock before firing. What attracted the rifle to shooters was the power of the cartridges it was chambered in. Until the 1886, all other lever-action rifles were chambered for pistol cartridges. As powerful as the .44-40 was in a handgun, in a rifle it was small stuff. But the Winchester 1886 burst onto the scene chambered in the .45-70 Government cartridge. Instead of a 200-grain bullet at 1,000 fps, hunters and explorers could have at their disposal a 500-grain bullet at 1,400 fps! Finally, a repeating rifle that could be used to hunt large game. The die was cast, and Winchester and Browning began a profitable business together. Profitable for Winchester because the Browning designs could not be equaled, and profitable for Browning because Winchester bought all his models, and patented them to keep them out of the hands of their competitors. The best estimate of how much Winchester paid Browning for the patent to the 1886 is $50,000. A nice chunk of change today, in 1886 it represented more money than the entire town of Ogden, Utah was worth. The President of Winchester and Browning came to view it almost as a game. Browning would show up at the Winchester office with a large satchel, and produce the rifle that T.G. Bennett, the President, had asked for. Once the agreed-on rifle was delivered, and the price settled, Browning would then produce one after another of a firearm that fit the same market niche, but had a different mechanical solution to the problem. Winchester would buy these models, too, in order to keep the patents out of the hands of their competitors.

The lever-action rifles that Browning designed swept all competitors before them.

Close on the heels of the huge 1886 came the compact Model 1892. The '92 is basically a scaled-down 1886, chambered for handgun cartridges. You might think this was a step backwards. After all, the '86 made it possible to have a repeating rifle in the most powerful common cartridge of the day. Why a lesser one? Then as now many shooters looked for convenience. A shooter who had a handgun and rifle chambered in the same cartridge had fewer supply problems. Getting ammunition from town was easier if there was only one to shop for. Getting ammo from the wholesalers to the town hardware store was easier. Not all problems required the

In the middle is the Model '92. It was chambered for the same cartridges as the Model 1873 on the left, while being much handier. On the right is the '94, smaller than the '73 and almost as handy as the '92.

With a rifle chambered in a handgun caliber, supply was easier. The '92 had enough power for day-to-day work (a century ago, rifles were a tool, like a laptop today) and was handy enough to keep close by all the time. (Photo courtesy U.S. Repeating Arms Co.)

Hollywood and its interpretation of the Western, brought about things that didn't actually exist back then. The "big-ring" loop on a '92 probably got its start when John Wayne used one in his role in "Stagecoach." (A brilliant western, if you haven't seen it, you should.) Once the movies had it, shooters had to have it. You can still have it today. (Photo courtesy U.S. Repeating Arms Co.)

Movie production departments loved the '92 because it was chambered for handgun cartridges. Despite all the revolvers and rifles in a movie, they could all be fed the same blanks. Oh, back when Winchester made them (this is a '73) the cartridges were .38 & .44 Winchester Center Fire. (W.C.F.)

power of the .45-70. The cost and recoil of a .45-70 were more than a hunter of the time needed to protect himself and his herds. A .44-40 was plenty good enough for wild dogs, wolves, bobcats and the occasional would-be rustler. The 1892 production immediately went into high gear in an effort to keep up with demand. So many '92s were produced that Hollywood production companies bought truckloads of them to use in Westerns. Hugely popular through the 1950s and into the 1960s, Westerns almost all required guns as props. If you look closely, you'll see that many of the lever-action rifles in those movies are 1892s. Even in movies set before the '92 was invented! In part, the popularity of the '92 with movie production departments came from the design of blanks. Called "five in one," they could be used in any revolver or rifle chambered in the most popular western calibers; .38-40, 44-40 and .45 Colt. By using rifles chambered in those pistol calibers, the gun wranglers and prop masters could make sure they never started a day's filming with the wrong ammo for the guns.

The late 1880s and early 1890s was a time of upheaval in ballistics. The new smokeless powders were the subject of

feverish inquiry and experimentation. No smoke! No fouling! Higher velocities! Why did my rifle blow up?

The newer powder was more dense and more powerful than black powder. Black powder cartridges had to be large to contain enough powder to propel the bullet. The same cartridges were now too large for the smaller amounts of smokeless that was needed. Where a black powder cartridge could be re-loaded by scooping black powder into the case until the powder rose to where the base of the bullet would be, doing so with smokeless created a compact bomb. The greater velocities of smokeless were gained by reaching to higher pressures. The softer steels that were suitable for black powder stretched under the load of smokeless powder.

The old designs would not do for the new powder.

Stepping into the picture with an updated old design was Browning. He took the lever-action he had made so smooth and elegant in the 1886 and 1892 rifles, and made it simpler. The simpler design made Winchester happy, for they could make the rifle for less money, and either make a higher profit or swamp the competition with larger production. He created the model 1894. The '94 Winchester went on to create generation after generation of hunters who viewed a hunting rifle as first and foremost a lever-action rifle. Now more than 100 years after its introduction, the '94 is just as suitable as a hunting rifle, and held in the same high regard by a large number of hunters.

The 1894 did away with the dual locking blots of the '86 and '92. Instead, as you closed the lever a single small locking block rose up behind the breechblock of the 94. The cartridge lifter hinged up to present each cartridge for feeding. The feed lips are separate blocks fastened to the receiver with a pair of screws. Caliber changes in production were simple for Winchester. A different barrel, a different lifter, and a pair of feed lips, and they had a different caliber to ship. On the Mauser '98 rifle, the feed lips are an integral part of the receiver. To change calibers requires a different machining set-up and a separate inventory of receivers. Mauser was selling rifles by the 10,000-rifle production batch to national armies. Winchester was selling rifles in 10's and 20's to hardware stores who sold them retail. Winchester could not afford to produce huge batches of one caliber or another, and the Browning design was perfect for their needs.

The Model 94 used a single locking block, rising up behind the bolt.

Here, in its upright and locked position, we see another Browning design inspiration. The locking block has a pin that connects the hammer to the firing pin. If the locking block is unlocked, the pin cannot transmit the force of the hammer to the firing pin. Unlocked, the rifle will not fire.

But many rifles have been easily produced and have not been successful in the marketplace. Why the '94? Being an early entry helps. When it first appeared smokeless powder and jacketed bullet technology were hotter and more unknown than the computer revolution in the early 1980s. No one knew if it would live up to the promises of power and velocity without some drawbacks. Could a .30-caliber bullet of half the weight do what a .45 had done? More than being early, the '94 had the advantage of being right. It was and is the right size, weight and balance for a hunting rifle. The flat receiver without knobs sticking out on the side made a handy package. It could be slid into a saddle scabbard or hung behind a wagon seat without getting hung up when it was needed. Its compact size was a blessing on the frontier. Despite the wide-open spaces, a standard rifle was too large. Packing a rifle on a horse, getting into and out of a log cabin, threading

The carbine '94 was flat, compact and handy. It could easily slide into a scabbard, and ride on a horse unnoticed until needed. (Photo courtesy U.S. Repeating Arms Co.)

through timber and thickets put a premium on a compact rifle. A standard bolt-action rifle with its 29-inch barrel and receiver and buttstock could top 50 inches. A '94 carbine held as many rounds and did it in a package that could be a foot shorter.

And as icing on the cake, the lever-action rifle was fast to fire. While the British were developing the double rifle into a portable combination art masterpiece and small cannon, the American hunter used a levergun. If you need to place a second shot into a fleeing deer, elk or moose, a lever-action rifle had all the advantages over a bolt-action. While the double rifle was faster still, who could afford one? Then as now double rifles were the property of the well-to-do. An American frontiersman could save every penny he made for years and still not be able to afford a double rifle. The levergun could be afforded from saving money for a few months. Ammunition was common and powerful, and the accuracy and rapidity of fire meant no potential game escaped the tired hunter with a family to feed. Hunting a century ago was not like hunting today. Many times game taken was game encountered almost at chance. A rifle had to be at hand to be of any use. It had to be chambered in a common caliber, and one suitable for the game at hand.

Although the Model 1894 was the most successful Browning lever rifle design, it was not the last. The Model 1895 solved a vexing problem for Winchester. The tube magazine of the lever-action rifle cannot use ammunition with pointed bullets. The nose of each cartridge rests against the primer of the cartridge ahead of it. If you use a pointed

The problem with a large, powerful rifle is hauling it around between the times you need it. One solution was to make a carbine model. Another was to make a take-down model. By using interrupted threads, this modern Model 1886 comes apart with half a turn. (Photo courtesy U.S. Repeating Arms Co.)

The Winchester Model 1895 solved one vexing problem with tube-fed rifles; the need to use flat-nosed bullets. Any attempt to use pointed bullets in a tubular magazine could detonate the primers under recoil. The '95 used a vertical magazine. (Photo courtesy U.S. Repeating Arms Co.)

bullet, you may detonate one or more of the cartridges under recoil. Even a round-nosed bullet that is hard and pointy enough may set a primer off. In the early 1890s, the U.S. Army adopted a new smokeless round. We later called it the .30-40 Krag, but then it was called the .30 Army or .30 Government. It was too powerful for the sleek little model 1894, and the full metal jacketed ammunition was dangerous to use in a tubular magazine.

John Browning delivered, and again he exceeded his mandate. The 1895 feeds from a stacked magazine. Not only would it easily utilize the .30 Army, it would handle the 7.62 Russian cartridge, a ballistic equal to the later .30-06. (Or should I say the later .30-06 equaled the Russian?) It was chambered in the .303 British. When the .30-03 and then .30-06 came along, the '95 handled those, too. And as icing on the cake, the '95 appeared in a new powerhouse, the .405 Winchester. The .405 started a 300-grain bullet at a listed 2,260 fps. Before you sneer at such "wimpy" ballistics, remember the then-current American military cartridge (the .30-40 Krag) launched its 220-grain bullet at a slightly slower speed. Winchester manufactured almost 300,000 rifles in 7.62 Russian for the Imperial Russian Army during World War I.

Winchester was so enamored of the lever-action that they commissioned Browning to design a lever-action shotgun. It was not popular, mostly because it was large and awkward in looks and handling. If you grew up with a double-barreled shotgun, you would not like the Winchester Model 1887 or its successor, the Model 1901. Browning didn't like it either, and he persisted in offering Winchester a pump shotgun, until they accepted his 1893.

Winchester was not the only maker offering lever-action rifles at the end of the 19th Century. Marlin got into the action, and offered several designs, designs that unwittingly corrected later problems with the Browning/Winchester rifles. The problem was the open-topped action and its vertical ejection. The Marlins, with their side-ejection, were a snap to drill and tap for a scope mount, when scopes became a required shooting accessory. The Marlin design remains almost the same today. If you want to know what an original Marlin Model 1893 looked like, go to your local gun shop and look at a modern Model 1894. Side ejection, flat bolt, external hammer, it is almost identical.

Not to be left out, Savage began making lever-action rifles at the end of the 19th Century. Their Model of 1899, later simply the '99, offered the one thing that Winchester didn't; a handy little rifle that could take pointed bullets. The rotary magazine of the '99 could not only take pointed bullets, but it handled the rimless ones without a hitch. Made today, if you want a lever gun chambered in a rimless cartridge handling pointed bullets, the Savage is your choice.

While the slow decline of the levergun began during the 1920s, it was popular then for a reason, and that reason was

Still hugely popular today with hunters, the lever-action rifle is seeing a new resurgence of interest in the sport of Cowboy Action Shooting. Competitors must wear appropriate period dress, and use nothing invented after 1898. (Photo courtesy U.S. Repeating Arms Co.)

Recognizing the desire of many hunters today to use optics, Winchester has offered the '94 for years already drilled and tapped for scope mounts. The stock on this Black Shadow has been designed with scope use in mind. (Photo courtesy U.S. Repeating Arms Co.)

The cross-bolt safety on the new Winchesters (and safeties on any rifle) should not be deactivated. (Photo courtesy U.S. Repeating Arms Co.)

The .30-30 was powerful in its day. It is still just as powerful (if anything, more!) but shooters expectations have grown. To handle a bigger cartridge, Winchester offers the Big Bore '94. The reinforcement of the rear of the receiver allows it to handle cartridges such as the .375 Winchester. (Photo courtesy U.S. Repeating Arms Co.)

eyesight. The best shooter around could not count on bringing down a deer, elk or moose beyond 200 yards, using iron sights. Within that distance, a lever-action rifle has the power and accuracy needed, and offers the fastest-possible second shot at a reasonable cost.

The lever-action rifle arrived a century and a half ago. The best designs sprang forth a century ago, and unless something disturbing happens, they will probably be with us for another century.

Having said so many good things about the lever-action rifle, it may seem strange to say that it can be improved, but few objects exist that can't be improved in looks or function. I would put on the short list Michelangelo's "David", the gull-wing Mercedes and the samurai sword. But even in the last two mentioned, some were better than others.

What are the shortcomings of the lever-action rifle? Power, sights, handiness, the buttplate and the lack of a sling. While the trigger pull of many rifles is quite good,

others are not so good. Most of the shortcomings inherent in the design can be overcome with a little gunsmithing. Additional power can be had by re-boring and chambering suitable rifles. One new trend should not be gunsmithed, and it is one that troubles old-time shooters. The new design on the block is the cross-bolt safety. Original lever-action rifles with external hammers used a half-cock notch as a safety. By lowering the hammer you made the rifle safe. This was not enough safety, and the designers have been compelled to add another safety. The cross-bolt safety blocks the hammer. When pushed on "Safe" the hammer cannot travel far enough to contact the firing pin. It is ugly. It is here to stay.

If you have a rifle with a cross-bolt safety, either live with it or trade it. Under no circumstances should you ever deactivate one of these for a buddy who promises "to be safe" with his rifle. If you do, you may come to regret it. "Maybe not now, or tomorrow, but soon, and for the rest of your life."

Glossary

Acetylene torch

A heating torch that uses acetylene from a tank and ambient oxygen. Hotter than propane, it is not hot enough to weld. Welding requires an oxy-acetylene torch.

Action

The heart of the rifle. The main part that all the rest of the parts are attached to, also called the receiver.

Assault Weapon

A technical and political category of rifle. A political category of shotgun and handgun. The technical description of an assault weapon is: "A select-fire rifle or carbine chambered in an intermediate caliber with a large detachable magazine issued to military units." The political category is: "A semi-automatic rifle manufactured or assembled after Sept 13, 1994, that has the capability of accepting a detachable magazine, and has at least two of the following: (i) a folding or telescoping stock (ii) a pistol grip that protrudes conspicuously beneath the action of the weapon (iii) a bayonet mount (iv) a flash suppressor or threaded barrel designed to accommodate a flash suppressor (v) a grenade launcher. Real assault weapons (machine guns, etc.) are strictly controlled under the National Firearms Act of 1934. The current semi-automatics can still be bought and sold, you just can't assemble a rifle that fits the description of the Crime Bill of 1994.

Bake-on

A paint or epoxy finish that is cured by heat. Protective, it is not as durable as some other finishes, but can be touched-up when it wears. A utilitarian finish used more by guides who lead clients to dangerous game, and by handgunners protecting personal protection carry guns.

Barrel channel

The groove through the forearm of the stock where the barrel rests.

Beanfield

A relatively new category of hunting rifle, used at long range from a blind or prepared shooting position. In a hunting context also called a "cross canyon" rifle. In police or military applications, a "tactical" or "precision" rifle.

Benchrest

A method of shooting using a bench for support, to determine the highest level of accuracy a rifle can deliver. Also a form of competition.

Blind magazine

One where the magazine or its parts do not protrude beneath the stock. A rifle with a blind magazine will have only a trigger guard underneath, two screws to secure the receiver to the stock, and wood or other stock material in between.

Bluing

A chemical treatment of the surface of steel or iron to provide some protection from corrosion. Bluing is a form of rust, and rust-removing chemicals will remove a blued finish.

Bowling pins

A variant of practical shooting that uses actual bowling pins as targets. The object of a bowling pin shoot is to knock a certain number of bowling pins off of a table. The fastest time wins. Rifle bowling pin shooting uses hinged steel cutouts of bowling pins, again, with the fastest time winning.

Brass

A single, empty cartridge case, or plural cases.

Bolt-action

A rifle that uses a turnbolt to feed and secure each cartridge in the chamber.

Boltface

The part of the bolt where the firing pin protrudes to ignite the primer.

Bore scope

A device to inspect the interior of a rifle barrel. While a useful tool, the bore scope is not the definitive authority on a barrels performance. A barrel that looks good through the scope may only be an average performer, while a barrel that shoots quite well could look very bad through the scope.

Bore sight

Aligning the bore and the sights or scope optically. Bore sighting can be done with the naked eye using a distant object or optically with a bore collimator.

Bore solvents

Used to chemically remove the copper, brass or lead form the bore of a rifle, often aided by brushing.

Bottom metal

The trigger guard, the magazine floorplate and the bottom of the magazine box. On some rifles such as the

Remington ADL, there is only a trigger guard as the magazine is blind. On other rifles, the bottom metal can be two or three pieces.

Bushing

Any sleeve that holds another part.

Butt

The stock rearwards from the wrist or pistol grip.

Caliber

A particular cartridge size and operating pressure. The caliber can be a numerical description; 5.56 X 45 or 7.62 X 39, it can be a numerical composite; .30-06 ("Caliber thirty, model of 1906") or it can be a name; .300 Winchester Magnum. Calibers can have several names; the .30-06 was called ".30 Gov't" and in Europe is known as "7.62 X 63". Cartridges of a caliber can be loaded to different pressures. The .257 Roberts is loaded to +P as well as standard pressure.

Cartridge

A single, loaded round of ammunition.

Chamber

The recess in the rear of a barrel where the cartridge rests during firing.

Chevy Truck

The "Chevy Truck Team Sportsmans Challenge" is an annual match held in Florida that involves three-man (or woman) teams using rifles, handguns and shotguns. The rifle commonly used is the Ruger 10/22.

Chrome

Also known as Hard Chrome or Industrial Hard Chrome, when properly plated onto a steel part it offers a hard and tough finish that is relatively inert to corrosion. Under sufficiently harsh conditions steel can rust underneath a chrome plating, but it is not common.

Cleaning

Removing the powder residue and jacket fouling from firing, or the dust and lint from storage. In extreme cases cleaning involves rust removal.

Cleaning rod

The rod used to clean the bore of a rifle. The threaded end allows changing from brushes to patch-holders.

Cleaning solvent

Solvents used to dissolve the powder residue or the jacket fouling from the bore.

Comb

The top of the stock, where the face rests during firing.

Compensator

A device that re-directs the gasses of combustion, to reduce felt recoil or muzzle rise. Also; muzzle brake.

Controlled feed

A rifle (usually bolt-action but not exclusively) with controlled feed has an extractor designed to grasp the rim of the cartridge during feeding. The CF action maintains control of the cartridge at all times, and will feed regardless of the position the rifle is held in. The Mauser, Springfield and Winchester Model 70 are examples of controlled feed rifles. See: Push feed.

Crown

The chamfering at the end of the barrel. A properly-crowned barrel evenly releases the bullet without disturbance, and aids accuracy.

Cryo

Cryogenic treatment of the barrel to relieve stress and improve the grain of the steel.

Dangerous game

A prey that has the capacity of inflicting injury on the hunter, even without mishap by the hunter. A whitetail deer may injure a hunter, but not because the deer intended to. Dangerous game is prey that objects strenuously to being hunted. While bears and African game are the obvious ones, wild boar are also dangerous. Hunting dangerous game usually requires larger than normal calibers, open sights or low-powered scopes, and ultra-reliable rifles.

Desiccant

A chemical substance that absorbs moisture. Desiccants come as two types, reversible and non-reversible. The N-R dessicants must be thrown out once they have absorbed water. The reversible ones can be dried out by heat or microwave, and used again. Used in a gun safe to keep the air dry for safe storage.

Disassembly

Taking a rifle apart in order to clean it or to work on it.

Disconnector

A part that removes the trigger from the firing linkage as the mechanism cycles. Prevents fully-automatic fire.

Double feed

A dangerous situation where a chambered round (or a fired case) remains in the chamber, and another round is attempting to feed. Controlled feed actions cannot double feed. On a CF rifle even if the bolt handle is not turned down the extractor will still pull the chambered round out.

Drop

The distance between the center of the bore and the top of the comb. The comb is the resting place for the face, and incorrect drop may interfere with the ability to use the sights or scope.

Elevation

Correction of bullet impact or sights in a vertical direction.

Ejector

A fixed post or spring-loaded plunger that tosses the empty brass out at the end of the firing cycle.

Epoxy

A synthetic adhesive made of two parts: resin and hardener. When the two are mixed, they chemically react to form a hard substance impervious to oils. Epoxy will stick to anything not protected by a release agent. Epoxy can be used to glue, repair or reinforce, and when mixed with a strengthening substance such as fiberglass or powdered metals, becomes strong enough to machine or file to shape.

Erosion

Wear in the leade and throat of a barrel, due to the hot gases of combustion. Once sufficiently worn, a barrel begins to lose accuracy.

Extractor

A hook or shelf that pulls cartridges out of the chamber. The appearance of an extractor is not always an indication of its strength or function. Remington extractors appear small, but have nearly as much gripping area as Mauser extractors. The Ruger extractor looks just like the Mauser, but earlier ones were not a controlled-feed extractor.

Feed lips

The top of a magazine, that parts that guide the top cartridge forward and upward, towards the chamber.

Feed ramp

The portion of the receiver between the magazine and the chamber.

Fire lapping

Lapping using a lapping compound on the surface of the bullet. The bullets passage down the bore laps the bore without the need for holding fixtures as in regular hand-lapping of bores during their manufacture.

Firing pin

The tip of the striker, the portion that protrudes from the bolt face.

Fluting

Parallel grooves machined down the ouside of a barrel, to lighten it. A fluted barrel is stiffer than another barrel of the same weight and length, and almost as stiff as one the full diameter of its maximum dimension. A fluted barrel also has more surface area than an unfluted barrel (greater than either its major or minor diameter) and will cool slightly faster because of the greater area.

Forearm

The portion of the stock forward of the receiver, grasped by the non-trigger-finger hand.

Glass bedding

The use of epoxy, or epoxy mixed with mechanical hardeners like fiberglass floc or powdered metals, to provide a solid and stable surface for the receiver to rest on within the stock.

Hammer

A pivoting part of the firing linkage that delivers the power of the mainspring to the firing pin. Seen mostly on lever-action rifles and single shots.

Headspace

The size of the chamber, plus and minus the allowable tolerances. Insufficient headspace leads to malfunctions. Excessive headspace is hazardous.

IPSC

The International Practical Shooting Confederation, the world organizing body for practical shooting and competition.

Laminated

A part built up by layers of material. A laminated stock is made of sheets of wood arranged in alternating grain direction, glued together. Very strong, if somewhat heavy.

Lap

The use of abrasive compounds in a carrier base, usually grease, to cut or polish the surface and make it conform to the shape or dimension of the lapping piece. Used to make scope rings concentric and to smooth bores during the barrel-making process.

Lever-action

A rifle that feeds the cartridges and locks the bolt by means of a lever underneath the receiver.

Lubricants

Petroleum oils or synthetic liquids used to reduce friction between moving parts. Except in extreme cases, rifles work better with lubricated working parts. Lubricants should not be left in the chamber or bore before firing.

Lug

Commonly a locking lug. The locking lugs of a bolt engage some surface of the receiver to keep the action closed during firing. On lever-action rifles, the locking lugs of the bolt and receiver require intermediate locking blocks that slide into place. Many lever-action rifles are not as strong as bolt-action rifles, and are not chambered for cartridges as strong. Some lever-action rifles are, such as the Winchester M-88 and the Browning BLR.

Magazine

Contains the cartridges in the rifle. Commonly, and mistakenly referred to as a "clip" in semi-automatic rifles. A magazine contains a spring for feeding, a clip does not.

Magazine box

The internal metal container that holds the cartridges in a bolt-action rifle. If the box dimensions do not correctly correspond to the cartridge dimensions, then the rifle will not feed well.

Magazine safety

A part of the firing linkage. If a pistol contains a magazine safety, and the magazine is not inserted into the pistol, the pistol will not fire. Not all pistols have magazine safeties. In those that do, it can be removed. When removed, the pistol will fire without a magazine in the frame. People have died as a result of accidents where they thought a magazine safety would prevent their being shot, and the MS had been removed. Rifles do not have magazine safeties mostly because rifles do not have detachable magazines. Current trends in legislation may change this in the future.

Mag-Na-Port

A process of recoil reduction involving slots burned through the barrel by Electrical Discharge Machining. The slots vent gas to counteract the effects of recoil.

Mainspring

The spring that powers the hammer or striker in firing. Also known as the striker spring.

MIG

"Metal-inert gas" welding. The inert gas flows through the rod holder and bathes the welded area, preventing oxygen in the air from forming slag in the weld.

Muzzle

The bullets exit point in the end of the barrel.

Muzzle brake

A device added to the muzzle of a rifle to scavenge and divert the combustion gases. The diverted gases counteract the effects of recoil. There is a direct relationship between the amount of gases diverted and the effectiveness of the brake. There is also a direct relationship between the amount of gases diverted and the increased noise experienced by the shooter and those next to him.

Night sight

Sights that glow in the dark. Commonly they contain small vials of Tritium, with a useful life of five to 10 years.

NRA

National Rifle Association. An association of the firearms owners of the U.S., that organizes competition, training, and political representation.

Oxy-acetylene

A torch that mixes oxygen from a pressurized tank with acetylene from another pressurized tank to create a very hot flame. The flame is hot enough to melt steel, thus enabling welding.

Parkerizing

A protective finish that involves the use of boiling phosphoric acid to create a zinc, magnesium or iron phosphate layer on the surface of the steel. Parkerizing makes a surface rougher, and hides toolmarks and other blemishes. Commonly used in military rifles by the United States.

Patches

Small cloth patches pushed down the bore to clean out powder residue, to apply bore solvent, and to remove solvent that has combined with fouling.

Peen

To move metal by striking it with a hammer. Peened parts are slightly distorted by the impact, and often have to be filed, stoned or lapped to fit properly. Used to fill small gaps between parts without welding or silver-soldering.

Pilot

A guide rod, used to keep a barrel in line with a cutting tool, or a cutting tool in line with the hole it will be reaming or chamfering.

Propane torch

A small torch commonly found at hardware stores, useful for soldering. To get enough heat to solder large jobs you may have to hold a propane torch in each hand.

Push feed

A push feed action pushes the cartridge ahead of it and into the chamber. Once the round is chambered, the extractor snaps over the rim as the bolt handle is being turned down. If the handle is not turned-down, then a double feed will result. The Remington 700 is a push-feed design.

Recoil

The reactive force of firing a rifle. The energy of propelling a bullet (and its propulsive gases) generates an equal and opposite force. This recoil must be accepted or redirected by the shooter.

Recoil spring

Found in semi-automatic rifles. The spring stores energy from the recoil, and uses it to feed the next cartridge into the chamber.

Recoil pad

A rubber or synthetic pad in the butt of a rifle to absorb recoil and make it less traumatic to the shooter.

Release agent

A substance sprayed or brushed onto a surface that prevents epoxy for adhering. The thin layer of release agent allows a faithful reproduction of the surface it protects, without allowing the epoxy to stick.

Reticle

Aiming marks in a scope.

Rifling

Spiral grooves cut or swaged into the bore of a barrel. The bullet passing down the barrel is rotated by the rifling, stabilizing the bullet for its trip to the target.

Scout rifle

A rifle design brought about by Jeff Cooper. The Scout is meant to be a general-purpose rifle able to be carried by a hunter or a scout long distances. It delivers enough energy to cleanly bag medium-sized game. It has enough accuracy to hit any target to 300 meters (more if the shooter is up to the task) and handles quickly enough to be used in a close-in emergency.

Soldering

Joining two pieces by heating them and introducing a different metal into their gap.

Swage

To move metal by cold-forming it, or pressing with a large and heavy bar shaped for the purpose.

TIG

"Tungsten inert gas". A method of welding using inert gas to prevent slag formation in the weld.

Trigger job

To adjust the trigger pull of a rifle (usually by making it lighter, but not always) either by adjusting the screws built into it, or replacing the trigger unit with an adjustable one.

USPSA

The United States Practical Shooting Association, the organizing body for practical shooting and competition in the US.

Varmint

A shooting sport/hunting endeavor that is less hunting and more marksmanship. Varmints are commonly small critters of various rodent branches of the mammal family.

The hunter fires from a prone and sandbagged position on an adjacent hilltop, firing into the "town" of burrows, with the intent to hit as many varmints as possible. The prolific rodents breed back faster than they can be shot, ensuring a never-ending supply of targets.

Welding

Joining two parts by heating their edges until the metal melts, and adding a filler to the joint.

Windage

Movement of the bullet or sights from side to side. Also the correction of sights side to side.

Wrist

The part of the stock grasped by the firing hand. Also; pistolgrip, where the pistolgrip is integral with the stock. When the stock and pistolgrip are separate, there is no wrist.

Suppliers

Accuracy Speaks, 3960 N. Usery Pass Rd., Mesa, AZ., (602)373-9499

Acra-Bond (Artistry in Wood), 134 Zimmerman Rd., Kalispell, MT., 59901, (406)257-9003

American Spirit Arms, 19401 North Cave Creek Rd., Suite 9, Phoenix, AZ., 85024, (888)486-5487 FAX(602)569-2487

Armalite, P.O. Box 299, Geneseo, IL, 61254 (309)944-6939 FAX(309)944-6949

Ashley Outdoors, Inc., 2401 Ludelle St., Fort Worth, TX., 76105 (817)536-0136 FAX(800)734-793

B-Square, P.O. Box 11281, 2708 St. Louis Ave., Fort Worth, TX., 76110 (817)923-0964 FAX(817)926-7012

Bald Eagle Precision Machine Co., 101-D Allison St., Lock Have, PA. 17745 (717)748-6772 FAX(717)748-4443

Blackstar, 437 Idaho St., Gooding, ID., 83330

Bore Tech, Inc., 2950-N Advance Lane, Colmar, PA., 18915 (215)997-9689 FAX(215)997-2371

Break Free, Inc., 1035 S. Linwood Ave., Santa Ana, CA. 92705 (714)953-1900 FAX(714)953-0402

Brownells, 200 S. Front St., Montezuma, IA., 50171 (515)623-5401 FAX(515)623-3896

Burris Co., Inc., P.O. Box 1747, Greeley, CO. 80631 (970)356-1670 FAX(970)356-8702

Butler Creek, 290 Arden Dr., Belgrade, MT., 59714 (406)388-1356 FAX(406)388-7204

Corbin, P.O. Box 2659, White City, OP., 87503 (541)826-5211 FAX(541)826-8669

Dewey Mfg. Co. Inc., P.O. Box 2014, Southbury, CT. 06488 (203)264-3064 FAX(203)262-6907

Douglas Barrels, Inc. 5504 Big Tyler Rd. Charleston, WV. 25313 (304)776-1341 FAX(304)776-8560

DPMS, 13983 industry Ave., Becker, MN. 55308 (612)261-5600 FAX(612)261-5599

Eley Ltd. P.O. Box 705, Witton, Birmingham, B6 7UT, England, 021-356-8899 FAX 021-331-4173

Federal Cartridge Co. 900 Ehlen Dr. Anoka, MN. 55303 (612)323-2300 FAX(612)323-2506

Flint 'N Frizzen Gun Shop (Bruce McArthur) (248)625-3333

Fred Wenig Stocks 103 North Market St., Lincoln, MO. 65338, (660)547-3334 FAX(660)547-2881

GG&G, 3602 East 42nd Stravenue, Tucson, AZ. 85713 (520)748-7167 FAX(520)748-7583

Gradient Lens Corp. 207 Tremont St., Rochester, NY. 14608 (716)235-2620 FAX(716)235-6645

Holland's Gunsmithing, P.O. Box 69 Powers, OR. 97466 (541)439-5155

Hornady Manufacturing Co. P.O. Box 1848, Grand Island, NE. 68802 (308)382-1390 FAX(308)382-5761

Iron Brigade Armory, 100 Radcliffe Circle, Jacksonville, NC. 28546 (910)455-3834 FAX(910)346-1134

JP Enterprises. P.O. Box 270005, St. Paul, MN. 55127 (651)486-9064 FAX(651)482-0970

L&R Manufacturing Co. 577 Elm St. Kearny, NJ. 07032-3604 (201)991-5330 FAX(201)991-5870

LaBounty Precision Reboring, Inc. 7968 Silver Lake Rd. P.O. Box 186, Maple Falls, WA. 98266 (360)599-2047 FAX(360)599-3018

LaFrance Specialties, P.O. Box 8733, San Diego, CA. 92138-7933 (619)293-3373 FAX(619)293-7087

Lahti Co. P.O. Box 453, Iron River, WI. 54847 (715)372-5188

Leupold & Stevens, Inc. P.O. Box 688 Beaverton, OR. 97075 (503)646-9171 FAX(503)526-1475

Lightforce USA, 19226 55th Ave S, Bldg L-103, Kent, WA, 98032, (425)656-1577 FAX(425)656-1578

Loon Lake Precision 8200 Embury Rd, Grand Blanc, MI. 48439 (810)953-0732 FAX(810)953-0735

Marlin Firearms Co. 100 Kenna Dr. North Haven, CT. 06473 (203)239-5621 FAX(203)234-7991

Midway P.O. Box 718-C, Columbia, MO. 65205 (573)445-6363 FAX(573)446-1018

Millett 16131 Gothard St., Huntington Beach, CA. 92647 (714)842-5575

Mountaindog Gunsmithing, Route 1, Box 58, Chama, NM. 87520 (505)756-2331

NECO, 536C Stone Rd, Benicia, CA, 94510, (707)747-0897 FAX(510)450-0421

New England Custom Gunsmiths, Brook Rd RR2, Box 122W, W. Lebanon, NH, 03784, (603)469-3450 FAX (603)469-3471

Nikon, Inc, 1300 Walt Whitman Rd, Melville, NY, 11747, (516)547-8623 FAX(516)547-0309

Olympic Arms, 620-625 Old Pacific Hwy SE, Olympia, WA. 98513 (360)459-7940 FAX(360)491-3447

Pac-Nor Barreling P.O. Box 6188, Brookings, OR. 97415 (541)469-7330 FAX(541)469-7331

Pachmayr 1875 Mountain Ave., Monrovia, CA. 91016 FAX(626)358-7251

Pacific Cryo, Box 1, Arvin, CA. 93203

Pentax, 35 Inverness Dr E., Englewood, CO. 80112 (303)799-8000 FAX(303)790-1131

Quality Parts/Bushmaster Firearms, 99 Roosevelt Trail, Windham, ME. 04062 (207)892-2005 FAX(207)892-8068

Remington Arms Co. P.O. Box 700, 870 Remington Dr. Madison, NC. 27025 (336)548-8581 FAX(336)548-7750

Savage Arms Co. 100 Springdale Rd., Westfield, MA. 01085 (413)568-7001 FAX(413)562-7764

Segway Industries, P.O. Box 783, Suffern, NY. 10901 (914)357-5510 FAX(914)357-4570

Shilen, Inc. P.O. Box 1300, 205 Metro Park Blvd., Ennis, TX. 75119 (972)875-5318 FAX(972)875-5402

Sierra Precision Rifles 24927 Bonanza Sr. Miwuk, CA. 95346 (209)586-6071 FAX(209)586-6555

Sinclair International, 2330 Wayne Haven St., Fort Wayne, IN. 46803 (219)749-5136

Smith Enterprises 1701 W. 10th St., Tempe, AZ. 85281 (602)964-1818 FAX(602)921-9987

Spec-Tech Industries, 1225 E. Sunset Dr. #617, Bellingham, WA. 98226 (360)366-2632

Spec-Tech Industries, Inc. 1225 E. Sunset Dr. #617, Bellingham, WA. 98226-3529 (360)366-2632 FAX(360)671-8297

Springfield Armory, 420 West Main, Geneseo, IL. 61254 (309)944-5631 FAX(309)944-3676

Sturm, Ruger & Co, Inc. 200 Ruger Road, Prescott, AZ. 86301 (520)541-8824 FAX(520)541-8850

Timney Triggers, 3940 W. Clarendon Ave., Phoenix, AZ. 85019 (602)274-2999 FAX(602)241-0361

U.S. Repeating Arms Co, 275 Winchester Ave., Morgan, UT. 84050 (801)876-3440 FAX(80-1)876-3737

Volquartsen Custom, Route 1 Box 33A, P.O. Box 271, Carroll, IA. 51401 (712)792-4238 FAX(712)792-2542

Weatherby, Inc. 3100 El Camino Real, Atascadero, CA. 93422 (805)466-1767 FAX(805)466-2527

Wenig Custom Gunstocks 103 North Market St, Lincoln, MO. 65338, (660)547-3334 FAX(660)547-2881

Winchester Shooting Products, 5875 W. Van Horn Tavern Rd. Columbia, MO. 65203 (573)446-6414 FAX(573)446-6606

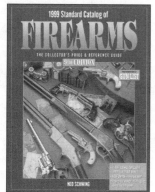

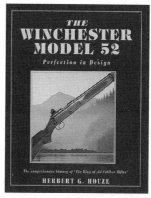